LANDMARKS
IN HUMANITIES

LANDMARKS
IN HUMANITIES

THIRD EDITION

GLORIA K. FIERO

Boston Burr Ridge, IL Dubuque, IA New York San Francisco St. Louis
Bangkok Bogotá Caracas Kuala Lumpur Lisbon London Madrid Mexico City
Milan Montreal New Delhi Santiago Seoul Singapore Sydney Taipei Toronto

The McGraw·Hill Companies

LANDMARKS

Published by McGraw-Hill, a business unit of The McGraw-Hill Companies, Inc. 1221 Avenue of the Americas, New York, NY 10020. Copyright © 2013, 2009, 2006 by The McGraw-Hill Companies, Inc. All rights reserved. Printed in the United States of America. No part of this publication may be reproduced or distributed in any form or by any means, or stored in a database or retrieval system, without the prior written permission of The McGraw-Hill Companies, Inc., including, but not limited to, in any network or other electronic storage or transmission, or broadcast for distance learning.

Some ancillaries, including electronic and print components, may not be available to customers outside the United States.

This book is printed on acid-free paper.

1 2 3 4 5 6 7 8 9 DOW/DOW 9 8 7 6 5 4 3 2 1

ISBN–13: 978-0-07-337664-6
MHID: 0-07-337664-7

Vice President Editorial: Michael Ryan
Publisher: Christopher Freitag
Director of Development: Rhona Robbin
Associate Sponsoring Editor: Betty Chen
Developmental Editor: Karen Dubno
Executive Marketing Manager: Stacy Ruel
Managing Editor: Christina Gimlin
Buyer II: Tandra Jorgensen

Library of Congress Cataloging-in-Publication Data

Fiero, Gloria K.
Landmarks in humanities / Gloria K. Fiero. -- 3rd ed.
p. cm.
ISBN-13: 978-0-07-337664-6 (pbk. : alk. paper)
ISBN-10: 0-07-337664-7 (pbk. : alk. paper)
1. Civilization--History--Textbooks. I. Title.
CB69.F54 2012
909--dc23
2011024217

This book was designed and produced by
Laurence King Publishing Ltd., London
www.laurenceking.com

Permissions Acknowledgments appear on pages 470–472, and on this page by reference. Every effort has been made to contact the copyright holders, but should there be any errors or omissions Laurence King Publishing Ltd. would be pleased to insert the appropriate acknowledgment in any subsequent printing of this publication.

Picture Research: Emma Brown
Design: Robin Farrow
Maps: Advanced Illustration, Cheshire
Literary Permissions: James Hodgson

FRONT COVER
Top to bottom:
- Stonehenge, Salisbury Plain, Wiltshire, England, ca. 3000–1800 B.C.E. Stone, diameter of circle 97 ft., tallest upright 22 ft. © Skyscan/Corbis
- Frank Gehry, Walt Disney Concert Hall, Los Angeles, California, 2003. Metal-clad stainless steel plates connected by aluminum panels, glass curtain wall, and skylights, area 270,000 sq. ft. © Rufus F. Folkks/Corbis

BACK COVER
Clockwise from top left:
- Colosseum, Rome (aerial view), 70–82 C.E. © Alinari Archives/Corbis
- *Shiva Nataraja, Lord of the Dance*, from Southern India, Chola period, eleventh century. Copper, height 3 ft. 77 in. © The Cleveland Museum of Art, 2011 Purchase from the J. H. Wade Fund, 1930.331
- The Kaaba, Mecca, Saudi Arabia. © Reuters/Corbis
- South rose window, Chartres Cathedral, France, thirteenth century. Sonia Halliday Photographs.

FRONTISPIECE
- Francisco Goya, *The Third of May, 1808: The Execution of the Defenders of Madrid*, 1814 (detail, see Figure 12.17). Oil on canvas, 8 ft. 6 in. x 10 ft. 4 in. Prado, Madrid.

Contents

Maps

Music Listening Excerpts

Preface

ALL TRAVELERS to foreign lands appreciate a guide, whether it be a tour leader who points out the important sights or a guidebook that orients the visitor with navigational tips. *LANDMARKS* guides students on a chronological journey through the history of culture. Focusing on prominent landmarks from prehistory to the present, the text introduces readers to the creative endeavors of the human imagination and to the prominent ideas and issues that have shaped the course and character of the world's various cultures. The landmarks that mark this journey are the great works of their place and time and, in some cases, of all time. They have been transmitted from generation to generation as a living legacy. In this edition, each chapter opens with "A First Look" at a landmark artwork that illustrates the key idea of the chapter and acts as a cultural guidepost to that chapter's overarching theme. This new feature explains the artwork's significance as a landmark in its own time as well as in ours.

LANDMARKS in Humanities is designed to help students understand and appreciate the relevance of historical works and ideas to their own daily lives.

LANDMARKS is interdisciplinary. It regards "Humanities" not as a collection of individual disciplines (literature, philosophy, music, and the visual arts), but as a discipline in itself: *the study of humankind in its creative and communicative dimensions*. As such, it emphasizes the *interrelatedness* of various modes of expression as they work to create, define, and reflect the unique culture of a given time and place.

LANDMARKS is thematic. It brings focus to each chapter by way of a *key idea*, presented in the chapter title and subtitle and discussed in the introductory paragraph. The key idea unifies the various landmarks included in the chapter and emphasizes their significance for their own time, as well as for ours. For instance, Chapter 1 ("Origins: The First Civilizations") surveys history's earliest cultures while considering universal strategies for dealing with the environment, the community, and the unknown. Chapter 4 ("Revelation: The Flowering of World Religions") compares three monotheistic world faiths—Judaism, Christianity, and Islam—that share a fundamental belief in revelation, while providing comparison with pantheistic Buddhism. Chapter 12 ("Romanticism: Nature, Passion, and the Sublime") examines the nineteenth-century phenomenon of Romanticism as a social and political movement, a style that sought inspiration in nature, and an attitude of mind that exalts the creative imagination.

LANDMARKS is selective. Some landmarks have been chosen for their universality, some for their singular beauty, and others for their iconic or symbolic value. Certain landmarks—the Statue of Liberty, the Mona Lisa, the sonnets of Shakespeare—meet more than one of these criteria. Although the author's choice of landmarks may differ from that of others, this book should encourage readers to choose and defend their own choice of landmarks.

Special Features

A First Look focuses on a full-page illustration of the work of art that introduces the chapter; it explains how that landmark relates to the key idea presented in the chapter title, subtitle, and introductory paragraph.

A First Look

On the outskirts of modern-day Cairo, at the ancient Egyptian funeral complex of Gizeh, stands the monumental figure of the Great Sphinx. A hybrid creature with the body of a crouching lion and the head of a human being, the Great Sphinx remains the largest monolithic statue in the world. It is crowned with the headdress of ancient Egypt's royal ruler, who bore the title of "pharaoh." The huge scale of the Great Sphinx expresses Egyptian belief in the pharaoh's superhuman power as an agent of the gods, mediating their influence over such natural occurrences as drought or a good harvest. Regal and serene, it looks eternally to the East: the place of renewal and rebirth associated with the rising sun, deified by the Egyptians as the major natural force in their life. A sphinx is generally regarded as a guardian figure that protects the entranceway to ancient tombs and temples. But scholars continue to dispute when and by whom this particular sphinx was built. Some suggest it embodies a tradition of sun-worship that goes back thousands of years before the rise of Egyptian civilization. The Great Sphinx reminds us that the study of our origins raises as many questions as it answers; as such, it is an appropriate landmark for this chapter.

Ideas and Issues examines a unique cultural or historical point of view, one that may be the subject of current debate or opinion. This feature may include quotations from *primary sources* (works original to the period under discussion). Questions are appended to this feature in order to provoke critical thought and discussion.

Ideas and Issues

KEEPING TRACK OF TIME

All dating systems are culture-bound: The Christian calendar fixes the year 1 with the birth of Jesus (see page 105), thus "A.D." abbreviates the Latin *anno domini nostri Jesu Christi* (the year of Our Lord Jesus Christ) and "B.C." "before Christ." However, the Hebrew calendar begins at the supposed date of creation, and the Muslim one starts with the year of Muhammad's flight to Medina (the Christian year 622). In an effort to find language for tracking time that might be acceptable to all faiths, historians have devised the designations "B.C.E." for "before the common era" and "C.E." for the "common era." While the actual dates of the Christian calendar are retained, the new wording offers an alternative to the Eurocentric and sectarian terminology of the older system.

Making Connections (formerly **Parallels**) explores the stylistic relationship between two or more images or ideas, or between text and image. This feature may suggest the universality or continuity of a landmark theme or motif, or compare the treatment of such themes or motifs in different time periods. Questions are appended to this feature in order to provoke critical thought and discussion.

Making Connections

MOTHER EARTH

In her role as childbearer, the female assures the continuity of humankind. Hence, in the prehistoric community, where survival was fragile, she assumed special importance. Perceived as life-giver, and identified with the mysterious powers of procreation, she was exalted as Mother Earth (Figure **1.3**). Her importance in the ancient world is confirmed by the great numbers of female statuettes uncovered by archaeologists throughout the world. Many of these objects show the female nude with pendulous breasts, large buttocks, and swollen abdomen, suggesting pregnancy. In the last century, the feminist movement inspired a revival of the imagery of Mother Earth. The twentieth-century sculptor Niki de Saint Phalle called her gigantic female figures "Nanas." These brightly painted polyester images (Figure **1.4**) are exuberant versions of the eternal Earth Mother.

Q Why might the Venus of Willendorf be considered a landmark and an inspiration to modern feminists?

Figure 1.3 (above) Venus of Willendorf, from Lower Austria, ca. 25,000–20,000 B.C.E. Limestone, height 4⅜ in. Museum of Natural History, Vienna.

Figure 1.4 Niki de Saint Phalle, *Black Venus*, 1965–1967. Painted polyester, 110 x 35 x 24 in. Whitney Museum of American Art, New York.

Beyond the West

MAO'S CHINA

THE history of totalitarianism is not confined to the West. In the course of the twentieth century, modern tyrants wiped out whole populations in parts of Cambodia, Vietnam, Iraq, Africa, and elsewhere. Of all the Asian countries, however, China experienced the most dramatic changes. Following World War II, communist forces under the leadership of Mao Zedong (1893–1976) rose to power, and in 1949 they formed the People's Republic of China.

Mao's ambitious reforms earned the support of the landless masses, but his methods for achieving his goals struck at the foundations of traditional Chinese culture. He tried to replace the old order, and especially the Confucian veneration of the family, with new socialist values that demanded devotion to the local economic unit—and ultimately to the state. Between 1949 and 1952, in an effort to make his reforms effective, Mao authorized the execution of some two to five million people, including the wealthy landowners themselves. To carry out his series of five-year plans for economic development in industry and agriculture, Mao also instituted totalitarian practices, such as indoctrination, exile, and repeated purges of the voices of opposition. His utopian views on cooperative social endeavor and self-discipline were broadcast by way of guidelines published in his *Quotations from Chairman Mao* (1963). Mao's "little red book" soon became the "bible" of the Chinese Revolution.

Mao directed writers to produce literature that celebrated the creative powers of the masses. The movement for a "people's literature" included the abandonment of ancient, classical modes of writing in favor of the language of common, vernacular speech—a style strongly influenced by Western literature and journalism. In the visual arts, the influence of Western printmakers contributed to the appearance of *Social Realism*—a style that presented socially significant subject matter in a lifelike manner (Figure **14.7**).

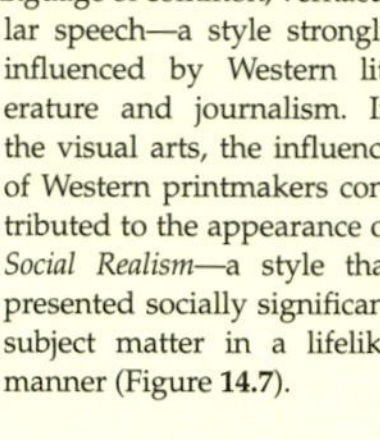

Figure 14.7 Li Hua, *Roar!* 1936. Woodcut, 8 x 6 in. Lu Xun Memorial, Shanghai.

Beyond the West considers the non-Western cultural landmarks that are contemporaneous with the materials presented in an individual chapter. Cross-cultural influences are also examined here. Along with these special features, **Key Topics** and **Timelines** can be found at the end of every chapter; the **Glossary** appears at the end of the book. The **Further Reading** appendix will assist those who wish to pursue additional research.

Key Topics

- prehistory
- Paleolithic/Neolithic cultures
- the birth of civilization
- counting/writing
- animism
- polytheism/monotheism/pantheism
- Mesopotamia: the literary epic
- Hammurabi: written law
- Egyptian theocracy
- Old Kingdom tombs
- Egyptian women
- perceptual/conceptual art
- lyric poetry
- New Kingdom temples
- India: Hinduism
- reincarnation
- China: the Mandate of Heaven
- Daoism

Pedagogical Enhancements to the Third Edition

- Study Questions added to **Making Connections** (formerly Parallels).
- Additional extended captions.
- Expanded Glossary.
- Additional Music Listening selections.
- Additional cross-references.

What's New in Each Chapter?

Chapter 1 Origins: The First Civilizations
- Archeological finds at Göbekli Tepe, Turkey
- Ishtar Gate
- **Ideas and Issues** box: The Out-of-India Debate

Chapter 2 Classicism: The Greek Legacy
- **Ideas and Issues** box: Plato's Ideal State
- The Golden Section

Chapter 4 Revelation: The Flowering of World Religions
- **Ideas and Issues** box: The Names of God
- **Making Connections** box: The Good Shepherd
- *Hadith*

Chapter 8 Reform: The Northern Renaissance and the Reformation
- Holbein's *Sir Thomas More*
- Baldung's *Witches*

Chapter 9 Encounter: Contact and the Clash of Cultures
- Benin bronzes
- African Architecture

Chapter 11 Enlightenment: Science and the New Learning
- Adam Smith's "invisible hand"
- Houdon and Voltaire

Chapter 13 Materialism: The Industrial Era and the Urban Scene
- Polynesian art of tattoo

Chapter 14 Modernism: The Assault on Tradition
- **Making Connections** box: Harlem
- **Making Connections** box: The Birth of Motion Pictures and the Visual Arts
- Copland's *Appalachian Spring*
- Mao's "little red book"

Chapter 15 Globalism: Information, Communication, and the Digital Revolution
- Media-shaped Globalism
- Adams' *I Was Looking at the Ceiling*
- The Interactive Spectator
- Serra's *Sequence*
- Neto's *Anthropodino*
- **Making Connections** box: Tradition and the Global Environment
- **Ideas and Issues** box: The Disappearing Art Object

Ancillaries

Teaching and learning resources to accompany *Landmarks in Humanities* can be found on the Online Learning Center at www.mhhe.com/fiero3e. Instructors will have access to an instructor's manual with study questions and strategies for lecture and discussions, a test bank, and *Connect Image Bank*, which houses numerous images from *LANDMARKS* and several other McGraw-Hill titles for download and for use in class. Students will have access to self-quizzes, videos, and core concepts in humanities resources.

A music CD-ROM (ISBN 978-0-07-760011-2) is available for packaging and standalone purchase. It includes mp3s of music excerpts marked by marginal music logos ♪ indicated in the text, listening guides, and other resources for further exploration and understanding of music.

For instructors looking to supplement their course with additional readings, Traditions: *Humanities Readings through the Ages* on McGraw-Hill's Create (http://create.mcgraw-hill.com/traditions/index.html#) allows instructors to choose from a database of over 100 selections.

CourseSmart, a new way for faculty to find and review eTextbooks, is also a useful option for students who are interested in accessing their course materials digitally.

Acknowledgments

As with previous editions, I am greatly indebted to James Hunter Dormon, who continues to serve as an intellectual sounding board for major ideas and remains a thoughtful critic of the written drafts. Special thanks go to Betty Chen, Jennie Katsaros, Rhona Robbin, and Karen Dubno at McGraw-Hill Higher Education, and to Susie May and the efficient editorial staff at Laurence King Publishing.

In preparing the third edition, I have benefited from the suggestions and comments generously offered by Peggy Brown, Collin College; Michael Flanagan, University of Wisconsin, Whitewater; Tami Gitto-Kania, Valencia Community College; Richard D. Hall, Texas State University, San Marcos; Linda Johnson, Modesto Junior College; P. Diane Knapp, Tulsa Community College; Carol Kramer, Germanna Community College; Janet Madden, El Camino College; Bruce McGraw, Southwestern Community College; Robert P. Mills, Liberty University; Bruce Naschak, San Diego Mesa College; Scott Olsen, Central Florida Community College; Carlos Sanabria, Hostos Community College; Bernadette Schwarz, Lansing Community College; Dennis P. Smith, Oklahoma State University; and Steven Woods, Tulsa Community College. I am particularly grateful to Eric C. Shiner and Larry Walsh for assistance in obtaining access to contemporary artworks.

Gloria K. Fiero

Chapter 1

Origins:

THE FIRST CIVILIZATIONS

ca. 25,000–330 B.C.E.

How and why did life originate? What is our purpose on earth? How might human beings survive the onset of flood, fire, drought, and other natural threats? How might they bring order to collective and communal life? Even before the dawn of writing—during the era known as "prehistory"—the earliest inhabitants of our planet must have asked such questions, for we know they made vigorous efforts to manipulate nature and to protect the members of their small and thriving communities. Just as in our own time, prehistoric men and women devised technologies for survival and strategies to protect the members of their struggling communities. Their answers and solutions come to us in the form of the artifacts they left behind: their tools and weapons, cave paintings, burial mounds, and stone sanctuaries.

More sophisticated evidence comes to us from humankind's first civilizations. Born in the river valleys of Mesopotamia, Egypt, India, and China, ancient cities left written records of trade contracts, law codes, religious hymns and prayers, as well as cast bronze artifacts, and monumental tombs and temples. Recently excavated sites in the Americas reveal some, but not all of the hallmarks of these early civilizations. The remains of early urban dwellers throughout the world present a complex picture of the ways in which our ancestors lived and died, how they dealt with each other in peace and war, and how they confronted the universal realities of natural disaster, illness, birth, and death.

A First Look

On the outskirts of modern-day Cairo, at the ancient Egyptian funeral complex of Gizeh, stands the monumental figure of the Great Sphinx. A hybrid creature with the body of a crouching lion and the head of a human being, the Great Sphinx remains the largest monolithic statue in the world. It is crowned with the headdress of ancient Egypt's royal ruler, who bore the title of "pharaoh." The huge scale of the Great Sphinx expresses Egyptian belief in the pharaoh's superhuman power as an agent of the gods, mediating their influence over such natural occurrences as drought or a good harvest. Regal and serene, it looks eternally to the East: the place of renewal and rebirth associated with the rising sun, deified by the Egyptians as the major natural force in their life. A sphinx is generally regarded as a guardian figure that protects the entranceway to ancient tombs and temples. But scholars continue to dispute when and by whom this particular sphinx was built. Some suggest it embodies a tradition of sun-worship that goes back thousands of years before the rise of Egyptian civilization. The Great Sphinx reminds us that the study of our origins raises as many questions as it answers; as such, it is an appropriate landmark for this chapter.

Figure 1.1 Great Sphinx at Gizeh, Egypt, ca. 2540–2514 B.C.E. Limestone, length 240 ft., height 65 ft. In the background is the pyramid of Khufu (Khefren), ca. 2650 B.C.E. (See also page 16.)

PREHISTORY

THE study of human development prior to the advent of written records helps us to understand our origins. During the late phases of prehistory, our earliest ancestors fashioned stone and bone tools and weapons to hunt, gather, and provide the means for their survival. Communities left signs and symbols deep inside caves; others constructed stone sanctuaries and burial sites. The sum total of those things created and transmitted by humankind, we call **culture**.

Not all phases of prehistoric culture developed at the same time; some persisted longer than others in certain parts of the globe. A few lasted well into the twentieth century, giving modern scholars a glimpse into the past. As food-producing slowly came to replace food-gathering, and hunters became farmers, communities of a very different sort emerged: Urban societies developed systems of writing, the technology of metallurgy, and complex forms of civic life.

Paleolithic Culture

The landmark event of Paleolithic culture was the making of tools and weapons. Toolmaking represents the beginning of culture, which, in its most basic sense, proceeds from the manipulation of nature. The making of tools—humankind's earliest technology—was prehistoric peoples' primary act of extending control over nature and a fundamental example of problem-solving behavior. The earliest Paleolithic tools and weapons, found in Africa and East Asia, included cleavers, chisels, spears, harpoons, hand-axes, and a wide variety of choppers. This hunting technology evolved during a period of climatic change called the Ice Age, which occurred between roughly three million and ten thousand years ago. In the face of glacial advances that covered the area north of the equator, Paleolithic people were forced either to migrate (following their prey) or adapt to changing conditions. By the end of the Ice Age, hunter-gatherers used fire to provide safety, warmth, and a means of preparing food.

The burial of the dead among some of our human ancestors and the practice of including tools, weapons, and other personal effects in the graves of the dead are evidence of a self-conscious population with memory and foresight. Their ritual preparation of the deceased suggests fear of the dead or anticipation of life after death. While toolmaking constitutes the landmark technology of Paleolithic culture, cave painting represents an enterprise whose meaning and function remain the subject of wide debate.

During the last sixty years, archeologists have discovered thousands of paintings and carvings on the walls of caves and the surfaces of rocks at Paleolithic sites in Europe, Africa, Australia, and North America. Over one hundred limestone cave dwellings in southwestern France and still others discovered as recently as 1996 in southeastern France contain mysterious markings and lifelike images of animals (bears, bison, elk, lions, and zebras, among others), birds, fish, and sea creatures. Executed between ten thousand and thirty thousand years ago, Paleolithic wall-paintings provide a visual record of such long-extinct animals as the hairy mammoth and the woolly rhinoceros (Figure **1.2**). They also reveal extraordinary technical sophistication and a high degree of **Naturalism** (fidelity to nature).

What were the purpose and function of these vivid images? It is unlikely that they were intended as decorations or even as records of the hunt, given that they were located in the most inaccessible regions of the caves and frequently drawn one over another, with no apparent regard for clarity of composition. Scholars have long

PREHISTORIC CULTURES

Paleolithic ("Old Stone")
ca. 6 million to 10,000 B.C.E.

- tribal hunters and gatherers
- crude stone and bone tools and weapons
- cave painting and sculpture

Mesolithic ("Transitional Stone")
ca. 10,000 to 8000 B.C.E.

- domestication of plants and animals
- stone circles and shrines

Neolithic ("New Stone")
ca. 8000 to 2000 B.C.E.

- farming and food production
- polished stone and bone tools and weapons
- architecture
- pottery and weaving

Figure 1.2 Hall of Bulls, left wall, Lascaux caves, Dordogne, France, ca. 15,000–10,000 B.C.E. Paint on limestone rock, length of individual bulls 13–16 ft. Executed in **polychrome** mineral pigments and shaded with bitumen and burnt coal, realistically depicted bison, horses, reindeer, and a host of other creatures are shown standing or running, often wounded by spears and lances.

Ideas and Issues

KEEPING TRACK OF TIME

All dating systems are culture-bound: The Christian calendar fixes the year 1 with the birth of Jesus (see page 105), thus "A.D." abbreviates the Latin *anno domini nostri Jesu Christi* (the year of Our Lord Jesus Christ) and "B.C." "before Christ." However, the Hebrew calendar begins at the supposed date of creation, and the Muslim one starts with the year of Muhammad's flight to Medina (the Christian year 622). In an effort to find language for tracking time that might be acceptable to all faiths, historians have devised the designations "B.C.E." for "before the common era" and "C.E." for the "common era." While the actual dates of the Christian calendar are retained, the new wording offers an alternative to the Eurocentric and sectarian terminology of the older system.

debated the meaning of so-called "cave art." Some hold that it served as part of a virtual hunting ritual in which the image of the animal was symbolically killed prior to the hunt itself. Others contend that the creatures pictured on cave walls may be **totems** (heraldic tribal emblems) or symbols of male and female forces. Still others read certain abstract markings as lunar calendars, notational devices used to predict seasonal change and the migration of animals.

Long associated with the procreative womb and cosmic underworld, the cave may have served as a ceremonial chamber or shrine in which rituals were orchestrated by **shamans**, that is, mediators between the natural and the spiritual world. On the other hand, it seems possible that cave paintings—like tools and weapons—served a vital function: The depiction of the animal, that is, its "capture" on the cave wall, may have been essential to the hunt itself. Well into the twentieth century, hunting tribes such as the Pygmies of the African Congo enacted the hunt prior to the actual event. They drew and then symbolically "killed" the animal by shooting arrows into the drawing. Such rituals of "sympathetic magic," virtual hunts that included chant, mime, and dance, were believed to ensure the success of the hunt. Might Paleolithic cave art have served a similar function?

Whatever actual purpose cave art served, it is evident that in the ancient world "art" was not intended primarily as decoration or entertainment as it is today. Rather, the arts held a sacred function related to communal well-being. Just as tools and weapons empowered our earliest ancestors in their manipulation of nature, so visual images, songs, and dance acted as powerful agents for petitioning superhuman forces and for shaping destiny.

Mesolithic and Neolithic Cultures

The evolution of human culture is difficult to date with any precision, especially because the technologies of survival varied from region to region over a long period of time. Following the end of the Ice Age, however, communities in some parts of the world began to domesticate plants and animals; hunters and gatherers gradually became farmers and food producers. A dynamic new culture emerged: the Neolithic. Food production freed people from a nomadic way of life. Farmers gradually settled in permanent communities, raising high-protein crops such as wheat and barley in Asia, rice in China, and maize and beans in the Americas. They raised goats, pigs, cattle, and sheep that provided regular sources of food and valuable by-products such as wool and leather. The transition from the hunting-gathering phase of human subsistence to the agricultural-herding phase was a revolutionary development in human social organization, because it marked the shift from a nomadic to a sedentary way of life.

Making Connections

MOTHER EARTH

In her role as childbearer, the female assures the continuity of humankind. Hence, in the prehistoric community, where survival was fragile, she assumed special importance. Perceived as life-giver, and identified with the mysterious powers of procreation, she was exalted as Mother Earth (Figure **1.3**). Her importance in the ancient world is confirmed by the great numbers of female statuettes uncovered by archeologists throughout the world. Many of these objects show the female nude with pendulous breasts, large buttocks, and swollen abdomen, suggesting pregnancy. In the last century, the feminist movement inspired a revival of the imagery of Mother Earth. The twentieth-century sculptor Niki de Saint Phalle called her gigantic female figures "Nanas." These brightly painted polyester images (Figure **1.4**) are exuberant versions of the eternal Earth Mother.

Q Why might the Venus of Willendorf be considered a landmark and an inspiration to modern feminists?

Figure 1.3 (above) "Venus" of Willendorf, from Lower Austria, ca. 25,000–20,000 B.C.E. Limestone, height $4\frac{3}{8}$ in. Museum of Natural History, Vienna.

Figure 1.4 Niki de Saint Phalle, *Black Venus*, 1965–1967. Painted polyester, 110 x 35 x 24 in. Whitney Museum of American Art, New York.

Neolithic sites excavated in Southwest Asia (a region also known as "the Near East" or "the Middle East," which includes Israel, Jordan, Turkey, Iran, and Iraq), East Asia (China and Japan), and (as late as 1000 B.C.E.) Meso-America, center on villages consisting of a number of mud- and limestone-faced huts—humankind's earliest architecture. At Jericho, in present-day Israel, massive defense walls surrounded the town, while tombs held the ornamented remains of local villagers. At Jarmo, in northern Iraq, a community of more than 150 people harvested wheat with stone sickles. Polished stone tools, some designed especially for farming, replaced the cruder tools of Paleolithic people. Ancient Japanese communities seem to have produced the world's oldest known pottery—handcoiled and fired clay vessels. But it is in Southwest Asia that some of the finest examples of painted pottery have come to light.

Agricultural life stimulated a new awareness of seasonal change and a profound respect for those life-giving powers, such as sun and rain, that were essential to the success of the harvest. The earth's fertility and the seasonal cycle were the principal concerns of the farming culture.

The overwhelming evidence of female statuettes found in many Neolithic graves suggests that the cult of the Earth Mother may have become important in the transition from food-gathering to food-production, when fertility and agricultural abundance were vital to the life of the community. Nevertheless, as with cave art, the exact meaning and function of the so-called "mother goddesses" remain a matter of speculation: They may have played a role in the performance of rites celebrating seasonal regeneration or they may have been associated with fertility cults that ensured successful childbirth. The symbolic association between the womb and Mother Earth played an important part in almost all ancient religions. In myth as well, female deities governed the earth, while male deities ruled the sky. From culture to culture, the fertility goddess herself took many different forms. In contrast with the Paleolithic "Venus" of Willendorf (see Figure 1.3), for instance, whose sexual characteristics are boldly exaggerated, the marble statuettes produced in great number on the Cyclades (the Greek islands of the Aegean Sea) are as streamlined and highly stylized as some modern sculptures (Figure **1.5**). Though lacking the pronounced sexual characteristics of the Venus, the Cycladic figure probably played a similar role in rituals that sought the blessings of Mother Earth.

Figure 1.5 (right) Female figure, early Cycladic II, Late Spedos type, ca. 2600–2400 B.C.E. Marble, height $24\frac{3}{4}$ in. The Metropolitan Museum of Art, New York.

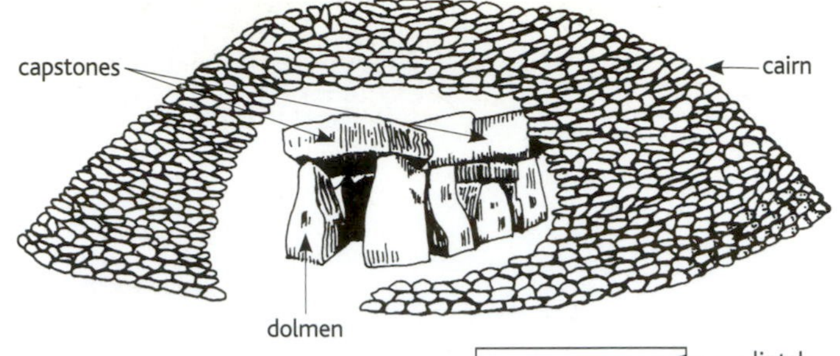

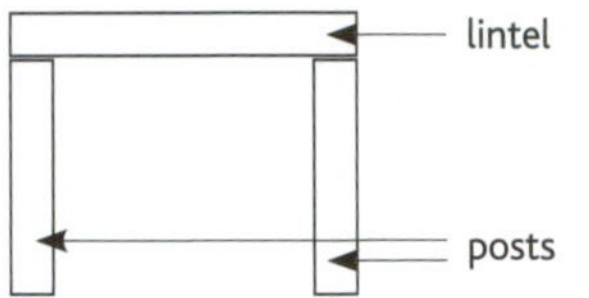

Figure 1.6 Dolmen site (above) and post-and-lintel construction (right). The dolmen tomb made use of the simplest type of architectural construction: the **post-and-lintel** principle.

To farming peoples, the seasonal cycle—a primary fact of subsistence—was associated with birth, death, and regeneration. The dead, whose return to the earth put them in closer touch with the forces of nature, received careful burial. Almost all early cultures regarded the dead as messengers between the world of the living and the spirit world. Neolithic folk marked graves with **megaliths** ("great stones"), upright stone slabs roofed by a capstone to form a stone tomb or **dolmen** (Figure **1.6**). At some sites, the tomb was covered over with dirt and rubble to form a mound, symbolic of the sacred mountain (the abode of the gods) and the procreative womb (the source of regenerative life). This distinctive shape prevails in sacred architecture that ranges from the Meso-American temple (see Figure 1.17) to the Buddhist shrine (see Figure 4.26).

Recently, archeologists have found a series of stone circles consisting of 10-ton megaliths dated as early as 9000 B.C.E. The oldest of these, at Göbekli Tepe in southeastern Turkey, belongs to a temple complex that probably functioned as a religious shrine (Figure **1.7**). Since only 5 percent of this site has been excavated, its significance for unraveling the history of our human origins is still to be determined. But the presence of such early stone structures in an area lacking water and farm-based villages suggests that ancient types of open-air shrines may have preceded the more complex agricultural communities traditionally associated with the so-called "Neolithic revolution."

At ceremonial centers and burial sites in Western Europe, larger megalithic complexes are found. Placed in multiple rows or in concentric circles, the upright stones are usually capped by horizontal slabs. A landmark example is the sanctuary at Stonehenge in southern England, where an elaborate group of stone circles, constructed in stages over a period of two thousand years, forms one of the most mysterious and impressive ritual spaces of the prehistoric world (Figure **1.8**).

Figure 1.7 Stone pillar, Göbekli Tepe ("Potbelly Hill"), southeastern Turkey. Farming areas have been detected no closer than forty miles from this site. No burial remains have been uncovered. The upright stones are T-shaped, and in height they range from 9 ft. 10 in. to 19 ft. 8 in. Some are carved with images of leopards, foxes, snakes, spiders, carrion birds, and human body parts.

To this windswept site, 20-foot megaliths, some weighing 25 tons each, were dragged from a quarry some 20 miles away, then shaped and assembled without metal tools to form a huge outer circle and an inner horseshoe of post-and-lintel stones. The smaller stones, originating in southwest Wales, were probably transported on wooden rollers and on water—a journey of some 200 miles. A special **stele** that stands apart from the complex of stone circles marks the point—visible from the exact center of the inner circle—at which the sun rises at the midsummer solstice (the longest day of the year). It is probable that Stonehenge served as a celestial observatory predicting the movements of the sun and moon, clocking the seasonal cycle, and thus providing information that would have been essential to an agricultural society.

Recent excavations at nearby Durrington Walls suggest that Stonehenge may also have functioned as the site of funerary rituals for the cremated dead. Dating from ca. 2600 B.C.E., the huge settlement at Durrington Walls includes hundreds of houses and a ceremonial complex of concentric stone rings. Along a wide avenue that connects Durrington with Stonehenge stand dwellings thought by archeologists to have housed religious shrines. Continuing excavation will no doubt unlock more of the mysteries of this Neolithic landmark.

Making Connections

STONE CIRCLES

Reviving the mysterious presence of such Neolithic shrines as Stonehenge (Figure 1.8), the American sculptor and environmentalist Nancy Holt (b. 1938) designed the contemporary concentric stone circles known as *Stone Enclosure* (Figure **1.9**). This earthwork is pierced by four arches that run north and south, calculated from the North Star used by celestial navigators. The circular holes in the rings are aligned with the points of the compass. While modern societies no longer depend on earthworks to predict celestial events, Environmental artists like Holt reassert the human role in reconfiguring space to reflect universal invariables.

Q Are there any monuments or sites in your area that reflect the human fascination with the circle as a sacred symbol?

Figure 1.8 (above) Stonehenge, Salisbury Plain, Wiltshire, England, ca. 3000–1800 B.C.E. Stone, diameter of circle 97 ft., tallest upright 22 ft.

Figure 1.9 (right) Nancy Holt, *Stone Enclosure: Rock Rings*, Western Washington University, 1977–1978. Brown Mountain stone, diameter of outer ring 40 ft., diameter of inner ring 20 ft., height of ring walls 10 ft.

THE BIRTH OF CIVILIZATION

THE birth of civilization (the word derives from the Latin *civitas*, or "city") marked the shift from rural to urban culture: the transition from the Neolithic village to the more complex form of social, economic, and political organization associated with urban life. In the ancient cities of Sumer in Mesopotamia, and along the Nile River (Map **1.1**), Neolithic villages had grown in population and productivity to become the bustling cities of a new era. Surplus amounts of food and goods were now traded with neighboring communities. Advances in technology, such as the wheel, the plow, the solar calendar, and bronze-casting, enhanced economic efficiency. Wheeled carts transported people and goods overland, while sailboats used the natural resources of wind and water for travel. Large-scale farming required artificial systems of irrigation, which, in turn, demanded more complex kinds of communal cooperation and organization.

By comparison with the self-sustaining Neolithic village, the early city reached outward. Specialization and the division of labor raised productivity and encouraged trade, which, in turn, enhanced the growth of the urban economy. Activities related to the production and distribution of goods could no longer be committed entirely to memory; they required an efficient system of accounting and record keeping.

From Counting to Writing

The landmark event of the first civilizations was the invention of writing. Writing made it possible to record and preserve information. More a process than an invention, writing evolved from counting. As early as 7500 B.C.E., merchants used tokens—pieces of clay molded into the shapes of objects—to represent specific commodities: a cone for a unit of grain, an egg shape for a unit of oil, and so on. Tokens were placed in hollow clay balls that accompanied shipments of goods. Upon arrival at their destination, the balls were broken open and the tokens—the "record" of the shipment—were counted. Eventually, traders began to stamp the tokens into wet clay to indicate the nature and amounts of the actual goods.

By 3100 B.C.E., pictorial symbols, or **pictographs**, had replaced the tokens. Using a stylus cut from a reed, scribes incised the pictographs on wet clay tablets. These marks assumed more angular and wedged shapes: **Cuneiform** (from *cuneus*, the Latin word for "wedge") became the type of script used throughout the Near East for well over three thousand years. Thousands of inscribed clay tablets have survived; the earliest of them come from Sumer in Mesopotamia. Most bear notations concerning production and trade, while others are inventories and business accounts, records of historical events, myths, prayers, and genealogies of local rulers.

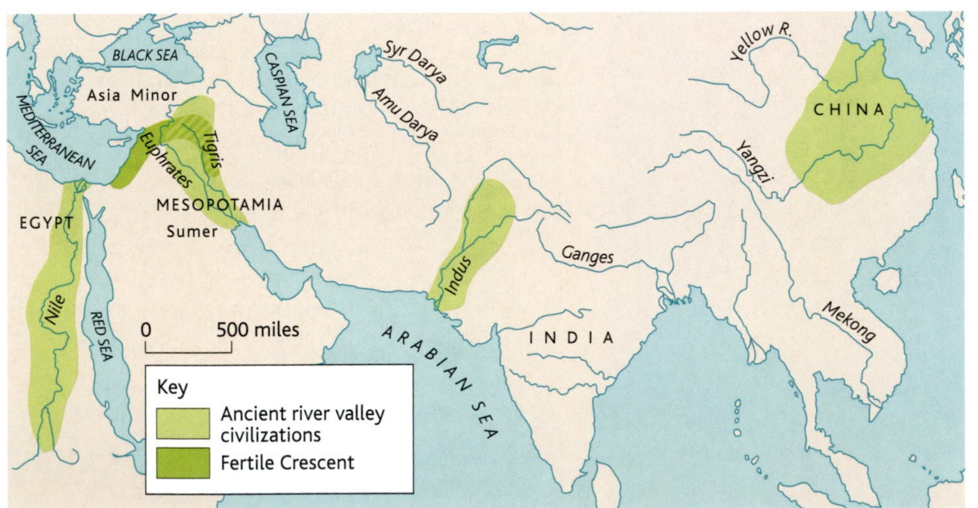

RIVER VALLEY CIVILIZATIONS
ca. 4000–2000 B.C.E.

- urban life
- political institutions
- specialization and division of labor
- trade and large-scale farming
- wheeled vehicles and sailboats
- metallurgy/bronze tools and weapons
- writing and record keeping
- solar calendar

Map 1.1 Ancient River Valley Civilizations. The first civilization of the ancient world emerged in Mesopotamia, a fertile area that lay between the Tigris and Euphrates rivers of the Southwest Asian land mass. Mesopotamia formed the eastern arc of the Fertile Crescent, which stretched westward to the Nile delta. At the southeastern perimeter of the Fertile Crescent, about a dozen cities collectively constituted Sumer, the very earliest civilization known to history. Shortly after the rise of Sumer, around 3500 B.C.E., Egyptian civilization emerged along the Nile River in northeast Africa. In India, the earliest urban centers appeared in the valley of the Indus River that runs through the northwest portion of the Indian subcontinent. Chinese civilization was born in the northern part of China's vast central plain, watered by the Yellow River. The appearance of these four river valley civilizations was not simultaneous. Fully a thousand years separates the birth of civilization in Sumer from the rise of cities in China.

Making Connections

THE INVENTION OF WRITING

The first of these texts, written in **hieroglyphs** ("sacred writing"), bears a curse against the tomb robbers that plagued Old Kingdom Egypt (Figure **1.10**). The tablet from Sumer, written in cuneiform, is a record of accounts listing the sale of animals and such commodities as bread and beer (Figure **1.11**). The Chinese oracle bone bears a calligraphic inscription that asks whether there will be a disaster in the week to come (Figure **1.12**). A later inscription notes that there was indeed a disaster in the form of a military invasion.

Figure 1.10 (above) Egyptian hieroglyphs: Lintel from the Tomb of Meni, Old Kingdom, sixth **dynasty**, ca. 2250 B.C.E. Limestone, $10\frac{5}{8}$ x $26\frac{3}{4}$ in. State Collection of Egyptian Art, Munich.

Figure 1.12 (left) Chinese **calligraphy**: Inscribed oracle bone, Shang dynasty, twelfth century B.C.E. 7 x $4\frac{1}{2}$ in. C. V. Starr East Asian Library, Columbia University.

Figure 1.11 (left) Cuneiform: Reverse side of pictographic clay tablet from Jamdat Nasr, near Kish, Iraq, ca. 3000 B.C.E. Height $4\frac{3}{8}$ in. Ashmolean Museum, Oxford.

Q How did each of these texts serve the practical concerns of the community?

Metallurgy: The Bronze Age

Along with writing, a landmark change in technology marked the birth of civilization: Metal began to replace stone and bone. **Metallurgy**, first practiced in Asia Minor shortly after 4000 B.C.E., afforded individuals greater control over nature by providing harder, more efficient tools and weapons. At the outset, copper ore was extracted from surface deposits, but eventually metalsmiths mined and smelted a variety of ores to produce bronze—an alloy of copper and tin that proved far superior to stone or bone in strength and durability. Since copper and tin ores were often located far apart, travel and trade were essential to Bronze Age cultures. The technology of bronze-casting, which required a high degree of specialization, spread from Mesopotamia throughout the ancient world. In India, complex metalwork techniques were used for the production of jewelry, musical instruments, horse fittings, and toys. But the master metallurgists of the ancient world were the Chinese, who used sectional clay molds to cast separate parts of bronze vessels, which they then soldered together. These bronze-cast vessels are among the great artforms of early history (Figure **1.13**).

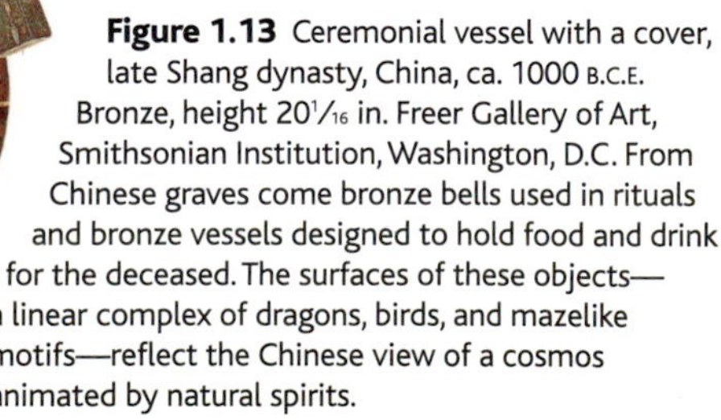

Figure 1.13 Ceremonial vessel with a cover, late Shang dynasty, China, ca. 1000 B.C.E. Bronze, height $20\frac{1}{16}$ in. Freer Gallery of Art, Smithsonian Institution, Washington, D.C. From Chinese graves come bronze bells used in rituals and bronze vessels designed to hold food and drink for the deceased. The surfaces of these objects—a linear complex of dragons, birds, and mazelike motifs—reflect the Chinese view of a cosmos animated by natural spirits.

MESOPOTAMIA

"Land Between the Rivers"

SUMER, humankind's earliest civilization, came to flourish around 3500 B.C.E. Located in present-day Iraq, where the Tigris and the Euphrates rivers empty into the Persian Gulf (Map **1.2**), Sumer enjoyed the rich soil that made possible agricultural life and the rise of urban culture. The Fertile Crescent formed by the two rivers, an area known as Mesopotamia—literally "land between the rivers"—was also, however, at the mercy of these rivers. They overflowed unpredictably, often devastating whole villages. Sumer consisted of a loosely knit group of city-states, that is, urban centers that governed the neighboring countryside. Because Sumer was the home of our earliest bronze technology, the first wheeled vehicles, and the cuneiform script used for the first written records, one might say that history began at Sumer.

In the individual city-states of Sumer, priest-kings ruled as agents of the gods. They led the army, regulated the supply and distribution of food, and provided political and religious leadership. However, the city-states were disunited and generally rivalrous, and thus vulnerable to invasion from tribal nomads who greedily threatened Sumer from the mountainous regions to the north of the Fertile Crescent.

Around 2350 B.C.E., the warrior Sargon of Akkad (Figure **1.14**) conquered the Sumerian city-states, uniting them under his command. But by 2000 B.C.E., Sargon's empire had fallen in turn to the attacks of a new group of invaders, who—establishing a pattern that dominated Mesopotamian history for three thousand years—would build a new civilization on the soil and the achievements of the very lands they conquered.

Myths, Gods, and Goddesses

Like their prehistoric ancestors, the people of Mesopotamia lived in intimate association with nature. They looked upon the forces of nature—sun, wind, and rain—as vital and alive, indeed, as inhabited by living spirits—a belief known as **animism**. Just as they devised tools to manipulate the natural environment, so they devised strategies by which to explain and control that environment. Myths—that is, stories that describe the workings of nature—were part of the ritual fabric of everyday life. In legends and myths, the living spirits of nature assumed human (and heroic) status: Deities of the wind and storm, sun and moon might be vengeful or beneficent, ugly or beautiful, fickle or reliable. Ultimately, they became a family of superhumans—gods and goddesses who very much resembled humans in their physical features and personalities, but whose superior strength and intelligence far exceeded that of human beings. The gods were also immortal, which made them the envy of ordinary human beings. Ritual sacrifice, prayer, and the enactment of myths honoring one or more of the gods accompanied seasonal celebrations, rites of passage, and almost every other significant communal event. In the early history of civilization, goddesses seem to have outnumbered

Figure 1.14 (above) Head of the Akkadian ruler Sargon I, from Nineveh, Iraq, ca. 2350 B.C.E. Bronze, height 12 in. Iraq Museum, Baghdad. Some scholars identify this portrait as Sargon's grandson. As with most ancient figural sculptures, the eyes, which once contained precious or semiprecious gemstones, were vandalized by thieves or destroyed by the ruler's enemies. The finely detailed bronze image remains, however, a landmark example of the **lost-wax** method of metal-casting, which originated in Mesopotamia.

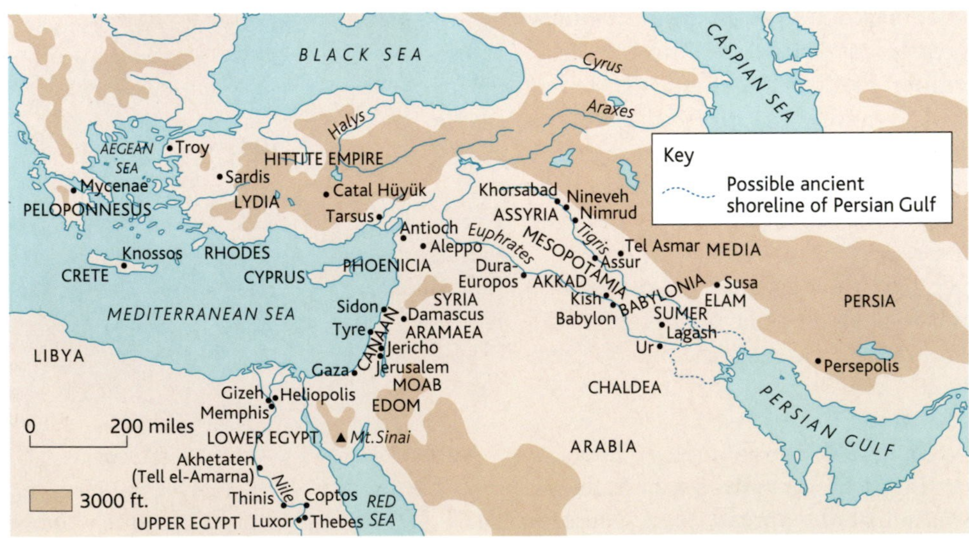

Map 1.2 (right) Southwest Asia (Near and Middle East).

Figure 1.15 Statuettes from the Abu Temple, Tell Asmar, Iraq, ca. 2900–2600 B.C.E. Marble, tallest figure ca. 30 in. Iraq Museum, Baghdad, and the Oriental Institute, University of Chicago. The enlarged eyes, inlaid with shell and black limestone, convey the impression of dread and awe—visual testimony to the sense of human apprehension in the face of divine power.

gods, and local deities reigned supreme within their own districts.

Mesopotamian **polytheism** (belief in many gods) was closely linked to nature and its forces. Much like the environment of the Fertile Crescent, its gods were fierce and capricious and its mythology filled with physical and spiritual woe, reflecting a **cosmology** (a view of the origin and structure of the universe) of chaos and conflict. *The Babylonian Creation*, humankind's earliest cosmological myth, illustrates all of these conditions. A Sumerian poem recited during the festival of the New Year, *The Babylonian Creation* celebrates the birth of the gods and the order of creation.

***The Babylonian Creation* (ca. early second millennium B.C.E.)**

It describes a universe that originated by means of spontaneous generation: At a moment when there was neither heaven nor earth, the sweet and bitter waters "mingled" to produce the first family of gods. As the story unfolds, chaos and discord prevail amid the reign of Tiamat, the Great Mother of the primeval waters, until Marduk, hero-god and offspring of Wisdom, takes matters in hand. He destroys the Great Mother and proceeds to establish a new order, bringing to an end the long and ancient tradition of matriarchy:

> Then Marduk made a bow and strung it to be his own weapon, he set the arrow against the bow-string, in his right hand he grasped the mace and lifted it up, bow and quiver hung at his side, lightnings played in front of him, he was altogether an incandescence.
>
> He netted a net, a snare for Tiamat; the winds from their quarters held it, south wind, north, east wind, west, and no part of Tiamat could escape. . . .
>
> He turned back to where Tiamat lay bound, he straddled the legs and smashed her skull (for the mace was merciless), he severed the arteries and the blood streamed down the north wind to the unknown ends of the world.
>
> When the gods saw all this they laughed out loud, and they sent him presents. They sent him their thankful tributes.
>
> The lord rested; he gazed at the huge body, pondering how to use it, what to create from the dead carcass. He split it apart like a cockle-shell; with the upper half he constructed the arc of sky, he pulled down the bar and set a watch on the waters, so they should never escape. . . .

Finally, Marduk founds the holy city of Babylon (literally, "home of the gods") and creates human beings, whose purpose it is to serve heaven's squabbling divinities.

Mesopotamia's Ziggurats

The **ziggurat**, a massive terraced tower made of rubble and brick, was the spiritual center of the Mesopotamian city-state. Serving as both a shrine and a temple (and possibly also a funerary site), it symbolized the sacred mountain that linked heaven and earth (see Figure 1.16). Ascended by a steep stairway, it provided a platform for sanctuaries dedicated to the local deities honored by priests and priestesses.

Shrine rooms located some 250 feet atop the ziggurat stored clay tablets inscribed with cuneiform records of the city's economic activities, its religious customs, and its rites. The shrine room of the ziggurat at Tell Asmar in Sumer also housed a remarkable group of statues representing men and women of various sizes, with large, staring eyes and hands clasped across their chests (Figure **1.15**). Carved out of soft stone, these cult images may represent the gods, but it is more likely that they are votive (devotional) figures that represent the townspeople of Tell Asmar in the act of worshipping their local deities. The larger figures may be priests, and the smaller figures, laypersons. Rigid and attentive, they stand as if in perpetual prayer.

Gilgamesh: The First Epic

Mesopotamia produced the world's first literary **epic**: the *Epic of Gilgamesh*. An epic is a long, narrative poem that recounts the deeds of a hero, one who undertakes some great quest or mission. Epics are usually tales of adventure that reflect the ideas and values of the community in which they originate. The *Epic of Gilgamesh* was recited orally for centuries before it was written down at Sumer in the late third millennium B.C.E. As literature, it precedes the Hebrew Bible and all the other major writings of antiquity. Its hero is a semihistorical figure who

***Epic of Gilgamesh* (ca. 2300 B.C.E.)**

probably ruled the ancient Sumerian city of Uruk around 2800 B.C.E. Described as two-thirds god and one-third man, Gilgamesh is blessed by the gods with beauty and courage. But when he spurns the affections of the Queen of Heaven, Ishtar (a fertility goddess not unlike the Egyptian Isis), he is punished with the loss of his dearest companion, Enkidu. Despairing over Enkidu's death, Gilgamesh undertakes a long and hazardous quest in search of everlasting life. Among his numerous adventures is his encounter with Utnapishtim, a mortal who (like Noah of the Hebrew Bible) saved humankind from a great and devastating flood. As his reward for this deed, the gods have granted Utnapishtim eternal life. Gilgamesh begs him to disclose the secret of life everlasting:

> "Oh, father Utnapishtim, you who have entered the assembly of the gods, I wish to question you concerning the living and the dead, how shall I find the life for which I am searching?"
>
> Utnapishtim said, "There is no permanence. Do we build a house to stand for ever, do we seal a contract to hold for all time? Do brothers divide an inheritance to keep for ever, does the flood-time of rivers endure? It is only the nymph of the dragon-fly who sheds her larva and sees the sun in his glory. From the days of old there is no permanence. The sleeping and the dead, how alike they are, they are like a painted death. What is there between the master and the servant when both have fulfilled their doom?"

The *Epic of Gilgamesh* is important not only as the world's first epic poem, but also as the earliest known literary work that tries to come to terms with death, or nonbeing. It reflects the profound human need for an immortality ideology—a body of beliefs that anticipates the survival of some aspect of the self in a life hereafter. Lamenting the brevity of life, Utnapishtim teaches Gilgamesh that all classes of people—the master and the servant—are equal in death. However, he generously guides Gilgamesh to the plant that miraculously restores lost youth. Although Gilgamesh retrieves the plant, he guards it poorly: while he sleeps, it is snatched by a serpent (a creature whose capacity for shedding its skin made it an ancient symbol of rebirth). Gilgamesh is left with the haunting vision of death as "a house of dust," and a destiny of inescapable sadness. The mythic hero has discovered his human limits, but he has failed to secure everlasting life.

Babylon: Hammurabi's Law Code

Shortly after 2000 B.C.E., rulers of the city-state of Babylon unified the neighboring territories of Sumer to establish the first Babylonian empire. In an effort to unite these regions politically and provide them with effective leadership, Babylon's sixth ruler, Hammurabi, called for a systematic codification of existing legal practices. He sent out

Making Connections

TEMPLE TOWERS

There are striking similarities between the mud-brick ziggurats of Mesopotamia (Figure **1.16**) and the stepped platform pyramids of the ancient Americas (Figure **1.17**). Erected atop rubble mounds, the temples of the Americas functioned as solar observatories, religious sanctuaries, and grave sites. Whether or not any historical link exists between the temple towers of these remote cultures remains among the many mysteries of ancient history.

Figure 1.16 (above) Ziggurat at Ur (partially reconstructed), third dynasty of Ur, Iraq, ca. 2150–2050 B.C.E. Base 210 x 150 ft., height ca. 100 ft.

Figure 1.17 Pyramid of the Sun, Teotihuacán, Mexico, begun before 150 C.E. Length of each side of base 768 ft., height 210 ft.

Q How do these structures compare in function and size?

envoys to collect the local statutes and had them consolidated into a single body of law. Hammurabi's Code—a collection of 282 clauses engraved on a 7-foot-high stele—is our most valuable index to life in ancient Mesopotamia (Figure **1.18**). The Code is not the first example of recorded law among the Babylonian rulers; it is, however, the most extensive and comprehensive set of laws to survive from ancient times. Although Hammurabi's Code addressed primarily secular matters, it bore the force of divine decree. This fact is indicated in the prologue to the Code, where Hammurabi claims descent from the gods.

Hammurabi's Code (ca. 1750 B.C.E.)

Written law represents a landmark advance in the development of human rights in that it protected the individual from the capricious decisions of monarchs. Unwritten law was subject to the hazards of memory and the eccentricities of the powerful. Written law, on the other hand, permitted a more impersonal (if more objective and impartial) kind of justice than did oral law. It replaced the flexibility of the spoken word with the rigidity of the written word. It did not usually recognize exceptions and was not easily or quickly changed. Ultimately, recorded law shifted the burden of judgment from the individual ruler to the legal establishment. Although written law necessarily restricted individual freedom, it safeguarded the basic values of the community.

Ideas and Issues

FROM HAMMURABI'S CODE

"**134** If a man has been taken prisoner, and there is no food in his house, and his wife enters the house of another; then that woman bears no blame.

138 If a man divorces his spouse who has not borne him children, he shall give to her all the silver of the bride-price, and restore to her the dowry which she brought from the house of her father; and so he shall divorce her.

141 If a man's wife, dwelling in a man's house, has set her face to leave, has been guilty of dissipation, has wasted her house, and has neglected her husband; then she shall be prosecuted. If her husband says she is divorced, he shall let her go her way; he shall give her nothing for divorce. If her husband says she is not divorced, her husband may espouse another woman, and that woman shall remain a slave in the house of her husband.

142 If a woman hate her husband, and says 'Thou shalt not possess me,' the reason for her dislike shall be inquired into. If she is careful and has no fault, but her husband takes himself away and neglects her; then that woman is not to blame. She shall take her dowry and go back to her father's house.

196 If a man has destroyed the eye of a free man, his own eye shall be destroyed.

198 If he has destroyed the eye of a plebeian, or broken the bone of a plebeian, he shall pay one mina of silver [approximately one pound of silver].

199 If he has destroyed the eye of a man's slave, or broken the bone of a man's slave, he shall pay half his value."

Q What limits to human equality are suggested in these laws?
Q How would you evaluate the rights of women?

Figure 1.18 Stele of Hammurabi, first Babylonian dynasty, ca. 1750 B.C.E. Basalt, entire stele 88½ x 25½ in. Louvre, Paris. At the top of this stele, carved in low **relief**, is the image of the sun god Shamash (right). Wearing a conical crown topped with bull's horns, and discharging flames from his shoulders, Shamash is enthroned atop a sacred mountain, symbolized by triangular markings beneath his feet. Like Moses atop Mount Sinai, Hammurabi (left) receives the law—here in the form of a staff—from the supreme deity.

Hammurabi's Code covers a broad spectrum of moral, social, and commercial obligations. Its civil and criminal statutes specify penalties for murder, theft, incest, adultery, kidnapping, assault and battery, and many other crimes. More important for our understanding of ancient culture, it is a storehouse of information concerning the nature of class divisions, family relations, and human rights.

Under Babylonian law, individuals were not regarded as equals. Human worth was defined in terms of a person's wealth and status in society. Violence committed by one free person upon another was punished reciprocally (clause 196), but the same violence committed upon a lower-class individual drew considerably lighter punishment (clause 198), and penalties were reduced even further if the victim was a slave (clause 199). Slaves, whether captives of war or victims of debt, had no civil rights under law and enjoyed only the protection of the household to which they belonged.

In Babylonian society, women were considered intellectually and physically inferior to men and—much like slaves—were regarded as the personal property of the male head of the household. A woman went from her father's house to that of her husband, where she was expected to bear children (clause 138). Nevertheless, as indicated by the Code, women enjoyed considerable legal protection (see clauses 134, 138, 141, and 142); their value both as childbearers and housekeepers was clearly acknowledged.

Iron Technology

In the course of the second millennium B.C.E., all of Mesopotamia felt the effects of a new technology: Iron was introduced into Asia Minor (present-day Turkey) by the Hittites, tribal nomads who built an empire lasting until ca. 1200 B.C.E. Cheaper to produce and more durable than bronze, iron represented new, superior technology. In addition to their iron weapons, the Hittites made active use of horse-drawn war chariots, which provided increased speed and mobility in battle. The combination of war chariots and iron weapons gave the Hittites clear military superiority over all of Mesopotamia.

As iron technology spread slowly throughout the Near East, it transformed the ancient world. Iron tools contributed to increased agricultural production, which in turn supported an increased population. In the wake of the Iron Age, numerous small states and vast **empires** came to flower.

Landmarks of the Iron Age

Cheaper and stronger weapons also meant larger, more efficient armies. By the first millennium B.C.E., war was no longer the monopoly of the elite. Iron technology encouraged the rapid rise of large and powerful empires: Equipped with iron weapons, the Assyrians (ca. 750–600 B.C.E.; Figure **1.19**), the Chaldeans (ca. 600–540 B.C.E.), and the Persians (ca. 550–330 B.C.E.) followed one another in conquering vast portions of Mesopotamia.

Under the leadership of Nebuchadnezzar (ca. 634–562 B.C.E.), the Chaldeans (or Neo-Babylonians) rebuilt the ancient city of Babylon (see Map 1.2). A huge ziggurat commissioned by Nebuchadnezzar is believed to be the "Tower of Babel" referred to in the Hebrew Bible, while the Ishtar Gate, one of Babylon's eight monumental portals, spanned the north entrance route into the city (Figure **1.20**). Faced with deep blue glazed bricks and adorned with rows of dragons and bulls, it is history's earliest round **arch** employed on a colossal scale. The Chaldean empire would play a major role in the history of the Hebrew people (see page 94); however, all three of the iron-wielding empires grew in size and authority by imposing military control over territories outside their own natural boundaries—a practice known as *imperialism*.

While iron itself represents a landmark in the technology of the ancient world, each of the era's small states would generate lasting cultural innovations. By 1500 B.C.E., the Phoenicians—an energetic, seafaring people located on the Mediterranean Sea (see Map 1.2)—developed a nonpictographic alphabet of twenty-two signs, which, like Hebrew and Arabic, consisted only of consonants. Traveling widely as merchants, the Phoenicians spread this alphabetic script throughout the Mediterranean area.

In Asia Minor the successors of the Hittites—a people known as Lydians—began the practice of minting coins. Easier to trade than bars of gold or silver, coin currency facilitated commercial ventures. The third of the small states, the Hebrew, would leave the world an equally significant but more intangible landmark: a religious tradition founded on ethical monotheism (see page 92).

Figure 1.19 King Ashurnasirpal II Killing Lions, from Palace of King Ashurnasirpal II, Nimrud, ca. 883–859 B.C.E. Alabaster relief, 3 ft. 3 in. x 8 ft. 4 in. British Museum, London. The Assyrians were the most militant of the iron-wielding Mesopotamian empires. On the walls of their citadels at Nimrud and Nineveh, they carved low-relief depictions of hunting and war, two closely related subjects that displayed the ruler's courage and physical might. The lion, a traditional symbol of power, falls to the king in this splendid scene of combat.

Figure 1.20 Ishtar Gate (reconstructed), from Babylon, ca. 575 B.C.E. Glazed brick. Staatliche Museen, Berlin. The gate was dedicated to Ishtar, the Akkadian goddess of love, fertility, and war (see page 10); dragons and bulls were sacred to the god Marduk (see page 9).

The Persian Empire

Among the Mesopotamian empires that rose to power during the first millennium B.C.E., Persia (modern-day Iran) was the largest. Swallowing up the region's small states, it reached (at its height) from the shores of the Mediterranean to India's Indus valley (see Map 1.1). Its linguistic and ethnic diversity made it the first multicultural civilization of the ancient world. At the ceremonial center of Persepolis, the Persians built a huge palace of elaborately carved stone. Persian craftsmen brought to perfection the art of metalworking: their utensils and jewelry display some of the most intricate techniques of goldworking in the history of this medium.

Persia's powerful monarchs, aided by efficient administrators, oversaw a vast network of roads that aided in operating an imperial postal system. Across some 1600 miles of terrain, fresh horses (located at post stations 14 miles apart) carried couriers "unhindered by snow, or rain, or heat, or by the darkness of night," according to the Greek historian Herodotus, who (unwittingly) provided the motto for the United States Postal Service.

The Persians devised a monotheistic religion based on the teachings of the prophet Zoroaster (ca. 628–ca. 551 B.C.E.). Zoroaster saw the universe as the product of two warring forces: Good and Evil. The Good, associated with light and with a place of ultimate reward known as Paradise, opposed Evil and darkness, represented by a powerful satanic spirit. By their freedom to make choices, human beings took part in this cosmic struggle; their choices determined their fate at the end of time. Zoroastrian beliefs, including the anticipation of last judgment and resurrection, would come to influence the evolution of three great world religions: Judaism, Christianity, and Islam (see chapter 4).

AFRICA: ANCIENT EGYPT

ANCIENT Egyptian civilization emerged along the banks of the Nile River in northeast Africa. From the heart of Africa, the thin blue thread of the Nile flowed some 4000 miles to its fan-shaped delta at the Mediterranean Sea. Along this river, agricultural villages thrived, coming under the authority of a sole ruler around 3150 B.C.E. Surrounded by sea and desert, Egypt was relatively invulnerable to foreign invasion (Map **1.3**), a condition that lent

Map 1.3 Ancient Egypt.

Figure 1.21 Scene from a Funerary Papyrus, *Book of the Dead*. Height 11¾ in. The Metropolitan Museum of Art, New York. Princess Entiu-ny stands to the left of a set of scales on which Anubis, the jackal-headed god, weighs her heart against the figure of Truth, while Osiris, Lord of the Dead, judges from his throne. His wife, Isis, stands behind the princess.

stability to Egyptian history. Unlike Mesopotamia, home to many different civilizations, ancient Egypt enjoyed a fairly uniform religious, political, and cultural life that lasted for almost three thousand years. Its population shared a common language and a common world view.

In the hot, arid climate of northeast Africa, where ample sunlight made possible the cultivation of crops, the sun god held the place of honor. Variously called Amon, Re (Ra), or Aten, this god was considered greater than any other deity in the Egyptian pantheon. His cult dominated the polytheistic belief system of ancient Egypt for three millennia. Equally important to Egyptian life was the Nile, the world's longest river. Egypt, called by the Greek historian Herodotus "the gift of the Nile," depended on the annual overflow of the Nile, which left fertile layers of rich silt along its banks. The 365-day cycle of the river's inundation became the basis of the solar calendar. In the regularity of the sun's daily cycle and the Nile's annual deluge, ancient Egyptians found security and a deep sense of order. From the natural elements—the sun, the Nile, and the mountainless topography of North Africa—they conceived Egypt's cosmological myth, which described the earth as a flat platter floating on the waters of the underworld. According to Egyptian mythology, at the beginning of time the Nile's primordial waters brought forth a mound of silt, out of which emerged the self-generating sun god; from that god, the rest of Egypt's gods were born.

Ancient Egyptians viewed the sun's daily ascent in the east as symbolic of the god's "rebirth"; his daily resurrection signified the victory of the forces of day, light, purity, goodness, and life over those of night, darkness, ignorance, evil, and death. In the cyclical regularity of nature evidenced by the daily rising and setting of the sun, the ancient Egyptians perceived both the inevitability of death and the promise of birth.

Second only to the sun as the major natural force in Egyptian life was the Nile River. Ancient Egyptians identified the Nile with Osiris, ruler of the underworld and god of the dead. According to Egyptian myth, Osiris was slain by his evil brother, Set, who chopped his body into pieces and threw them into the Nile. But Osiris' loyal wife Isis, Queen of Heaven, gathered the fragments and restored Osiris to life. The union of Isis and the resurrected Osiris produced a son, Horus, who ultimately avenged his father by overthrowing Set and becoming ruler of Egypt. The Osiris myth vividly describes the idea of resurrection that was central to the ancient Egyptian belief system. Although the cult of the sun in his various aspects dominated the official religion of Egypt, local gods and goddesses—more than two thousand of them—made up the Egyptian pantheon. These deities, most of whom held multiple powers, played protective roles in the daily lives of the ancient Egyptians. The following invocation to Isis, however, found inscribed on a sculpture of the goddess, suggests her central role among the female deities of Egypt:

> Praise to you, Isis, the Great One
> God's Mother, Lady of Heaven,
> Mistress and Queen of the Gods.

A painted **papyrus** scroll called the *Book of the Dead*, a collection of funerary prayers (see page 93), illustrates the last judgment: The enthroned Osiris, god of the underworld (far right) and his wife Isis (far left) oversee the ceremony in which the heart of the deceased Princess Entiu-ny is weighed against the figure of Truth (Figure **1.21**). Having made her testimony, the princess watches as the jackal-headed god of death, Anubis, prepares her heart for the ordeal. "Grant thou," reads the prayer to Osiris, "that I may have my being among the living, and that I may sail up and down the river among those who are in thy following." If the heart is not "found true by trial of the Great Balance," it will be devoured by the monster, Ament, thus meeting a second death. If pure, it might sail with the sun "up and down the river," or flourish in a realm where wheat grows high and the living souls of the dead enjoy feasting and singing.

Theocracy and the Cult of the Dead

From earliest times, political power was linked with spiritual power and superhuman might. The Egyptians held that divine power flowed from the gods to their royal agents. In this **theocracy** (rule by god or god's representative), the reigning **monarch**, called "pharaoh" (literally "great house"), represented heaven's will on earth.

Ancient Egyptians venerated the pharaoh as the living representative of the sun god. They believed that on his death, the pharaoh would join with the sun to govern Egypt eternally. His body was prepared for burial by means of a special, ten-week embalming procedure that involved removing all of his internal organs (with the exception of his heart) and filling his body cavity with preservatives. His intestines, stomach, lungs, and liver were all embalmed separately; the brain was removed and discarded. The king's corpse was then wrapped in fine linen and placed in an elaborately ornamented coffin, which was floated down the Nile on a royal barge to a burial site located at Gizeh, near the southern tip of the Nile delta (see Map 1.3). Guarding the entrance to the funerary complex at Gizeh was the Great Sphinx (see Figure 1.1), a recumbent creature bearing what scholars believe to be the portrait head of the Old Kingdom pharaoh Khafre (ca. 2600 B.C.E.) and the body of a lion, king of beasts. This hybrid symbol of superhuman power and authority

Making Connections

PYRAMIDS ANCIENT AND MODERN

The Great Pyramid of Khufu, which stands as part of a large walled burial complex at Gizeh (Figure **1.22**), consists of more than two million stone blocks rising to a height of approximately 480 feet and covering a base area of 13 acres. It inspired the Chinese-born architect I. M. Pei for his commission in the mid-1980s to provide a monumental entrance for the Louvre Museum in Paris. The angle of the slope of Pei's glass structure (Figure **1.23**) is almost identical to that of the Pyramid of Khufu.

Q How does the transposition of materials (from stone to glass) affect the visual impact of Pei's modern Pyramid?

Figure 1.22 (above) Great Pyramids of Gizeh: from left to right, Menkure, ca. 2575 B.C.E., Khufu (Khefren), ca. 2650 B.C.E., Khafre, ca. 2600 B.C.E.

Figure 1.23 I. M. Pei & Associates, Louvre Pyramid, Paris, 1988.

Figure 1.24 Egyptian cover of the Coffin of Tutankhamen (portion), from the Valley of the Kings, ca. 1323 B.C.E. Gold with inlay of enamel, carnelian, lapis lazuli, and turquoise. Egyptian Museum, Cairo. The body of Tutankhamen was enclosed in the innermost of three nested coffins. This innermost coffin, the most elaborate of the three, consisted of several hundred pounds of solid gold. Its surface is incised with hieroglyphic prayers and embellished with enamelwork and gemstones. Like Osiris in Figure 1.21, the pharaoh holds the traditional symbols of authority: the crook (a shepherd's staff signifying leadership) and the flail (a threshing instrument that doubles as a whip).

Facial reconstructions based on computer tomography (CT) scans of Tutenkhamen's remains undertaken in 2005 show indisputable similarities to the ancient portraits of the pharaoh, including that seen on this gold coffin. Modern science thus confirms that despite its abstract qualities, Egyptian art was grounded in keen observation of the natural world.

is antiquity's earliest and largest surviving colossal sculpture. It is carved from a single outcropping of sandstone left from quarrying the surrounding rock.

Khafre and other fourth-dynasty pharaohs built tombs in the shape of a pyramid representing the mound of silt from which the primordial sun god arose. Constructed between 2600 and 2500 B.C.E., the pyramids are technological wonders, as well as symbols of ancient Egypt's endurance through time (see Figure 1.22). A work force of some fifty thousand men (divided into gangs of twenty-five) labored almost thirty years to raise the Great Pyramid of Khufu. According to recent DNA analysis of the workers found buried at Gizeh, the pyramid builders were Egyptians, not foreign slaves, as was previously assumed. This native workforce quarried, transported, and assembled thousands of mammoth stone blocks, most weighing between 2 and 50 tons. These they lifted from tier to tier by means of levers—though some historians speculate they were slid into place on inclined ramps of sand and rubble. Finally, the laborers faced the surfaces of the great tombs with finely polished limestone. All of these feats were achieved with copper saws and chisels, and without pulleys or mortar.

The royal burial vault, hidden within a series of chambers connected to the exterior by tunnels, was prepared as a home for eternity—a tribute to communal faith in the eternal benevolence of the pharaoh. Its chambers were fitted with his most cherished possessions: priceless treasures of jewelry, weapons, and furniture, all of which he might require in the life to come. The chamber walls were painted in **fresco** and carved in relief with images recreating everyday life on earth (see Figure 1.26). Hieroglyphs formed an essential component of pictorial illustration, narrating the achievements of Egypt's rulers, listing the grave goods, offering perpetual prayers for the deceased and issuing curses against tomb robbers (see also Figure 1.10). Carved and painted figures carrying provisions—loaves of bread, fowl, beer, and fresh linens—accompanied the pharaoh to the afterlife. Additionally, death masks or "reserve" portrait heads of the pharaoh might be placed in the tomb to provide the king's *ka* (life force or soul) with safe and familiar dwelling places.

Intended primarily as homes for the dead, the pyramids were built to assure the ruler's comfort in the afterlife. However, in the centuries after their construction, grave robbers greedily despoiled them, and their contents were largely plundered and lost. Middle and Late Kingdom pharaohs turned to other methods of burial, including interment in the rock cliffs along the Nile and in unmarked graves in the Valley of the Kings west of Thebes. In time, these too were pillaged. One of the few royal graves to have escaped vandalism was that of a minor fourteenth-century-B.C.E. ruler named Tutankhamen (ca. 1341–1323 B.C.E.). Uncovered by the British archeologist Howard Carter in 1922, the tomb housed riches of astonishing variety, including the pharaoh's solid gold coffin, inlaid with semiprecious carnelian and lapis lazuli (Figure **1.24**).

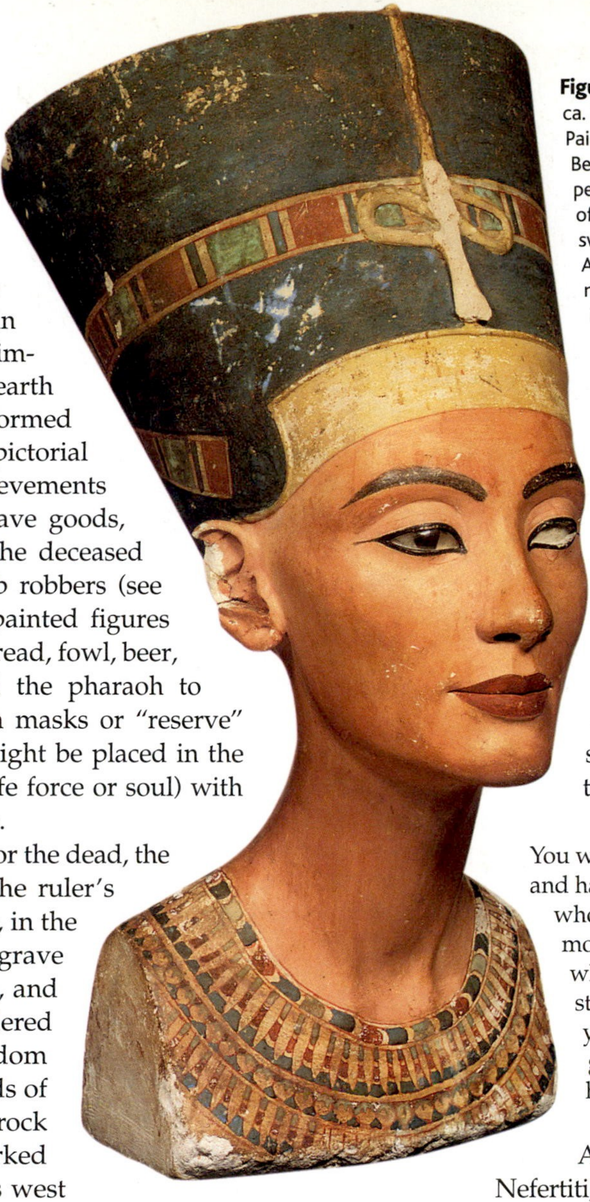

Akhenaten's Reform

Throughout the dynastic history of Egypt, the central authority of the pharaoh was repeatedly contested by local temple priests, all of whom held religious and political sway in their own regions along the Nile. Perhaps in an effort to consolidate his authority against such encroachments, the New Kingdom pharaoh Amenhotep IV (ca. 1385–1336 B.C.E.) defied the tradition of polytheism by elevating Aten (God of the Sun Disk) to a position of supremacy over all other gods. Changing his own name to Akhenaten ("Shining Spirit of Aten"), the pharaoh abandoned the political capital at Memphis and the religious center at Thebes to build a new palace midway between the two at a site at Tell el-Amarna on the east bank of the Nile. It was called Akhetaten ("Place of the Sun Disk's Power") (see Map 1.3). Akhenaten's famous "Hymn to the Aten," which drew on earlier Egyptian songs of praise, exalts the sun as the source of light and heat, and as the proactive life force:

> You who have placed seed in woman
> and have made sperm into man,
> who feeds the son in the womb of his mother,
> who quiets him with something to stop his crying;
> you are the nurse in the womb,
> giving breath to nourish all that has been begotten. . . .

Figure 1.25 Portrait of head of Queen Nefertiti, ca. 1355 B.C.E. New Kingdom, eighteenth dynasty. Painted limestone, height 20 in. State Museums, Berlin. This painted limestone portrait bust is perhaps the most famous icon in the history of Egyptian art. Nefertiti's conical crown and swanlike neck contribute to her regal elegance. At the same time, her half-closed eyes and musing smile convey a mood of contemplative introspection.

Akhenaten's chief wife, Queen Nefertiti, along with her mother-in-law, assisted in organizing the affairs of state. The mother of six daughters, Nefertiti is often pictured as Isis, the goddess from whom all Egyptian queens were said to have descended. The great number of portraits immortalizing the queen suggests either that she played a major role in the political life of her time or that she was regarded as an exceptional beauty. Some of these sculpted likenesses are striking in their blend of realism and abstraction (Figure **1.25**).

Akhenaten's **monotheistic** reform lasted only as long as his reign. In the years following his death, Egypt's conservative priests and rulers, including Akhenaten's successor, Tutankhamen, returned to the polytheism of their forebears.

Egyptian Women

Throughout their long history, ancient Egyptians viewed the land as sacred. It was owned by the gods, ruled by the pharaohs, and farmed by the peasants with the assistance of slaves. By divine decree, the fruits of each harvest were shared according to the needs of the community. This type of *theocratic socialism* provided Egypt with an abundance

Figure 1.26 Scene of Fowling, from the tomb of Neb-amon at Thebes, Egypt, ca. 1400 B.C.E. Fragment of a **fresco secco**, height 32¼ in. British Museum, London. Egyptian artists adhered to a set of guidelines by which they might "capture" the most characteristic and essential aspects of the subject matter: In depicting the human figure the upper torso is shown from the front, while the lower is shown from the side; the head is depicted in profile, while the eye and eyebrow are frontal. This method of representation is *conceptual*—that is, based on ideas—rather than *perceptual*—that is, based on visual evidence. In contrast with the human figures, however, the tawny cat, birds, fish, and tiger butterflies are based on close observation.

of food and a surplus that encouraged widespread trade. The land itself, however, passed from generation to generation not through the male line but through the female—that is, from the king's daughter to the man she married. For the pharaoh's son to come to the throne, he would have to marry his own sister or half-sister (hence the numerous brother–sister marriages in Egyptian dynastic history). This tradition, probably related to the practice of tracing parentage to the childbearer, lasted longer in Egypt than anywhere else in the ancient world.

Possibly because all property was inherited through the female line, Egyptian women seem to have enjoyed a large degree of economic independence, as well as civil rights and privileges. Women who could write and calculate might go into business. Women of the pharaoh's harem oversaw textile production, while others found positions as shopkeepers, midwives, musicians, and dancers.

While Egypt's rulers were traditionally male, women came to the throne three times. The most notable of all female pharaohs, Hatshepsut (ca. 1500–1447 B.C.E.), governed Egypt for twenty-two years. She is often pictured in male attire, wearing the royal wig and false beard, and carrying the crook and the flail—traditional symbols of rulership.

Egyptian Art

Egyptian art—at least that with which we are most familiar—comes almost exclusively from tombs and graves. Such art was not intended as decoration; rather, it was created to replicate the living world for the benefit of the dead and the lands they continued to protect.

Stylistically, Egyptian art mirrors the deep sense of order and regularity that dominated ancient Egyptian life. Over a period of three thousand years, Egyptian artists followed a set of stylistic conventions that dictated the manner in which subjects should be depicted. In representations of everyday life, figures are usually sized according to a strict hierarchy, or graded order: Upper-class individuals are shown larger than lower-class ones, and males usually outsize females and servants (Figure **1.26**).

The Egyptian painter's approach to space was also conceptual. Spatial depth is indicated by placing one figure above (rather than behind) the next, often in horizontal registers, or rows. Cast in this timeless matrix, Egyptian figures shared the symbolic resonance of the hieroglyphs by which they are framed. Nowhere else in the ancient world do we see such an intimate and intelligible conjunction of images and words—a union designed to immortalize ideas rather than imitate reality. This is not to say that Egyptian artists ignored the world of the senses. Their love for realistic detail is evident, for example, in the hunting scene from the tomb of Neb-amon at Thebes, where fish and fowl are depicted with such extraordinary accuracy that individual species of each can be identified (see Figure 1.26). It is in the union of the particular and the general that Egyptian art achieves its defining quality.

Some of ancient Egypt's most memorable artworks take the form of monumental sculpture. Carved from

EGYPT	MESOPOTAMIA
Early Dynastic (Dynasties I–II) ca. 3100–2700 B.C.E.	Early Dynastic (Sumerian) ca. 3500–2350 B.C.E.
Old Kingdom (Dynasties III–VI) ca. 2700–2150 B.C.E.	Sargon's Empire (Akkadian) ca. 2350–2230 B.C.E.
Middle Kingdom (Dynasties XI–XII) ca. 2050–1785 B.C.E.	Babylonian Empire ca. 2000–1600 B.C.E. Hammurabi rules ca. 1790–1750 B.C.E.
New Kingdom (Dynasties XVIII–XX) ca. 1575–1085 B.C.E. Akhenaten rules ca. 1353–1336 B.C.E.	Hittite Empire ca. 1450–1200 B.C.E.

Figure 1.27 Pair Statue of Mycerinus and Queen Kha-merer-nebty II, Gizeh, Mycerinus, fourth dynasty, ca. 2599–1571 B.C.E. Slate schist, height 4 ft. 6½ in. (complete statue). Museum of Fine Arts, Boston. In monumental sculptures of Egyptian royalty, the chief wife of the pharaoh is usually shown the same size as her husband.

stone or wood, these figures—usually portraits of Egypt's political and religious leaders—reflect a sensitive balance between gentle, lifelike **realism** and powerful stylization. In the freestanding sculpture of the Old Kingdom pharaoh Mycerinus, the queen stands proudly at his side, one arm around his waist and the other gently touching his arm (Figure **1.27**). A sense of shared purpose is conveyed by their lifted chins and confident demeanor.

New Kingdom Temples

Temples were built by the Egyptians from earliest times, but most of those that have survived date from the New Kingdom. The basic plan of the temple mirrored the central features of the Egyptian cosmos: The **pylons** (two truncated pyramids that made up the gateway) symbolized the mountains that rimmed the edge of the world, while the progress from the open courtyard through the **hypostyle** hall into the dark inner sanctuary housing the cult statue represented the voyage from light to darkness (and back) symbolic of the sun's cyclical journey. Oriented on an east–west axis, the temple received the sun's morning rays, which reached through the sequence of hallways into the sanctuary.

The Great Temple of Amon-Ra at Karnak was the heart of a 5-acre religious complex that included a sacred lake, a sphinx-lined causeway, and numerous **obelisks** (commemorative stone pillars). The temple's hypostyle hall is adorned with painted reliefs that cover the walls and the surfaces of its 134 massive columns shaped like budding and flowering papyrus—these plants were identified with the marsh of creation (Figure **1.28**). Decorated with stars and other celestial images, the ceiling of the

Figure 1.28 Hypostyle Hall, Great Temple of Amon-Ra, Karnak, ca. 1220 B.C.E.

hall symbolized the heavens. Such sacred precincts were not intended for communal assembly—in fact, commoners were forbidden to enter. Rather, Egyptian temples were sanctuaries in which priests performed daily rituals of cosmic renewal on behalf of the pharaoh and the people. Temple rituals were celebrations of the solar cycle, associated not only with the birth of the sun god but with the regeneration of the ruler upon whom universal order depended.

Literature and Music

Ancient Egypt did not produce any literary masterpieces. Nevertheless, from tomb and temple walls, and from papyrus rolls, come prayers and songs, royal decrees and letters, prose tales, and texts that served to educate the young. These offer valuable glimpses into everyday life. One school text, which reflects the fragile relationship between oral and written traditions, reads, "Man decays, his corpse is dust,/All his kin have perished;/But a book makes him remembered,/ Through the mouth of its reciter." The so-called "wisdom literature" of Egypt, which consists of advice and instruction, anticipates parts of the Hebrew Bible. As Egypt's empire expanded and its government grew in size, greater emphasis was placed on the importance of writing. The *Satire of Trades,* a standard exercise text for student scribes, argues that the life of a government clerk is preferable to that of a farmer, soldier, baker, metalworker, and even a priest: "Behold," it concludes, "there is no profession free of a boss—except for the scribe: he is the boss!"

From the New Kingdom came a very personal type of poetry defined as **lyric** (literally, accompanied by the **lyre** or harp). A lovesick Egyptian boy expresses his secret passion thus:

> I will lie down within
>   and feign to be ill, and then
> my neighbors will come to see.
>   My [mistress] will enter with them.
> She'll put the physicians to shame,
>   for she will understand
> that I am sick for love.

Throughout the history of ancient Egypt, song and poetry were interchangeable (hymns praising the gods were chanted, not spoken). Musical instruments, including harps, flutes, pipes, and sistrums (a type of rattle)—often found buried with the dead—accompanied song and dance. Greek sources indicate that Egyptian music was based in theory; nevertheless, we have no certain knowledge how that music actually sounded. Visual representations confirm, however, that music had a special place in religious rituals, in festive and funeral processions, and in many aspects of secular life. Such representations also confirm the importance of Egyptian women in musicmaking.

AFRICA: WESTERN SUDAN

The Nok Terracottas

While East Africa's ancient Egyptian civilization was known to the world as early as the eighteenth century, the western parts of the continent were not fully investigated by modern archeologists until the mid-twentieth century. In 1931, near a farming village called Nok, located along the Niger River in the western Sudan (see Map 1.3), tin miners accidentally uncovered a large group of **terracotta** sculptures (Figure **1.29**). Dating from the first millennium B.C.E., these hand-modeled animal figurines and portrait-like heads, possibly once joined to life-sized bodies, are the earliest known three-dimensional artworks of sub-Saharan Africa. They are true landmarks: the first evidence of the long tradition of realistic portraiture in African art (see page 244). The Nok heads, most of which display clearly individualized personalities, probably represent tribal rulers or ancestral chieftains.

Figure 1.29 Head, Nok culture, ca. 500 B.C.E.–200 C.E. Terracotta, height $14^{3}/_{16}$ in. National Museum, Lagos, Nigeria. Holes found in the hair designs of the Nok heads might once have held ornamental beads or feathers.

THE AMERICAS

Native cultures in the Americas had their beginnings at least twenty thousand years ago, when groups of nomads migrated from Asia across a land bridge that once linked Siberia and Alaska at the Bering Strait. Over a long period of time, many different peoples came to settle in North, South, and Meso- (or Middle) America—parts of present-day Mexico and Central America. The earliest populations formed a mosaic of migrant cultures (see Map 9.3). In the centuries prior to the late fifteenth century, when Europeans first made contact with the Americas, some one thousand agricultural societies and civilizations flourished.

Until recently, it was believed that the earliest civilization in the Americas dated from the middle of the second millennium B.C.E. However, in 2001, archeologists at Caral, a 150-acre complex near Lima, Peru, established a date of 2627 B.C.E. for the site's oldest artifacts; and in 2008, the ruins of yet another ancient Peruvian stone complex at Sechin Bajo were dated as early as ca. 3500 B.C.E. Located northwest of Lima, near the Pacific coast, these oldest known settlements in the Americas may be as old as (or older than) the Egyptian pyramids.

At Caral, six pyramids with stone and mud mortar walls, wide plazas, a sunken amphitheater, and numerous residences served an urban community with a population that probably exceeded three thousand (Figure **1.30**). The largest of the pyramids, the size of four football fields, boasts a wide staircase and is topped with shrine rooms. This type of stepped temple (compare Figures 1.17 and 9.15) prevailed for centuries in the civilizations of the Olmec, Maya, Aztec, and Inka peoples, the last of which flourished some three thousand years later in Peru. The remains of cotton nets at Caral indicate that fishing complemented native agricultural cultivation. Flutes made of bird bones and cornets created from deer and llama bones suggest a musical culture.

The dating of Caral raises many questions concerning the origins and development of ancient civilizations in the Americas. Capable of erecting mammoth temple structures, Caral's inhabitants must have reached a level of political and social complexity beyond that of the average Neolithic village. Yet, they had no draft animals, no wheeled vehicles, and no metal tools and weapons (although gold was worked as early as 2000 B.C.E., copper and bronze did not come into use in the Americas until the ninth century C.E.). There is no evidence of ceramics, nor of written records. Hence, while Caral may indeed be the birthplace of "New World" civilization, it differs dramatically from the first civilizations in Mesopotamia, Egypt, India, and China. Ongoing excavation at Caral (and nineteen nearby sites) will surely provide more information about this fascinating site.

Figure 1.30 Amphitheater, Caral, Peru, ca. 2627 B.C.E.

Around 1200 B.C.E., Meso-America was the site of one of the largest and most advanced cultures: that of the Olmecs. They were called "Olmecs" ("rubber people") by the Aztecs, who named the substance derived from the trees that flourished in their region. On the coast of the Gulf of Mexico south of the modern Mexican city of Veracruz, the Olmecs built ceremonial centers from which priestly rulers governed on behalf of the gods. The elite cadre of priests oversaw the spiritual life of the community—a population consisting of farmers and artisans at the lower end of the class structure and a ruling nobility at the upper end. Probably to honor their rulers, the Olmecs carved colossal stone heads weighing some 20 tons (Figure **1.31**). Producing massive sculptures and monumental pyramids required the labor of thousands and a high degree of civic organization. Olmec culture flourished until ca. 400 B.C.E., but their political, religious, and artistic traditions survived for centuries in the civilizations of the Maya and the Aztecs (see pages 251–252).

Figure 1.31 Colossal Olmec head, from San Lorenzo, Veracruz, Mexico, ca. 1000 B.C.E. Basalt, height 5 ft. 10⅞ in. Regional Museum of Veracruz, Jalapa, Mexico. The Olmecs paid homage to their rulers in the form of publicly displayed portraits. These heads are carved in basalt and are colossal in size, ranging in height from 5 to 12 feet and approximately 8 feet in diameter.

Beyond the West

ANCIENT INDIA

Indus Valley Civilization (ca. 2709–1500 B.C.E.)

India's earliest known civilization was located in the lower Indus valley of northwest India, an area called Sind—from which the words "India" and "Hindu" derive (Map **1.4**). At Mohenjo-daro and Harappa (both in modern-day Pakistan) , a sophisticated Bronze Age culture flourished before 2500 B.C.E. India's first cities were planned communities: Their streets, lined with fired-brick houses, were laid out in a grid pattern, and their covered sewage systems were unmatched in other parts of the civilized world. Bronze Age India also claimed a form of written language, although the four hundred pictographic signs that constitute their earliest script are still undeciphered. There is little evidence of temple or tomb architecture, but a vigorous sculptural tradition existed in both bronze and stone (Figure **1.32**).

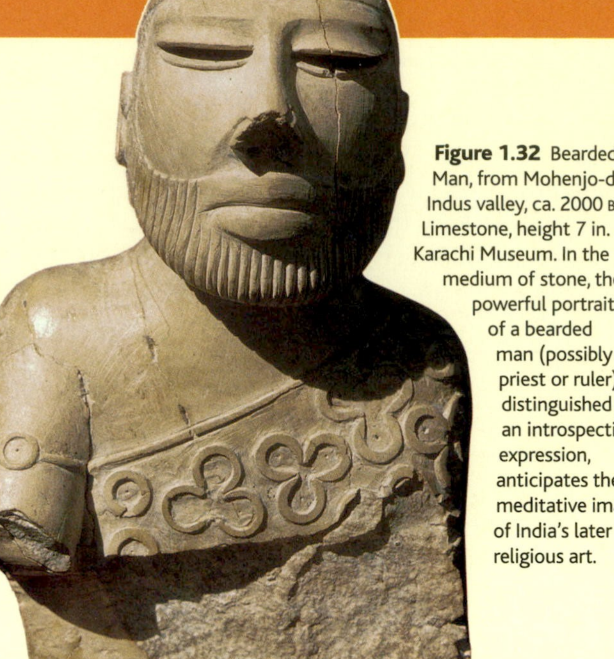

Figure 1.32 Bearded Man, from Mohenjo-daro, Indus valley, ca. 2000 B.C.E. Limestone, height 7 in. Karachi Museum. In the medium of stone, the powerful portrait of a bearded man (possibly a priest or ruler), distinguished by an introspective expression, anticipates the meditative images of India's later religious art.

The Vedic Era (ca. 1500–322 B.C.E.)

Between ca. 1700 and 1500 B.C.E. the decline of the Indus valley's urban centers coincided with a cultural transformation from which two major features emerged: the introduction of Sanskrit, the classic language of India; and a set of societal divisions known as the **caste system**. While a hierarchical order marked the social systems of all ancient civilizations, India developed the most rigid kind of class stratification, which prevailed until modern times. By 1000 B.C.E., there were four principal castes: priests and scholars, rulers and warriors, artisans and merchants, and unskilled workers. Slowly, these castes began to subdivide according to occupation. At the very bottom of the social order—or, more accurately, outside it—lay those who held the most menial and degrading occupations. They became known as Untouchables.

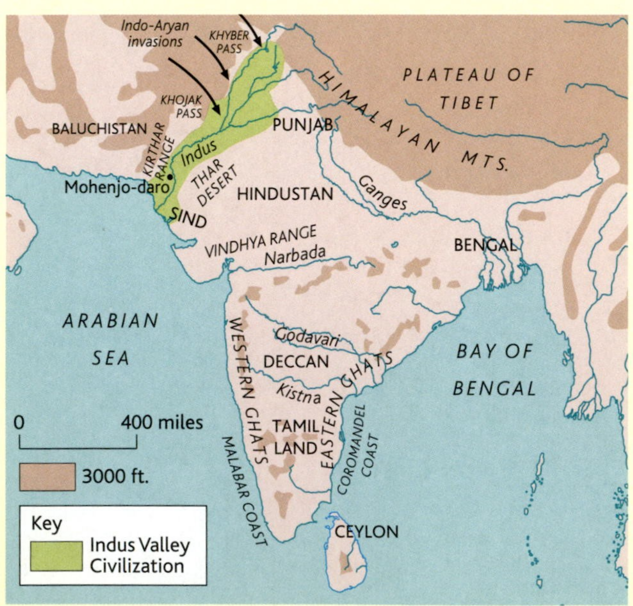

Map 1.4 Ancient India.

Writing in ancient Sanskrit, the bards of this era recorded stories of bitter tribal warfare. These stories were the basis for India's two great epics—the *Mahabharata* (*Great Deeds of the Bharata Clan*) and the *Ramayana* (*Song of Prince Rama*), transmitted orally for generations but not recorded until the eighth century B.C.E. The *Mahabharata*—the world's longest epic—recreates the ten-year-long struggle for control of the Ganges valley that occurred around the year 1000 B.C.E. Along with the *Ramayana*, this epic assumed a role in the cultural history of India not unlike that of the *Iliad* and the *Odyssey* in Hellenic history. Indeed, the two epics have been treasured resources for much of the poetry, drama, and art produced throughout India's long history.

India's oldest devotional texts, the *Vedas* (literally, "sacred knowledge"), also originate in (and give their name to) the thousand-year period after 1500 B.C.E. The *Vedas* are a collection of prayers, sacrificial formulae, and hymns. Transmitted orally for centuries, they reflect a blending of ancient traditions of the Indus valley. Among the chief Vedic deities were the sky gods Indra and Rudra (later known as Shiva), the fire god Agni, and the sun god Vishnu. The *Vedas* provide a wealth of information concerning astronomical phenomena. The study of the stars, along with the practice of surgery and dissection, mark the beginnings of scientific inquiry in India.

Vedas **(ca. 1500–1000 B.C.E.);**
Mahabharata **(*Great Deeds of the Bharata Clan*) (ca. 750 B.C.E.);**
Ramayana **(*Song of Prince Rama*) (ca. 750 B.C.E.)**

Ideas and Issues

THE OUT-OF-INDIA-DEBATE

Two theories dominate the explanation of India's early history: One holds that warlike seminomadic tribes known as "Aryans" (people belonging to the Indo-European language family) invaded the Indus valley around 1500 B.C.E., enslaving or removing the native population and initiating the extraordinary culture of the Vedic era. More recently, a group of scholars has offered evidence denying that such an invasion occurred; they argue that the Indo-Europeans were native to the Indian subcontinent. This second ("out-of-India") theory regards Indians as a single people descended from two ancient populations: Dravidian and Indo-European.

Citing environmental change as responsible for the decline of Indus Valley civilization, the new theory holds that Vedic beliefs and the Vedas themselves emerged in the Indus Valley prior to ca. 1500 B.C.E., when Sanskrit became the dominant language. It argues that the caste system grew out of tribal-like organizations and that India's great epics were the product of native tribal warfare. To date, the available evidence—archeological, linguistic, and genetic—is insufficient to fully resolve either explanation of India's origins; nevertheless, the subject remains hotly debated.

Hindu Pantheism

From the Indus valley civilization came the most ancient of today's world religions: Hinduism. Hinduism is markedly different from the religions of the West. It identifies the sacred not as a superhuman personality, but as an objective, all-pervading cosmic Spirit. **Pantheism**, the belief that divinity inheres in all things, is basic to the Hindu view that the universe itself is sacred. While neither polytheistic nor monotheistic in the traditional sense, Hinduism venerates all forms and manifestations of the all-pervasive Spirit. Hence, Hinduism embraces all the Vedic gods, who themselves take countless forms. Hindus believe in the oneness of Spirit, but worship that Spirit by way of a multitude of deities, who are perceived as emanations of the divine. In the words of the *Rig Veda*, "Truth is one, but the wise call it by many names."

Hinduism is best understood by way of the religious texts known as the *Upanishads*, some 250 prose commentaries on the *Vedas*. Like the *Vedas* themselves, the *Upanishads* were first orally transmitted and only later recorded in Sanskrit. While the *Vedas* teach worship through prayer and sacrifice, the *Upanishads* teach enlightenment through meditation. They predicate the concept of the single, all-pervading cosmic force called **Brahman**. Unlike the nature deities of Egypt and Mesopotamia, Brahman is infinite, formless, and ultimately unknowable. Unlike the Hebrew Yahweh (see page 92), Brahman assumes no personal and contractual relationship with humankind. Brahman is the Absolute Spirit, the Uncaused Cause, and the Ultimate Reality.

Upanishads (ca. eighth to sixth centuries B.C.E.)

In every human being, there resides the individual manifestation of Brahman: the Self, or **Atman**, which, according to the *Upanishads*, is "soundless, formless, intangible, undying, tasteless, odorless, without beginning, without end, eternal, immutable, [and] beyond nature." Although housed in the material prison of the human body, the Self (Atman) seeks to be one with the Absolute Spirit (Brahman). The (re)union of Brahman and Atman—a condition known as ***nirvana***—is the goal of the Hindu. This blissful reabsorption of the Self into Absolute Spirit must be preceded by one's gradual rejection of the material world, that is, the world of illusion and ignorance, and by the mastery of the techniques of meditation:

> By the purified mind alone is the indivisible Brahman to be attained. Brahman alone is—nothing else is. He who sees the manifold universe, and not the one reality, goes evermore from death to death.

Essentially a literature of humility, the *Upanishads* offer no guidelines for worship, no moral injunctions, and no religious dogma. They neither exalt divine power, nor do they interpret it. They do, however, instruct the individual Hindu on ***dharma*** (right conduct) and on the subject of death and rebirth. *Dharma* governs one's duties based on one's caste and station in life. The Hindu anticipates a succession of lives: that is, the successive return of the Atman in various physical forms. The physical form, whether animal or human and of whatever species or class, is determined by the level of spiritual purity that the Hindu has achieved by the time of his or her death. The Law of ***Karma*** holds that the collective spiritual energy gained from accumulated deeds determines one's physical state in the next life. Reincarnation, or the Wheel of Rebirth, is the fate of Hindus until they achieve *nirvana*. In this ultimate state, the enlightened Atman is both liberated from the endless cycle of death and rebirth and absorbed into the Absolute Spirit—a process that may be likened to the dissolution of a grain of salt in the vast waters of the ocean.

The fundamentals of Hinduism are issued in the sacred text known as the *Bhagavad-Gita* (*Song of God*). In this lengthy verse episode from the *Mahabharata*, a dialog takes place between the warrior-hero, Arjuna, and Krishna, the incarnation of the god Vishnu, himself a divine manifestation of Brahman. Facing the prospect of shedding his kinsmen's blood in the impending battle, Arjuna seeks to reconcile his duty as a soldier with his respect for life. Krishna's response—a classic statement of resignation, right conduct, and renunciation—represents the essence of Hindu thought as distilled from the *Upanishads*.

Bhagavad-Gita (_Song of God_) (ca. 500–100 B.C.E.)

ANCIENT CHINA

ANCIENT Chinese civilization emerged in the fertile valleys of two great waterways: the Yellow and the Yangzi rivers (Map **1.5**). As early as 3500 B.C.E., the Neolithic villages of China were producing silk, a commodity that would bring wealth and fame to Chinese culture, but the hallmarks of civilization—urban centers, metallurgy, and writing—did not appear until the second millennium B.C.E. By 1750 B.C.E., the Chinese had developed a calligraphic script (see Figure 1.12) that employed some 4500 characters (each character representing an individual word), some of which are still used today. Combining pictographic and phonetic elements, Chinese characters became the basis for writing throughout East Asia. It is likely that China's dynastic system was in place well before the appearance of writing. But not until the rise of the warrior tribe known as the Shang is there evidence of a fully developed urban civilization in Bronze Age China.

Map 1.5 Ancient China.

The Shang Dynasty (ca. 1520–1027 B.C.E.)

Shang rulers were hereditary kings who were regarded as intermediaries between the people and the spirit world. Limited in power by councils consisting of China's landholding nobility, they claimed their authority from the Lord on High (Shang-di). Hence, as in Egypt, they ruled by divine right. Royal authority was symbolized by the dragon, a hybrid beast that stood for strength, fertility, and life-giving water (Figure **1.33**). Occupants of the "dragon throne," China's early kings defended their position by way of a powerful bureaucracy and huge armies of archer-warriors recruited from the provinces. The king's soldiers consisted of peasants, who, in peacetime, farmed the land with the assistance of slaves captured in war. The Chinese social order is clearly articulated in Shang royal tombs, where the king is surrounded by the men and women who served him. Royal graves also include several hundred headless bodies, probably those of the slaves who built the tombs. As in Egypt and Mesopotamia, China's royal tombs were filled with treasures, most of which took the form of carved jade and magnificently worked bronze objects (Figure **1.34**; see also Figure 1.13).

Figure 1.33 Ritual disk, Zhou dynasty, fifth to third century B.C.E. Jade, diameter 6½ in. Nelson-Atkins Museum of Art, Kansas City, Missouri. Beginning in Neolithic times and throughout ancient Chinese history, large numbers of jade objects—especially jade disks—were placed in royal graves. The meaning and function of these objects is a matter of some speculation. The Chinese used jade for tools, but also for carved insignias and talismans probably related to ceremonial ritual. As well as for its durability, jade was prized by the Chinese for its musical qualities, its subtle, translucent colors, and its alleged protective powers—it was thought to prevent fatigue and delay the decomposition of the body.

The Aristocracy of Merit

From ancient China comes our earliest evidence of an aristocracy of merit, that is, leadership based on the principle of excellence, tied directly to a system of education and testing. Since order governs all of nature,

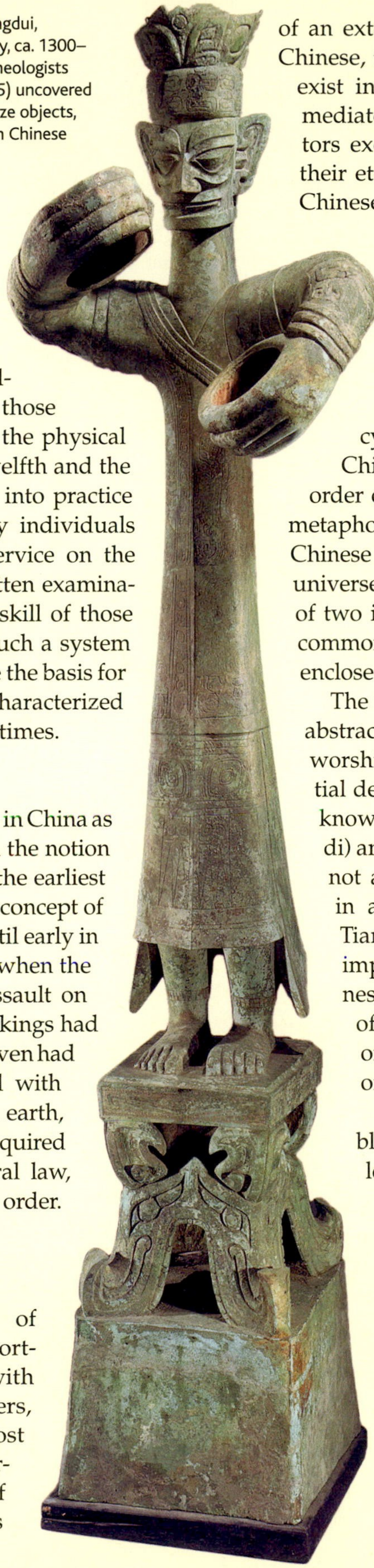

Figure 1.34 Standing figure, from Pit 2, Sanxingdui, Guanghan, Sichuan Province, late Shang dynasty, ca. 1300–1100 B.C.E. Bronze, height 8 ft. 7 in. In 1986, archeologists working in the Upper Yangzi region (see Map 1.5) uncovered graves containing more than two hundred bronze objects, including the earliest life-sized human figures in Chinese art. Whether these are votive images (compare Figure 1.15), representations of mythological characters, or surrogate royal servants remains unanswered; however, these finds suggest that the early history of China is still largely hidden from us.

argued the Chinese, it must also govern human intelligence and ability. Those with greater abilities, then, should govern, while those with lesser abilities should fulfill the physical needs of the state. Between the twelfth and the eighth centuries B.C.E., China put into practice the world's first system whereby individuals were selected for government service on the basis of merit and education. Written examinations tested the competence and skill of those who sought government office. Such a system persisted for centuries and became the basis for an aristocracy of merit that has characterized Chinese culture well into modern times.

The Mandate of Heaven

The sacred right to rule was known in China as the Mandate of Heaven. Although the notion of divine-right kingship began in the earliest centuries of China's dynasties, the concept of a divine mandate was not fixed until early in the Zhou era (ca. 1027–256 B.C.E.), when the rebel Zhou tribe justified their assault on the Shang by claiming that Shang kings had failed to rule virtuously; hence, heaven had withdrawn its mandate. Charged with maintaining the will of heaven on earth, the king's political authority required obedience to pre-established moral law, which in turn reflected the natural order.

Spirits, Gods, and the Natural Order

The agricultural communities of ancient China venerated an assortment of local spirits associated with natural forces, and with rivers, mountains, and crops. But the most powerful of the personalized spirits of ancient China were those of deceased ancestors, the members of an extended familial community. According to the Chinese, the spirits of deceased ancestors continued to exist in heaven, where they assumed their role as mediators between heaven and earth. Since the ancestors exerted a direct influence upon human affairs, their eternal welfare was of deep concern to ancient Chinese families. They buried the dead in elaborate tombs, regularly made sacrifices to them, and brought offerings of food and wine to their graves.

The dead and the living shared a cosmos animated by spirits and regulated by the natural order—a holistic and primordial arrangement. In the regularity of the seasonal cycle and the everyday workings of nature, the Chinese found harmony and order. Signifying the order of nature most graphically is the cosmological metaphor of the *yin/yang*. This principle, which ancient Chinese emperors called "the foundation of the entire universe," interprets all nature as the dynamic product of two interacting cosmic forces, or modes of energy, commonly configured as twin interpenetrating shapes enclosed within a circle (Figure **1.35**).

The natural order might be symbolized by way of abstract symbols, such as the circle, but it was also worshipped in the form of nature spirits and celestial deities. The creative principle, for instance, was known interchangeably as the Lord on High (Shang-di) and, more abstractly, as heaven (Tian). Although not an anthropomorphic deity of the kind found in ancient Egypt and Mesopotamia, Shang-di/Tian regulated the workings of the universe and impartially guided the destinies of all people. Chinese mythology described cosmic unity in terms of the marriage of Tian (the creative principle, or heaven) and Kun (the receptive principle, or earth).

The ancient Chinese perception of an inviolable natural order dominated all aspects of China's long and productive history. Unlike the civilizations of Egypt and Mesopotamia, China left no mythological tales or heroic epics. Rather, China's oldest text, the *I jing* (*The Book of Changes*), is a directory for interpreting the operations of the universe. *The Book of Changes*, which originated in the Shang era but was not recorded until the sixth century B.C.E. (see page 43), consists of cryptic symbols and commentaries on which diviners drew to predict the future. Order derived

***I jing* (*The Book of Changes*) (ca. 1000–500 B.C.E.)**

Beyond the West

Figure 1.35 The yin and the yang as interpenetrating shapes in a circle. The interaction of yang, the male principle (associated with lightness, hardness, brightness, warmth, and the sun) and yin, the female principle (associated with darkness, softness, moisture, coolness, the earth, and the moon) describes the creative energy of the universe and the natural order itself.

from the balance between the four seasons, the five elements (wood, fire, earth, metal, and water), and the five powers of creation (cold, heat, dryness, moisture, and wind). For the Chinese, the cosmic and human order was a single sacred system. This holistic viewpoint identified ***qi*** (pronounced "chee") as the substance of the universe and, thus, the vital energy that pervades the human body.

Daoism: The Philosophy of the Way

The most profound expression of the natural order is the ancient Chinese practice known as Daoism. As much a philosophy as a religion, Daoism embraces a universal natural principle: the Dao, or Way. Daoism resists all intellectual analysis. It manifests itself in the harmony of things and may be understood as the unity underlying nature's multiplicity and the wellspring of yin and yang. Only those who live in total simplicity, in harmony with nature, can be one with the Dao. Daoists seek to cultivate tranquility, spontaneity, compassion, and spiritual insight. They practice meditation and breath control and observe special life-prolonging dietary regulations. While Daoism has its roots in Chinese folk religion, no one knows where or when it originated. The basic Daoist text is the *Dao de jing* (*The Way and Its Power*). This five-thousand-word "scripture" associated with the name Lao Zi ("the Old One") is a landmark work that has influenced every aspect of Chinese culture.

Dao de jing
(*The Way and Its Power*)
(ca. mid-sixth century B.C.E.)

The following excerpt from the *Dao de jing* illustrates the unity of thing and nothing that typifies the Way:

Thirty spokes will converge
In the hub of a wheel;
But the use of the cart
Will depend on the part
Of the hub that is void.
With a wall all around
A clay bowl is molded;
But the use of the bowl
Will depend on the part
Of the bowl that is void.
Cut out windows and doors
In the house as you build;
But the use of the house
Will depend on the space
In the walls that is void.
So advantage is had
From whatever is there;
But usefulness rises
From whatever is not.

Afterword

Civilization emerged not in a fleeting moment of change, but in a slow process of urban growth and by the operation of an increasingly refined intelligence. By dint of individual ingenuity and communal cooperation, the peoples of ancient Mesopotamia, Africa, the Americas, India, and China generated a cultural heritage whose traditions would be passed from generation to generation. The landmarks of these cultures—from writing to metallurgy, from epic poetry to codes of conduct, and from lavish tombs to the temples and palaces of empires—provided the foundations for future civilizations, including and most immediately, those of Classical antiquity.

Key Topics

- prehistory
- Paleolithic/Neolithic cultures
- the birth of civilization
- counting/writing
- animism
- polytheism/monotheism/pantheism
- Mesopotamia: the literary epic
- Hammurabi: written law
- Egyptian theocracy
- Old Kingdom tombs
- Egyptian women
- perceptual/conceptual art
- lyric poetry
- New Kingdom temples
- India: Hinduism
- reincarnation
- China: the Mandate of Heaven
- Daoism

THE FIRST CIVILIZATIONS TIMELINE

	HISTORICAL EVENTS: MESOPOTAMIA	HISTORICAL EVENTS: AFRICA	HISTORICAL EVENTS: ASIA AND THE AMERICAS	LANDMARKS IN THE VISUAL ARTS	LITERARY LANDMARKS
25,000 B.C.E.				• "Venus" of Willendorf (ca. 25,000–20,000) • Lascaux cave paintings (ca. 15,000–10,000)	
4000 B.C.E.	• Bronze metallurgy (ca. 4000) • Sumerian civilization (ca. 3500–2350) • Akkadian civilization (ca. 2350–2230) **Figure 1.18** Stele of Hammurabi, see p. 11	• Predynastic Nile valley civilization (ca. 3500–3150) • Unification of Egypt (ca. 3150) • Egypt: Old Kingdom (ca. 2700–2150) **Figure 1.22** Great Pyramids of Gizeh, see p. 15	• Yellow River valley civilization (ca. 3500–1520) • Indus valley civilization (ca. 2700–1500) • Caral, Peru (ca. 2600)	• Stonehenge (ca. 3000–1800) **Figure 1.8** Stonehenge, see p. 5 • Pyramids, Gizeh (ca. 2650–2575) • Mycerinus and queen (ca. 2599–1571) • Head of Sargon I (ca. 2350) • Ziggurat at Ur (ca. 2150–2050)	• Egyptian *Book of the Dead* (from 4000) • Invention of writing: pictographs (ca. 3100) • *Epic of Gilgamesh* (ca. 2300)
2000 B.C.E.	• Hittites introduce iron to Asia Minor (ca. 2000) • Babylonian Empire (ca. 2000–1600)	• Egypt: Middle Kingdom (ca. 2050–1785)		• Bearded man, from Mohenjo-daro (ca. 2000) • Stele of Hammurabi (ca. 1750)	• *The Babylonian Creation* (ca. 2000) • Hammurabi's Code (ca. 1750)
1500 B.C.E.	• Hittite Empire (ca. 1450–1200)	• Egypt: New Kingdom (ca. 1575–1085)	• Shang era in China (ca. 1520–1027) • Vedic era in India (ca. 1500–322) • Olmec, Mexico (ca. 1200–400)	• Queen Nefertiti (ca. 1355) • Shang standing figure (ca. 1300–1100) • Great Temple of Amon-Ra, Karnak (ca. 1220)	• Phoenicians develop nonpictographic alphabet (ca. 1500) • *Vedas* (ca. 1500–1000)
1000 B.C.E.			• Zhou era in China (ca. 1027–256)	• Shang ceremonial vessel (ca. 1000) • Assyrian reliefs, from Nimrud (ca. 883–859)	• *I jing* (ca. 1000–500) • *Upanishads* (ca. 900–500)
750 B.C.E	• Assyrian Empire (ca. 750–600) • Chaldean Empire (ca. 600–540) • Persian Empire (ca. 550–330)			• Ishtar Gate (ca. 575)	• *Mahabharata* (ca. 750) • *Ramayana* (ca. 750) • *Dao de jing* (ca. 550)
500 B.C.E.		• Western Sudan: Nok culture (ca. 500–200)			

(All dates on this timeline are before the common era—B.C.E.)

Chapter 2

Classicism:

THE GREEK LEGACY

ca. 1200–30 B.C.E.

When we call something a "classic"—whether it be a car, a film, or a novel—we mean that it is recognized as first-ranking or the best of its kind. A classic outlives the time in which it was created and sets the standard for future achievement. The civilization of ancient Greece produced classics in almost all genres of creative expression: literature, philosophy, music, the visual arts, and architecture. These classics advanced the aesthetic principles of clarity, simplicity, balance, regularity, and harmonious proportion. As a style, Classicism is characterized by these aesthetic principles and by the related ideals of reason, moderation, and dignity.

The foundations of Classicism were laid during the Bronze Age in the maritime civilizations that flourished in and around the Aegean Sea, but it was not until the fifth century B.C.E. that the Greek city-state of Athens ushered in a Golden Age of artistic productivity. The Hellenic (Greek) phase of Classical creativity was followed by an era in which Alexander the Great spread the Classical style throughout much of the civilized world, a phase of antiquity known as Hellenistic (Greek-like). The Romans, in turn, preserved the Classical style, which continued to provide inspiration for recurring Neoclassical (new classical) revivals.

A First Look

Millions of tourists travel to Greece each year to see the Parthenon, the outstanding architectural landmark of Greek Classicism. Balance, regularity, and geometric simplicity—defining features of the Classical style—are united here in harmonious design. Overlooking Athens from the highest point of the citadel known as the Acropolis, the Parthenon served the people of ancient Athens as a sacred shrine, dedicated to Athena, the goddess of wisdom and war. It also functioned as a treasury and a civic meeting place. Unlike Egypt's pyramids and Mesopotamia's ziggurats, the Parthenon was constructed in gleaming marble, adorned with lifelike sculptures, and conceived according to human proportions (see pages 52–56). Despite its monumental grandeur, it does not impress us as awesome or colossal; rather, it reminds us of the churches and banks we find in our own towns and cities. This is no accident, since centuries of Western architects have taken this temple as a model of perfect design. Now a noble ruin, partially destroyed by warfare, pollution, and neglect, the Parthenon remains symbolic of Greek achievement, a landmark revered and imitated well into the present.

Figure 2.1 West end of the Parthenon, Athens, 447–432 B.C.E. Pentelic marble, height of columns 34 ft.

ANCIENT GREEK CIVILIZATION

THE nineteenth-century British poet Percy Bysshe Shelley once proclaimed, "We are all Greeks." By this he meant that modern humankind—profoundly influenced by Hellenic notions of reason, beauty, and the good life—bears the stamp of ancient Greece. Few civilizations have been so deeply concerned with the quality of human life as that of the ancient Greeks. And few have been so committed to the role of the individual intellect in shaping the destiny of the community. Because their art, their literature, and their religious beliefs celebrate human interests and concerns, the Greeks have been called the humanists of the ancient world. The worldliness and robust optimism that mark Hellenic culture are evident in landmark works that have endured the test of time.

Aegean Civilizations (ca. 3000–1200 B.C.E.)

The Bronze Age culture of Mycenae was not known to the world until the late nineteenth century, when an amateur German archeologist named Heinrich Schliemann uncovered the first artifacts of ancient Troy (see Map 2.1). Schliemann's excavations brought to light the civilization of an adventuresome tribal people, the Mycenaeans, who had established themselves on the Greek mainland around 1600 B.C.E. In the early twentieth century, the British archeologist Sir Arthur Evans found an even earlier pre-Greek civilization located on the island of Crete in the Aegean Sea. He called it "Minoan" after the legendary King Minos, celebrated in ancient Greek legend. This maritime civilization flourished between around 2000 and 1400 B.C.E., when it seems to have been absorbed or destroyed by the Mycenaeans.

Centered in the Palace of Minos at Knossos on the island of Crete (Figure **2.2**), Minoan culture was prosperous and seafaring. The absence of protective walls around the palace complex suggests that the Minoans enjoyed a sense of security. The three-story palace at Knossos was a labyrinthine masonry structure with dozens of rooms and corridors built around a central courtyard. The interior walls of the palace bear magnificent frescoes illustrating natural and marine motifs, ceremonial processions, and other aspects of Cretan life. The most famous of the palace frescoes, the so-called "bull-leaping" fresco, shows two women and a man, the latter vigorously somersaulting over the back of a bull (Figure **2.3**). Probably associated with the cult of the bull—ancient symbol of virility—the ritual game prefigures the modern bullfight, the "rules" of which were codified in Roman times by Julius Caesar. Minoan artifacts suggest the persistence of ancient fertility cults honoring gods traditionally associated with procreation. The small statue of a bare-breasted female

Figure 2.2 Palace of Minos, Knossos, Crete, ca. 1500 B.C.E.

Figure 2.3 (above) Bull-leaping fresco, from the Palace of Minos, Knossos, Crete, ca. 1500 B.C.E. Height 32 in. Archeological Museum, Heraklion, Crete. Since 1979, when modern archeologists uncovered the evidence of human sacrifice in Minoan Crete, historians have speculated on the meaning of ancient bull-vaulting (a sport still practiced in Portugal), and its possible relationship to rituals of blood sacrifice. Nevertheless, the significance of the representation lies in the authority it bestows upon the players: Human beings are pictured here not as pawns in a divine game, but, rather, as challengers in a contest of wit and physical agility.

brandishing snakes (ancient symbols of rebirth) may represent a popular fertility goddess; or it may depict a priestess performing specific cult rites (Figure **2.4**). Minoan writing (called by Evans "Linear A") has not yet been deciphered, but a later version of the script ("Linear B") found both at Knossos and on mainland Greece appears to be an early form of Greek.

Modern archeologists were not the first to prize Minoan culture; the Greeks immortalized the Minoans in myth and legend. The most famous of these legends describes a Minotaur—a monstrous half-man, half-bull hybrid born of the union of Minos' queen and a sacred white bull. According to the story, the clever Athenian hero Theseus, aided by the king's daughter Ariadne, threaded his way through the Minotaur's labyrinthine lair to kill the monster, thus freeing Athens from its ancient bondage to the Minoans. Around 1700 B.C.E., some three centuries before mainland Greece absorbed Crete, an earthquake brought devastation to Minoan civilization.

Mycenaean Civilization (ca. 1600–1200 B.C.E.)

By 1600 B.C.E., the Mycenaeans had established themselves in the Aegean. By contrast with the Minoans, the Mycenaeans were a militant and aggressive people: Their warships challenged other traders for control of the eastern Mediterranean. On mainland Greece at Tiryns and Mycenae (Map **2.1**), the Mycenaeans constructed heavily fortified citadels and walls so massive that later generations thought they had been built by a mythical race of giants known as the Cyclops. These "cyclopean" walls were guarded by symbols of royal power: In the triangular arch above the entrance gate to the citadel, two 9-foot-high stone lions flank a

Figure 2.4 Priestess with Snakes, Minoan, ca. 1600 B.C.E. **Faience**, height 13½ in. Archeological Museum, Heraklion, Crete. The head and the snake in the figure's left hand are modern fabrications. Recent scholarship questions the authenticity of this reconstruction. Nevertheless, many other Eastern Mediterranean artifacts of this era show females flanked by or holding snakes or animals.

Map 2.1 Ancient Greece.

column that rests on a Minoan-style altar (Figure **2.5**). Master stonemasons, the Mycenaeans buried their rulers in beehive-shaped tombs. The royal graves, uncovered by Schliemann in 1876, are filled with weapons and jewelry fit for an Egyptian pharaoh. These items, and in particular a gold death mask that once covered the face of the deceased, Schliemann mistakenly identified as belonging to Agamemnon (Figure **2.6**), the legendary king who led the ancient Greeks against the city of Troy. This tale is immortalized in the first of the Greek epic poems, the *Iliad*. Although later archeologists have proved Schliemann wrong—the tombs are actually some three hundred years earlier than he thought—the legends and the myths of the Greek world would flower in Mycenaean soil.

Around 1200 B.C.E., the Mycenaeans attacked Troy ("Ilion" in Greek), a commercial stronghold on the northwest coast of Asia Minor. The ten-year-long war between Mycenae and Troy would provide the historical context not only for the *Iliad*, but also for the second of the two great epic poems of the ancient Greeks: the *Odyssey*.

Figure 2.5 Lion Gate, Citadel at Mycenae, ca. 1500–1300 B.C.E. Limestone, height of relief 9 ft. 6 in. Huge, rough-cut blocks of stone were set in projecting layers to hold in place the triangular relief. The heads of the lions, carved separately, are missing.

Figure 2.6 Funerary mask, ca. 1500 B.C.E. Gold, height 12 in. National Archeological Museum, Athens. Death masks are frequently found in ancient graves going back to prehistory. Bound to the head of the mummified corpse, the mask was a kind of portrait that preserved the identity of the dead person in the afterlife.

The Heroic Age
(ca. 1200–750 B.C.E.)

Soon after 1200 B.C.E., more powerful, iron-bearing tribes of Dorians, a Greek-speaking people from the north, destroyed Mycenaean civilization. During the long period of political and social turmoil that followed, storytellers kept alive the history of early Greece, the adventures of the Mycenaeans, and the tales of the Trojan War, passing them orally from generation to generation. It was not until at least the ninth century B.C.E. that these stories were transcribed; and it was yet another three hundred years before they reached their present form. The *Iliad* and the *Odyssey* became the "national" poems of ancient Greece, uniting Greek-speaking people by giving literary authority to their common heritage. Although much of what is known about the early history of the Greeks comes from these landmark epics, little is known about the blind poet Homer, to whom they are traditionally attributed. Scholars are not sure when or where he lived, or, indeed, if he existed at all. It is unlikely that Homer actually composed the poems, though legend has it that he memorized the whole of each one. The only fact of which we can be fairly certain is that Homer represents the culmination of a long and vigorous tradition in which oral recitation—possibly to instrumental accompaniment—was a popular kind of entertainment.

The *Iliad* takes place in the last days of the Trojan War. It is the story of the Achaean (ancient Greek) hero Achilles (or Achilleus), who, moved to anger by an affront to his honor, refuses to join the battle against Troy alongside his Achaean comrades. Wearing Achilles' armor, the hero's dearest friend, Patroclus, routs the Trojans and slays many of their allies (Figure 2.7). Only after Patroclus is killed by Hector (leader of the Trojan forces) does Achilles finally and vengefully go to war. He confronts and kills Hector, stripping him of his armor and dragging his nude body before the walls of Troy. Hector's father, King Priam, is forced to humble himself before the victorious Achilles and request the return and proper burial of his son; the epic closes with Hector's funeral.

Homer, *Iliad* (ca. 850 B.C.E.)

The *Odyssey*, the second of the two epics, recounts the long, adventure-packed sea journey undertaken by Odysseus, the clever and resourceful hero of the Trojan War, in his effort to return to his home and family and reassume his authority as King of Ithaca. Like the *Epic of Gilgamesh*, the *Iliad* and the *Odyssey* belong to the dynamic history of a rugged young culture, but whereas the *Epic of*

Homer, *Odyssey* (ca. 850 B.C.E.)

Figure 2.7 Euphronios and Euxitheos, *Death of Sarpedon*, ca. 515 B.C.E. Ceramic krater with red figure decoration, height 18 in. Etruscan Museum, Villa Giulia, Rome. The legendary warrior and Trojan ally Sarpedon was killed by Patroclus in the course of the war. He is shown on this **krater** (a vessel used for mixing wine and water) being carried from the battlefield by the winged figures of Hypnos (Sleep) and Thanatos (Death). Central to the lyrically balanced composition is the figure of Hermes, messenger of the gods, who guides the dead to the underworld.

Gilgamesh takes as its theme the pursuit of everlasting life, the Greek epics deal with the quest for individual honor and glory.

Almost sixteen thousand lines long, the *Iliad* is a robust tale of war; but its true subject is Achilles, the offspring of Peleus, King of Thessaly, and the sea goddess Thetis. (Later legends report that his mother, having dipped her infant son in the River Styx, made him invulnerable except for the heel by which she held him.) Like Gilgamesh, Achilles is the personification of youthful bravery, a superhero who embodies the ideals of his people; but he is a more psychologically complex character than Gilgamesh. The emotions he exhibits—anger, love, rage, and grief—are wholly human. His pettiness ("the wrath of Achilles" cited in the first line of the *Iliad*) is balanced by his unflinching courage in battle. Like the poem itself, the hero brings to light the terrible blend of brutality and compassion that remains a universal constant of war. Achilles' humanity, his effort to reconcile personal pride and moral virtue is illustrated in the following lines from Book 24, in which Achilles, describing to King Priam the fate of humankind at the hands of the gods, reflects on his own failed obligations:

> Let us put our griefs to rest in our own hearts,
> rake them up no more, raw as we are with mourning.
> What good's to be won from tears that chill the spirit?
> So the immortals spun our lives that we, we wretched men
> live on to bear such torments—the gods live free of sorrows.
> There are two great jars that stand on the floor of Zeus' halls
> and hold his gifts, our miseries one, the other blessings.
> When Zeus who loves the lightning mixes gifts for a man,
> now he meets with misfortune, now good times in turn.
> When Zeus dispenses gifts from the jar of sorrows only,
> he makes a man an outcast—brutal, ravenous hunger
> drives him down the face of the shining earth,
> stalking far and wide, cursed by gods and men.
> So with my father, Peleus. What glittering gifts
> the gods rained down from the day that he was born!
> He excelled all men in wealth and pride of place,
> he lorded the Myrmidons,[1] and mortal that he was,
> they gave the man an immortal goddess for a wife.
> Yes, but even on him the Father piled hardships,
> no powerful race of princes born in his royal halls,
> only a single son he fathered, doomed at birth,
> cut off in the spring of life—
> and I, I give the man no care as he grows old
> since here I sit in Troy, far from my fatherland,
> a grief to you, a grief to all your children.
>
> (from the *Iliad*, Book 24, ll. 226–250)

The Greek Gods

The ancient Greeks envisioned their gods as a family of immortals who intervened in the lives of human beings. Originating in the cultures of Crete and Mycenae, the Greek pantheon exalted Zeus, the powerful sky god, and his wife, Hera, as the ruling deities. Among the lesser gods were Poseidon, god of the sea; Apollo, god of light, medicine, and music; Dionysus, god of wine and vegetation; Athena, goddess of wisdom and war; and Aphrodite, goddess of love, beauty, and procreation. Around these and other deities there emerged an elaborate mythology.

Many Greek myths look back to the common pool of legends and tales that traveled throughout the Mediterranean and the Near East. In the *Theogony* (*The Birth of the Gods*), a poem recounting the history and genealogy of the gods, Homer's contemporary Hesiod (fl. 700 B.C.E.) describes the origins of the universe and the birth of the gods.

Hesiod, *Theogony* (*The Birth of the Gods*) (ca. 700 B.C.E.)

The Greeks traced their origins to events related to the fury of Zeus: Angered by human evil, Zeus decided to destroy humankind by sending a flood. Deucalion, the Greek Noah, built a boat for himself and his wife and obeyed an oracle that commanded them to throw the "bones" of Mother Earth overboard. From these stones sprang up human beings, the first of whom was Hellen, the legendary ancestor of the Greeks, or "Hellenes."

The Greeks also had their own version of the Isis/Osiris myth. When Hades, god of the underworld, abducts the beautiful Persephone, her mother, Demeter, rescues her; tricked by Hades, however, this goddess of vegetation is forced to return annually to the underworld, leaving the earth above barren and desolate. Cults based in myths of death and rebirth offered their devotees the hope of personal regeneration. However, the promise of life after death did not hold a central place in Greek religious thought.

Although immortal, the Greek gods were much like the human beings who worshipped them: They were amorous, capricious, and quarrelsome. They lived not in some remote heaven, but (conveniently enough) atop a mountain in northern Greece—that is, among the Greeks themselves. From their home on Mount Olympus, the gods might take sides in human combat (as they regularly do in the *Iliad*), seduce mortal women, and meddle in the lives of ordinary people. The Greek gods were not always benevolent or just. They set forth no clear principles of moral conduct and no guidelines for religious worship. Popular Greek religion produced neither a sacred scripture nor any written doctrine—a circumstance that may have contributed to the freedom of intellectual inquiry for which the ancient Greeks became famous.

Priests and priestesses of local cults tended the temples and shrines and oversaw rituals, including human and animal sacrifice, performed to win divine favor. The most famous of the Hellenic shrines, the shrine of Apollo, was located at Delphi, a site the Greeks identified as the center of the universe and the "navel" of the earth. Here the priestess of Apollo sat on a tripod over a fissure in

[1] Warriors who followed Peleus and Achilles.

Making Connections

IN THE BEGINNING

The first excerpt is from Hesiod's *The Birth of the Gods*, a Greek poem composed ca. 700 B.C.E., while the second is from the first book of the Hebrew Bible (see p. 94).

"First of all, the Void came into being, next broad-bosomed Earth, the solid and eternal home of all, and Eros [Desire], the most beautiful of the immortal gods, who in every man and every god softens the sinews and overpowers the prudent purpose of the mind. Out of Void came Darkness and black Night, and out of Night came Light and Day, her children conceived after union in love with Darkness. Earth first produced starry Sky, equal in size with herself . . ."

(Book II, lines 116–123)

"[1]In the beginning God created the heavens and the earth. [2]The earth was without form and void, and darkness was upon the face of the deep; and the Spirit of God was moving over the face of the waters. [3]And God said, 'Let there be light'; and there was light. [4]And God saw that the light was good; and God separated the light from the darkness. [5]God called the light Day, and the darkness he called Night. And there was evening and there was morning, one day."

(Genesis 1:1–5)

Q What is the relationship between nature and divine agency in each of these versions of creation? What roles do males and females play in each?

the rock, and, in a state of ecstasy (which recent archeologists attribute to hallucinogenic fumes from narcotic gases in two geologic faults below), uttered inscrutable replies to the questions of seekers from near and far. The oracle at Delphi remained the supreme source of prophecy and mystical wisdom until the temple-shrine was destroyed in late Roman times.

Greek City-States and the Persian Wars (ca. 750–480 B.C.E.)

Homer speaks of the Greeks as Achaeans (see page 33), but the Greeks of the Classical era called their country "Hellas" and themselves "Hellenes," after their mythical ancestor Hellen. Toward the end of the Heroic Age, the Greeks formed small rural colonies that gradually grew into urban communities, mainly through maritime trade. Geographic conditions—a rocky terrain interrupted by mountains, valleys, and narrow rivers—made overland travel and trade difficult. At the same time, Greek geography encouraged the evolution of the independent city-state (in Greek, *polis*). Ancient Greece—the English word derives from the Roman place-name *Graecus*—consisted of a constellation of some two hundred city-states, a few as large as 400 square miles and others as tiny as 2 square miles. Many of these (Athens, for instance) were small enough that a person might walk around their walls in only a few hours. Although all of the Greek city-states shared the same language, traditions, and religion, each *polis* governed itself, issued its own coinage, and provided its own military defenses. The autonomy of the Greek city-states—so unlike the monolithic Egyptian state—fostered fierce competition and commercial rivalry. However, like the squabbling members of a family who are suddenly menaced by aggressive neighbors, the Greek city-states united in self-defense when confronted by the rising power of Persia.

By the sixth century B.C.E., the Persian Empire had conquered most of the territories between the western frontier of India and Asia Minor. Advancing westward, Persia annexed Ionia, the Greek region on the coast of Asia Minor (see Map 2.1), a move that clearly threatened mainland Greece. Thus, when in 499 B.C.E. the Ionian cities revolted against Persian rule, their Greek neighbors came to their aid. In retaliation, the Persians sent military expeditions to punish the rebel cities of the Greek mainland. In 490 B.C.E., on the plain of Marathon, near Athens, a Greek force of eleven thousand men met a Persian army with twice its numbers and defeated them, losing only 192 men. Persian casualties exceeded six thousand. Legend has it that the Greek herald who brought news of

THE PRINCIPAL GREEK GODS

Greek Name	Roman Name	Signifies
Aesclepius	Vejovis	Medicine, healing
Aphrodite	Venus	Love, beauty, procreation
Apollo	Phoebus	Solar light, medicine, music
Ares	Mars	War
Artemis	Diana	Hunting, wildlife, the moon
Athena	Minerva	Wisdom, war
Demeter	Ceres	Agriculture, grain
Dionysus	Bacchus	Wine, vegetation, seasonal regeneration
Eros	Amor/Cupid	Erotic love, desire
Hades	Pluto	Underworld
Helios	Phoebus	Sun
Hephaestus	Vulcan	Fire, metallurgy
Hera	Juno	Queen of the gods
Heracles	Hercules	Strength, courage
Hermes	Mercury	Male messenger of the gods
Hestia	Vesta	Hearth, domestic life
Nike	Victoria	Victory
Persephone	Proserpina	Underworld
Poseidon	Neptune	Sea
Selene	Diana	Moon
Zeus	Jupiter	King of the gods, sky

the victory at Marathon to Athens died upon completing the 26-mile run. (Hence the word "marathon" has come to designate a long-distance endurance contest.) But the Greeks soon realized that without a strong navy even the combined land forces of all the city-states could not hope to oust the Persians. They thus proceeded to build a fleet of warships which, in 480 B.C.E., ultimately defeated the Persian armada at Salamis, one of the final battles of the Persian Wars.

The story of the Persian Wars intrigued the world's first known historian, Herodotus (ca. 485–425 B.C.E.), the "father of history." Writing not as an eyewitness to the wars, but a half-century later, Herodotus nevertheless brought keen critical judgment to sources that included hearsay as well as record. His sprawling narrative, *The Persian Wars*, is filled with fascinating anecdotes and colorful digressions, including a "travelogue" of his visits to Egypt and Asia—accounts that remain among our most detailed sources of information about ancient African and West Asian life. The chapters on Africa, filled with numerous comparisons between Greek and Egyptian social practices and religious beliefs, show Herodotus as an early investigator of what would today be called "comparative culture." By presenting various (and often contradictory) pieces of evidence and weighing them before arriving at a conclusion, Herodotus laid the basis for the historical method. His procedures and his writings established a boundary between myth and history. *The Persian Wars*, which followed the Homeric poems by some three hundred years, remains significant as the Western world's first major work in prose.

Herodotus, *The Persian Wars* (ca. 430 B.C.E.)

Figure 2.8 Bust inscribed with the name of Pericles, from Tivoli. Roman copy after a bronze original of 450–425 B.C.E. Marble, height 23 in. British Museum, London. The helmet resting on Pericles' head signifies his role as a military general in the campaigns of the Peloponnesian War.

ATHENS AND THE GOLDEN AGE (CA. 480–430 B.C.E.)

ALTHOUGH all of the city-states had contributed to expelling the Persians, it was Athens that claimed the crown of victory. Indeed, in the wake of the Persian Wars, Athens assumed political dominion among the city-states, as well as commercial supremacy in the Aegean Sea. The defeat of Persia inspired a mood of confidence and a spirit of vigorous chauvinism. This spirit ushered in an age of drama, philosophy, music, art, and architecture. In fact, the period between 480 and 430 B.C.E., known as the Greek Golden Age, was one of the most creative in the history of the world. In Athens, it was as if the heroic idealism of the *Iliad* had bloomed into civic patriotism.

Athens, the most cosmopolitan of the city-states, was unique among the Greek communities, for the democratic government that came to prevail there was the exception rather than the rule in ancient Greece. In its early history, Athens—like most of the other Greek city-states—was an **oligarchy**, that is, a government controlled by an elite minority. But a series of enlight-ened rulers who governed Athens between roughly 600 and 500 B.C.E. introduced reforms that placed increasing authority in the hands of its citizens. The Athenian statesman, poet, and legislator Solon (ca. 638–558 B.C.E.) fixed the democratic course of Athenian history by abolishing the custom of debt slavery and encouraging members of the lower classes to serve in public office. By broadening the civic responsibilities of Athenians, Solon educated citizens of all classes in the activities of government. By 550 B.C.E., the Popular Assembly of Citizens (made up of all citizens) was operating alongside the Council of Five Hundred (made up of aristocrats who handled routine state business) and the Board of Ten Generals (an annually elected executive body). When, at last, in the year 508 B.C.E., the Popular Assembly acquired the right to make laws, Athens became the first direct democracy in world history.

The word "**democracy**" derives from Greek words describing a government in which the people (*demos*) hold power (*kratos*). In the democracy of ancient Athens, Athenian citizens exercised political power directly, thus—unlike the United States, where power rests in the hands of representatives of the people—the citizens of Athens themselves held the authority to make the laws and approve state policy. Athenian democracy was, however, highly exclusive. Its citizenry included only landowning males over the age of eighteen. Of an estimated population of 250,000, this probably constituted some forty thousand people. Women, children, resident aliens, and slaves did not qualify as citizens. Athenian women could not inherit or own property and had few legal rights. (Slaves, as in earlier civilizations, arrived at their unfree condition as a result of warfare or debt, not race or skin color.) Clearly, in the mind of the Athenian, Hellenes were superior to non-Greeks (or outsiders, whom the Greeks called *barbaros*, from which comes the English word "barbarians"), Athenians were superior to non-Athenians, Athenian males were superior to Athenian females, and all classes of free men and women were superior to slaves.

Golden Age Athens stands in vivid contrast to those ancient civilizations whose rulers—the earthly representatives of the gods—held absolute power while citizens held none. Athens also stands in contrast to its rival, Sparta, the largest *polis* on the Peloponnesus (see Map 2.1). In Sparta, an oligarchy of five officials, elected annually, held tight reins on a society whose male citizens (from the age of seven on) were trained as soldiers. All physical labor fell to a class of unfree workers called *helots*, the captives of Sparta's frequent local wars. Spartan soldiers were renowned for their bravery; their women, expected to live up to the ideals of a warrior culture, enjoyed a measure of freedom that was unknown in Athens. Yet the history of Sparta would be one in which a strict social order left little room for creativity, in government or in the arts.

The Athens of Pericles

The leading proponent of Athenian democracy was the statesman Pericles (ca. 495–429 B.C.E.) (Figure **2.8**), who dominated the Board of Ten Generals for more than thirty years until his death. An aristocrat by birth, Pericles was a democrat at heart. In the interest of broadening the democratic system, he initiated some of Athens' most sweeping domestic reforms, such as payment for holding public office and a system of public audit in which the finances of outgoing magistrates were subject to critical scrutiny. In Pericles' time many public offices were filled by lottery—a procedure that invited all citizens to seek governmental office, and one so egalitarian as to be unthinkable today. Pericles' foreign policy was even more ambitious than his domestic policies. In the wake of the Persian Wars, he encouraged the Greek city-states to form a defensive alliance against future invaders. At the outset, the league's collective funds were kept in a treasury on the sacred island of Delos (hence the name "Delian League"). But, in a bold display of chauvinism, Pericles moved the fund to Athens and expropriated its monies to rebuild the Athenian temples that had been burned by the Persians.

Pericles' high-handed actions, along with his imperialistic efforts to dominate the commercial policies of league members, led to antagonism and armed dispute between Athens and a federation of rival city-states led by Sparta. The ensuing Peloponnesian War (431–404 B.C.E.), which culminated in the defeat of Athens, brought an end to the Greek Golden Age. Our knowledge of the Peloponnesian War is based mainly on the account written by the historian Thucydides (ca. 460–400 B.C.E.), himself a general in the combat. Thucydides went beyond merely recording the events of the war to provide insights into its causes and a firsthand assessment of its political and moral consequences. Thucydides' terse, graphic descriptions and his detached analyses of events distinguish his style from that of Herodotus. In his *History of the Peloponnesian War*, Thucydides recounts a landmark speech given by Pericles in honor of those who died in its first battles. Here, his focus is the greatness of Athens and the superiority of the Athenian citizen. Nowhere are the values of humanism and individualism more closely linked to civic patriotism than in this speech.

Thucydides, *History of the Peloponnesian War* (ca. 410 B.C.E.)

The Olympic Games

Describing Athens, Pericles makes proud reference to the "regular games" that provide Athenians with "relaxations from toil." But, in fact, the most famous of the "games" were athletic contests in which all the city-states of Greece participated. These games were the chief feature of the Panhellenic ("all-Greek") Festival, instituted in 776 B.C.E. in honor of the Greek gods. Located in Olympia, one of the great religious centers of Greece, the festival took place at midsummer every four years, even during wartime: A sacred truce guaranteed safe conduct to all visitors. So significant were the games that they became the basis for the reckoning of time. While Egypt and Mesopotamia calculated time according to the rule of dynasties and kings, the ancient Greeks marked time in "Olympiads,"

Ideas and Issues

PERICLES: THE GREATNESS OF ATHENS

"For we are lovers of the beautiful, yet with economy, and we cultivate the mind without loss of manliness. Wealth we employ, not for talk and ostentation, but when there is a real use for it. To avow poverty with us is no disgrace; the true disgrace is in doing nothing to avoid it. An Athenian citizen does not neglect the state because he takes care of his own household; and even those of us who are engaged in business have a very fair idea of politics. We alone regard a man who takes no interest in public affairs, not as a harmless, but as a useless character; and if few of us are originators, we are all sound judges of a policy. The great impediment to action is, in our opinion, not discussion, but the want of that knowledge which is gained by discussion preparatory to action. . . .

To sum up: I say that Athens is the school of Hellas, and that the individual Athenian in his own person seems to have the power of adapting himself to the most varied forms of action with the utmost versatility and grace. This is no passing and idle word, but truth and fact; and the assertion is verified by the position to which these qualities have raised the state."

(from Thucydides, *History of the Peloponnesian War*)

Q What are the unique virtues of the Athenian citizen, according to Pericles?

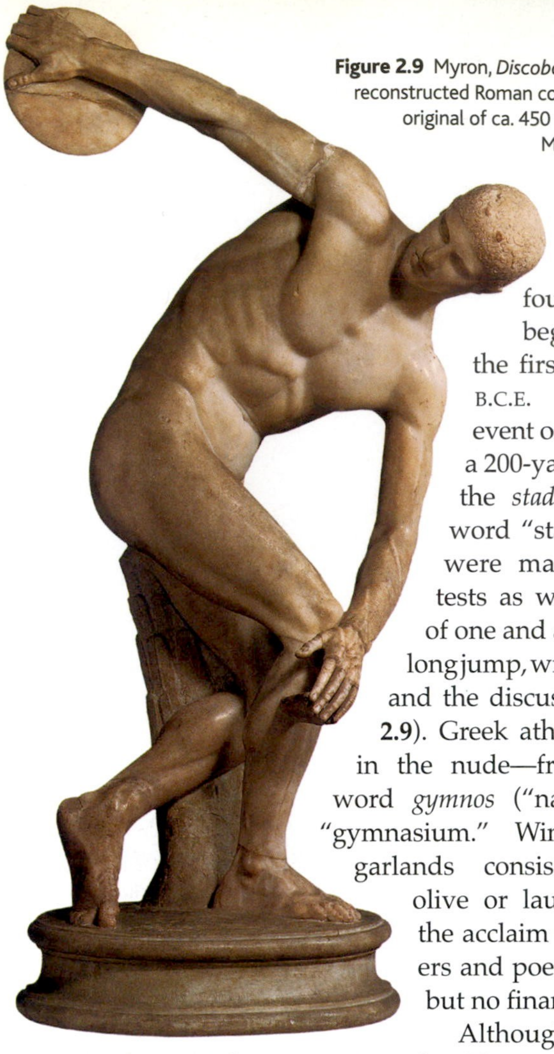

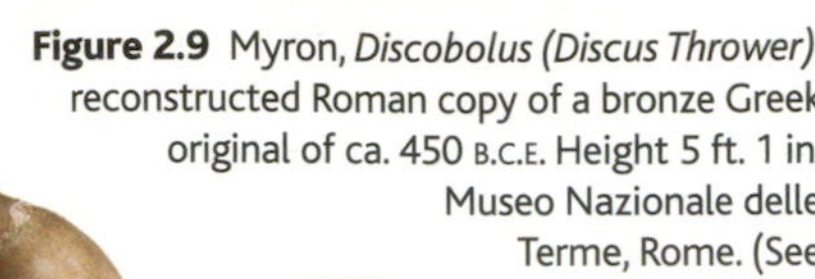

Figure 2.9 Myron, *Discobolus (Discus Thrower)*, reconstructed Roman copy of a bronze Greek original of ca. 450 B.C.E. Height 5 ft. 1 in. Museo Nazionale delle Terme, Rome. (See also page 51.)

four-year periods beginning with the first games in 776 B.C.E. The central event of the games was a 200-yard sprint called the *stadion* (hence the word "stadium"). There were many other contests as well: a foot race of one and a half miles, the long jump, wrestling, boxing, and the discus-throw (Figure **2.9**). Greek athletes competed in the nude—from the Greek word *gymnos* ("naked") we get "gymnasium." Winners received garlands consisting of wild olive or laurel leaves and the acclaim of Greek painters and poets (Figure **2.10**), but no financial reward.

Although women were not permitted to compete in the Olympics (as these games have come to be known), they could hold games of their own. Prowess rather than cunning was valued in all games: In wrestling, hair-pulling and finger-bending were permitted, but biting and finger-breaking were forbidden. A match terminated when either wrestler gave up, lost consciousness, or fell dead. True "sport" was that which gave athletes an opportunity to rival the divinity of the gods. Nevertheless, the Olympics were a national event that, typically, promoted both individual excellence and communal pride.

Figure 2.10 Attributed to the Euphiletos painter, Greek black-figured Panathenaic prize amphora showing foot race, from Vulci, ca. 530 B.C.E. Terracotta, height 24½ in. The Metropolitan Museum of Art, New York. Victors in the Panathenaic Games were awarded an amphora filled with olive oil from the sacred groves of Attica.

Greek Drama

While the Olympic Games were held only once in four years, theatrical performances in the city of Athens occurred twice annually. Like the games, Greek drama was a form of play that addressed the dynamic relationship between the individual, the community, and the gods. The ancient Greeks were the first masters in the art of drama, the literary **genre** that tells a story through the imitation of action. Recitation and chant, music, dance, and mime animated the enactment of myths that celebrated rites of passage or marked seasonal change. Ceremonial drama was designed to bring about favorable results in warfare, farming, and in ensuring the survival of the community.

Greek theater grew out of a complex of rituals associated with the worship of Dionysus, god of wine, vegetation, and seasonal regeneration. In early Homeric times, religious rites performed in honor of Dionysus featured a dialog between two choruses or between a leader (originally perhaps the shaman or priest) and a chorus (the worshippers or ritual participants). With the advent of the poet Thespis (fl. 534 B.C.E.), actor and chorus (the performers) seem to have become separate from those who witnessed the action (the audience). At the same time, dramatic action assumed two principal forms: *tragedy* and *comedy*. Although the origins of each are still the subject of speculation among scholars, tragedy probably evolved from fertility rituals surrounding the death and decay of the crops, while comedy seems to have developed out of village revels celebrating seasonal rebirth.

The two annual festivals dedicated to Dionysus were the occasion for the performances of tragedies and comedies, and on each occasion (lasting several days) the author of the best play in its category received a prize. By the fifth century B.C.E. Greece had become a mecca for theater, and while hundreds of plays were performed during the century in which Athenian theater flourished, only forty-four have survived. (All of the Greek plays in English translation may be found at the website http://classics.mit.edu.) They are the products of only four playwrights: Aeschylus (ca. 525–456 B.C.E.), Sophocles (496–406 B.C.E.), Euripides (480–406 B.C.E.), and Aristophanes (ca. 450–ca. 388 B.C.E.). Their plays were staged in the open-air theaters built into the hillsides at sacred sites throughout Greece (Figure **2.11**). These acoustically superb structures, which seated between thirteen thousand and twenty-seven

Figure 2.11 (above) Polycleitus the Younger, Theater at Epidaurus, Greece, ca. 350 B.C.E. This view shows the great size (thirteen thousand capacity) typical of Greek theaters. Nevertheless, actors and chorus could be heard even from the top row. The great theater at Epidaurus was dedicated to Aesclepius, the god of medicine. Like the more ancient theater of Dionysus in Athens, it stood adjacent to a chief sanctuary for the worship of the god of healing. These facts suggest that drama was related to the healing cults of ancient Greece.

thousand people, featured a *proscenium* (the ancient "stage"), an *orchestra* (the circular "dancing space" in front of the stage), a *skene* (an area that functioned as a stage set and dressing room), and an *altar* dedicated to the god Dionysus (Figure **2.12**). Music, dance, and song were essential to dramatic performance; scenery and props were few; and actors (all of whom were male) wore elaborate costumes, along with masks that served to amplify their voices.

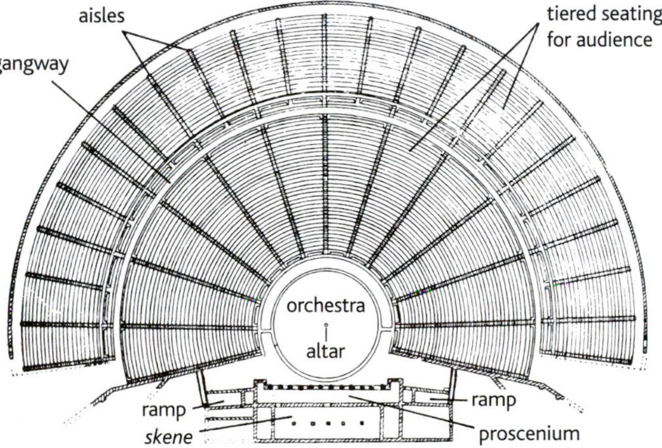

Figure 2.12 Plan of the theater at Epidaurus.

The tragedies of Aeschylus, Sophocles, and Euripides deal with human conflicts as revealed in Greek history, myth, and legend. Since such stories would have been generally familiar to the average Greek who attended the Dionysian theater, the way in which the playwright intrigued the theater-goer would depend upon his treatment of the story or the manner in which the story was enacted. The tragic drama concentrated on issues involving a specific moment of friction between the individual and fate, the gods, or the community. The events of the play unfolded by way of dialog spoken by individual characters but also through the commentary of the chorus. Aeschylus, the author of the oldest surviving Western tragedy, introduced a second actor and gave the chorus a principal role in the drama. He brought deep religious feeling to his tragedies, the most famous of which is the series of three plays, or trilogy, known as the *Oresteia* (Orestes plays). These plays deal with the history of the family of Agamemnon, who led the Greeks to Troy, and whose murder at the hands of his wife upon his return from Troy is avenged by their son, Orestes.

LANDMARKS OF GREEK TRAGEDY

- Aeschylus, *The Oresteia* trilogy (sixth century B.C.E.)
- Sophocles, *Antigone; Oedipus Rex; Electra; Oedipus at Colonus* (fifth century B.C.E.)
- Euripides, *Medea; Electra; The Trojan Women; The Bacchae* (fifth century B.C.E.)

While Aeschylus advanced the story of the play by way of sonorous language, Sophocles, the second of the great tragedians, developed his plots through the actions of the characters. He modified the ceremonial formality of earlier Greek tragedies by individualizing the characters and introducing moments of great psychological intimacy. Euripides, the last of the great tragedians, brought even greater realism to his characters; his striking psychological portraits explore the human soul in its experience of grief.

In modern parlance, the word "tragedy" is often used to describe a terrible act of fate that befalls an unwitting individual. With regard to drama, however, the word (and the form it describes) has a very different meaning. As a literary genre, tragedy deals not so much with catastrophic events as with *how* these events work to affect individuals in shaping their character and in determining their fate. The protagonist becomes a tragic hero not because of what befalls him, but rather as a result of the manner in which he confronts his destiny. In the *Poetics*, the world's first treatise on literary criticism, the Greek philosopher Aristotle (384–322 B.C.E.), whom we will meet again later in this chapter, describes tragedy as an imitation of an action involving incidents that arouse pity and fear. Tragic action, he argues, should involve an error in judgment made by an individual who is "better than the ordinary man" but with whom the audience may sympathize.

Aristotle, *Poetics* (ca. 340 B.C.E.)

The *Poetics* further clarifies the importance of "proper construction": The play must have a balanced arrangement of parts, and the action of the story should be limited to the events of a single day. The plot should consist of a single action made up of several closely connected incidents (without irrelevant additions). These concepts became known as "unities" of time and action; later, seventeenth-century playwrights would add "unity of place."

Tragedy, which gave formal expression to the most awful kinds of human experience—disaster and death—invited the spectator to participate vicariously in the dramatic action, thus undergoing a kind of emotional liberation. Comedy, on the other hand, drew its ability to provoke laughter from incongruity and the unexpected. Probably originating in association with fertility rites, comedy involved satires and parodies of sexual union and erotic play of the kind found to this day in seasonal festivals and carnivals such as Mardi Gras. Obscene jokes, grotesque masks, fantastic costumes, and provocative dance and song were common to ancient comedy, as they are in various forms of modern slapstick and burlesque.

In the history of ancient Greek drama, the only comic plays to survive are those of Aristophanes. His inventive wit, sharply directed against Athenian politics and current affairs, is best revealed in the landmark comedy *Lysistrata*, the oldest of his eleven surviving works. In *Lysistrata*, written in the wake of the bitter military conflict between Athens and Sparta, the playwright has the leading character—the wife of an Athenian soldier—launch a "strike" that will deprive all husbands of sexual satisfaction until they agree to refrain from war. As timely today as it was in ancient Athens, *Lysistrata* is a hilarious attack on the idealized, heroic image of armed combat.

Aristophanes, *Lysistrata* (ca. 411 B.C.E.)

Greek Poetry

In Classical Greece, as in other parts of the ancient world, distinctions between various forms of artistic expression were neither clear-cut nor definitive. A combination of the arts prevailed in most forms of religious ritual and in public and private entertainment. In *Antigone*, for instance, Sophocles used choric pantomime and dance to complement dramatic poetry. And in processions and festivals, music, poetry, and the visual arts all served a common purpose. The intimate relationship between music and poetry is revealed in the fact that many of the words we use to describe lyric forms, such as "**ode**" and "**hymn**," are also musical terms. The word *lyric*, meaning "accompanied by the lyre," describes verse that was meant to be sung, not read silently. Lyric poetry was designed to give voice to deep emotions.

Hellenic culture produced an impressive group of lyric poets, the greatest of whom was Sappho (ca. 610–ca. 580 B.C.E.). Her personal life remains a mystery. Born into an aristocratic family, she seems to have married, mothered a daughter, and produced some nine books of poetry, of which only fragments remain. She settled on the island of Lesbos, where she led a group of young women dedicated to the cult of Aphrodite. At Lesbos, Sappho trained women in the production of love poetry and music. Her homoerotic attachment to the women of Lesbos, as expressed in the poem below, reflects the realities of ancient Greek culture, in which bisexuality and homosexuality were commonplace both in life and as subject matter in the arts. Inspired by love and loss, Sappho's poems are frank and confessional, passionate and tender. They are marked by inventive combinations of sense and sound and by a powerful economy of expression—that is, an ability to convey profound sentiments with few, choice words—features that are particularly difficult to convey in English translation. The following poem offers a glimpse into a body of poetry that inspired Sappho's contemporaries to call her "the female Homer."

He Is More Than a Hero

He is more than a hero
He is a god in my eyes
the man who is allowed
to sit beside you—he

who listens intimately
to the sweet murmur of
your voice, the enticing
laughter that makes my own
heart beat fast. If I meet
you suddenly, I can't

speak—my tongue is broken;
a thin flame runs under
my skin; seeing nothing.

Hearing only my own ears
drumming, I drip with sweat;
trembling shakes my body

and I turn paler than
dry grass. At such times
death isn't far from me.

GREEK PHILOSOPHY

IN the ancient world, where most people saw themselves at the mercy of forces they could not comprehend, shamans and priestesses explored the unknown by means of sympathetic magic, myth, and ritual. During the sixth century B.C.E., a small group of Greek thinkers offered an intellectual alternative that combined careful observation, systematic analysis, and the exercise of pure reason. These individuals, whom we call philosophers (literally, "lovers of wisdom"), laid the foundations for Western scientific and philosophic inquiry. Instead of making nature the object of worship, they made it the object of study. To those who interpreted disasters such as earthquakes and lightning as expressions of divine anger, they submitted that such events might have natural, not supernatural, causes. Challenging all prevailing myths, the Greek philosophers made the speculative leap from supernatural to natural explanations of the unknown.

Naturalist Philosophy: The Pre-Socratics

The earliest of the Greek philosopher–scientists lived just prior to the time of Socrates in the city of Miletus on the Ionian coast of Asia Minor (see Map 2.1). Although their senses reported a world of constant change, they reasoned that there must be a single, unifying substance that formed the basic "stuff" of nature. They asked, "What is everything made of?" "How do things come into existence?" and "What permanent substance lies behind the world of appearance?" Thales (ca. 625–ca. 547 B.C.E.), history's first philosopher, held that water was the fundamental substance and source from which all things proceeded. Water's potential for change (from solid to liquid to gas) and its pervasiveness on earth convinced him that water formed the primary matter of the universe. His followers challenged this view: "Air," said one, "fire," countered another, and still others identified the basic substance as a mixture of the primordial elements.

The concept that a single, unifying substance underlay reality drew opposition from some of the pre-Socratics. The universe, argued Heraclitus of Ephesus (ca. 540–ca. 480 B.C.E.), has no permanence, but, rather, is in constant process or flux. Heraclitus defended the idea that change itself was the basis of reality. "You cannot step twice into the same river," he wrote, "for fresh waters are ever flowing in upon you." Yet, Heraclitus believed that an underlying Form or Guiding Force (in Greek, *logos*) permeated nature, an idea that resembles Hindu pantheism and anticipates the Christian concept (found in the Gospel of John) of a Great Intelligence governing the beginning of time. For Heraclitus the Force was impersonal, universal, and eternal.

Around 500 B.C.E., Leucippus of Miletus theorized that physical reality consisted of minute, invisible particles that moved ceaselessly in the void. These he called *atoms*, the Greek word meaning "indivisible." Democritus (ca. 460–370 B.C.E.), a follower of Leucippus and the best known of the naturalist philosophers, developed the atomic theory of matter. For Democritus, the mind consisted of the same indivisible physical substances as everything else in nature. According to this materialist view, atoms moved constantly and eternally according to chance in infinite time and space. The atomic theory survived into Roman times, and although forgotten for two thousand years thereafter, it was validated by physicists of the early twentieth century.

Yet another pre-Socratic thinker, named Pythagoras (ca. 580–ca. 500 B.C.E.), advanced an idea that departed from both the material and nonmaterial views of the universe. Pythagoras believed that proportion, discovered through number, was the true basis of reality. According to Pythagoras, all universal relationships may be expressed through numbers, the truths of which are eternal and unchanging. The formula in plane geometry that equates the square of the hypotenuse in right angle triangles to the sum of the square of the other two sides—a theorem traditionally associated with Pythagoras—is an example of such an unchanging and eternal truth, as is the simplest of mathematical equations: $2 + 2 = 4$. Pythagoras was the founding father of pure mathematics. He was also the first to demonstrate the relationship between musical harmonics and numbers. His view that number gives order and harmony to the universe is basic to the principles of balance and proportion that dominate Classical art and music.

In contrast with the Egyptians and the Mesopotamians, who deified the sun, the rivers, and other natural elements, the pre-Socratics stripped nature of all supernatural associations. They made accurate predictions of solar and lunar eclipses, plotted astronomical charts, and hypothesized on the processes of regeneration in plants and animals.

Hippocrates (ca. 460–377 B.C.E.), the most famous of the Greek physicians and so-called "father of medicine," investigated the influence of diet and environment on general health and advanced the idea that an imbalance among bodily "humors"—blood, phlegm, black bile, and yellow bile—was the cause of disease. He insisted on the necessary relationship of cause and effect in matters of physical illness, and he raised questions concerning the influence of the mind on the body. He may also be deemed the "father of medical ethics": To this day, graduating physicians are encouraged to practice medicine according to the precepts of the Hippocratic Oath (probably not written by Hippocrates himself), which binds them to heal the sick and abstain from unprofessional medical practices.

The separation of the natural from the supernatural was as essential to the birth of medical science as it was to speculative philosophy. And although no agreement as to the nature of reality was ever reached among the pre-Socratics, these intellectuals laid the groundwork and the methodology for the rational investigation of the universe. Their efforts represent the beginnings of Western science and philosophy as formal disciplines.

The Sophists

The naturalist philosophers were concerned with describing physical reality in terms of the unity that lay behind the chaos of human perceptions. The philosophers who followed them pursued a different course: They turned their attention from the world of nature to the world of the mind, from physical matters to moral concerns, and from the gathering of information to the cultivation of wisdom. Significantly, these thinkers fathered the field of inquiry known as *metaphysics* (literally, "beyond physics"), that branch of philosophy concerned with abstract thought. They asked not simply "*What* do we know (about nature)?" but "*How* do we know what we know?" The transition from the examination of matter to the exploration of mind established the humanistic direction of Greek philosophy for at least two centuries.

The first humanist philosophers were a group of traveling scholar-teachers called Sophists. Masters of formal debate, the Sophists were concerned with defining the limits of human knowledge. The Thracian Sophist Protagoras (ca. 485–410 B.C.E.) believed that knowledge could not exceed human opinion, a position summed up in his memorable dictum: "Man is the measure of all things." His contemporary Gorgias (ca. 483–ca. 376 B.C.E.) tried to prove that reality is incomprehensible and that even if one could comprehend it, one could not describe the real to others. Such skepticism was common to the Sophists, who argued that truth and justice were relative: What might be considered just and true for one individual or situation might not be just and true for another.

Socrates and the Quest for Virtue

Athens' foremost philosopher, Socrates (ca. 470–399 B.C.E.), vigorously opposed the views of the Sophists. Insisting on the absolute nature of truth and justice, he described the ethical life as belonging to a larger set of universal truths and an unchanging moral order. For Socrates, virtue was not discovered by means of clever but misleading argumentation—a kind of reasoning that would come to be called (after the Sophists) *sophistry*, nor was it relative to individual circumstances. Rather, virtue was a condition of the *psyche*, the seat of both the moral and intellectual faculties of the individual. ("*Psyche*" is often translated as "soul," but it is more accurately understood as the site of intelligence and individual personality.) Hence, understanding the true meaning of virtue was preliminary to acting virtuously: To know good was to do good.

The question of right conduct was central to Socrates' life and teachings. A stonemason by profession, Socrates preferred to roam the streets of Athens and engage his fellow citizens in conversation and debate. Insisting that the unexamined life was not worth living, he challenged his peers on matters of public and private virtue, constantly posing the question, "What is the greatest good?" In this pursuit, Socrates employed a rigorous question-and-answer technique known as the **dialectical method**. Unlike the Sophists, he refused to charge fees for teaching: He argued that wealth did not produce excellence; rather, wealth derived *from* excellence. Socrates described himself as a large horsefly, alighting upon and pestering the well-bred but rather sluggish horse—that is, Athens. So Socrates "alighted" on the citizens of Athens, arousing, persuading, and reproaching them and—most important—demanding that they give rational justification for their actions.

His style of intellectual cross-examination—the question-and-answer method—proceeded from his first principle of inquiry, "Know thyself." Meanwhile the progress of his analysis moved from specific examples to general principles, and from particular to universal truths, a type of reasoning known as *inductive*. (To compare *deductive* reasoning, see pages 296–297.)The inductive method requires a process of abstraction: a shift of focus from the individual thing (the city) to all things (cities) and from the individual action (just or unjust) to the idea of justice. Central to Socratic inquiry was discourse. The notion that talk itself humanizes the individual is typically Greek and even more typically Socratic. Indeed, the art of conversation—the dialectical exchange of ideas—united the citizens of the *polis*.

As gadfly, Socrates won as many enemies as he won friends. The great masses of Greek citizens found comfort in the traditional Greek gods and goddesses. They had little use for Socrates' religious skepticism and stringent methods of self-examination. Outspoken in his commitment to free inquiry, Socrates fell into disfavor with the reactionary regime that governed Athens after its defeat in the Peloponnesian War. Although he had fought bravely in the war, he vigorously opposed the new regime and the moral chaos of postwar Athens. In the year 399 B.C.E., when he was over seventy years old, he was brought to trial for subversive behavior, impiety, and atheism. The Athenian jury found him guilty by a narrow margin of votes and sentenced him to death by drinking hemlock, a poisonous herb (Figure **2.13**).

Beyond the West

CHINESE PHILOSOPHY

Confucius

While Socrates is regarded as the founder of philosophy in the West, no one holds a more important place in China's philosophic tradition than his near contemporary, Confucius (the Latin name for Kong-fuzi) (551–479 B.C.E.). China's most notable thinker was a self-educated man who pursued the career of teacher, local administrator, and social reformer. According to tradition, Confucius was the compiler and editor of the five Chinese classics, the earliest of which was *The Book of Changes* (see page 25). Like Socrates, however, Confucius wrote nothing. He earned renown through the force of his teachings, which his disciples transcribed after his death. This collection of writings came to be known as the *Analects*.

Confucius, *Analects* (ca. 450 B.C.E.)

The *Analects* comment on matters as diverse as marriage, music, and death, but their central concern is with matters of proper conduct. They articulate the ancient Chinese conviction that human beings must obey a moral order that is fixed in nature. Confucius maintains that behavior, not birth, determines the worth of the individual. Like the Greek philosophers, he has little to say about gods and spirits; on the other hand, he makes no effort to identify the primary matter of the universe, as do the pre-Socratics, nor does he formulate a novel system of abstract thought, as do Socrates and the Greek metaphysicians. Confucius emphasizes obedience to tradition, filial piety (respect for one's elders), and the exercise of proper conduct. The good influence and high moral status of the ruler—a figure much like Plato's philosopher-king (see page 45)—is central to the Confucian concept of the well-ordered society. For Confucius, as for Plato, moral and political life are one. Such precepts were basic to humanist thought in China for well over two thousand years.

Ideas and Issues

CONFUCIUS: MORAL ADVICE

"**4.11** The Master said: 'A gentleman seeks virtue; a small man seeks land. A gentleman seeks justice; a small man seeks favors.'

4.16 The Master said: 'A gentleman considers what is just; a small man considers what is expedient.'

4.21 The Master said: 'Always keep in mind the age of your parents. Let this thought be both your joy and your worry.'

4.24 The Master said: 'A gentleman should be slow to speak and prompt to act.'

15.9 The Master said: 'A righteous man, a man attached to humanity, does not seek life at the expense of his humanity; there are instances where he will give his life in order to fulfill his humanity.'

15.12 The Master said: 'A man with no concern for the future is bound to worry about the present.'

15.13 The Master said: 'The fact remains that I have never seen a man who loved virtue as much as sex.'

15.15 The Master said: 'Demand much from yourself, little from others, and you will prevent discontent.'

15.18 The Master said: 'A gentleman takes justice as his basis, enacts it in conformity with the ritual, expounds it with modesty, and through good faith, brings it to fruition. This is how a gentleman proceeds.'

15.19 The Master said: 'A gentleman resents his incompetence; he does not resent his obscurity.'

15.20 The Master said: 'A gentleman worries lest he might disappear from this world without having made a name for himself.'

15.21 The Master said: 'A gentleman makes demands on himself; a vulgar man makes demands on others.'

15.24 Zigong asked: 'Is there any single word that could guide one's entire life?' The Master said: 'Should it not be *reciprocity*? What you do not wish for yourself, do not do to others.'"

(from Confucius, *Analects*)

Q Describe the Confucian gentleman; how might he compare with Plato's philosopher-king?

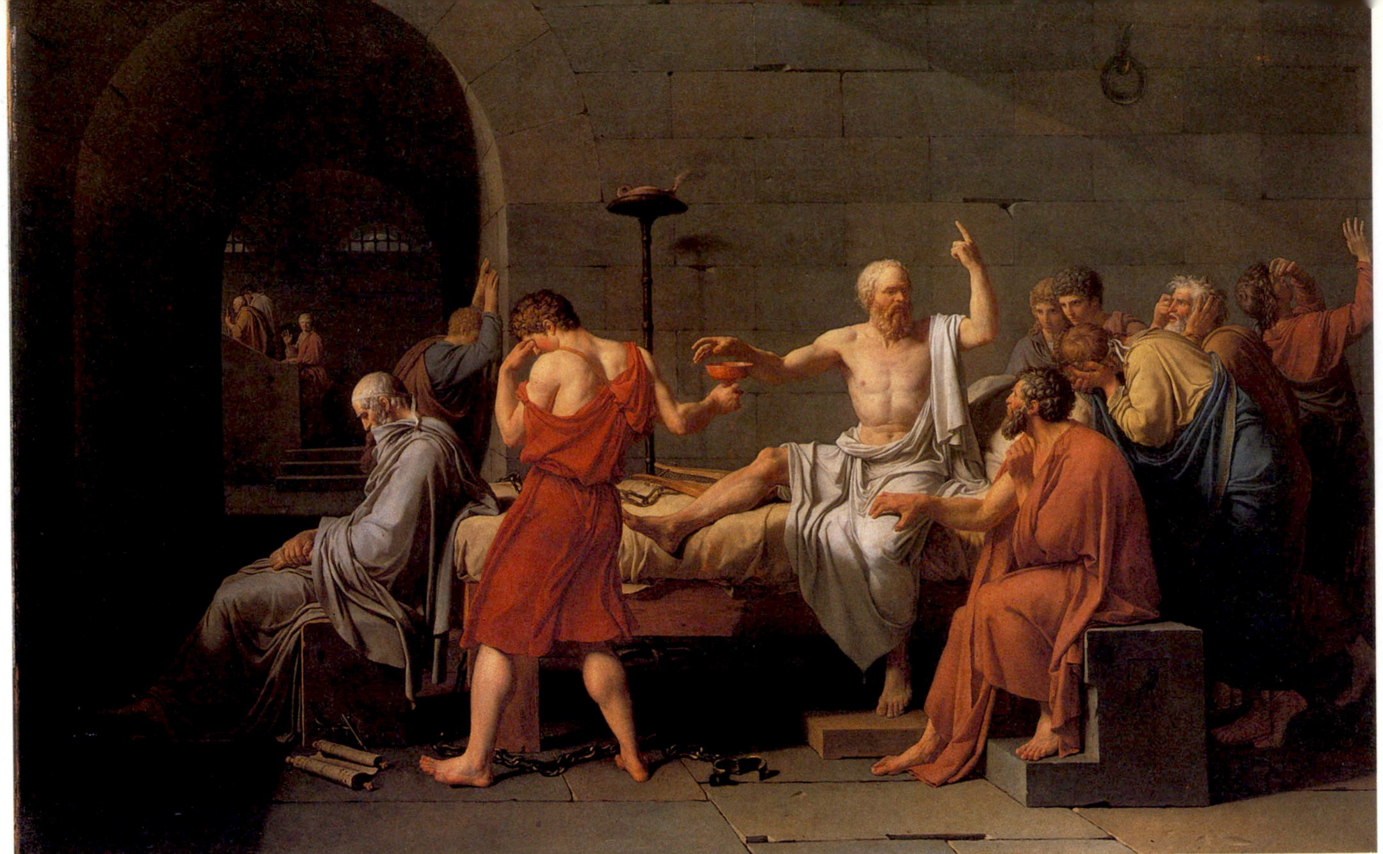

Figure 2.13 Jacques-Louis David, *The Death of Socrates*, 1787. Oil on canvas, 4 ft. 3 in. x 6 ft. 5¼ in. The Metropolitan Museum of Art, New York. Heroic themes drawn from antiquity characterized the Neoclassical ("new classical") revival of the eighteenth century. Here, David visually recreates the noble death of the "father of philosophy." "Everything in moderation," taught Socrates. Yet, his passionate loyalty to the state led him to abide by the will of the jury that condemned him to death. In his lifetime, Socrates wrote no books or letters. What we know of his teachings comes from the writings of his pupil Plato.

Plato and the Theory of Forms

Socrates' teachings were an inspiration to his pupil Plato (ca. 428–ca. 347 B.C.E.). Born in Athens during the Peloponnesian War, Plato reaped the benefits of Golden Age culture along with the insecurities of the postwar era. In 387 B.C.E., more than a decade after the death of his master, he founded the world's first school of philosophy, the Academy. Plato wrote some two dozen treatises, most of which were cast in the dialog or dialectical format that Socrates had made famous. Some of the dialogs may be precise transcriptions of actual conversations, whereas others are clearly fictional, but the major philosophical arguments in almost all of Plato's treatises are put into the mouth of Socrates. Since Socrates himself wrote nothing, it is almost impossible to distinguish between the ideas of Plato and those of Socrates.

Plato, *Republic* (ca. 375 B.C.E.)

Plato's landmark treatise, the *Republic*, asks two central questions: "What is the meaning of justice?" and "What is the nature of a just society?" In trying to answer these questions, Plato introduces a theory of knowledge that is both visionary and dogmatic. It asserts the existence of a two-level reality, one consisting of constantly changing particulars available to our senses, the other consisting of unchanging eternal truths understood by way of the intellect. According to Plato, the higher reality—eternal truths that he calls Forms—is distinct from the imperfect and transient objects of sensory experience. Plato's Theory of Forms proposes that all sensory objects are imitations of the Forms, which, like the simplest mathematical equations, are imperishable and forever true. For example, the circle and its three-dimensional counterpart, the sphere, exist independent of any *particular* circle and sphere. They have always existed and will always exist. But the beach ball I toss in the air, an imperfect copy of the sphere, is transitory. Indeed, if all of the particular beach balls in the world were destroyed, the Universal Form—Sphere—would still exist. Similarly, suggests Plato, Justice, Love, and Beauty (along with other Forms) stand as unchanging and eternal models for the many individual and particular instances of each in the sensory world.

According to Plato, Forms descend from an ultimate Form, the Form of the Good. Plato never locates or defines the Ultimate Good, except by analogy with the sun. Like the sun, the Form of the Good illuminates all that is intelligible and makes possible the mind's perception of Forms as objects of thought. The Ultimate Good, knowledge of which is the goal of dialectical inquiry, is the most difficult to teach.

The "Allegory of the Cave"

In the *Republic*, Plato uses a literary device known as **allegory** to illustrate the dilemma facing the *psyche* in its ascent to knowledge of the imperishable and unchanging Forms.

By way of allegory—the device by which the literal meaning of the text implies a figurative or "hidden" meaning—Plato describes a group of ordinary mortals chained within an underground chamber (the *psyche* imprisoned within the human body). Their woeful position permits them to see only the shadows on the walls of the cave (the imperfect and perishable imitations of the Forms that occupy the world of the senses), which the prisoners, in their ignorance, believe to be real (Figure **2.14**). The "Allegory of the Cave" illustrates some key theories in the teachings of Plato. The first of these is **idealism**, the theory that holds that reality lies in the realm of unchanging Forms, rather than in sensory objects. Platonic idealism implies a dualistic (spirit-and-matter or mind-and-body) model of the universe: The *psyche* belongs to the world of the eternal Forms, while the *soma* (body) belongs to the sensory or material world. Imprisoned in the body, the mind forgets its once-perfect knowledge of the Forms. The mind is, nevertheless, capable of recovering its prenatal intelligence. The business of philosophy is to educate the *psyche*, to draw it out of its material prison so that it can regain perfect awareness.

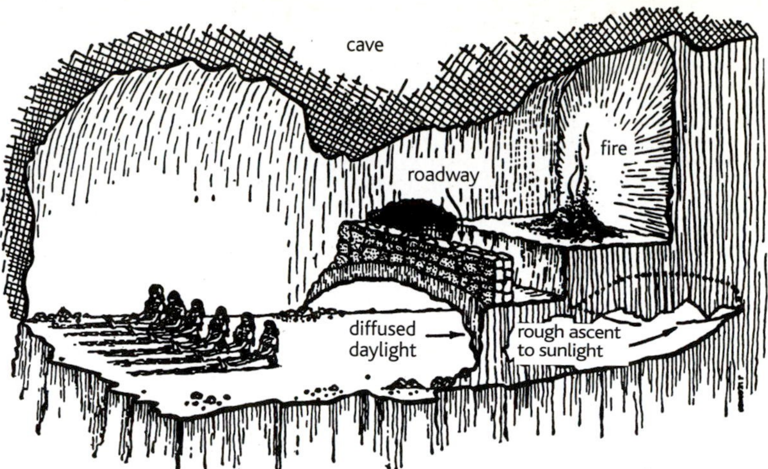

Figure 2.14 "Allegory of the Cave" from *The Great Dialogs of Plato*. Those chained in place see only the shadows of the figures on the roadway behind them. When one of the prisoners—the philosopher-hero—ascends to the domain of light (that is, knowledge of the Forms), it becomes evident that what the cave-dwellers perceive as truth is nothing more than shadows of Reality.

In the *Republic*, Plato proposes a practical system of education (by which one might arrive at knowledge of the Good), and a set of social requirements for everyday life and conduct. Plato's utopian community permits no private property and little family life, but exalts education as fundamental to society, and available to both men and women. If women are to be employed in the same duties as men, argues Plato, we must give them the same instruction, which would include music, gymnastics, and military training. In Book 5 of the *Republic*, Socrates says:

> ... none of the occupations which comprehend the ordering of the state belong to woman as woman, nor yet to man as man: but natural gifts are to be found here and there in both sexes alike, and so far as her nature is concerned, the woman is admissible to all pursuits as well as the man, though in all of them the woman is weaker than the man.

While all are educated equally, each person's abilities would determine his or her place within the community. Thus the duties of all citizens—laborers, soldiers, or governors—would be consistent with their mental and physical abilities. Plato has little use for democracy of the kind practiced in Athens. Governing, according to Plato, should fall to guardians who are the most intellectually able. Those who have most fully recovered a knowledge of the Forms are obliged to act as "king-bees" in the communal hive. (Plato might have been surprised to discover that the ruling bee in a beehive is female.) The life of contemplation carries with it heavy responsibilities, for in the hands of the philosopher-kings lies "the welfare of the commonwealth as a whole."

Ideas and Issues

PLATO'S IDEAL STATE

"... the law is not concerned to make any one class specially happy, but to ensure the welfare of the commonwealth as a whole. By persuasion or constraint it will unite the citizens in harmony, making them share whatever benefits each class can contribute to the common good; and its purpose in forming men of that spirit was not that each should be left to go his own way, but that they should be instrumental in binding the community into one.

... the truth is that you can have a well-governed society only if you can discover for your future rulers a better way of life than being in office; only then will power be in the hands of men who are rich, not in gold, but in the wealth that brings happiness, a good and wise life. All goes wrong when, starved for lack of anything good in their own lives, men turn to public affairs hoping to snatch from thence the happiness they hunger for. They set about fighting for power, and this internecine conflict ruins them and their country. The life of true philosophy is the only one that looks down upon offices of state; and access to power must be confined to men who are not in love with it; otherwise rivals will start fighting. So whom else can you compel to undertake the guardianship of the commonwealth, if not those who, besides understanding the best principles of government, enjoy a nobler life than the politician's and look for rewards of a different kind?"

(from Plato, *Republic*, Book VII)

Q What role does the law play in shaping society?
Q What kind of ruler does Plato envision for the ideal state?
Q What might Plato say of our contemporary political leaders?

Aristotle and the Life of Reason

Among Plato's students at the Academy was a young Macedonian named Aristotle (see page 40), whose contributions to philosophy ultimately rivaled those of his teacher. After a period of travel in the eastern Mediterranean and a brief career as tutor to the young prince of Macedonia (the future Alexander the Great), Aristotle returned to Athens and founded a school known as the Lyceum. Aristotle's habit of walking up and down as he lectured gave him the nickname the "peripatetic philosopher." His teachings, which exist only as lecture notes compiled by his students, cover a wider and more practical range of subjects than those of Plato. Aristotle argued that Plato's Forms had to be grounded in matter. Insisting that mind and matter could not exist independently of each other, he rejected Plato's notion of an eternal *psyche*. Nevertheless, he theorized that a portion of the soul identified with reason (and with the impersonal force he called the Unmoved Mover) might be immortal.

Aristotle's interests spanned many fields, including those of biology, physics, politics, poetry, drama, logic, and ethics. The son of a physician, Aristotle was inspired by his education to gather specimens of plant and animal life and classify them according to their physical similarities and differences. Over five hundred different animals, some of which Aristotle himself dissected, are mentioned in his zoological treatises. Though he did little in the way of modern scientific experimentation, Aristotle followed the practice of basing conclusions on careful observation, thus advancing the **empirical method**—a method of inquiry dependent on direct experience. He brought to his analysis of political life, literature, and human conduct the same principles he employed in classifying plants and animals: objectivity, clarity, and consistency. Before writing the *Politics*, he examined the constitutions of more than 150 Greek city-states. And in the *Poetics* he defined the various genres of literary expression (see page 40). In the fields of biology, astronomy, and physics, Aristotle's conclusions (including many that were incorrect) remained unchallenged for centuries. For instance, Aristotle theorized that in sexual union, the male was the "generator" and the female the "receptacle," while procreation involved the imposition of life-giving form (the male) on chaotic matter (the female). In short, Aristotle's views on the female role in reproduction led centuries of scholars to regard woman as an imperfect and incomplete version of man.

Aristotle's application of scientific principles to the reasoning process was the basis for the science of logic. Aristotelian logic requires, first, the division of an argument into individual terms and, second, a method of reasoning—in Socratic fashion—from the general to the specific (the **syllogism**).

Not the least of Aristotle's contributions was that which he made to **ethics**, the branch of philosophy that sets forth the principles of human conduct. Proceeding from an examination of human values, Aristotle hypothesizes that happiness or "the good life" (the Greek word *eudaimonia* means both) is the only human value that might be considered a final goal or end (*telos*) in itself, rather than a means to any other end. Is not happiness the one goal to which all human beings aspire? If so, then how does one achieve it? The answer, says Aristotle, lies in fulfilling one's unique function. The function of any thing is that by which it is defined: The function of the eye is to see; the function of the racehorse is to run fast; the function of a knife is to cut, and so on. How well a thing performs is synonymous with its excellence or virtue (in Greek, the word *arete* denotes both): The excellence of the eye, then, lies in seeing well; the excellence of a racehorse lies in how fast it runs; the excellence of a knife depends on how well it cuts, and so on. The unique function of the human being, observes Aristotle, is the ability to reason; hence, the excellence of any human creature lies in the exercise of reason.

In the *Ethics*, edited by Aristotle's son Nicomachus, Aristotle examines the Theory of the Good Life and the Nature of Happiness. He explains that action in accordance with reason is necessary for the acquisition of excellence, or virtue. Ideal conduct, suggests Aristotle, lies in the Golden Mean—the middle ground between any two extremes of behavior. Between cowardice and recklessness, for instance, one should seek the middle ground: courage. Between boastfulness and timidity, one should cultivate modesty. The Doctrine of the Mean rationalized the Classical search for moderation and balance. In contrast with the divinely ordained moral texts of other ancient cultures, Aristotle's teachings required individuals to reason their way to ethical conduct.

Aristotle, *Ethics* (ca. 340 B.C.E.)

Aristotle and the State

While the Golden Mean gave every individual a method for determining right action, Aristotle was uncertain that citizens would put it to efficient use in governing themselves. Like Plato, he questioned the viability of the democratic state. Political privilege, argued Aristotle, was the logical consequence of the fact that some human beings were naturally superior to others: From the hour of their birth some were marked out for subjection and others for rule. In the *Politics*, he defends the point of view that all human beings are *not* created equal:

Aristotle, *Politics* (ca. 350 B.C.E.)

> . . . between male and female the former is by nature superior and ruler, the latter inferior and subject. And this must hold good of mankind in general. . . . For the 'slave by nature' is he that can and therefore does belong to another, and he that participates in reason so far as to recognize it but not so as to possess it (whereas the other animals obey not reason but emotions). The use made of slaves hardly differs at all from that of tame animals: They both help with their bodies to supply our essential needs. It is then part of nature's intention to make the bodies of free men to differ from those of slaves, the latter strong enough to be used for necessary tasks, the former erect and useless for that kind of work, but well suited for the life of a citizen of a state, a life which is in turn divided between the requirements of war and peace.

Ideas and Issues

THE SYLLOGISM

All men are mortal.
a:b
Socrates is a man.
c:a
Therefore, Socrates is mortal.
∴ c = b

Aristotle formulated the syllogism, a deductive scheme that presents a major and a minor premise from which a conclusion may be drawn. As a procedure for reasoned thought without reference to specific content, the syllogism is a system of notation that is similar to mathematics.

Q Formulate a syllogism of your own based on the above model. Can a deductive "proof" be false?

Aristotle insisted that governments must function in the interest of the state, not in the interest of any single individual or group. He criticized democracy because, at least in theory, it put power in the hands of great masses of poor people who might rule in their own interests. He also pointed out that Athenian demagogues were capable of persuading the Assembly to pass less-than-worthy laws. He concluded that the best type of government was a constitutional one ruled by the middle class.

Aristotle defined the human being as a *polis*-person (the term from which we derive the word "political"). Humans are, in other words, political creatures, who can reach their full potential only within the governing framework of the state. Only beasts and gods, he noted, have no need for the state—he gracefully excluded women from such considerations.

Ideas and Issues

MAN IS A POLITICAL ANIMAL

"[The] state is by nature clearly prior to the family and to the individual, since the whole is of necessity prior to the part. . . . The proof that the state is a creation of nature and prior to the individual is that the individual, when isolated, is not self-sufficing; and therefore he is like a part in relation to the whole. But he who is unable to live in society, or who has no need because he is sufficient for himself, must be either a beast or a god: he is no part of a state. A social instinct is implanted in all men by nature, and yet he who first founded the state was the greatest of benefactors.

For man, when perfected, is the best of animals, but, when separated from law and justice, he is the worst of all; since armed injustice is the more dangerous, and he is equipped at birth with arms, meant to be used by intelligence and virtue, he is the most unholy and the most savage of animals, and the most full of lust and gluttony. But justice is the bond of men in states, for the administration of justice, which is the determination of what is just, is the principle of order in political society."

(from Aristotle, *Politics*)

Q What is the role of justice in Aristotle's "political society"?

THE CLASSICAL STYLE

Key Features

The quest for harmonious order was the driving force behind the evolution of the Classical style. Pythagoras, for example, tried to show that the order of the universe could be understood by observing proportion (both geometric and numerical) in nature: He produced a taut string that, when plucked, sounded a specific pitch; by pinching that string in the middle and plucking either half he generated a sound exactly consonant with (and one **octave** higher than) the first pitch. Pythagoras claimed that relationships between musical sounds obeyed a natural symmetry that might be expressed numerically and geometrically. If music was governed by proportion, was not the universe as a whole subject to similar laws? And, if indeed nature itself obeyed laws of harmony and proportion, then should not artists work to imitate them?

Among Greek artists and architects, such ideas generated the search for a **canon**, or set of rules for determining physical proportion. To arrive at a canon, the artist fixed on a **module**, or standard of measurement, that governed the relationships between all parts of the work of art and the whole. The size of the module was not absolute, but varied according to the subject matter. In the human body, for instance, the distance from the chin to the top of the forehead, representing one-tenth of the whole body height, constituted a module by which body measurements might be calculated. The Greek canon made active use of that principle of proportion known as *symmetry*, that is, correspondence of opposite parts in size, shape, or position, as is evident in the human body.

While proportion and order are two guiding principles of the Classical style, other features informed Greek Classicism from earliest times. One of these is *humanism*. Greek art is said to be humanistic not only because it observes fundamental laws derived from the human physique, but because it focuses so consistently on the actions of human beings. Greek art is fundamentally *realistic*, that is, faithful to nature; but it refines nature in a process of *idealization*, that is, the effort to achieve a perfection that surpasses nature. Humanism, realism, and idealism are hallmarks of Greek art.

Greek Painting

Because almost all evidence of Greek wall-painting has disappeared, decorated vases are our main source of information about Greek painting. During the first three hundred years of Greek art—the *Geometric period* (ca. 1000–700 B.C.E.)—artists painted their ceramic wares with flat, angular figures and complex geometric patterns organized according to the shape of the vessel (Figure **2.15**). By the *Archaic period* (ca. 700–480 B.C.E.), figures painted in

Figure 2.15 Funerary krater with "Geometric" decoration, ca. 750 B.C.E. Terracotta, height 3 ft. 4½ in. The Metropolitan Museum of Art, New York. This large krater shows a funeral bier mounted on a horse-drawn cart. The funerary procession, which is repeated on the lower register, shows warriors in chariots, suggesting that the deceased was a soldier.

black or brown, and scenes from mythology, literature, and everyday life, came to dominate the central zone of the vase (Figure **2.16**; see also Figure 2.10). Water jars, wine jugs, storage vessels, drinking cups, and bowls all reflect the keen enjoyment of everyday activities among the Greeks: working, dancing, feasting, fighting, and gaming. In these compositions, little if any physical setting is provided for the narrative action. Indeed, in their decorative simplicity, human figures often resemble the abstract shapes that ornament the rim, handle, and foot of the vessel. The principles of order and proportion that typify the Geometric style remain evident in the decoration of later vases, where a startling clarity of design is produced by the striking interplay of figure and ground.

By the *Classical period* (480–323 B.C.E.), artists had replaced the black-figured style with one in which the human body was left the color of the clay and the ground was painted black (Figure **2.17**; see also Figures 2.7 and 2.35). They refined their efforts to position figures and objects to complement the shape of the vessel. However, a newly developed red-figured style allowed artists to delineate physical details on the buff-colored surface, thereby making the human form appear more lifelike. Although still flattened and aligned side by side, figures are posed naturally. *Realism*, that is, fidelity to nature, has overtaken the decorative aspect of the Geometric and Archaic styles. At the same time, artists of the Classical period moved toward aesthetic *idealism*. Socrates is noted for having described the idealizing process: He advised the painter Parrhasius to reach beyond the flawed world of appearances by selecting and combining the most beautiful details of many different models. The artist must simplify the subject matter, free it of incidental detail, and impose the accepted canon of proportion to achieve the ideal form. Accordingly, the art object will surpass the imperfect and transient objects of sensory experience. Like Plato's Ideal Forms, the artist's imitations of reality are lifelike in appearance, but they improve upon sensory reality to achieve absolute perfection. Among the Greeks, as it had been among the Egyptians, conception played a large part in the process of making art; with the Greeks, however, the created object was no longer an abstract form, but a dynamic reconstruction of the physical world.

Figure 2.16 Exekias, Black-figured amphora with Achilles and Ajax Playing Dice, ca. 530 B.C.E. Height 24 in. Vatican Museums, Rome. The landmark painting by Exekias shows two legendary warriors fully armed, as if ready for battle, but intent on the board-game they are playing. Crispness of line, clarity of form, and powerful geometric composition contribute to creating both tension and harmony.

Figure 2.17 Epictetus, Cup (detail), ca. 510 B.C.E. Terracotta, diameter 13 in. British Museum, London. The graceful solo dance by a cult follower of Dionysus is accompanied by the music of a double **aulos** (a set of reed pipes) held in place by leather straps.

Greek Sculpture: The Archaic Period (ca. 700–480 B.C.E.)

Nowhere is the Greek affection for the natural beauty of the human body so evident as in Hellenic sculpture, where the male nude form assumed landmark importance as a subject. Freestanding Greek sculptures fulfilled the same purpose as Egyptian and Mesopotamian votive statues: They paid perpetual homage to the gods. They also served as cult statues, funerary monuments, and memorials designed to honor the victors of the athletic games. Since athletes both trained and competed in the nude, representation of the unclothed body was completely appropriate. Ultimately, however, the centrality of the nude in Greek art reflects the Hellenic regard for the human body as nature's perfect creation. (The fig leaves that cover the genitals of some Greek sculptures are additions dating from the Christian era.)

As in painting, so in sculpture, the quest for realism was offset by the will to idealize form. Achieving the delicate balance between real and ideal was a slow process, one that had its beginnings early in Greek history. During the Archaic phase of Greek sculpture, freestanding representations of the male youth (***kouros***) still resembled the blocklike statuary of ancient Egypt (see Figure 2.18). A *kouros* from Attica is rigidly posed, with arms close to its sides and its body weight distributed equally on both feet (see Figure 2.19).

Produced some fifty years after the Attica *kouros*, the *Calf-Bearer* is more gently and more realistically modeled—note especially the abdominal muscles and the sensitively carved bull calf (Figure **2.20**; see also Figure 4.5). The hollow eyes of the shepherd once held inlays of semiprecious stones (mother-of-pearl, gray agate, and lapis lazuli) that would have given the face a strikingly realistic appearance. Such lifelike effects were enhanced by the brightly colored paint (now almost gone) that enlivened the lips, hair, and other parts of the figure.

Making Connections

THE SCULPTURED MALE FORM

Greece was probably in close commercial contact with ancient Egypt, which provided the model for the sculptured male form. The rigidity seen in both traditional Egyptian statuary (Figure **2.18**) and Archaic Greek sculpture (Figure **2.19**) may derive from efforts to carve organic forms out of rigid wooden tree trunks and unyielding blocks of stone. Details freed from the stone such as the nose, the genitalia, and the fingers were easily broken off, as we know from the remains of many Greek statues.

Q What are the most notable similarities and differences between these two sculptures?

Figure 2.18 (below) Standing figure of Sepa, from Saqqara, Egypt, third dynasty, 2700–2620 B.C.E. Limestone with traces of paint, height 5 ft. 5 in. Louvre, Paris.

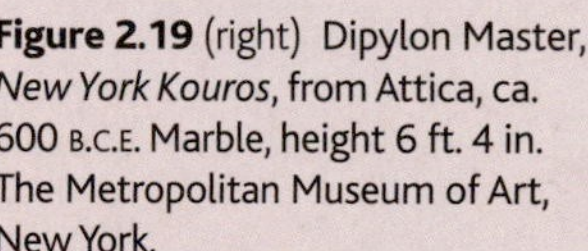

Figure 2.19 (right) Dipylon Master, *New York Kouros*, from Attica, ca. 600 B.C.E. Marble, height 6 ft. 4 in. The Metropolitan Museum of Art, New York.

Greek Sculpture: The Classical Period (480–323 B.C.E.)

By the mid-fifth century B.C.E., Greek sculptors had arrived at the natural positioning of the human body that would characterize the Classical style: The human torso turns on the axis of the spine, and the weight of the body shifts from equal distribution on both legs to greater weight on the left leg—a kind of balanced opposition that is at once natural and graceful. (This counterpositioning would be called ***contrapposto*** by Italian Renaissance artists.) The muscles are no longer geometrically schematized, but protrude subtly at anatomical junctures. And the face is no longer smiling, but instead solemn and contemplative. The new poised stance, along with a complete mastery of human anatomy and proportion, are features of the High Classical style that flourished between ca. 480 and 400 B.C.E. At mid-century, Polycleitus brought that style to perfection with the *Doryphorus* (*Spear-Bearer*; Figure **2.21**). Known today only by way of Roman copies, the *Doryphorus* is widely regarded as the embodiment of the canon of ideal human proportions. The figure, who once held a spear in his left hand, strides forward in a manner that unites motion and repose, energy and poise, male confidence and grace—the qualities of the ideal warrior-athlete.

There is little to distinguish man from god in the bronze statue of Zeus (or Poseidon) hurling a weapon (Figure **2.22**). The work of an unknown sculptor, this nude, which conveys the majesty and physical vitality of a mighty Greek deity, might just as well represent a victor of the Olympic Games. While the lost-wax method of bronze-casting originated in Mesopotamia (see Figure 1.14), the Greeks were the first to employ this ancient technique for

Figure 2.20 *Calf-Bearer*, ca. 575–550 B.C.E. Marble, height 5 ft. 6 in. Acropolis Museum, Athens. The rigidity of this archaic sculpture gave way to the more natural stance of High Classical figures.

Figure 2.21 Polycleitus, *Doryphorus* (*Spear-Bearer*), Roman copy after a bronze Greek original of ca. 450–440 B.C.E. Marble, height 6 ft. 11½ in. National Museum, Naples. Most freestanding Greek sculptures survive only in Roman copies, and what remains is a fraction of what once existed. The balance fell to the ravages of time and barbarian peoples, who pulverized marble statues to make mortar and melted down bronze sculptures to mint coins and cast cannons.

large-sized artworks. Lost-wax casting allowed sculptors to depict more vigorous physical action and to include greater detail than was possible in the more restrictive medium of marble. Dynamically posed—the length of the arms is deliberately exaggerated—the figure appears fixed at the decisive moment just before the action, when every muscle in the body is tensed, ready to achieve the mark. The sculptor has also idealized the physique in the direction of geometric clarity. Hence the muscles of the stomach are indicated as symmetrical trapezoids, and the strands of the hair and beard assume a distinctive pattern of parallel wavy lines.

Few bronze sculptures survived the High Classical era, but some of the most treasured works come to us in marble copies made by the Romans. One such masterpiece is the *Discobolus* (*Discus Thrower*), originally executed in bronze by Myron around 450 B.C.E. (see Figure 2.9). Like the Zeus, the *Discobolus* captures the crucial moment in which intellect guides the impending physical action: here, the flight of the discus from the athlete's hand. Composed as a complex of two intersecting arcs (one created by the arms and shoulders, the other by the curve of the body from head to knee), the figure tempers physical vigor with reasoned restraint.

The evolution of the Classical female figure (*kore*) underwent a somewhat different course from that of the male. Early *korai* were fully clothed and did not appear in the nude until the fourth century B.C.E. Female statues of the Archaic period were ornamental, columnar, and (like their male counterparts) smiling (Figure **2.23**). Not until the Late Classical Age (400–323 B.C.E.) did Greek sculptors arrive at the sensuous female nudes that so inspired Hellenistic, Roman, and (centuries later) Renaissance

Figure 2.22 (right) Zeus (or Poseidon), ca. 460 B.C.E. Bronze, height 6 ft. 10 in. National Archeological Museum, Athens.

Figure 2.23 (right) *Kore* from Chios (?), ca. 520 B.C.E. Marble with traces of paint, height approx. 22 in. (lower part missing). Acropolis Museum, Athens. This is one of the few Greek sculptures on which traces of the original brightly colored paint have survived.

artists. The *Aphrodite of Knidos* (Figure **2.24**) by Praxiteles established a model for the ideal female nude: tall and poised, with small breasts and broad hips. Regarded by the Romans as the finest statue in the world, Praxiteles' goddess of love exhibits a subtle counterposition of shoulders and hips, smooth body curves, and a face that bears a dreamy, melting gaze. She is distinguished by the famous Praxitelean technique of carving that coaxed a translucent shimmer from the fine white marble.

A careful study of Greek statuary from the Archaic through the Late Classical Age reflects increasing refinements to realism and idealism: All imperfections (wrinkles, warts, blemishes) have been purged in favor of a radiant flawlessness. The Classical nude is neither very old nor very young, neither very thin nor very fat. He or she is eternally youthful, healthy, serene, dignified, and liberated from all accidents of nature. This synthesis of humanism, realism, and idealism in the representation of the freestanding nude was one of Greek art's great achievements. Indeed, the Hellenic conception of the nude defined the standard of beauty in Western art for centuries. The Classical conception of beauty has had a profound influence on Western cultural expression. Its mark is most visible in the numerous Neoclassical revivals that have flourished over the centuries, beginning with the Renaissance in Italy (see page 192).

Greek Architecture: The Parthenon

The great monuments of Classical architecture were designed to serve the living, not—as in Egypt—the dead. In contrast with the superhuman scale of the Egyptian pyramid, the Greek temple was proportioned according to the human body (see page 55). Greek theaters (see Figures 2.11 and 2.12) celebrated life here on earth rather than the life in the hereafter, and Greek temples served as shrines for the gods and depositories for civic and religious treasures. Both theaters and temples functioned as public meeting places. Much like the Mesopotamian ziggurat, the Greek temple was a communal symbol of reverence for the gods, but, whereas the ziggurat enforced the separation of priesthood and populace, the Greek temple instead united religious and secular domains.

The landmark architectural achievement of Golden Age Athens is the Parthenon (Figures **2.25** and **2.26** and see Figure 2.1), a temple dedicated to Athena, the goddess of war and of wisdom, and the patron of the arts and crafts. The name Parthenon derives from the Greek word *parthenos* ("maiden"), a popular epithet for Athena. Built in glittering Pentelic marble upon the ruins of an earlier temple burned during the Persian Wars, the Parthenon overlooks Athens from the highest point on the Acropolis (Figure **2.28**). Athens' preeminent temple was commissioned by Pericles, who freely drew on Delian League funds to restore the wooden temples burned by the Persians during their attack on Athens in 480 B.C.E. The Parthenon was designed by the architects Ictinus and Kallicrates, and embellished by the sculptor Phidias (fl. ca. 490–430 B.C.E.) who directed and supervised its construction over a period of more than ten years, from 448 to 432 B.C.E. In the tradition of Egyptian builders, Greek architects used no mortar. Rather, they employed bronze clamps and dowels to fasten the individually cut marble segments.

The Parthenon represents the culmination of a long history of post-and-lintel temple building among the Greeks. That history, like the history

Figure 2.24 Praxiteles, *Aphrodite of Knidos*, Roman copy of Greek original of ca. 350 B.C.E. Marble, height 6 ft. 8 in. Vatican Museums, Rome. This celebrated female nude is a Roman copy of a lost Greek original. The bar bracing the hip, probably added to give support to the freestanding marble figure, suggests that the original may have been executed in bronze (where no such support would have been needed). There exist today some sixty versions of this famous Classical icon, ranging from full-sized statues to miniature figures.

Figure 2.25 (above) Ictinus and Kallicrates, west end of the Parthenon, Athens, 448–432 B.C.E. Pentelic marble, height of columns 34 ft.

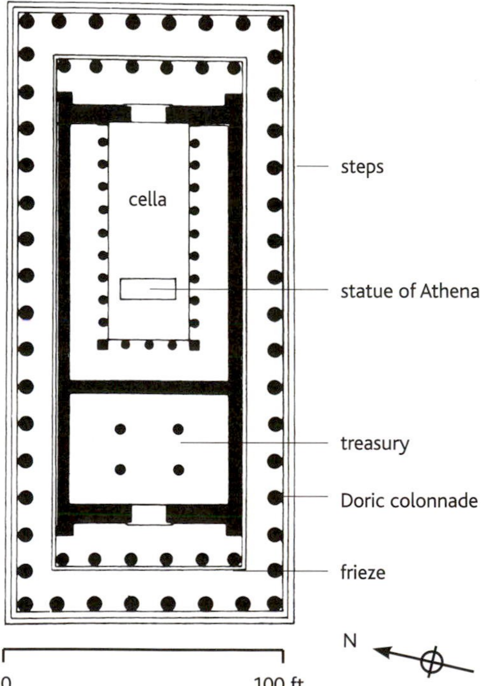

Figure 2.26 Plan of the Parthenon, Athens. The plan of the temple, a rectangle delimited on all four sides by a colonnaded walkway, reflects the typically Classical reverence for clarity and symmetry.

Making Connections

GREEK CLASSICISM AND NEOCLASSICISM

This nineteenth-century example of Greek revival architecture (Figure **2.27**) is a simplified version of the Parthenon (see Figure 2.25), though its interior features a Roman-style rotunda. A Doric "temple" raised on the spot in which George Washington took the oath of office as president in 1789, Federal Hall (once a U.S. Customs house and a branch of the Treasury) offers clear evidence of the use of Classical models to convey the dignity, stability, and authority that American Neoclassicists associated with the Hellenic world.

Q What stylistic features contribute to the dignity of this American landmark?

Figure 2.27 A. J. Davis and Ithiel Town, Federal Hall, 28 Wall Street, New York City, 1842.

Figure 2.28 Model of the Classical Acropolis at Athens. American School of Classical Studies at Athens: Agora Excavations.
1 Erechtheion
2 picture gallery
3 Propylaia (entrance gate)
4 Sacred Way
5 Temple of Athena Nike
6 Chalkotheke (armory)
7 Parthenon (Temple of Athena Parthenos)

of Greek painting and sculpture, entailed a search for clarity, regularity, balance, and harmonious proportion—the hallmarks of the Classical style. Freestanding columns (each 34 feet tall) make up the exterior, while two further rows of columns on the east and west ends of the temple provide inner **porticos** (see Figure 2.30). The interior of the Parthenon is divided into two rooms, a central hall (or *cella*), which held the colossal cult statue of Athena, and a smaller room used as a treasury. It was here that the much-disputed Delian League funds were stored. Entirely elevated on a raised, stepped platform, the Parthenon invited the individual to move around it, as if it were a piece of monumental sculpture. Indeed, scholars have suggested that the Parthenon was both a shrine to Athena and a victory monument.

The Parthenon makes use of the Doric **order**, one of three programs of architectural design developed by the ancient Greeks (Figure **2.29**). Each of the orders—Doric, Ionic, and (in Hellenistic times) Corinthian—prescribes a fundamental set of structural and decorative parts that stand in fixed relation to each other. Each order differs in details and in the relative proportions of the parts. The Doric order, which originated on the Greek mainland, is simple and severe. In the Parthenon it reached its most refined expression. The Ionic order, originating in Asia Minor and the Aegean Islands, is more delicate and ornamental. Its slender columns terminate in capitals with paired volutes or scrolls. The Ionic order is employed in some of the small temples on the Acropolis (see Figure 2.28 No. 5). The Corinthian, the most ornate of the orders, is characterized by capitals

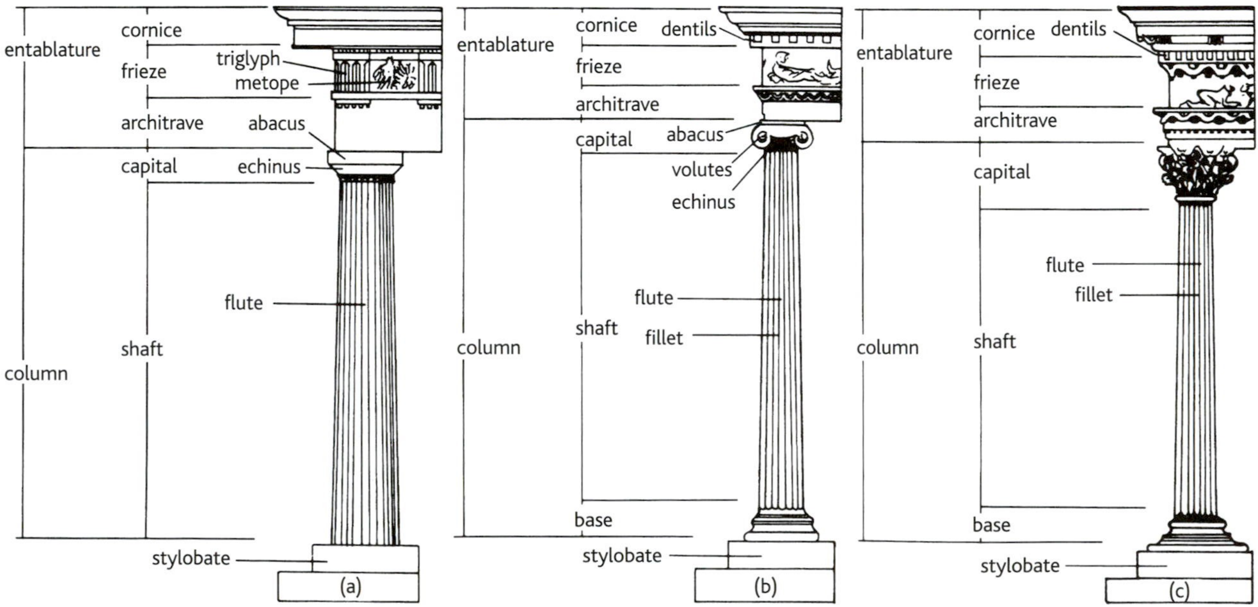

Figure 2.29 The Greek orders: (a) Doric, (b) Ionic, and (c) Corinthian.

consisting of acanthus leaves. It is often found on victory monuments, in **tholos** (circular) sanctuaries and shrines, as well as in various Hellenistic and Roman structures (see Figures 3.8 and 3.11).

If an ideal system governed the parts of the Greek building, a similar set of laws determined its proportions. The precise canon of proportion adopted by Phidias for the construction of the Parthenon is still, however, the subject of debate. Most scholars agree that the design was governed by the adoption of a system of "divine proportion" known as the "Golden Section." This system of geometric proportion is expressed numerically by the ratio of 1.618:1 or approximately as 8:5. The ratio, which is found in the ground plan of the Parthenon (see Figure 2.26), represents an aesthetic ideal found in nature and in human anatomy. As such,

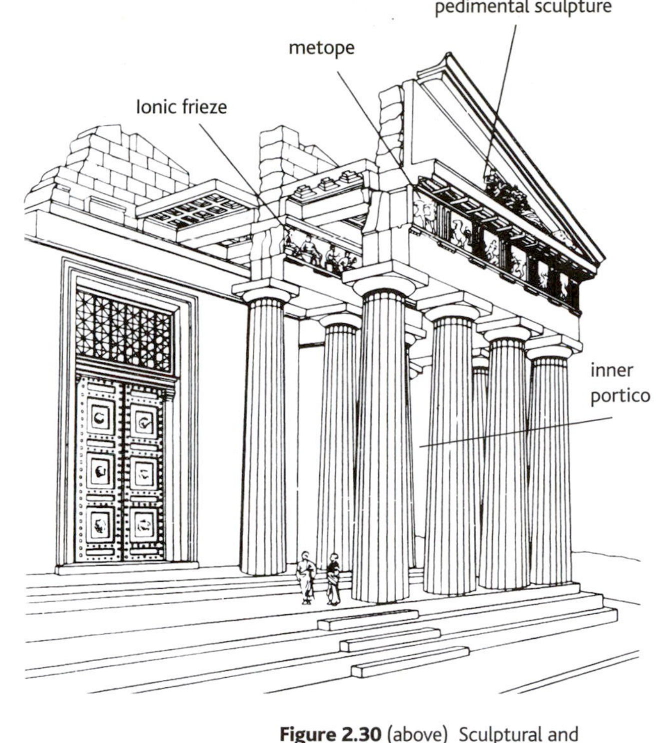

Figure 2.30 (above) Sculptural and architectural detail of the Parthenon. **Frieze**, a decorative band along the top of a wall; **metopes**, segmented spaces on a frieze; **pediment**, a **gable**; portico, a roofed porch.

Figure 2.31 (above) Three Goddesses: Hestia, Dione, Aphrodite, from east pediment of the Parthenon, Athens, ca. 437–432 B.C.E. Marble, over life-size. British Museum, London.

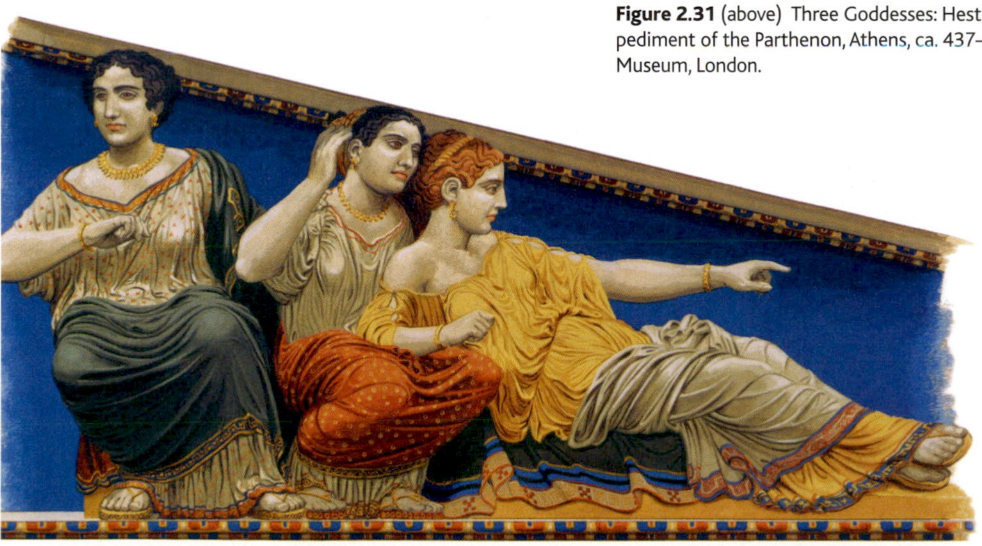

Figure 2.32 A reconstruction of the three goddesses in Figure 2.31.

the Parthenon embraces the humanism and the rationalism of the Classical style.

Regarding the actual construction of the Parthenon, it is often said that there are virtually no straight lines in the entire building. Its Doric columns, for instance, swell out near the center to counter the optical effect of thinning that occurs when the normal eye views an uninterrupted set of parallel lines. All columns tilt slightly inward. Corner columns are thicker than the others to compensate for the attenuating effect produced by the bright light of the sky against which the columns are viewed, and also to ensure their ability to bear the weight of the terminal segments of the superstructure. The top step of the platform on which the columns rest is not parallel to the ground, but rises four and a quarter inches at the center, allowing for rainwater to run off the convex surface even as it corrects the optical impression of sagging along the extended length of the platform. Consistently, the architects of the Parthenon corrected negative optical illusions produced by strict conformity to geometric regularity. Today the Parthenon stands as a noble ruin, the victim of an accidental gunpowder explosion in the seventeenth century, followed by centuries of vandalism, air pollution, and unrelenting tourist traffic.

The Sculpture of the Parthenon

Between 448 and 432 B.C.E. Phidias and the members of his workshop executed the sculptures that would appear in three main locations on the Parthenon: in the pediments of the roof gables, on the metopes or square panels between the beam ends under the roof, and in the area along the outer wall of the *cella* (Figure **2.30**). Brightly painted, as were some of the decorative portions of the building, the Parthenon sculptures relieved the stark angularity of the post-and-lintel structure. In subject matter, the temple sculptures paid homage to the patron deity of Athens: The east pediment narrates the birth of Athena with gods and goddesses in attendance (Figures **2.31** and **2.32**). The west pediment shows the contest between Poseidon and Athena for domination of Athens. The ninety-two metopes that occupy the frieze illustrate scenes of combat between the Greeks (the bearers of civilization) and Giants, Amazons, and Centaurs (the forces of barbarism; Figure **2.33**). Carved in high relief, each metope is a masterful depiction of two contestants, one human and the other bestial. Appropriate to a temple honoring the goddess of wisdom, the sculptural program of the Parthenon celebrates the victory of intellect over unbridled passion, hence, barbarism.

Figure 2.33 Lapith Overcoming a Centaur, south metope 27, Parthenon, Athens, 447–438 B.C.E. Marble, height 4 ft. 5 in. British Museum, London. The Centaurs, a fabulous race of creatures (part-horse and part-human), attacked their neighbors, the Lapiths, and tried to carry off their women. In the ensuing battle, the Lapiths were defeated and driven out of their home near Mount Pelion.

Figure 2.34 A Group of Young Horsemen, from the north frieze of the Parthenon, Athens, 447–438 B.C.E. Marble, height 3 ft. 7 in. British Museum, London. The figures move with graceful rhythms, in tempos that could well be translated into music. Once brightly painted and ornamented with metal details, the horsemen must have looked impressively lifelike. To increase this effect and satisfy a viewpoint from below, Phidias graded the relief, cutting the marble more deeply at the top than at the bottom.

Ideas and Issues

THE BATTLE OVER ANTIQUITIES

Only one half of the Parthenon's original sculptures survive today. Half of these are on display at the British Museum in London, and the rest are scattered in museums throughout the world. In 1687, while the Ottoman Turks ruled Greece (see page 208), an enemy firebomb ignited an Ottoman gunpowder supply stored in the Parthenon. Between 1801 and 1805, England's ambassador to the Ottoman Empire, Thomas Bruce, the seventh Earl of Elgin, rescued the sculptures from rubble and ruin and shipped them to England. A few years later, the trustees of the British Museum bought the marbles with money funded by Parliament. Since achieving independence in 1832, the Greeks have demanded the return of the sculptures. Britain, however, claims legitimate ownership, and the issue remains in dispute today.

Similar debates are currently raging over the question of "cultural patrimony": Do antiquities (and other artworks) belong to the country in which they were produced, or do they belong to those individuals and institutions who have bought them for private collections or for public display? The issue is complicated by the fact that many works of art, both ancient and modern, were looted from ancient graves or taken forcibly from their owners during wartime. Some museum curators and art dealers now face trial for buying and selling objects that were illegally excavated from foreign soil. Recently, the Metropolitan Museum in New York City returned the landmark Euphronios krater (see Figure 2.7) to Rome after the courts determined that the work of art had been looted and had to be repatriated by the year 2008. How other of these cases are resolved will have a major effect on the global art market, and on the availability of visual landmarks for public display in the world's museums.

Q Should the Elgin marbles be returned to Greece?

Completing Phidias' program of architectural decoration for the Parthenon is the continuous frieze that winds around the outer wall of the *cella* where that wall meets the roofline. The 524-foot-long sculptured band is thought to depict the Panathenaic Festival, a celebration held every four years in honor of the goddess Athena. Hundreds of figures—a cavalcade of horsemen (Figure **2.34**), water bearers, musicians, and votaries—are shown filing in calm procession toward an assembled group of gods and goddesses. This masterpiece of the Greek Golden Age reveals the harmonious reconciliation of humanism, realism, and idealism that is typical of the Classical style.

Greek Music and Dance

The English word *music* derives from *muse*, the Greek word describing any of the nine mythological daughters of Zeus and the goddess of memory. According to Greek mythology, the muses presided over the arts and the sciences. Pythagoras observed that music was governed by mathematical ratios and therefore constituted both a science and an art. As was true of the other arts, music played a major role in Greek life. However, we know almost as little about how Greek music sounded as we do in the cases of Egyptian or Sumerian music. The ancient Greeks did not invent a system of notation with which to record instrumental or vocal sounds. Apart from written and visual descriptions of musical performances, there exist only a few fourth-century-B.C.E. treatises on music theory and some primitively notated musical works. The only complete piece of ancient Greek music that has survived is an ancient song found chiseled on a first-century-B.C.E. gravestone. It reads: "So long as you live, be radiant, and do not grieve at all. Life's span is short and time exacts the final reckoning." Both vocal and instrumental music were commonplace, and contests between musicians, like those between playwrights, were a regular part of public life. Vase paintings reveal that the principal musical instruments of ancient Greece were the lyre, the **kithara**—both belonging to the harp family and differing only in shape, size, and number of strings (Figure **2.35**)—and the aulos, a flute or reed pipe (see Figure 2.17). Along with percussion devices often used to accompany dancing, these string and wind instruments were probably inherited from Egypt.

Figure 2.35 The Berlin painter, red-figure amphora, ca. 490 B.C.E. Terracotta, height of vase 16³⁄₈ in. The Metropolitan Museum of Art, New York. Accompanying himself on the kithara (the larger counterpart of the lyre), the young man sings ecstatically. The lyre was the primary instrument for the cult of Apollo.

The Greeks devised a system of **modes**, or types of **scales** characterized by fixed patterns of pitch and tempo within the octave. (The sound of the ancient Greek Dorian mode is approximated by playing the eight white keys of the piano beginning with the white key two notes above middle C.) Modified variously in Christian times, the modes were preserved in Gregorian chant and Byzantine church hymnology. Although the modes themselves may have been inspired by the music of ancient India, the diatonic scale (familiar to Westerners as the series of notes C, D, E, F, G, A, B, C) originated in Greece.

Greek music lacked harmony as we know it. It was thus **monophonic**, that is, confined to a single unaccompanied line of melody. The strong association between poetry and music suggests that the human voice had a significant influence in both melody and rhythm.

From earliest times, music was believed to hold magical powers and therefore exercise great spiritual influence. Greek and Roman mythology describes gods and heroes who used music to heal or destroy. Following Pythagoras, who equated musical ratios with the unchanging cosmic order, many believed that music might put one "in tune with" the universe. The planets, which Pythagoras described as a series of spheres moving at varying speeds in concentric orbits around the earth, were said to produce a special harmony, the so-called *music of the spheres*. The Greeks believed, moreover, that music had a moral influence. This argument, often referred to as the "Doctrine of Ethos," held that some modes strengthened the will, whereas others undermined it and thus damaged the development of moral character. In the *Republic*, Plato encouraged the use of the Dorian mode, which settled the temper and inspired courage, but he condemned the Lydian mode, which aroused sensuality. Because of music's potential for affecting character and mood, both Plato and Aristotle recommended that the types of music used in the education of young children be regulated by law. As with other forms of Classical expression, music was deemed essential to the advancement of the individual and the well-being of the community.

Inseparable from music, dance played an important role in communal ceremonial rites and in theatrical presentations. Dance was prized for its moral value, as well as for its ability to give pleasure and induce good health. For Plato the uneducated man was a "danceless" man. Both Plato and Aristotle advised that children be instructed at an early age in dancing. However, both men distinguished noble dances from ignoble ones—Dionysian and comic dances, for instance. These they considered unfit for Athenian citizens and therefore inappropriate to the educational curriculum. Nevertheless, the scantily clad dancing *maenad*, a cult follower of Dionysus, was a favorite symbol of revelry in ancient Greece (see Figure 2.17).

THE HELLENISTIC AGE (323–30 B.C.E.)

THE fourth century B.C.E. was a turbulent era marked by rivalry and warfare among the Greek city-states. Ironically, however, the failure of the Greek city-states to live in peace would lead to the spread of Hellenic culture throughout the civilized world. Manipulating the shifting confederacies and internecine strife to his advantage, Philip of Macedonia eventually defeated the Greeks in 338 B.C.E. When he was assassinated two years later, his twenty-year-old son Alexander (356–323 B.C.E.) assumed the Macedonian throne (see Figure 2.36). A student of Aristotle, Alexander brought to his role as ruler the same kind of far-reaching ambition and imagination that his teacher had exercised in the intellectual realm. Alexander was a military genius: Within twelve years, he created an empire that stretched from Greece to the borders of modern India (Map **2.2**). To all parts of his empire, but especially to the cities he founded—many of which he named after himself—Alexander carried Greek language and culture. Greek art and literature made a major impact on civilizations as far east as India, where it influenced Buddhist art and Sanskrit literature (see page 117).

Alexander carved out his empire with the help of an army of thirty-five thousand Greeks and Macedonians equipped with weapons that were superior to any in the ancient world. Siege machines such as catapults and battering rams were used to destroy the walls of the best-defended cities of Asia Minor, Egypt, Syria, and Persia. Finally, in northwest India, facing the prospect of confronting the formidable army of the King of Ganges and his force of five thousand elephants, Alexander's troops refused to go any further. Shortly thereafter, the thirty-two-year-old general died (probably of malaria), and his empire split into three segments: Egypt governed by the Ptolemy dynasty, Persia under the leadership of the Seleucid rulers, and Macedonia-Greece governed by the family of Antigonus the One-Eyed (see Map 2.2, inset).

The era that followed, called Hellenistic ("Greek-like"), lasted from 323 to 30 B.C.E. The defining features of the Hellenistic Age were cosmopolitanism, urbanism, and the blending of Greek, African, and Asian cultures. Trade routes linked Arabia, east Africa, and central Asia, bringing great wealth to the cities of Alexandria, Antioch,

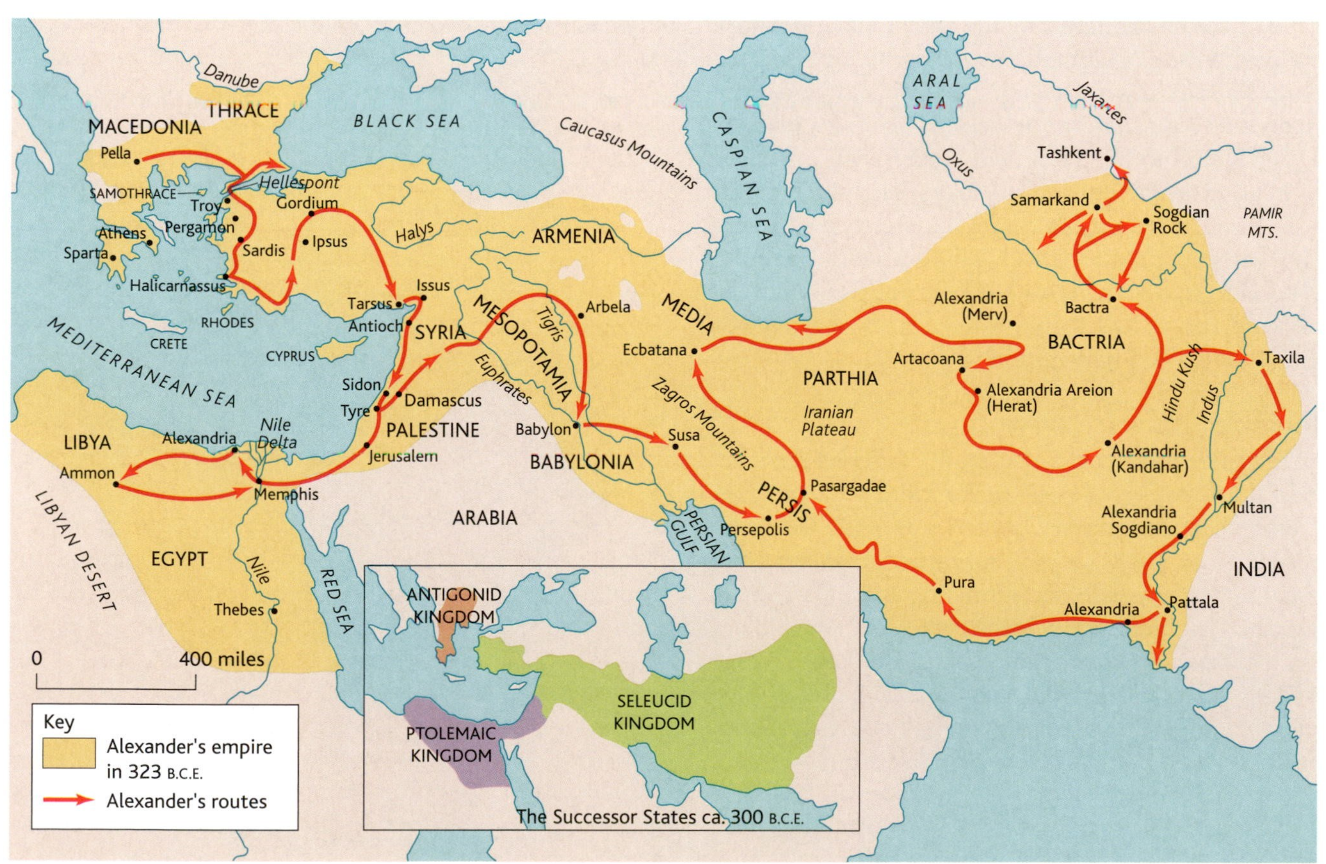

Map 2.2 The Hellenistic World. Pergamon, Antioch, Alexandria, and Rhodes were vital urban centers. After Alexander's death, the empire broke into three successor states located in the regions of Greece, Egypt, and Persia.

Pergamon, and Rhodes. Alexandria, which replaced Athens as a cultural center, boasted a population of more than one million people and a library of half a million books (the collection was destroyed by fire when Julius Caesar besieged the city in 47 B.C.E.). The Great Library, part of the cultural complex known as the Temple of the Muses (or "Museum"), was an ancient "think tank" that housed both scholars and books. At the rival library of Pergamon (with some 200,000 books), scribes prepared sheepskin to produce "pergamene paper," that is, parchment, the medium that would be used for centuries of manuscript production prior to the widespread dissemination of paper. Textual criticism and the editing of Classical manuscripts produced the scholarly editions of Homer's epics and other "classics" that would be passed on to generations of Western readers.

The Hellenistic Age made important advances in geography, astronomy, medicine, and mathematics. Euclid, who lived in Alexandria during the late fourth century B.C.E., produced a textbook of existing geometric learning that systematized the theorems of plane and solid geometry. Aristarchus of Samos, who was active in the third century B.C.E., proposed that the earth and all the planets revolved around the sun, a (heliocentric) theory of the solar system that would not be confirmed until the seventeenth century. Archimedes of Syracuse, who flourished in the third century B.C.E., calculated the value of *pi* (the ratio of the circumference of a circle to its diameter). An engineer as well as a mathematician, he invented the compound pulley, a windlass for moving heavy weights, and many other mechanical devices. "Give me a place to stand," he is said to have boasted, "and I shall move the earth." Legend describes Archimedes as the typical absent-minded scientist, who often forgot to eat; upon realizing that the water he displaced in his bathtub explained the law of specific gravity, he is said to have jumped out of the bathtub and run naked through the streets of Syracuse, shouting "*Eureka*" ("I have found it!").

Hellenistic Schools of Thought

The Hellenistic world was considerably different from the world of the Greek city-states. In the latter, citizens identified with their community, which was itself the state; but in Alexander's vast empire, communal loyalties were unsteady and—especially in sprawling urban centers—impersonal. The intellectuals of the Hellenistic Age did not formulate rational methods of investigation in the style of either Plato or Aristotle; rather they espoused philosophic schools of thought that guided everyday existence: Skepticism, Cynicism, Epicureanism, and Stoicism.

The *Skeptics*—much like the Sophists of Socrates' time—denied the possibility of knowing anything with certainty: They argued for the suspension of all intellectual judgment. The *Cynics* held that spiritual satisfaction was only possible if one renounced societal values, conventions, and material wealth. The *Epicureans*, followers of the Greek thinker Epicurus (341–270 B.C.E.), taught that happiness depended on avoiding all forms of physical excess; they valued plain living and the perfect union of body and mind. Epicurus held that the gods played no part in human life, and that death was nothing more than the rearrangement of atoms of which the body and all of nature consisted. Finally, the *Stoics* found tranquility of mind in a doctrine of detachment that allowed them to accept even the worst of life's circumstances. The aim of the Stoics was to bring the individual will into complete harmony with the will of nature, which they believed was governed by an impersonal intelligence. The Stoics also advanced the notion of universal equality. All four of these schools of thought placed the personal needs and emotions of the individual over and above the good of the community at large; in this, Hellenistic inquiry constituted a practical and radical departure from the Hellenic quest for universal truth.

Hellenistic Art

The shift from city-state to empire that accompanied the advent of the Hellenistic era was reflected in larger, more monumental forms of architecture and in the construction of utilitarian structures, such as lighthouses, theaters, and libraries. Circular sanctuaries and colossal Corinthian temples with triumphant decorative friezes embellished the cities of the Hellenistic world.

Figure 2.36 Head of Alexander, from Pergamon, Hellenistic portrait, ca. 200 B.C.E. Marble, height 16 in. Archeological Museum, Istanbul.

In freestanding Hellenistic sculpture, the new emphasis on personal emotion and individuality gave rise to portraits that were more intimate and less idealized than those of Hellenic Greece. A marble portrait of Alexander manifests the new effort to capture fleeting mood and momentary expression (Figure **2.36**). Hellenistic art is also notable for its sensuous male and female nudes, and fondness for erotic expression is especially evident in works carved in the tradition of Praxiteles (see Figure 2.24). A landmark example of the new sensuousness is the male nude statue known as the *Apollo Belvedere* (Figure **2.37**). A comparison of this figure with its Hellenic counterpart, the *Spear-Bearer* (see Figure 2.21), reveals a subtle move away from High Classical austerity to a more animated, feminized, and self-conscious figural style. One of the most popular icons of Classical beauty, this Roman copy of a Hellenistic work was destined to exercise a major influence in Western art from the moment it was recovered in Rome in 1503.

Hellenistic artists broadened the range of subjects to include young children and old, even deformed, people. Refining the long tradition of technical virtuosity, they introduced new carving techniques that produced dynamic contrasts of light and dark, dramatic displays of vigorous movement, and a wide range of expressive details. All of these features characterize the monumental *Laocoön and his Sons* (Figure **2.38**). This sculpture recreates the dramatic moment, famous in Greek legend, when Laocoön, the Trojan priest of Apollo, and his two sons succumb to the strangling attack of sea serpents sent by gods friendly to the Greeks to punish Laocoön for his effort to warn the Trojans of the Greek ruse—the wooden horse filled with the Achaean soldiers that would destroy Troy, bringing an end to the Trojan War. The writhing limbs, strained muscles, and anguished expressions of the doomed figures contribute to a sense of turbulence and agitation that sharply departs from the dignified restraint of Hellenic art. Indeed, Laocoön is the landmark of an age in which Classical idealism had already become part of history.

Figure 2.37 *Apollo Belvedere*, Roman copy of a Greek original, late fourth century B.C.E. Marble, height 7 ft. 4 in. Vatican Museums, Rome. The *Apollo Belvedere* became the symbol of Classical beauty for artists of the High Renaissance, as well as for later Neoclassicists, one of whom called it "the most sublime of all the statues of antiquity."

Figure 2.38 Agesander, Polydorus, and Athenodorus of Rhodes, *Laocoön and His Sons*, second to first century B.C.E. or a Roman copy of the first century C.E. Marble, height 7 ft. 10½ in. Vatican Museums, Rome.

Afterword

Alexander the Great bestowed upon the civilized world the ideas and artifacts of Hellenic antiquity—a legacy that would come to be called "Classical." After some three hundred years, in 30 B.C.E., Hellenistic civilization came to an end, but the landmarks of Classicism—in drama, poetry, philosophy, music, and the visual arts—endured. In the centuries to follow, the creative achievements of the ancient Greeks would continue to inspire the cultures of the West, beginning with that of the great Roman Empire.

Key Topics

- Aegean civilizations
- the Heroic Age
- the Greek gods
- the *polis*
- Athenian democracy
- the Olympic Games
- Greek drama
- Greek poetry
- the pre-Socratics
- Socrates
- Plato's *Republic*
- "Allegory of the Cave"
- Aristotle's *Ethics*
- the Classical style
- the Parthenon
- Greek music and dance
- Hellenistic culture
- Confucian thought

ANCIENT GREECE TIMELINE

	HISTORICAL EVENTS	LANDMARKS IN THE VISUAL ARTS	LITERARY LANDMARKS	MUSIC LANDMARKS
2000 B.C.E.	• Minoan civilization (ca. 2000–1400) • Mycenaean civilization (ca. 1600–1200) • Trojan War (ca. 1200) • Heroic Age (ca. 1200–750) • Olympic Games instituted (776)	• Minoan Priestess with Snakes (ca. 1600) • Palace of Minos, Knossos (ca. 1500) • Mycenaean funerary mask (ca. 1500)	• Homer, *Iliad* (ca. 850); *Odyssey* (ca. 850)	
750 B.C.E.	• Greek city-states (ca. 750–480)	• "Geometric" funerary krater (ca. 750)	• Hesiod, *Theogony* (ca. 700)	• System of modes (from 750) • Choral odes in drama (from 750)
600 B.C.E.	**Figure 2.6** Funerary mask, see p. 33	• Black-figured ceramics (ca. 600–530) • *Calf-Bearer* (ca. 575–550) • Red-figured ceramics (ca. 530–300)	• Sappho, Lyric poems (ca. 580) • Aeschylus, *Oresteia* trilogy (fifth century) • Sophocles, *Antigone*; *Oedipus Rex*; *Electra*; *Oedipus at Colonus* (fifth century) • Euripides, *Medea*; *Trojan Women*; *Electra*; *The Bacchae* (fifth century)	• Pythagoras: music theory (ca. 550)
500 B.C.E.	• Athens becomes the first direct democracy (508) • Persian Wars against Greece (499–480) • Peloponnesian War (431–404)	• Zeus (or Poseidon) (ca. 460) • Polycleitus, *Spear-Bearer* (ca. 450–440) • Myron, *Discobolus* (ca. 450) • Parthenon, Athens (448–432)	• Herodotus, *The Persian Wars* (ca. 430) • Aristophanes, *Lysistrata* (ca. 411) • Thucydides, *History of the Peloponnesian War* (ca. 410)	
400 B.C.E.	• Philip of Macedonia defeats Greeks (338) • Rule of Alexander the Great (336–323) • Persia comes under rule of Seleucids (323) • Macedonia-Greece governed by family of Antigonus the One-Eyed (323) • Egypt ruled by Ptolemy dynasty (323–30)	• Theater at Epidaurus (ca. 350) • Praxiteles, *Aphrodite of Knidos* (ca. 350) • *Apollo Belvedere* (late fourth century)	• Plato, *Republic* (ca. 375) • Aristotle, *Politics* (ca. 350); *Ethics* (ca. 340); *Poetics* (ca. 340)	**Figure 2.22** Zeus, see p. 51
300 B.C.E.	**Figure 2.25** Parthenon, see p. 53	• Head of Alexander, from Pergamon (ca. 200) • *Laocoön and His Sons* (second to first century)	**Figure 2.16** Black-figured amphora, see p. 48	

(All dates on this timeline are before the common era—B.C.E.)

PAVLVS III PONT. MAX. STATVAM AENEAM
EQVESTREM A. S. P. Q. R. M. ANTONINO PIO ETIAM
TVM VIVENTI STATVTAM VARIIS DEIN VRBIS
CASIB. EVERSAM ET A SIXTO IIII PONT. MAX. AD
LATERAN. BASILICAM REPOSITAM VT MEMO
RIAE OPT. PRINCIPIS CONSVLERET PATRIAEQ.
DECORA ATQ. ORNAMENTA RESTITVERET
EX HVMILIORI LOCO IN AREAM CAPITOLINAM
TRANSTVLIT ATQ. DICAVIT
ANN. SAL. M. D XXXVIII
AVGVSTINVS TRINCIVS IACOBVS BVCCA BELLA
CAESAR DE MAGISTRIS CONSERVATORES CVR

Chapter 3

Empire:

THE POWER AND GLORY OF ROME

ca. 500 B.C.E.–500 C.E.

The word "empire" comes from the Latin *imperium*, the absolute authority held by the rulers of ancient Rome. By sheer military force, Rome created the West's largest and longest-lasting empire: a world state embracing many different lands and peoples. Rome was not the first of antiquity's empires; from Sargon and Hammurabi of Mesopotamia to the kings of Assyria and Persia, territorial ambitions drove the course of empire. However, Rome's influence outlasted that of its predecessors by centuries. By adopting and then adapting the best features of the cultures it conquered—Etruscan, Egyptian, Greek, and Asian—Rome became the fountainhead of urban civilization. While the Roman transmission of the Greek legacy was crucial to the success of Classicism, Rome's original contributions to language, law, and architecture remain imprinted on the humanistic tradition of the West.

During the centuries in which imperial Rome came to dominate the West, East Asia saw the rise of an equally vast and powerful empire, that of ancient China. Just as Rome's achievements came to shape the West, so Chinese culture, especially that of the Han dynasty, would have a lasting and formative impact on the lands of East Asia.

A First Look

Seated astride his spirited horse, the Roman emperor Marcus Aurelius (121–180 C.E.) addresses his troops and the people of Rome. He raises his right hand in the magisterial gesture of *imperator* (from which the word "emperor" derives): army general and supreme commander. Wearing a short tunic and a cloak fastened by a brooch at his shoulder, he holds the reins of his charger in his left hand. (Saddles and stirrups were not yet in use.) This imperial monument, conceived by an unknown artist, is the only surviving bronze equestrian sculpture from the Classical era. It probably celebrates Rome's victory over the Parthians in Mesopotamia.

Most antique bronzes were melted down after the fall of Rome in the fifth century of the Christian era; however, this sculpture escaped destruction because it was mistakenly thought to represent the emperor Constantine, the first pagan ruler to officially adopt Christianity. As such, it was interpreted as reflecting Rome's continuity of power from the pagan to the Christian world. Even before the sixteenth century, when Michelangelo designed its oval base, the equestrian statue of Marcus Aurelius was an inspiration to dozens of Renaissance artists, and it has remained the model for scores of modern victory monuments. The original (seen here) was moved in 1981 from the Piazza del Campidoglio in Rome to the nearby Capitoline Museums. A replica, made from a mold created with computer-generated photographs, now stands in its place.

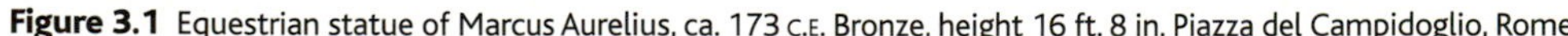

Figure 3.1 Equestrian statue of Marcus Aurelius, ca. 173 C.E. Bronze, height 16 ft. 8 in. Piazza del Campidoglio, Rome.

THE ROMAN RISE TO EMPIRE

Rome's Early History

Rome's origins are to be found among the tribes of Iron Age folk called *Latins*, who invaded the Italian peninsula just after the beginning of the first millennium B.C.E. By the mid-eighth century B.C.E., these people had founded the city of Rome in the lower valley of the Tiber River, a spot strategically located for control of the Italian peninsula and for convenient access to the Mediterranean Sea (see Map 3.1). While central Italy became the domain of the Latins, the rest of the peninsula received a continuous infusion of eastern Mediterranean people—Etruscans, Greeks, and Phoenicians—who brought with them cultures richer and more complex than that of the Latins.

The Etruscans, whose origins are unknown (and whose language remains undeciphered), established themselves in northwest Italy. A sophisticated, Hellenized people with commercial contacts throughout the Mediterranean, they were experts in the arts of metallurgy, town building, and city planning. The Greeks, who colonized the tip of the Italian peninsula and Sicily, were masters of philosophy and the arts. And the Phoenicians, who settled on the northern coast of Africa, brought westward their alphabet and their commercial and maritime skills. From all of these peoples, but especially from the first two groups, the Latins borrowed elements that would enhance their own history. From the Etruscans, the Romans absorbed the fundamentals of urban planning, chariot racing, the toga, bronze and gold crafting, and the most ingenious structural principle of Mesopotamian architecture—the arch. The Etruscans provided their dead with tombs designed to resemble the lavish dwelling places of the deceased. On the lids of the **sarcophagi** (stone coffins) that held the remains of the dead, Etruscan artists carved their portraits, depicting husbands and wives relaxing and socializing on their dining couch, as if still enjoying a family banquet (Figure **3.2**).

From the Greeks, the Romans borrowed a pantheon of gods and goddesses, linguistic and literary principles, and the aesthetics of the Classical style. As the Latins absorbed Etruscan and Greek culture, so they drew these and other peoples into what would become the most powerful world state in ancient history.

The Roman Republic (509–133 B.C.E.)

For three centuries, Etruscan kings ruled the Latin population, but in 509 B.C.E. the Latins overthrew the Etruscans. Over the next two hundred years, monarchy slowly gave way to a government "of the people" (***res publica***). The agricultural population of ancient Rome consisted of a powerful class of large landowners, the *patricians*, and a more populous class of farmers and small landowners called *plebeians*. The plebeians constituted the membership of a Popular Assembly. Although this body conferred civil and military authority (the ***imperium***) upon two elected magistrates (called *consuls*), its lower-class members had

Figure 3.2 Sarcophagus from Cerveteri, ca. 520 B.C.E. Painted terracotta, length 6 ft. 7 in. National Museum of Villa Giulia, Rome. Etruscan funerary art, with its lively, life-sized representations of the dead, probably influenced Roman portrait sculpture. These remarkable Etruscan sculptures made original use of Greek and Egyptian traditions by bringing to life the image of the mummified corpse.

Map 3.1 The Roman Republic in 44 B.C.E. and the Roman Empire in 180 C.E.

little voice in government. The wealthy patricians—life members of the Roman Senate—controlled the lawmaking process. But step by step, the plebeians gained increasing political influence. Using as leverage their service as soldiers in the Roman army and their power to veto laws initiated by the Senate, the plebeians—through their leaders, the *tribunes*—made themselves heard. Eventually, they won the freedom to intermarry with the patricians, the right to hold executive office, and, finally, in 287 B.C.E., the privilege of making laws. The stern and independent population of Roman farmers had arrived at a *res publica* by peaceful means. But no sooner had Rome become a Republic than it adopted an expansionist course that would erode these democratic achievements.

Obedience to the Roman state and service in its powerful army were essential to the life of the early Republic. Both contributed to the rise of Roman imperialism, which proceeded by means of long wars of conquest similar to those that had marked the history of earlier empires. After expelling the last of the Etruscan kings, Rome extended its power over all parts of the Italian peninsula. By the middle of the third century B.C.E., having united all of Italy by force or negotiation, Rome stood poised to rule the Mediterranean. A longstanding distrust of the Phoenicians, and rivalry with the city of Carthage, Phoenicia's commercial stronghold in northeastern Africa, led Rome into the Punic (Latin for "Phoenician") Wars—a 150-year period of intermittent violence that ended with the destruction of Carthage in 146 B.C.E.

With the defeat of Carthage, Rome assumed naval and commercial leadership in the western Mediterranean, the sea they would come to call *mare nostrum* ("our sea"). But the ambitions of army generals and the impetus of a century of warfare fueled the fire of Roman imperialism. Rome seized every opportunity for conquest, and by the end of the first century B.C.E. the Empire included most of North Africa, the Iberian peninsula, Greece, Egypt, much of southwest Asia, and the territories constituting present-day Europe as far as the Rhine River (Map **3.1**).

Despite the difficulties presented by the task of governing such far-flung territories, the Romans proved to be efficient administrators. They demanded from their foreign provinces taxes, soldiers to serve in the Roman army, tribute, and slaves. Roman governors, appointed by the Senate from among the higher ranks of the military, ruled within the conquered provinces. Usually, local customs and even local governments were permitted to continue unmodified, for the Romans considered tolerance of provincial customs politically practical. The Romans introduced the Latin language and Roman law in the provinces. They built paved roads, freshwater aqueducts, bridges, and eventually granted the people of their conquered territories Roman citizenship.

Rome's highly disciplined army was the backbone of the Empire. During the Republic, the army consisted of citizens who served two-year terms, but by the first century C.E., the military had become a profession to which all free men might devote twenty-five years (or more) of their lives. Since serving for this length of time allowed a non-Roman to gain Roman citizenship for himself and his children, military service acted as a means of Romanizing foreigners. The Roman army was the object of fear and admiration among those familiar with Rome's rise to power.

The Collapse of the Republic (133–30 B.C.E.)

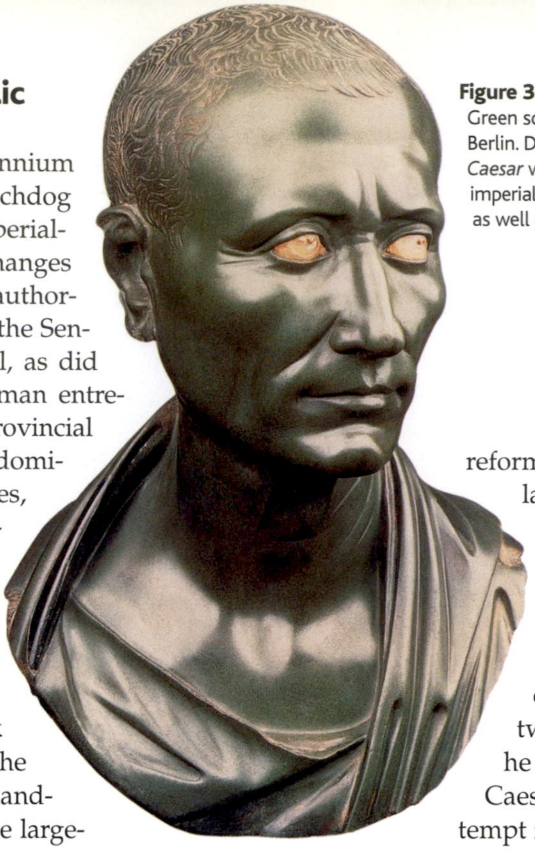

By the beginning of the first millennium C.E., Rome had become the watchdog of the ancient world. Roman imperialism, however, worked to effect changes within the Republic itself. By its authority to handle all military matters, the Senate became increasingly powerful, as did a new class of men, wealthy Roman entrepreneurs who filled the jobs of provincial administration. The army, by its domination of Rome's overseas provinces, also became more powerful. Precious metals, booty, and slaves from foreign conquests brought enormous wealth to army generals and influential patricians; corruption became widespread. Captives of war were shipped back to Rome and auctioned off to the highest bidders, usually patrician landowners, whose farms soon became large-scale plantations (*latifundia*) worked by slaves. The increased agricultural productivity of the plantations gave economic advantage to large landowners who easily undersold the lesser landowners and drove them out of business. Increasingly, the small farmers were forced to sell their farms to neighboring patricians in return for the right to remain on the land. Or, they simply moved to the city to join, by the end of the first century B.C.E., a growing unemployed population. The disappearance of the small farmer signaled the decline of the Republic.

As Rome's rich citizens grew richer and its poor citizens poorer, the patricians fiercely resisted efforts to redistribute wealth more equally. But reform measures failed and political rivalries increased. Ultimately, Rome fell victim to the ambitions of army generals, who, having conquered in the name of Rome, now turned to conquering Rome itself. The first century B.C.E. was an age of military dictators, whose competing claims to power fueled a spate of civil wars. As bloody confrontations replaced reasoned compromises, the Republic crumbled.

In 46 B.C.E., the extraordinary army commander Gaius Julius Caesar (Figure **3.3**) triumphantly entered the city of Rome and established a dictatorship. Caesar, who had spent nine years conquering Gaul (present-day France and Belgium), was as shrewd in politics as he was brilliant in war. These campaigns are described in his prose *Commentaries on the Gallic War*. His brief but successful campaigns in Syria, Asia Minor, and Egypt—where his union with the Egyptian Queen Cleopatra (69–30 B.C.E.) produced a son—inspired his famous boast: *Veni, vidi, vici* ("I came, I saw, I conquered"). A superb organizer, Caesar took strong measures to restabilize Rome: He reformed and consolidated the laws, regulated taxation, reduced debts, sent large numbers of the unemployed proletariat to overseas colonies, and inaugurated public works projects. He also granted citizenship to non-Italians and reformed the Western calendar to comprise 365 days and twelve months (one of which—July—he named after himself). Threatened by Caesar's populist reforms and his contempt for republican institutions, a group of his senatorial opponents, led by Marcus Junius Brutus, assassinated him in 44 B.C.E.

Figure 3.3 Bust of Julius Caesar, first century B.C.E. Green schist, height 16$^{1}/_{8}$ in. State Museums, Berlin. Despite Caesar's inglorious death, the name *Caesar* would be used as an honorific title by all his imperial successors well into the second century C.E., as well as by many modern-day dictators.

The Roman Empire: *Pax Romana* (30 B.C.E.–180 C.E.)

Following the assassination of Julius Caesar, a struggle for power ensued between Caesar's first lieutenant, Mark Antony (ca. 80–30 B.C.E.), and his grandnephew (and adopted son) Octavian (63 B.C.E.–14 C.E.). The contest between the two was resolved at Actium in 31 B.C.E., when Octavian's navy routed the combined forces of Mark Antony and Queen Cleopatra. The alliance between Antony and Cleopatra, like that between Cleopatra and Julius Caesar, advanced the political ambitions of Egypt's most seductive queen, who sought not only to unite the eastern and western portions of Rome's great empire, but to govern a vast Roman world state. That destiny, however, would fall to Octavian.

In 43 B.C.E., Octavian usurped the consulship and gained the approval of the Senate to rule for life. Although he called himself "first citizen" (*princeps*), his title of Emperor betrayed the reality that he was first and foremost Rome's army general (*imperator*). After the Roman Senate bestowed on him the title *Augustus* ("the Revered One") in 27 B.C.E., he was known by that honorific title (Figure **3.4**). Augustus shared legislative power with the Senate, but retained the right to veto legislation. Thus, to all intents and purposes, the Republic was defunct. The destiny of Rome lay once again in the hands of a military dictator.

Augustus' reign ushered in an era of peace and stability, a *Pax Romana* ("Roman peace"). From 30 B.C.E. to 180 C.E. the Roman peace prevailed throughout the Empire, and Rome enjoyed active commercial contact with all parts of the civilized world, including India and China. The *Pax Romana* was also a time of artistic and literary productivity. An enthusiastic patron of the arts, Augustus commissioned literature, sculpture, and architecture. He boasted that he had come to power when Rome was a city of brick and would leave it a city of marble. In most cases, this meant a veneer of marble that was, by standard Roman building practices, laid over the brick surface. In a city blighted by crime, noise, poor hygiene, and a frequent scarcity of food and water, Augustus initiated many new public works (including three new aqueducts and some five hundred fountains) and such civic services as a police force and a fire department. The reign of Augustus also witnessed the birth of a new religion, Christianity, which, in later centuries, would spread throughout the Empire (see page 99).

Augustus put an end to the civil wars of the preceding century, but he revived neither the political nor the social equilibrium of the early Republic. Following his death, Rome continued to be ruled by military officials. Since there was no machinery for succession to the imperial throne, Rome's rulers held office until they either died or were assassinated. Government by and for the people had been the hallmark of Rome's early history, but the enterprise of imperialism ultimately overtook these lofty republican ideals.

Roman Law

Against this backdrop of conquest and dominion, it is no surprise that Rome's contributions to the history of culture were practical rather than theoretical. The sheer size of the Roman Empire inspired engineering programs, such as bridge and road building, that united all regions under Roman rule. Law—a less tangible means of unification—was equally important in this regard. The development of a system of law was one of Rome's most original landmark achievements.

Roman law (the Latin *jus* means both "law" and "justice") evolved out of the practical need to rule a world state, rather than—as in ancient Greece—as the product of a dialectic between the citizen and the *polis*. Inspired by the laws of Solon, the Romans published their first civil code, the Twelve Tables of Law, in around 450 B.C.E. They placed these laws on view in the Forum, the public meeting area for the civic, religious, and commercial activities of Rome. The Twelve Tables of Law provided Rome's basic legal code for almost a thousand years. To this body of law were added the acts of the Assembly and the Senate, and public decrees of the emperors. For some five hundred years, *praetors* (magistrates who administered justice) and *jurisconsults* (experts in the law) interpreted the laws, bringing commonsense resolutions to private disputes. Their interpretations constituted a body of "case law." In giving consideration to individual needs, these magistrates cultivated the concept of equity, which puts the spirit of the law above the letter of the law. The decisions of Roman jurists became precedents that established comprehensive guidelines for future judgments. Thus, Roman law was not fixed, but was an evolving body of opinions on the nature and dispensation of justice.

Figure 3.4 Augustus of Primaporta, early first century C.E., after a bronze of ca. 20 B.C.E. Marble, height 6 ft. 8 in. Vatican Museums, Rome. In this freestanding, larger-than-life statue from Primaporta, Augustus raises his arm in a gesture of leadership and imperial authority (see also Figure 3.1). He wears a breastplate celebrating his victory over the Parthians in 20 B.C.E. At his feet appear Cupid and a dolphin, reminders of his alleged divine descent from Venus—the mother of Aeneas, Rome's legendary founder. Augustus's stance and physical proportions are modeled on the *Doryphorus* by Polycleitus (see Figure 2.21). His handsome face and tall, muscular physique serve to complete the heroic image. In reality, however, Augustus was 5 feet 4 inches tall—the average height of the Roman male.

ROMAN LITERATURE

Latin Prose Literature

Roman literature reveals a masterful use of Latin prose for the purposes of entertainment, instruction, and record keeping. Ever applying their resources to practical ends, the Romans found prose the ideal vehicle for compiling and transmitting information. Rome gave the West its first geographies and encyclopedias, as well as some of its finest biographies, histories, and manuals of instruction. In the writing of history, in particular, the Romans demonstrated their talent for the collection and analysis of factual evidence. Although Roman historians tended to glorify Rome and its leadership, their attention to detail often surpassed that of the Greek historians. One of Rome's greatest historians, Titus Livius ("Livy," ca. 59 B.C.E.–17 C.E.), wrote a history of Rome from the eighth century B.C.E. to his own day. Although only a small portion of Livy's original 142 books survives, this monumental work—commissioned by Augustus himself—constitutes our most reliable account of political and social life in the days of the Roman Republic.

The Romans were masters, as well, in **oratory**, that is, the art of public speaking, and in the writing of **epistles** (letters). In both of these genres, the statesman Marcus Tullius Cicero (106–43 B.C.E.) excelled. A contemporary of Julius Caesar, Cicero produced more than nine hundred letters—sometimes writing three a day to the same person—and more than one hundred speeches and **essays**. Clarity and eloquence are the hallmarks of Cicero's prose style, which Renaissance humanists hailed as the model for literary excellence (see page 184). While Cicero was familiar with the theoretical works of Aristotle and the Stoics, his writings reflect a profound concern for the political realities of his own day. In his essay *On Duty* (44 B.C.E.), for instance, he evaluates the benefits of diplomacy versus war:

> . . . diplomacy in the friendly settlement of controversies is more desirable than courage in settling them on the battlefield; but we must be careful not to take that course merely for the sake of avoiding war rather than for the sake of public expediency. War, however, should be undertaken in such a way as to make it evident that it has no other object than to secure peace.

In his lifetime, Cicero served Rome as consul, statesman, and orator; his carefully reasoned speeches helped to shape public opinion. While he praised Julius Caesar's literary style, he openly opposed his patron's dictatorship. (Caesar congenially confessed to Cicero, "It is nobler to enlarge the boundaries of human intelligence than those of the Roman Empire.") During the tumultuous period following Caesar's assassination, Cicero too was murdered, his head and hands put on public display in the Forum.

Philosophic Thought

More a practical than a speculative people, the Romans produced no systems of philosophic thought comparable to those of Plato and Aristotle. Yet they respected and preserved the writings of Hellenic and Hellenistic thinkers. Educated Romans admired Aristotle and absorbed the works of the Epicureans and the Stoics. The Latin poet Lucretius (ca. 95–ca. 55 B.C.E.) popularized the materialist theories of Democritus and Leucippus, which describe the world in purely physical terms and deny the existence of the gods and other supernatural beings. Since all of reality, including the human soul, consists of atoms, he argues in his only work, *On the Nature of Things*, there is no reason to fear death: "We shall not feel because we shall not be."

In the vast, impersonal world of the Empire, many Romans cultivated the attitude of rational detachment popular among the Stoics (see page 60). Like their third-century-B.C.E. forebears, Roman Stoics believed that an impersonal force (Providence or Divine Reason) governed the world, and that happiness lay in one's ability to accept one's fate. Stoics rejected any emotional attachments that might enslave them. The ideal spiritual condition and the one most conducive to contentment, according to the Stoic point of view, depended on the subjugation of the emotions to reason.

Stoicism was especially popular among Roman intellectuals and moralists. Among these was the noted playwright and essayist Lucius Annaeus Seneca (ca. 4 B.C.E.–65 C.E.) and the emperor Marcus Aurelius (121–180 C.E.), both of whom wrote stimulating treatises on the subject. Seneca's *On Tranquility of*

Seneca, *On Tranquility of Mind* (ca. 40 C.E.)

Ideas and Issues

STOIC DETACHMENT AND ACCEPTANCE

"All life is bondage. Man must therefore habituate himself to his condition, complain of it as little as possible, and grasp whatever good lies within his reach. No situation is so harsh that a dispassionate mind cannot find some consolation in it. If a man lays even a very small area out skillfully it will provide ample space for many uses, and even a foothold can be made livable by deft arrangement. Apply good sense to your problems; the hard can be softened, the narrow widened, and the heavy made lighter by the skillful bearer. . . ."

(from Seneca, *On Tranquility of Mind*)

Q Do you find Seneca's advice practical or impractical?

Mind argues that one may achieve peace of mind by avoiding burdensome responsibilities, gloomy companions, and excessive wealth. Stoicism offered a reasoned retreat from psychic pain and moral despair, as well as a practical set of solutions to the daily strife between the self and society.

Epic Poetry

While the Romans excelled in didactic prose, they also produced some of the world's finest verse. Under the patronage of Augustus, Rome enjoyed a Golden Age of Latin literature whose most notable representative was Virgil (Publius Vergilius Maro, 70–19 B.C.E.). Rome's foremost poet-publicist, Virgil wrote the semilegendary epic that immortalized Rome's destiny as world ruler. The *Aeneid* was not the product of an oral tradition, as were the Homeric epics; rather, it was a literary epic, undertaken to rival the epics of Homer. The hero of Virgil's poem is Rome's mythical founder, the Trojan-born Aeneas. The instrument of destiny, Aeneas founds the settlement of Latium and sets the course on which Rome will establish itself as world ruler. As is typical of the epic hero, he undertakes a long journey, filled with adventures that test his prowess. The first six books of the *Aeneid* recount his voyage from Troy to Italy and his love affair with a beautiful Carthaginian princess, Dido. The second six books describe the Trojan conquest of Latium and the establishment of the Roman state. While Virgil wrote the *Aeneid* to glorify the imperial achievements of Augustus, he infused the poem with an epic theme that reflects the sober ideals of ancient Rome: the primacy of duty—that of the citizen, of the warrior, and of the state. Rome's duty to rule is proclaimed by Aeneas' father, Anchises, whom the hero meets in the underworld (described in Book 6):

Virgil, *Aeneid* (ca. 20 B.C.E.)

Others, no doubt, will better mold the bronze
To the semblance of soft breathing, draw from marble,
The living countenance; and others please
With greater eloquence, or lean to measure
Better than we, the pathways of the heavens,
The risings of the stars: remember, Roman,
To rule the people under law, to establish
The way of peace, to battle down the haughty,
To spare the meek. Our fine arts, these forever.

No summary of the *Aeneid* can represent adequately the monumental impact of this landmark work, which became the foundation for education in the Latin language. Its poetry and its patriotic theme—the origins, history, and destiny of Rome—inspired generations of writers, including the late medieval Tuscan poet Dante Alighieri, who in his own epic poem, the *Commedia* (see page 148), embraced Virgil as his guide to the underworld and his master in the literary arts.

Lyric Poetry and Satire

While Virgil is best known for the *Aeneid*, he also wrote pastoral poems, or **eclogues**, that glorify the natural landscape and its rustic inhabitants. Virgil's *Eclogues* found inspiration in the pastoral sketches of Theocritus, a third-century-B.C.E. Sicilian poet. Many Classicists besides Virgil looked to Hellenic prototypes. The poetry of Catullus (ca. 84–54 B.C.E.), for instance, reflects familiarity with the art of Sappho of Lesbos, whose lyrics he admired. The greatest of the Latin lyric poets, Catullus came to Rome from Verona. A young man of some wealth and charm, he wrote primarily on the subjects that consumed his short but intense life: friendship, love, and sex. Some of his finest poems were inspired by his passionate affair with Clodia (whom he names Lesbia in reference to Sappho), the adulterous wife of a Roman consul. These trace the trajectory from the poet's first fevered amorous passions to his despair and bitterness at the collapse of the affair. Candid and deeply personal, they strike us with the immediacy of a modern, secular voice. One example of Catullus' seductive *Poems to Lesbia* will serve to illustrate:

Catullus, *Poems to Lesbia* (ca. 60 B.C.E.)

Come, Lesbia, let us live and love,
nor give a damn what sour old men say.
The sun that sets may rise again
but when our light has sunk into the earth,
it is gone forever.
Give me a thousand kisses,
then a hundred, another thousand,
another hundred
and in one breath
still kiss another thousand,
another hundred.
O then with lips and bodies joined
many deep thousands;
confuse
their number,
so that poor fools and cuckolds (envious
even now) shall never
learn our wealth and curse us
with their
evil eyes.

The poetry of Catullus notwithstanding, passion and personal feeling were not typical of Latin literature, which inclined more usually toward instruction. One of Rome's most notable poets, Publius Ovidius Naso, or Ovid (43 B.C.E.–17 C.E.), earned centuries of fame for his narrative poem, the *Metamorphoses*. This vast collection of stories about Greek and Roman gods develops the theme of supernatural transformation. Ovid himself pursued a career of poetry and love. Married three times, he seems to have been a master in the art of seduction. His witty guide on the subject, *The Art of Love*, brought him

Ovid, *Metamorphoses* (ca. 5 C.E.); *The Art of Love* (ca. 10 C.E.)

Ideas and Issues

HORACE: "*CARPE DIEM*" ("SEIZE THE DAY")

Pry not in forbidden lore,
Ask no more, Leuconoë,
How many years—to you?—to me?—
The gods will send us
Before they end us;
Nor, questing, fix your hopes
On Babylonian horoscopes.
Learn to accept whatever is to be:
Whether Jove grant us many winters,
Or make of this the last, which splinters
Now on opposing cliffs the Tuscan sea.

Be wise; decant your wine; condense
Large aims to fit life's cramped circumference.
We talk, time flies—you've said it!
Make hay today,
Tomorrow rates no credit.

Q What personal advantages or disadvantages might follow from embracing this maxim?

into disfavor with Augustus, who (finding the work morally threatening) sent Ovid into exile. Though written with tongue in cheek, *The Art of Love* swelled an already large canon of misogynist, or antifemale, Classical literature. In this humorous "handbook," Ovid offers vivid glimpses into everyday life in Rome, but he clearly holds that the greatest human crimes issue from women's lust, which, according to the poet, is "keener, fiercer, and more wanton" than men's.

Roman poets were moralizers. Augustus' poet laureate, Quintus Haeredes Flaccus, better known as Horace (65–8 B.C.E.), wrote some of the most popular verse of his time, much of which took a critical view of Roman life. The son of a freed slave who sought his son's advancement, Horace was educated in Rome and Athens. His poetry won him the friendship of Virgil and the patronage of Maecenas, Augustus' chief minister of state. Lacking the grandeur of Virgil and the virtuosity of Ovid, Horace wrote verses that exposed various types of human folly—self-indulgence, vanity, ambition, and greed—by pointing up the contradictions between practical realities and abstract ideals. These lyric poems reflect the Roman affection for **satire**, a literary genre that uses humor to denounce human vice and folly. Satire—another of Rome's landmark contributions to world literature—is a kind of moralizing in which human imperfection is not simply criticized, but, rather, mocked by way of biting wit and comic exaggeration. While Horace brings a satiric eye to such subjects as war, patriotism, and everyday conduct, he celebrates the enjoyment of life and laments its brevity. In a poem from the *Odes*, he discloses his Stoic disbelief in human perfection, advising us to "seize the day" and to "learn to accept whatever is to be."

Horace, *Odes* (ca. 23 B.C.E.)

While Horace's lyrics are, for the most part, genial, those of Rome's most famous satirist, Juvenal (Decimus Junius Juvenalis, ca. 60–130 C.E.), are bitter and devastating. Juvenal came to Rome from the provinces. His subsequent career as a magistrate and his experience of poverty and financial failure contributed to his negative perception of Roman society, which he describes in his sixteen *Satires* as swollen with greed and corruption. Juvenal's attack on the city of Rome paints a picture of a noisy, dirty, and crowded urban community inhabited by selfish, violent, and self-indulgent people. Juvenal was especially hostile toward foreigners and women. His sixth *Satire*, "Against Women," is one of the most hostile antifemale diatribes in the history of Western literature and a landmark in the long history of misogyny. In this excerpt, the poet laments the disappearance of the chaste Latin woman whose virtues, he submits, have been corrupted by luxury:

Juvenal, *Satires* (ca. 125 C.E.)

There's nothing a woman won't do, nothing she thinks
is disgraceful
With the green gems at her neck, or pearls distending
her ear lobes.
Nothing is worse to endure than your Mrs. Richbitch,
whose visage
Is padded and plastered with dough, in the most
ridiculous manner.
Furthermore, she reeks of unguents, so God help her
husband
With his wretched face stunk up with these, smeared by
her lipstick.
To her lovers she comes with her skin washed clean. But
at home
Why does she need to look pretty? Nard[1] is assumed for
the lover,
For the lover she buys all the Arabian perfumes.
It takes her some time to strip down to her face,
removing the layers
One by one, till at last she is recognizable, almost,
Then she uses a lotion, she-asses' milk; she'd need herds
Of these creatures to keep her supplied on her
northernmost journeys.
But when she's given herself the treatment in full, from
the ground base
Through the last layer of mud pack, from the first wash
to a poultice,
What lies under all this—a human face, or an ulcer?

[1] Spikenard, a fragrant ointment.

The women of imperial Rome did not have many more civil rights than did their Golden Age Athenian sisters. They could neither vote nor hold public office. However, they could own property, and they were free to manage their own legal affairs. Roman girls were educated along with boys, and most middle-class women could read and write. Some female aristocrats were active in public life, and the consorts of Rome's rulers often shaped matters of succession and politics by way of their influence on their husbands and sons. Roman records confirm that in addition to the traditional occupations of women in food and textile production and in prostitution, Roman women held positions as musicians, painters, priestesses, midwives, and gladiators.

Although Juvenal's bias against womankind strikes a personal note, it is likely that he was reflecting the public outcry against the licentiousness that was widespread in his own day. Increasingly during the second century, men openly enjoyed concubines, mistresses, and prostitutes. Infidelity among married women was on the rise, and divorce was common, as were second and third marriages for both sexes.

Roman Drama

Roman tragedies were roughly modeled on those of Greece. They were moral and didactic in intent, and their themes were drawn from Greek and Roman history. Theatrical performances in Rome did not share, however, the religious solemnity of those in Greece. Rather, they were a form of entertainment offered along with the public games that marked the major civic festivals known as *ludi*. Unlike the rituals and athletic contests of the Greeks, *ludi* featured displays of armed combat and other violent amusements. The nature of these public spectacles may explain why many of the tragedies written to compete with them were bloody and ghoulish in character. The lurid plays of the Stoic writer Seneca drew crowds in Roman times and were to inspire—some 1500 years later—such playwrights as William Shakespeare.

The Romans seem to have preferred comedies to tragedies, for most surviving Roman plays are of the comic genre. Comic writers employed simple plots and broad (often obscene) humor. The plays of Plautus (ca. 250–184 B.C.E.) and Terence (ca. 185–159 B.C.E.) are filled with stock characters, such as the good-hearted prostitute, the shrewish wife, and the clever servant. The characters engage in farcical schemes and broad slapstick action of the kind common to today's television situation comedies. In the comic theater of the Romans, as in Roman culture in general, everyday life took precedence over fantasy, and the real, if imperfect, world was the natural setting for down-to-earth human beings.

ART AND EMPIRE

Roman Architecture

Rome's architecture reflected the practical needs of a sprawling empire whose urban centers suffered from the congestion, noise, and filth described by Juvenal. To link the provinces that ranged from the Atlantic Ocean to the Euphrates River, Roman engineers built fifty thousand miles of paved roads, many of which are still in use today. The need to house, govern, and entertain large numbers of citizens inspired the construction of tenements, meeting halls, baths, and amphitheaters. Eight- and nine-story tenements provided thousands with cheap (if often rat-infested) housing.

Superb engineers, the Romans employed the structural advantages of the arch (the knowledge of which they inherited from the Etruscans) to enclose greater volumes of uninterrupted space than any previously known. The arch constituted a clear technical advance over the post-and-lintel construction used by the Greeks in buildings like the Parthenon (see Figure 2.25). The Romans adapted this structural principle inventively. They placed arches back to back to form a barrel or tunnel **vault**, at right angles to each other to form a cross or groined vault, and around a central point to form a dome (Figure **3.5**). Roman bridges and tunnels defied natural barriers, while some eighteen aqueducts brought fresh water to Rome's major cities (Figure **3.6**). The aqueducts, some of which delivered well over forty million gallons of water per day to a single site, were the public works that the Romans considered their most significant technological achievement.

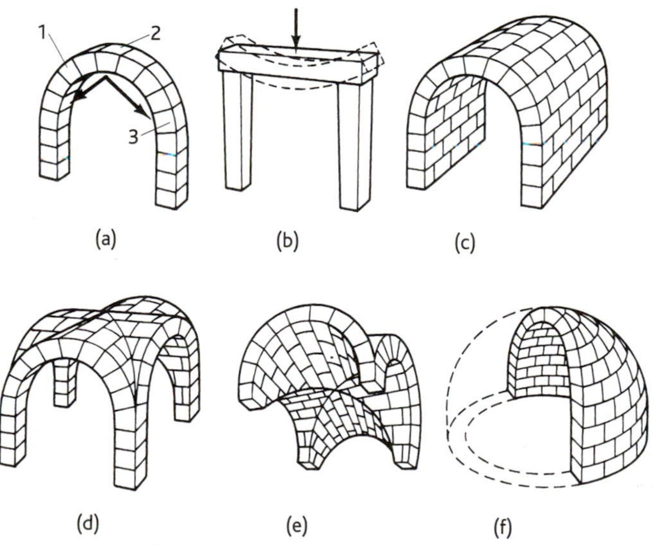

Figure 3.5 Arch principle and arch construction. (a) Arch consisting of *voussoirs*, wedge-shaped blocks (1, 2, 3); (b) Post-and-lintel; (c) Barrel or tunnel vault; (d) and (e) Cross or groined vault; (f) Dome.

Figure 3.6 Pont du Gard, near Nîmes, France, ca. 20–10 B.C.E. Stone, height 180 ft., length ca. 900 ft. One of Rome's most spectacular large-scale engineering projects is the 900-foot-long Pont du Gard, part of a 25-mile-long aqueduct that brought fresh water to the city of Nîmes in southern France. Built of 6-ton stones and assembled without mortar, the structure reflects the practical function of arches at three levels, the bottom row supporting a bridge and the second row undergirding the top channel through which water ran by gravity to its destination.

Roman building techniques reveal a combination of practicality and innovation: The Romans were the first to use concrete (an aggregate of sand, lime, brick-and-stone rubble, and water), a medium that made possible cheap large-scale construction. They laid their foundations with concrete, raised structures with brick, rubble, and stone, and finished exterior surfaces with veneers of marble, tile, bronze, or plaster.

Roman architecture and engineering were considered one and the same discipline. Vitruvius' *Ten Books on Architecture*, the oldest and most influential work of its kind, includes instructions for hydraulic systems, city planning, and mechanical devices. For the Roman architect, the function of a building determined its formal design. The ground plans for villas, theaters, and temples received the same attention to detail as that given to hospitals, fortresses, and military camps.

The sheer magnitude of such Roman amphitheaters as the Circus Maximus, which seated 200,000 spectators, and the Colosseum, which covered 6 acres and accommodated fifty thousand (Figure **3.7**), is a reminder that during the first century C.E. Rome's population exceeded one million people. Many of them were the impoverished recipients of relief in the form of wheat and free entertainment, hence the phrase "bread and circuses." The Roman amphitheaters testify to the popular taste for entertainments that included chariot races, mock sea battles, gladiatorial contests, and a variety of brutal blood sports. At the Colosseum, three levels of seating rose above the arena floor. Beneath the floor was a complex of rooms and tunnels from which athletes, gladiators, and wild animals emerged to entertain the cheering crowd. To provide shade from the sun, an awning at the roof level could be extended by means of a system of pulleys. On each level of the exterior, arches were framed by a series of decorative, or engaged, columns displaying the three Greek orders: Doric (at ground level), Ionic, and Corinthian. The ingenious combination of arch and post-and-lintel structural elements in the design of the Colosseum would be widely imitated for centuries, and especially during the Italian Renaissance (see Chapter 7).

Roman architectural genius may be best illustrated by the Pantheon, a temple whose structural majesty depends on the combination of Roman technical ingenuity and inventive spatial design. Dedicated to the seven planetary deities, the Pantheon was built in the early second century C.E. Its monumental exterior—once covered with a veneer of white marble and bronze—features a portico with eight Corinthian columns originally elevated by a flight of stairs that now lies buried beneath the city street (Figure **3.8**). One of the few buildings from Classical antiquity to have remained almost intact, the Pantheon boasts a 19-foot-thick rotunda that is capped by a solid dome consisting of 5000 tons of concrete. The interior of the dome, once painted blue and gold to resemble the vault of heaven, is pierced by a 30-foot-wide *oculus*, or "eye," that admits light and air (Figure **3.9**). The proportions of the Pantheon observe the Classical principles of symmetry and harmony as described by Vitruvius: The height from the floor to the apex of the dome (143 feet) equals the diameter of the rotunda. A landmark even in its own time, the Pantheon has inspired more works of architecture than any other monument in Greco-Roman history (Figure **3.10**).

Figure 3.7 Colosseum, Rome (aerial view), 70–82 C.E. The longstanding influence of this Roman amphitheater is apparent in the design of the modern sports arena.

Figure 3.8 (left) The Pantheon, Rome, ca. 118–125 C.E. Dome height 143 ft.

Figure 3.9 (opposite) Giovanni Paolo Panini, *The Interior of the Pantheon*, ca. 1734–1735. Oil on canvas, 4 ft. 2½ in. x 3 ft. 3 in. National Gallery of Art, Washington, D.C. In the mid-eighteenth century, artists not only looked to Classical Rome for models in the arts; they also traveled to major Roman sites, where they documented the glories of the Classical past with Neoclassical fervor. Panini specialized in the production of detailed drawings, paintings, and prints of Roman monuments such as the Pantheon.

Making Connections

ROMAN CLASSICISM AND NEOCLASSICISM

The Roman Pantheon awed and delighted such eminent late eighteenth-century Neoclassicists as Thomas Jefferson, who used it as the model for many architectural designs, including those of the Rotunda of the University of Virginia (Figure **3.10**) and his own residence at Monticello (see Figure 11.23). The Rotunda, which served originally as the university library, was constructed at two-thirds the size of the Pantheon. It is unadorned and faithful to the design of its Roman model, except for the use of Corinthian (rather than Doric) columns.

Q What is suggested by the fact that Jefferson drew on a religious structure as the model for a library, a secular building designed as the focal point of what he called the "academical village"?

Figure 3.10 Thomas Jefferson, the Rotunda, University of Virginia, Charlottesville, Virginia, 1822–1826.

DOMINVM IN SANCTIS EIVS
LAVS EIVS IN EC

Figure 3.11 Maison Carrée, Nîmes, France, ca. 19 B.C.E. The epitome of Classical refinement, the Maison Carrée inspired numerous European and American copies, including the Virginia State Capitol, designed by Thomas Jefferson.

The Pantheon is distinctly Roman in its ingenious utilization of the arch; however, other Roman buildings imitated Greek models. The temple in Nîmes, France, for instance, known as the Maison Carrée, stands like a miniature Greek shrine atop a high podium (Figure **3.11**). A stairway and a colonnaded portico accentuate the single entranceway and give the building a frontal "focus" usually lacking in Greek temples. The Corinthian order (see Figure 2.29) appears in the portico, and engaged columns adorn the exterior wall.

If temples such as the Pantheon and the Maison Carrée served the spiritual life of the Romans, the baths, such as those named for the emperor Caracalla, satisfied some of their physical needs. Elaborate structures fed by natural hot springs (Figure **3.12**), the baths provided a welcome refuge from the noise and grime of the city streets. In addition to rooms in which pools of water were heated to varying degrees, such spas often included steam rooms, exercise rooms, art galleries, shops, cafés, reading rooms, and chambers for physical intimacy. Though most baths

Figure 3.12 Great Bath, Roman bath complex, Bath, England, 54 C.E. Part of the finest group of Roman remains in England, this sumptuous pool is still fed by natural hot springs.

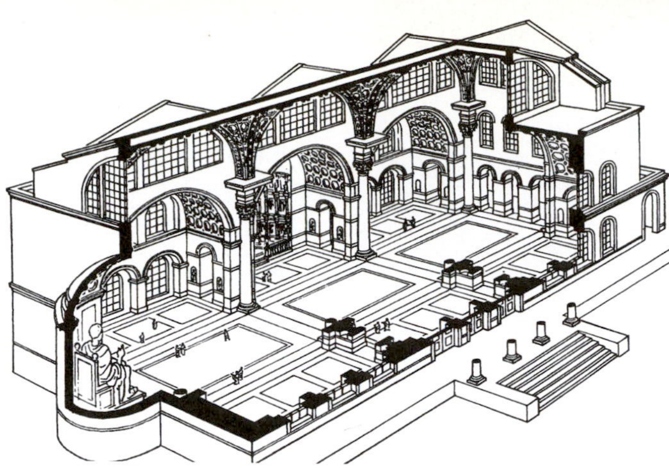

Figure 3.13 Reconstruction drawing of the Basilica of Constantine and Maxentius.

had separate women's quarters, many permitted mixed bathing. The popularity of the baths is reflected in the fact that by the third century C.E. there were more than nine hundred of them in the city of Rome.

Roman baths centered on a **basilica**, a rectangular colonnaded hall commonly used for public assemblies. The basilica was the ideal structure for courts of law, meeting halls, and marketplaces, all of which might be found in the Roman Forum. Typically, a basilica consisted of a long central **nave**, side-aisles, and a semicircular recess called an **apse** (Figure **3.13**). The Roman basilica might be roofed by wooden beams or by gigantic stone vaults. In a basilica completed by the Emperor Constantine in the fourth century C.E., these enormous vaults rested on brick-faced concrete walls some 20 feet thick.

Roman Sculpture

Like its imperialistic predecessors, Rome advertised its political power and its military achievements in monumental public works. These consisted mainly of triumphal arches and victory columns, which, like the obelisks of Egyptian pharaohs, commemorated the conquests of strong rulers. The 100-foot-tall marble column erected in 113 C.E. by Emperor Trajan to celebrate his victory over the Dacians includes 2500 figures arranged on a huge spiraling picture scroll carved in brilliant low relief (Figures **3.14** and **3.15**). Here, as in many other Roman narrative reliefs, a sense of action is achieved by the piling up of figures in illusionistic space, and by numerous realistic details that describe Roman military fortifications, tactics, and weaponry.

The triumphal arch was the most popular and widely used symbol of Roman imperial victory. More rightly classed with sculpture than with architecture (where arches serve to enclose interior space), this distinctive concrete structure, usually faced with marble, functioned

Figure 3.14 Trajan's Victory Column, Rome, 113 C.E. Marble, height (with base) 125 ft. (See also Figure 3.15.)

Figure 3.15 Detail from Trajan's Victory Column, Rome (after restoration), 113 C.E. Marble. (See also Figure 3.14.)

as visual propaganda and as a monumental gateway through which triumphant armies marched, often carrying the spoils of war. Commemorative arches were first used by Augustus to celebrate military triumphs. Some thirty-four—almost all embellished with sculpture and inscriptions—were raised in Rome. Many more still standing throughout what was the Empire immortalized the power and geographic reach of imperial Rome. The Arch of Titus, marking the upper end of the Roman Forum, commemorates the final days of the Jewish Wars (66–70 C.E.) fought by the emperors Vespasian and Titus (Figure **3.16**; see also Figure 4.4).

Roman sculpture served an essentially public function, advertising the regal authority of the emperor, often shown leading his troops to victory. During the second century, this tradition of portraiture assumed a heroic dimension in the image of the ruler on horseback. The **equestrian** portrait of Emperor Marcus Aurelius depicts the general with the thoughtful demeanor appropriate to a figure who was both a military man and a beloved philosopher, the author of the Stoic treatise *Meditations*. At the same time, the sculpture is a brilliant example of technical prowess and skillful realism, visible in the detailed mastery of the veins and muscles that seem to burst from beneath the skin of the massive horse (see Figure 3.1). Scholars have debated the question of whether a conquered warrior once lay under the horse's raised right hoof.

While public portrayal of the ruler usually demanded a degree of flattering idealization, images intended for private use invited realistic detail. The Roman taste for realism is perhaps best illustrated in three-dimensional portraits of Roman men and women, often members of the ruling class or wealthy patricians. In contrast to the idealized portraits of Golden Age Greece (see Figure 2.8), many Roman likenesses reflect obsessive fidelity to nature. So true to life seem some Roman portrait heads that scholars

Figure 3.16 Arch of Titus, Rome, ca. 81 C.E. Marble, height approx. 50 ft., width approx. 40 ft. The Latin inscription on the superstructure proclaims that the Senate and the Roman people (SPQR) dedicate the arch to Titus, son of Vespasian Augustus. Narrative relief panels on the interior of the vault depict the triumphal procession celebrating the Roman destruction of Jerusalem (see Figure 4.4).

Figure 3.17 (below) Roman aristocrat holding portrait busts of his ancestors, late first century B.C.E. Marble, height 5 ft. 5 in. Capitoline Museums, Rome. Sculptured likenesses of the deceased would have been displayed and venerated at special altars and shrines within the Roman home.

suspect they may have been executed from wax death masks. Roman portrait sculpture tends to reflect the personality and character of the sitter, a fact perhaps related to the ancient custom of honoring the "genius" or indwelling spirit of the dead ancestor. The lifelike portrait bust of Julius Caesar, carved in green schist with inset crystal eyes, captures the spirit of resolute determination for which he was famous (see Figure 3.3). It is the record of a particular person at a particular time in his life; as such it conveys a depth of psychological insight absent from most Classical Greek portraits. In that portrait sculpture served much as our photographs do today—as physical reminders of favorite relatives and friends—this emphatic naturalism is understandable. The balding patrician who carries two portrait busts of his ancestors (Figure **3.17**) reminds us that the Roman family placed extraordinary emphasis on its lineage and honored the father of the family (*paterfamilias*), along with those who preceded him.

Figure 3.18 Mosaic portrait of a woman, from Pompeii, first century C.E. This portrait was used as the centerpiece for a patterned marble floor. By introducing shading on one side of the face and under the eyes, the artist achieved a level of illusionism that is uncommon in the mosaic medium, which, by its nature, tends to flatten forms.

Roman Painting and Mosaic

A similar taste for realism appears in the frescoes with which the Romans decorated their meeting halls, baths, and country villas. Possibly inspired by Greek murals, of which only a few examples survive, Roman artists painted scenes drawn from literature, mythology, and everyday life. Among the finest examples of Roman frescoes are those found in and around Pompeii and Herculaneum, two southern Italian cities that attracted a population of wealthy Romans.

Pompeii and Herculaneum remain the showcases of Roman suburban life: Both cities were engulfed and destroyed by a mountain of ash from the volcanic eruption of Mount Vesuvius in 79 C.E., but the lava from the disaster preserved many of the area's suburban homes, along with their contents. In an effort to create casts of the victims, modern archeologists have poured concrete into their incinerated body cavities. But the inhabitants of these devastated cities remain alive by way of the ancient images on their walls and floors, created by means of paint and in **mosaic**, a technique by which small pieces of stone or glass are embedded into wet cement surfaces. The striking portrait of a Roman matron, radiant in her finest earrings and necklace, remains as fresh and immediate as yesterday's artworks (Figure **3.18**).

The residential villas of Pompeii were usually constructed around an **atrium**, a large central hall open to the sky (Figure **3.19**). The surrounding walls are painted with frescoes designed to give viewers the impression that they are looking out upon gardens and distant buildings or at shelves laden with goods. Such illusionism is a kind of visual artifice known by the French phrase ***trompe l'oeil*** ("fool the eye"). Designed to deceive the eye, they reveal the artist's competence in mastering *empirical perspective*, the technique of achieving a sense of three-dimensional space on a two-dimensional surface. Other devices, such as light and shade, are also employed to seduce the eye into believing it perceives real objects in deep space: In the extraordinary *Still Life with Eggs and Thrushes*, for instance, one of a series of frescoes celebrating food and found in a villa at Pompeii, light seems to bounce off the metal pitcher, whose shiny surface contrasts with the densely

Figure 3.19 Atrium, House of the Silver Wedding, Pompeii, first century C.E.

Figure 3.20 *Still Life with Eggs and Thrushes*, from the House (or Villa) of Julia Felix, Pompeii, Italy, before 79 C.E. Fresco, 35 x 48 in.

textured towel and the ceramic plate holding ten lifelike eggs (Figure **3.20**). Roman artists integrated illusionistic devices in ways that would not be seen again in Western art for a thousand years.

The invention of still life as an independent genre (or type) of art confirmed the Roman fondness for the tangible things of the material world. Similarly, their affection for nature led them to pioneer the genre of landscape painting. Evident in Roman landscapes is a deep affection for the countryside and for the pleasures of nature. Arcadia, the mountainous region in the central Peloponnesus inhabited by the peace-loving shepherds and nymphs of ancient Greek legend, provided the model for the Classical landscape, which celebrated (as did Greek and Latin **pastoral** poetry) a life of innocence and simplicity. The glorification of bucolic freedom—the "Arcadian Myth"—reflected the Roman disenchantment with city life. The theme was to reappear frequently in the arts of the West, especially during periods of rising urbanization.

Roman Music

While Roman civilization left abundant visual and literary resources, the absence of surviving examples in music makes it almost impossible to evaluate the Roman contribution in this domain. Passages from the writings of Roman historians suggest that Roman music theory was adopted from the Greeks, as were most Roman instruments. In drama, musical interludes replaced the Greek choral odes—a change that suggests the growing distance between drama and its ancient ritual function. Music was, however, essential to most forms of public entertainment and also played an important role in military life; for the latter, the Romans developed brass instruments, such as trumpets and horns, and drums for military processions. From Hellenistic musicians, the Romans borrowed the water organ, a harsh-sounding hydraulic device that used water to force air through a set of bronze pipes. This instrument, resembling a calliope, was employed in both the Roman theater and the public sports arenas.

The Fall of Rome

Why and how the mighty empire of Rome came to collapse in the fifth century C.E. has intrigued scholars for centuries. A great number of theories have been advanced, ranging from soil exhaustion and lead-poisoning to the malaria epidemic of the third century. In reality, it is likely that no one problem was responsible. Rather, slow decline was likely caused by a combination of internal circumstances: the difficulties of governing so huge an empire, the decline of the slave trade, and an increasing gap between the rich and the poor—during the *Pax Romana*, one-third to one-half of the population of Rome received some form of public welfare. These internal problems were made all the worse by repeated attacks on Rome's borders by Germanic tribes (see page 122) and by unchecked corruption in Roman government. Between 335 and 385, some twenty-six different emperors ruled Rome. Only one of them died a natural death. The emperors Diocletian (245–316) and Constantine (ca. 274–337) attempted to stem the decline (see page 99), but they failed. In 476, a Germanic army commander deposed the reigning Roman emperor in the West, Romulus Augustulus. The great Empire had fallen.

CHINA'S RISE TO EMPIRE

WHILE the Roman Empire dominated the West, a comparable empire arose on the eastern end of the Asian landmass (Map **3.2**). Rome and China traded overland, by way of Asian intermediaries, but neither reflects the direct influence of the other. Nevertheless, the two empires have much in common. Both brought political stability and cultural unity to vast reaches of territory. Both were profoundly secular in their approach to the world and to the conduct of human beings. Han China and imperial Rome each inherited age-old practices in religion, law, literature, and the arts, which they self-consciously preserved and transmitted to future generations.

The Qin Dynasty (221–210 B.C.E.)

The first great period of unity in China came about under the Qin (pronounced "chin"), the dynasty from which the English name "China" derives. Like the Roman rulers, the militant Qin created an empire by defeating all rival states and assuming absolute responsibility for maintaining order. The self-titled "First Emperor," Shih Huang Di (ca. 259–210 B.C.E.), appointed a large, salaried bureaucracy, ordered a census of China's population (the first of its kind in world history), oversaw the standardization of written Chinese, and divided China into the provinces that exist to this day. He created a uniform coinage, a system of weights and measures, and, in a move whose practicality rivaled that of the ancient Romans, he standardized the width of all axles so that Chinese wagons would fit the existing ruts in Chinese roads (thus speeding travel and trade).

Royal promotion of the silk industry attracted long-distance merchants and brought increasing wealth to China. While imperial policies fostered the private ownership of land by peasant farmers, the new system permitted the governors to tax those farmers, which they did mercilessly. Peasant protest was a constant threat to imperial power, but the most serious challenge to Qin safety came from the repeated invasions by the nomadic Central Asian Huns along China's northern borders. To discourage invasion, the Qin commissioned the construction (and in some stretches the reconstruction) of the 1500-mile-long Great Wall of China (Figure **3.21**). This spectacular

Figure 3.21 The Great Wall, near Beijing, China, begun third century B.C.E. Length approx. 1500 miles, height and width approx. 25 ft. This photo shows watch towers placed strategically along the wall.

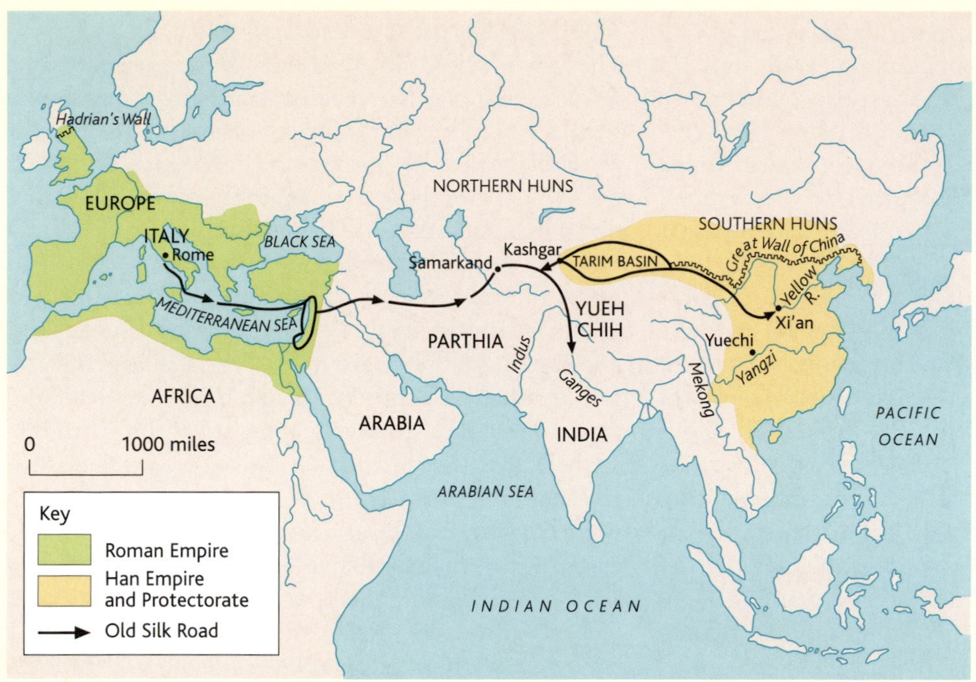

Map 3.2 Han and Roman Empires, ca. 180 C.E. The Roman Empire reached its geographic extent by 180 C.E. Two hundred years earlier, Han emperors had extended their authority throughout most of East Asia.

Figure 3.22 Terracotta army of soldiers, horses, and chariots, tomb of the first emperor of the Qin dynasty, 221–210 B.C.E. The bodies of the ceramic warriors seem to have been mass-produced from molds, but the faces, no two of which are exactly alike, were individually carved and painted.

engineering feat may be compared with the wall built by the Roman emperor Hadrian: Hadrian's Wall, only 73 miles long, would be raised in the early second century in an effort to deter attacks on Roman Britain's northernmost border. Like Hadrian's Wall, the Great Wall of China could not stop an army on foot; rather, it discouraged mounted men, wagons, and the like from making raids across the borders.

The landmark expression of Qin power is Emperor Shi Huang Di's tomb built by some 700,000 workers over a period of eleven years. The entranceway, part of a 21-square-mile burial site, provides an immortal record of the Qin military machine: It contains almost eight thousand life-sized terracotta armed soldiers, accompanied by horse-drawn chariots (Figure **3.22**). Standing at strict attention, foot soldiers and cavalry guard the emperor's tomb, which archeologists have not yet opened. The figures, mass-produced but individually carved and painted, probably replaced the living sacrifices that went to the grave with earlier Chinese rulers. In their lifelike intensity, these sculptures (Figure **3.23**) resemble Roman portrait busts. However, the Roman images were created for the living, while the Chinese images, like those of ancient Egypt, were designed to protect the dead. Nevertheless, the subterranean legions of the First Emperor glorify a military force that the Romans might have envied.

The Han Dynasty (210 B.C.E.–220 C.E.)

The Qin dynasty survived only eleven years, but under the leadership of succeeding dynasties, China's empire would last more than four centuries. Just as the Roman Empire marked the culmination of Classical civilization in the West, so the Han dynasty represented the high point and the classical phase of Chinese civilization. The intellectual and cultural achievements of the Han, which would remain in place for two thousand years, made an indelible mark on the history of neighboring Korea, Vietnam, and Japan, whose cultures adopted Chinese methods of writing and the Confucian precepts of filial piety and propriety. The Chinese have long regarded the era of the Han as their classical age and to this day refer to themselves as the "children of the Han." Han intellectual achievements ranged from the literary and artistic to the domains of **cartography**, medicine, mathematics, and astronomy. The invention of paper, block printing, the seismograph, the crossbow, the horse collar, and the wheelbarrow are but a few of the technological advances of the late Han era.

Han rulers tripled the size of the empire they inherited from the Qin. At its height, the Han Empire was roughly equivalent to that of Rome in power and prestige, but larger in actual population—a total of fifty-seven million people, according to the census of 2 C.E. Improvements in farming and advances in technology ensured economic prosperity, which

Figure 3.23 Terracotta soldier, tomb of the first emperor of the Qin dynasty, 221–210 B.C.E. Height 4ft.

LITERARY LANDMARKS

THE FIVE CHINESE CLASSICS (CA. 1000–500 B.C.E.)*

1 *The Book of Changes* (*I jing*)—a text for divination
2 *The Book of History* (*Shu jing*)—government records: speeches, reports, and announcements by rulers and ministers of ancient China
3 *The Book of Songs* (*Shi jing*)—an anthology of some three hundred poems: folk songs, ceremonial and secular poems
4 *The Book of Rites* (*Li chi*)—a collection of texts centering on rules of conduct for everyday life
5 *The Spring and Autumn Annals* (*Chun-chiu*)—commentaries that chronicle events up to the fifth century B.C.E.

*A sixth classic, on music, is no longer in existence.

in turn stimulated vigorous long-distance trade. Camel caravans traveled the 5000-mile-long "Silk Road" that stretched from the Mediterranean Sea to the Pacific Ocean. While the Chinese imported from the West glassware, wool, linen, jade, and silver, the Romans eagerly sought gems, spices, and the luxurious fabrics produced by those they called *Seres*, the "Silk People."

Visual Arts and Music

Because the Chinese built primarily in the impermanent medium of wood, nothing remains of the grand palaces of the Qin and Han eras. And while the Chinese produced no monumental architecture comparable to that of Rome, the Great Wall and the royal tombs (themselves replicas of the royal palaces) testify to the high level of Chinese building skills. Like their Shang predecessors (see pages 24–25), the Han excelled in bronze-casting and ceramics. Han craftspeople also produced exquisite works in jade, gold, lacquered wood, and silk. The numerous polychromed ceramic figures found in the royal tombs of the Han and their followers leave a record of daily life that ranges from horseback riding to musicmaking (Figure **3.24**).

While dancers and musicians (often female) appear frequently in the imperial tombs, so do the musical instruments themselves. A set of sixty-five bronze bells, seven large **zithers**, two panpipes, three flutes, three drums, and other musical instruments accompanied one fifth-century-B.C.E. emperor to his grave. The large sets of bells offered a range of several octaves, each containing up to ten notes (Figure **3.25**).

Han Literature

Imperial China left a body of landmark writings that continued to influence Chinese culture into modern times. The Han restored Confucianism, rejuvenating the five Chinese classics—works in which many of ancient China's oldest moral and religious precepts are preserved. Han rulers also revived the ancient practice of appointing government officials based on merit and education (see pages 24–25). The Chinese placed a high value on record keeping, and the tradition of writing chronicles, already evident in the commentaries on the classics, took on even greater emphasis in imperial China. Although some of the

Figure 3.24 Musicians, Northern Wei dynasty, 386–534 C.E. Mold-pressed clay with traces of unfired pigments, height 11 in. Nelson-Atkins Museum of Art, Kansas City, Missouri. Scenes of threshing, baking, juggling, musicmaking, game-playing, and other everyday activities appear routinely in three-dimensional ceramic models recovered from ancient Chinese funerary chambers.

Figure 3.25 Bells, from the tomb of the Marquis Yi of Zeng, Hubei province, fifth century B.C.E. Bronze, height of largest nearly 5 ft. This spectacular set of bells was discovered in the central chamber of the tomb of the Marquis Yi of Zeng, ruler of a small Chinese state. The names of the two notes each bell could produce (depending on where it was struck) are inscribed on it in gold. The bodies of Yi's servants or concubines, who probably played these instruments, were found in an adjacent chamber.

chronicles kept by court historians were lost in the wars and notorious "book-burnings" of the Qin era, Han historians kept a continuous record of rulership. The landmark work in this genre is the *Shiji* (*Records of the Grand Historian*), a prose narrative by Sima Qian (145–90 B.C.E.), which rivals those of Livy in scope and sharp detail.

Sima Qian, *Records of the Grand Historian* (ca. 100 B.C.E.)

The Chinese left neither epics nor heroic poems comparable to those of Greece and Rome. However, imperial China produced a long and rich history of poetry, especially lyric poetry, much of which was written by women. Rather than glorify individual prowess and valorous achievement, Han poetry reflects gently on the human experience. In its emphasis on the personal and the contemplative, Han poetry rivals that of Sappho, Catullus, and Horace.

Afterword

Although a direct comparison of the Roman and Chinese empires reveals many differences, their similarities are equally remarkable. At either end of the great Asian continent, these two extraordinary civilizations amassed great empires whose many cultural achievements became classics. Nevertheless, in the centuries following the fall of Rome, Classical rationalism and its secular agenda would be challenged by the impact of three world religions that would come to shape the course of cultural history.

Key Topics

- the Roman republic
- Rome's rise to empire
- Caesar's Rome
- the *Pax Romana*
- Roman law
- Roman literature
- Stoicism
- satire
- Roman women
- Roman architecture
- art as propaganda
- Roman portraiture
- Roman painting and mosaics
- Rome's decline
- China's rise to empire
- China's royal tombs
- Han culture and technology

ANCIENT ROME TIMELINE

	HISTORICAL EVENTS	LANDMARKS IN THE VISUAL ARTS	LITERARY LANDMARKS	BEYOND THE WEST
1000 B.C.E.		• Etruscan sarcophagus from Cerveteri (ca. 520 B.C.E.)		• *The Five Chinese Classics* (ca. 1000–500 B.C.E.)
500 B.C.E.	• Roman Republic (509–133 B.C.E.) • Twelve Tables of Law (ca. 450 B.C.E.)			• Bronze bells of Marquis Yi (fifth century B.C.E.) • Confucius, *Analects* (ca. 450 B.C.E.)
300 B.C.E.	• Plebeians win the right to make laws (287 B.C.E.) • Punic Wars (264–146 B.C.E.) • Collapse of Roman Republic (133–30 B.C.E.)			• Great Wall of China (begun third century B.C.E.) • Qin dynasty (221–210 B.C.E.) • Terracotta army, tomb of Emperor Shih Huang Di (221–210 B.C.E.) • Han dynasty (210 B.C.E.–220 C.E.)
100 B.C.E.	• Assassination of Julius Caesar (44 B.C.E.) • *Pax Romana* (30 B.C.E.–180 C.E.) • Roman Empire (30 B.C.E.–476 C.E.)	• Augustus of Primaporta (ca. 20 B.C.E.) • Pont du Gard, Nîmes (ca. 20–10 B.C.E.) • Maison Carrée, Nîmes (ca. 19 B.C.E.)	• Cicero, *Letters* (ca. 70–40 B.C.E.), *On Duty* (44 B.C.E.) • Catullus, *Poems to Lesbia* (ca. 60 B.C.E.) • Horace, *Odes* (ca. 23 B.C.E.) • Virgil, *Aeneid* (ca. 20 B.C.E.)	• Sima Qian, *Records of the Grand Historian* (ca. 100 B.C.E.)
0	• Jewish Wars (66–70 C.E.) • Eruption of Mount Vesuvius (79 C.E.)	• Roman bath complex, Bath (54 C.E.) • Pompeii frescoes and mosaics (ca. 62–79 C.E.) • Colosseum, Rome (70–82 C.E.) • Arch of Titus, Rome (ca. 81 C.E.)	• Ovid, *Metamorphoses* (ca. 5 C.E.), *The Art of Love* (ca. 10 C.E.) • Seneca, *On Tranquility of Mind* (ca. 40 C.E.)	
100 C.E.		• Trajan's Victory Column, Rome (113 C.E.) • Pantheon, Rome (ca. 118–125 C.E.) • Equestrian statue of Marcus Aurelius, Rome (ca. 173 C.E.)	• Juvenal, *Satires* (ca. 125 C.E.)	
200 C.E.				

Figure 3.23
Terracotta soldier, see p. 86

Figure 3.4
Augustus of Primaporta, see p. 69

Figure 3.6
Pont du Gard, see p. 74

Figure 3.14
Trajan's Victory Column, see p. 79

Chapter 4

Revelation:

THE FLOWERING OF WORLD RELIGIONS

ca. 1300 B.C.E.–1000 C.E.

Why does religion play such a central role in the lives of human beings? An understanding of the evolution and development of three great world religions—Judaism, Christianity, and Islam—may help us to answer this question. All three faiths are based in a belief in *revelation*: the divine disclosure of sacred knowledge. All three religions hold to the idea that a Supreme Being passed a set of holy injunctions to humankind by way of a prophet (literally, "one who speaks for God"), an agent of God on earth. To Abraham in Canaan, to Moses on Mount Sinai, to Jesus at the river Jordan, and to Muhammad in the Arabian desert came the holy message that inspired the teachings of these founding figures.

The birth of Judaism, the oldest of these religions, occurred in the second millennium B.C.E., a thousand years prior to the onset of the Classical civilizations of Greece and Rome. During the reign of the Roman emperor Octavian, in the Roman province of Judea, Jesus and his followers kindled the flame of Christianity. Islam, the youngest of these three world faiths, did not appear until the seventh century C.E. It flourished in the region of Southwest Asia that had nurtured Judaism and Christianity.

Buddhism provides a contrast with those world faiths based in revelation. Born in India in the fifth century B.C.E., Siddhartha Gautama, its founder, known as "the Buddha" ("the enlightened one"), achieved spiritual illumination not by divine decree but by meditation and the practice of humility. While some Asian sects came to perceive the Buddha as a savior, others subscribe to the original message of the founder, who charted a unique moral path to enlightenment.

A First Look

Revelation, while emanating from God, may be channeled through various celestial messengers, such as angels, saints, and those endowed with the gift of prophecy. In the ninth-century ivory plaque reproduced here, the Holy Spirit—pictured as a dove—whispers the divine message in the ear of the early Church Father and Pope, Gregory the Great (see page 101). Gregory is traditionally regarded as the author of the reformed liturgy of the Catholic Mass adopted under the Holy Roman Emperor Charlemagne. He is seen transcribing the text for which this carved ivory plaque probably served as a book cover. The Church Father labors at his desk in the *scriptorium* (writing room) of the monastery depicted in the upper part of the panel. Three scribes below busily prepare copies of manuscripts that will serve the priesthood in ministering to the faithful. In the centuries following the legalization of Christianity, the transition from the spoken to the written word was monopolized by educated members of the clergy. The parchment scrolls of Antiquity became bound manuscripts that were lavishly ornamented with brightly colored pigments and "illuminated" with gold leaf. The covers of such manuscripts, equally precious, were masterpieces of ivory, leather, or wood, often covered with silver gilt, cloisonné, and precious stones (see Figure 5.9).

Figure 4.1 *Gregory the Great and Three Scribes*, carved panel from West Germany or Lorraine, Carolingian, late ninth century C.E. Ivory relief, 8 x 5 in. Museum of Art History, Vienna.

JUDAISM

The Hebrews

The Hebrews, a tribal people from Mesopotamia, abandoned the polytheism of the ancient world. They worshipped a single all-powerful god, a Supreme Being whose revelations would become the basis for Western religious belief. The idea of a single, all-powerful creator-god had appeared already around 1350 B.C.E., when the pharaoh Amenhotep IV (Akhenaten) made the sun god Aten the sole deity of Egypt (see page 17). However, in transcending nature and all natural phenomena, the Hebrew deity differed from Aten and other ancient gods. As Supreme Creator, the Hebrew god preceded the physical universe, shaping its design, and establishing a set of moral laws to govern human behavior. Hebrew monotheism stood apart from other ancient conceptions of divinity in yet another way: its ethical thrust. The Hebrews envisioned their god as the source of moral law and the arbiter of social justice. *Ethical monotheism*, the belief that a single, benevolent, all-knowing god requires obedience to divine laws of right conduct, would become the fundamental tenet of three great world religions: Judaism, Christianity, and Islam.

Almost everything we know about the Hebrews comes from the Bible (Latin *biblia*, meaning "books")—the word derives from the Greek name for the ancient Phoenician city of Byblos (Map **4.1**), where the earliest papyrus books were produced. In addition to the Bible, archeological research of the Fertile Crescent offers considerable information by which the history of the Hebrew people has been reconstructed. The tribes called by their neighbors "Hebrews" originated in Sumer. They shared the geographic and cultural environment that produced the first written code of law under Hammurabi (see pages 10–11). Sometime after 2000 B.C.E., under the leadership of Abraham of Ur, they migrated westward across the Fertile Crescent and settled in Canaan along the Mediterranean Sea (see Map 4.1). In Canaan, according to the Book of Genesis—the first book of the Hebrew Bible—God revealed to Abraham that his descendants would inhabit that land to become a "great nation." God's promise to Abraham established the Hebrew claim to Canaan (modern-day Israel). The special bond between God and the Hebrews ("I will be your God; you will be my people," Genesis 17:7–8) was the first of many divine revelations that distinguished the Hebrews as a "chosen" (or holy) people. This contract or **covenant** bound the Hebrews to God in return for God's protection.

Map 4.1 Ancient Israel, eighth century B.C.E. The area corresponds to the biblical territory known as Canaan.

Ideas and Issues

THE NAMES OF GOD

In the earliest transcriptions of the Hebrew Bible, the name of God was spelled with four Hebrew letters (*Yodh*, *He*, *Waw*, and *He*). Commonly transcribed in English as YHWH (consonants, because ancient Hebrew does not have written letters for vowel sounds) this word is similar to the Hebrew verb "to be." Scholars therefore suggest that the name of the Hebrew deity means "I am," or "He who brings all into existence" (see Exodus 3: 13–14, where God replies to Moses: "I am who am").

Reverence for the name of God led the ancient Hebrews to resist uttering it aloud. This may be the reason for the variety of Hebrew names for the deity: *Ha Shem* ("The Name"), *Elohim* ("God"), and *Adonai* ("Lord"). All of these names, including *Yahweh* (from YHWH, and the Latinate *Jehovah*) appear in English transcriptions of religious texts. Some scholars hold that the various names for God reflect a variety of biblical authors. Others point out that the practice of calling a single god by many different names (each of which expressed a different aspect of his or her power) was common in the ancient world.

Q What names for God can be found in Christian and Muslim texts?

Making Connections

CODES OF CONDUCT

The ancient Egyptian *Book of the Dead* (see Figure 1.21), a collection of funerary prayers originating as far back as 4000 B.C.E., prepared each individual for final judgment. In the presence of the gods Osiris and Isis, dead souls were expected to recite a lengthy confession attesting to their purity of heart. Like the Ten Commandments found in the Hebrew Bible (Exodus 20:1–17), the Egyptian recitation is framed in the negative; and neither code specifies the consequences of violating moral conduct.

Ancient Egypt's *Book of the Dead*

I have not done iniquity.
I have not robbed with violence.
I have not done violence [to any man].
I have not committed theft.
I have not slain man or woman.
I have not made light the bushel.
I have not acted deceitfully.
I have not uttered falsehood.
I have not defiled the wife of a man.
I have not stirred up strife.
I have not cursed the god.
I have not increased my wealth, except with
such things as are my own possessions.

The Hebrew Decalogue (Ten Commandments)

[1]Then God spoke all these words. He said. [2]'I am Yahweh your God who brought you out of Egypt,
where you lived as slaves.
[3]'You shall have no other gods to rival me.
[4]'You shall not make yourself a carved image or any likeness of anything in heaven above or on earth
beneath or in the waters under the earth.
[5]'You shall not bow down to them or serve them. For I, Yahweh your God, am a jealous God and I
punish a parent's fault in the children, the grandchildren, and the great grandchildren among those
who hate me, [6]but I act with faithful love towards thousands of those who love me and keep my
commandments.
[7]'You shall not misuse the name of Yahweh your God, for Yahweh will not leave unpunished anyone
who misuses his name.
[8]'Remember the Sabbath day and keep it holy. [9]For six days you shall labor and do all your work,
[10]but the seventh day is a Sabbath for Yahweh your God. You shall do no work that day, neither you nor
your son nor your daughter nor your servants, men or women, nor your animals nor the alien living
with you. [11]For in six days Yahweh made the heavens, earth and sea and all that these contain, but on
the seventh day he rested, that is why Yahweh has blessed the Sabbath day and made it sacred.
[12]'Honor your father and your mother so that you may live long in the land that Yahweh your God is
giving you.
[13]'You shall not kill.
[14]'You shall not commit adultery.
[15]'You shall not steal.
[16]'You shall not give false evidence against your neighbor.
[17]'You shall not set your heart on your neighbor's house. You shall not set your heart on your
neighbor's spouse, or servant, man or woman, or ox, or donkey, or any of your neighbor's possessions.'

(Exodus 20:1–17)

Q What aspects of ethical monotheism are unique to the Decalogue?

Sometime after 1700 B.C.E., the Hebrews migrated into Egypt, where, some four centuries later, they fell subject to political turmoil and were reduced to the status of state slaves. Around 1300 B.C.E., a charismatic leader named Moses led the Hebrews out of Egypt and back toward Canaan—an event enshrined in the second book of the Hebrew Bible, Exodus (literally, "the going out"). Since Canaan was now occupied by local tribes with a sizable military strength, the Hebrews settled in the arid region near the Dead Sea. During a forty-year period that archeologists place sometime between 1300 and 1150 B.C.E., the Hebrews forged the fundamentals of their faith, as revealed to Moses in a mystical encounter with Yahweh at Mount Sinai. Here, Yahweh revealed to Moses the essence of the covenant in a set of ten laws or commandments. The Ten Commandments (or Decalogue) define the proper relationship between God and the faithful, and between, and among, all members of the Hebrew community. There is no mention of retribution in an afterlife, nor of heaven or hell—only the terrible warning that God will punish those who do not "keep the commandments," as well as their children's children "to the third and fourth generation" (Exodus 20:5). Reward and punishment, that is, occur here on earth and may be read in the history of the chosen people themselves.

HISTORY OF THE EARLY HEBREW STATE

- ca. 1040–1000 B.C.E.
  King Saul
- ca. 1000–960 B.C.E.
  King David
- ca. 960–920 B.C.E.
  King Solomon

(Division of the Hebrew Kingdom: North = Israel and South = Judah)

- 722 B.C.E.
  Fall of Israel to Assyria
- 586 B.C.E.
  Fall of Judah to Chaldea
- 586–539 B.C.E.
  Babylonian Captivity
- 538–516 B.C.E.
  Restoration of Solomon's Temple

The Hebrew State

The history, legends, and laws of the Hebrews were transmitted orally for hundreds of years; they would not be written down until the young Hebrew state emerged, around 1000 B.C.E. The first monarchy was established only after the Hebrew tribes reasserted the ancient patriarchal claim to Canaan (the "Promised Land") and defeated the powerful Philistines, "sea peoples" who had occupied these territories during the twelfth century B.C.E. The first three Hebrew kings shaped Canaan into a fortified state defended by armies equipped with iron war-chariots. King David, whose name is associated with the composition of the Hebrew songs of praise known as the Psalms, located his court in Jerusalem. His son, Solomon, constructed a royal palace and a magnificent

Figure 4.2 Reconstruction of Solomon's Temple. Destroyed by the Babylonians in 586 B.C.E., the temple was rebuilt in 516 B.C.E., following the Jews' return from Babylon to Jerusalem. The Second Temple, lavishly embellished by Herod between 19 and 4 B.C.E., was burned and looted by the Romans in 70 C.E. A portion of the surviving western outer wall, known as the "Wailing Wall," has become a place of prayer and a sacred symbol of the Jewish national identity. Since the seventh century a Muslim shrine, the Dome of the Rock, has stood on the Temple site (see Figure 4.23).

temple that was prized as God's residence (Figure **4.2**). The temple's innermost chamber, the Holy of Holies, housed the Ark of the Covenant—the receptacle bearing the stone tablets inscribed with the Ten Commandments (Figure **4.3**). After the death of King Solomon, the nation assumed two administrative divisions (see Map 4.1): a northern kingdom called Israel, and a southern kingdom known as Judah (hence the name "Jews"). In 722 B.C.E. the northern kingdom of Israel fell to the Assyrians, and its people, the so-called "Lost Tribes of Israel," were dispersed. Judah survived until 586 B.C.E., when the Chaldeans, led by Nebuchadnezzar (see page 12), attacked Jerusalem, destroying Solomon's Temple and taking the Hebrews into bondage. The event ushered in the forty-seven-year period of Jewish exile known as the Babylonian Captivity.

The Hebrew Bible

The vast collection of recitations that constitutes the Hebrew Bible found its way into writing sometime after 1000 B.C.E.: The earliest portions of this scriptural landmark are the five books known as the **Torah** ("instruction" or "law"). Considered the founding religious document of Judaism, the Torah consists of legends, historical narratives, and an ethical code that is unique among the societies of the ancient world.

A second group of writings, that of the prophets, appeared between the eighth and sixth centuries B.C.E. In the period that followed the death of Solomon, as Judah and Israel struggled with the trials of urban life and the military assaults of foreign powers, moral leadership fell to such figures as Isaiah and Jeremiah. Known as **prophets** ("those who speak for another"), these zealous preachers denounced moral laxity, defended social justice, and reminded the Hebrews of their ancient covenant with God. Less than a century after the fall of Israel to the Assyrians in 722 B.C.E., the prophet Jeremiah warned the

Figure 4.3 The Ark of the Covenant and sanctuary implements, Hammath, near Tiberias, Israel, fourth century C.E. Mosaic. Israel Antiquities Authority, Jerusalem. This decorative mosaic pictures the curtained Ark that sheltered the Torah, the parchment scroll on which the *Pentateuch* (the first five books of the Hebrew Bible) was written. It also shows such sacramental objects as the **menorah** (seven-branched candelabrum) and the **shofar** or ram's horn, which is used to call the faithful to prayer.

people of Judah that, failing to obey the laws of God as taught by Moses, they would suffer a similar fate, the expression of God's wrath. From the writings of the prophets, two fundamental ideas emerge: first, that history—the destiny of a people—is divinely directed; and second, that God punishes or rewards the actions of humankind not in a hereafter, but here on earth.

A large portion of the Hebrew Bible was recorded after the sixth century B.C.E., though some of its most lyrical books, such as the Psalms, were probably transmitted orally from the time of Solomon. Of these later writings, the Book of Job is especially significant. It deals with the question of unjustified suffering in a universe governed by a loving god. A devoted and lifelong servant of God, Job—the "blameless and upright"—is tested mercilessly by the loss of his possessions, his family, and his health. Friends encourage him both to acknowledge his sinfulness and to renounce his faith in God, but Job protests that he has given God no cause for anger. The Book of Job tests the promise of Jeremiah's message. It asks the universal question: "If there is no heaven (and thus no reward after death), how can a good man's suffering be justified?" Or put more simply, "Why do bad things happen to good people?"

THE HEBREW BIBLE

The Torah
Genesis
Exodus
Leviticus
Numbers
Deuteronomy

The Prophets
Joshua
Judges
Samuel I and II
Kings I and II
Isaiah
Jeremiah
Ezekiel
Twelve Minor Prophets

The Writings
Psalms
Proverbs
Job
Song of Songs
Ruth
Lamentations
Ecclesiastes
Esther
Daniel
Ezra
Nehemiah
Chronicles I and II

Scholars suggest that the Book of Job was probably written in the years after the Babylonian Captivity, which began in 586 B.C.E. Freed by the Persians in 539 B.C.E., the post-exile Jews returned to Judah, where they reconstructed their communities and rebuilt the Temple. Under the direction of the scholar and teacher known as Ezra (fl. 428 B.C.E.), the books of the Bible became ever more central in shaping the Jewish identity. But it was not until 90 C.E. that a select group of **rabbis** (Jewish teachers) drew up the authoritative (or "**canonic**") list of books that would constitute the Hebrew Bible. The history of settlement and conquest at the hands of a foreign power followed by dispersion, known as the **Diaspora** ("scattering"), runs through Hebrew history and informs much of the contemplative "wisdom" literature of the Bible.

Following the eastward expansion of Alexander the Great (see pages 59–60), the revived Hebrew nation was "Hellenized," and by the second century B.C.E. a Greek transcription of Hebrew scriptures appeared. Called the *Septuagint* ("Seventy"), as it was reputed to have been translated by seventy scholars in a period of seventy-two days. This is the first known translation of a sacred book into another language.

A tradition of biblical interpretation has marked Hebrew history. In the centuries following the Diaspora, the rabbis of the Hebrew community continued to debate and interpret the scriptural ordinances, and by the second century C.E. that oral tradition was recorded in a book of commentary known as the *Mishna* ("oral instruction"). The *Mishna* became part of the *Talmud* ("learning"), a larger body of commentaries, interpretations of civil and religious law, and thought-provoking maxims that collectively reflect the intellectual vitality of Judaism.

The Hebrew Bible provided the religious and ethical foundations for Judaism, and, almost two thousand years after the death of Abraham, for two other world faiths: Christianity and Islam. Biblical teachings, including the belief in a single, personal, caring deity who intervenes on behalf of the faithful, have become fundamental to Western thought. And Bible stories—from Genesis to Job—have inspired some of humankind's greatest works of art, music, and literature. *Ethical monotheism*, adherence to a contractual moral system set forth by an all-powerful god, is more than a doctrine; it is the cornerstone of a universal system of social justice.

The Arts of the Hebrews

The biblical injunction against carved images discouraged representation in three-dimensional art among the early Hebrews. The implication of this rule went beyond any concern that the Hebrews might worship pagan idols; it reflected the view that human efforts to create such images showed disrespect to God as Supreme Creator. Nevertheless, in early **synagogues** (houses of worship), frescoes of major biblical events occasionally appear, along with decorative mosaics picturing the symbols of Hebrew ritual and prayer (see Figure 4.3).

In Hebrew culture, music was closely tied to prayer and worship: **Cantors** chanted biblical passages as part of the Hebrew **liturgy** (the rituals for public worship), and members of the congregation participated in the singing of psalms. Prayers were performed in various ways: In the **responsorial** style, the congregation answered the voice of the cantor; in the **antiphonal** practice, the cantor and the congregation sang alternate verses. Generally, the rhythm of the words dictated the rhythm of the music. The texture of sacred music was monophonic (consisting of a single line of melody). Musical settings might be **syllabic**, that is, using one note for each text syllable, or **melismatic**, a more florid style in which many notes were sung to each syllable. Since no method of notating music existed prior to the ninth century C.E., the music of the Hebrews (and of most other ancient cultures) was committed to memory, and, like the Bible itself, passed orally from generation to generation. The close relationship between music and prayer was shared by Judaism, Christianity, and Islam.

CHRISTIANITY

THE soil in which Christianity came to flower was an amalgam of many local traditions. The Greco-Roman world was polytheistic, dominated by strongly secular values. Throughout the East Roman Empire, more mystical forms of worship—the mystery cults—honored a variety of gods and goddesses associated with fertility and regeneration. Finally, in the birthplace of Jesus himself, the Hebrews practiced an exclusive form of ethical monotheism. The faith that would come to be called Christianity had roots in these three major traditions: Greco-Roman, Near Eastern, and Jewish.

The Greco-Roman Background

Roman religion, like Roman culture itself, was a blend of native and borrowed traditions. Ancient pagan religious rituals marked seasonal change and celebrated seedtime and harvest. Augury, the interpretation of omens (a practice borrowed from the Etruscans), was important to Roman religious life as a means of predicting future events. As with the Greeks, Rome's favorite deities were looked upon as protectors of the household, the marketplace, and the state. The Romans welcomed the gods of non-Roman peoples and honored them along with the greater and lesser Roman gods. This tolerance contributed to the lack of religious uniformity in the Empire, as well as to wide speculation concerning the possibility of life after death. Roman poets pictured a shadowy underworld in which the souls of the dead survived (similar to the Greek Hades and the Hebrew Sheol), but Roman religion promised neither retribution in the afterlife nor the reward of eternal life.

Mystery Cults

Throughout much of the Near East, agricultural societies celebrated seasonal change by way of symbolic performances of the birth, death, and rebirth of the gods. The cults of Isis in Egypt, Cybele in Phrygia, Dionysus in Greece, and Mithra in Persia are known collectively as "mystery cults," because their initiation rituals were secret (*mysterios*). These cults embraced symbolic acts of spiritual death and rebirth, such as ritual baptism and a communal meal at which the flesh and blood of the god was consumed. Mithraism, the most widespread of the mystery cults, looked back to ancient Persia's Zoroastrian belief in the rival forces of Light and Dark (Good and Evil). Devotees of Mithra, the god of light, anticipated spiritual deliverance and everlasting life. Mithraism required strict initiation rites, periods of fasting, ritual baptism, and a communal meal of bread and wine. Mithra's followers celebrated his birth on December 25th, that is, at the winter solstice that marked the sun's annual "rebirth." The cult of Mithraism excluded women but was enormously popular among Roman soldiers, who identified with Mithra's heroic prowess and self-discipline.

Judea Before Jesus

The young Jewish preacher and healer known as Joshua (Greek, *Jesus*) was born in the city of Bethlehem during the reign of the Roman emperor Octavian. The territory in which he lived had become the Roman province of Judea in 63 B.C.E., when Pompey had captured Jerusalem. These were troubled times for the Jewish population—the Romans required imperial taxes and loyalty to the emperor, while monotheistic Judaism forbade the worship of Rome's ruler and its gods. The spiritual values of a deeply religious community were now threatened by the militant forces of the most powerful secular empire in history. It is no wonder that the Roman presence in Judea stirred mutual animosity and discord, conditions that would culminate in the Roman destruction of Jerusalem and its Second Temple in 70 C.E. (Figure **4.4**).

There was discord as well within the Jewish community, as rabbis debated the meaning of certain parts of Scripture. Many awaited the arrival of a **Messiah** (Greek, *Christos*), the deliverer anticipated by the Hebrew prophets. The Sadducees, a group of Jews who followed a strict and literal interpretation of the Torah, envisioned the Messiah as a temporal leader who would rescue the Jews from political bondage to Rome. Others, whose beliefs reflected the religious traditions of the mystery cults of ancient Egypt and Persia, looked forward to deliverance in the form of liberation of the immortal soul from the earthly body. The Pharisees, a scribal class of rabbis, anticipated the advent of a spiritual redeemer who would usher the righteous to eternal salvation and the wicked to damnation. The Essenes, a minor religious sect living in small monastic communities near the Dead Sea, renounced worldly possessions and practiced a life of strict self-denial. These **ascetics** may have been responsible for the preservation of some of the oldest parts of the Hebrew Bible—the Dead Sea Scrolls (so named for having been found in the caves of Qumran near the Dead Sea), fragments of which forecast an apocalyptic age marked by the coming of a Teacher of Truth. In Judea, then, the climate of religious expectation was altogether receptive to the appearance of a charismatic leader.

The Coming of Jesus

The historical Jesus is an elusive figure. His name is not mentioned in the non-Christian literature until almost the end of the first century C.E. The Christian writings that

Figure 4.4 Spoils from the Temple in Jerusalem. Relief from the Arch of Titus, Rome, ca. 81 C.E. Marble, height approx. 7 ft. This narrative relief panel, carved on the interior vault of the Arch of Titus (see Figure 3.16), depicts the destruction of Jerusalem following the pillage of the Second Temple of Solomon. Crowned with laurel wreaths, the Roman soldiers carry the huge menorah and other spoils of war through the city gate.

describe his life and teaching, known as the Gospels (literally "Good News"), date from at least forty years after his death. And since the Gospel authors or evangelists—Matthew, Mark, Luke, and John—gave most of their attention to the last months of Jesus' life, these books are not biographies in the full sense of the word. Nevertheless, the Gospels recount the revelations of God to Jesus, the first of which occurs after Jesus is baptized by John at the Jordan in Galilee: "And when Jesus was baptized, he went up immediately from the water," writes Matthew, "and behold, the heavens were opened and he saw the Spirit of God descending like a dove, and alighting on him; and lo, a voice from heaven saying, 'This is my beloved Son, with whom I am well pleased'" (Matthew 3:16–17).

Written in Greek and Aramaic, the Gospels describe the life of an inspired teacher and healer—a charismatic reformer of Judaism, who proclaimed his mission to "complete" Hebrew law and the lessons of the prophets. While the message of Jesus embraced the ethical demands of traditional Judaism, it gave new emphasis to the virtues of pacifism and antimaterialism. It warned of the perils of wealth and the temptations of the secular world. In simple and direct language, embellished with parables (stories that illustrated a moral), Jesus urged the renunciation of material goods ("do not lay up for yourselves treasures on earth"), not simply as a measure of freedom from temporal enslavement, but as preparation for eternal life and ultimate reward in "the kingdom of heaven." Criticizing the Judaism of his day, with its emphasis on strict observance of ritual, Jesus stressed the fundamentals of faith and compassion that lay at the heart of the Hebrew covenant: love of God and love of one's neighbor (Matthew 22:34–40). The God of this new revelation was stern but merciful, loving, and forgiving. In the landmark Sermon on the Mount, as recorded by Matthew, Jesus sets forth the injunctions of an uncompromising ethic: Love your neighbor as yourself, accept persecution with humility, pass no judgment on others, and treat others as you would have them treat you. This ideal, unconditional love is linked to an equally lofty directive: "You must . . . be perfect, just as your heavenly Father is perfect" (Matthew 5:48).

Word of the Jewish preacher from Nazareth, his family home, and stories of his miraculous acts of healing spread like wildfire throughout Judea. While the Roman authorities viewed his presence in Jerusalem as subversive, the Pharisees and the Sadducees accused Jesus of violating Jewish law. Many Jews also questioned his legitimacy as

Making Connections

THE GOOD SHEPHERD

Early Christians found Classical realism ill-suited to express the teachings of Jesus and the miracles of the new faith. Moreover, Christians observed the biblical prohibition against "graven images." Consequently, for at least five centuries after the death of Jesus, very little was produced in the way of freestanding religious sculpture. Nevertheless, as this comparison reveals, the strength of Classical tradition persisted in Early Christian art. The archaic Greek *Calf-Bearer*, dedicated on the Acropolis in Athens in the sixth century B.C.E., carries on his shoulders a handsome, young sacrifice to the gods (Figure **4.5**). Similarly, the youthful Jesus is pictured bearing a sacrificial lamb (Figure **4.6**), a symbol of his own sacrifice (as Lamb of God, John 1:29) and of his role as Good Shepherd—minister to the faithful and guardian of the flock (John 10:11). Stylistically, the Good Shepherd preserves the graceful *contrapposto* stance that characterized High Classical Greek sculpture (see page 50) and its Roman followers.

Q How does the fresco of Christ as Good Shepherd in the Catacombs of Saints Pietro and Marcellino (see Figure 4.8) compare with the marble version in Figure 4.6?

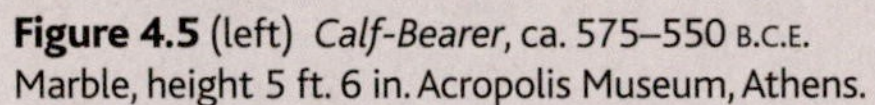

Figure 4.5 (left) *Calf-Bearer*, ca. 575–550 B.C.E. Marble, height 5 ft. 6 in. Acropolis Museum, Athens.

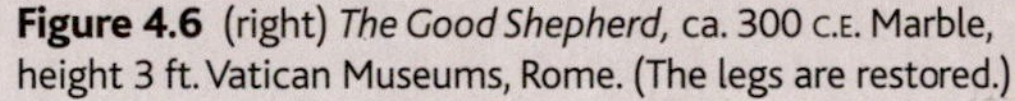

Figure 4.6 (right) *The Good Shepherd*, ca. 300 C.E. Marble, height 3 ft. Vatican Museums, Rome. (The legs are restored.)

the biblical Messiah. Finally, the Romans condemned him as a threat to imperial stability. By the authority of the Roman governor Pontius Pilate, Jesus was put to death by crucifixion, the humiliating and horrific public punishment dispensed to thieves and traitors to Rome. All four of the gospels report that Jesus rose from the dead on the third day after his death, and that he appeared to his disciples before ascending into heaven. This event, the resurrection of Jesus, became fundamental to the Christian faith. In the earliest representations of Jesus, however, it is not his death on the Cross, or the reports of his miraculous resurrection, but his role as redeemer and protector—hence as Good Shepherd—that is immortalized (see Figure 4.6).

Paul: Co-Founder of Christianity

The immediate followers of Jesus, a group of disciples or **apostles**, claimed not only that Jesus rose bodily from the dead, but that this resurrection anticipated a Second Coming in which all who followed the Messiah would be delivered to the Kingdom of Heaven. Despite the missionary activities of the apostles, only a small part of the Judean population—scholars estimate between 10 and 15 percent—became "Christians," that is, followers of Jesus, in the first hundred years after his death. However, through the efforts of the best known of the apostles, Paul (d. 65 C.E.), the view of Jesus as a reformer of Judaism gave way to an image of him as Redeemer and Son of God, and the fledgling sect of Christians was transformed into a new and vibrant faith.

A Jewish tentmaker from Tarsus in Asia Minor, Paul received schooling in both Greek and Hebrew. Following a personal experience in which Jesus revealed himself to Paul, he became a passionate convert to his teachings. Paul is believed to have written ten to fourteen of the twenty-seven books that comprise the Christian Scriptures, called by Christians the "New Testament" to distinguish it from the Hebrew Bible, which they refer to as

Ideas and Issues

JESUS' SERMON ON THE MOUNT

The Beatitudes

"[1]Seeing the crowds, he went onto the mountain. And when he was seated his disciples came to him. [2]Then he began to speak. This is what he taught them:
[3]How blessed are the poor in spirit:
the kingdom of Heaven is theirs.
[4]Blessed are the gentle:
they shall have the earth as inheritance.
[5]Blessed are those who mourn:
they shall be comforted.
[6]Blessed are those who hunger and thirst for uprightness:
they shall have their fill.
[7]Blessed are the merciful:
they shall have mercy shown to them.
[8]Blessed are the pure in heart:
they shall see God.
[9]Blessed are the peacemakers:
they shall be recognized as children of God.
[10]Blessed are those who are persecuted in the cause of uprightness:
the kingdom of Heaven is theirs.
[11]Blessed are you when people abuse you and persecute you and speak all kinds of calumny against you falsely on my account. [12]Rejoice and be glad, for your reward will be great in heaven; this is how they persecuted the prophets before you."

(from Matthew 5:1–12)

Q What are the qualities of the blessed, according to Jesus?

the "Old Testament." Through Paul's writings, the message of Jesus gained widespread appeal. By preaching to non-Jews in Greece, Asia Minor, and Rome, Paul "universalized" Jesus' message, earning the title "Apostle to the Gentiles [non-Jews]." Moreover, Paul explained the messianic mission of Jesus and the reason for his death: He saw Jesus as a living sacrifice who died to atone for the sins of humankind, and specifically for the original sin that had entered the world through Adam's defiance of God in the Garden of Eden. For Paul, the death of Jesus was the act of atonement that rescued humankind from its sinful condition. As the New Adam, Jesus would redeem his followers. His resurrection confirmed the promise of eternal salvation. By their faith, promised Paul, the faithful would be rewarded with everlasting life.

Paul's writings separated Christianity from its parent faith, Judaism, and from the Greco-Roman culture that glorified heroic individualism and the secular world. The view of Jesus as sacrifice for human sin accommodated ancient religious beliefs in which guilt for communal or individual transgression was ritually displaced by a living sacrifice. Like the mystery cults, Paul's Christianity promised eternal life as the reward for devotion to a savior deity. Paul's focus on moral renewal and redemption, however, set Christianity apart from the mystery religions. So important was Paul's contribution to the foundations of the new faith that he is rightly called "the co-founder of Christianity."

THE SPREAD OF CHRISTIANITY

THE last great Roman emperors, Diocletian (245–316 C.E.) and Constantine (ca. 274–337 C.E.), made valiant efforts to restructure the Empire and reverse military and economic decline. Resolved to govern Rome's sprawling territories more efficiently, Diocletian divided the Empire into western and eastern halves and appointed a coemperor to share the burden of administration and defense. After Diocletian retired, Constantine levied new taxes and made unsuccessful efforts to revive a money economy. However, in 330 C.E., having failed to breathe new life into the waning Empire, he moved the seat of power from the beleaguered city of Rome to the eastern capital of the Empire, Byzantium, which he renamed Constantinople (modern Istanbul). This city Constantine envisioned as "the new Rome."

A variety of historical factors contributed to the slow but growing receptivity to Christianity within the Roman Empire. The decline of the Roman Republic had left in its wake large gaps between the rich and the poor. Octavian's efforts to restore the old Roman values of duty and civic pride had failed to offset increasing impersonalism and bureaucratic corruption. Furthermore, as early as the second century B.C.E., Germanic tribes had been migrating into the West and assaulting Rome's borders. Repeatedly, these nomadic people put Rome on the defensive and added to the prevailing sense of insecurity. Amid widespread oppression and grinding poverty, Christianity promised redemption from sins, personal immortality, and a life to come from which material adversities were absent. The message of Jesus was easy to understand, free of cumbersome regulations (characteristic of Judaism) and costly rituals (characteristic of the mystery cults), and, in contrast to Mithraism, it was accessible to all—male and female, rich and poor, free and enslaved. The unique feature of the new faith, however, was its historical credibility, that is, the fact that Jesus—unlike the elusive gods of the mystery cults or the remote Hebrew god—had actually lived among men and women and had practiced the morality he preached.

THE NEW TESTAMENT (ca. 50–150 C.E.)

Gospels
Matthew
Mark
Luke
John

Acts of the Apostles

Letters of Paul
Romans
I Corinthians
II Corinthians
Galatians
Ephesians
Philippians
Colossians
I Thessalonians
II Thessalonians
I Timothy
II Timothy
Titus
Philemon
Hebrews

Letters of
James
I Peter
II Peter
I John
II John
III John
Jude

The Book of Revelation (The Apocalypse)

Nevertheless, at the outset the new religion failed to win official approval. While both Roman religion and the mystery cults were receptive to many gods, Christianity—like Judaism—professed monotheism. Christians not only refused to worship the emperor as divine but also denied the existence of the Roman gods. Even more threatening to the state was the Christian refusal to serve in the Roman army. While the Romans dealt with the Jews by destroying Jerusalem, how might they annihilate a people whose kingdom was in heaven? During the first century, Christian converts were simply expelled from the city of Rome, but during the late third century—a time of famine, plague, and war—Christians who refused to make sacrifices to the Roman gods of state suffered horrific forms of persecution: They were tortured, burned, beheaded, or thrown to wild beasts in the public amphitheaters. Christian martyrs astonished Roman audiences by going to their deaths joyously proclaiming their anticipation of a better life in the hereafter.

Not until 313 C.E., when the emperor Constantine issued the Edict of Milan, did the public persecution of Christians come to an end. The Edict, which proclaimed religious toleration in the West, not only liberated Christians from physical and political oppression, but also encouraged the development of Christianity as a legitimate faith. Christian leaders were free to establish a uniform doctrine of belief, an administrative hierarchy, the guidelines for worship, and a symbolic vocabulary for religious expression. By the end of the fourth century, the minor religious sect called Christianity had become the official religion of the Roman Empire.

Ideas and Issues

THE NON-CANONICAL GOSPELS

In 325 C.E. the Council of Nicaea established the canon of twenty-seven writings known as the New Testament. However, from the years prior to Nicaea, and especially between 60 and 150 C.E., come dozens of apocryphal writings that describe the life and teachings of Jesus. Some of these, such as the Gospel of Thomas, the Gospel of Mary Magdalene, and the Gospel of Judas, record detailed conversations between Jesus and his disciples. In the Gospel of Thomas, for instance, Jesus instructs his followers:

> "... the Kingdom [of Heaven] is inside you and outside you. When you know yourselves, then you will be known, and you will understand that you are children of the living Father. But if you do not know yourselves, then you live in poverty, and you are poverty."

Whether or not the noncanonical writings are reliable, they offer valuable insight into the beliefs of Jesus' immediate followers. In an effort to unify and consolidate the young faith, early Church leaders either rejected or suppressed these writings, some of which have only recently been translated into English.

Q How does Jesus' message to Thomas compare with the Beatitudes in Jesus' Sermon on the Mount?

The Christian Identity

In the first centuries after the death of Jesus, there was considerable diversity of belief and practice among those who called themselves Christians. But after the legalization of the faith in 313 C.E., the followers of Jesus moved toward resolving the issues of leadership, doctrine, and liturgy. In an effort to resolve disagreements on such issues, Constantine invited bishops throughout the empire to attend an **ecumenical** (worldwide) council, which met at Nicaea, near Constantinople, in 325 C.E. At the Council of Nicaea, a consensus of opinion among church members laid the basis for Christian doctrine in the landmark Nicene Creed—a statement of Christian belief in such miraculous phenomena as virgin birth, the resurrection of the dead, and a mystical **Trinity** (the union of the Father, the Son, and the Holy Ghost in a single divine Godhead).

As Rome had been the hub of the Western Empire, so it became the administrative center of the new faith, especially as the bishop of Rome rose to prominence in the newly established Church—the Roman Catholic Church. From Rome, Church leaders in the West took the Latin language, the Roman legal system (which would become the basis for Church, or **canon**, **law**), and Roman methods of architectural construction. The Church retained the Empire's administrative divisions, appointing archbishops to oversee the provinces, bishops in the dioceses, and priests in the parishes.

While in the West the Roman Catholic Church came to replace the Roman Empire as the ministerial agency of spiritual and secular order, in the eastern portion of the Empire the Greek Orthodox Church assumed supreme religious authority. Between the fourth and sixth centuries, under the leadership of each of these two Churches, Christianity grew from a small, dynamic sect into a fully fledged religion.

Christian Monasticism

Even before the coming of Christ, communal asceticism (self-denial) was a way of life among those who sought an environment for study and prayer, and an alternative to the decadence of urban life. The earliest Christian monastics (the word comes from the Greek *monos*, meaning "alone") pursued sanctity in Syria and the deserts of the Near East. Fasting, poverty, and celibacy were the essential features of the ascetic lifestyle eventually instituted by the Greek bishop Basil of Caesarea (ca. 329–379 C.E.) at his monastic settlement at Pontus (in present-day Turkey) and still followed by monastics of the Eastern Church.

In the West, the impulse to retreat from the turmoil of secular life became more intense as the last remnants of Classical civilization disappeared. In 529 C.E., the same year that Plato's Academy closed its doors in Athens, the first Western monastic community was founded at Monte Cassino in southern Italy. Named after its founder, Benedict of Nursia (ca. 480–547 C.E.), the Benedictine rule required that its members take vows of poverty (the renunciation of all material possessions), chastity (abstention from sexual activity), and obedience to the governing **abbot**, or "father" of the monastic community. Benedictine monks followed a routine of work that freed them from dependence on the secular world, balanced by religious study and prayer: the daily recitation of the Divine Office, a cycle of prayers that marked eight devotional intervals in the twenty-four-hour period. This program of *ora et labora* ("prayer and work") gave structure and meaning to the daily routine, and provided a balanced standard best expressed by the Benedictine motto, *mens sana in corpore sano* ("a sound mind in a sound body").

The Benedictine Rule (529 C.E.)

Monastics and church fathers alike generally regarded women as the daughters of Eve—inherently sinful and dangerous as objects of sexual temptation. The Church therefore prohibited women from holding positions of Church authority and from receiving ordination as **secular clergy** (priests). However, women were not excluded from joining the ranks of the religious. In Egypt, some twenty thousand women—twice the number of men—lived in monastic communities as nuns. In the West, aristocratic women often turned their homes into Benedictine nunneries, where they provided religious education for women of all classes. Benedict's sister, Scholastica (d. 543 C.E.), became abbess of a monastery near Monte Cassino. A refuge for female intellectuals, the convent offered women an alternative to marriage.

From the fifth century on, members of the **regular clergy** (those who follow the rule of a monastic order) played an increasingly important role in Western intellectual history. As Greek and Roman sources of education dried up and fewer men and women learned to read and write, the task of preserving the history and literature of the past fell to the monasteries. Benedictine monks and nuns hand-copied and illustrated Christian as well as Classical manuscripts, and stored them in their libraries (see Figure 4.1). Over the centuries, Benedictine monasteries provided local education, managed hospices, sponsored sacred music and art, and provided a continuous stream of missionaries, mystics, scholars, and Church reformers.

The Latin Church Fathers

In the formation of Christian **dogma** and liturgy in the West, the most important figures were four Latin scholars who lived between the fourth and sixth centuries C.E.: Jerome, Ambrose, Gregory, and Augustine. Saint Jerome (ca. 347–420 C.E.), a Christian educated in Rome, translated into Latin both the Hebrew Bible and the Greek books of the New Testament. This mammoth task resulted in the **Vulgate**, the Latin edition of Scripture that became the official Bible of the Roman Catholic Church. Although Jerome considered pagan culture a distraction from the spiritual life, he admired the writers of Classical antiquity and did not hesitate to plunder the spoils of Classicism to build the edifice of a new faith.

Ideas and Issues

NEOPLATONISM

Neoplatonism was a school of philosophy developed in Alexandria, Egypt, that took as its inspiration some of the principal ideas in the writings of Plato and his followers. It anticipated a mystical union between the individual soul and "the One" or Ultimate Being—comparable with Plato's Form of Goodness. According to the third-century C.E. Egyptian thinker Plotinus, union with the One could be achieved only by the soul's ascent through a series of levels or degrees of spiritual purification. Neoplatonism's view of the soul as eternal and divine, and its perception of the universe as layered in ascending degrees of perfection, would have a shaping influence on early Christian thought.

Q What features of Neoplatonism remind you of Plato's "Allegory of the Cave"? (See pages 44–45.)

Like Jerome, Ambrose (339–397 C.E.) fused Hebrew, Greek, and Southwest Asian traditions in formulating Christian doctrine and liturgy. A Roman aristocrat who became bishop of Milan, Ambrose wrote some of the earliest Christian hymns for congregational use.

The contribution of the Roman aristocrat Gregory the Great (ca. 540– 604 C.E.) was vital to the development of early Church government. Elected to the papacy in 590 C.E., Gregory established the administrative machinery by which all subsequent popes would govern the Church of Rome. A born organizer, Gregory sent missionaries to convert England to Christianity; he extended the temporal authority of the Roman Church throughout Western Europe. Despite a lack of historical evidence, Gregory's name is associated with the codification of the body of chants that became the liturgical music of the early Church (see Figure 4.1).

The most profound and influential of all the Latin church fathers was Augustine of Hippo (354–430 C.E.). A native of Roman Africa, Augustine converted to Christianity at the age of thirty-three. Intellectually, he came under the spell of both Paul and Plotinus, a third-century C.E. Egyptian-born neoplatonist. His treatises on the nature of the soul, free will, and the meaning of evil made him the greatest philosopher of Christian antiquity. Before his conversion to Christianity, Augustine had enjoyed a sensual and turbulent youth, marked by womanizing, gambling, and fathering an illegitimate child. Augustine's lifelong conflict between his love of worldly pleasures, dominated by what he called his "lower self," and his love of God, exercised by the "higher part of our nature," is the focus of his fascinating and self-scrutinizing autobiography known as the *Confessions*. In the *Confessions*, Augustine makes a fundamental distinction between physical and spiritual modes of personal experience. His perception of the human being as the site of warring elements—the "unclean body" and the "purified soul"—drew heavily on the neoplatonist duality of Matter and Spirit and on the Pauline promise that the sin of Adam might be cleansed by the sacrifice of Jesus. Augustine's dualistic model—matter and spirit, body and soul, earth and heaven, Satan and God, state and Church—governed Western thought for centuries. The conception of the visible world (matter) as an imperfect reflection of the divine order (spirit) determined the allegorical character of Christian culture. According to this model, matter was the matrix in which God's message was hidden. In Scripture, and in every natural and created thing, God's invisible order might be discovered. For Augustine, the Hebrew Bible was a symbolic guide to Christian belief, and history itself was a cloaked message of divine revelation.

Augustine, *Confessions* (ca. 400 C.E.); *City of God* (413–426 C.E.)

A living witness to the decline of the Roman Empire, Augustine defended his faith against recurrent pagan charges that Christianity was responsible for Rome's downfall. In his multivolume work the *City of God*, he distinguishes between the earthly city of humankind and the heavenly city that is the eternal dwelling place of the Christian soul. Augustine's earthly abode, a place where "wise men live according to man," represents the Classical world prior to the coming of Jesus. By contrast, the heavenly city—the spiritual realm where human beings live according to divine precepts—is the destiny of those who embrace the "New Dispensation" of Christ.

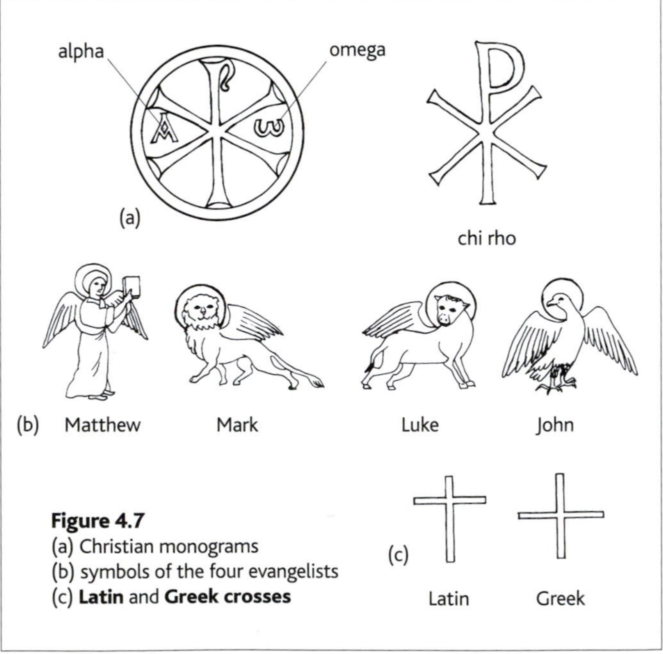

Figure 4.7
(a) Christian monograms
(b) symbols of the four evangelists
(c) **Latin** and **Greek crosses**

Symbolism and Early Christian Art

Christian signs and symbols link the visible to the invisible world. They work by analogy, and—similar to allegory—they bear hidden meanings. In Christian art, the symbolic value of a representation is often more significant than its literal meaning. Hence the study of the meaning of these symbols (a discipline known as **iconography**) is essential to an understanding of Christian art. Before Christianity was legalized in 313 C.E., visual symbols served the practical function of identifying the converts to the faith among themselves. Followers of Jesus adopted the sign of the fish because the Greek word for fish (*ichthys*) is an acrostic combination of the first letters of the Greek words "Jesus Christ, Son of God, Savior." They also used the first and last letters of the Greek alphabet, *alpha* and *omega*, to designate Christ's presence at the beginning and the end of time. Roman converts to Christianity saw in the Latin word for peace, *pax*, a symbolic reference to Christ, since the last and first letters could also be read as *chi* and *rho*, the first two letters in the Greek word *Christos*. Indeed, *pax* was emblazoned on the banner under which the emperor Constantine was said to have defeated his enemies. Such symbols soon found their way into Christian art.

In early Christian art, music, and literature, almost every number and combination of numbers was thought to bear allegorical meaning. The number 3, for example, signified the Trinity, 4 signified the evangelists, 5 symbolized the wounds of Jesus, 12 stood for the apostles, and so on. The evangelists were usually represented by four winged creatures: the man for Matthew, the lion for Mark, the ox for Luke, and the eagle for John (Figure **4.7**). Prefigured in the Book of Revelation (4:1–8), each of the four creatures came to be associated with a particular Gospel. The lion, for example, was appropriate to Mark because in his Gospel he emphasized the royal dignity of Jesus; the heaven-soaring eagle suited John, who produced the most lofty and mystical of the Gospels. The halo, a zone of light used in Roman art to signify dignity or holiness, became a favorite symbolic device in the visual representation of Jesus, the evangelists, Christian martyrs, and others whom the Church canonized as saints (holy persons capable of interceding for sinners).

Some of the earliest evidence of Christian art comes from the **catacombs**, subterranean burial chambers outside the city of Rome. These vast networks of underground galleries and rooms include gravesites whose walls are covered with frescoes illustrating scenes from the Old and New Testaments. Figure **4.8** takes up the popular image of Jesus as Good Shepherd (see Figure 4.6), symbolizing Jesus' role not only as savior-protector (shepherd) but also as sacrificial victim (lamb). As such, it evokes the early Christian theme of deliverance.

Figure 4.8 *Christ as Good Shepherd*, mid-fourth century C.E. Fresco. Catacombs of Saints Pietro and Marcellino, Rome. As late as the fourth century, depictions of Jesus had not taken on any standard, recognizable form. Jesus might be shown in the guise of a bearded Roman emperor or as a youthful shepherd. Crucifixion, a method of punishment traditionally used by Romans for traitors and thieves, did not appear in early Christian art until the fifth century, when the manner in which Jesus died began to lose its ignoble associations.

Early Christian Architecture

The legalization of Christianity made possible the construction of monumental houses for public religious worship. In the West, the early Christian church building was modeled on the Roman basilica. As with the sacred temples of Egypt and Greece, the Christian church consisted of a hierarchy of spaces that ushered the devotee from the chaos of the everyday world to the security of the sacred interior and, ultimately, to the ritual of deliverance. One entered Rome's earliest Christian basilicas, Saint Peter's and Saint Paul's, through the unroofed atrium that was surrounded on three sides by a covered walkway or **ambulatory**, and on the fourth side (directly in front of the church entrance) by a vestibule, or **narthex**. This outer zone provided a transition between temporal and spiritual realms. Having crossed the vestibule and entered through the west portal, one proceeded down the long, colonnaded central hall or **nave**, flanked on either side by two aisles; the upper wall of the nave consisted of the **gallery** and the **clerestory** (Figure **4.9**). The gallery was often decorated with mosaics or frescoes, while the clerestory was pierced by windows through which light entered the basilica.

Toward the east end of the church, lying across the axis of the nave, was a rectangular area called the **transept**. The north and south arms of the transept, which might be extended to form a Latin cross, might provide entrances additional to the main doorway at the west end of the church. Crossing the transept, one continued toward the triumphal arch that framed the apse, the semicircular space beyond the transept. In the apse, at an altar that stood on a raised platform, one received the sacrament of Holy Communion. As in ancient Egypt, which prized the eastern horizon as the site of the sun's daily "rebirth," so in Christian ritual, the most important of the sacraments was celebrated in the east. The Christian pilgrimage from the secular world to the church altar thus symbolized the soul's progress from sin to salvation.

Early Christian churches served as places of worship, but they also entombed the bones of Christian martyrs,

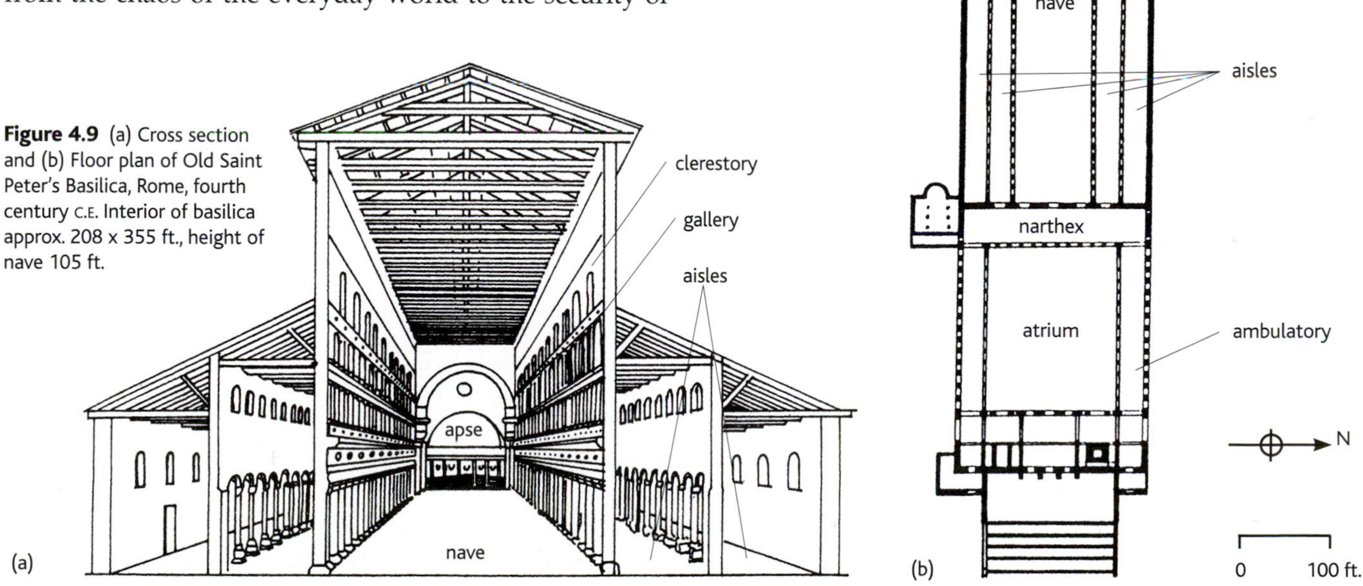

Figure 4.9 (a) Cross section and (b) Floor plan of Old Saint Peter's Basilica, Rome, fourth century C.E. Interior of basilica approx. 208 x 355 ft., height of nave 105 ft.

TEODOSIVS CEPIT PERFECIT ONORIVS AVLAM
DOCTORIS MVNDI SACRATAM CORPORE PAVLI

Figure 4.10 (opposite) Interior of the nave of Saint Paul Outside the Walls, Rome (after reconstruction), begun 386 C.E. Resembling the triumphal arches of Rome (see Figure 3.16), the arch that separates the apse from the nave is supported by Ionic columns. Above the arch, Jesus is shown in the guise of a Roman emperor: bearded and robed in purple. The halo or nimbus surrounding his head suggests his divinity and his authority as *Pantocrator* (a Greek title meaning "Ruler of All").

usually beneath the altar. Hence church buildings were massive shrines, as well as settings for the performance of the liturgy. Their spacious interiors—Old Saint Peter's basilica was approximately 355 feet long and 208 feet wide (see Figure 4.9)—accommodated thousands of Christian pilgrims. However, the wood-trussed roofs of these churches made them especially vulnerable to fire. None of the great early Christian structures has survived, but the heavily restored basilica of Saint Paul Outside the Walls (Figure **4.10**) offers some idea of the magnificence of the early church interior.

The Latin cross plan became the model for medieval churches in the West. The church exterior, which clearly reflected the functional divisions of the interior, was usually left plain and unadorned, but the interior was lavishly decorated with mosaics. While the Romans had used the technique largely to decorate the floors of public or private buildings (see Figure 3.18), it became the ideal means of conveying the transcendental character of the Christian message.

Byzantine Art and Architecture

In the five centuries after the birth of Jesus, while the Roman Empire languished in the West, the East Roman, or Byzantine, Empire flourished (Map **4.2**). Located at the crossroads of Europe and Asia, Constantinople was the hub of a vital trade network and the heir to the cultural traditions of Greece, Rome, and Asia. Byzantine rulers formed a firm alliance with the Greek Orthodox Church, whose leaders converted the Slavic regions of Eastern Europe (including Russia). While the West Roman Empire would fall to Germanic invaders in 459 C.E., its eastern portion survived until 1453.

The first Golden Age in Byzantine culture took place under the leadership of the emperor Justinian (481–565 C.E.). Assuming the throne in 527 C.E., Justinian tried to restore the power and prestige of ancient Rome. Directing his ambassadors to smuggle silkworm eggs out of China, he initiated a luxury industry that came to compete with Eastern markets, providing financial resources for his imperial ambitions. Justinian is best known for his revision and codification of Roman law. The so-called Code of Justinian, which compiled laws along with summaries of the opinions of jurists, had enormous influence on legal and political history in the West. During the Middle Ages, this landmark code became the basis for the legal systems in most of the European states.

Under Justinian's inspired leadership, Constantinople enjoyed an ambitious program of church building. In church construction, Byzantine architects favored the Greek cross plan by which all four arms of the structure were of equal length. The crowning architectural glory and principal church of Byzantium was Hagia Sophia ("Holy Wisdom"), which Justinian commissioned in 532 C.E.

Ideas and Issues

THE CHRISTIAN CALENDAR

The little-known sixth-century abbot Dionysius Exiguus (Denis the Little, fl. 525 C.E.) was responsible for establishing the calendar that is most widely used in the world to this day. In an effort to fix the Church timetable for the annual celebration of Easter, Dionysius reckoned the birth of Jesus at 754 years after the founding of Rome. Although he was inaccurate by at least three years, he applied his chronology to establish the year one as *Anno domini nostri Jesu Christi* ("the Year of Our Lord Jesus Christ"). This method of dating became the standard practice in the West after the English abbot and scholar known as the Venerable Bede (673–735 C.E.) employed the Christian calendar in writing his monumental history of England.

Q What is the year according to the Jewish calendar? And what is the year according to the Muslim calendar?

Map 4.2 The Byzantine World Under Justinian, 565 C.E.

Figure 4.11 (left) Anthemius of Tralles and Isidorus of Miletus, Hagia Sophia, from the southwest, Constantinople, Turkey, 532–537 C.E. Dome height 184 ft., diameter 112 ft. The body of the original church is now surrounded by later additions, including the minarets built after 1453 under the Ottoman Turks.

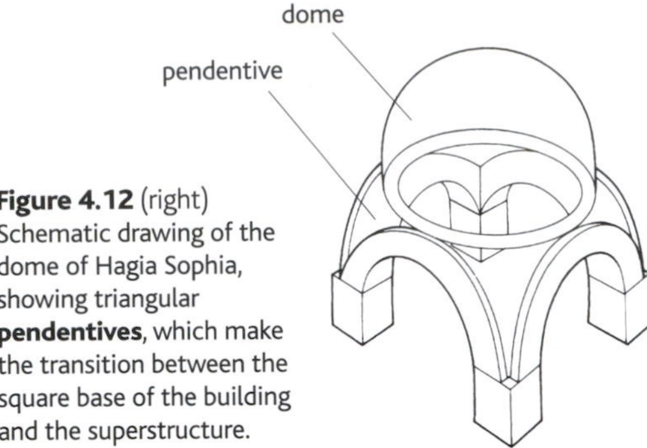

Figure 4.12 (right) Schematic drawing of the dome of Hagia Sophia, showing triangular **pendentives**, which make the transition between the square base of the building and the superstructure.

(Figures **4.11** and **4.12**). Over the center of this enormous church, a large and imposing dome rises 41 feet higher than the Pantheon in Rome (see Figure 3.8). Light filtering through the forty closely set windows at the base of the dome works to give the illusion that the great canopy is floating miraculously above the massive substructure (Figure **4.13**). Originally decorated with lavish mosaics,

Figure 4.13 Hagia Sophia, Constantinople. After the fall of Constantinople to the Turks in 1453, the Muslims transformed Hagia Sophia into a mosque and whitewashed its mosaics (in accordance with the Islamic prohibition against figurative images). In 1934, the first president of the Turkish republic, Mustafa Kemal Ataturk, turned the building into a museum. Modern Turkish officials have been restoring some of the original mosaics for the last century.

Hagia Sophia's interior must have produced breathtaking visual effects. It is no wonder that Justinian is said to have boasted that in the construction of this holy edifice, he had "surpassed" Solomon.

The last of the great Roman emperors, Justinian tried unsuccessfully to reunite the eastern and western halves of the Empire. His western outpost, established in Ravenna, on the east coast of Italy (see Map 4.2), still bears the hallmarks of his ambitious vision. The octagonal, domed church of San Vitale is one of the small gems of Byzantine architecture in Ravenna (Figure **4.14**). The drab exterior hardly prepares one for the radiant interior, the walls of which are embellished with polychrome marble, carved alabaster columns, and some of the most magnificent mosaics in the history of world art. The mosaics on either

Figure 4.14 San Vitale, Ravenna, Italy, ca. 526–547 C.E.

side of the altar show Justinian and his consort Theodora, each carrying offerings to Christ (Figures **4.15** and **4.16**). The iconography of the Justinian representation illustrates the bond between Church and state that characterized Byzantine history: Justinian is flanked by twelve companions, an allusion to Jesus and the apostles. On his right are his soldiers, the defenders of Christ (note the *chi* and *rho* emblazoned on the shield), while on his left are representatives of the clergy, who bear the instruments of the liturgy: crucifix, book, and incense vessel. Crowned by a

Figure 4.15 (above) *Emperor Justinian and His Courtiers*, ca. 547 C.E. Mosaic. San Vitale, Ravenna.

Figure 4.16 (below) *Empress Theodora and Retinue*, ca. 547 C.E. Mosaic. San Vitale, Ravenna. Justinian and his empress reenact the ancient rite of royal donation, a theme underscored by the illustration of the Three Magi on the hem of Theodora's robe. The style of the mosaic conveys the solemn formality of the event: Justinian and his courtiers stand grave and motionless, as if frozen in ceremonial attention. They are slender, elongated, and rigidly positioned—like the notes of a musical score—against a gold background that works to eliminate spatial depth. Minimally shaded, these "paper cutout" figures with small, flapperlike feet seem to float on the surface of the picture plane, rather than stand anchored in real space.

Figure 4.17 *Jesus Calling the First Apostles, Peter and Andrew*, early sixth century C.E. Mosaic. Detail of upper register of north wall, Sant' Apollinare Nuovo, Ravenna.

solar disk or halo—a device often used in Persian and late Roman art to indicate divine status—Justinian assumes the sacred authority of Christ on earth, thus uniting temporal and spiritual power in the person of the emperor.

At San Vitale and the other Byzantine churches, the mosaic technique reached its artistic peak. Favored by early Christian artisans, the mosaic medium called forth flat, simple shapes and radiant color patterns. Small pieces of glass backed with gold leaf added visual splendor to the presentation. As daylight or candlelight moved across church walls, the imagery of a young and mystical faith was transformed into ethereal apparitions of otherworldly glory (Figure **4.17**).

The Byzantine Icon

Although religious imagery was essential to the growing influence of Christianity, a fundamental disagreement concerning the role of **icons** (images) in divine worship led to conflict between the Roman Catholic and Eastern Orthodox Churches. Most Roman Catholics held that visual representations of God the Father, Jesus, the Virgin, and the saints worked to inspire religious reverence. On the other hand, **iconoclasts** (those who favored the destruction of icons) held that such images were no better than pagan idols, which were worshipped in and of themselves. During the eighth century C.E., Byzantine iconoclasm resulted in the wholesale destruction of images, while the Iconoclastic Controversy, which remained unresolved until the middle of the ninth century C.E., generated a schism between the Eastern and Western Churches. Nevertheless, for over a thousand years, Byzantine monastics produced solemn portraits of Jesus, Mary, and the saints. The faithful regarded these devotional images as sacred; indeed, some icons were thought to have supernatural and miraculous powers. The idea of the icon as epiphany or "appearance" was linked to the belief that the image (usually that of Mary) was the tangible confirmation of the Blessed Virgin's miraculous appearance (Figure **4.18**). The anonymity of icon painters and the formulaic quality of the image from generation to generation reflect the unique nature of the icon as an archetypal image—one that cannot be altered by the human imagination.

Following the conversion of Russia to Orthodox Christianity in the tenth century, artists brought new splendor to the art of the icon, often embellishing the painted panel with gold leaf and semiprecious jewels, or enhancing the garments of the saint with thin sheets of hammered gold or silver. To this day, the icon assumes a special importance in the Eastern Orthodox Church and home, where it may be greeted with a kiss, a bow, and the sign of the Cross.

Early Christian Music

Early Christians distrusted the sensuous and emotional powers of music, especially instrumental music. Augustine of Hippo noted the "dangerous pleasure" of music and confessed that on those occasions when he was more "moved by the singing than by what was sung" he felt that he had "sinned criminally." For such reasons, the Early Church was careful to exclude all forms of individual expression from liturgical music. Ancient Jewish religious ritual, especially the practice of chanting daily prayers and singing psalms, directly influenced Church music. Hymns of praise such as those produced by Ambrose, bishop of Milan, were sung by the Christian congregation led by a cantor (chief solo singer). But the most important music of Christian antiquity, and that which became central to the liturgy of the Church, was the music of the Mass.

The most sacred rite of the Christian liturgy, the Mass celebrated the sacrifice of Christ's body and blood as enacted at the Last Supper. The service culminated in the sacrament of Holy Communion (or Eucharist), by which Christians symbolically shared the body and blood of their Redeemer. In the West, the service called High Mass featured a series of Latin chants known as either plainsong, plainchant, or Gregorian chant—the last because Gregory the Great was said to have codified and made uniform the many types of religious chant that existed in early Christian times. The invariable or "ordinary" parts of the Mass—that is, those used regularly throughout the church year—included "Kyrie eleison" ("Lord have mercy"), "Gloria" ("Glory to God"), "Credo" (the affirmation of the

Gregorian chant (ca. 590–604 C.E.)

Nicene Creed), "Sanctus" ("Holy, Holy, Holy"), "Benedictus" ("Blessed is He that cometh in the name of the Lord") and "Agnus Dei" ("Lamb of God"). Eventually, the "Sanctus" and the "Benedictus" appeared as one chant, making a total of five ordinary parts of the Mass.

One of the oldest bodies of liturgical song still in everyday use, Gregorian chant stands among the landmarks of Western music. Like early Christian hymnody, it is monophonic; that is, it consists of a single line of melody. Sung ***a cappella*** (without instrumental accompaniment), the plainsong of the early Christian era was performed by the clergy and by choirs of monks rather than by members of the congregation. Both hymns and plainsong might be performed in the responsorial and antiphonal styles, and in the syllabic or melismatic textures, that typified Hebrew chant. And, as with the liturgical music of the Hebrews, the rhythm of the words determined the rhythm of the music. Lacking methods of musical notation, choristers depended on memory and on **neumes**—tiny marks entered above the words of the text to indicate the rise or fall of the voice. The duration and exact pitch of each note, however, was committed to memory. The free rhythms of Gregorian chant must have produced an otherworldly, hypnotic effect as the music echoed in the cavernous interiors of early Christian churches.

Figure 4.18 *Virgin and Child with Saints and Angels*, second half of sixth century C.E. Icon: encaustic on wood, 27 x 18⅞ in. Monastery of Saint Catherine, Mount Sinai, Egypt. Executed in glowing colors and gold paint on small, portable panels, Byzantine icons usually featured the Virgin as Mother of God (alone or surrounded by saints) seated frontally in a formal, stylized manner.

ISLAM

ISLAM, the world's youngest major religion, emerged among the tribal people of the Arabian peninsula. For centuries, the desert Arabs were polytheistic and politically diverse. The birth of the prophet Muhammad in 570 C.E., in the city of Mecca (in modern Saudi Arabia), would bring dramatic changes to these circumstances.

The Coming of Muhammad

Orphaned at the age of six, Muhammad received little formal education. He traveled with his uncle on caravan journeys that brought him into contact with communities of Jews and Christians. At the age of twenty-five, he married Khadijah, a wealthy widow fifteen years his senior, and assisted her in running a flourishing caravan trade. Long periods of solitary meditation in the desert, however, led to a transformation in Muhammad's career. According to Muslim teachings, one night the Angel Gabriel appeared to Muhammad and commanded him to proclaim his role as the prophet of Allah (the Arabic word for "God"). Now forty-one years old, Muhammad declared himself the final messenger in a history of religious revelation that had begun with Abraham and continued through Moses and Jesus. Muhammad's followers—called Muslims ("those who submit")—were to recognize him as a prophet, human rather than divine, and to acknowledge Allah as the one god, identical with the god of the Jews and that of the Christians. Fulfilling the long Judeo-Christian tradition of deliverance, Islam ("submission to God's will") would complete God's revelation to humankind.

How then did that revelation and the ensuing religion of Islam differ from those of Judaism and Christianity? Most of Allah's revelations to Muhammad, including the doctrine of final judgment and resurrection, the promise of personal immortality, and the certainty of heaven and hell, were staples of Christianity. Other aspects of the faith, such as an uncompromising monotheism, a strict set of social and ethical injunctions, and special dietary laws, were fundamental to Judaism. Muhammad preached no new doctrines of faith. Rather, he emphasized the centrality of the bond between Allah and his believers, a community (*umma*) of the faithful whose gratitude toward God would govern every aspect of their lives and every dimension of their conduct. Addressed to all people, the message of Islam holds: "There is no god but Allah [God], and Muhammad is the Messenger of Allah." This declaration of faith is the first of the so-called "Five Pillars" of Muslim religious practice.

At the outset, the message of Muhammad commanded few followers. Tribal loyalties among the polytheistic Meccans ran deep, and armed conflict between tribes was common. In 622 C.E., after twelve years of indecisive battles

Figure 4.19 The *Kaaba*, Mecca, Saudi Arabia. Nomadic Arabs were an animistic people who worshipped some three hundred different nature deities. Idols of these gods, along with the sacred Black Stone (probably an ancient meteorite), were housed in the *Kaaba*, a cubical sanctuary located in the city of Mecca. The origins of the *Kaaba* are variously explained. According to Muslim tradition, it was built by Abraham and his son Ishmael; the shrine is also said to be the sacred spot where, at God's command, Abraham had prepared to sacrifice his son Isaac. Both stories reflect the ties that bound the fledgling Muslim faith to biblical Judaism. All Muslims are expected to make a *hajj* (pilgrimage) to the *Kaaba* at least once during their lifetime. Some two million pilgrims throng to Mecca annually to take part in the ritual procession that encircles the *Kaaba* seven times.

with the Meccan opposition, Muhammad abandoned his native city. Along with some seventy Muslim families, he emigrated to Medina (see Map 4.3)—a journey known as the ***hijra*** ("migration"). Before the population of Medina was converted, eight more years, marked by sporadic warfare, were to elapse. When Muhammad returned to Mecca with a following of ten thousand men, the city opened its gates to him. Muhammad conquered it and destroyed the idols in the ancient sanctuary, the ***Kaaba***, with the exception of the Black Stone (Figure **4.19**). Thereafter, Muhammad, commonly known as "the Prophet," assumed spiritual and political authority—a position that united religious and secular realms in a manner not unlike that of the early Hebrew theocracy. By the time Muhammad died in 632 C.E., the entire Arabian peninsula was united in its commitment to Islam. Since the history of Muhammad's successful missionary activity began with the *hijra* in 622 C.E., that date is designated as the first year of the Muslim calendar.

The *Qur'an*

Muhammad himself wrote nothing, but his disciples memorized the revelations that came to him over a period of twenty-three years and recorded them within ten years of his death. Written in Arabic, the *Qur'an* (Arabic for "recitation") is the Holy Book of Islam (Figure **4.20**). The Muslim guide to spiritual and secular life, the *Qur'an* consists of 114 chapters (*suras*) arranged in order of length, beginning with the longer ones dealing with legal and social issues, and ending with the shorter and more poetic ones that date from the earliest portion of Muhammad's career. Each *sura* begins with an invocation to Allah. Many of the chapters are directly related to events in Mohammad's life; some of the strict ethical injunctions (like those of Moses and Hammurabi) reflect the customs of the tribal desert culture out of which Muhammad emerged.

The *Qur'an* (ca. 650 C.E.)

Muslim holy scripture reveals the nature of God and the inevitability of judgment and resurrection. It teaches that human beings are born in the purity of God's design, free of Original Sin. To the righteous, those who practice submission, humility, and reverence, it promises a hereafter that resembles the garden of paradise, filled with cool rivers and luscious fruit trees. To the wicked and to **infidels** (nonbelievers), it promises the terrifying punishments of hell—as hot and dusty as the desert itself. The following passage from the *Qur'an* deals with the nature of reward and punishment in the hereafter:

Judgment

"*In the Name of God, the Compassionate, the Merciful*
Does there not pass over man a space of time when his life is a blank?

We have created man from the union of the two sexes so that We may put him to the proof. We have endowed him with hearing and sight and, be he thankful or oblivious of Our favours, We have shown him the right path.

For the unbelievers We have prepared fetters and chains, and a blazing Fire. But the righteous shall drink of a cup tempered at the Camphor Fountain, a gushing spring at which the servants of God will refresh themselves: they who keep their vows and dread the far-spread terrors of Judgment-day; who, though they hold it dear, give sustenance to the poor man, the orphan, and the captive, saying: 'We feed you for God's sake only; we seek of you neither recompense nor thanks: for we fear from God a day of anguish and of woe.'

God will deliver them from the evil of that day and make their faces shine with joy. He will reward them for their steadfastness with robes of silk and the delights of Paradise. Reclining there upon soft couches, they shall feel neither the scorching heat nor the biting cold. Trees will spread their shade around them, and fruits will hang in clusters over them.

They shall be served with silver dishes, and beakers as large as goblets; silver goblets which they themselves shall measure: and cups brim-full with ginger-flavoured water from the Fount of Salsabil ['Seek the Way']. They shall be attended by boys graced with eternal youth, who to the beholder's eyes will seem like sprinkled pearls. When you gaze upon that scene you will behold a kingdom blissful and glorious.

They shall be arrayed in garments of fine green silk and rich brocade, and adorned with bracelets of silver. Their Lord will give them pure nectar to drink.

Thus you shall be rewarded; your high endeavors are gratifying to God.

We have made known to you the *Qur'an* by gradual revelation; therefore wait with patience the judgment of your Lord and do not yield to the wicked and the unbelieving. Remember the name of your Lord morning and evening; in the nighttime worship Him: praise Him all night long.

The unbelievers love this fleeting life too well, and thus prepare for themselves a heavy day of doom. *We* created them, and endowed their limbs and joints with strength; but if We please We can replace them by other men.

This is indeed an admonition. Let him that will, take the right path to his Lord. Yet you cannot will, except by the will of God. God is wise and all-knowing.

He is merciful to whom He will: but for the wrongdoers He has prepared a woeful punishment . . ."

(*Sura* 76.1–26)

THE FIVE PILLARS

- Confession of faith: repetition of the *shahadah* ("creed"), "There is no god but Allah, Muhammad is the Messenger of Allah."
- Prayer: recitation of prayers five times a day (dawn, midday, mid-afternoon, sundown, and evening)
- Alms: charitable contribution (at least $^1/_{40}$ of a Muslim's assets and income) to the poor and needy, or for the welfare of the Islamic community
- Fasting: abstaining from food, tobacco, and sexual intercourse from sunrise to sundown during the sacred month of Ramadan
- ***Hajj***: the pilgrimage to Mecca undertaken during the twelfth month of the Muslim calendar, required at least once in every Muslim's lifetime

The Muslim guide to proper worship and belief, the *Qur'an* provides a system of social justice that emphasizes equality among all members of the Islamic community. Although men and women are considered equal before God (*Sura* 4.3–7), men are described as being "a degree higher than women," and women are enjoined to veil their bodies from public view (*Sura* 24.31). A husband has unrestricted rights of divorce and can end a marriage by renouncing his wife publicly. Nevertheless, Muhammad's voice worked to raise the status of women by condemning female infanticide, by according women property rights, and by ensuring their financial support in an age when such protections were rarely guaranteed.

Muslims consider the *Qur'an* the eternal and absolute word of God, and centuries of Muslim leaders have governed according to its precepts. Unlike the histories of Judaism and Christianity, in which religion and the secular state have come to occupy separate domains, Muslim

Figure 4.20 Kufic calligraphy from the *Qur'an*, from Persia, ninth–tenth centuries C.E. Ink and gold leaf on vellum, 8½ x 21 in. Nelson-Atkins Museum of Art, Kansas City, Missouri. Crucial to Arab culture and to Islamic civilization, the *Qur'an* is the primary text for the study of the Arabic language. Muslim scripture is considered untranslatable, not only because its contents are deemed holy, but because it is impossible to capture in other languages the musical nuances of the original Arabic. As sacred poetry, the *Qur'an* is intended to be chanted or recited, not read silently.

Ideas and Issues

THE *QUR'AN* IN TRANSLATION

The *Qur'an* is said to be untranslatable; even non-Arabic Muslims often learn the *Qur'an* in the original Arabic. Nevertheless, there exist numerous versions in English and other languages. Most translations adhere closely to the classical Arabic used at the time of Muhammad, while some attempt to accommodate modern Arabic usage. As with all efforts to translate foreign-language literature, clarity and accuracy of meaning are major goals. Word choice, however, inevitably results in varying interpretation. In the case of works that are said to be divinely revealed, accurate translation becomes especially significant. The following excerpt is from the chapter titled "Women," which deals with family relations and the rights and obligations of men and women in perpetuating righteous behavior. Like both ancient Jewish and Christian cultures, Muslim society was patriarchal. The parallel translations of Sura 4:34 offer instructions as to how Muslim men should deal with disobedient wives, but the differences between the two illustrate the problematic relationship between translation and interpretation:

> 1) "Men are the protectors and maintainers of women, because Allah has given the one more (strength) than the other, and because they support them from their means. Therefore the righteous women are devoutly obedient, and guard in (the husband's) absence, what Allah would have them guard. As to those women on whose part ye fear disloyalty and ill-conduct, admonish them (first), (next), refuse to share their beds, (and last) beat them (lightly); but if they return to obedience, seek not against them Means (of annoyance): For Allah is Most High, great (above you all)."
>
> Translated by Abdullah Yusuf Ali (1934)

> 2) "Men are supporters of wives because God has given some of them an advantage over others and because they spend of their wealth. So the ones who are in accord with morality are the ones who are morally obligated, the ones who guard the unseen of what God has kept safe. But those whose resistance you fear, then admonish them and abandon them in their sleeping place then go away from them; and if they obey you, surely look not for any way against them; truly God is Lofty, Great."
>
> Translated by Laleh Bakhtiar (2006)

Q What major differences do you detect between these two translations?

history (and most modern Muslim states) has held fast to the theocratic model of the early Islamic community. *Qur'an*-based theocracy is still the generally accepted governing order throughout the Islamic world.

Hadith

While the *Qur'an* is Islam's central text, the ***hadith*** ("reports") constitute a second source of Muslim religious and legal tradition. The *hadith* are the words and deeds of Muhammad as reported by his followers. Transmitted orally for decades, they were recorded gradually a century or more after his death. Expanding on the *Qur'an*, the *hadith* provide Muslims with an all-embracing code of ethical conduct known as the ***sharia*** ("the path to follow").

Like the *Qur'an*, the *hadith* are believed to have been divinely revealed to Muhammad, but their wide range of subjects (including diplomacy, warfare, personal hygiene, diet, dress, and the treatment of wives), and their variant and often contradictory content have been subject to continued interpretation. Whereas, for instance, the *Qur'an* (like the Hebrew Bible) calls simply for modesty in women's dress and behavior, there are numerous *hadith* that address the veiling of women, a circumstance that has led to considerable controversy as to whether and to what extent the Muslim woman's body should be covered or veiled. Compare, for instance, *hadith* #282 "They [women] should draw their veils over their necks and bosoms" and *hadith* #641 "Allah does not accept the prayer of a woman who has reached puberty unless she wears a veil."

Map 4.3 The Expansion of Islam, 622–ca. 750 C.E. In just ten years, from 622 to 632 C.E., Muhammad's conquests spread Islam throughout Arabia. Under the first four caliphs, from 632 to 661 C.E., the new faith penetrated Egypt and Persia. Under the Umayyads, from 661 to 750 C.E., Islam reached India on the eastern extreme, and spread across North Africa and into Europe to the west. Thereafter, under the Abbasid caliphate (750–1055), with its capital at Baghdad on the Tigris, the Islamic Empire dominated the Near and Middle East.

THE SPREAD OF ISLAM

ISLAM'S success in becoming a world faith is a remarkable historical phenomenon, one that is explained in part by the fact that, at the outset, religious, political, and military goals were allied—somewhat as with Christianity after the Edict of Milan. However, other factors were crucial to the success of Islam. The new faith offered rules of conduct that were easy to understand and to follow—a timely alternative, perhaps, to the complexities of Jewish ritual and Christian theology. In contrast with Christianity and Judaism, Islam remained unencumbered by a priestly hierarchy. Spiritual supervision fell into (and remains to this day in) the hands of prayer leaders (***imams***) and scholars trained in Muslim law (***mullahs***), whose duty it was (and is) to interpret the *sharia*. Orthodox Muslims venerated no intercessors and regarded the Christian cult of saints as a form of polytheism.

Following the death of Muhammad, Islam unified the tribal population of Arabia in a common religious and ethnic bond that propelled Muslims into East Asia, Africa, and the West. The young religion assumed a sense of historical mission much like that which drove the ancient Romans and medieval Christian warriors like Charlemagne. The militant expansion of Islam—like the militant expansion of the Christian West (see page 134)—was the evangelical counterpart of aggressive religious zeal. ***Jihad***, or fervent religious struggle, describes the nature of Muslim expansion. Usually translated (too narrowly) as "holy war," the word signifies all aspects of the Muslim drive toward moral and religious perfection, including the defense and spread of Islam. Although there are multiple interpretations of this term in Muslim thought and practice, its dual aspect may be understood in Muhammad's distinction between "the lesser *jihad*" (war) and "the greater *jihad*" (self-control, or struggle to contain lust, anger, and other forms of indulgence). Muslims would have agreed with Augustine that a "just cause" made warfare acceptable in the eyes of God. Indeed, Christian soldiers looked forward to Paradise if they died fighting for the faith, while Muslims anticipated heavenly rewards if they died in the service of Allah.

Generally speaking, early Muslim expansion succeeded not so much by the militant coercion of foreign populations as it did by the economic opportunities Muslims offered conquered people. Unlike Christianity, Islam neither renounced nor condemned material wealth. Converts to Islam were exempt from paying a poll tax levied on all non-Muslim subjects. Into the towns that would soon become cultural oases, Muslims brought expertise in navigation, trade, and commercial exchange. They fostered favorable associations between Arab merchants and members of the ruling elite (in Africa, for instance) and rewarded converts with access to positions of power and authority. While many subject people embraced Islam out of genuine spiritual conviction, others found clear commercial and social advantages in conversion to the faith of Muhammad.

Muhammad never designated a successor; hence, after his death, bitter controversies arose concerning Muslim leadership. Rival claims to authority produced major divisions within the faith that still exist today; the Sunni consider themselves the orthodox of Islam. Their name derives from the Arabic word *sunna* ("customary practice"), which refers to both the ancestral body of social and legal customs and to the sayings and actions of Muhammad. Representing approximately 90 percent of the modern Muslim world population, the Sunni hold that religious rulers should be chosen by the faithful. By contrast, the Shiites or Shiah-i-Ali ("partisans of Ali", the majority population in present-day Iran and Iraq) claim descent through Muhammad's cousin and son-in-law Ali. The Shiites hold that only the direct descendants of Ali should rule.

After Muhammad's death, the **caliphs**, theocratic successors to Muhammad, were appointed by his followers. The first four caliphs, who ruled until 661 C.E., assumed political and religious authority, and their success in carrying Islam outside of Arabia (Map **4.3**) resulted in the establishment of a Muslim Empire. Damascus fell to Islam in 634 C.E., Persia in 636 C.E., Jerusalem in 638 C.E., and Egypt in 640 C.E. Within another seventy years, all of North Africa and Spain also lay under Muslim rule. Two rounds of violent civil wars between Shiite and Sunni partisans raged during the second half of the seventh century. Nevertheless, the Muslim advance upon the West encountered only two significant obstacles: The first was Constantinople, where Byzantine forces equipped with "Greek fire" (an incendiary compound catapulted from ships) deterred repeated Arab attacks. The second was in southwest France near Tours, where, in 732 C.E., Frankish soldiers led by Charles Martel (the grandfather of Charlemagne) turned back the Muslims, barring the progress of Islam into Europe. Nevertheless, in less than a century, Islam had won more converts than Christianity had gained in its first three hundred years.

Islam in Africa

Followers of Muhammad may have entered the African continent even before his *hijra* in the early seventh century. On the edges of the Sahara Desert and in North Africa, Muslim traders came to dominate commerce in salt (essential for the preservation of food), gold, and slaves. They soon commanded the trans-Saharan network that linked West Africa to Cairo and continued through Asia via the Silk Road to China (see Maps 3.2 and 9.2). Islam would quickly become Africa's fastest growing religion, mingling with various aspects of local belief systems as it attracted a following primarily among the ruling elite of the continent's burgeoning kingdoms: in West Africa,

Figure 4.21 Niche (*mihrab*) showing Islamic calligraphy, from Iran. 135 1/16 x 113 11/16 in. The Metropolitan Museum of Art, New York.

Ghana, Mali, and Songhai (see Map 9.2). The kings of Mali incorporated Islamic rituals into local African ceremonies; adopted the Arabic language for administrative purposes; hired Muslim scribes and jurists; and underwrote the construction of **mosques** (see Figure 9.3) and universities, the greatest of which was located at Timbuktu. In East Africa, as elsewhere, rulers who converted to Islam did not actively impose the religion on their subjects, so that only the larger African towns and centers of trade became oases of Islamic culture.

Islam's Golden Age

Between 661 and 750 C.E., Damascus (in modern Syria) served as the political center of the Muslim world. However, as Islam spread eastward under the leadership of a new Muslim dynasty—the Abbasids—the capital shifted to Baghdad (in modern Iraq). In Baghdad, a multiethnic city of more than 300,000 people, a Golden Age would come to flower. Between the eighth and tenth centuries C.E., the city became an international trade center and expansive commercial activity enriched the growing urban population. In the ninth century C.E., no city in the world could match the breadth of educational instruction or boast a library as large as that of Baghdad. Al-Yaqubi, a late ninth-century C.E. visitor to Baghdad, called it "the navel of the earth" and "the greatest city, which has no peer in the east or the west of the world in extent, size, prosperity, abundance of water, or health of climate. . . ."

From its beginnings, Islam assumed the status of a state-sponsored religion that held the *Qur'an* (as interpreted by Muslim scholars) as the sole source of the law. Yet, by the ninth century, a reaction against the growing complexity of religious doctrine and the increasing worldliness and luxury of cities like Baghdad resulted in the rise of a new, mystical branch of Islam known as Sufism (see page 146). Seeking the direct, personal experience of God, Sufi mystics renounced material prosperity and embraced religious traditions that exalted Truth as central to belief.

The cosmopolitan centers of the Muslim world—Cairo, Córdoba, and Baghdad—boasted levels of wealth and culture that far exceeded those of early medieval Western Christendom. Even after invading Turkish nomads gained control of Baghdad in the eleventh century, the city retained its cultural primacy. The city of Córdoba in medieval Spain enjoyed a culture of tolerance among Jews, Christians, and Muslims. In Egypt an independent Islamic government ruled until the sixteenth century. Visiting fourteenth-century Egypt, the Tunisian historian and political theorist, Ibn Khaldun (1332–1406), called Cairo "the mother of the world" and the mainspring of the arts and sciences. Until the mid-fourteenth century, Muslims dominated a system of world trade that stretched from Europe to China.

The diversity of Islam is the product of its assimilation of many different cultures and peoples. Some one and a half billion Muslims now live in fifty to sixty countries worldwide. The principal languages of the Islamic world are Arabic, Persian, and Turkish, but dozens of other languages, including Berber, Swahili, Kurdish, Tamil, Malay, and Javanese, are spoken by Muslims. As Islam expanded, it absorbed many different styles from the arts of non-Arab cultures. "Islamic," then, is a term used to describe the culture of geographically diverse regions—Arab and non-Arab—dominated by Islam.

Early Islamic Art and Architecture

Five times a day, at the call of ***muezzins*** (criers) usually located atop **minarets** (tall, slender towers; see Figure 4.11), Muslims are summoned to interrupt their activities to kneel and pray facing Mecca. Such prayer is required whether believers are in the heart of the desert or in their

homes. The official Muslim place of worship, however, is the mosque: a large, columned hall whose square or rectangular shape derives from the simple urban house made of sun-dried bricks. The design of the mosque is not, as with the early Christian church, determined by the needs of religious liturgy. Rather, the mosque is first and foremost a place of prayer. Every mosque is oriented toward Mecca, and that direction is marked by a niche (***mihrab***) located in the wall (Figure **4.21**). Occasionally, the niche holds a lamp that symbolizes Allah as the light of the heavens and the earth (*Sura* 24:35). To the right of the *mihrab* is a small, elevated platform (***minbar***) at which the *Qur'an* may be read.

The Great Mosque in Córdoba, Spain, begun in 784 C.E. and enlarged over a period of three hundred years, is one of the noblest landmarks of early Islamic architecture. Its interior consists of more than five hundred double-tiered columns that originally supported a wooden roof. Horseshoe-shaped arches, consisting of contrasting wedges of white marble and red sandstone, crown a forest of ornamental pillars (Figure **4.22**). In parts of the interior and exterior, six-leafed arches make a rhythmic pattern on which horseshoe arches are set in a "piggyback" fashion. Within the spacious interior of the Great Mosque (now a Catholic cathedral), arches seem to "flower" like palm fronds from column "stems."

Figure 4.22 Columns in the Moorish part of the Great Mosque, Córdoba, Spain, 784–987 C.E. White marble and red sandstone. The unbounded and diffused ground plan of the Great Mosque suggests the all-pervasiveness of the faith (as described in the *Qur'an*). It provides a sharp contrast with the typical interior of the early Christian basilica (see Figures 4.9 and 4.10), which prompts the worshipper to move in a linear fashion from portal to altar, symbolically from sin to salvation.

Islam was self-consciously resistant to imagemaking. Like the Jews, Muslims condemned the worship of pagan idols and considered making likenesses of living creatures an act of pride that "competed" with the Creator God. Hence, in Islamic religious art, there is almost no three-dimensional sculpture, and, with the exception of occasional depictions of the Muslim Paradise, no pictorial representation of the kind found in Christian art. Islamic art also differs from Christian art in its avoidance of symbols. But such self-imposed limitations did not prevent Muslims from creating one of the richest bodies of visual ornamentation in the history of world art.

Such ornamentation, in frescoes, carpets, ivories, manuscripts, textiles, and ceramics, combines geometric, **arabesque**, and calligraphic motifs. Since in Muslim art the written word takes precedence over the human form, calligraphy often dominates the design (see Figure 4.21). In manuscripts of the *Qur'an*, as in the walls of the mosque, the written word—that is, the record of revelation—becomes both sacramental and ornamental. Calligraphy

Figure 4.23 Dome of the Rock, Jerusalem, Israel, ca. 687–691 C.E. Constructed on a 35-acre plateau in east Jerusalem, the Dome of the Rock (also known as the Mosque of Omar) is capped by a gilded dome. While much of the exterior has been refaced with glazed pottery tiles, the interior still shelters the original dazzling mosaics of glass and mother-of-pearl. Both in its harmonious proportions and its lavishly ornamented surfaces, the structure is a landmark of the Muslim faith.

often alternates with the arabesque, a type of linear ornamentation drawn from plant and flower forms. Whether vegetal, floral, or geometric, Islamic motifs are usually repeated in seemingly infinite, rhythmic extension, bound only by the borders of the frame. "Meander and frame"—an expression of the universal theme of variety and unity in nature—is a fundamental principle of the Islamic decorative tradition.

Complex surface designs executed in mosaics and polychrome patterned glazed tiles regularly transform the exteriors of mosques and palaces into shimmering veils of light and color. Indeed, the bold use of color in monumental buildings is one of the unique achievements of Islamic architects over the centuries. At the Dome of the Rock (Figure **4.23**), the earliest surviving Islamic sanctuary, Qur'anic inscriptions in gold mosaic cubes on a blue ground wind around the spectacular octagon. The shrine is believed to crown the site of the creation of Adam and mark the spot from which Muhammad ascended to heaven. It is also said to be the site of the biblical Temple of Solomon and the spot at which Abraham prepared to sacrifice Isaac. Hence, the Dome of the Rock is a sacred monument, a landmark whose historical significance—like that of Jerusalem itself—is shared, but also bitterly contested, by Jews, Muslims, and Christians.

Early Islamic Music

Just as early Christians regarded music as a forbidden pleasure, so did Muslims. For the devout Muslim, there was no religious music other than the sound of the chanted *Qur'an* and the *muezzin*'s call to prayer. Nevertheless, Muslims made landmark contributions in the development of solo songs, in instrumental music for secular entertainment, and in music composition and theory (see page 135). Essentially monophonic, the line of Muslim religious song weaves and wanders, looping and repeating themes in a kind of aural arabesque that resembles the overall design pattern in Islamic visual arts. The voice, which follows the rhythms of the spoken word, may slide and intone in subtle and hypnotic stretches. This vocal pattern has much in common with that of Hebrew, Christian, and Buddhist chant.

Making Connections

JESUS AND THE BUDDHA: HUMILITY

Jesus' Sermon on the Mount

You have heard how it was said: *Eye for eye and tooth for tooth.* But I say this to you: offer no resistance to the wicked. On the contrary, if anyone hits you on the right cheek, offer him the other as well; if someone wishes to go to law with you to get your tunic, let him have your cloak as well.

(from Matthew 5:38–40; recorded ca. 100 C.E.)

The Buddha's Sermon on Abuse

And the Buddha said: "If a man foolishly does me wrong, I will return to him the protection of my ungrudging love; the more evil comes from him, the more good shall go from me; the fragrance of goodness always comes to me, and the harmful air of evil goes to him."

(recorded ca. 100 B.C.E.)

Q What are the similarities and the differences between these two messages?

Beyond the West

BUDDHISM

SIDDHARTHA Gautama, known as the Buddha (Sanskrit, "Enlightened One"), lived in India some three to five centuries before Jesus—scholars still disagree as to whether his life spanned the years 560–480 or 440–360 B.C.E. Born into a princely Hindu family, Siddhartha was well educated and protected from the pain and suffering that were widespread among lower-class Hindus. At the age of nineteen, Siddhartha married his cousin and fathered a son. Years later, upon venturing outside the sheltered pleasure gardens of the royal palace, Siddhartha encountered the physical suffering of ordinary people. Devastated by his discovery of the three "truths" of existence—sickness, old age, and death—the twenty-nine-year-old Siddhartha renounced his wealth, abandoned his family, and took up the quest for enlightenment. With shaven head, yellow robe, and begging bowl, he followed the way of the Hindu ascetic. After six years of rigorous self-denial, however, he came to reject the life of an itinerant monk. Turning inward, Siddhartha began the work of meditation that ultimately brought him to inner illumination. Sitting beneath a *bo* (fig) tree, he arrived at the full perception of reality that became the basis of his teaching (Figure **4.24**). He would continue to teach for more than forty years, dying (after eating a dish of spoiled food) at the age of eighty.

Figure 4.24 *Teaching Buddha*, from Sarnath, India, Gupta dynasty, fifth century C.E. Sandstone, height 5 ft. 2 in. Archeological Museum, Sarnath. The Buddha's prohibition of idolatry influenced early Buddhist art, which was dominated by symbols of the Buddha, such as his footprints, the fig tree, and the wheel (signifying the Wheel of the Law). By the fourth century C.E., however, the image of the Buddha assumed its classic form: Siddhartha is seated cross-legged on a lotus (the symbol of procreative life) in a position of yoga meditation. His head, framed by a halo, features a mounded protuberance (symbolizing spiritual wisdom), elongated earlobes (a reference to his princely origins), and a third eye, symbolic of spiritual vision. His hands form one of many ***mudras*** (hand gestures; Figure **4.25**) that make reference to his teachings.

In his first sermon, the Buddha "set in motion the Wheel of the Law" by explaining the Four Noble Truths: (1) suffering is universal, (2) desire causes suffering, (3) ceasing to desire relieves suffering, and (4) escape from suffering is provided by the Eightfold Path.

The reward of the Buddhist is not the achievement of personal immortality, but, rather, the attainment of *nirvana*, that is, release from the endless cycle of death and rebirth that binds all Hindus (see page 23). The Buddha held that enlightenment might be reached by every individual; it was not the exclusive domain of upper-class Hindus. Rejecting both the popular Vedic gods and the existing forms of Hindu worship, he urged his followers to work out their own salvation. Meditation, not revelation, lay at the heart of this spiritual journey.

The Spread of Buddhism

Buddhism, with its emphasis on nonattachment, humility, and meditation, was as indebted to ancient Hinduism as Christianity was to early Judaism. Like Jesus, Siddhartha was an eloquent teacher whose concerns were profoundly ethical. Like Jesus and Muhammad, the Buddha himself wrote nothing: His disciples passed on his sermons, which were not recorded until the first century B.C.E. As with Jesus, the life of the Buddha came to be surrounded by miraculous tales, which, along with his sermons, were preserved and transcribed in Pali (an ancient Indic language). Buddhist scribes compiled stories of his birth (the *Jataka*) and preserved his sayings in a collection of 423 verses known as the *Dhammapada* ("moral path"), which became an essential part of the Buddhist canon.

During the third century B.C.E., under the rule of the Emperor Asoka (273–232 B.C.E.), Buddhism became the state religion of India. Asoka initiated official policies, such as nonviolence (*ahimsa*), vegetarianism, and egalitarianism, and built shrines and monuments honoring the Buddha. Buddhist missionaries helped to spread the faith throughout China, Japan, and Southeast Asia.

By the first century C.E. there were as many as five hundred major and minor Buddhist sects in India alone. One of the many permutations of Buddhism—Mahayana Buddhism—gave the Buddha divine status. Mahayana Buddhists believed that the Buddha was a god who had come to earth in the form of a man in order to provide a clear path to salvation. Other gods, such as those in the Hindu pantheon, were seen as **avatars** (incarnations) of the Buddha, who himself had appeared in various bodily forms in his previous lives. Moreover, Mahayana Buddhism taught that other compassionate beings, who lived both before and after the Buddha, had voluntarily postponed reaching *nirvana* in order to help suffering humankind. These prospective Buddhas, or ***bodhisattvas***, were the heroes of Buddhism, and, much like the Christian saints, they became cult figures.

Early Buddhist Architecture

Buddhist texts relate that upon his death, the body of the Buddha was cremated and his ashes divided and enshrined in eight burial mounds or ***stupas***. When Asoka made Buddhism the state religion of India, he further divided the ashes, distributing them among some sixty thousand shrines. The most typical Buddhist structure, the *stupa* is a beehivelike mound of dirt and rubble encased by brick or stone (Figure **4.26**). Derived from the prehistoric burial mound (see Figure 1.6), the *stupa* symbolizes at once the world mountain, the dome of heaven, and the hallowed womb of the universe. A hemisphere set atop a square base, the shrine is the three-dimensional realization of the cosmic ***mandala***—a diagrammatic map of the universe used as a visual aid to meditation. Separating the shrine from the secular world are stone balustrades. Four gates mark the cardinal points of the compass; both walls and gates are carved with symbols of the Buddha and his teachings. As they pass through the east gate and circle the *stupa* clockwise, Buddhist pilgrims make the sacred journey that awakens the mind.

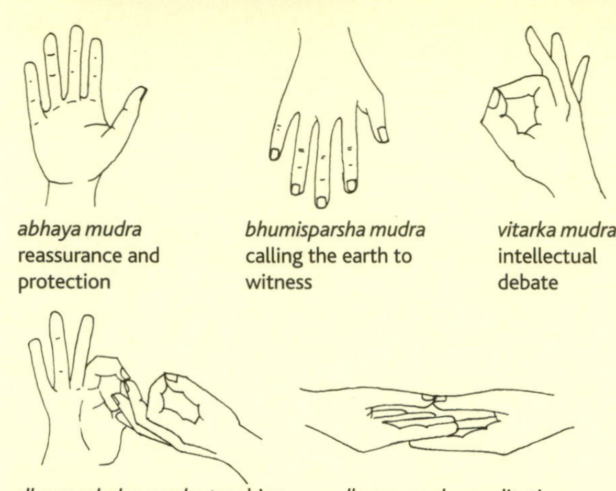

Figure 4.25 (above) *Mudras.*

Figure 4.26 (below) West gateway, the Great Stupa, Sanchi, central India, Shunga and early Andhra periods, third century B.C.E.–early first century C.E. Shrine height 50 ft., diameter 105 ft. The Great Stupa at Sanchi was one of Asoka's foremost achievements. Elevated on a 20-foot drum and surrounded by a circular stone railing, the shrine is surmounted by a series of ***chatras***—umbrellalike shapes that signify the sacred *bo* tree under which the Buddha reached *nirvana*. The *chatras* also symbolize the levels of human consciousness through which the soul ascends in seeking enlightenment.

Afterword

From the part of Asia modern Westerners call "the Near East" came three world faiths. All were religions founded on divine revelation; all called upon their followers to worship a single omnipotent god; all commanded a way of life governed by strict codes of behavior recorded in holy scripture. The history of the West, well into our own times, would be shaped by the interaction—as well as the conflicts—between and among these three monumental faiths.

Buddhism arose in India but found its greater following in China and other parts of East Asia. It stands apart from the three world religions not by the Buddha's other ethical teachings, which resemble those of Judaism, Christianity, and Islam, but by its emphasis on the attainment of spiritual enlightenment, and by the absence of a tradition of revelation. Unlike the other world faiths, Buddhism has no history of religious warfare.

Key Topics

- ethical monotheism
- the Hebrew Bible
- Babylonian Captivity
- the arts of the Hebrews
- Pharisees/Sadducees/Essenes
- mystery cults
- Jesus and Paul
- the Gospels
- Christian monasticism
- Latin church fathers
- Christian symbolism
- Early Christian art and architecture
- Byzantine art and architecture
- Muhammad and the *Qur'an*
- Muslim expansion
- Islamic art and architecture
- religious music and liturgy
- the Buddha and Buddhism

WORLD RELIGIONS TIMELINE

JUDAISM

- Migration of Hebrews to Canaan (after 2000 B.C.E.)
- Moses leads Hebrews out of Egypt (ca. 1300 B.C.E.)
- Reign of King Saul (ca. 1040–1000 B.C.E.)
- Reign of King David (ca. 1000–960 B.C.E.)
- Reign of King Solomon (ca. 960–920 B.C.E.)
- Hebrew Bible (ca. 950–150 B.C.E.)
- Division of Hebrew kingdom: Israel and Judah (ca. 920 B.C.E.)
- Fall of Israel to Assyria (722 B.C.E.)
- Fall of Judah to Chaldea (586 B.C.E.)
- Babylonian Captivity (586–539 B.C.E.)
- Restoration of Solomon's Temple (538–516 B.C.E.)
- Herod embellishes Solomon's Temple (19–4 B.C.E.)
- Romans destroy Jerusalem and its Second Temple (70 C.E.)

BUDDHISM

- Birth of Siddhartha Gautama (the Buddha) (560 B.C.E.[?])
- Great Stupa, Sanchi (begun third century B.C.E.)
- Asoka makes Buddhism the state religion of India (273–232 B.C.E.)
- Sermons of the Buddha (recorded first century B.C.E.)
- *Teaching Buddha,* from Sarnath (fifth century C.E.)

1300 B.C.E. · 1000 B.C.E. · 800 B.C.E. · 600 B.C.E. · 400 B.C.E. · 200 B.C.E. · 0

Figure 4.15
Emperor Justinian and His Courtiers, see p. 107

CHRISTIANITY

- Birth of Jesus (4 B.C.E.)
- New Testament (ca. 50–150 C.E.)
- Death of Paul (65 C.E.)
- *The Good Shepherd* (ca. 300 C.E.)
- Emperor Constantine: Edict of Milan (313 C.E.)
- Old Saint Peter's basilica, Rome (fourth century C.E.)
- Council of Nicaea (325 C.E.)
- Catacomb frescoes, Rome (mid-fourth century C.E.)
- Jerome produces Vulgate (ca. 400 C.E.)
- Augustine, *Confessions* (ca. 400 C.E.), *City of God* (413–426 C.E.)
- Founding of Benedictine order (529 C.E.)
- Hagia Sophia, Constantinople (532–537 C.E.)
- Code of Justinian (534 C.E.)
- Mosaics of San Vitale, Ravenna (ca. 547 C.E.)
- Pope Gregory the Great (r. 590–604 C.E.): Gregorian chant

Figure 4.6
The Good Shepherd, see p. 98

ISLAM

Figure 4.23
Dome of the Rock, see p. 116

- Birth of Muhammad (570 C.E.)
- Muhammad's *hijra* to Medina (622 C.E.)
- First year of Muslim calendar (622 C.E.)
- Death of Muhammad (632 C.E.)
- Rule of first four caliphs (632–661 C.E.)
- *Qur'an* (ca. 650 C.E.)
- *Hadith* (ca. 650 C.E.)
- Umayyad dynasty (661–750 C.E.)
- Dome of the Rock, Jerusalem (ca. 687–691 C.E.)
- Abbasid dynasty (750–1258)
- Great Mosque, Córdoba (784–987 C.E.)

0 · 300 · 400 · 500 · 600 · 650 · 700

ADERVNT
SIM

Chapter 5

Synthesis:

THE RISE OF THE WEST

ca. 500–1100

The thousand-year period between the fall of the Roman Empire (476 C.E.) and the European Renaissance (ca. 1400) is generally known as "the Middle Ages." *Synthesis* (the combining of individual parts to form a whole) describes the first phase of this era, roughly 500 to 1100 C.E., when three distinctive cultures—Classical, Christian, and Germanic—came together to fuel the rise of the West. In the territories that would come to be called "Europe," the geographic contours of modern Western states took shape. Isolated from the rest of the world by the westward expansion of Islam, early medieval culture generated unique political, religious, and linguistic traditions that survive today.

The empire created by the Germanic chieftain Charlemagne (Charles the Great) provides an excellent example of the process of synthesis that characterized the rise of the West. Carolingian culture integrated Classical, Christian, and Germanic traditions to form the fabric of medieval life. Feudalism, a political and military system, established patterns of social rank and status that dominated early medieval society. The landmark artworks of this period are animated by a spirit of rugged warfare, the bonds of feudal loyalty, and a rising tide of Christian piety and belief.

A First Look

The Bayeux Tapestry is a unique record of a major historical event: the Norman conquest of England. This landmark artwork is not, in fact, a woven tapestry, but an embroidery, created to ornament a banquet hall or to line the choir walls of Bayeux Cathedral in northwestern France. Sewn into a roll of bleached linen cloth, some 20 inches high and 231 feet long—two-thirds the length of a football field—the lively visual narrative chronicles the incidents leading up to and including the Battle of Hastings, the outcome of which gave William of Normandy control of England in 1066. Some seventy-nine scenes unroll continuously, in the manner of an ancient parchment scroll, a Roman historical narrative (see Figure 3.14), or a modern comic strip. Above and alongside each scene, Latin captions identify the characters, places, and events. Real and imaginary birds and animals populate the borders above and below, and in the battle scenes, fallen warriors clutter the earth. Epic in scope and robust in style, the Bayeux Tapestry presents a picture of an age in which Christianity became a militant force in the West. It provides a vivid visual record of feudal life, colored by scenes of combat that constitute a veritable encyclopedia of medieval battle gear (seen in this detail): kite-shaped shields, conical iron helmets, chain mail, battle axes, and double-edged swords.

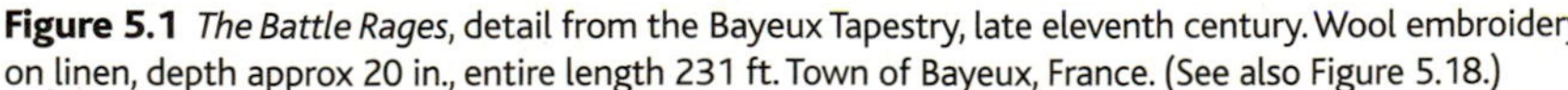

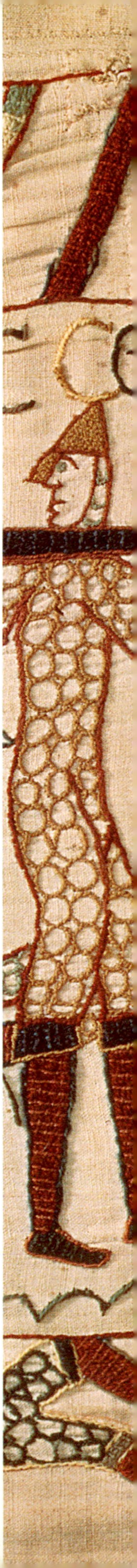

Figure 5.1 *The Battle Rages*, detail from the Bayeux Tapestry, late eleventh century. Wool embroidery on linen, depth approx 20 in., entire length 231 ft. Town of Bayeux, France. (See also Figure 5.18.)

THE GERMANIC TRIBES

THE Germanic peoples were a tribal folk who followed a migratory existence. Dependent on their flocks and herds, they lived in pre-urban village communities throughout Asia and frequently raided and plundered nearby lands for material gain; yet they settled no territorial state. As early as the first century B.C.E., a loose confederacy of Germanic tribes began to threaten Roman territories, but it was not until the fourth century C.E. that these tribes, driven westward by the fierce Central Asian nomads known as Huns, pressed into the Roman Empire. Lacking the hallmarks of civilization—urban settlements, monumental architecture, and the art of writing—the Germanic tribes struck the Romans as inferiors, as outsiders, hence, as "barbarians."

The Germanic language family, dialects of which differed from tribe to tribe, included East Goths (Ostrogoths), West Goths (Visigoths), Franks, Vandals, Burgundians, Angles, and Saxons—to name but a few. The Ostrogoths occupied the steppe region between the Black and Baltic seas, while the Visigoths settled in territories closer to the Danube River (Map **5.1**). As the tribes pressed westward, an uneasy alliance was forged: The Romans allowed them to settle on the borders of the Empire, but in exchange the Germanic warriors had to afford Rome protection against other invaders. Antagonism between Rome and the West Goths led to a military showdown. At the Battle of Adrianople (130 miles northwest of Constantinople, near modern Edirne in Turkey) in 378 C.E., the Visigoths defeated the "invincible" Roman army, killing the East Roman emperor Valens and dispersing his army. Almost immediately thereafter, the Visigoths swept across the Roman border, raiding the cities of the declining West, including Rome itself in 410 C.E.

Germanic Culture

Germanic culture differed dramatically from that of Rome: In the agrarian and essentially self-sufficient communities of these nomadic peoples, fighting was a way of life and a highly respected skill. Armed with javelins and shields, Germanic warriors fought fiercely both on foot and on horseback. Superb horsemen, the Germanic cavalry would come to borrow from the Mongols spurs and foot stirrups—devices (originating in China) that firmly secured the rider in his saddle and improved his driving force. In addition to introducing to the West superior methods of fighting on horseback, the Germanic tribes imposed their own longstanding traditions on medieval Europe. Every Germanic chieftain retained a band of warriors that followed him into battle, and every warrior

Map 5.1 The Early Christian World and the Barbarian Invasions, ca. 500 C.E.

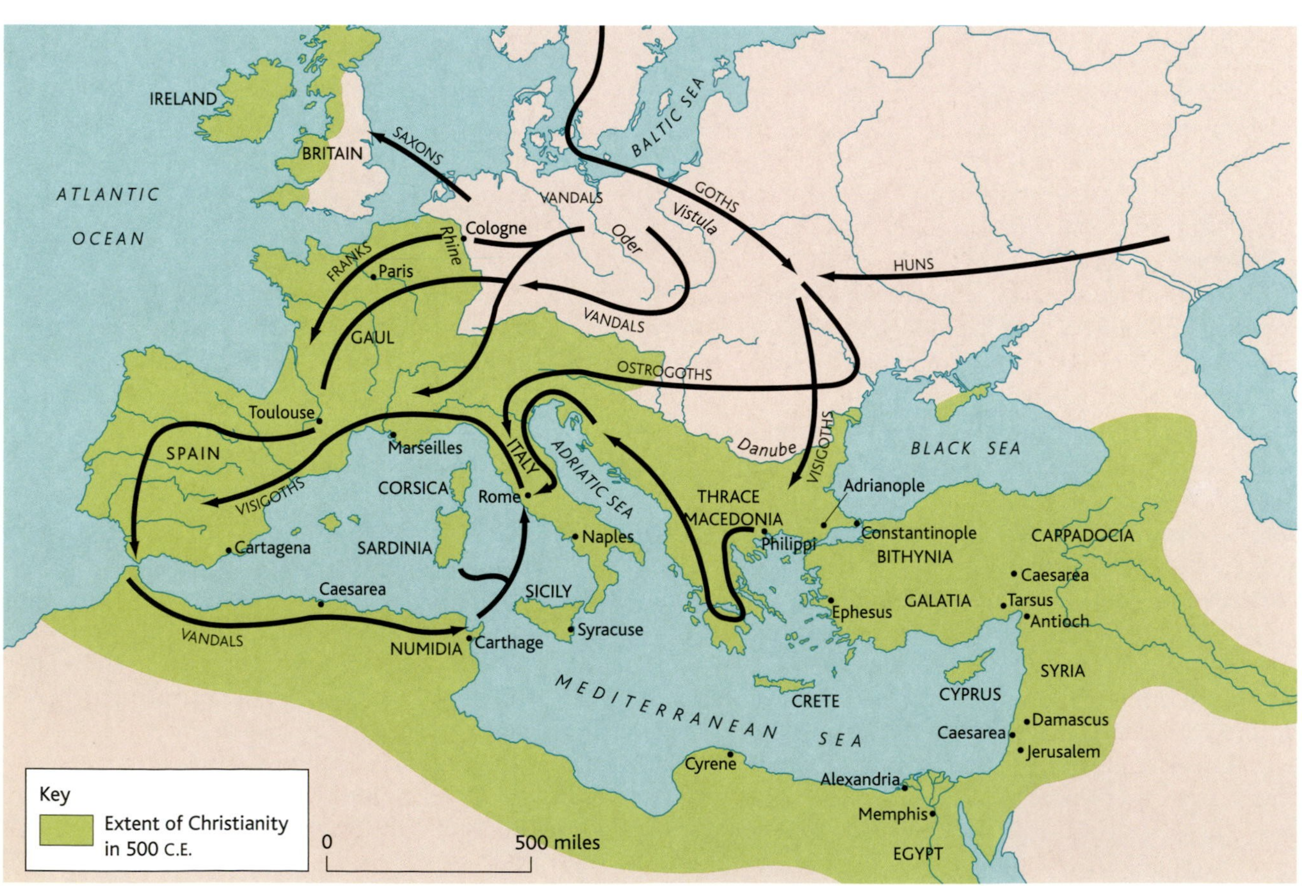

anticipated sharing with his chieftain the spoils of victory. The bond of **fealty**, or loyalty between the Germanic warrior and his chieftain, and the practice of rewarding the warrior would become fundamental to the medieval practice of **feudalism**.

Germanic law was not legislated by the state, as in Roman tradition, but was, rather, a collection of customs passed orally from generation to generation. The Germanic dependence on custom would have a lasting influence on the development of law, and especially **common law**, in parts of the West. As in most ancient societies—Hammurabi's Babylon, for instance—penalties for crimes varied according to the social standing of the guilty party. Among the Germanic tribes, however, a person's guilt or innocence might be determined by an ordeal involving fire or water; such trials reflected the faith Germanic peoples placed in the will of nature deities. Some of the names of these gods came to designate days of the week; for example, the English word "Wednesday" derives from "Woden's day" and "Thursday" from "Thor's day."

Germanic Literature

Germanic traditions, including those of personal valor and heroism associated with a warring culture, are reflected in the epic poems of the early Middle Ages. The three most famous of these, *Beowulf*, *The Song of the Nibelungs*, and *The Song of Roland*, were transmitted orally for hundreds of years before they were written down sometime between the tenth and thirteenth centuries. *Beowulf* originated among the Anglo-Saxons and was recorded in Old English—the Germanic language spoken in part of the British Isles between the fifth and eleventh centuries. *The Song of the Nibelungs*, a product of the Burgundian tribes, was recorded in Old German; and the Frankish *Song of Roland*, in Old French. Celebrating the deeds of warrior-heroes, these three epic poems have much in common with the *Iliad*, the *Mahabharata*, and other orally transmitted adventure poems.

Beowulf (ca. 700 C.E.)

The three-thousand-line epic known as *Beowulf* is the first monumental literary composition in a European vernacular language—the everyday language of the people. The tale of a daring Scandinavian prince, *Beowulf* brings to life the heroic world of the Germanic people with whom it originated. In unrhymed Old English verse embellished with numerous two-term metaphors known as **kennings** ("whale-path" for "sea," "ring-giver" for "king"), the poem recounts three major adventures: Beowulf's encounter with the monster Grendel, his destruction of Grendel's hideous and vengeful mother, and (some five decades later) his efforts to destroy the fire-breathing dragon that threatens his people. These adventures—the stuff of legend, folk tale, and fantasy—immortalize the mythic origins of the Anglo-Saxons. Composed in the newly Christianized England of the eighth century, the poem was not written down for another two centuries.

Germanic Art

The artistic production of nomadic peoples consists largely of easily transported objects such as carpets, jewelry, and weapons. Germanic folk often buried the most lavish of these items with their chieftains in boats that were cast out to sea (as described in *Beowulf*). In 1939, archeologists at Sutton Hoo in eastern England excavated a seventh-century C.E. Anglo-Saxon grave that contained weapons, coins, utensils, jewelry, and a small lyre. These landmark treasures were packed, along with the corpse of the chieftain, into an 89-foot-long ship that served as a tomb. Among the remarkable metalwork items found at Sutton Hoo was a 5-pound gold belt buckle richly ornamented with a dense pattern of interlaced snakes with beaked, birdlike heads (Figure **5.2**). The high quality of so-called "barbarian" art, as evidenced at Sutton Hoo and elsewhere, shows that technical sophistication and artistic originality were by no means the monopoly of "civilized" societies. Such artifacts also demonstrate the continuous diffusion and exchange of styles across Asia and into Europe.

As the Germanic tribes poured into Europe, their art and their culture comingled with that of the people with whom they came into contact. A classic example is the fusion of Celtic and Anglo-Saxon styles. The Celts were a non-Germanic, Iron Age folk that had migrated throughout Europe between the fifth and third centuries B.C.E., settling in the British Isles before the time of Jesus. A great flowering of Celtic art and literature occurred in Ireland and England following the conversion of the Celts to Christianity in the fifth century C.E. The instrument of this conversion was the fabled Patrick (ca. 385–461 C.E.), the British monk who is said to have baptized more than 120,000 people and founded three hundred churches in Ireland, for which he is revered as Ireland's patron saint. In the centuries thereafter, Anglo-Irish monasteries produced a number of extraordinary Christian manuscripts, whose decorative style is closely related to the dynamic linear ornamentation of the Sutton Hoo artifacts.

The Germanic ornamental vocabulary influenced not only the illumination of Christian manuscripts but also the decoration of Christian liturgical objects, such as the **paten** (Eucharistic plate) and the **chalice** (Eucharistic cup). Used in the celebration of the Mass, these objects usually commanded the finest and most costly materials; and, like the manuscripts prepared for the sacred rite itself, they received inordinate care in their execution. Even as the Germanic tribes slowly converted to Christianity, Germanic art entered the mainstream of medieval art, where it fused with Greco-Roman artforms to flower eventually in the great age of cathedrals (see pages 157–164).

Making Connections

INTERLACE: SECULAR AND SACRED

The visual landmark of an otherwise bleak era in the West is the Book of Kells, an eighth-century Latin Gospel book. Produced by monks at the Irish monastery of Kells, this manuscript is the most richly illuminated of all Celtic prayer books. The initial page, where Matthew's account of the Nativity starts, features the first two Greek letters of the word "Christ," *chi* and *rho* (Figure **5.3**). Like a sheet of metal engraved with the decorative devices of Germanic ornamental art (see Figure 5.2), the surface of the parchment page is covered with a profusion of spirals, interlaced snakes, knots, scrolls, and, here and there, human and animal forms. As early as the eleventh century, this superb manuscript was called "the chief relic of the Western world."

Q How does the Book of Kells reflect the synthesis of Germanic, Christian, and Classical traditions?

Figure 5.2 Buckle, from Sutton Hoo, first half of seventh century C.E. Gold and **niello**, length 5¼ in., weight 5 lb. British Museum, London. Monsters and serpents, which figure in the Germanic epic *Beowulf*, were associated with the dark forces of nature, while knots and braids were often seen as magical devices. Nevertheless, it is unlikely that there is any specific symbolism associated with the zoomorphic ornamentation of this superbly crafted belt buckle.

Figure 5.3 Monogram XPI, first page of Matthew's Gospel, Book of Kells, ca. 800 C.E. Manuscript illumination, 13 x 9½ in. Trinity College Library, Dublin. Because of its similarities to the techniques and devices of Germanic metalwork, this and other folios in the Book of Kells have inspired historians to dub its artist "the Goldsmith."

THE AGE OF CHARLEMAGNE

FROM the time he came to the throne in 768 C.E., until his death in 814 C.E., the Frankish chieftain Charles the Great (in French, "Charlemagne"; Figure **5.4**) pursued the dream of restoring the Roman Empire under Christian leadership. A great warrior and an able administrator, the fair-haired heir to the Frankish kingdom conquered vast areas of land in what would later come to be called "Europe" (Map **5.2**). His holy wars—the Christian equivalent of the Muslim *jihad*—resulted in the forcible conversion of the Saxons east of the Rhine River, the Lombards of northern Italy, and the Slavic peoples along the Danube. Charlemagne's campaigns also pushed the Muslims back beyond the Pyrenees into Spain.

Figure 5.4 Equestrian statuette of Charlemagne, from Metz, ninth century C.E. Bronze with traces of gilt, height 9½ in. Louvre, Paris. Carolingian artists revived the ancient Roman techniques of bronze-casting. Despite its small size—less than 10 inches high—the equestrian statuette of Charlemagne calls to mind the monumental sculpture of Emperor Marcus Aurelius (see Figure 3.1).

In the year 800 C.E., Pope Leo III crowned Charlemagne "Emperor of the Romans," thus establishing a firm relationship between Church and state. But, equally significantly, Charlemagne's role in creating a Roman Christian or "Holy" Roman Empire cast him as the prototype of Christian kingship. For the more than thirty years during which he waged wars in the name of Christ, Charlemagne sought to control conquered lands by placing them in the hands of local administrators—on whom he bestowed the titles "count" and "duke"—and by periodically sending out royal envoys to carry his edicts abroad. He revived trade with the East, stabilized the currency of the realm, and even pursued diplomatic ties with Baghdad, whose caliph, Harun al-Rashid, graced Charlemagne's court with the gift of an elephant.

The Carolingian Renaissance

Charlemagne's imperial mission was driven by a passionate interest in education and the arts. Like most Germanic warrior chieftains, Charlemagne could barely read and write—his sword hand was, according to his biographers, so callused that he had great difficulty forming letters. Nevertheless, admiring his Classical predecessors, he sponsored the Carolingian (from *Carolus*, Latin for Charles) **renaissance**, or rebirth, of learning and literacy. To oversee his educational program, he invited to his court missionaries and scholars from all over Europe. The most notable of these was Alcuin of York, an Anglo-Saxon monk whose work as a teacher and translator fostered a glorious revival of learning. With Alcuin's assistance, Charlemagne established a school at his palace in Aachen (see Map 5.2), and similar schools at Benedictine monasteries throughout the Empire. Here, monks and nuns copied religious manuscripts, along with Classical texts on medicine, drama, and other secular subjects. Carolingian copyists replaced the difficult-to-decipher Roman script, which lacked punctuation and spaces between words, with a neat, uniform writing style known as the Carolingian *minuscule*—the model for modern typography. The long-term importance of Charlemagne's renaissance is best reflected in the fact that 80 percent of our oldest Classical Latin manuscripts survive in Carolingian copies.

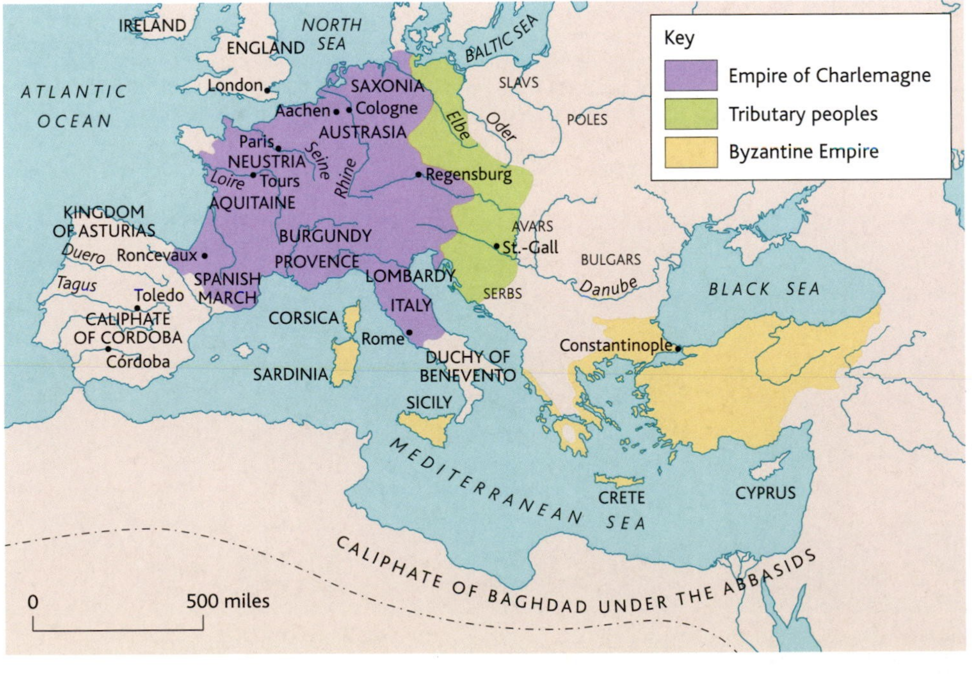

Map 5.2 The Empire of Charlemagne, 814 C.E.

The Monastic Complex

The heart of Charlemagne's educational revival was the monastery. In the course of his reign, Charlemagne authorized the construction of numerous Benedictine monasteries, or abbeys—communities for prayer and the preservation of Christian and Classical learning. Monks and (in female convents) nuns lived and worked within these religious precincts. Central to each monastic complex was a church that served as a place of worship and as a shrine that housed the sacred relics—a bone, skull, or shank of hair exhumed from the Roman catacombs—of Christian saints and martyrs. Both the floor plan of the abbey church and the organization of the monastic complex as a whole manifest the Classical principles of symmetry and order. At the same time, the complex provided all the necessities of daily life isolated from the outside world. The plan for an ideal monastery (Figure **5.5**) found in a manuscript in the library of the monastery of Saint-Gall, Switzerland, reflects these concerns. Each part of the complex, from the **refectory** (dining hall) to the cemetery, is disposed on a gridlike plan. Monks gained access to the church by means of both the adjacent dormitory, where they slept, and the cloister—the covered walkway that opened to a courtyard or garden where they might grow plants and herbs. At the abbey church of Saint-Gall, the many chapels along the aisles and transepts of the church were to house the relics of saints and martyrs.

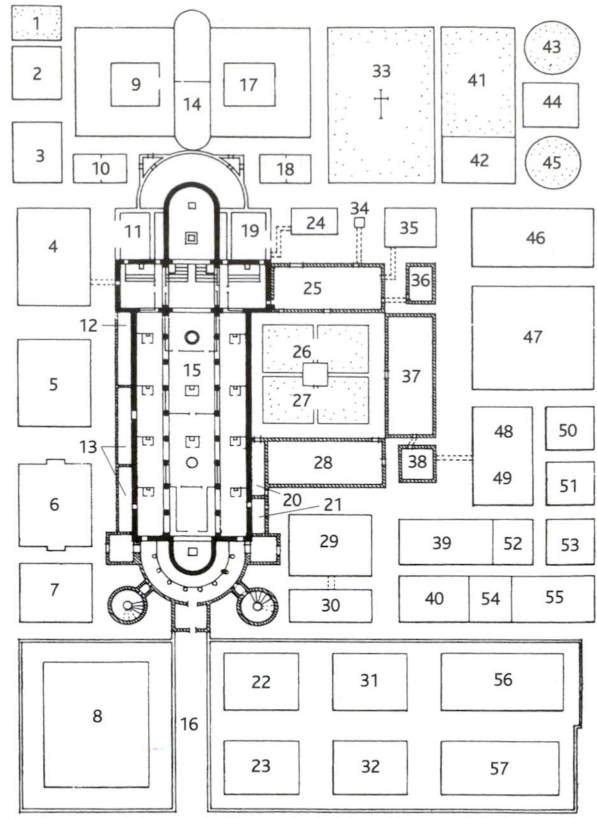

Figure 5.5 Plan for an ideal Benedictine monastery, ninth century C.E. 13½ x 10¼ in. Monastery Library of Saint-Gall.

Making Connections

THE MONASTIC COMPLEX EAST AND WEST

The Christian West was not the only part of the world in which religion inspired the construction of sanctuaries graced with monumental temples and shrines (Figure **5.6**). In Japan, Buddhism was introduced in the sixth century C.E. Absorbing the Shinto nature worship of the ancient Japanese, Buddhism became the spiritual force that united the emperor of Japan, the nobility, and growing communities of monks. As in the West, religious and political authority worked together to create impressive religious complexes furnished with religious icons. The seventh- and eighth-century C.E. Buddhist monastery of Horyu-ji at Nara—the site of the oldest wooden buildings in the world—was home to hundreds of monks (Figure **5.7**). Its graceful five-tiered pagoda, a landmark of Japanese architecture, is derived from a synthesis of the Buddhist *stupa* (see page 118) and the Chinese defense tower, and preserves unique timber-construction techniques that originated in China. Roughly contemporaneous with the Carolingian era, the Nara period in Japan (646–794 C.E.) witnessed a flowering of culture that included the writing of the earliest histories of Japan and the first collections of Japanese poetry.

Q Why might men and women in both the East and the West have chosen to withdraw from secular life to live in religious communities?

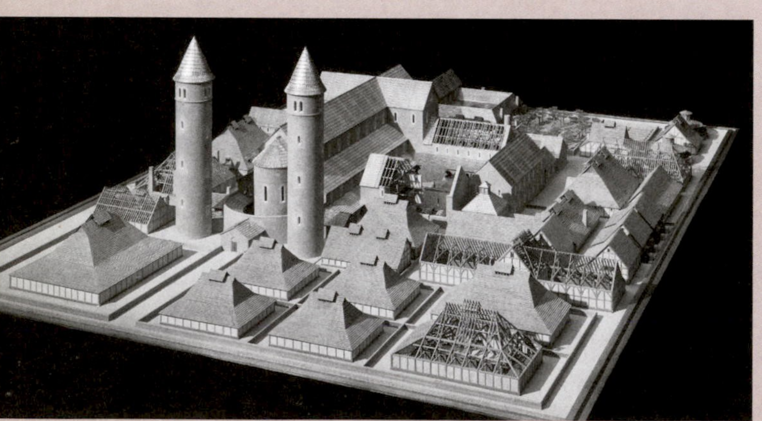

Figure 5.6 Reconstruction model of Saint-Gall Monastery, Switzerland.

Figure 5.7 Horyu-ji, Nara, Japan, seventh and eighth centuries C.E.

1 herbs
2 physician
3 leeching
4 abbot's house
5 school
6 guest house
7 kitchen, brew, & bakehouse for guests
8 hostel (?)
9 infirmary
10 kitchen & bath
11 scriptorium library
12 visiting monks
13 school & guest masters
14 chapel
15 church nave
16 entranceway
17 novitiate
18 kitchen & bath
19 sacristy vestry
20 parlor
21 hospice master
22 sheep
23 servitors
24 preparation of sacramental elements
25 calefactory; dormitory above
26 cloister
27 garth
28 cellar
29 almonry
30 kitchen, brew, & bakehouse for almonry
31 goats
32 pigs
33 orchard cemetery
34 chimney
35 latrine
36 bath
37 refectory
38 kitchen
39 turners, coopers
40 servitors' mares
41 garden
42 gardener
43 geese
44 caretakers of fowl
45 chickens
46 barn threshing floor
47 shops
48 brew house
49 monks' bakery
50 mill
51 press
52 brewery grain
53 kiln or drying house
54 stable
55 servitors' bulls
56 cows
57 horses

The Medieval Book

The Middle Ages was the great era of book production. Carolingian books were prepared for and by monks and clerics rather than for laypeople, most of whom could neither read nor write. Pre-Carolingian manuscripts appeared as continuous rolls, but by the ninth century they took the form of bound pages. Manuscripts were handwritten on parchment (sheepskin) or vellum (calfskin) and hand-decorated, or "illuminated"—that is, ornamented with gold leaf or gold paint and brightly colored pigments. The opening letter of each section of a book was often **historiated**—that is, embellished by a narrative representation appropriate to the subject of the text (Figure **5.8**). Medieval bibles and liturgical books were lavishly ornamented, as befitting their sacred character. Much like devotional objects (see Figure 6.10), they were often sheathed in costly materials, such as ivory, tooled leather, and precious metals. Dating from the decades after Charlemagne's death, the book cover for the Lindau Gospels testifies to the superior technical abilities of Carolingian metalsmiths (Figure **5.9**). The integration of stylistic traditions evident here typifies the Carolingian Renaissance, the glories of which would not be matched for at least three centuries.

Figure 5.8 *The Ascension*, from the Sacramentary of Archbishop Drogo of Metz, ca. 842 C.E. National Library, Paris.

Figure 5.9 Back cover of the Lindau Gospels, ca. 870 C.E. Silver gilt with ***cloisonné*** enamel and precious stones, $13\frac{3}{8} \times 10\frac{3}{8}$ in. J. Pierpont Morgan Library, New York.

HOLY BOOKS AND MANUSCRIPTS

Because of religious prohibitions against the visual representation of humans and animals, Hebrew and Muslim holy books were embellished with abstract ornamentation consisting of Hebrew or Arabic script. Between the eighth and twelfth centuries C.E., as the format of *Qur'an* manuscripts shifted from horizontal (see Figure 4.20) to vertical, there developed a new style of composition featuring elegant, elongated forms of Kufic calligraphy (Figure **5.10**).

The world's first printed books were produced in China. The earliest of these, *The Diamond Sutra*, dated 868 C.E., is a Buddhist text produced from large woodcut blocks (Figure **5.11**). In contrast with medieval European manuscripts, executed on parchment or vellum (see Figure 5.8), the two holy books pictured here were prepared on paper.

Q Why might damaging, stealing, or destroying a religious book be considered sacrilegious?

Figure 5.10 (right) Page of a *Qur'an*, from Iran, twelfth century. Ink, colors, and gold on paper, $11^{3}/_{4} \times 8^{3}/_{4}$ in. The Metropolitan Museum of Art, New York.

Figure 5.11 (below) *The Diamond Sutra*, the world's earliest printed book, dated 868 C.E. Paper, 30 x 72 in. British Library, London.

Beyond the West

JAPAN

The Birth of the Novel

During the eighth century C.E., the Fujiwara clan ascended to the imperial Japanese throne. For roughly four centuries thereafter (794–1185), a sophisticated Japanese aristocracy dominated the capital city of Heian (modern Kyoto), from which came Japan's first wholly original literature: the prose narrative form known as the **novel**. Murasaki Shikibu (978–1016), the author of the world's first novel, was one of a group of female writers who were members of Heian court society. Her achievement is all the more remarkable in that she—like every Japanese female—was excluded from the opportunity for scholarly education and, hence, from training in written Chinese, the literary language of Japan. Nevertheless, using a system of phonetic symbols derived from Chinese characters, Murasaki left a record of her culture, both in her *Diary* and in her landmark novel, *The Tale of Genji* (Figure **5.12**). This Japanese classic tells the story of a young Heian prince, his life and loves at court, as well as his moods, tastes, and desires. Murasaki wrote the world's first psychological novel; in doing so, she painted a detailed picture of daily life among the Heian aristocrats with their elegant silk robes, refined manners, affection for music, and poetic versatility—features that prefigure by five hundred years the elegant culture of the Renaissance West.

Murasaki, *The Tale of Genji* (ca. 1004)

Ideas and Issues

HANDWRITING AS AN ART

"The competition [to produce beautiful handwritten script] was intense. Genji secluded himself as before in the main hall. The cherry blossoms had fallen and the skies were soft. Letting his mind run quietly through the anthologies, he tried several styles with fine results, formal and cursive [flowing script] Chinese and the more radically cursive Japanese 'ladies' hand.' He had with him only two or three women whom he could count on for interesting comments. They ground ink for him and selected poems from the more admired anthologies. Having raised the blinds to let the breezes pass, he sat out near the veranda with a booklet spread before him, and as he took a brush meditatively between his teeth the women thought that they could gaze at him for ages on end and not tire. His brush poised over papers of clear, plain reds and whites, he would collect himself for the effort of writing, and no one of reasonable sensitivity could have failed to admire the picture of serene concentration which he presented."

(from Murasaki, *The Tale of Genji*)

Q Why was handwriting considered an art in Japan and elsewhere in the medieval world?

Figure 5.12 Attributed to Tosa Tokayoshi, *Prince Genji Visiting His Wife*, illustration for *The Tale of Genji* by Murasaki Shikibu, Heian period, early eleventh century. Colors on paper. Private collection, Paris.

FEUDAL SOCIETY

WHEN Charlemagne died in 814 C.E., the short-lived unity he had brought to Western Europe died with him. Although he had turned the Frankish kingdom into an empire, he failed to establish any legal and administrative machinery comparable with that of imperial Rome. There was no standing army, no system of taxation, and no single code of law to unify the widely diverse population. Inevitably, following his death, the fragile stability of the Carolingian Empire was shattered by Scandinavian seafarers known as Vikings. Charlemagne's sons and grandsons could not repel the raids of these fierce invaders, who ravaged the northern coasts of the Empire; at the same time, neither were his heirs able to arrest the repeated forays of the Muslims along the Mediterranean coast. Lacking effective leadership, the Carolingian Empire disintegrated.

In the mid-ninth century C.E., Charlemagne's three grandsons divided the Empire among themselves, separating French- from German-speaking territories. Increasingly, however, administration and protection fell to members of the local ruling aristocracy—heirs of the counts and dukes whom Charlemagne had appointed to administer portions of the realm, or simply those who had taken land by force. The fragmentation of the Empire and the insecurity generated by the Viking invasions caused people at all social levels to attach themselves to members of a military nobility who were capable of providing protection. These circumstances enhanced the growth of a unique system of political and military organization known as *feudalism*.

The Feudal Contract

Derived from Roman and Germanic traditions of rewarding warriors with the spoils of war, feudalism involved the exchange of land for military service. In return for the grant of land, known as a **fief** or *feudum* (the Germanic word for "property"), a **vassal** owed his **lord** a certain number of fighting days (usually forty) per year. The contract between lord and vassal also involved a number of other obligations, including the lord's provision of a court of justice, the vassal's contribution of ransom if his lord were captured, and the reciprocation of hospitality between the two. In an age of instability, feudalism provided a rudimentary form of local government, while answering the need for security against armed attack.

Those engaged in the feudal contract constituted roughly the upper 10 percent of European society. The feudal nobility, which bore the twin responsibilities of military defense and political leadership, was a closed class of men and women whose superior status was inherited at birth. A male member of the nobility was first and foremost a mounted man-at-arms—a *chevalier* (from the French *cheval*, for "horse") or knight (from the Germanic *Knecht*, a youthful servant or soldier). The medieval knight was a cavalry warrior equipped with stirrups, protected by **chain mail** (flexible armor made of interlinked metal rings), and armed with such weapons as broadsword and shield.

The knight's conduct and manners in all aspects of life were guided by a strict code of behavior called **chivalry**. Chivalry demanded that the knight be courageous in battle, loyal to his lord and fellow warriors, and reverent toward women. Feudal life was marked by ceremonies and symbols almost as extensive as those of the Christian Church. For instance, a vassal received his fief by

Making Connections

FEUDALISM EAST AND WEST

Though not identical in character with European feudalism, the Japanese feudal system provides a valid comparison. Between the ninth and twelfth centuries C.E., Japan's powerful aristocratic clans overthrew the imperial regents of the Heian dynasty. The political strength of the clans depended on the allegiance of *samurai* (Japanese, "those who serve") warriors who held land in return for military service to local landholders. Outfitted with warhorses and elaborate armor made of iron plated with lacquer (Figure **5.13**) and trained in the arts of archery and swordsmanship, *samurai* clans competed for position and power. The *samurai* embraced values similar to those of European feudal lords and vassals (Figure **5.14**). Their code, known as *bushido* ("the way of the warrior"), exalted selflessness in battle, fierce loyalty to one's overlord, and a disdain for death. The Japanese code of honor, however, called for ritual suicide (usually by disembowelment) if the *samurai* fell into dishonor.

Q Which aspects of these costumes convey social status? Which reflect the function of these warriors on the battlefield?

Figure 5.13 Yoshihisa Matahachiro's Suit of Armor. Muromachi period, ca. 1550. Steel, blackened and gold-lacquered; flame-colored silk braid, gilt bronze, stenciled deerskin, bear pelt, and gilt wood; approx. height 5 ft. 6 in., approx. weight 48 lb. The Metropolitan Museum of Art, New York. Japanese armor was notable for its flexibility, which contrasted with the rigidity of European plate armor.

Figure 5.14 Matthew Paris, *Vassal Paying Homage to His Lord*, from the Westminster Psalter, ca. 1250. British Library, London. Medieval European chain mail consisted of thousands of individually joined metal links. Plate mail did not appear until the fourteenth century (see page 175). The rank and status of the European soldier was usually indicated by heraldic devices painted or incised on his shield or helmet.

an elaborate procedure known as **investiture**, in which oaths of fealty were formally exchanged (see Figure 5.14). In warfare, adversaries usually fixed the time and place of combat in advance. Medieval warfare was both a profession and a pastime, as knights entertained themselves with **jousts** (personal combat between men on horseback) or war games that imitated the trials of combat.

The Lives of Medieval Serfs

Although the feudal class monopolized land and power within medieval society, this elite group represented only a tiny percentage of the total population. The majority of people—more than 90 percent—were unfree peasants or **serfs** who, along with freemen, farmed the soil. Medieval serfs lived quite differently from their landlords. Bound to large farms or manors (Figure **5.15**), they, like the farmers of the old Roman *latifundia* (see page 68), provided food in exchange for military protection furnished by the nobility. They owned no property. They were forbidden to leave the manor, although, on the positive side, they could not be evicted. Their bondage to the soil assured them the protection of feudal lords who, in an age lacking effective central authority, were the sole sources of political authority.

During the Middle Ages, the reciprocal obligations of serfs and lords and the serf's continuing tenure on the land—a system known as **manorialism**—became firmly fixed. At least until the eleventh century, the interdependence between the two classes was generally beneficial to both; serfs needed protection, and feudal lords, whose position as gentleman-warriors excluded them from menial toil, needed food. For upper and lower classes alike, the individual's place in medieval society was inherited and bound by tradition.

By comparison with the Greeks and Romans, whose dependence on a readily available slave market made the invention of labor-saving devices unnecessary, medieval people made landmark advances in technology. The tandem harness increased the farmer's "horsepower" in the field; the heavy-wheeled plow, in use by the eleventh century, enhanced agricultural productivity. Equally significant was the invention of the spinning wheel and the lathe, and the widespread construction of wind- and watermills. By the thirteenth century, England and France boasted tens of thousands of watermills, used to grind grain, prepare cloth, make beer, and forge iron.

The Norman Conquest

As early as the eighth century C.E. the seafarers known as Vikings (but also as Norsemen, Northmen, and, later, Normans) had moved beyond the bounds of their Scandinavian homelands. They constructed long wooden ships equipped with sailing gear that allowed them to tack into the wind. Expert shipbuilders, sailors, and navigators, they soon came to control the North Atlantic. The western Vikings were the first to colonize Iceland, and they set up a colony in Greenland before the year 1000. The eastern Vikings sailed across the North Sea to establish trading centers at Kiev and Novgorod. Known among Arab traders of the area as "rus," they gave their name to Russia. They traded animal hides, amber, and other valued items, including captive Eastern Europeans—Slavs—from which the English word "slave" derives.

The Vikings began their raids on England with an attack on the Lindisfarne monastery in 793 C.E., and by the end of the ninth century C.E. they had settled throughout northern Europe. Within one hundred years, these aggressive Normans made Normandy one of the strongest fiefs

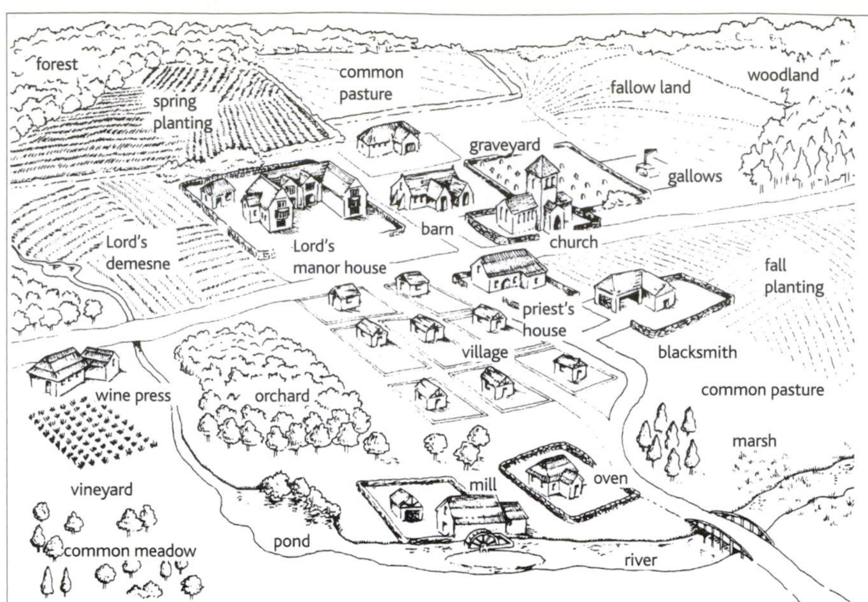

Figure 5.15 The Medieval Manor. A medieval fief usually included one or more manors. The average manor community comprised fifteen to twenty families, while a large manor of 5000 acres might contain some fifty families. The typical manor consisted of farmlands, woodland, and pasture, and included a common mill, wine press, and oven.

in France. In 1066, under the leadership of William of Normandy, some five thousand men crossed the English Channel; at the Battle of Hastings, William defeated the Anglo-Saxon King Harold and seized the throne of England. The Norman Conquest had enormous consequences for the histories of England and France, for it marked the transfer of power in England from Anglo-Saxon rulers to Norman noblemen who were already vassals of the king of France. The Normans brought feudalism to England. To raise money, William ordered a detailed census of all property in the realm—the *Domesday Book*—which laid the basis for the collection of taxes. King William controlled all aspects of government with the aid of the *Curia Regis*—the royal court and council consisting of his feudal barons. Under the Norman kings, England would become one of Europe's leading medieval states.

The Norman Castle

The Normans led the way in the construction of stone castles and churches. Atop hills and at such vulnerable sites as Dover on the southeast coast of England, Norman kings erected austere castle-fortresses (Figure **5.16**). The castle featured a **keep** (square tower) containing a dungeon, a main hall, and a chapel, and incorporated a central open space with workshops and storehouses (Figure **5.17**). The enclosing stone walls were usually surmounted by turrets with **crenellations** that provided archers with protection in defensive combat. A **moat** (a trench usually filled with water) often surrounded the castle walls to deter enemy invasion.

The brilliance of the Normans' achievements in architecture, apparent in their fortresses and in some of the earliest Romanesque churches (see page 154), lies in

Figure 5.16 Dover Castle, Kent, England, twelfth century. Aerial view from the northwest.

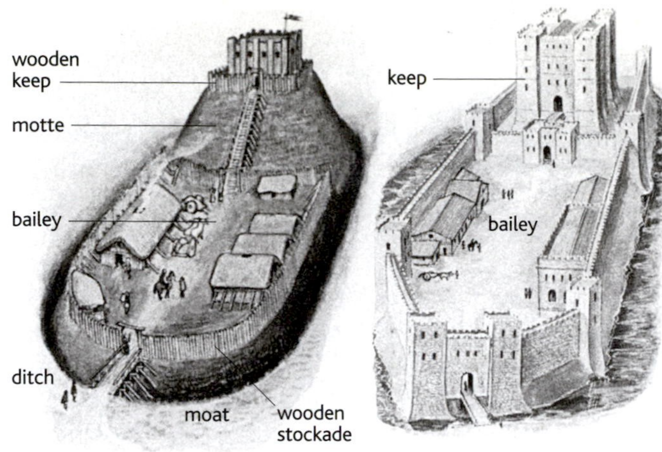

Figure 5.17 The Norman Castle. At first (left), Norman castles in England had two parts, a flattened area called a bailey and a large mound called a motte. Buildings were of wood. Later castles (right) were built of stone. There was no motte, for the heavy keep had to stand on flat, firm earth that would not collapse.

the use of stone to replace earlier timber fortifications and in the clarity with which the design of the building reflects its function.

The Bayeux Tapestry

One of the most notable landmarks of the early Middle Ages is the eleventh-century C.E. embroidered wall-hanging known as the Bayeux Tapestry (see Figure 5.1). The only surviving medieval narrative textile, it depicts the political and military events leading up to and including the battle that gave William of Normandy control of England. Woven with eight colors of wool yarn, its 626 figures, 190 horses, and over 500 other real and fantastic animals make up a richly detailed narrative that unrolls in the manner of an earlier victory landmark: the column of Trajan (see Figure 3.14). Like the historical narratives of Roman art, it is a victor's version of events.

The portion of the textile shown here (Figure **5.18**) describes the crossing of the English Channel: The ships are laden with some of the five to seven thousand vassals that are said to have made up William's fighting force. Above the scene are the last words of the Latin caption, "Here Duke William in a great ship is crossing the sea." Probably commissioned by William's half-brother, Bishop Odo of Bayeux (see Map 6.1), the design and execution of the Bayeux Tapestry remain a subject of debate. Some scholars contend that it was executed in France, while others argue for Canterbury, England. However, since embroidery was almost exclusively a female occupation, it is likely that wherever it originated, it is the work of women—although women are depicted only four times in the entire piece.

Figure 5.18 *William Duke of Normandy's Fleet Crossing the Channel*, detail from the Bayeux Tapestry, late eleventh century. Wool embroidery on linen, depth approx. 20 in., entire length 231 ft. Town of Bayeux, France. The ships pictured here are typical of the wooden vessels built by the Vikings to ply the North and Mediterranean seas. Some 70 feet in length, they were propelled by sails and oars. Carvings of fierce animals and serpents ornamented both ship and prow. Vessels similar to this were also used as burial chambers—the treasures unearthed at Sutton Hoo were packed inside such a ship, along with the body of the deceased chieftain (see page 123).

The Crusades

During the eleventh century, numerous circumstances contributed to a change in the character of medieval life. The Normans effectively pushed the Muslims out of the Mediterranean Sea and, as the Normans and other marauders began to settle down, Europeans enjoyed a greater degree of security. At the same time, rising agricultural productivity and surplus encouraged trade and travel. The Crusades of the eleventh to thirteenth centuries were directly related to these changes. They were both a cause of economic revitalization and a symptom of the increased freedom and new mobility of Western Europeans during the High Middle Ages (ca. 1000–1300).

The Crusades began in an effort to rescue Jerusalem from Muslim Turks who were threatening the Byzantine Empire and denying Christian pilgrims access to the Holy Land. At the request of the Byzantine emperor, the Roman Catholic Church launched a series of military expeditions designed to regain territories dominated by the Turks. The First Crusade, called by Pope Urban II in 1095, began in the spirit of a holy war, but, unlike the Muslim *jihad,* the primary intention was to recover land, not to convert pagans. Thousands of people—both laymen and clergy—"took up the Cross" and marched overland through Europe to the Byzantine East (Figure **5.19**).

It soon became apparent, however, that the material benefits of the Crusades outweighed the spiritual ones, especially since the campaigns provided economic and military opportunities for the younger sons of the nobility. While the eldest son of an upper-class family inherited his father's fief under the principle of **primogeniture**, his younger brothers were left to seek their own fortunes. The Crusades stirred the ambitions of these disenfranchised young men. Equally ambitious were the Italian city-states. Eager to expand their commercial activities, they encouraged the Crusaders to become middlemen in trade between Italy and the East. In the course of the Fourth Crusade, Venetian profit seekers persuaded the Crusaders to sack Constantinople and capture trade ports in the Aegean. Moral inhibitions failed to restrain greedy ambition, and, in 1204, the Fourth Crusade deteriorated into a contest for personal profit. A disastrous postscript to the Fourth Crusade was the Children's Crusade of 1212, in which thousands of children aged between ten and fourteen set out to recapture Jerusalem. Almost all died or were taken into slavery before reaching the Holy Land.

Aside from such economic advantages as those enjoyed by individual Crusaders and the Italian city-states, the gains made by the Crusades were slight. In the first of the four major expeditions, the Crusaders did retake some important cities, including Jerusalem. But by 1291, all recaptured lands were lost again to the Muslims. Indeed, in over two hundred years of fighting, the Crusaders did not secure any territory permanently, nor did they stop the westward advance of the Turks. Constantinople finally fell in 1453 to a later wave of Muslim Turks.

Despite their failure as religious ventures, the Crusades had enormous consequences for the West: The revival of trade between East and West enhanced European commercial life, encouraging the rise of towns and bringing great wealth to the Italian cities of Venice, Genoa, and Pisa. Then, too, in the absence or at the death of crusading noblemen, feudal lords (including emperors and kings) seized every opportunity to establish greater authority over the lands within their domains, thus consolidating and centralizing political power in the embryonic nation-states of England and France. Finally, renewed contact with Byzantium promoted an atmosphere of commercial and cultural receptivity that had not existed since Roman times.

Figure 5.19 *French Knights under Louis IX Besieging Damietta, Egypt*, Seventh Crusade, 1249. National Library, Paris. Over a period of some two hundred years, there were seven major Crusades (and various smaller expeditions) to the Holy Land. After the Muslims recaptured Jerusalem in 1244, King Louis IX of France (better known as "Saint Louis") led the last major Crusade, capturing the Egyptian seaport of Damietta in 1249. But the following year the Egyptians trapped the Crusaders by opening sluice gates for reservoirs on the Nile and surrounding them with floodwater. To secure their escape, Louis had to surrender Damietta and pay a large ransom.

FEUDAL-AGE LITERATURE

The Song of Roland

The ideals of the fighting nobility in the feudal age are best captured in the oldest and greatest French epic poem, *The Song of Roland*. It is based on an event that took place in 778 C.E.—the ambush at the "Gate of Spain," a narrow pass in the Pyrenees, of Charlemagne's rear guard, led by Charlemagne's nephew Roland as they returned from an expedition against the Muslims. This four-thousand-line ***chanson de geste*** ("song of heroic deeds") was transmitted orally for more than three centuries after the event before being written down. Generation after generation of ***jongleurs*** (professional entertainers) wandered from court to court chanting the story (and possibly embellishing it with episodes of folklore) to the accompaniment of a lyre. Although the music for the poem has not survived, it is likely that it consisted of a single and highly improvised line of melody. The tune was probably syllabic (setting one note to each syllable) and—like folk song—dependent on simple repetition.

The Song of Roland (ca. early twelfth century)

As with other works in the oral tradition (the *Epic of Gilgamesh* and the *Iliad*, for instance), *The Song of Roland* is grandiose in its dimensions and profound in its lyric power. Its rugged Old French verse describes a culture that prized the performance of heroic deeds, which brought honor to the warrior, his lord, and his religion. The strong bond of loyalty between vassal and chieftain that characterized the Germanic way of life resonates in Roland's declaration of unswerving devotion to his temporal overlord, Charlemagne. Roland's willingness to die for his religious beliefs, fired by the archbishop's promise of admission into Paradise for those who fall fighting the infidels (in this case, the Muslims), suggests that the militant fervor of Muslims was matched by that of early medieval Christians. The following stanza (91) captures this warring spirit and suggests the powerful antagonism between Christians and Muslims that dominated medieval history:

At Roncevaux[1] Count Roland passes by,
Riding his charger, swift-running Veillantif.[2]
He's armed for battle, splendid in shining mail.
As he parades, he brandishes his lance.
Turning the point straight up against the sky,
And from the spearhead a banner flies, pure white,
With long gold fringes that beat against his hands.
Fair to behold, he laughs, serene and gay.
Now close behind him comes Oliver, his friend,
With all the Frenchmen cheering their mighty lord.
Fiercely his eyes confront the Saracens[3];
Humbly and gently he gazes at the Franks,
Speaking to them with gallant courtesy:
'Barons, my lords, softly now, keep the pace!
Here come the pagans looking for martyrdom.
We'll have such plunder before the day is out,
As no French king has ever won before!'
And at this moment the armies join in war.

AOI[4]

The Poetry of the *Troubadours*

During the early Middle Ages, few men and women could read or write. But by the eleventh century, literacy was spreading beyond the cathedral schools and monasteries. The popularity of such forms of vernacular literature as lyric poetry, the chronicle, and the romance gives evidence of increasing lay literacy among upper-class men and women. To entertain the French nobility, *trouvères* (in the north) and *troubadours* (in the south) composed and performed poems devoted to courtly love, chivalry, religion, and politics. The most famous collection of such lyric poems, the *Carmina burana*, came from northern France. In German-speaking courts, *Minnesingers* provided a similar kind of entertainment, while *Meistersingers*, masters of the guilds of poets and musicians, flourished somewhat later in German towns.

Carmina burana (ca. 1180)

Unlike the minstrels of old, *troubadours* were usually men and women of noble birth. Similar to the *chansons* of the early Middle Ages, their poems were monophonic and syllabic. However, they were more expressive in content and more delicate in style, betraying their indebtedness to Arab poetic forms. Often, *troubadours* (or the professional musicians who recited their poems) accompanied themselves on a lyre or a lute.

The pear-shaped wooden string instrument known as the lute (Arabic, *ud*, meaning "wood") was invented by the Arabs at the end of the sixth century C.E. It was used to accompany vocal performance and soon found its way into the West, probably via Muslim Spain (Figure **5.20**). The widespread tradition of song in the Islamic world gave rise to a twenty-one-volume encyclopedia, the *Great Book of Songs*, composed by the Arab scholar Abu al-Faraj al-Isfahani (897–967 C.E.). The *Great Book* remained for centuries the principal source of information about Islamic music and poetry. Similar to the secular songs of Arab composers, many of the 2,600 extant *troubadour* poems exalt the passionate affection of a gentleman for a lady, or, as in those written by the twenty identifiable *trobairitzes* (female *troubadours*), the reverse. The countess of Dia (often called "Beatriz") was a twelfth-century *trobairitz*; her surviving four songs (one of which follows) are

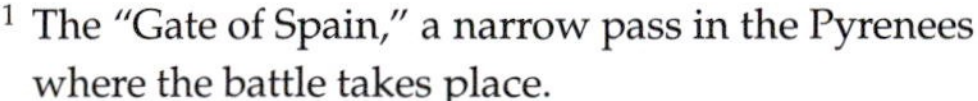

1 The "Gate of Spain," a narrow pass in the Pyrenees where the battle takes place.

2 Roland's horse.

3 Muslims.

4 The letters "AOI" have no known meaning, but they probably signify a musical appendage or refrain that occurred at the end of some stanzas.

Figure 5.20 Lute with nine strings. Miniature from the *Cantigas de Santa Maria*, 1221–1289. El Escorial de Santa Maria, Spain. The forerunner of the guitar, the lute has a right-angled neck and is played with a small quill.

filled with impassioned enticements of physical pleasure (Figure **5.21**) and laments for lost love:

I've been in great anguish

I've been in great anguish
over a noble knight I once had,
and I want everyone to know, for all time,
that I loved him—too much!
Now I see I'm betrayed
because I didn't yield my love to him.
For that I've suffered greatly,
both in my bed and when I'm fully clad.
How I'd yearn to have my knight
in my naked arms for one night!
He would feel a frenzy of delight
only to have me for his pillow.
I'm more in love with him
than Blancheflor ever was with Floris[1].
To him I'd give my heart, my love,
my mind, my eyes, my life.
Beautiful, gracious, sweet friend,
when shall I hold you in my power?
If I could lie with you for one night,
and give you a kiss of love,
you can be sure I would desire greatly
to grant you a husband's place,
as long as you promised
to do everything I wished!

The Medieval Romance and the Code of Courtly Love

The Crusades inspired the writing of chronicles that were a mixture of historical fact, Christian lore, and stirring fiction. As such histories had broad appeal in an age of increasing upper-class literacy, they came to be written in the vernacular, rather than in Latin. The Crusades also contributed to the birth of the **medieval romance**, a fictitious tale of love and adventure that became the most popular form of literary entertainment in the West between the years 1200 and 1500. Medieval romances first appeared in twelfth-century France in the form of rhymed verse, but later ones were written in prose. While romances were probably recited before a small, courtly audience rather than read individually, the development of the form coincided with the rise of a European "textual culture"—that is, a culture dependent on written language rather than oral tradition. In this textual culture, vernacular language gained importance for intimate kinds of literature, while Latin remained the official language of Church and state.

The "spice" of the typical medieval romance was an illicit relationship or forbidden liaison between a man and woman of the upper class. During the Middle Ages, marriage among members of the nobility was usually an alliance formed in the interest of securing land. In fact, noble families might arrange marriages for offspring who were still in the cradle. Given such circumstances, romantic love was more likely to flourish outside marriage. An adulterous affair between Lancelot, a knight of King Arthur's court, and Guinevere, the king's wife, is central to the popular verse romance *Lancelot*. Written in vernacular French by Chrétien de Troyes (d. ca. 1183), *Lancelot* belongs to a cycle of stories associated with a semilegendary sixth-century Welsh chieftain named Arthur. Chrétien's poem stands at the beginning of a long tradition of Arthurian romance literature. Filled with bloody combat, supernatural events, and romantic alliances, medieval romances introduced a new and complex picture of human conduct and courtship associated with the so-called code of courtly love. With its careful construction and nuanced, idealized portrait of courtly behavior, *Lancelot* is a landmark of the medieval romance genre.

Chrétien de Troyes, *Lancelot* (ca. 1170)

The courtly love tradition contributed to shaping modern Western concepts of gender and courtship. It also worked to define the romantic perception of women as objects, particularly objects of reward for the performance of brave deeds. For although courtly love elevated the woman (and her prototype, the Virgin Mary) as worthy of adoration, it defined her exclusively in terms of the interests of men. Nevertheless, the medieval romance, which flattered and exalted the aristocratic lady as an object of desire, was directed toward a primarily female audience. A product of the aristocratic (and male) imagination, the lady of the medieval romance had no counterpart in the lower classes of society, where women worked side by side with men in the fields and in a variety of trades. Despite its artificiality, however, the theme of courtly love and the romance itself had a significant influence on Western literary tradition. In that tradition, even into modern times, writers have tended to treat love as a spiritual awakening or as an emotional affliction rather than as a condition of true affection and sympathy between the sexes.

[1] The lovers in a popular medieval romance.

EARLY MEDIEVAL MUSIC

THE major musical developments of the early Middle Ages came out of the monasteries. In Charlemagne's time, monastic reforms in Church liturgy and in sacred music accompanied the renaissance in the visual arts. Early Church music took the form of unaccompanied monophonic chant (see pages 108–109), a solemn sound that inspired one medieval monk to write in the margin of his songbook, "The tedious plainsong grates my tender ears." Possibly to remedy such complaints, the monks at Saint-Gall enlarged on the range of expression of the classical Gregorian chant by adding **antiphons**, or verses sung as responses to the religious text. Carolingian monks also embellished plainsong with the **trope**, an addition of music or words to the established liturgical chant. Thus, "Lord, have mercy upon us" became "Lord, omnipotent Father, God, Creator of all, have mercy upon us." A special kind of trope, called a **sequence**, added words to the long, melismatic passages—such as the alleluias and amens—that occurred at the end of each part of the Mass.

Liturgical Drama

By the tenth century, singers began to divide among themselves the parts of the liturgy for Christmas and Easter, now embellished by tropes and sequences. As more and more dramatic incidents were added to the texts for these Masses, full-fledged music-drama emerged. Eventually, liturgical plays broke away from the liturgy and were performed in the intervals between the parts of the Mass. Such was the case with the eleventh-century *Play of Herod*, whose dramatic "action" brought to life the legend of the three Magi and the massacre of the innocents by King Herod of Judea—incidents surrounding the Gospel story of the birth of Christ appropriate to the Christmas season. By the twelfth century, spoken dialog and possibly musical instruments were introduced. Eventually, such plays were removed from the church interior and performed in the town square (see pages 147–148).

***Play of Herod* (ca. 1050)**

Figure 5.21 *Konrad von Altstetten Smitten by Spring and His Beloved*, from the Manesse Codex, Zürich, ca. 1300. Manuscript illumination, 14 x 9⅞ in. University Library, Heidelberg, Germany. Influenced by Islamic verse, *troubadour* poems generally manifest a positive, even joyous, response to physical nature and the world of the senses. An eleventh-century poem by William IX, Duke of Aquitaine and one of the first *troubadours*, compares the anticipation of sexual fulfillment with the coming of spring. It opens with these high-spirited words:

In the sweetness of the new season
when woods burst forth and birds
sing, each in its own voice
to the lyrics of a new song,
then should one seize
the pleasures one most desires.

Beyond the West

CHINA

Tang and Song

In the Middle Ages, while Eastern Europe consisted mainly of cow pastures and random villages, China, under the centralized rule of the Tang dynasty (618–907 C.E.) and the subsequent Song dynasty (960–1279), boasted a sophisticated urban culture with city populations that often reached one million (Figure **5.22**). The Tang Empire dwarfed the Carolingian Empire in the West not only in terms of its geographic size and population but also with respect to its intellectual and educational accomplishments. Tang bureaucrats, steeped in Confucian traditions and rigorously trained in the literary classics, were members of an intellectual elite that rose to service on the basis of merit. Beginning in the seventh century C.E. (but rooted in a long tradition of leadership based on education and ability), every government official was subject to a rigorous civil service examination (see page 25). A young man gained a political position by passing three levels of examinations (district, provincial, and national) that tested his familiarity with the Chinese classics as well as his grasp of contemporary political issues. For lower-ranking positions, candidates took exams in law, mathematics, and calligraphy. As in the Islamic world and the Christian West, higher education in China required close familiarity with the basic religious and philosophical texts. But because Chinese characters changed very little over the centuries, students could read 1500-year-old texts as easily as they could read contemporary ones. Chinese classics were thus accessible to Chinese scholars in a way that the Greco-Roman classics were not accessible to Western scholars. Training for the arduous civil service examination required a great degree of memorization and a thorough knowledge of China's literary tradition, but originality was also important: Candidates had to prove accomplishment in the writing of prose and poetry as well as in the analysis of administrative policy. Strict standards applied to grading, and candidates who failed the exams (only one to 10 percent passed the first level) could take them over and over, even into their middle and old age.

During the seventh century C.E., the imperial college in the capital city of Chang'an (present-day Xi'an) prepared some three thousand men for the civil service examinations. (As in the West, women were excluded from education in colleges and universities.) Such scholar officials constituted China's highest social class. And while the vast population of Chinese peasants lived in relative ignorance and poverty, the aristocratic bureaucrats of the Tang generally enjoyed lives of wealth and position. Nowhere else in the world of the ninth and tenth centuries C.E. (except perhaps Baghdad) was such prestige attached to scholarship and intellectual achievement. Despite instances in which family connections influenced political position, the imperial examination system remained the main route to official status in China well into the twentieth century.

Chinese Technology

Chinese civilization is exceptional in the extraordinary number of its technological inventions, many of which came into use elsewhere in the world only long after their utilization in China. A case in point is printing, which originated in ninth-century C.E. China (see page 128 and Figure 5.11) but was not perfected in the West until the fifteenth century.

Figure 5.22 Chang Tse-Tuan, detail from *Life Along the River on the Eve of the Ch'ing Ming Festival*, late eleventh to early twelfth century. Handscroll, ink on silk. Palace Museum, Beijing. Chinese cities boasted a variety of restaurants, teahouses, temples, gardens, and shops, including bookstores and pet shops. City dwellers enjoyed conditions of safety that are enviable even today—in Hangzhou, the streets were patrolled at night, and bridges and canals were guarded and fitted with balustrades to prevent drunken revelers from falling into the water.

Chinese technology often involved the intelligent application of natural principles to produce labor-saving devices. Examples include the watermill (devised to grind tea leaves and to provide power to run machinery), the wheelbarrow (used in China from at least the third century C.E. but not found in Europe until more than ten centuries later), the foot stirrup (in use well before the fifth century C.E.), the stern-post rudder, the magnetic compass, and the processes of iron and steel casting. Gunpowder, invented as early as the seventh century C.E. and used in firework displays, was employed in the form of fire-arrow incendiaries for military purposes in the mid-tenth century, but did not arrive in the West until the fourteenth century.

Chinese Porcelain

By 700 C.E., the Chinese, whose ceramic tradition reached back thousands of years, had perfected the manufacture of **porcelain**—a hard, translucent ceramic ware fired at extremely high heat. Glazed with delicate colors and impervious to water, porcelain vessels represent a landmark in ceramic technology. The level of technical sophistication achieved in the manufacture of porcelain objects was matched only by their stylistic elegance. Based on natural forms, such as the lotus blossom, Chinese porcelains are marvels of calculated simplicity (Figure 5.23). Observing the sparkle of water through porcelain bowls of the Tang era, one ninth-century C.E. merchant marveled that they were "as fine as glass." Exported along with silks, lacquerware, and carved ivories, porcelain became one of the most sought-after of Chinese luxury goods—especially popular in the West, where it came to be called, simply, "china."

Chinese Landscape Painting

Landscape painting, the visual record of the natural world, was born in China. While Roman artists used realistic depictions of nature as background settings, the Chinese made landscape a subject in its own right. Some of the earliest and finest Chinese landscapes come from the Tang and Song eras, a Golden Age of painting and poetry. In landscape painting, as in poetry, the Chinese sought to evoke a mood, rather than to provide a literal, objective record of reality. On leaves and scrolls made of silk or paper,

Figure 5.23 (left) Lobed Yue-ware bowl, Tang dynasty, ca. tenth century. Stoneware with pale green glaze. Victoria and Albert Museum, London.

Beyond the West

calligraphic brushstrokes and thin washes of muted color capture a sense of vast space that dwarfs the human presence. Such paintings are not settings for heroic endeavors; rather, they offer a contemplative approach to nature and an all-embracing, pantheistic view of the world shared by Daoists (see page 26), Hindus (see page 23), and Buddhists (see page 117). Similar to the poems often inscribed on the margins of these scrolls, these paintings are executed with an astonishing economy of line. Mountains (symbols of immortality) and valleys, trees and streams, temples and bridges are enshrouded by an all-enveloping mist that invites the eye to wander between foreground, middle ground, and background (Figure **5.24**).

Figure 5.24 Attributed to Li Cheng, *A Solitary Temple Amid Clearing Peaks*, Northern Song dynasty, ca. 950 C.E. Ink and slight color on silk hanging scroll, 44 x 22 in. Nelson-Atkins Museum of Art, Kansas City, Missouri. There is no single viewpoint from which to observe all elements in this cosmic view of nature. Rather, we contemplate the whole from what one eleventh-century Chinese art critic called "the angle of totality." The lofty mountains and gentle waterfalls seem protective of the infinitely smaller temples, houses, and people.

Both the spirit and the subject matter of this landscape are captured in a poem by Li Bo (ca. 700–762), one of the finest of China's Golden Age of poets:

Watching the Mount Lushan Waterfall

Incense-Burner Peak shimmers
in the sun,
Purple mist slowly rising.
A flying stream, seen from below,
Hangs like clouds down the crag.

The waterfall pours itself
Three thousand feet
straight down,
Roaring like the Milky Way
Tumbling from high heaven.

Afterword

The thousand years following the fall of Rome was a time in which Classical, Christian, and Germanic traditions coalesced to usher in the rise of the West. Unlike the more highly developed Chinese at the eastern reaches of the Asian continent, Western Europeans developed a rugged, warring society, tempered by feudal loyalties and the otherworldly ideals of Roman Catholic Christianity. The synthesis of earlier traditions gave the early Middle Ages its fundamental character and its prominent landmarks. These, in turn, would anticipate the vibrant culture of medieval Christendom.

Key Topics

- Germanic tribes
- Germanic literature and art
- the Carolingian renaissance
- the monastic complex
- the medieval book
- feudalism
- medieval serfs
- the Norman Conquest
- the Bayeux Tapestry
- Norman castles
- the Crusades
- *The Song of Roland*
- *troubadour* verse
- the medieval romance
- the code of courtly love
- Japan's court culture
- Tang and Song China
- Chinese technology and arts

EARLY MIDDLE AGES TIMELINE

	HISTORICAL EVENTS	LANDMARKS IN THE VISUAL ARTS	LITERARY LANDMARKS	MUSIC LANDMARKS	BEYOND THE WEST
350	Visigoths defeat Romans at battle of Adrianople (378)				
400	Saint Patrick converts Celts to Christianity (fifth century)				
600		Sutton Hoo artifacts (early seventh century)		Antiphons, tropes, and sequences (from 600)	Horyu-ji monastery, Nara, Japan (seventh and eighth centuries) Tang dynasty in China (618–907) Nara period in Japan (646–794)
700	Rule of Charlemagne (768–814): revival of learning Carolingian *minuscule* replaces Roman script (late eighth century)	Saint-Gall monastery (eighth century)	*Beowulf* (ca. 700)		Chinese porcelains (from eighth century) Li Bo (ca. 700–762), Golden Age poems Heian (Fujiwara family) period in Japan (794–1185)
800	Viking invasions (ca. 800–1100)	Book of Kells (ca. 800) Lindau Gospels (ca. 870)			First printed book (China): *The Diamond Sutra* (868)
900					Li Cheng, *A Solitary Temple* (ca. 950) Song dynasty in China (960–1279)
1000	Norman Conquest (1066) Christian Crusades (from 1095)	Bayeux Tapestry (late eleventh century)	*Troubadour* poems (ca. 1050–1200)	*Play of Herod* (ca. 1050)	First novel (Japan): Murasaki Shikibu, *The Tale of Genji* (ca. 1004)
1100		Dover Castle, England (twelfth century) Manesse Codex (ca. 1300)	*The Song of Roland* (ca. 1100) Chrétien de Troyes, *Lancelot* (ca. 1170) *Carmina burana* (ca. 1180) *The Song of the Nibelungs* (ca. 1180)		

Figure 5.2
Buckle, from Sutton Hoo, see p. 124

Figure 5.23
Lobed Yue-ware bowl, see p. 139

Figure 5.18
Bayeux Tapestry, see p. 133

Figure 5.16
Dover Castle, see p. 132

Chapter 6

Christendom:

EUROPE IN THE AGE OF FAITH

ca. 1000–1300

Christendom, the Christian community of the Middle Ages, assumed its distinctive character between roughly 1000 and 1300. Ushered in by the Crusades, the era witnessed the rise of Europe's urban centers, the founding of universities, and the construction of majestic cathedrals. The Roman Catholic Church dominated Christendom. The authority and eminence of the Church rivaled that of the royal monarchs in Europe's young nation-states, and its patronage was responsible for some of the greatest landmarks of the era. The Church shaped medieval culture and values; it governed the life of the individual Christian from cradle to grave. Aspirations to follow the Christian way from sin to salvation inspired medieval morality plays, the writings of mystics, poets, and preachers, and the music of praise and redemption. By the thirteenth century, urban culture enjoyed the patronage of a rising merchant class. The Gothic cathedral, the spiritual heart of the medieval city, embodied a new architectural style. A multitude of sculptures, radiant stained glass windows, devotional altarpieces, and a rich new style of polyphonic music proclaimed the irrepressible fervor of the Age of Faith.

A First Look

On the night of June 10, 1194, a catastrophe befell Christendom: Fire swept through the renowned cathedral of Chartres, southwest of Paris, France, leaving only the crypt, the towers, and the newly constructed west façade. The ruined church, the victim of recurring conflagrations since the eighth century, had been skillfully enlarged only a few decades earlier in recognition of the need to accommodate the increasing numbers of pilgrims flocking to worship at the shrine of the Virgin. Not only did this holy shrine bring great prestige to Chartres; it was also a welcome source of civic revenue. It was with great joy, therefore, when, on June 13, the townspeople, assembled before the smoking ruins of the cathedral, learned that its famous holy relic, the tunic that Mary was said to have worn at the birth of Jesus, had survived intact. The miraculous incident inspired all of Christendom: Clerics and kings, burghers and laborers contributed financially and physically to the massive program of rebuilding hailed as testament to the faith. The new cathedral rose to an unprecedented height and could be seen as a tangible as well as a spiritual beacon for miles around the agricultural countryside. Chartres cathedral continues to awe us. Its monumental stone façade, its elegant rose window, its towering spires, and its breathtaking integration of pointed arches, rib vaults, and stained glass windows (see Figure 6.21), have made it a landmark of the Gothic style (see pages 157–164).

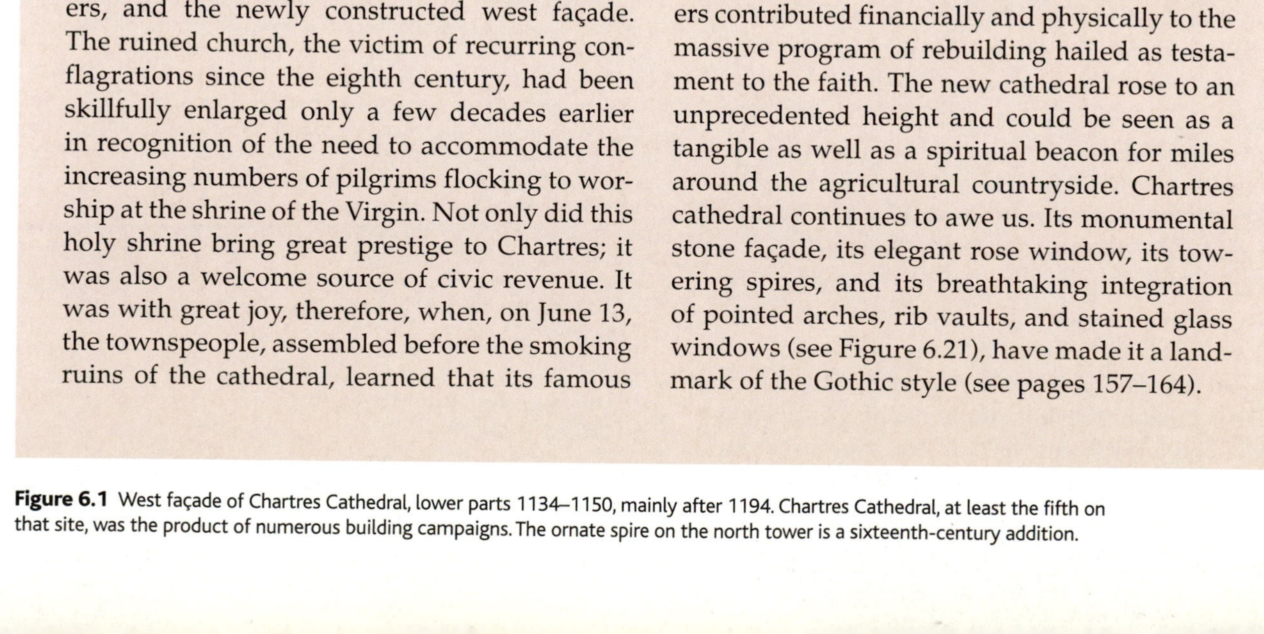

Figure 6.1 West façade of Chartres Cathedral, lower parts 1134–1150, mainly after 1194. Chartres Cathedral, at least the fifth on that site, was the product of numerous building campaigns. The ornate spire on the north tower is a sixteenth-century addition.

THE MEDIEVAL CHURCH

THE Roman Catholic Church formed the bedrock of medieval European culture. It exercised great power and authority not only as a religious force, but also as a political institution. Against the rising tide of European monarchies, the papacy took measures to ensure its independence and its dominance. In 1022, for instance, the Church rid itself of secular influence by founding the College of Cardinals as the sole body responsible for the election of the pope. Medieval pontiffs functioned much like secular monarchs, governing a huge and complex bureaucracy incorporating financial, judicial, and disciplinary branches. The Curia, the papal council and highest Church court, headed a vast network of ecclesiastical courts, while the Camera (the papal treasury) handled financial matters. The medieval Church was enormously wealthy. Over the centuries, Christians had donated and bequeathed to Christendom so many thousands of acres of land that, by the end of the twelfth century, the Catholic Church was the largest single landholder in Western Europe.

Among lay Christians of every rank the Church commanded religious obedience. It enforced religious conformity by means of such spiritual penalties as **excommunication** (exclusion from the sacraments) and **interdict**, the excommunication of an entire city or state—used to dissuade secular rulers from opposing papal policy. In spite of these spiritual weapons, **heresy** (denial of the revealed truths of the Christian faith) spread rapidly within the increasingly cosmopolitan centers of twelfth-century Europe. Such anticlerical groups as the Waldensians (followers of the French thirteenth-century reformer Peter Waldo) denounced the growing worldliness of the Church. Waldo proposed that lay Christians administer the sacraments and that the Bible—sole source of religious authority—should be translated into the vernacular.

Condemning such views as threats to civil and religious order, the Church launched antiheretical crusades that were almost as violent as those advanced against the Muslims. Further, in 1233, the pope established the Inquisition, a special court designed to stamp out heresy. The Inquisition brought to trial individuals whom local townspeople denounced as heretics. The accused were deprived of legal counsel and were usually tried in secret. Inquisitors might use physical torture to obtain confession, for the Church considered injury to the body preferable to the eternal damnation of the soul. If the Inquisition failed to restore accused heretics to the faith, it might impose such penalties as exile or excommunication, or it might turn over the defendants to the state to be hanged or burned at the stake—the latter being the preferred punishment for female heretics. With the same energy that the Church persecuted heretics, it acted as a civilizing agent. It preserved order by enforcing periods in which warfare was prohibited. It assumed moral and financial responsibility for the poor, the sick, and the homeless; and it provided for the organization of hospitals, refuges, orphanages, and other charitable institutions.

Church and State

A key issue in medieval history was the rivalry between Church and state for supreme authority in Christendom. The slow development of nationhood in France and England depended on the monarch's ability to wrest land and power from his vassals, some of whom were members of the clergy. Between the eleventh and thirteenth centuries, the establishment of royal courts and other agencies of central government gave the kings of France and England increasing influence and prestige (see page 175). While the Church, in the person of such august pontiffs as Gregory VII (r. 1073–1085) and Innocent III (r. 1198–1216), claimed ultimate authority as the caretaker of the soul, the monarchs of the rising nation-states often came into conflict with church leaders over issues of taxation, the dispensation of justice, and the selection and ordination of priests. It was not until the sixteenth century that the European West would acknowledge a clear separation of the roles of Church and state in governing human affairs.

Sin and Salvation

Christianity addressed the question of personal salvation more effectively than any other world religion. Through the **sacraments**, a set of sacred acts that impart **grace** (the free and unearned favor of God), medieval Christians were assured of the soul's redemption from sin and, ultimately, of eternal life in the world to come. The

Ideas and Issues

THE SUPREMACY OF THE CHURCH

"... every Christian king when he approaches his end asks the aid of a priest as a miserable suppliant that he may escape the prison of hell, may pass from darkness into light and may appear at the judgment seat of God freed from the bonds of sin. But who, layman or priest, in his last moments has ever asked the help of any earthly king for the safety of his soul? And what king or emperor has power through his office to snatch any Christian from the might of the Devil by the sacred rite of baptism, to confirm him among the sons of God and to fortify him by the holy chrism [consecrated oil]? Or—and this is the greatest thing in the Christian religion—who among them is able by his own word to create the body and blood of the Lord? Or to whom among them is given the power to bind and loose in Heaven and upon earth? From this it is apparent how greatly superior in power is the priestly dignity."

(from Gregory VII, *Letters*)

Q How does Pope Gregory VII justify the superiority of the Church over the state?

seven sacraments—the number fixed by the Fourth Lateran Council of 1215—touched every significant phase of human life: At birth, *baptism* purified the recipient of Original Sin; *confirmation* admitted the baptized to full church privileges; *ordination* invested those entering the clergy with priestly authority; *matrimony* blessed the union of man and woman; *penance* acknowledged repentance of sins and offered absolution; *Eucharist*—the central and most important of the sacraments—joined human beings to God by means of the body and blood of Jesus; and finally, just prior to death, *extreme unction* provided final absolution from sins.

By way of the sacraments, the Church participated in virtually every major aspect of the individual's life, enforcing a set of values that determined the collective spirituality of Christendom. Since only church officials could administer the sacraments, the clergy held a "monopoly" on personal salvation. Medieval Christians thus looked to representatives of the Mother Church as shepherds guiding the members of their flock on their long and hazardous journey from cradle to grave. Their conduct on earth determined whether their souls went to heaven, hell, or Purgatory (the place of purification from sins). But only by way of the clergy might they receive the gifts of grace that made salvation possible.

By the twelfth century, the Christian concepts of sin and divine justice had become ever more complex: Church councils defined Purgatory as an intermediate realm occupied by the soul after death (and before the Last Judgment). In Purgatory punishment was imposed for the unexpiated but repented sins committed in mortal life. While ordinary Christians might suffer punishment in Purgatory, they might also benefit from prayers and good works offered on their behalf. The role of the priesthood in providing such forms of remission from sin would give the medieval Church unassailable power and authority.

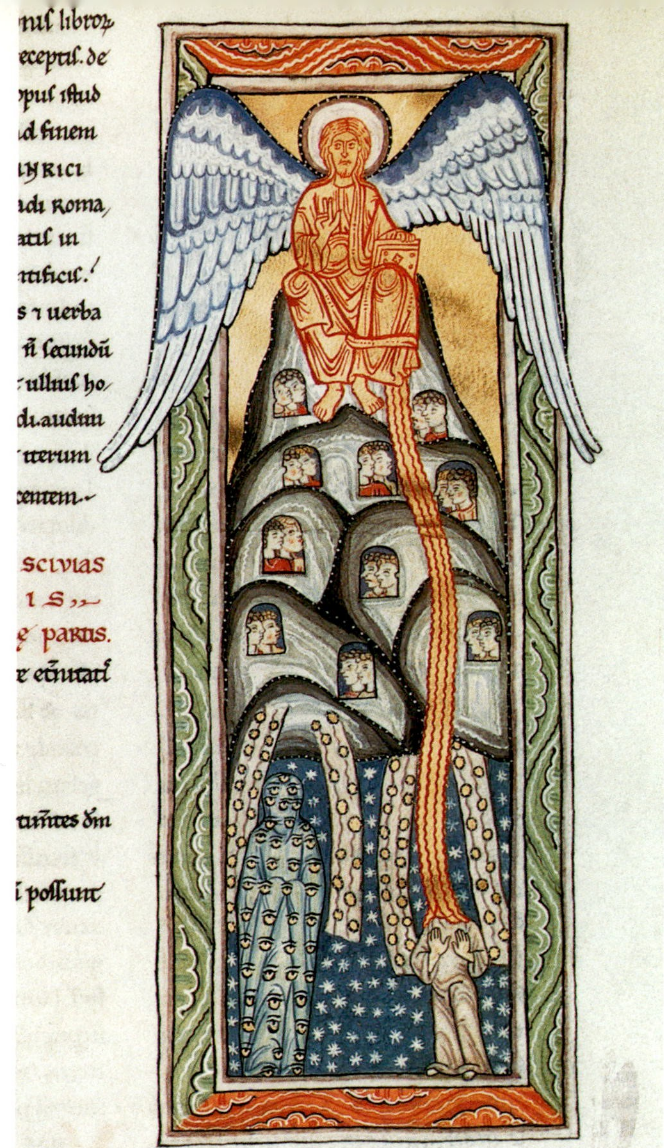

Figure 6.2 Hildegard of Bingen, *Scivias*, ca. 1146. Landesbibliothek, Wiesbaden. This miniature—like all of those that illustrate her manuscripts—was supervised by Hildegard herself. Its imagery illustrates the contents of the excerpt from the *Scivias* found in Making Connections on page 146.

The Literature of Mysticism

Most of the religious literature of the Middle Ages was didactic—that is, it served to teach and instruct. Visionary literature, however, functioned in two other ways. In that it recorded one's intuitive and direct knowledge of God, it operated as a kind of autobiography; and, owing to its vivid images of the supernatural, it provided a vocabulary by which the unknowable might be known. The writings of Hildegard of Bingen (1098–1179), the leading mystic of the twelfth century, reflect these features.

Hildegard entered a Benedictine convent at the age of eight, eventually becoming its abbess. A scholar of both Latin and her native German, she penned treatises on natural science, medicine, and the treatment of disease. Her writings on the nature of the universe, the meaning of Scripture, and the destiny of the Christian soul are among the most eloquent expressions of the Age of Faith. Hildegard was the first woman composer for whom an entire body of music survives. Her seventy-seven songs offer praise for the Virgin Mary, for womankind, and for the virgin saints; and her *Ordo virtutum* (*Play of the Virtues*) became history's first music-drama (see page 148).

At the age of 42, Hildegard began to experience intense visions that inspired her to write a number of visionary tracts. In her landmark treatise, *Scivias* (short for *Scitos vias Domini* [*Know the Ways of the Lord*]), she recounts the ecstatic revelations that "stunned" her vision (Figure **6.2** and see Making Connections on page 146). While Hildegard has been hailed as the first female visionary, she actually follows a long line of mystics whose history begins in antiquity (most famously represented by the priestesses of Delphi). Nevertheless, Hildegard remains one of the first great Christian mystics.

Hildegard of Bingen, *Scivias* (ca. 1146)

Saint Francis: Medieval Humanist

The growing wealth and worldliness of the Roman Catholic Church and many of its monastic communities inspired movements of reform devoted to reviving the early Christian ideals of poverty, chastity, and humility. One of the landmark figures in this humanist wave that swept medieval Christendom was a young Italian named Giovanni Bernardone (1181–1226), whose father nicknamed him "Francesco." The son of a wealthy cloth merchant from Assisi, Francis drew an immediate following when, at the age of twenty-four, he dramatically renounced a life of wealth and comfort, dedicating himself

Making Connections

MYSTICISM: CHRISTIAN AND MUSLIM

All world religions have produced mystics—individuals inspired to reveal truths that lie beyond human understanding. Before the eighth century C.E., some of Muhammad's followers began to pursue a world-renouncing religious life of poverty and chastity similar to that of Christian and Buddhist monks. The Sufi, so-called for their coarse wool (Arabic, *suf*) garments, sought mystical union with God through meditation, fasting, and prayer. Sufism placed emphasis on visionary experience and the intensification of physical sensation through music, poetry, and dance. Religious rituals featuring whirling dancers known as "dervishes" transported the pious to a state of ecstasy (Figure **6.3**).

The Sufi mystic and poet Jalal al-Din Rumi (ca. 1207–1273), like Hildegard of Bingen, drew on the intuitive, nonrational dimensions of religious experience to compose inspired verses that have become landmarks of Muslim literature. As with the writings of Hildegard, radiant, truth-giving light is a frequent image in his poems. In "The One True Light," Rumi rehearses an ancient parable: While religions are many, God is One.

Hildegard of Bingen: "The Iron-Colored Mountain and the Radiant One"

I saw what seemed to be a huge mountain having the color of iron. On its height was sitting One of such great radiance that it stunned my vision. On both sides of him extended a gentle shadow like a wing of marvelous width and length. And in front of him at the foot of the same mountain stood a figure full of eyes everywhere. Because of those eyes, I was not able to distinguish any human form.

In front of this figure there was another figure, whose age was that of a boy, and he was clothed in a pale tunic and white shoes. I was not able to look at his face, because above his head so much radiance descended from the One sitting on the mountain. From the One sitting on the mountain a great many living sparks cascaded, which flew around those figures with great sweetness. In this same mountain, moreover, there seemed to be a number of little windows, in which men's heads appeared, some pale and some white.

And see! The One sitting on the mountain shouted in an extremely loud, strong voice, saying: "O frail mortal, you who are of the dust of the earth's dust, and ash of ash, cry out and speak of the way into incorruptible salvation! Do this in order that those people may be taught who see the innermost meaning of Scripture, but who do not wish to tell it or preach it because they are lukewarm and dull in preserving God's justice. Unlock for them the mystical barriers. For they, being timid, are hiding themselves in a remote and barren field. You, therefore, pour yourself forth in a fountain of abundance! Flow with mystical learning, so that those who want you to be scorned because of the guilt of Eve may be inundated by the flood of your refreshment!"

(from Hildegard of Bingen, *Scivias*, Book 1, Vision 1)

Rumi: "The One True Light"

The lamps are different, but the Light is the same: it comes from Beyond.
If thou keep looking at the lamp, thou art lost: for thence arises the appearance of number and plurality.
Fix thy gaze upon the Light, and thou art delivered from the dualism inherent in the finite body.
O thou who art the kernel of Existence, the disagreement between Moslem, Zoroastrian and Jew depends on the standpoint.

Some Hindus brought an elephant, which they exhibited in a dark shed.
As seeing it with the eye was impossible, every one felt it with the palm of his hand.
The hand of one fell on its trunk: he said, "This animal is like a water-pipe."
Another touched its ear: to him the creature seemed like a fan.
Another handled its leg and described the elephant as having the shape of a pillar.
Another stroked its back. "Truly," said he, "this elephant resembles a throne."
Had each of them held a lighted candle, there would have been no contradiction in their words.

(from Rumi, *Love is a Stranger*)

Q How does light function in each of these mystical "visions"?

Figure 6.3 Detail of *Dancing Dervishes*, from a manuscript of the *Diwan* (*Book of Poems*) of Hafiz, Herat School, Persia, ca. 1490. Colors and gilt on paper, whole leaf 11¾ x 7⅞ in. The Metropolitan Museum of Art, New York.

Figure 6.4 Giotto, *Sermon to the Birds*, ca. 1290. Fresco. Upper Church of San Francesco, Assisi, Italy. The famous series of frescoes in the Upper Church of Assisi, painted by Giotto (see page 180) at the end of the thirteenth century, was based on the biography of Francis written by Bonaventura, a Franciscan theologian. Francis' reverence for nature is reflected in his sermon to the birds and his song of praise to "Brother Sun."

instead to preaching and serving the poor. Imitating the first apostles, Francis practiced absolute poverty, begging for food and lodging on his travels throughout Christendom. Unlike the cloistered monks, Francis evangelized among the citizens of the rapidly growing Italian towns. His mendicant (begging) lifestyle emphasized simplicity and humility; and his efforts among the poor and sickly rejuvenated the compassionate idealism of early Christianity and of Jesus himself.

As word of Francis spread, he came to be known as a missionary to all of God's creatures, hence the popular depiction of the saint—he was canonized in 1228—sermonizing among beasts and birds (Figure **6.4**). At the same time, Francis would be regarded as a mystic: Legends written after his death credit him with numerous miracles and cures. One of the most popular legends relates that toward the end of his life, during a period of withdrawal and fasting, his spiritual identity with Jesus was confirmed by his reception of the *stigmata*—the physical marks of the Crucifixion.

MEDIEVAL TOWNS

THE rise of towns in the period following the First Crusade (1095) was a landmark development of medieval Christendom. Driven by increased agricultural production and the reopening of trade routes, merchants (often the younger sons of the nobility) engaged in commercial enterprises that promoted the growth of local markets. Usually established near highways or rivers, outside the walls of a fortified castle (*bourg* in French, *burg* in German, and "borough" in English), the trade market became an essential part of medieval life. As these local markets became permanent, they slowly grew in size to become urban communities, enticing farmers and artisans to buy freedom from the lord of the manor—or simply run away from the manor. Over the years, then, there emerged a new class of people, a middle class ("midway" between serfs and feudal lords). "City air makes a man free" was the cry of those who had discovered an urban alternative to manorial life.

In the newly established towns, the middle class pursued profit from commercial exchange. Merchants and craftspeople in like occupations formed **guilds** for the mutual protection of buyers and sellers. The guilds regulated prices, fixed wages, established standards of quality in the production of goods, and provided training for newcomers in each profession. During the eleventh and twelfth centuries, urban dwellers purchased charters of self-government from lords in whose fiefs their towns were situated. These charters allowed townspeople (*bourgeois* in French, *burghers* in German) to establish municipal governments and regulate their own economic activities. Such commercial centers as Milan, Florence, and Venice became completely self-governing city-states similar to those of ancient Greece and Rome. The self-governing Flemish cities of Bruges and Antwerp exported fine linen and wool to England and to towns along the Baltic Sea. The spirit of urban growth was manifested in the construction of defensive stone walls that protected the citizens and in the building of cathedrals and guildhalls that flanked the open marketplace. Although by the twelfth century town dwellers constituted less than 15 percent of the total European population, the middle class continued to expand, and ultimately it came to dominate Western society.

Medieval Drama

The heart of the medieval town was the cathedral and its adjacent town square. On religious holidays and feast days, the space that usually held a bustling market became an open-air theater for the enactment of Christian history and legend. Medieval drama, like Greek drama, had its roots in religious performance: specifically, the Catholic Mass. Early church plays, such as the *Play of Herod* (see page 137), became popular as musical dramatizations of the Catholic liturgy. Between the eleventh and thirteenth centuries, as such plays expanded in staging techniques (to include more performers, sets, costumes, and incidental and often boisterous interludes), performances moved from the choir to the church doorway, and then into the town square. As laymen (often members of the individual guilds) took on the roles that had been played by members of the clergy, vernacular languages came to replace Latin. By the thirteenth century, medieval plays were performed on roofed (often two-story) wagon-stages known as **pageants** that were rolled into the town square. Theater soon became a civic enterprise with town guilds overseeing and supporting the production and performance aspects of each play.

While medieval plays were a popular form of entertainment, they were principally didactic, functioning as sources of instructive entertainment. Three types of medieval drama emerged: The **mystery play** dramatized aspects of biblical history from the fall of Lucifer to the Last Judgment. A favorite stage device for this type of play was the hell's mouth (Figure **6.5**), a gaping monster's jaw big enough for actors to pass through, often animated with smoke and fire and peopled with lively, costumed devils. The **miracle play** enacted stories from the Life of Christ, the Virgin Mary, or the saints. The third type of medieval drama, the **morality play**, dealt with the struggle between good and evil, and the destiny of the soul in the hereafter. The morality play had clear precedents in allegorical poetry and sermon literature. Allegory—a literary device already encountered in Plato's *Republic* (see page 44) and in Augustine's *City of God* (see page 102)—employs symbols to stand for a person, thing, or idea. In the same manner, the characters in the morality play are personifications of abstract qualities and universal conditions.

The earliest existing morality play, *Ordo virtutum* (*Play of the Virtues*), was written by Hildegard of Bingen. In this allegorical music-drama, the Virtues contest with the Devil for the Christian Soul. The Devil's lines are spoken, not sung, consistent with Hildegard's belief that satanic evil was unable to know the harmony and order of music itself. It is likely that this play was performed by the nuns of Hildegard's convent.

Hildegard of Bingen, *Ordo virtutum* (*Play of the Virtues* ca. 1151)

The most popular morality play of the Middle Ages was the allegorical drama known as *Everyman*. Surviving in fifteenth-century Dutch and English editions, *Everyman* dramatizes the pilgrimage of the Christian soul from earthly existence to Last Judgment: On God's instruction, Death has come to take Everyman. Unprepared and frightened, the Christian pilgrim desperately looks to his family (Kindred), his friends (Fellowship), his worldly possessions (Goods), and all he has treasured in life to accompany him to the grave. He soon learns that Knowledge, Wits, Beauty, and Discretion may point the way to redemption, but they cannot save him. Ultimately, his only ally is Good Deeds, which, with the assistance of the Catholic priesthood, will help him achieve salvation. *Everyman* teaches that life is transient, that all things contributing to worldly pleasure are ultimately valueless, and that sin can be mitigated solely by salvation earned by means of good works and through God's grace as dispensed by the Church.

***Everyman* (ca. 1490)**

Dante's *Divine Comedy*

The medieval view of life on earth as a valley of tears was balanced by a triumphant belief in the divine promise of deliverance and eternal bliss. By far the most profound and imaginative statement of these ideas is the landmark epic poem known as the *Commedia Divina* or *Divine Comedy*. Written by the Florentine poet Dante Alighieri (1265–1321), the *Commedia* records, on the literal level, an adventure-packed journey through the realm of the dead (Figure **6.6**). On a symbolic level, the poem describes the spiritual pilgrimage of the Christian soul from sin (hell), through purification (Purgatory), and ultimately to salvation (Paradise). The *Divine Comedy* is the quintessential expression of the medieval mind in that it gives dramatic form to the fundamental precepts of the Christian way of life and death. The structure of the poem reflects the medieval view of nature as the mirror of

Dante, *Divine Comedy* (ca. 1320)

Figure 6.5 Gislebertus, detail of *Last Judgment*, ca. 1130–1135. Autun Cathedral, France. In this section of the **tympanum** (the semicircular space within the arch of the portal) of the Romanesque cathedral in Autun (see Figures 6.14 and 6.15), the Archangel Michael weighs the soul of a Christian to determine its fate, a motif that recalls Egyptian art (see Figure 1.21). The demon on the right tries to tip the scale toward hell. The hell's mouth at the right holds in its jaws a demon who snatches the souls of the damned below.

Figure 6.6 Domenico di Michelino, *Dante and His Poem*, 1465. Fresco, 10 ft. 6 in. x 9 ft. 7 in. Florence Cathedral, Italy. Dante, with an open copy of the *Commedia*, points to hell with his right hand. Mount Purgatory with its seven terraces is behind him. Florence's cathedral (with its newly finished dome) represents Paradise on the poet's left.

God's plan, while the content of the poem provides an invaluable picture of the ethical, political, and theological concerns of Dante's own time.

Every aspect of Dante's *Commedia* carries symbolic meaning. For instance, Dante is accompanied through hell by the Roman poet Virgil, who stands for human reason. Dante deeply admired Virgil's great epic, the *Aeneid*, and was familiar with the hero's journey to the underworld included in the sixth book of the poem. As Dante's guide, Virgil may travel only as far as the top of Mount Purgatory, for while human reason serves as the pilgrim's initial guide to salvation, it cannot penetrate the divine mysteries of the Christian faith. In Paradise, Dante is escorted by Beatrice, the symbol of Divine Wisdom, modeled on a Florentine woman who, throughout the poet's life, had been the object of his physical desire and spiritual devotion.

Well versed in both Classical and Christian literature, Dante had written Latin treatises on political theory and on the origins and development of language. But for the poem that constituted his epic masterpiece, he rejected the Latin of clerics and scholars and wrote in his native Italian, the language of everyday speech. Dante called his poem a comedy because the piece begins with affliction (hell) and ends with joy (heaven). Later admirers added the adjective "divine" to the title, not simply to mark its religious character, but also to praise its sublime poetry and its artful composition.

Sacred numerology—especially the number 3, symbolic of the Trinity—permeates the design of the *Commedia*. The poem is divided into three canticles (books) that correspond to the Aristotelian divisions of the human psyche: reason, will, and love. They also represent the potential moral conditions of the Christian soul: perversity, repentance, and grace. Each canticle has thirty-three **cantos**, to which Dante added one introductory canto to total a sublime one hundred (the number symbolizing plenitude and perfection). Each canto consists of stanzas composed in *terza rima*—interlocking lines that rhyme a/b/a, b/c/b, c/d/c. There are three guides to escort Dante, three divisions of hell and Purgatory, three main rivers in hell. Three squared (9) are the regions of sinners in hell, the circles of penitents in Purgatory, and the spheres of heaven.

The elaborate numerology of the *Commedia* is matched by multivalent symbolism that draws into synthesis the theological, scientific, and historical information based in ancient and medieval sources. Given this wealth of symbolism, it is remarkable that the language of the poem is so sharply realistic. For, while the characters in the *Commedia*, like those in *Everyman*, serve an allegorical function, they are, at the same time, convincing flesh-and-blood creatures. The inhabitants of Dante's universe are real people, some drawn from history and legend, others from his own era—citizens of the bustling urban centers of Italy through which Dante had wandered for nineteen years following political exile from his native Florence. By framing the poem on both a literal level and an allegorical one, Dante reinforces the medieval (and essentially Augustinian) view of the bond between the City of Man and the City of God. At the same time, he animates a favorite theme of medieval sermons: the warning that actions in this life bring inevitable consequences in the next.

The most lively of the canticles, and the one that best manifests Dante's talent for creating realistic images, is the "Inferno," the first book of the *Commedia*. With grim moral logic, Dante assigns each sinner to one of the nine rings in hell (Figure **6.7**), where each is punished according to the nature of his or her sins. The violent are immersed for eternity in boiling blood and the gluttons wallow like pigs in their own excrement. By the law of symbolic retribution, the sinners are punished not *for* but *by* their sins. Those condemned for sins of passion—the least grave of sins—inhabit the conical rings at the top of hell, while those who have committed sins of the will lie farther down. Those guilty of sins of the intellect are imprisoned still lower, deep within the pit ruled by Satan (Figure **6.8**). Thus, Dante's hell proclaims a moral hierarchy and a divinely graded system in which the damned suffer their proper destiny.

Ideas and Issues

DANTE: "THE NINTH CIRCLE OF HELL"

"'On march the banners of the King of Hell,'
my Master [Virgil] said. 'Toward us. Look straight ahead:
can you make him out at the core of the frozen shell?'

Like a whirling windmill seen afar at twilight,
or when a mist has risen from the ground—
just such an engine rose upon my sight

stirring up such a wild and bitter wind
I cowered for shelter at my Master's back
there being no other windbreak I could find.

I stood now where the souls of the last class
(with fear my verses tell it) were covered wholly:
they shone below the ice like straws in glass.

Some lie stretched out; others are fixed in place
upright, some on their heads, some on their
soles; another, like a bow, bends foot to face.

When we had gone so far across the ice
that it pleased my Guide to show me the foul creature
which once had worn the grace of Paradise,

he made me stop, and, stepping aside, he said:
'Now see the face of Dis! This is the place
where you must arm your soul against all dread.'

Do not ask, Reader, how my blood ran cold
and my voice choked up with fear. I cannot write it:
this is a terror that cannot be told.

I did not die, and yet I lost life's breath:
imagine for yourself what I became,
deprived at once of both my life and death.

The Emperor of the Universe of Pain
jutted his upper chest above the ice;
and I am closer in size to the great mountain

the Titans make around the central pit,
than they to his arms. Now starting from this part,
imagine the whole that corresponds to it.

If he was once as beautiful as now
he is hideous, and still turned on his Maker,
well may he be the source of every woe!

With what a sense of awe I saw his head
towering above me! for it had three faces:
one was in front, and it was fiery red,

the other two, as weirdly wonderful,
merged with it from the middle of each shoulder
to the point where all converged at the top of the skull;

the right was something between white and bile;
the left was about the color that one finds
on those who live along the banks of the Nile.

Under each head two wings rose terribly,
their span proportioned to so gross a bird:
I never saw such sails upon the sea.

They were not feathers—their texture and their form
were like a bat's wings—and he beat them so
that three winds blew from him in one great storm:

it is these winds that freeze all Cocytus. [The final pit of Hell.]
He wept from his six eyes, and down three chins
the tears ran mixed with bloody froth and pus.

In every mouth he worked a broken sinner
between his rake-like teeth. Thus he kept three
in eternal pain at his eternal dinner.

For the one in front the biting seemed to play
no part at all compared to the ripping: at times
the whole skin of his back was flayed away.

'That soul that suffers most,' explained the Guide,
'is Judas Iscariot, he who kicks his legs
on the fiery chin and has his head inside.

Of the other two, who have their heads thrust forward
the one who dangles down from the black face
is Brutus: note how he writhes without a word.

And there, with the huge and sinewy arms, is the soul
of Cassius. But the night is coming on
and we must go, for we have seen the whole.'"

(from Canto 34)

Notes

line 1 *On march the banners of the King*: The hymn ("Vexilla regis prodeunt") was written in the sixth century C.E. by Venantius Fortunatus, bishop of Poitiers. The original celebrates the Holy Cross, and is part of the service for Good Friday to be sung at the moment of uncovering the cross.

line 17 *the foul creature*: Satan.

line 38 *three faces*: Numerous interpretations of these three faces exist. What is essential to all explanations is that they be seen as perversions of the qualities of the Trinity.

line 54 *bloody froth and pus*: The gore of the sinners he chews, which is mixed with his slaver.

line 62 *Judas*: Note how closely his punishment is patterned on that of the Simoniacs [those who buy or sell pardons or church offices].

line 67 *huge and sinewy arms*: The Cassius who betrayed Caesar was more generally described in terms of Shakespeare's "lean and hungry look." Another Cassius is described by Cicero (Catiline III) as huge and sinewy. Dante probably confused the two.

line 68 *the night is coming on*: It is now Saturday evening.

Q What features in Dante's description of Satan provoke a sense of awe? For what offenses are the sinners in the ninth circle punished?

The Medieval University

Of the many landmark contributions of medieval Christendom to modern Western society—including trial by jury and the Catholic Church itself—one of the most significant was the university. Education in medieval Europe was almost exclusively a religious enterprise, and monastic schools had monopolized learning for many centuries. By the twelfth century, however, spurred by the resurgence of economic activity, the rise of towns, and the influx of previously unavailable texts, education shifted from monastic and parish settings to cathedral schools located in the new urban centers of Western Europe. Growing out of these schools, groups of students and teachers formed

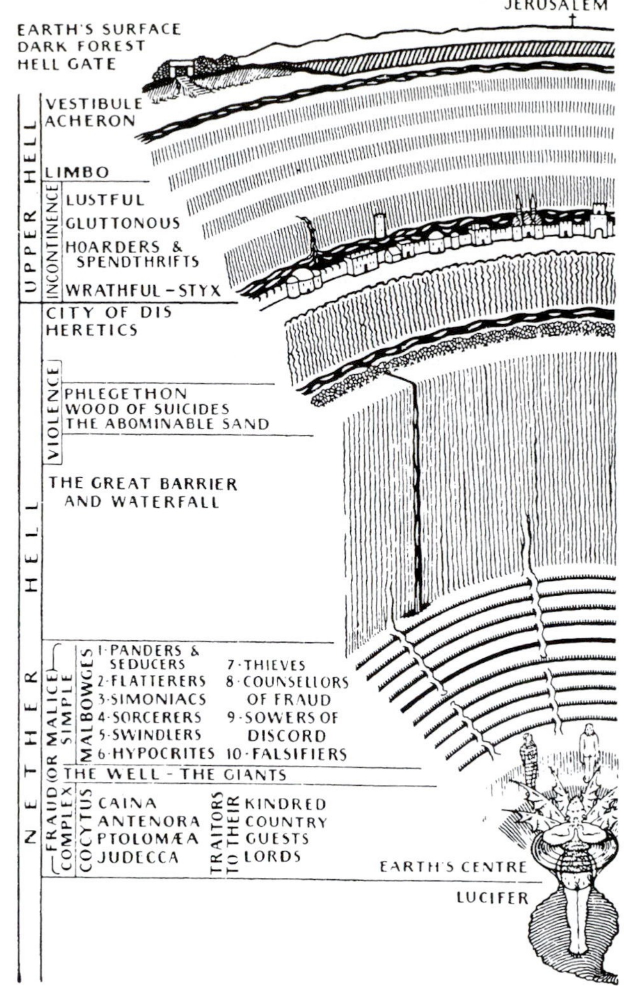

Figure 6.7 Plan of Dante's "Inferno."

guilds for higher learning. The guild of teachers and students was known by the Latin word *universitas.*

In medieval Europe, as in our own day, universities were arenas for intellectual inquiry and debate (**Figure 6.9**). At Bologna, Paris, Oxford, and Cambridge, to name but four among some eighty universities founded during the Middle Ages, the best minds of Europe grappled with the compelling ideas of their day, often testing those ideas against the teachings of the Church. The universities offered a basic Liberal Arts curriculum divided into two parts: the *trivium,* consisting of grammar, logic, and rhetoric; and the *quadrivium,* which included arithmetic, geometry, astronomy, and music. Programs in professional disciplines, such as medicine, theology, and law, were also available. Exams for the bachelor of arts (B.A.) degree, usually taken upon completion of a three- to five-year course of study, were oral. Beyond the B.A. degree, one might pursue additional study leading to mastery of a specialized field. The master of arts (M.A.) degree qualified the student to teach theology or practice law or medicine. Still another four years of study were usually required for the doctoral candidate, whose efforts culminated in his defense of a thesis before a board of learned masters. (Tradition required the successful candidate to honor his examiners with a banquet.)

Among the first universities was that founded at Bologna in northern Italy in 1159. Bologna was a center for the study of law. Its curriculum was run by students who hired professors to teach courses in law and other fields. University students brought pressure on townsfolk to maintain reasonable prices for food and lodging. They controlled the salaries and teaching schedules of their professors, requiring a teacher to obtain permission from his students for even a single day's absence and docking his pay if he was tardy.

In contrast to the student-run university at Bologna, the university in Paris was a guild of teachers organized primarily for instruction in theology. This institution, which grew out of the cathedral school of Notre Dame, became independent of Church control by way of a royal charter issued in the year 1200. Its respected degree in theology drew an international student body that made Paris the intellectual melting pot of the medieval West.

Until the thirteenth century, upper-class men and women received basically the same kinds of formal education. But with the rise of the university, women were excluded from receiving a higher education, much as they were forbidden from entering the priesthood. Ranging between the ages of seventeen and forty, students often held minor orders in the Church. The intellectual enterprise of the most famous of the theologically trained scholars (or *scholastics,* as they came to be called) inspired an important movement in medieval intellectual life known as Scholasticism.

Figure 6.8 *Satan Eating and Excreting the Souls of the Damned in Hell.* Louvre, Paris.

Medieval Scholasticism

Before the twelfth century, intellectuals (as well as ordinary men and women) considered Scripture and the writings of the church fathers the major repositories of knowledge. Faith in these established sources superseded rational inquiry and preempted the empirical examination of the physical world. Indeed, most intellectuals upheld the Augustinian credo that faith preceded reason. They maintained that since both faith and reason derived from God, the two could never stand in contradiction.

When, in the late twelfth century, Arab transcriptions of the writings of Aristotle and Arab commentaries on his works filtered into the West from Muslim Spain and Southwest Asia, a new intellectual challenge confronted clergy and scholars. How were they to reconcile Aristotle's rational and dispassionate views of physical reality with the supernatural truths of the Christian faith? The Church's initial reaction was to ban Aristotle's works (with the exception of the *Logic*, which had long been available in the West), but by the early thirteenth century, all of the writings of the venerated Greek philosopher were in the hands of medieval scholars. For the next hundred years, the scholastics engaged in an effort to reconcile the two primary modes of knowledge: faith and reason, the first as defended by theology, the second as exalted in Greek philosophy.

Even before the full body of Aristotle's works was available, a brilliant logician and popular teacher at the University of Paris, Peter Abelard (1079–ca. 1144), had inaugurated a rationalist approach to Church dogma. In his treatise *Sic et Non* (*Yes and No*), written several years before the high tide of Aristotelian influence, Abelard put into practice one of the principal devices of the scholastic method—that of balancing opposing points of view. *Sic et Non* presents 150 conflicting opinions on important religious matters from such sources as the Old Testament, the Greek philosophers, the Latin church fathers, and the decrees of the Church. Abelard's methodical compilation of Hebrew, Classical, and Christian thought is an expression of the scholastic inclination to collect and reconcile vast amounts of information. This impulse toward synthesis also inspired the many *compendia* (collections), *specula* ("mirrors" of knowledge), and *summa* (comprehensive treatises) that were written during the twelfth and thirteenth centuries.

Figure 6.9 *University Lecture by Henry of Germany*, from a medieval German edition of Aristotle's *Ethics*, second half of fourteenth century. Manuscript illumination, parchment, 7 x 8¾ in. State Museums, Berlin. Textbooks—that is, handwritten manuscripts—were expensive and difficult to obtain; therefore, teaching took the form of oral instruction, and students took copious notes based on class lectures.

Ideas and Issues

AQUINAS: WHETHER WOMAN SHOULD HAVE BEEN MADE IN THE FIRST PRODUCTION OF THINGS

"Reply Objection 1. As regards the individual nature, woman is defective and misbegotten, for the active power in the male seed tends to the production of a perfect likeness according to the masculine sex; while the production of woman comes from a defect in the active power, or from some material indisposition, or even from some external influence, such as that of a south wind, which is moist, as the Philosopher [Aristotle] observes. On the other hand, as regards universal human nature, woman is not misbegotten, but is included in nature's intention as directed to the work of generation. Now the universal intention of nature depends on God, Who is the universal Author of nature. Therefore, in producing nature, God formed not only the male but also the female. . . ."

(from Aquinas, *Summa Theologica*)

Q Based on this passage, why might women have been excluded from the medieval university?

The greatest of the scholastics and the most influential teacher of his time was the Dominican theologian Thomas Aquinas (1225–1274). Aquinas lectured and wrote on a wide variety of theological and biblical subjects, but his landmark contribution was the *Summa Theologica*, a vast compendium of virtually all of the major theological issues of the High Middle Ages. In this unfinished work, which exceeds Abelard's *Sic et Non* in both size and conception, Aquinas poses 631 questions on topics ranging from the nature of God to the ethics of money lending. The comprehensiveness of Aquinas' program is suggested by the following list of queries drawn arbitrarily from the *Summa*:

Aquinas, *Summa Theologica* (1274)

Whether God exists
Whether God is the highest good
Whether God is infinite
Whether God wills evil
Whether there is a trinity in God
Whether it belongs to God alone to create
Whether good can be the cause of evil
Whether angels assume bodies
Whether woman should have been made in the first production of things
Whether woman should have been made from man
Whether the soul is composed of matter and form
Whether man has free choice
Whether paradise is a corporeal place
Whether man can merit eternal life without grace
Whether it is lawful to sell a thing for more than it is worth

In dealing with each question, Aquinas follows Abelard's method of marshaling opinions that seem to oppose or contradict each other. But where Abelard merely mediates, Aquinas offers carefully reasoned answers; he brings to bear all the intellectual ammunition of his time in an effort to prove that the truths of reason (those proceeding from the senses and from the exercise of logic) are compatible with the truths of revelation (those that have been divinely revealed).

The scholastics aimed at producing a synthesis of Christian and Classical learning, but the motivation for and the substance of their efforts were still largely religious. Despite their attention to Aristotle's writings and their respect for his methods of inquiry, medieval scholastics created no system of knowledge that completely dispensed with supernatural assumptions. Nevertheless, the scholastics were the humanists of the medieval world; they held that the human being, the noblest of God's creatures, was the link between the created universe and divine intelligence. They believed that human reason was the servant of faith, and that reason—though incapable of transcending revelation—was essential to the understanding of God's divine plan.

THE PILGRIMAGE CHURCH

IF the Catholic Church was the major source of moral and spiritual instruction in medieval Christendom, it was also the wellspring of artistic productivity and the patron of some of the most glorious artworks ever created. Christians anticipated the return of Jesus in the year 1000, at the end of the first millennium; when this event did not take place, Christendom was reconciled to the advent of a new age. Spearheading a revival of church construction that accompanied a program of monastic reform was the Benedictine abbey of Cluny in southeastern France (Map **6.1**). Within a period of 150 years, more than one thousand monasteries and abbey churches were raised throughout Western Europe. Many of the new churches enshrined relics collected locally or brought back from the Holy Land by the Crusaders. These relics—the remains of saints and martyrs (see page 126), a piece of the Cross on which Jesus was crucified, and the like—became objects of holy veneration. They were housed in ornamented containers, or **reliquaries**, that were often shaped to replicate the person of the saint (Figure **6.10**) or the body part of the saint they enshrined. The monastic churches that housed the holy relics of saints and martyrs attracted thousands of Christian pilgrims. Some traveled to the shrine to seek pardon for sins or pay homage to a particular saint. Suppliants afflicted with blindness, leprosy, and other illnesses often slept near the saint's tomb in hope of a healing vision or a miraculous cure.

Four major pilgrimage routes linked the cities of France with the favorite shrine of Christian pilgrims: the cathedral of Santiago de Compostela in northwestern Spain (see Map 6.1). Santiago—that is, Saint James Major (brother of John the Evangelist)—was said to have brought Christianity to Spain and was thereafter martyred upon his return to Judea. His body was miraculously recovered in the early ninth century C.E. and buried at Compostela, where repeated miracles made his shrine a major pilgrimage center. Along the roads that carried pilgrims from Paris across to the Pyrenees, old churches were rebuilt and new churches erected, prompting one eleventh-century chronicler to observe, "The whole world seems to have shaken off her slumber, cast off her old rags, and clothed herself in a white mantle of new churches."

Like the Crusades, pilgrimages were an expression of increased mobility and economic revitalization. Since pilgrims, like modern tourists, constituted a major source of revenue for European towns and churches, parishes competed for them by enlarging church interiors and by increasing the number of reliquary chapels. The practical requirement for additional space in which to house these relics safely and make them accessible to Christian pilgrims determined the character of the pilgrimage church. In the early Christian church, as in the Carolingian abbey, the width of the nave was limited by the size and availability of roofing timber, and the wooden superstructure itself was highly susceptible to fire. The use of cut stone as the primary vaulting medium provided a solution to both of these problems. Indeed, the medieval architect's return to stone barrel and groin vaults of the kinds first used by the Romans (see Figure 3.5) inaugurated the *Romanesque style*.

Romanesque Architecture

Romanesque architects employed round arches and a uniform system of stone vaults in the upper zones of the nave and side-aisles. While the floor plan of the typical Romanesque church followed the Latin cross design of early Christian and Carolingian churches, the new system of stone vaulting allowed medieval architects to build on a grander scale than ever before. To provide additional space for shrines, architects enlarged the eastern end of the church to include a number of radiating chapels. They also extended the side-aisles around the transept and behind the apse to form an ambulatory (walkway). The ambulatory allowed lay visitors to move freely into the chapels without disturbing the monks at the main altar.

Most Romanesque churches belonged to a monastic complex (see Figure 5.5); however, some, like the church of Saint-Sernin at Toulouse, were urban cathedrals. Located on the southernmost pilgrimage route to Compostela, Saint-Sernin is one of the largest of the French pilgrimage churches (Figures **6.11–6.13**). Its formal design follows rational and harmonious principles: The square represented by the crossing of the nave and transept is the module for the organization of the building and its parts. Each nave **bay** (vaulted compartment) equals one-half the module, while each side-aisle bay equals one-fourth of the module. Clarity of design is also visible in the ways in which the exterior reflects the geometry of the interior: At the east end of the church, for instance, five reliquary chapels protrude uniformly from the ambulatory, while at the crossing of the nave and transept, a tower (enlarged in the thirteenth century) rises as both a belfry and a beacon to approaching pilgrims. Constructed of magnificent pink granite, Saint-Sernin's spacious nave is covered by a barrel vault divided by ornamental transverse arches (see Figure 6.13). Beneath the vaults over the double side-aisles, a gallery that served weary pilgrims as a place of overnight refuge provided additional lateral buttressing.

Romanesque Sculpture

Pilgrimage churches of the eleventh and twelfth centuries heralded the revival of monumental stone sculpture—a medium that, for the most part, had been abandoned since Roman antiquity. Scenes from the Old and New

Figure 6.10 Reliquary statue of Sainte Foy, Conques, France, late tenth to eleventh century. Gold and gemstones over a wooden core, height 33½ in. This life-sized reliquary held the cranium of the female child martyr and favorite local saint of Conques. On feast days, the image, sheathed in thin sheets of gold and semiprecious stones, was carried through the streets in sacred procession.

Figure 6.11 Saint-Sernin, Toulouse, France, ca. 1080–1120 (tower enlarged in the thirteenth century). Massive and stately in its exterior, dignified and somber in its interior, Saint-Sernin conveys the concept of a monumental spiritual fortress.

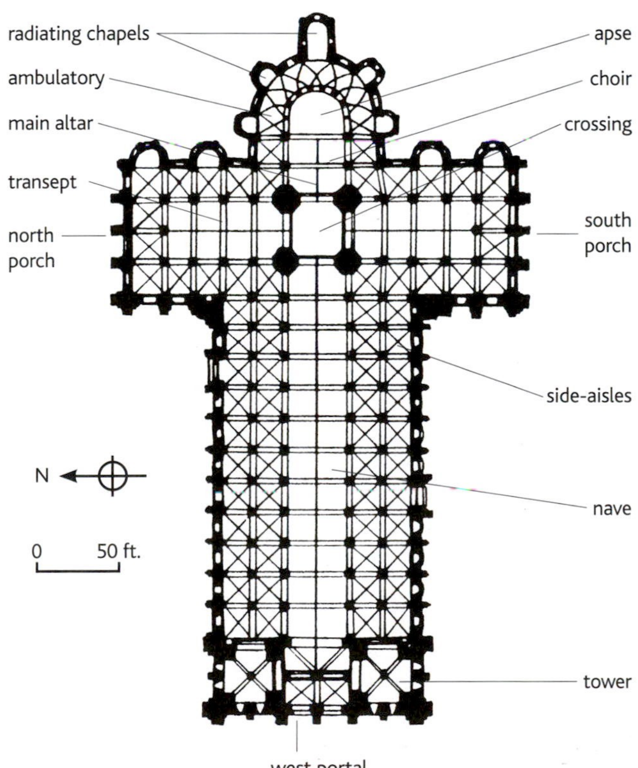

Figure 6.12 (above) Plan of Saint-Sernin, Toulouse.

Figure 6.13 (right) Nave and choir of Saint-Sernin, Toulouse. Pink granite, length of nave 377 ft. 4 in. Thick stone walls and heavy piers carry the weight of the vault and provide lateral (sideways) support. Since window openings might have weakened the walls that buttressed the barrel vault, the architects of Saint-Sernin eliminated the clerestory.

Map 6.1 Romanesque and Gothic Sites in Western Europe.

Testaments—carved in high relief and brightly painted—usually appeared on the entrance portals of the church, as well as in the capitals of columns throughout the basilica and its cloister. The entrance portal, normally located at the west end of the church, marked the dividing point between the earthly city and the City of God. Passage through the portal marked the beginning of the symbolic journey from sin (darkness/west) to salvation (light/east).

At the church of Saint Lazarus at Autun in France, medieval Christians were powerfully reminded of the inevitability of sin, death, and judgment. The forbidding image of Christ as Judge greeted them from the center of the tympanum just above their heads (Figures **6.14** and **6.15**) as they entered at the west end of the building. Framed by an almond-shaped halo, Jesus displays the wounds of his crucifixion and points to the realms of the afterlife: heaven (on his right) and hell (on his left). Surrounding the awesome Christ, flamelike saints and angels and grimacing devils (see Figure 6.5) await the souls of the resurrected. They are pictured rising from their graves in the **lintel** (the horizontal band below the tympanum). In the **archivolts** that frame the tympanum are roundels with signs of the zodiac and depictions of the labors of the months, symbols of the calendar year and the passage of time between the First and Second Coming of Christ. Like a medieval morality play, the tympanum at Autun served as a ***memento mori*** ("remember death"), reminding Christians of their mortality. Indeed, beneath his signature, the artist Gislebertus added the warning, "Let this terror frighten those bound by earthly sin."

Figure 6.14 (left) Gislebertus, *Last Judgment*, ca. 1130–1135. West tympanum, Cathedral Church of Saint Lazarus, Autun. Gislebertus carved his figures to fit the shapes of the stone segments that comprise the portal. These lively, elongated figures bend and twist, as if animated by the restless energy that suffused the age. The architectural divisions of the portal appear in the diagram below.

Diagram of a portal.

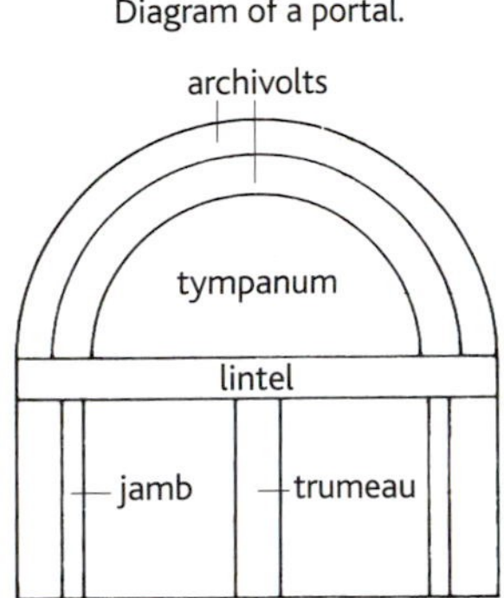

Figure 6.15 (left) Labeled diagram of the west tympanum, Autun Cathedral.

THE GOTHIC CATHEDRAL

SEVENTEENTH-CENTURY Neoclassicists coined the term "Gothic" to describe the "rude and barbarous" architectural style that followed the Romanesque. While Romanesque architects employed Greco-Roman principles and techniques for churches that hugged the ground, Gothic architects developed new ways to make these monumental sanctuaries soar upward to the heavens. Modern critics soon recognized the Gothic cathedral as a majestic expression of the Age of Faith.

Like other Christian churches, the Gothic cathedral was a sanctuary for the celebration of the Mass. But it was also the administrative seat (Latin, *cathedra*) of a bishop, the site of ecclesiastical authority, and an educational center—a fount of theological doctrine and divine precept. The typical Gothic cathedral honored one or more saints, including and especially the Virgin Mary—the principal intercessor

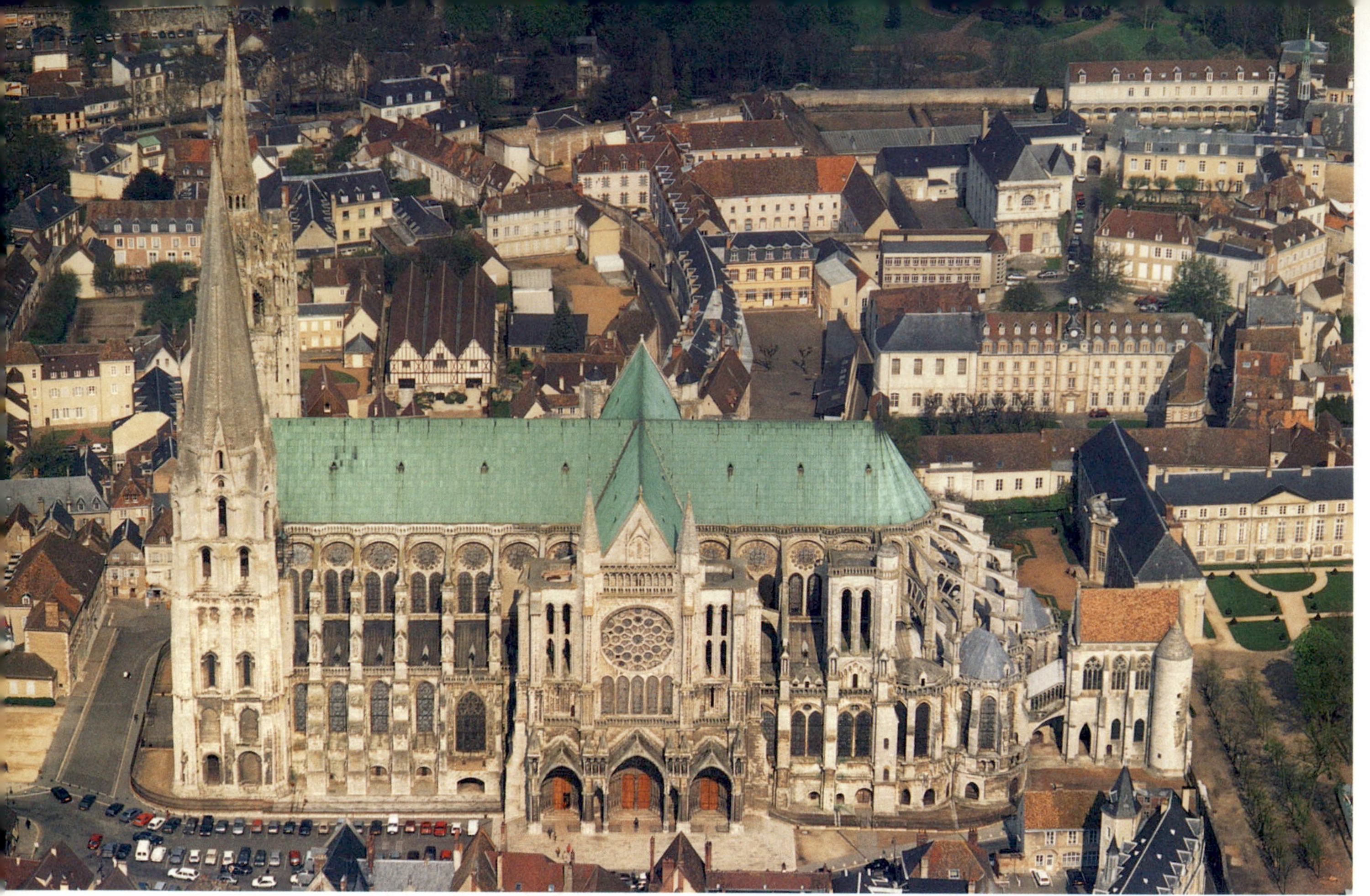

between God and the Christian believer. Indeed, most of the prominent churches of the Middle Ages were dedicated to Notre Dame ("Our Lady"). On a symbolic level, the church was both the Heavenly Jerusalem (the City of God) and a model of the Virgin as Womb of Christ and Queen of Heaven. In the cathedral, the various types of religious expression converged: Sculpture appeared in its portals, capitals, and choir screens; stained glass diffused divine light through its windows; painted altarpieces embellished its chapels; medieval plays were enacted both within its walls and outside its doors; liturgical music filled its choirs.

Finally, the Gothic cathedral, often large enough to hold the entire population of a town, was the municipal center. While the Romanesque church usually constituted a rural retreat for monastics and pilgrims, the Gothic cathedral, the seat of a bishop, served as the focal point for an urban community. Physically dominating the town, its spires soaring above the houses and shops below (Figure **6.16**), the cathedral attracted civic events, public festivals, and even local business.

The Gothic Style

The *Gothic style* was born in northern France and spread quickly throughout medieval Europe. In France alone, eighty Gothic cathedrals and nearly five hundred cathedral-class churches were constructed between 1170 and

Figure 6.16 (above) Chartres Cathedral, France, begun 1194. The actual construction of a Gothic cathedral was a town effort, supported by the funds and labors of local citizens and guild members, including stonemasons, carpenters, metalworkers, and glaziers.

1270. The definitive features of the Gothic style were first assembled near Paris at the monastic church of Saint-Denis. The burial place of French kings and queens, this abbey also sheltered the relics of the patron saint of France, Denis the martyr, first bishop of Paris. Between 1122 and 1144, Abbot Suger (1085–1151), a personal friend and adviser of the French kings Louis VI and VII, enlarged and remodeled the old Carolingian structure. Suger's designs for the east end of the church called for a combination of three architectural innovations that had been employed in previous decades only occasionally or experimentally: the pointed arch, the rib vault, and stained glass windows. The result was a spacious choir and ambulatory, free of heavy stone supports and flooded with light (Figure **6.17**).

Suger exalted stained glass as a medium that filtered the light of divine truth. To the medieval mind, light was a symbol of Jesus, who had proclaimed to his apostles, "I am the light of the world" (John 8:12). Drawing on this mystical bond between Jesus and light, Suger identified

Figure 6.17 (opposite) Choir and ambulatory of the Abbey Church of Saint-Denis, France, 1140–1144. On the wall of the ambulatory at Saint-Denis, Abbot Suger had these words inscribed: "That which is united in splendor, radiates in splendor/And the magnificent work inundated with the new light shines."

the *lux nova* ("new light") of the Gothic church as the symbolic equivalent of God and the windows as mediators of God's love. But for Suger, light—especially as it passed through the stained glass windows of the church—also signified the sublime knowledge that accompanied the progressive purification of the ascending human spirit. Suger's mystical interpretation of light, inspired by his reading of neoplatonic treatises, sustained his belief that contemplation of the "many-colored gems" of church glass could transport the Christian from "the slime of this earth" to "the purity of heaven."

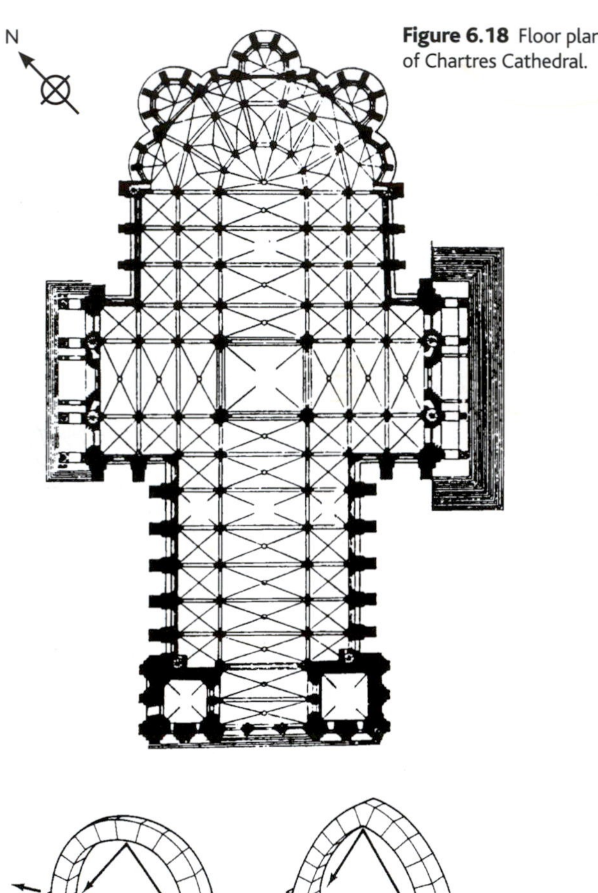

Figure 6.18 Floor plan of Chartres Cathedral.

While Gothic cathedrals followed Saint-Denis in adopting a new look, their floor plan—the Latin cross—remained basically the same as that of the Romanesque church; only the transept might be moved further west to create a larger choir area (Figure **6.18**). The ingenious combination of rib vault and pointed arch, however, had a major impact on the size and elevation of Gothic structures. Stone ribs replaced the heavy stone masonry of Romanesque vaults, and pointed arches raised these vaults to new heights. Whereas the rounded vaults of the Romanesque church demanded extensive lateral buttressing, the steeply pointed arches of the Gothic period, which directed weight downward, required only the combination of slender vertical piers and thin lateral ("flying") buttresses (Figures **6.19** and **6.20**).

In place of masonry, broad areas of glass filled the small intervening spaces of this "cage" of stone. The nave wall consisted of an arcade of pier bundles that swept from floor to ceiling, an ornamental **triforium** gallery (the arcaded passage between the nave arcade and the clerestory), and a large clerestory consisting of **rose** (from the French *roue*, "wheel"; see Figure 6.25) and **lancet** (vertically pointed) windows (see Figure 6.20). Above the clerestory hung elegant canopies of **quadripartite** (four-part; Figure **6.21**) or **sexpartite** (six-part) rib vaults. Lighter and more airy than Romanesque churches, Gothic interiors seem to expand and unfold in vertical space. The pointed arch, the rib vault, and stained glass windows, along with the flying buttress (first used at the cathedral of Notre Dame in Paris around 1170), became the fundamental ingredients of the Gothic style.

If the interior of the Gothic cathedral was unique in the history of church design, so was the exterior: Architects

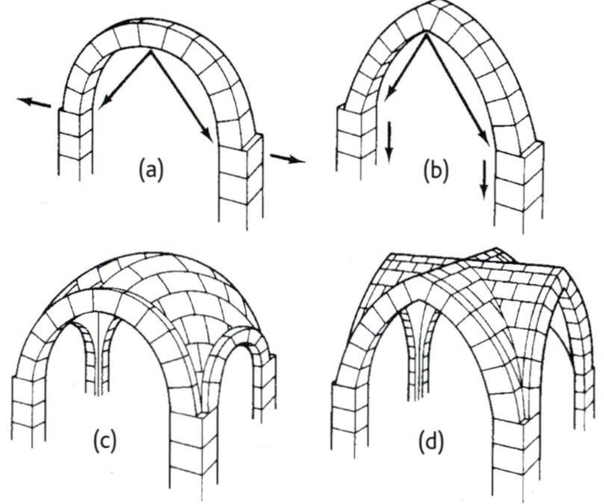

Figure 6.19 Round and pointed arches and vaults. The round arch (a) spreads the load laterally, while the pointed arch (b) thrusts its load more directly toward the ground. The pointed arch can rise to any height while the height of the semicircular arch is governed by the space it spans. Round arches create a dome-shaped vault (c). The Gothic rib vault (d) permits a lighter and more flexible building system with larger wall openings that may accommodate windows.

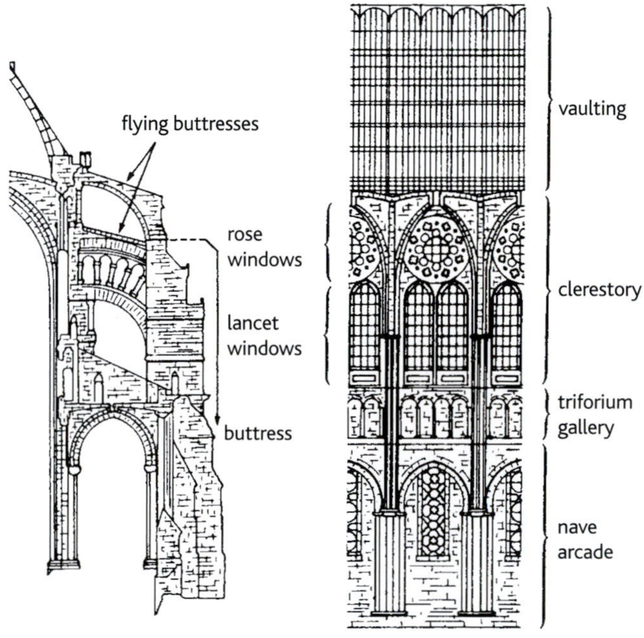

Figure 6.20 Diagram of vaulting and section of nave wall, Chartres Cathedral.

Figure 6.21 (left) Nave facing east, Chartres Cathedral, nave completed in 1220. Height of nave 122 ft. Medieval towns competed with one another in the grandeur of their cathedrals. At Chartres, the nave rose to a height of 122 feet; architects at Amiens (see Figure 6.27) took the space from floor to vault to a breathtaking 144 feet; at Beauvais, the 157-foot vault of the choir collapsed twelve years after its completion and was reconstructed over a period of forty years.

embellished the structural extremities of the cathedral, including the flying buttresses, with stone **crockets** (stylized leaves) and **finials** (ornamental details). To the upper parts of the building, they added **gargoyles**—grotesque human beings or hybrid beasts that were believed to ward off evil (Figure **6.22**).

Figure 6.22 (right) Grotesques and a gargoyle waterspout on a tower terrace of Notre Dame, Paris, as restored in the nineteenth century. Gargoyles may have held symbolic meaning for medieval people. From a purely practical point of view, however, some functioned as downspouts that drained the building of rainwater.

Chartres Cathedral: Gothic Landmark

While the abbey church at Saint-Denis constitutes a landmark in the evolution of the Gothic style, it is at the church of Our Lady of Chartres, located southwest of Paris, that all of the most characteristic features of the Gothic style—architecture, sculpture, and stained glass—reach a classic synthesis (see Figure 6.1). In the twelfth century, this church would become one of Christendom's most beloved shrines. From earliest times, the church at Chartres had housed the tunic that the Virgin Mary was said to have worn at the birth of Jesus. When this tunic survived the devastating fire that destroyed most of the old cathedral in 1194, it was taken as a miracle indicating the Virgin's desire to see the cathedral gloriously rebuilt. Contributions for its reconstruction poured in from all of Christendom. And while construction in some parts of the cathedral lasted for centuries, the beautifully proportioned nave was completed in 1220 (see Figure 6.21).

On the exterior at Chartres, as at most medieval cathedrals, thousands of individually carved figures required the labor of many sculptors (and sculptural workshops) over a period of many decades. The sculptural program—that is, the totality of its carved representations—is a compendium of Old and New Testament history, Classical learning, and secular legend and lore, laid out in its entirety by clerical scholars. While clerics, who were familiar with the vocabulary of Christian symbolism, took from the church façade a profound didactic message, less educated Christians saw in the stones the story of their faith and a mirror of daily experience. Designed to be "read," Chartres was both a "bible in stone" and an encyclopedia of religious and secular life.

As with most Gothic cathedrals, the image of the Virgin Mary dominated the iconographic program. In the west portal—called the Royal Portal for its figures of kings and queens from the Old Testament and from French history—the central tympanum features the image of Christ in Majesty surrounded by symbols of the four evangelists (Figure **6.23**). But the right tympanum is dedicated to the Mother of God, who is honored as Queen of the Liberal Arts. Elsewhere, she is shown carrying the Christ Child, crowned by angels, or sharing with Jesus the throne of heaven.

Figure 6.23 Royal Portal, west façade of Chartres Cathedral, ca. 1140–1150. The Royal Portal retains the linear severity of the Romanesque style. In the central tympanum sits a rigidly posed Christ in Majesty flanked by symbols of the four evangelists and framed by the Elders of the Apocalypse in the outer archivolts. In the lintel below, the apostles are ordered into formal groups of three.

Figure 6.24 *Notre Dame de la Belle Verrière* ("Our Lady of the Beautiful Glass"), Chartres Cathedral, twelfth century. Stained glass. In one of Chartres' oldest windows, whose vibrant combination of red and blue glass inspired the title "Our Lady of the Beautiful Glass."

At Chartres, the medieval cult of the Virgin reached its peak. From the earliest years of its establishment as a religion, Christianity exalted the Virgin Mary as an object of veneration. Long revered as "the new Eve," Mary was honored for having delivered humankind from damnation and death brought on by the disobedience of the "old Eve." An ideal type, the Virgin was seen as the paragon of virtue and chastity. But during the twelfth century, as increasing emphasis came to be placed on the humanity of Jesus, Mary was more frequently exalted as a compassionate, "motherly" intercessor. Her praises were sung by Hildegard of Bingen (see page 145) and others, but at Chartres most specifically in stone sculpture and stained glass. One of Chartres' oldest stained glass windows, the central portion of which survived the fire of 1194, is known as *Notre Dame de la Belle Verrière* ("Our Lady of the Beautiful Glass"). Here, in a striking composition of vibrant reds and blues, the Virgin appears in her dual role as Mother of God and Queen of Heaven. Holding the Christ Child on her lap, she also represents the Seat of Wisdom (Figure **6.24**).

Chartres Cathedral surpasses all other Gothic cathedrals as a landmark in the art of stained glass. Replacing the stone walls of former churches, the windows at Chartres filter light that constantly changes in color and intensity (see Figures 6.24 and **6.25**). Chartres' 175 surviving glass panels, with representations of more than four thousand figures, comprise a cosmic narrative of humankind's religious and secular history. The windows, which were removed for safekeeping during World War II and thereafter returned to their original positions, follow a carefully organized theological program designed, as Abbot Suger explained, "to show simple folk . . . what they ought to believe."

Stained glass was to the Gothic cathedral what mosaics were to the early Christian church: a source of religious edification, a medium of divine light, and a delight to the eye. Produced on the site of the cathedral by a process of mixing metal oxides into molten glass, colored sheets of glass were cut into fragments to fit preconceived designs. They were then fixed within lead bands, bound by a grid of iron bars, and set into stone **mullions** (vertical frames). Imprisoned in this lacelike armature, the glass vibrated with color, sparkling in response to the changing natural light and casting rainbows of color that seemed to dissolve the stone walls. The faithful of Christendom regarded the cathedral windows as precious objects—glass tapestries that clothed the House of God with radiant light. They especially treasured the windows at Chartres with their rich blues, which, in contrast to other colors, required a cobalt oxide that came from regions outside France. Legend had it that Abbot Suger produced blue glass by grinding up sapphires—a story that, although untrue, reflects the popular equation of precious gems with sacred glass.

Medieval Painting: The Gothic Altarpiece

Medieval paintings, unlike modern ones, were not created to decorate domestic or public interiors. Rather, they took the form of visual illustrations for medieval manuscripts (see page 127), didactic (often biblical) frescoes for medieval church walls, or panel paintings that were assembled as church altarpieces. The upsurge of Gothic architecture in the thirteenth century was accompanied by a burst of productivity in the creation of painted altarpieces. Often consisting of many panels, such altarpieces were installed in chapels dedicated to the Virgin or to one of the saints. Elevated above and behind the altar itself, the altarpiece might display scenes from the life of Jesus, the life of the Virgin, or depict a favorite saint or martyr. On saints' days and church holidays, the altarpiece might be carried through the streets of the town.

The typical Gothic altarpiece consisted of a wooden panel or panels smoothed and covered with **gesso** (a chalky white plaster), on which images were painted in **tempera** (a powdered pigment made with egg yolk). The dry, flat surface colors provided a rich contrast with motifs such as halos and backgrounds that were brightly embellished with gold leaf that reflected the light of altar candles. Panels painted in Italian cities, many of which had remained in close commercial contact with the East, reflect the stark and expressive Byzantine style that typified the icons of Greek Orthodox Christendom (see Figure 4.18). One late thirteenth-century altarpiece by the Florentine painter Cimabue (1240–1302) is a landmark example of this style (Figure **6.26**).

Against a brilliant gold background, Cimabue painted the Virgin and Child—more a miniature adult than an infant—elevated on a monumental seat that is at once throne and tower. The angels on either side are stacked one above the other, creating a flat, two-dimensional pattern. Beneath the Virgin's feet, four Hebrew prophets display scrolls predicting the coming of Jesus. As in Egyptian art, where figures of great importance are shown larger than those of minor significance, the image of the Virgin, radiant in her gold-flecked dark blue tunic, outsizes the attendant angels and prophets.

Figure 6.25 (opposite) South rose window and lancets, Chartres Cathedral, France, thirteenth century. The window centers on the image of the enthroned Christ, surrounded by the evangelists, censing angels, and the elders of the Apocalypse. In the lancet windows, the Virgin and Child stand between four Old Testament prophets carrying on their shoulders the four New Testament evangelists, a motif symbolizing the Old Dispensation's "support" of the New. The donors and their coats-of-arms are shown at the base of the windows.

Figure 6.26 (right) Cimabue, *Madonna Enthroned*, ca. 1280–1290. Tempera on wood, 12 ft. 7½ in. x 7 ft. 4 in. Uffizi Gallery, Florence. Cimabue's lavishly gilded devotional image has a schematic elegance: Line creates the sharp, metallic folds of the Virgin's dark blue mantle, the crisp wings of the angels, the chiseled features of the Christ child, and the decorative surface of the throne.

Making Connections

TEMPLE-SHRINES: CHRISTIAN AND HINDU

The thirteenth-century cathedral of Notre Dame at Amiens is one of the most profusely ornamented Gothic churches in France (Figure **6.27**). Like Amiens, the Kandariya Mahadeo temple in Khajuraho (central North India)—one of twenty-five remaining Hindu temple-shrines—rises like a beehive-shaped stone mountain, its façades embellished by a multitude of high-relief sculptures drawn from Hindu lore and literature (Figures **6.28** and **6.29**). Yet no two artistic enterprises could stand further apart in their imagery: Whereas the medieval Church discouraged the representation of nudity as symbolic of sexual desire and sinfulness, Hinduism invited the display of sculptured nudes, often erotically posed. The exaltation of the body as a vessel of abundance, prosperity, and regeneration, so evident in Hindu temple sculpture, reflects the Hindu respect for the union of human and divine love.

Q What are the differences in form and function between the medieval cathedral and the Hindu temple? What are the similarities?

Figure 6.27 (right) West façade of Notre Dame at Amiens, France, ca. 1220–1288. Height of nave 144 ft.

Figure 6.28 (below left) Kandariya Mahadeo temple, Khajuraho, India, ca. 1000. Height approx. 102 ft.

Figure 6.29 (below right) Celestial deities, Kandariya Mahadeo temple, Khajuraho, ca. 1000. Stone.

MEDIEVAL MUSIC

Medieval Musical Notation

Musical notation was invented in the monasteries. During the eleventh century, Benedictine monks at the monastery of Cluny, in southern France, devised the first efficient Western system of musical notation, thus facilitating the performance and transmission of liturgical music. They arranged the tones of the commonly used scale in progression from A through G and developed a formal system of notating pitch. The Italian Benedictine Guido of Arezzo (ca. 990–ca. 1050) introduced a staff of colored lines (yellow for C, red for F, etc.) on which he registered *neumes*—notational signs traditionally written above the words to indicate tonal ascent or descent. Guido's landmark system established a precise means of indicating shifts in pitch. Instead of relying on memory alone, singers could consult songbooks inscribed with both words and music. Such advances encouraged the kinds of compositional complexity that characterized medieval music after 1100.

Medieval Polyphony

Polyphony (music consisting of two or more lines of melody) was a Western invention; it did not make its appearance in Asia until modern times. The earliest polyphonic compositions consisted of Gregorian melodies sung in two parts simultaneously, with both voices moving note-for-note in parallel motion (parallel **organum**), or with a second voice moving in contrary motion (free organum), perhaps also adding many notes to the individual syllables of the text (melismatic organum). Consistent with rules of harmony derived from antiquity, and with the different ranges of the voice, the second musical part was usually pitched a fourth or a fifth above or below the first, creating a pure, hollow sound.

Throughout the High Middle Ages, northern France—and the city of Paris in particular—was the center of polyphonic composition. From the same area that produced the Gothic cathedral came a new musical style that featured several lines of melody arranged in counterpoised rhythms. The foremost Parisian composer of the twelfth century was Pérotin (ca. 1160–1240). A member of the Notre Dame School, Pérotin enhanced the splendor of the Christian Mass by writing three- and four-part polyphonic compositions based on Gregorian chant. Pérotin's music usually consisted of a principal voice or "tenor" (from the Latin *tenere*, meaning "to hold") that sang the chant or "fixed song" (Latin, *cantus firmus*) and one or more voices that moved in shorter phrases and usually faster tempos. The combination of two or three related but independent voices, a musical technique called **counterpoint**, enlivened late twelfth- and thirteenth-century music. Like the cathedral itself, the polyphonic Mass was a masterful synthesis of carefully arranged parts—a synthesis achieved in *time* rather than in *space*.

Pérotin, Three- and Four-Part Mass (ca. 1200)

The "Dies Irae"

"Dies irae" (ca. 1250)

While polyphony was the landmark musical development of its time, a specific hymn known as the "Dies irae" ("Day of Wrath") reflected the new spirit of dramatic expression in medieval Christendom. This fifty-seven-line hymn, which originated among the Franciscans during the thirteenth century, was added to the Roman Catholic **requiem** (the Mass for the Dead) and quickly became a standard part of the Christian funeral service. Invoking a powerful vision of the end of time, the "Dies irae" is the musical counterpart of the apocalyptic sermons and Last Judgment portals (see Figure 6.14) that issued solemn warnings of final doom. The hymn opens with the words:

> Day of Wrath! O day of mourning!
> See fulfilled the prophets' warning,
> Heaven and earth in ashes burning!

But, as with most examples of apocalyptic art, including Dante's *Commedia*, the hymn holds out hope for absolution and deliverance:

> With Thy favored sheep, oh, place me!
> Nor among the goats abase me,
> But to Thy right hand upraise me.
> While the Wicked are confounded,
> Doomed to flames of woe unbounded,
> Call me, with Thy saints surrounded.

Like so many other forms of medieval expression, the "Dies irae" brings into vivid contrast the destinies of sinners and saints. In later centuries, it inspired the powerful requiem settings of Mozart, Berlioz, and Verdi, and its music became a familiar symbol of death and damnation.

The Motet

The thirteenth century also witnessed the invention of a new religious musical genre, the **motet**—a short, polyphonic choral composition based on a sacred text. Performed both inside and outside the church, it was the most popular kind of medieval religious song. Like the trope (see page 137), the motet (from the French *mot*, meaning "word") developed from the practice of adding words to the melismatic parts of a melody. Medieval motets usually juxtaposed two or more uncomplicated themes, each with its own lyrics and metrical pattern, in a manner that was lilting and lively. Motets designed to be sung outside the church often borrowed secular tunes with vernacular words. A three-part motet might combine a love song in the vernacular, a well-known hymn of praise to the Virgin, and a Latin liturgical text in the *cantus firmus*. Thirteenth-century motets were thus polytextual as well as polyphonic and polyrhythmic.

Beyond the West

INDIA AND CHINA

Religious Icons

The religious life of Hindus in India and Buddhists in China inspired a body of devotional artifacts that may be compared to those produced in the Christian West. These objects of veneration found a place in the homes or temples of the faithful. During the eleventh to thirteenth centuries, at the time when Christendom filled churches and shrines with statues of the Virgin Mary and the saints, bronze-crafters in southern India forged a variety of important Hindu icons, the most famous of which is *Shiva Nataraja, Lord of the Dance* (Figure **6.30**).

Hinduism teaches the oneness of nature: that individual aspects of being are part of the One (known as Brahman); however, the gods of ancient India have long been worshipped as avatars (incarnations) of the One (see page 23). Shiva, one of the principal gods of the Hindu pantheon, is venerated as a god of destruction and creation, a regenerative force associated with birth, death, and rebirth. Embodying the rhythms of the universe, he is famously pictured as Lord of the Dance. Encircled by a celestial ring of fire, the four-armed deity embodies the five activities of the godhead: creation, protection, destruction, release from destiny, and enlightenment.

Figure 6.30 *Shiva Nataraja, Lord of the Dance*, from southern India, Chola period, eleventh century. Copper, height 3 ft. 7⁷/₈ in. Cleveland Museum of Art. Shiva's earrings are mismatched to represent the god's dual role: male and female. The small drum in his right hand is a symbol of creation, a second right arm is wreathed by a snake, symbolic of regeneration, while the hand makes the *mudra* of protection (see Figure 4.25); his outstretched left hand holds the flame of destruction; a second left hand points to his feet, one raised to indicate "release from worldliness," the other crushing the demon-dwarf of egotism and ignorance. Bronze icons of India's popular Lord of the Dance were produced in great numbers during the eleventh century.

In China and other parts of Buddhist East Asia, one of the most revered religious icons is the *bodhisattva* Guanyin (known in Japan as Kannon). *Bodhisattvas* are beings who have chosen to postpone their own entry into *nirvana* in order to assist others in reaching enlightenment (see page 118). Like Christendom's Virgin Mary, Guanyin is venerated as a figure of compassion and mercy. She protects the Buddhist against the calamities of nature. Brightly painted and gilded, the wood-carved Guanyin wears sumptuous robes, an ornate headdress, and a profusion of jewels (Figure **6.31**). This fashionable costume, which would seem contrary to the Buddha's teachings on the renunciation of worldliness, signifies the *bodhisattva's* high status in secular society. The gentle and benign icon, a feminized male figure, reflects the profound humanism of Buddhist art in twelfth-century China.

Figure 6.31 *Seated Guanyin Bodhisattva*, Liao dynasty, eleventh to early twelfth century. Wood with multiple layers of paint, 7 ft. 11 in. x 5 ft. 5 in. Nelson-Atkins Museum of Art, Kansas City, Missouri.

A stock of melodies was available to musicians for use in secular and sacred songs, and the same one might serve both types of song.

Instrumental Music

Musical instruments first appeared in religious music not for the purpose of accompanying songs, as with *troubadour* poems and folk epics, but to substitute for the human voice in polyphonic compositions. Medieval music depended on **timbre** (tone color) rather than volume for its effect, and most medieval instruments produced sounds that were gentle and thin by comparison with their modern (not to mention electronically amplified) counterparts.

Medieval string instruments included the harp, the **psaltery**, and the lute (all three are plucked), and bowed fiddles such as the vielle and the rebec (Figure **6.32**). Wind instruments included portable pipe **organs**, recorders, and bagpipes. Percussion was produced by chimes, cymbals, bells, tambourines, and drums. Instrumental music performed without voices accompanied medieval dancing. Percussion instruments established the basic rhythms for a wide variety of high-spirited dances, including the *estampie*, a popular round dance consisting of short, repeated phrases.

Figure 6.32 Music and Her Attendants, from Boethius, *De Arithmetica*, fourteenth century. Holding a portable pipe organ, the elegant lady who symbolizes the civilized art of courtly music is surrounded by an ensemble of female court musicians. In the circle at the top, the biblical king David plays a psaltery, the instrument named after the Psalms (Psaltery) of David. Clockwise from right: lute, clappers, trumpets, nakers (kettledrums), bagpipes, shawm, tambourine, rebec (viol).

Afterword

From the Western point of view, the period between ca. 1000 and 1300 may be called the Age of Faith: During that time, Christian beliefs and practices infused virtually every aspect of life. Medieval Christendom left a number of institutions and artifacts that have come to shape the culture of the West: in political life, the beginnings of European monarchy; in economic life, the rise of towns; in higher education, the university; in religion, the Roman Catholic Church; and in the arts, a flowering of masterworks ranging from allegorical drama and epic poetry to Gothic cathedrals and polyphonic music. The centuries to follow would witness a transition from medieval to modern values, as Christendom encountered increasing secularism and a revival of Classical humanism.

Key Topics

- the medieval Church
- medieval mystics
- medieval towns
- medieval drama
- Dante's *Commedia*
- medieval universities
- Scholasticism
- the pilgrimage church
- the Romanesque style
- the Gothic style
- Chartres Cathedral
- the painted altarpiece
- medieval polyphony
- instrumental music
- temple-shrines: Christian and Hindu
- religious icons: Hindu and Buddhist

HIGH MIDDLE AGES TIMELINE

	HISTORICAL EVENTS	LANDMARKS IN THE VISUAL ARTS	LITERARY LANDMARKS	MUSIC LANDMARKS	BEYOND THE WEST
1000	• Catholic Church founds College of Cardinals (1022)	• Reliquary of Sainte Foy (late tenth to eleventh century) • Romanesque style (ca. 1000–1150)		• Guido of Arezzo introduces staff for notation (ca. 1020)	• Song dynasty in China (960–1279) • Kandariya Mahadeo temple, Khajuraho, India (ca. 1000) • *Shiva Nataraja* (eleventh century)
1050	• Rise of towns and guilds (eleventh and twelfth centuries)	• Saint-Sernin, Toulouse (ca. 1080–1120)			• *Seated Guanyin Bodhisattva* (eleventh to early twelfth century)
1100		• Gislebertus, *Last Judgment*, Autun Cathedral (ca. 1130–1135) • Abbey Church of Saint-Denis (1140–1144) • *Notre Dame de la Belle Verrière*, Chartres (twelfth century)	• Hildegard of Bingen, *Scivias* (ca. 1146)		
1150	• Bologna University founded (1159)	• Gothic style (ca. 1150–1300) • Chartres Cathedral (mainly 1194–1220)		• Hildegard of Bingen, *Ordo virtutum* (*Play of the Virtues*) (ca. 1151)	
1200	• Canonization of Francis of Assisi (1228) • Pope Gregory IX establishes Inquisition (1233)	• Notre Dame, Paris (ca. 1200–1250)		• Pérotin, Three- and Four-Part Mass (ca. 1200) • Motet (thirteenth century)	• Rumi, *Love is a Stranger* (thirteenth century)
1250		• Cimabue, *Madonna Enthroned* (ca. 1280–1290)	• Aquinas, *Summa Theologica* (1274)	• "Dies irae" (ca. 1250)	
1300			• Dante, *Divine Comedy* (ca. 1320)		
1400			• *Everyman* (ca. 1490)		

Figure 6.10 Reliquary statue of Sainte Foy, see p. 154

Figure 6.5 Gislebertus, *Last Judgment*, see p. 148

Figure 6.1 Chartres Cathedral, see p. 142

Figure 6.26 Cimabue, *Madonna*

Chapter 7

Rebirth:

THE AGE OF THE RENAISSANCE
ca. 1300–1600

The Renaissance—meaning "rebirth"—was the turning point between medieval and modern times. It marks the revival of Greco-Roman culture, a movement that spread from its birthplace in Florence, Italy, to all parts of the European West. More generally, it describes the broader intellectual renewal that produced a wealth of new technologies and ideas, from the printing press to the formulation of linear perspective and other techniques for achieving pictorial naturalism, and from mapmaking to ingenious systems of record keeping. The Age of the Renaissance, the period from roughly 1300 to 1600, witnessed a spirit of self-conscious individualism in political and economic life, as well as in the arts. Money, fame, and power were the motivating forces of the men and women who, like their modern-day counterparts, easily reconciled their worldly pursuits with their religious beliefs.

The Age of the Renaissance opened with a century of European warfare and devastating plague. Nevertheless, the fifteenth and sixteenth centuries saw the growth of the European nation-states, the rise of a prosperous middle class, the advancement of Classically based education, as well as the celebrated revival of Greco-Roman principles in art and architecture. An optimistic view of the human potential for knowledge and pleasure inspired this European rebirth that left the world many of its most glorious landmarks.

A First Look

The mysterious smile of the woman in this sixteenth-century portrait by Leonardo da Vinci (1453–1519) has intrigued viewers for centuries. Identified by modern scholars as the wife of the wealthy Florentine merchant Francesco del Gioconda and called "La Gioconda," she is better known as Mona Lisa (see page 198). The most famous female image in the history of Western art, she has been idealized in love songs, implicated in modern mystery capers, and subjected to thousands of commercial abuses. She was even given a mustache by the twentieth-century Dada artist Marcel Duchamp (see Figure 14.26). For centuries, admirers have tried to interpret the meaning of Mona Lisa's enigmatic smile. But she is a landmark figure for other reasons as well: She was among the first to be portrayed in a landscape setting, rather than in the traditional domestic interior. Her lifelike presence is achieved by means of the techniques of aerial perspective and *sfumato*, the subtle blurring of contours for which Leonardo, who is said to have worked on the portrait for three years, was famous. The prime example of the rebirth of naturalistic portraiture in the West, the Mona Lisa has become symbolic of the individualism and humanism that marked the Age of the Renaissance.

Figure 7.1 Leonardo da Vinci, *Mona Lisa*, ca. 1503–1505. Oil on panel, 30¼ x 21 in. Louvre, Paris.

TRANSITION: MEDIEVAL TO RENAISSANCE

THE fourteenth century was a period of transition marked by a number of dramatic developments: the struggle for survival against the devastating bubonic plague, the trials of a long and debilitating war between England and France, and the decline of the Roman Catholic Church. These phenomena—the Black Death, the Hundred Years' War, and the Great Schism—radically altered all aspects of Western European life and culture. In the arts of this era, there are clear signs of a revived self-consciousness, a growing preoccupation with gender and class, and spirited efforts to represent the world with greater objectivity.

The Black Death

The most devastating natural catastrophe of the fourteenth century, the bubonic plague, struck Europe in 1347. Within less than a century it destroyed one-third to one-half of its population. Originating in China and spread by the Mongol tribes that dominated that vast area, the disease devastated East Asia and the Middle East, interrupting long-distance trade and cross-cultural encounters that had flourished for two centuries. The plague was carried into Europe by flea-bearing black rats infesting the commercial vessels that brought goods to Mediterranean ports. In its early stages, it was transmitted by the bite of either the infected flea or the host rat; in its more severe stages, it was passed on by those infected with the disease. The symptoms of the malady were terrifying: Buboes (or abscesses) that began in the lymph glands of the groin or armpits of the afflicted slowly filled with pus, turning the body a deathly black, hence the popular label "the Black Death." Once the boils and accompanying fever appeared, death usually followed within two to three days. Traditional treatments, such as the bleeding of victims and fumigation with vapors of vinegar, proved useless. No connection was perceived between the rats and the plague itself, and in the absence of a clinical understanding of bacterial infection, the medical profession of the day was helpless. (Indeed, the bacillus of the bubonic plague was not isolated until 1894.)

The plague hit hardest in the towns, where the concentration of population and the lack of sanitation made the disease more difficult to contain. Four waves of bubonic plague spread throughout Europe between 1347 and 1375, infecting some European cities several times and nearly wiping out their entire populations (Figure 7.2). If the psychological impact of the Black Death was traumatic, its economic effects were equally devastating. Widespread death among the poor caused a shortage of labor, which in turn created a greater demand for workers. The bargaining power of those who survived the plague was thus improved. In many parts of Europe, workers pressed to raise their status and income. Peasants took advantage of opportunities to become tenant farmers on lands leased by lords in need of laborers. Others fled their rural manors for cities, where jobs were readily available. This exodus from the countryside spurred urban growth and contributed to the slow disintegration of manorialism, the economic system that bound medieval serfs to the land (see page 131).

Figure 7.2 Hans Holbein the Younger, *Dance of Death*, ca. 1490. Woodcut. Library of Congress, Washington, D.C. Of all the plague-related themes depicted in the arts, the most popular was the "Dance of Death" or *danse macabre*. Set forth in both poetry and the visual arts, it portrayed Death as a grinning skeleton or cadaver shepherding a parade of victims to the grave. The procession (which might have originated in conjunction with popular dances) included men, women, and children from all walks of life and social classes: Peasants and kings, schoolmasters and merchants, priests and nuns—all succumb to Death's ravishment.

All of Europe, however, was disadvantaged by climatic disasters that caused frequent crop failure and famine, and by the continuing demands of financially threatened feudal overlords. Violent working-class revolts—the first examples of labor rebellion in Western history—broke out in France and England in the mid-fourteenth century. In 1358, French peasants (known as *jacques*) staged an angry protest (the *Jacquerie*) that took the lives of hundreds of noblemen before it was suppressed by the French king. In England, the desperation of the poor was manifested in the Peasants' Revolt of 1381, led by Wat Tyler and described in the *Chronicles* of the French historian Jean Froissart (1338–1410). Despite their ultimate failure, these revolts left their imprint on the social history of the West. They frightened landowners everywhere and lent an instability to class relationships that hastened the demise of the old feudal order.

The Rise of Constitutional Monarchy

While the peasant rebellions achieved no immediate reforms, the lower classes had taken a major step toward equality with the rest of society. England's laborers were not the first, however, to have contested the absolute authority of the English monarch. As early as 1215, the barons of the realm had forced King John of England (1167–1216) to sign the landmark document called the Magna Carta (Latin, meaning "great charter"), which forbade the king to levy additional feudal taxes without the consent of his royal council. The Magna Carta, which was also interpreted as guaranteeing such other freedoms as trial by jury, is regarded as a constitutional landmark because it asserted the primacy of law over the will of the ruler—a principle that paved the way for the development of constitutional monarchy.

Only fifty years after the signing of the Magna Carta, the English nobility, demanding equal authority in ruling England, imprisoned King Henry III (1207–1272) and invited middle-class representatives to participate in the actions of the Great Council (Parliament), thus initiating the first example of representative government among the burgeoning nation-states of the West. During the fourteenth century, as Parliament met frequently to raise taxes for England's wars with France, it bargained for greater power, including the right to initiate legislation. Peasants and laborers still exercised no real political influence, but by the end of the century the English had laid the groundwork for a constitutional monarchy that would bridge the gap between medieval feudalism and modern democracy.

The Hundred Years' War

In France, the ills of plague, famine, and civil disturbance were compounded by a war with England that lasted more than one hundred years (1337–1453) and that was fought entirely on French soil. Larger and more protracted than any previous medieval conflict, the Hundred Years' War was the result of a longstanding English claim to continental lands: From the time of the Norman Conquest, the kings of England had held land in France, a situation that caused chronic resentment among the French. But the immediate cause of the war was the English claim to the French throne, occasioned by the death of Charles IV (1294–1328), the last of the male heirs in a long line of French kings that had begun with Hugh Capet in 987 C.E.

The war that began in 1337 was marked by intermittent battles, in many of which the French outnumbered the English by three or four to one. Nevertheless, the English won most of the early battles of the war, owing to their use of three new "secret" weapons: the foot soldier, the longbow, and gunpowder—the invisible enemy that would ultimately eliminate the personal element in military combat. Along with the traditional cavalry, the English army depended heavily on foot soldiers armed with longbows. The thin, steel-tipped arrows of the 6-foot longbow could be fired more quickly and at a longer range than those of the traditional crossbow. Because the thin arrows of the longbow easily pierced the finest French chain mail, plate mail soon came to replace chain mail. However, within the next few centuries, even plate mail became obsolete, since it proved useless against artillery that employed gunpowder.

Introduced into Europe by the Muslims, who acquired it from the Chinese, gunpowder was first used in Western combat during the Hundred Years' War. In the first battle of the war, however, the incendiary substance proved too potent for the poorly cast English cannons, which issued little more than terrifying noise. Still, gunpowder, which could lay waste a city, constituted a landmark advance in military technology.

Although the English repeatedly devastated the French armies throughout the Hundred Years' War, the financial and physical burdens of garrisoning French lands ultimately proved too great for the English. Facing a revitalized French army under the charismatic leadership of Joan of Arc, the English finally withdrew from France in 1450. Of peasant background, the seventeen-year-old Joan begged the French king to allow her to obey the voices of the Christian saints who had directed her to expel the English. Donning armor and riding a white horse, she led the French into battle (Figure **7.3**). Her success forced the English to withdraw from Orléans but initiated her martyrdom. Betrayed by her supporters, in 1431 she was condemned as a heretic and burned at the stake.

The Hundred Years' War dealt a major blow to feudalism. By the mid-fifteenth century the French nobility was badly depleted. Hand-to-hand combat and the "rules" of medieval chivalry were outmoded by the dramatically impersonal technology of gunpowder. In France, feudal allegiances were soon replaced by a system of national conscription. In the decades following England's withdrawal

Figure 7.3 Joan of Arc, from Antoine Dufour's *Lives of Famous Women*, French manuscript, 1504. Dobrée Museum, Nantes, France. Manuscripts illustrating the lives of famous women became increasingly popular in the Renaissance. Here, even in the relatively limited space of a manuscript miniature, the anonymous artist includes picturesque details and a convincing architectural setting.

from France, both countries began to move in separate directions, ultimately becoming independent nation-states.

The Decline of the Church

The growth of the European nation-states contributed to the weakening of the Christian commonwealth, especially where Church and state competed for influence and authority. The two events that proved most damaging to the prestige of the Catholic Church were the Avignon Papacy (1309–1377) and the Great Schism (1378–1417). The term "Avignon Papacy" describes the relocation of the papacy from Rome to the city of Avignon in southern France (see Map 6.1) in response to political pressure from the French king Philip IV ("the Fair"; 1268–1314). Attempting to compete in prestige and political influence with the secular rulers of Europe, the Avignon popes established a luxurious and powerful court using stringent (and occasionally corrupt) means to accomplish their purpose. The increasing need for Church revenue led some of the Avignon popes to sell Church office (a practice known as **simony**), to levy additional taxes upon the clergy, to elect members of their own families to ecclesiastical office, and to step up the sale of **indulgences** (pardons from temporal penalties for sins committed by lay Christians). From the twelfth century on, the Church had sold these certificates of grace—drawn from the "surplus" of good works left by the saints—to lay Christians who bought them in order to speed their own progress to heaven or to benefit their relatives and friends in Purgatory. While the seven popes who ruled from Avignon were able administrators, their unsavory efforts at financial and political aggrandizement damaged the reputation of the Church.

The return of the papacy to Rome in 1377 was followed by one of the most devastating events in Church history, the Great Schism: A rift between French and Italian factions of the College of Cardinals led to the election of two popes, one who ruled from Avignon, the other from Rome. For more than thirty years there were two conflicting claims to universal sovereignty and bitter controversy within the Church. As each pope excommunicated the other, laypeople questioned whether any Christian soul might enter heaven. The Great Schism proved even more detrimental to Church prestige than the Avignon Papacy, for while the latter had prompted strong anticlerical feelings—even shock—in Christians who regarded Rome as the traditional home of the papacy, the Schism violated the very sanctity of the Holy Office.

THE ARTS IN TRANSITION

FOURTEENTH-CENTURY Europeans manifested an unprecedented preoccupation with differences in class, gender, and personality. Both in literature and in art, there emerged a new fidelity to nature and to personal experience in the everyday world. This close, objective attention to human society and social interaction may be described as "social realism." This new realism is apparent in the many woodcuts of the Dance of Death (see Figure 7.2), where class differences are clearly drawn. It is also evident in the landmark works of three notable fourteenth-century writers: Giovanni Boccaccio, Christine de Pisan, and Geoffrey Chaucer.

Boccaccio

The virulence of the plague and the mood of mounting despair horrified the Florentine poet and humanist Giovanni Boccaccio (1313–1375). A prolific writer of Italian prose romances and lyric poetry, Boccaccio was also the first biographer of Dante and the author of many Latin treatises and textbooks. But his landmark work is the celebrated collection of short stories known as the *Decameron*. The framework for the *Decameron* is provided by the plague itself: Eager to escape contagion, seven young women and three young men retreat to a villa in the suburbs of Florence, where, to pass the time, each tells a story on each of ten days. The stories, designed as distractions from the horrors of the pandemic, are, in effect, amusing secular entertainments. They provide insight, however, into the social concerns and values of both their fictional narrators and Boccaccio's reading public.

Boccaccio, *Decameron* (1351)

Boccaccio borrowed many stories in the *Decameron* from popular fables, *fabliaux* (humorous narrative tales), and contemporary incidents. His characters resemble neither the allegorical figures of *Everyman* nor the courtly stereotypes of *Lancelot*. Rather, they are realistically conceived, high-spirited individuals who prize cleverness, good humor, and the world of the flesh over the classic medieval virtues of chivalry, piety, and humility. The *Decameron* must have had special appeal for men and women who saw themselves as the heroes of unstable and rapidly changing times. Toward the end of his life, Boccaccio repented writing what he himself called his "immoral tales"; nevertheless, his stories remain a lasting tribute to the varieties of human affection and desire.

Christine de Pisan

The world's first feminist writer, Christine de Pisan (1364–1428?), emerged in France. The daughter of an Italian physician, Christine wedded a French nobleman when she was fifteen—medieval women usually married in their mid- to late teens. Ten years later, when her husband died, Christine was left to support three children, a task she met by becoming the first female professional writer. Christine attacked the long antifemale tradition that had demeaned women and denied them the right to a university education. Her **feminism** is all the more significant because it occurred at a time in which men were making systematic efforts to restrict female inheritance of land and female membership in the guilds. In an early poem, the "Epistle to the God of Love" (1399), she protested the persistent antifemale bias of clerics and scholars with these words:

> Some say that many women are deceitful,
> Wily, false, of little worth:
> Others that too many are liars,
> Fickle, flighty, and inconstant;
> Still others accuse them of great vices,
> Blaming them much, excusing them nothing,
> Thus do clerics, night and day,
> First in French verse, then in Latin,
> Based on who knows what books
> That tell more lies than drunkards do.

Christine was keenly aware of the fact that Western literary tradition did not offer a representative picture of women's importance to society. Eager to correct this inequity, she became a spokesperson for female achievements and talents. Inspired by Boccaccio's *On Famous Women* (1374), a collection of 106 biographies of historical and mythological women, Christine wrote the allegorical *Book of the City of Ladies*, an attack on male misogyny and a sound defense of the female's right to education.

Christine de Pisan, *Book of the City of Ladies* (1405)

Chaucer

Geoffrey Chaucer (1340–1400), a contemporary of Boccaccio and Christine de Pisan, was one of the greatest masters of fourteenth-century vernacular literature. Writing in the everyday language of his time (Middle English), Chaucer shaped the development of English literature much as Dante, a century earlier, had influenced the course of Italian poetry.

A middle-class civil servant, soldier in the Hundred Years' War, a diplomat, and a citizen of the bustling city of London, Chaucer left an indelible image of his time in a group of stories known as the *Canterbury Tales*. Modeled broadly on Boccaccio's *Decameron*, this versified human comedy was framed by Chaucer in the setting of a pilgrimage whose participants tell stories to entertain each other while traveling to the shrine of Saint Thomas à Becket in Canterbury. Chaucer's twenty-nine pilgrims, who include a miller, a monk, a plowman, a

Chaucer, *Canterbury Tales* (ca. 1390)

Making Connections

THE NEW REALISM IN LITERATURE AND ART

Chaucer: The Wife of Bath

"There was a good Wife from near Bath, but she was somewhat deaf, which was a shame. She had such skill in clothmaking that she surpassed the weavers of Ypres and Ghent. In all her parish there was no woman who could go before her to the offertory; and if someone did, the Wife of Bath was certainly so angry that she lost all charitable feeling. Her kerchiefs were of fine texture; those she wore upon her head on Sunday weighed, I swear, ten pounds. Her fine scarlet hose were carefully tied, and her shoes were uncracked and new. Her face was bold and fair and red. All of her life she had been an estimable woman: she had had five husbands, not to mention other company in her youth—but of that we need not speak now. And three times she had been to Jerusalem; she had crossed many a foreign river; she had been to Rome, to Bologna, to St. James' shrine in Galicia, and to Cologne. About journeying through the country she knew a great deal. To tell the truth she was gap-toothed. She sat her gentle horse easily, and wore a fine headdress with a hat as broad as a buckler or a shield, a riding skirt about her large hips, and a pair of sharp spurs on her heels. She knew how to laugh and joke in company, and all the remedies of love, for her skill was great in that old game."

This excerpt from the Preface to the *Canterbury Tales* illustrates Chaucer's use of descriptive detail to bring zesty realism to his characters. The Wife of Bath, one of the liveliest of his twenty-nine pilgrims, comes to life by way of his pen. Similarly, the artists Jean, Pol, and Herman Limbourg—who illustrated the prayer book known as the *Très Riches Heures* (*Very Precious Hours*) for Jean, duke of Berry and brother of the French king—introduced a new level of descriptive detail to the art of manuscript illumination. At the turn of the fifteenth century, the Limbourgs explored the mundane activities and labors peculiar to each month of the year. For the month of February, they depicted the first snowscape in Western art. Three peasants warm themselves by a fire, while others hurry to complete their chores (Figure **7.4**). The Limbourg brothers show a fascination with visual details: Dovecote and beehives are topped with new-fallen snow, smoke curls from a chimney, and two female laborers lift their skirts immodestly before the fire.

Q Which of Chaucer's descriptive details work to create a realistic portrait? Which visual details in the Limbourg miniature work to create a realistic scene?

Figure 7.4 Jean, Pol, and Herman Limbourg, *February*, plate 3 from the *Très Riches Heures* (*Very Precious Hours*) *du Duc de Berry*, ca. 1413–1416. Illumination, 8¾ x 5$^{5}/_{16}$ in. Condé Museum, Chantilly, France.

Figure 7.5 Giotto, Arena Chapel (Cappella Scrovegni), Padua, Italy, interior looking toward the choir. Height 42 ft., width 27 ft. 10 in., length 96 ft. Enrico Scrovegni, a Paduan banker and moneylender, dedicated this chapel to the Virgin to atone for his worldliness. He commissioned Giotto to decorate the barrel-vaulted interior with frescoes illustrating the Life of Christ beginning with the history of Mary—a cycle of narratives that unfolds under a star-studded sky.

knight, a priest, a scholar, and a prioress, provide a literary cross section of late medieval society. Although they are type characters, they are also individual personalities. (The Pardoner, for instance, is portrayed as effeminate, while the Wife of Bath is lusty.) Chaucer characterizes each pilgrim by description by their lively and humorous conversations, and by the twenty stories they tell, which range from moral tales and beast fables to *fabliaux* of the most risqué and bawdy sort.

Like his medieval predecessors, Chaucer tended to moralize, reserving special scorn for clerical abuse and human hypocrisy. But unlike his forebears, whose generalized view of human nature often produced stereotypes, Chaucer brought his characters to life by means of memorable details.

Giotto's New Realism

The pioneer in painting on the eve of the Renaissance was the Florentine artist Giotto (1266–1337). Giotto's art represents a landmark in a new era because it introduced a natural and lifelike style that anticipated Italian Renaissance picture-making. Giotto broke with the decorative formality of Byzantine painting (see Figure 4.18), which had strongly influenced the style of the late medieval altarpiece (see Figure 6.26). In place of the flat, stylized saints of the Byzantine icon, he introduced weighty, robust figures that are solemnly posed and set in shallow but convincing space. Modeling form through gradations of light and shade (a technique known as ***chiaroscuro***), he gave his figures a three-dimensional presence not seen since Roman times. Giotto brought this new realism to his panel paintings, and most notably to the famous cycle of frescoes he executed for the family chapel of the wealthy Enrico Scrovegni in Padua (Figure **7.5**).

On the walls of the chapel, Giotto illustrated familiar episodes from the lives of the Virgin and Jesus. While wholly traditional in subject matter, in style Giotto took a new direction, giving weight and volume to figures whose nobility and dignity call to mind Classical sculpture. In the *Lamentation over Jesus* (Figure **7.6**), where the mourners are theatrically set in shallow but carefully defined space, Giotto subtly varied the gestures and degrees of sorrow

Figure 7.6 Giotto, *Lamentation over Jesus*, 1305–1306. Fresco, 7 ft. 7 in. x 7 ft. 9 in. Arena Chapel, Padua. The medium of fresco involved the application of pigments mixed in water and applied to damp lime plaster. The colors bonded to the wall as the plaster dried, and the tonal differences from area to area may indicate where a single day's painting ended.

ranging from the stoic despair of the Virgin Mother to the grief-stricken anguish of the angels that flutter above the scene. Like the characters in Boccaccio's *Decameron* and Chaucer's *Canterbury Tales*, Giotto's figures are convincingly human: While not individualized to the point of portraiture, neither are they stereotypes. They anticipate the direction of art in the age of rebirth.

The *Ars Nova* in Music

Imagination and diversity characterized fourteenth-century music, which composers of that era self-consciously labeled the ***ars nova*** ("new art"). The music of the *ars nova* featured increased rhythmic complexity and aural expressiveness, achieved in part by **isorhythm** (literally, "same rhythm"): the close repetition of identical rhythmic patterns in different portions of a composition. Isorhythm, which reflected a new interest in the manipulation of pitches and rhythms, gave unprecedented unity to musical compositions. At the same time, unexpected variations in rhythmic patterns might be achieved by way of a new musical effect known as **syncopation**, which shifted the accent from the normally strong beat to the weaker beat.

In France, the leading proponent of the *ars nova* was the French poet, priest, and composer Guillaume de Machaut (1300–1377). In his day, Machaut was more widely known and acclaimed than Chaucer and Boccaccio. Machaut held commissions from such members of the French aristocracy as the duke of Berry, patron of the Limbourg Brothers (see Figure 7.4). Machaut penned hundreds of poems, including a verse drama interspersed with songs. His most important musical achievement, however, was his *Messe de Notre Dame* (*Mass of Our Lady*). Departing from the medieval tradition of treating the Mass as five separate compositions (based on Gregorian chant), he unified the textually fixed portions of the Mass into a single polyphonic composition, and added a sixth movement, the "Ite missa est." Machaut's effort at coherence of design is clear evidence that composers had begun to rank musical effect as equal to liturgical function. This landmark treatment of the Catholic liturgy set a precedent for such composers as the sixteenth-century Palestrina and the baroque master Johann Sebastian Bach (see page 287).

Machaut, *Mass of Our Lady* (ca. 1350)

Machaut's sacred compositions represent only a small part of his total musical output. His numerous secular works include 142 polyphonic **ballades** (secular songs); these look back to the music of the *trouvères*, but their attention to expressive detail is unique. They introduce new warmth and lyricism, as well as vivid poetic imagery—features that parallel the humanizing currents in fourteenth-century art and literature. "One who does not compose according to feelings," wrote Machaut, "falsifies his work and his song."

THE ITALIAN RENAISSANCE

THE new realism in the arts, increasing secularism, and the spirit of criticism that accompanied the decline of the Church—all features of the transitional fourteenth century—came into focus in the cities of the Italian peninsula. Italy was the homeland of Roman antiquity, the splendid ruins of which stood as reminders of the greatness of Classical civilization. The least feudalized part of the medieval world and Europe's foremost commercial and financial center, Italy had traded with Southwest Asian cities even in the decades that followed the fall of Rome. It had also maintained cultural contacts with Byzantium, the heir to Greek culture. The cities of Italy, especially Venice and Genoa (Map **7.1**), had profited financially from the Crusades and—despite the ravages of the plague—continued to enjoy a high level of commercial prosperity. But it was in Florence, dominated by its landmark cathedral, that the Renaissance would come to flower (Figure **7.7**). In fourteenth-century Florence, shopkeepers devised a practical system (based on Arab models) of tracking debits and credits: Double-entry bookkeeping helped merchants to maintain systematic records of transactions in what was the soundest currency in the West, the Florentine gold florin. Fifteenth-century handbooks on arithmetic, foreign currency, and even good penmanship encouraged the commercial activities of traders and bankers.

The pursuit of money and leisure, rather than a preoccupation with feudal and chivalric obligations, marked the lifestyle of merchants and artisans who lived in the bustling city-states of Italy. Middle-class men and women challenged canonical sources of authority that frowned upon profit-making and the accumulation of wealth. In this materialistic and often only superficially religious society, the old medieval values no longer made sense, while those of pre-Christian antiquity seemed more compatible with the secular interests and ambitions of the rising merchant class. The ancient Greeks and Romans were ideal historical models for the enterprising citizens of the Italian city-states. In Italy, the movement to recover the culture of Classical antiquity would become the dominant feature of the Renaissance.

Politically, Renaissance Italy had much in common with ancient Greece. Independent and disunited, the city-states of Italy, like those of ancient Greece, were fiercely competitive. As in Golden-Age Greece, commercial rivalry among the Italian city-states led to frequent civil wars. In Italy, however, such wars were not always fought by citizens (who, as merchants, were generally ill-prepared for combat), but by ***condottieri*** (professional soldiers) whose loyalties, along with their services, were bought for a price. The papacy, a potential source of political leadership, made

Map 7.1 Renaissance Italy.

little effort to unify the rival Italian communes. Rather, as temporal governors of the Papal States (the lands located in central Italy), Renaissance popes joined in the game of power politics, often allying themselves with one group of city-states against another.

The Medici

Italian Renaissance cities were ruled either by members of the petty nobility, by mercenary generals, or—as in the case of Florence and Venice—by wealthy middle-class families. In Florence, a city of some fifty thousand people, some one hundred families dominated political life. The most notable of these was the Medici, a wealthy banking family that rose to power during the fourteenth century and gradually assumed the reins of state. Partly because the commercial ingenuity of the Medici enhanced the material status of the Florentine citizens, and partly because strong, uninterrupted leadership guaranteed local economic stability, the Medici ruled Florence for four generations. The Medici merchant-princes, especially Cosimo (1389–1464) and Lorenzo "the Magnificent" (1449–1492) (Figure **7.8**), supported scholarship and patronized the arts. Affluence coupled with intellectual discernment and refined taste inspired the Medici to commission works from such artists as Brunelleschi, Botticelli, Verrocchio, and Michelangelo, who produced some of the West's most brilliant art. For almost two centuries, scholars, poets, painters, and civic leaders shared common interests, acknowledging one another as leaders of a vigorous cultural revival.

Figure 7.7 Florence Cathedral, Italy.

RENAISSANCE HUMANISM

CLASSICAL humanism, the revival of Greco-Roman culture, was a major feature of the Italian Renaissance and a phenomenon that gave the period its distinctly secular stamp. Classical culture did not disappear altogether with the fall of Rome in 476 C.E. It was preserved by countless Christian and Muslim scholars, revived by Charlemagne in the early Middle Ages, and championed by such medieval intellectuals as Aquinas (who took Aristotle as his master) and Dante (who chose Virgil as his guide). But the Classical revival of the fourteenth to sixteenth centuries—the age of the Renaissance—generated new and more all-embracing attitudes toward Greco-Roman antiquity than any that had preceded it.

Renaissance humanists advocated the recovery and uncensored study of the entire body of Greek and Latin manuscripts and the self-conscious imitation of Classical art and architecture. They regarded Classical authority not exclusively as a means of clarifying Christian truths, but as the basis for a new appraisal of the role of the individual in the world order. Thus, although Renaissance humanists still prized the Liberal Arts as the basis for intellectual advancement, they approached the classics from a different point of view than that of their scholastic predecessors. Whereas the scholastics had studied the Greco-Roman legacy as the foundation for Christian dogma and faith, Renaissance humanists discovered in the Greek and Latin classics a rational guide to the fulfillment of human potential. Additionally, the Renaissance revival of humanism differed from earlier revivals because it attracted the interest of a broad base of the population and not a mere handful of theologians, as was the case, for instance, in Carolingian or later medieval times.

The humanists of the Renaissance were the cultural archeologists of their age. They uncovered new evidence of the splendor of Greco-Roman antiquity and consumed the fruits of their Western heritage. Unattached to any single school or university, this new breed of humanists pursued what the ancient Romans had called *studia humanitatis*, a program of study that embraced grammar, rhetoric, history, poetry, and moral philosophy. These branches of learning fostered training in moral and aesthetic values—the very subjects with which this textbook is concerned. While such an educational curriculum was assuredly not antireligious—indeed, most Renaissance humanists were devout Catholics—its focus was secular rather than religious. For these humanists, life on earth was not a valley of tears but, rather, an extended occasion during which human beings might cultivate their unique talents and abilities. Classical humanists saw no conflict, however, between humanism and religious belief. They viewed their intellectual mission as both pleasing to God and advantageous to society in general. Humanism, then, grounded in a reevaluation of Classical literature and art, represented a shift in emphasis rather than an entirely new pursuit; it involved a turning away from exclusively otherworldly preoccupations to a robust, this-worldly point of view.

Figure 7.8 Andrea del Verrocchio, *Lorenzo de' Medici*, ca. 1478. Terracotta, 25⅞ x 23¼ x 12⅞ in. National Gallery of Art, Washington, D.C. Grandson of Cosimo de' Medici, Lorenzo "the Magnificent" governed Florence from 1471 to his death in 1492. A supporter of humanists and artists, he himself was a prolific poet whose verses were inspired by neoplatonic thought.

Petrarch: "Father of Humanism"

The most famous of the early Florentine humanists was the poet and scholar Francesco Petrarch (1304–1374). Often called the "father of humanism," Petrarch devoted his life to the recovery, copying, and editing of Latin manuscripts. In quest of these ancient sources of wisdom, he traveled all over Europe, hand-copying manuscripts he could not beg or buy from monastic libraries, borrowing others from friends, and gradually amassing a private library of more than two hundred volumes. Petrarch was a tireless popularizer of Classical studies. Reviving the epistolary (letter-writing) tradition that had practically disappeared since Roman times, he wrote hundreds of letters describing his admiration for antiquity and his enthusiasm for the classics, especially the writings of the Roman statesman Cicero (see page 70). In his letters, Petrarch eulogized and imitated Cicero's polished prose style, which stood in refined contrast to the corrupt Latin of his own time. Petrarch's affection for Cicero was matched only by his devotion to Augustine of Hippo and his writings (see pages 101–102). Indeed, in their introspective tone and their expression of intimate feelings and desires, Petrarch's letters reveal the profound influence of Augustine's *Confessions*, a work that Petrarch deeply admired.

Torn between Christian piety and his passion for Classical antiquity, Petrarch experienced recurrent psychic conflict. In his writings there is a gnawing and unresolved dissonance between the dual imperatives of his heritage: the Judeo-Christian will to believe and the Classical will to reason. Such self-torment—evident in Petrarch's poems, over three hundred examples of which make up the *Canzoniere* (*Songbook*)—implies that Petrarch remained, in part, a medieval man. Yet it did not prevent him from pursuing worldly fame. At Rome in 1341, he proudly received the laurel crown for outstanding literary achievement. The tradition, which looks back to the ancient Greek practice of honoring victors in the athletic games with wreaths made from the foliage of the laurel tree, survives in our modern honorary title "poet laureate."

Petrarch, *Canzoniere* (*Songbook*) (ca. 1350)

The object of Petrarch's affection and the inspiration for the *Canzoniere* was a married Florentine woman named Laura de Sade. To Laura, Petrarch dedicated hundreds of love lyrics, many of which were written after she died of bubonic plague in 1348. While Petrarch used Latin, the language of learning, for his letters and essays, he wrote his poems and songs in vernacular Italian. His favorite poetic form was the **sonnet**, a fourteen-line lyric poem. The sonnet form originated among the poets of Sicily, but it was Petrarch who brought it to perfection. He favored a rhyme scheme (difficult to replicate in faithful English translation) of *abab/abab* for the octave and *cde/cde* for the sestet. Influenced by the "sweet style" of his Italian forebears and, more generally, by *troubadour* songs and Islamic lyric verse, Petrarch's sonnets are a record of his struggle between the flesh and the spirit. In their self-reflective and even self-indulgent tone, they are strikingly modern, especially where they explore Petrarch's love for Laura—and for love itself. Petrarch's Sonnet No. 134 follows:

> I find no peace, yet I am not at war;
> I fear and hope, I burn and freeze;
> I rise to heaven, and fall to earth's floor
> Grasping at nothing, the world I seize.
>
> She imprisons me, who neither jails nor frees,
> Nor keeps me for herself, nor slips the noose;
> Love does not kill, nor set me free,
> Love takes my life, but will not set me loose.
>
> I have no eyes yet see, no tongue yet scream;
> I long to perish, and seek release;
> I hate myself, and love another.
>
> I feed on grief, and in my laughter weep;
> Both death and life displease me;
> Lady, because of you I suffer.

Ficino: The Platonic Academy

The effort to recover, copy, and produce accurate editions of Classical writings dominated the early history of the Renaissance in Italy. By the middle of the fifteenth century, almost all of the major Greek and Latin manuscripts of antiquity were available to scholars.

After the fall of Constantinople to the Ottoman Turks in 1453, Greek manuscripts and Byzantine scholars poured into Italy, contributing to the efflorescence of what the humanist philosopher Marsilio Ficino (1433–1499) called "a Golden Age." Encouraged by the availability of Greek resources and supported by his patron Cosimo de' Medici, Ficino translated the entire corpus of Plato's writings from Greek into Latin, making them available to Western scholars for the first time since antiquity. Ficino's translations and the founding of the Platonic Academy in Florence (financed by Cosimo) launched a reappraisal of Plato and the neoplatonists that had major consequences in the domains of art and literature. Plato's writings—especially the *Symposium*, the dialog in which love is exalted as a divine force—advanced the idea, popularized by Ficino, that "platonic" (or spiritual) love attracts the soul to God. Platonic love became a major theme among Renaissance poets and painters, who held that spiritual love was inspired by physical beauty.

Pico della Mirandola: The Dignity of Man

While Ficino was engaged in popularizing Plato, one of his most learned contemporaries, Giovanni Pico della Mirandola (1463–1494), undertook the translation of various ancient literary works in Hebrew, Arabic, Latin, and Greek. Humanist, poet, and theologian, Pico sought not only to bring to light the entire history of human thought, but to prove that all intellectual expression shared the same divine purpose and design. This effort to discover a "unity of truth" in all philosophic thought—similar to but more comprehensive than the medieval quest for synthesis and so dramatically different from our own modern pluralistic outlook—dominated the arts and ideas of the Renaissance.

Both in personality and in academic ambition, Pico typified the activist spirit of Renaissance *individualism*—the affirmation of the unique, self-fashioning potential of the human being. In Rome, at the age of twenty-four, Pico boldly challenged the Church to debate some nine hundred propositions that disputed the institutional Church on a variety of theological and philosophical matters. The young scholar did not get the opportunity to debate his theses; indeed, he was persecuted for heresy and forced to flee Italy.

As an introduction to the disputation, Pico had prepared the Latin text that has come to be called the *Oration on the Dignity of Man* (1486). In this landmark "manifesto of humanism," Pico drew on a wide range of literary sources to build an argument for free will and the perfectibility of the individual. Schooled in neoplatonism (see page 101, Ideas and Issues), Pico described humanity's position as only "a little lower than the angels," on the hierarchical "chain of being" that linked the divine and earthly realms. While this proposition followed Ficino and the humanists of the Platonic Academy, Pico emphasized the individual's moral freedom to fashion one's own nature and thus determine one's destiny. The Renaissance view that the self-made individual occupies the center of a rational universe is nowhere better described than in the excerpt reproduced here.

Ideas and Issues

PICO: FREE WILL AND HUMAN PERFECTIBILITY

"At last, the Supreme Maker decreed that this creature, to whom He could give nothing wholly his own, should have a share in the particular endowment of every other creature. Taking man, therefore, this creature of indeterminate image, He set him in the middle of the world and thus spoke to him:

'We have given you, Oh Adam, no visage proper to yourself, nor any endowment properly your own, in order that whatever place, whatever form, whatever gifts you may, with premeditation, select, these same you may have and possess through your own judgment and decision. The nature of all other creatures is defined and restricted within laws which We have laid down: you, by contrast, impeded by no such restrictions, may, by your own free will, to whose custody We have assigned you, trace for yourself the lineaments of your own nature. I have placed you at the very center of the world, so that from that vantage point you may with greater ease glance round about you on all that the world contains. We have made you a creature neither of heaven nor of earth, neither mortal nor immortal, in order that you may, as the free and proud shaper of your own being, fashion yourself in the form you may prefer. It will be in your power to descend to the lower, brutish forms of life; [or] you will be able, through your own decision, to rise again to the superior orders whose life is divine.'"

(from Pico, *Oration on the Dignity of Man*)

Q Do you find Pico's views on human perfectibility realistic or idealistic? Why?

Q What role does God play in the ascent of the individual?

Castiglione: The Well-Rounded Person

By far the most provocative analysis of Renaissance individualism is that found in *The Book of the Courtier*, a treatise written by the Italian diplomat and humanist writer Baldassare Castiglione (1478–1529) (Figure **7.9**). Castiglione's *Courtier* was inspired by a series of conversations that had taken place among a group of sixteenth-century aristocrats at the court of Urbino, a mecca for humanist studies located in central Italy. The subject of these conversations, which Castiglione probably recorded from memory, concerns the qualifications of the ideal Renaissance man and woman. Debating this subject at length, the members of the court arrive at a consensus that affords the image of *l'uomo universale*, the well-rounded person. Castiglione reports that the ideal man should master all the skills of the medieval warrior and display the physical proficiency of a champion athlete. But, additionally, he must possess the refinements of a humanistic education. He must know Latin and Greek (as well as his own native language), be familiar with the classics, speak and write well, and be able to compose verse, draw, and play a musical instrument. Moreover, all that the Renaissance gentleman does, he should do with an air of nonchalance and grace, a quality summed up in the Italian word *sprezzatura*. This unique combination of breeding and education would prepare the individual to serve a very special end: the perfection of the state. For, as Book Four of *The Courtier* explains, the primary duty of the well-rounded gentleman is to influence the ruler to govern wisely.

Castiglione, *The Book of the Courtier* (1513–1518)

Although, according to Castiglione, the goal of the ideal gentleman was to cultivate his full potential as a human being, such was not the case with the Renaissance gentlewoman. The Renaissance woman should have a knowledge of letters, music, and art—that is, like the gentleman, she should receive a humanistic education—but in no way should she violate that "soft and delicate tenderness that is her defining quality." Castiglione's peers agreed that "in her ways, manners, words, gestures, and bearing, a woman ought to be very unlike a man." Just as the success of the courtier depends on his ability to influence those who rule, the success of the lady rests with her skills in entertaining the male members of the court.

Castiglione's handbook of Renaissance etiquette was based on the views of a narrow, aristocratic segment of society. But despite its selective viewpoint, it was immensely popular: It was translated into five languages and went through fifty-seven editions before the

Ideas and Issues

THE RENAISSANCE GENTLEMAN

"[Count Ludovico de Canossa says:] 'I think that what is chiefly important and necessary for the Courtier, in order to speak and write well, is knowledge; for he who is ignorant and has nothing in his mind that merits being heard, can neither say it nor write it.

Next he must arrange in good order what he has to say or write; then express it well in words, which (if I do not err) ought to be precise, choice, rich and rightly formed, but above all, in use even among the masses; because such words as these make the grandeur and pomp of speech, if the speaker has good sense and carefulness, and knows how to choose the words most expressive of his meaning, and to exalt them, to mold position and order that they shall at a glance show and make known their dignity and splendor, like pictures placed in good and proper light. . . .

I would have him more than passably accomplished in letters, at least in those studies that are called the humanities, and conversant not only with the Latin language but with the Greek, for the sake of the many different things that have been admirably written therein. Let him be well versed in the poets, and not less in the orators and historians, and also proficient in writing verse and prose, especially in this vulgar tongue [common speech, that is, Italian] of ours; for besides the enjoyment he will find in it, he will by this means never lack agreeable entertainment with ladies, who are usually fond of such things. And if other occupations or want of study prevent his reaching such perfection as to render his writings worthy of great praise, let him be careful to suppress them so that others may not laugh at him. . . .'"

THE RENAISSANCE LADY

"[Giuliano de' Medici says: 'The Lady] must have not only the good sense to discern the quality of him with whom she is speaking, but knowledge of many things, in order to entertain him graciously; and in her talk she should know how to choose those things that are adapted to the quality of him with whom she is speaking, and should be cautious lest occasionally, without intending it, she utter words that may offend him. Let her guard against wearying him by praising herself indiscreetly or by being too prolix. Let her not go about mingling serious matters with her playful or humorous discourse, or jests and jokes with her serious discourse. Let her not stupidly pretend to know that which she does not know, but modestly seek to do herself credit in that which she does know—in all things avoiding affectation, as has been said. In this way she will be adorned with good manners, and will perform with perfect grace the bodily exercises proper to women; her discourse will be rich and full of prudence, virtue and pleasantness; and thus she will be not only loved but revered by everyone, and perhaps worthy to be placed side by side with this great Courtier as well in qualities of the mind as in those of the body. . . .

And to repeat in a few words part of what has been already said, I wish this Lady to have knowledge of letters, music, painting, and to know how to dance and make merry; accompanying the other precepts that have been taught the Courtier with discreet modesty and with the giving of a good impression of herself. And thus, in her talk, her laughter, her play, her jesting, in short, in everything, she will be very graceful, and will entertain appropriately, and with witticisms and pleasantries befitting her, everyone who shall come before her. . . .'"

(from Castiglione, *The Book of the Courtier*)

Q How do the personalities of Castiglione's Renaissance man and woman differ? How are they similar?
Q What contemporary figures fit the description of *l'uomo universale*?

year 1600. Historically, *The Book of the Courtier* is an index to cultural changes that were taking place between medieval and early modern times. It departs from exclusively feudal and Christian educational ideals and formulates a program for the cultivation of both mind *and* body that has become fundamental to modern Western education. Representative also of the shift from medieval to modern values is Castiglione's preoccupation with manners rather than morals, that is, with *how* individuals act and how their actions may impress their peers, rather than with the intrinsic moral value of those actions.

The Printing Press

In 1527, the Aldine Press in Venice printed *The Courtier* in an edition of more than one thousand copies. Indeed, the humanist enterprise in general was greatly aided by a landmark in Renaissance technology: the printing press. Block printing originated in China during the ninth century C.E. and movable type in the eleventh. But print technology did not reach Western Europe until the fifteenth century. By 1450, Johann Gutenberg (ca. 1400–1468), a German goldsmith working in the city of Mainz, perfected a press with movable metal type that made it possible to fabricate books cheaply, rapidly, and in great numbers. The first printed book, the Gutenberg Bible (Saint Jerome's Latin translation), was published in 1455 (see page 216).

By the end of the century, print shops appeared in hundreds of European cities: seventy-seven in Italy alone. Texts that had been laboriously prepared by hand over a period of months were now reproduced in only days. Information became a commodity for mass production, as vast areas of knowledge—heretofore the exclusive domain of clerics and scholars—were readily available to the literate public. The printing press revolutionized learning and communication: The major vehicle in the spread of humanist writings, it facilitated the rise of popular education, even as it encouraged readers to form opinions for themselves.

Machiavelli and Power Politics

The modern notion of progress as an active process of improvement was born during the Renaissance. Civic humanists argued that society's leaders must exercise *virtù*, that is, the self-confident vitality of the self-made individual. *Virtù*, not to be confused with the English word "virtue"), was the quality by which powerful personalities (usually men) mastered Fate (usually personified as a woman). Balanced against humanist ideals of *virtù* and human perfectibility, however, were the realities of greed, ignorance, and cruelty. Personal ambition and commercial competition fueled frequent armed conflicts between Italy's city-states. Gunpowder and other technological innovations made warfare increasingly impersonal, while

Figure 7.9 Raphael, *Portrait of Baldassare Castiglione*, ca. 1515. Oil on canvas, approx. 30¼ x 26½ in. Louvre, Paris.

the swollen ambitions of local and national rulers occasioned the worst kinds of aggression and brute force. Even the keepers of the spiritual kingdom on earth—the leaders of the Church of Rome—had become notorious for their self-indulgence and greed, as some Renaissance popes actually took mistresses, led armed attacks upon neighboring states, and lived at shocking levels of luxury.

The most acute critic of these realities was the Florentine diplomat and statesman Niccolò Machiavelli (1469–1527). A keen political observer and a student of Roman history, Machiavelli lamented Italy's disunity in the face of continuous rivalry among the city-states. He anticipated that outside powers might try to take advantage of Italy's internal weaknesses. The threat of foreign invasion became a reality in 1494, when French armies marched into Italy, thus initiating a series of wars that left Italy divided and impoverished. Exiled from Florence upon the collapse of the republican government he had served from 1498 to 1512, and eager to win favor with the Medici now that they had returned to power, Machiavelli penned *The Prince*, a political treatise that called for the unification of Italy under a powerful and courageous leader. This notorious

Machiavelli, *The Prince* (1513)

little book laid out the guidelines for how an aspiring ruler might gain and maintain political power.

In *The Prince,* Machiavelli argued that the need for a strong state justified strong rule. He pictured the secular prince as one who was schooled in war and in the lessons of history. The ruler must trust no one, least of all mercenary soldiers. He must imitate the lion in his fierceness, but he must also act like a fox to outsmart his enemies. Finally, in the interest of the state, he must be ruthless, and, if necessary, he must sacrifice moral virtue. In the final analysis, the end—that is, the preservation of a strong state—will justify any means of maintaining power, however cunning or violent. Machiavelli's profound grasp of past and present history, which he summed up as his "knowledge of the actions of man," made him both a critic of human behavior and modern Europe's first political scientist.

Widely circulated, *The Prince* was hailed not simply as a cynical examination of political expediency, but as an exposé of real-life politics—so much so that the word "Machiavellian" soon became synonymous with the idea of political duplicity. Only the master of power politics, argues the Machiavellian, can ensure the survival of the state. History's tyrants have heeded this message.

Ideas and Issues

WHETHER IT IS BETTER TO BE LOVED THAN FEARED

"[We now consider] the question whether it is better to be loved rather than feared, or feared rather than loved. It might perhaps be answered that we should wish to be both; but since love and fear can hardly exist together, if we must choose between them, it is far safer to be feared than loved. For of men it may generally be affirmed that they are thankless, fickle, false, studious to avoid danger, greedy of gain, devoted to you while you are able to confer benefits upon them, and ready, as I said before, while danger is distant, to shed their blood, and sacrifice their property, their lives, and their children for you; but in the hour of need they turn against you. The Prince, therefore, who without otherwise securing himself builds wholly on their professions is undone. For the friendships which we buy with a price, and do not gain by greatness and nobility of character, though they be fairly earned are not made good, but fail us when we have occasion to use them.

Moreover, men are less careful how they offend him who makes himself loved than him who makes himself feared. For love is held by the tie of obligation, which, because men are a sorry breed, is broken on every whisper of private interest; but fear is bound by the apprehension of punishment which never relaxes its grasp.

Nevertheless a Prince should inspire fear in such a fashion that if he [does] not win love he may escape hate. For a man may very well be feared and yet not hated, and this will be the case so long as he does not meddle with the property or with the women of his citizens and subjects. And if constrained to put any to death, he should do so only when there is manifest cause or reasonable justification. But, above all, he must abstain from the property of others. For men will sooner forget the death of their father than the loss of their property."

(from Machiavelli, *The Prince*)

Q Do you agree with Machiavelli that a ruler cannot be both loved and feared? Why might it be safer to be feared?

EARLY RENAISSANCE ART

THE Renaissance produced a flowering in the visual arts rarely matched in the annals of world culture. Artists embraced the natural world with an enthusiasm that was equalled only by their ambition to master the lessons of Classical antiquity. The result was a unique and sophisticated body of art that set the standards for most of the painting, sculpture, and architecture produced in the West until the late nineteenth century.

Italian Renaissance art is usually divided into two periods: Early Renaissance (ca. 1400–1490) and High Renaissance (ca. 1490–1520). In the earlier period, a time of experimentation with new techniques of representation, productivity was centered in Florence. In the later decades, when these techniques reached new levels of refinement, both patronage and productivity shifted to Rome and Milan. Renaissance art was a tangible expression of increasing wealth. Artists looked not solely to traditional sources of patronage, such as the Catholic Church, but to merchants and petty despots, to middle-class patrons and urban guilds, for lavish commissions that brought prestige to their businesses, families, and communities. Those who supported the arts did so at least in part with an eye on leaving their mark upon society or immortalizing themselves for posterity. Thus art became evidence of material well-being as well as a visible extension of the ego in an age of individualism.

Active patronage enhanced the social and financial status of Renaissance artists. Such artists were first and foremost craftspeople, apprenticed to studios in which they might achieve mastery over a wide variety of techniques, including the grinding of paints, the making of brushes, and the skillful copying of images. While trained to observe firmly established artistic conventions, the more innovative among them moved to create a new visual language. Indeed, for the first time in Western history, artists came to wield influence as humanists, scientists, and poets: A new phenomenon of the artist as hero and genius was born. The image of the artist as hero was promoted by the self-publicizing efforts of these artists, as well as by the adulation of their peers. The Italian painter, architect, and critic Giorgio Vasari (1511–1574) immortalized hundreds of Renaissance artists in his monumental biography *The Lives of the Most Excellent Painters, Architects, and Sculptors*. Vasari drew to legendary proportions the achievements of notable Renaissance figures, many of whom he knew personally.

Vasari, *The Lives of the Most Excellent Painters, Architects, and Sculptors* (1550)

Early Renaissance Architecture

Early Renaissance architects were devoted to the principles laid out by the Roman architect and engineer Vitruvius Pollio (see page 74). Among these principles was the Classical notion that human proportions mirrored the universal order. The human *microcosm* (the "lesser world") was the natural extension of the divine *macrocosm* (the "greater world"). Accordingly, the study of nature and an understanding of its harmonious design put one in touch with the universe. Rational architecture, reflecting natural laws, according to Renaissance theorists, would cultivate rational individuals; and harmoniously proportioned buildings would produce ideal citizens.

Brunelleschi The revival of Classical architecture was inaugurated by the architect, sculptor, and theorist Filippo Brunelleschi (1377–1446). In 1420, Brunelleschi won a civic competition for the design of the dome of Florence Cathedral (see Figures 7.7 and 7.10). His dome—the largest since that of the Pantheon in Rome (see Figure 3.8)—consists of two octagonal shells. Each incorporates eight curved panels joined by massive ribs that soar upward from the octagonal **drum**—the section immediately beneath the dome—to converge at an elegant **lantern** through which light enters the interior. In the space between the two shells, Brunelleschi designed an interlocking system of ribs that operate like hidden flying buttresses (Figure **7.10**). At the base of the dome, reinforced by stone chains, he constructed a double wall made of sandstone bricks laid in herringbone fashion. To raise the dome he devised new methods of hoisting stone, and ingenious masonry techniques, all of which won him acclaim in Florence. Brunelleschi's colleague Alberti hailed the completed dome as "a feat of engineering . . . unknown and unimaginable among the ancients." Brunelleschi's dome became a legend in its time; it remains an architectural landmark, the defining feature of the Florentine skyline.

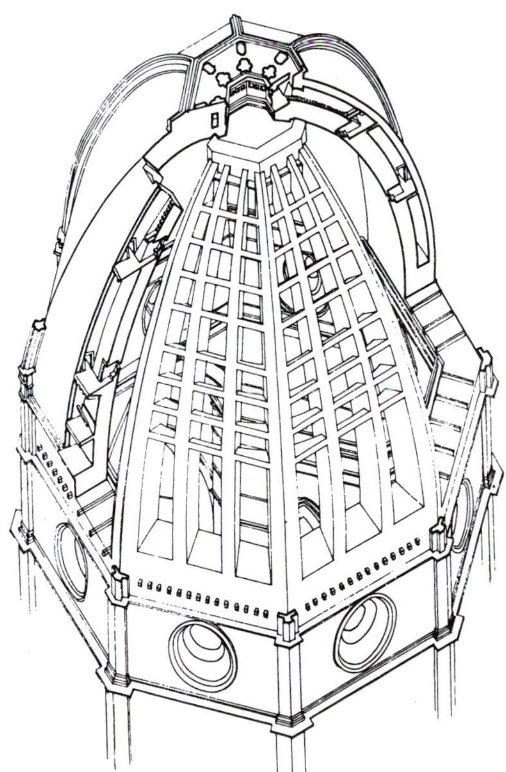

Figure 7.10 Axonometric section of the dome of Florence cathedral. Cross section at base 11 ft. x 7 ft.

Brunelleschi was among the first architects of the Renaissance to defend Classical principles of symmetry and proportion in architectural design. In the graceful little chapel he produced for the Pazzi family of Florence in the cloister of the Franciscan basilica of Santa Croce (Figure **7.11**), he placed a dome over the central square of the inner hall and buttressed the square with two short barrel vaults. Since the exterior of this self-contained structure was later modified by the addition of a portico, it is in the interior that Brunelleschi's break with the medieval past is fully realized (Figure **7.12**). Gray stone moldings and gray Corinthian **pilasters**—shallow, flattened, rectangular columns that adhere to the wall surface—emphasize the "seams" between the individual segments of the stark white interior, producing a sense of order and harmony that is unsurpassed in Early Renaissance architecture. Whereas the medieval cathedral coaxes one's gaze heavenward, the Pazzi Chapel fixes the beholder decisively on earth.

Alberti Brunelleschi's enthusiasm for an architecture of harmonious proportions was shared by his younger colleague, the multitalented Florentine humanist Leon Battista Alberti (1404–1474). Alberti's scientific treatises on painting, sculpture, and architecture reveal his admiration for Roman architecture and his familiarity with the writings of the Roman engineer Vitruvius. In his *Ten Books on Architecture* (modeled after Vitruvius' work of the same title), Alberti argued that architectural design should proceed from the square and the circle, the two most perfect geometric shapes. This proposition was the guiding precept for all of Alberti's buildings (a total of only six); it would become the definitive principle of High Renaissance composition.

Alberti, *Ten Books on Architecture* (1452)

In the townhouse Alberti designed for the wealthy Rucellai family of Florence (Figure **7.13**)—a structure for which there were no direct antique precedents—each story is ornamented with a different Classical order (see Figure 2.29). Rows of crisply defined arcaded windows appear on the upper stories, while square windows placed well above the street (for safety and privacy) accent the lowest level. From the Roman Colosseum (see Figure 3.7), Alberti borrowed the device of alternating arches and engaged columns, flattening the latter into pilasters. Here the principles of clarity and proportion prevail.

Figure 7.11 (above left) Filippo Brunelleschi, Pazzi Chapel, cloister of Santa Croce, Florence, ca. 1441–1460.

Figure 7.12 (left) Filippo Brunelleschi, Pazzi Chapel, interior, Santa Croce, Florence, ca. 1441–1460. Geometric design dominates this intimate chapel, every part of which is immediately accessible to the eye. The effect of rationalized space is emphasized by the cool tones of gray and white.

Figure 7.13 (above) Leon Battista Alberti (designer) and Bernardo Rossellino (architect), Rucellai Palace, Florence, 1446–1451. Alberti employs the traditional three-story *palazzo* design but, adhering to Classical principles of balance, the stories are of equal height. The Rucellai coat-of-arms is seen over some of the windows on the second level.

Early Renaissance Painting

In painting, Renaissance artists pioneered a new pictorialism that took inspiration from both Classical antiquity and from the evidence of the human eye. Empirical perspective and the reliance on direct observation of the physical world were already evident in Roman painting (see pages 82–83). Roman efforts to recreate the "look" of nature by way of various illusionistic techniques were revived by Renaissance artists: Working from live models, they studied human and animal anatomy and analyzed the effects of natural light on objects in space. But, in pursuing a rational analysis of the natural world, Renaissance artists moved beyond empirical devices to introduce scientific methods for the representation of objects in space,

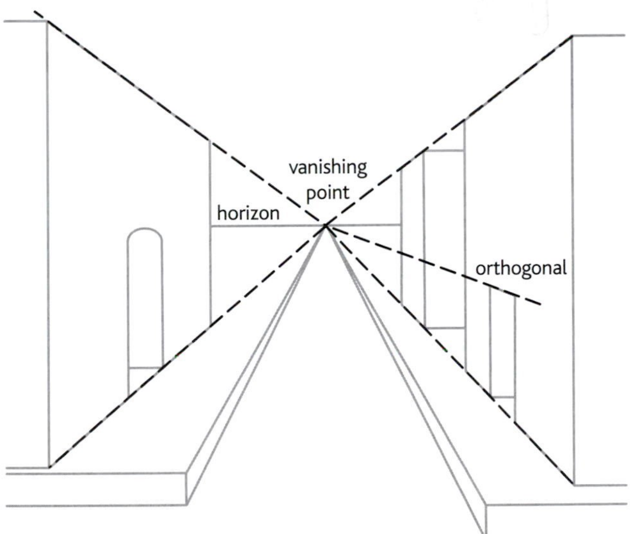

Figure 7.14 Linear perspective. Brunelleschi projected the picture plane as a cross section through which diagonal lines (orthogonals) connected the eye of the beholder with objects along those lines and hence with the vanishing point.

Figure 7.15 (above) Masaccio, *The Tribute Money*, ca. 1425. Fresco (after restoration), 8 ft. 4 in. x 19 ft. 8 in. Brancacci Chapel, Santa Maria del Carmine, Florence. Masaccio worked from live models as well as from the available antique sources. From Classical statuary such as the *Apollo Belvedere* (see Figure 2.37) he borrowed the graceful stance of the Roman tax collector, who is shown twice in the fresco—viewed from front and back. Antique sculpture also probably inspired the Roman togas and the head of John the Evangelist (on the right of Jesus).

thus transforming the painting into a window on nature: The **picture plane**, that is, the two-dimensional surface of the panel or canvas, was conceived as a transparent glass or window through which one perceives the three-dimensional world. Various techniques aided artists in the task of recreating the illusion of reality. The most notable of these was the invention of **linear** or **one-point perspective,** an ingenious tool for the translation of three-dimensional space onto a two-dimensional surface. Around 1420, inspired, in all likelihood, by Latin translations of Arab-Muslim treatises on optics and optical devices, Brunelleschi formulated the first laws of linear perspective. These laws describe the manner by which all parallel lines in a given visual field appear to converge at a single vanishing point on the horizon (an illusion familiar to anyone who, from the rear of a train, has watched railroad tracks "merge" in the distance) (Figure **7.14**). Linear perspective satisfied the Renaissance craving for an exact and accurate description of the physical world. It also imposed a fixed relationship—both in time and space—between the image and the eye of the beholder, making the latter the exclusive point of reference within the spatial field and thus, metaphorically, placing the individual at the center of the macrocosm.

Masaccio The first artist to master Brunelleschi's new spatial device was the Florentine painter Tommaso Guidi, called Masaccio, or "Slovenly Tom" (1401–1428). Before his untimely death (possibly by poison) at age twenty-seven, Masaccio demonstrated his remarkable artistic talent in frescoes he painted for the churches of Florence. His cycle of frescoes at the Brancacci Chapel in Santa Maria del Carmine in Florence represents an elaborate synthesis of illusionistic techniques. In *The Tribute Money* (Figure **7.15**), a scene based on the Gospel story in which Jesus honors the demands of the Roman state by paying a tax or "tribute," the artist depicted Jesus instructing the apostle Peter to gather the money from the mouth of a fish, an event seen at the left; at the right, Peter is shown delivering the coins to the Roman tax collector. Masaccio's application of linear perspective—the orthogonals of the building

on the right meet at a vanishing point just behind the head of Jesus—provides spatial unity to the three separate episodes. Tonal unity is provided by means of **aerial perspective**—the subtle blurring of details and diminution of color intensity in objects perceived at a distance. Refining the innovative techniques explored by Giotto at the Arena Chapel in Padua (see Figures 7.5 and 7.6), Masaccio also made use of light and shade (*chiaroscuro*) to model his figures as though they actually stood in the light of the chapel window located to the right of the fresco. In the Brancacci Chapel frescoes, Masaccio anticipated the three principal features of Early Renaissance painting: the adaptation of Classical prototypes (see caption 7.15), the empirical study of nature, and the application of the new techniques of spatial illusionism.

Botticelli Masaccio's follower, Sandro Botticelli (1445–1510), was less interested in achieving illusionistic effects. Primarily a painter of religious subjects, he was nevertheless inspired by the physical beauty of the Classical nude. His landmark painting, the *Birth of Venus* (Figure **7.16**), features an idealized image of womankind based on an antique model, possibly a statue in the Medici collection (see Figure 2.24). Rendered in tempera on a large canvas, the composition depends largely on the harmonious integration of line and pastel colors: The figures are only minimally shaded, so that (unlike Masaccio's) they seem weightless, suspended in space.

Figure 7.16 Sandro Botticelli, *Birth of Venus*, after 1482. Tempera on canvas, 5 ft. 9 in. x 9 ft. ½ in. Uffizi Gallery, Florence. An undulating line animates the windblown hair, the embroidered robes, and the delicate flowers that lie on the tapestrylike surface of the canvas. Gold accents and pastel colors (including the delicious lime of the water) further remove this idyllic vision from association with the mundane world.

The painting is memorable as a tribute to physical and spiritual beauty. Following the Greek poet Hesiod, Botticelli shows Venus born of sea foam and floating toward the island of Cythera on a pearlescent scallop shell. To her right are two wind gods locked in sensuous embrace, while to her left is the welcoming figure of Pomona, the ancient Roman goddess of fruit trees and fecundity. Many elements in the painting—water, wind, flowers, trees—suggest procreation and fertility, powers associated with Venus as goddess of earthly love. But Botticelli, inspired by a contemporary neoplatonic poem honoring Aphrodite/Venus as goddess of divine love, renders Venus also as an object of ethereal beauty and spiritual love. He pictorializes ideas set forth at the Platonic Academy of Florence, particularly the neoplatonic notion that objects of physical beauty move the soul to desire union with God, divine fount of beauty and truth. Botticelli's wistful goddess assumes the double role accorded her by the neoplatonists: goddess of earthly love and goddess of divine (or Platonic) love.

Early Renaissance Sculpture

The art of the Early Renaissance was never a mere imitation of antique models, as was the case with Roman copies of Greek art. Rather, it was an original effort to reinterpret Greco-Roman themes and principles. Such originality, evident in the architecture of Brunelleschi and the paintings of Botticelli, reaches dramatic heights in Renaissance sculpture of the fifteenth century.

Donatello The most creative force in Early Renaissance sculpture was the Florentine artist Donato Bardi, known as Donatello (1386–1466). With Brunelleschi, Donatello traveled to Rome to study antique statuary. His efforts thereafter, in both marble and bronze, set the benchmark for technical proficiency and the expression of emotional intensity in three-dimensional representation. Donatello's idealized likeness of the biblical hero David, completed in 1432, was the first freestanding, life-sized nude since antiquity (Figure **7.17**). While not an imitation of any single Greek or Roman statue, this landmark work reveals an indebtedness to Classical models in its correct anatomical proportions and gentle *contrapposto* stance (compare the *Doryphorus*, Figure 2.21). However, the sensuousness of the youthful figure, especially apparent in the surface modeling, surpasses that of any antique statue. While Donatello's subject is biblical, hence religious, his style—seductive and sensuous—celebrates the beauty of the physical, hence secular, world. Indeed, in this tribute to male beauty, Donatello rejected the medieval view of the nude as the wellspring of sin. Rather, he anticipated the modern Western exaltation of the body as the seat of pleasure.

Figure 7.17 Donatello, *David*, completed 1432. Bronze, height 5 ft. 2 in. National Museum of the Bargello, Florence. Standing on the head of Goliath, David wears a shepherd's hat crowned with laurel, a traditional symbol of victory. The slim, somewhat effeminate youth is caught in a moment of proud yet private meditation.

Ghiberti Donatello's friend and contemporary Lorenzo Ghiberti (1378–1455) was a goldsmith and a sculptor. Winning the competition for a set of bronze relief panels for the north door of the Florence Baptistry of San Giovanni in 1402, he went on to prepare another set for the east doorway of the building (Figure **7.18**). In the second group of panels, completed in 1452, Ghiberti achieved astonishingly dramatic effects by applying the laws of linear perspective to humanized narratives marked by figural grace and atmospheric detail. Overwhelmed by the beauty of the doors, the great sculptor of the next generation, Michelangelo, would comment that they were worthy of being the Gates of Paradise.

Figure 7.18 Lorenzo Ghiberti, "Gates of Paradise," 1425–1452. The east portal of the Florentine Baptistry of San Giovanni once held Ghiberti's immense (18 ft. 6 in. tall) gilt-bronze doors, brilliantly sculpted in low relief. After a massive flood in 1966, the "Gates" underwent painstaking restoration. The original panels (seen here) were replaced with copies in 1990, and are now in a hermetically sealed, oxygen-free case at the Museo dell'Opera del Duomo in Florence.

Figure 7.19 Lorenzo Ghiberti, *Meeting of Solomon and Sheba* (single panel of the "Gates of Paradise"; see Figure 7.18). Gilt-bronze relief, 31¼ x 31¼ in. Museo dell'Opera del Duomo, Florence. The vanishing point in this scene lies just above and between the heads of the two principal characters, whose meeting is related in the Hebrew Bible (1 Kings 10:1–13). The figures in the foreground are more deeply cut than those in the background, an effect that adds to the illusion of deep space.

On the east portal ten Old Testament scenes, from Creation to the Reign of Solomon, are depicted. The bottom panel on the right, which illustrates the biblical meeting of Solomon and Sheba (Figure **7.19**), makes use of one-point perspective to emphasize the central characters and draw the eye into deep space. Other panels bring to life key biblical events in similarly complex architectural settings or verdant, mountainous landscapes—compositions that would profoundly influence Renaissance art for the next hundred years. Ghiberti "signed" his landmark work with a portrait bust of himself that protrudes from a roundel midway down the inner frame of the left door (see Figure 7.18).

Figure 7.20 (left and above) Andrea del Verrocchio (completed by Alessandro Leopardi). Equestrian statue of Bartolommeo Colleoni, ca. 1481–1496. Bronze, height approx. 13 ft. Campo Santi Giovanni e Paolo, Venice. Verrocchio (a nickname meaning "true eye") worked mainly in bronze, marble, and terracotta. Considered the greatest Italian sculptor between Donatello and Michelangelo, he brought a sense of dynamic movement to many of his sculptures.

Verrocchio Portraiture, the likeness of a specific individual, was a favorite Renaissance genre, inspiring such famous paintings as the *Mona Lisa* (see Figure 7.1) and the *Arnolfini Marriage* (see Figure 8.10). Three-dimensional renderings of the physical self had held an important place in the cultures of Greece (see Figures 2.6 and 2.36) and Rome, where civic leaders and notable personalities (see Figures 3.3 and 3.4) were honored or commemorated, along with one's own ancestors (see Figure 3.17).

The revival of portraiture during the Renaissance was, similarly, an expression of two impulses: the desire to immortalize the self by means of a lifelike replication of one's physical appearance (a service provided in the modern world by the medium of photography), and the wish to advertise publicly the greatness of a civic leader or notable personality. Like the literary genres biography and autobiography—both of which were also revived by Renaissance humanists—portraiture and self-portraiture were hallmarks of a new self-consciousness and growing civic pride.

The sculpted likeness of Florence's late fifteenth-century eminent ruler and patron of the arts, Lorenzo de' Medici (see Figure 7.8), was the work of one of the most notable Florentine artists, Andrea del Verrocchio (1435–1488). A follower of Donatello, Verrocchio ran a large workshop that trained many artists, including the young Leonardo da Vinci. The terracotta likeness of Lorenzo, painted to enhance its lifelike presence, was prized by the humanist himself.

Even more monumental is Verrocchio's equestrian statue of the *condottiere* Bartolommeo Colleoni (Figure **7.20**), a life-sized bronze commissioned by the rulers of Venice to commemorate Colleoni's military victories on behalf of the city. This landmark sculpture, which recalls the Roman statue of Marcus Aurelius on horseback (see Figure 3.1), provides yet another example of the Renaissance admiration for Classical art. However, compared with its predecessor, Verrocchio's equestrian portrait displays an unprecedented degree of scientific naturalism and an obsessive attention to anatomical detail—note the bulging muscles of Colleoni's mount. Verrocchio moreover makes his towering mercenary twist dramatically in his saddle and scowl fiercely. Such expressions of *terribilità*, or awe-inspiring power, typify the aggressive spirit that fueled the Renaissance.

HIGH RENAISSANCE ART

BY the end of the fifteenth century, Renaissance artists had mastered all of the fundamental techniques of visual illusionism, including linear and aerial perspective and the use of light and shade. Between roughly 1490 and 1520, the period known as the High Renaissance, they employed these techniques in ever more heroic and monumental ways. To the techniques of scientific illusionism they wedded the Classical principles of design that would typify the Grand Style of High Renaissance art.

High Renaissance Architecture

During the High Renaissance, the center of artistic activity shifted from Florence to Rome as the popes undertook a campaign to restore that ancient city to its original grandeur as the capital of Christendom. When Pope Julius II commissioned Donato Bramante (1444–1514) to rebuild Saint Peter's Cathedral, the architect designed a monumentally proportioned, centrally planned church to be capped by an immense dome. Bramante's plan was much modified in the 120 years it took to complete the new Saint Peter's. But his ideal of a building organized so that all structural elements were evenly disposed around a central point took shape on a smaller scale in his Tempietto, the "little temple" that marked the site of Peter's martyrdom in Rome (Figure **7.21**). Modeled on the Classical *tholos* (round temple), Bramante's shrine is ringed by a simple colonnade, and topped by a dome elevated upon a niched drum. Although the interior affords little light and space, the exterior gives the appearance of an elegant marble reliquary, a perfect structure from which nothing can be added or subtracted without damage to the whole.

Figure 7.21 Donato Bramante, Tempietto, San Pietro in Montorio, Rome, 1502. Height 46 ft., external diameter 29 ft.

The Renaissance passion for harmonious design had an equally powerful influence on the history of domestic architecture, a circumstance for which the Italian architect Andrea Palladio (1518–1580) was especially responsible. In his *Four Books on Architecture*, published in Venice in 1570, Palladio defended symmetry and centrality as the controlling elements of architectural design. He put his ideals into practice in a number of magnificent country houses he built for patrons in northern Italy. The Villa Rotonda near Vicenza—a centrally planned, thirty-two-room country house—is a perfectly symmetrical structure featuring a central room (or rotunda) covered by a dome (Figure **7.22**). All four façades of this landmark residence are identical, featuring a projecting Ionic portico approached by a flight of steps (Figure **7.23**).

Leonardo da Vinci

The Florentine artist Leonardo da Vinci (1452–1519) exercised the curiosity, talent, and inventiveness that typified the age of rebirth. A "Renaissance man," Leonardo impressed Vasari as a scientist, an artist, a skilled mathematician, a composer, and an inventor:

> He might have been a scientist if he had not been so versatile. But the instability of his character caused him to take up and abandon many things. In arithmetic, for example, he made such rapid progress during the short time he studied it that he often confounded his teacher by his questions. He also began the study of music and resolved to learn to play the lute, and as he was by nature of exalted imagination, and full of the most graceful vivacity, he sang and accompanied himself most divinely, improvising at once both verses and music. He studied not one branch of art only, but all. Admirably intelligent, and an excellent geometrician besides, Leonardo not only worked in sculpture . . . but, as an architect, designed ground plans and entire buildings; and, as an engineer, was the one who first suggested making a canal from Florence to Pisa by altering the river Arno. Leonardo also designed mills and water-driven machines. But, as he had resolved to make painting his profession, he spent most of his time drawing from life. . . .

Figure 7.22 Andrea Palladio (Andrea di Pietro Gondola), Villa Rotonda, Vicenza, Italy, completed 1569. In its geometric clarity, its cool elegance, and its dominance over its landscape setting, the Villa Rotonda represents the Renaissance distillation of Classical principles as applied to secular architecture. With this building, Palladio established the definitive ideal in domestic housing for the wealthy and provided a model of solemn dignity that would inspire generations of Neoclassical architects in England and America.

Figure 7.23 (below) Plan of the Villa Rotonda, Vicenza.
1 Columns
2 Steps
3 Portico
4 Central domed space

More than any other Renaissance figure, Leonardo fulfilled the ideal of the artist as creative genius. "I wish to work miracles," he wrote in his notes, amid designs for sculptures, paintings, military fortifications, and mechanical devices. Among his fewer than twenty surviving paintings is the portrait that may be the world's most famous painting, the *Mona Lisa* (see Figure 7.1). Mona Lisa ("Mona" is the abbreviation of "Madonna" or "Madame") was the young wife of a Florentine merchant, Francesco del Gioconda. She is shown in three-quarter view, seated on a stone balcony. While Early Renaissance artists usually represented their sitters in domestic interiors, Leonardo situated his subject outdoors, as if to suggest human compatibility with nature. The pyramidal shape of the sitter is echoed in the rugged mountains; the folds of her tunic are repeated in the curves of distant roads and rivers. Soft golden tones highlight the figure, which, like the landscape, is modeled in melting, smoky (*sfumato*) gradations of light and shade. The imaginary setting, a rocky and ethereal wilderness, is as elusive as the sitter, whose eyes and mouth are delicately blurred to produce a facial expression that is almost impossible to decipher, a smile both melancholic and mocking. While the sitter's shaved eyebrows and plucked hairline are typical of fifteenth-century female fashion, the image resists classification by age and—in the opinion of some—by gender (some scholars see Leonardo's own face in the portrait). Praised by Renaissance artists for its "lifelikeness," the *Mona Lisa* has remained a beloved icon well into our own time.

Ideas and Issues

RESTORATION OR RUIN?

Slow in his working methods, Leonardo rejected the traditional (fast-drying) fresco technique in which paint is applied to the wet plaster on the wall. Instead, he experimented with a mixture of oil, tempera, and varnish on a dry wall, a technique that proved to be nondurable. The use and abuse of the refectory over the centuries—especially after it was hit by an Allied bomb in 1943—further precipitated the deterioration of the painting. Between the eighteenth and twentieth centuries, the fresco underwent many cleanings, retouchings, and repaintings, the most recent of which was a twenty-year Italian-led rehabilitation (completed in 1999) that made use of various new technologies but left many of the figures with no facial features.

Bitter controversy has followed on the heels of this and similar work on other landmark paintings (such as the Sistine Chapel ceiling; see Figure 7.30). While some scholars praise the recent restoration of the *Last Supper* (Figure **7.24**), many critics claim that the enterprise has done additional damage to the painting and has distorted Leonardo's original colors beyond repair.

Some art historians vehemently refuse to show the restored version in their books and classrooms, claiming that the precleaned painting (Figure **7.25**) is closer to Leonardo's intentions. Most agree, however, that what is left of this landmark is not much more than a ghost of the original.

Q What advantages might there be in restoring landmark artworks? What disadvantages?

Figure 7.24 Leonardo da Vinci, *Last Supper*, ca. 1485–1498. Fresco: oil, tempera, and varnish on plaster, 15 ft. 1⅛ in. x 28 ft. 10½ in. Refectory, Santa Maria delle Grazie, Milan. This shows the fresco after the restoration completed in 1999.

Figure 7.25 Leonardo da Vinci, *Last Supper*, ca. 1485–1498. This shows the same painting as Figure 7.24 as it looked before restoration.

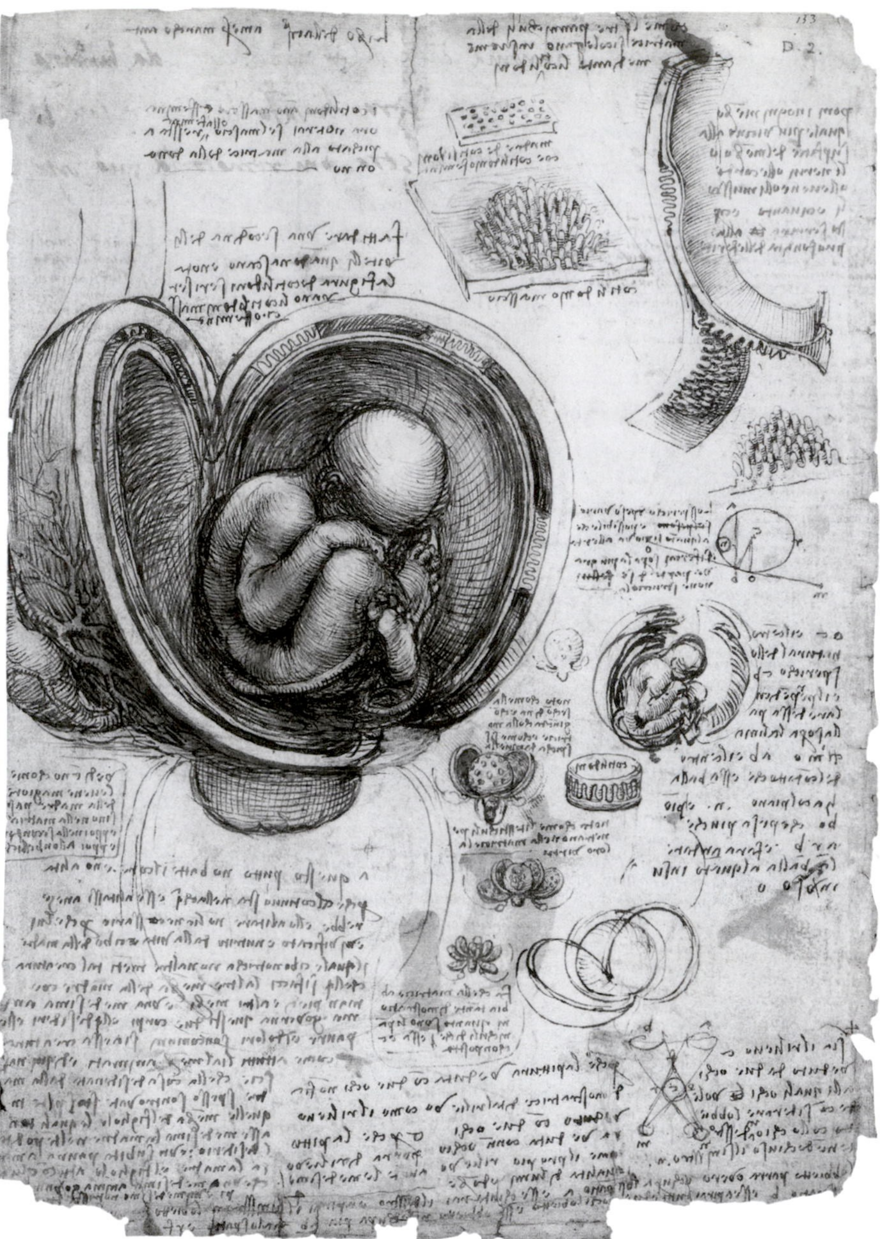

Figure 7.26 Leonardo da Vinci, *Embryo in the Womb*, ca. 1510. Pen and brown ink, 11¾ x 8½ in. The Royal Collection, Royal Library, Windsor Castle. Although Leonardo never established a strict methodology for the formulation of scientific laws, his insistence on direct experience and experimentation made him the harbinger of the Scientific Revolution that would sweep through Western Europe during the next two centuries.

While Leonardo's portraits were among his most notable commissions, his few (and largely unfinished) religious paintings brought him further notoriety. In his classic fresco the *Last Supper*, Leonardo fused narrative and symbolic content to achieve an ordered, grand design. This landmark work was executed in the late 1490s to adorn the wall of the refectory (the monastery dining room) of Santa Maria delle Grazie in Milan (see Figures 7.24 and 7.25). The *Last Supper* is one of the great religious paintings of all time. Leonardo intended that the sacred event *appear* to take place within the monastic dining room: The receding lines of the ceiling beams and side niches in the fresco create a sense of spatial depth and link the scene illusionistically with the interior walls of the refectory. Leonardo fixed the vanishing point at the center of the composition directly behind the head of Jesus so that the orthogonals of the composition radiate out from the apex of the figure. Topped by a pediment, the open doorway (one of three, symbolic of the Trinity) acts as a halo, reinforcing the centrality of Christ and his mission as "light of the world." The formal elements of the composition thereby underscore the symbolic aspects of the religious narrative. To this masterful rationalization of space, Leonardo added high drama: He divided the apostles into four groups of three who interact in agitated response to their leader's declaration that one of them would betray him (Matthew 26:21). Jesus' meditative composure and submissive gesture (indicating the bread and wine as symbols of the Eucharist) is countered by the reactions of the apostles—astonishment, anger, disbelief—appropriate to their biblical personalities. (The angry Peter, for instance—fifth from the left—wields the knife he later uses to cut off the ear of Jesus' assailant, Malchus.)

More than any other artist of his time, Leonardo exalted the importance of empirical study for discovering the general rules of nature. Critical of abstract speculation bereft of direct observation, he held that the human eye was the most dependable instrument for obtaining true knowledge of nature. A diligent investigator of natural phenomena, Leonardo examined the anatomical and organic functions of plants, animals, and human beings (Figure **7.26**). He also studied the properties of wind and water and invented several hundred ingenious mechanical devices, including an armored tank, a diving bell, and a flying machine, most of which never left the notebook stage. Between 1489 and 1518, Leonardo produced thousands of drawings accompanied by notes written in mirror-image script (devised perhaps to discourage imitators and plagiarists). This annotated record of the artist-scientist's passion to master nature includes anatomical drawings whose accuracy remained unsurpassed until 1543, when the Flemish physician Andreas Vesalius published the first medical illustrations of the human anatomy.

Raphael

The second of the great High Renaissance artists was Urbino-born Raphael (Raffaello Sanzio; 1483–1520). Less devoted to scientific speculation than Leonardo, Raphael was first and foremost a master painter. His fashionable portraits were famous for their accuracy and incisiveness. A case in point is the portrait of Raphael's lifelong friend Baldassare Castiglione (see Figure 7.9), which captures the self-confidence and thoughtful intelligence of this celebrated Renaissance personality.

Raphael's compositions are notable for their clarity, harmony, and unity of design. In *The Alba Madonna* (**Figure 7.27**), one of Raphael's many renderings of the Madonna and Child, he seats the Virgin on the ground, as a traditional Madonna of Humility. However, she is clothed in Classical robes and set in an idealized landscape framed by the picturesque hills of central Italy. Using clear, bright colors and precise draftsmanship, Raphael organized the composition according to simple geometric shapes: the triangle (formed by the Virgin, Child, and the infant John the Baptist), the circle (the painting's basic shape and the head of the Virgin), and the trapezoid (one length of which is formed by the Virgin's outstretched leg). In its mannered sweetness and clarity of form, the Raphaelesque Madonna became one of the most frequently reproduced Christian images in the history of Western art.

In 1510, Pope Julius II, the greatest of Renaissance Church patrons, commissioned Raphael to execute a series of frescoes for the Vatican Stanza della Segnatura—the pope's personal library and the room in which official Church papers were signed. The paintings were to represent the four domains of human learning: theology, philosophy, law, and the arts. To illustrate philosophy, Raphael painted *The School of Athens* (**Figure 7.28**). In this landmark fresco, the artist immortalized with unsurpassed dignity the company of the great philosophers and scientists of ancient history. At the center of the composition appear, as if in scholarly debate, the two giants of Classical philosophy: Plato, who points heavenward to indicate his view of reality as fixed in universal Forms, and Aristotle, who points to the earth to indicate that universal truth depends on the study of nature. Framed by a series of receding arches, the two philosophers stand against the bright sky, beneath the lofty vaults of a Roman basilica that resembles the newly remodeled Saint Peter's Cathedral. Between their heads lies the invisible vanishing point at which all the principal lines of sight converge. On either side of the great hall appear historical figures belonging to each of the two philosophic "camps": the Platonists (left) and the Aristotelians (right).

In the restrained nobility of the near life-sized figures and the measured symmetry of the composition, Raphael's *School of Athens* marked the culmination of a style

Figure 7.27 Raphael, *The Alba Madonna*, ca. 1510. Oil on wood transferred to canvas, diameter 37¼ in. National Gallery of Art, Washington, D.C. Despite the dignity of the composition and the nobility of the figures, the scene might be construed as a record of an ordinary woman with two children in a landscape, for Raphael has avoided obvious religious symbolism, such as the traditional halo.

Figure 7.28 Raphael, *The School of Athens*, 1509–1511. Fresco, 26 ft. x 18 ft. Stanza della Segnatura, Vatican, Rome. *The School of Athens* is a portrait gallery of Renaissance artists whose likenesses Raphael borrowed to depict his Classical heroes. The stately, bearded Plato is an idealized portrait of Leonardo. The balding Euclid, seen bending over his slate in the lower right corner of the composition, resembles Raphael's good friend, the architect Bramante. In the far right corner, Raphael himself (wearing a dark hat and looking at the viewer) appears discreetly among the Aristotelians.

1 Apollo
2 Alcibiades or Alexander
3 Socrates
4 Plato (Leonardo)
5 Aristotle
6 Minerva
7 Sodoma
8 Raphael
9 Ptolemy
10 Zoroaster (Pietro Bembo?)
11 Euclid (Bramante)
12 Diogenes
13 Heraclitus (Michelangelo)
14 Parmenides, Xenocrates or Aristossenus
15 Francesco Maria della Rovere
16 Telauges
17 Pythagoras
18 Averhöes
19 Epicurus
20 Federigo Gonzaga
21 Zeno

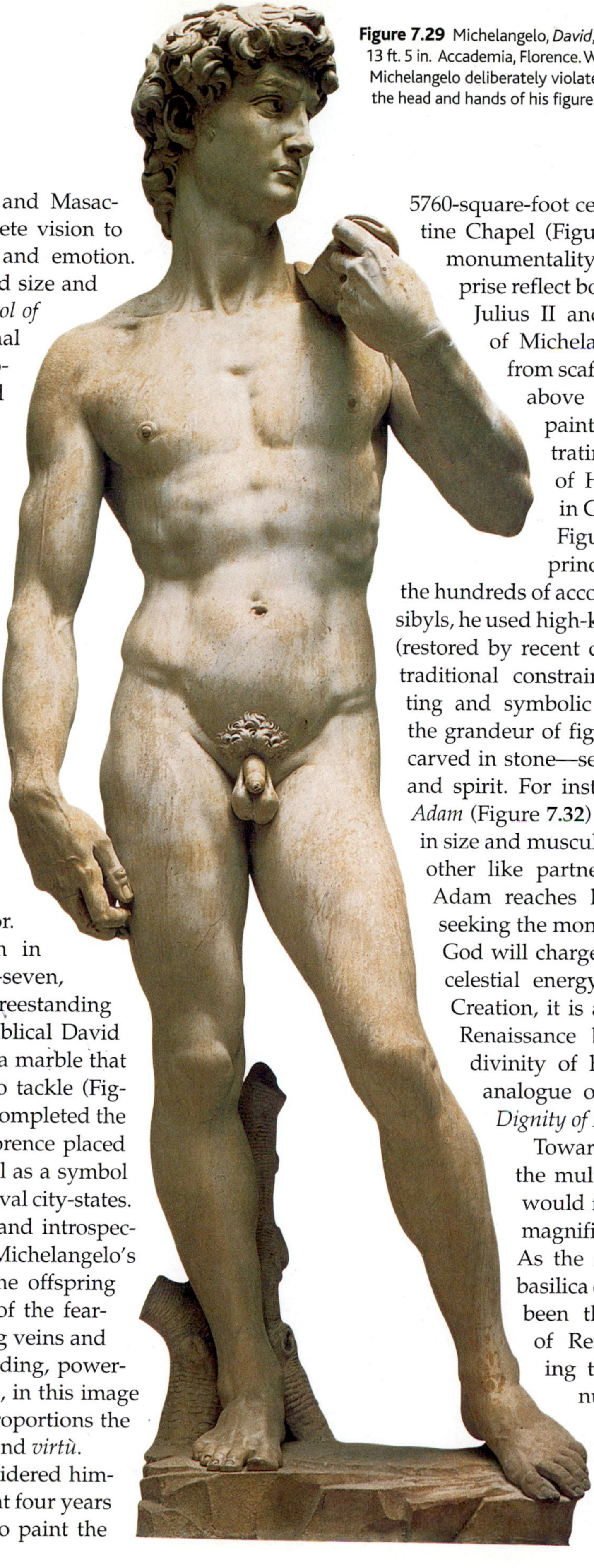

Figure 7.29 Michelangelo, *David*, 1501–1504. Marble, height 13 ft. 5 in. Accademia, Florence. While indebted to Classical tradition, Michelangelo deliberately violated Classical proportions by making the head and hands of his figure too large for the trunk.

that had begun with Giotto and Masaccio; here, Raphael gave concrete vision to a world purged of accident and emotion. Monumental in conception and size and flawless in execution, *The School of Athens* advanced a set of formal principles that came to epitomize the Grand Style: spatial clarity, decorum (that is, propriety and good taste), balance, unity of design, and grace (the last especially evident in the subtle symmetries of line and color). These principles remained touchstones for Western academic art until the late nineteenth century.

Michelangelo

The works of the High Renaissance master Michelangelo Buonarroti (1475–1564) are some of the most celebrated in Renaissance art. An architect, poet, painter, and engineer, Michelangelo regarded himself first and foremost as a sculptor. He established his reputation in Florence at the age of twenty-seven, when he undertook to carve a freestanding larger-than-life statue of the biblical David from a gigantic block of Carrara marble that no other sculptor had dared to tackle (Figure **7.29**). When Michelangelo completed the statue in 1504, the rulers of Florence placed it at the entrance to the city hall as a symbol of Florentine vigilance against rival city-states. Compared to Donatello's lean and introspective youth (see Figure 7.17), Michelangelo's *David* is a defiant presence—the offspring of a race of giants. The body of the fearless adolescent, with its swelling veins and taut muscles, is tense and brooding, powerful rather than graceful. Indeed, in this image Michelangelo drew to heroic proportions the Renaissance ideals of *terribilità* and *virtù*.

Although Michelangelo considered himself primarily a sculptor, he spent four years fulfilling a papal commission to paint the 5760-square-foot ceiling of the Vatican's Sistine Chapel (Figure **7.30**). The scope and monumentality of this landmark enterprise reflect both the ambitions of Pope Julius II and the grand aspirations of Michelangelo himself. Working from scaffolds poised some 70 feet above the floor, Michelangelo painted a vast scenario illustrating the Creation and Fall of Humankind as recorded in Genesis (1:1 through 9:27; Figure **7.31**). In the nine principal scenes, as well as in the hundreds of accompanying prophets and sibyls, he used high-keyed, clear, bright colors (restored by recent cleaning). Overthrowing traditional constraints, he minimized setting and symbolic detail and maximized the grandeur of figures that—like those he carved in stone—seem superhuman in size and spirit. For instance, in the *Creation of Adam* (Figure **7.32**) God and Adam—equal in size and muscular grace—confront each other like partners in the divine plan. Adam reaches longingly toward God, seeking the moment of fulfillment when God will charge his languid body with celestial energy. If the image depicts Creation, it is also a metaphor for the Renaissance belief in the potential divinity of humankind—the visual analogue of Pico's *Oration on the Dignity of Man.*

Toward the end of his career, the multitalented Michelangelo would further contribute to the magnificence of papal Rome. As the seat of the papacy, the basilica of Saint Peter's had long been the principal landmark of Renaissance Rome. During the sixteenth century a number of artists, including Bramante and Raphael, prepared plans for the renovation of both the cathedral's basilica and its dome,

David and Goliath	Zacharias	Judith and Holofernes
Joel	Drunkenness of Noah	Delphic Sybil
Zorobabel	The Flood	Josiah
Eritrean Sibyl	Sacrifice of Noah	Isaiah
Ozias	Temptation and Expulsion	Ezekias
Ezekiel	Creation of Eve	Cumaean Sibyl
Roboam	Creation of Adam	Asa
Persian Sibyl	Separation of Land from Water	Daniel
Salmon	Creation of Sun, Moon, Planets	Jesse
Jeremiah	Separation of Light from Darkness	Libyan Sibyl
Death of Haman	Jonah	Moses and the Serpent of Brass

Figure 7.30 (above) Michelangelo, Sistine Chapel ceiling (after cleaning), Vatican, Rome, 1508–1512. Fresco, 45 ft. x 128 ft. Lifelike Old Testament prophets and Roman sibyls appear in niches surrounding the narrative scenes in the ceiling, the whole framed by illusionistic cornices. Beginning in 1980, controversy among scholars raged for over a decade as the ceiling was cleaned and restored. Some believe the restoration was too radical; they argue that the bright colors that were uncovered were originally muted by a subtle glaze applied by Michelangelo.

Figure 7.31 (opposite) Sistine Chapel ceiling, plan of scenes (after Hibbard).

but these projects were aborted. In 1546, Michelangelo accepted the papal commission to design the dome and east end of the new cathedral; and, in the year of his death, he finally mounted an elliptically shaped dome on a huge drum ornamented with double columns of the "colossal order" (Figure **7.33**). Rising some 450 feet from the floor of the nave to the top of its tall lantern, Michelangelo's dome was heroic in size and dramatic in contour. But its enormous double shell of brick and stone proved impractical: Cracks in the substructure appeared less than ten years after completion, and the superstructure had to be bolstered repeatedly over the centuries, most recently by means of chains.

Figure 7.32 Michelangelo, *Creation of Adam* (after cleaning), Sistine Chapel ceiling, Vatican, Rome, 1508–1512. Fresco. (See also Figures 7.30 and 7.31.)

Figure 7.33 Michelangelo, dome of Saint Peter's, Vatican, Rome, ca. 1546–1564 (view from the south). Dome completed by Giacomo della Porta, 1590. The great dome inspired numerous copies, such as that of Saint Paul's Cathedral in London (see Figure 10.12) and the United States Capitol in Washington, D.C.

The High Renaissance in Venice

While the most notable paintings of the Early Renaissance came from Florence, those of the High Renaissance were produced elsewhere in Italy. Florence suffered severe political upheavals at the end of the fifteenth century as the cities of Rome, Milan, and Venice flourished. Venice, the Jewel of the Adriatic and a thriving center of trade, was a cluster of islands whose main streets consisted of canals lined with richly ornamented palaces. The pleasure-loving Venetians, governed by a merchant aristocracy, regularly imported costly tapestries, jewels, and other luxury goods from all parts of Asia. During the sixteenth century, Venice outshone all the other city-states of Italy in its ornate architecture and its taste for pageantry.

Renaissance Venice produced an art of color and light. Where the Florentines depended primarily on line as fundamental to design, the Venetians delighted in producing form by way of sumptuous color. In preference to fresco painting and tempera-on-wood panels, Venetian artists favored the oil medium, which had been perfected in Northern Europe (see pages 226–227). By this means they could apply fine color glazes to rough canvas surfaces.

The most prominent sixteenth-century Venetian artist was Tiziano Vecelli, called Titian (ca. 1488–1576). A painter of both religious and secular subjects, he produced seductive female nudes that were a favorite subject of aristocratic patrons seeking sensuous or erotic art for private enjoyment. The most famous of such commissions, the so-called *Venus of Urbino* (Figure **7.34**), was painted for Guidobaldo della Rovere, the duke of Urbino, from whom it takes its name. Titian enhanced the sensuality of the image by means of exquisitely painted surfaces: the delicate nuances of creamy skin modeled with glowing pinks, the reddish-blond locks of hair, the deep burgundies of tapestries and cushions, and the cooler bluish whites of the sheets—all bathed in a pervasive golden light. Titian, who worked almost exclusively in oils, applied paint loosely, using semitransparent glazes to build up forms whose contours seem to melt into each other, a technique best described as "painterly." He preferred broken and subtle tones of color to the flat, bright hues favored by such artists as Raphael. Titian's style, as represented in the *Venus of Urbino*, became the definitive expression of Venetian High Renaissance painting.

Figure 7.34 Titian, *Venus of Urbino*, 1538–1539. Oil on canvas, 3 ft. 11 in. x 5 ft. 5 in. Uffizi Gallery, Florence. Here, a curvaceous nude reclines on a bed in the curtained alcove of a typical upper-class Venetian palace. The tiny roses in her hand, the myrtle plant (a symbol of Venus, goddess of love and fertility) on the window sill, the faithful dog at her feet, and the servants who rummage in the nearby wedding chest all suggest impending marriage. Her pose and arresting gaze are manifestly seductive. The painting is a landmark of the new genre of eroticized female portraits that became popular in sixteenth-century Italy and, more generally, in Western art.

THE GLORIES OF THE OTTOMAN EMPIRE

IN the fourteenth century, a Central Asian clan of Muslim Turks known as Ottoman (the name derives from their tribal founder, Osman) swept westward, threatening Byzantine lands. In 1453, the highly disciplined Ottoman infantry took the Byzantine city of Constantinople (renamed Istanbul); and by 1529, at the gates of Vienna, Ottoman forces so aggressively challenged the security of the West that the French king Francis I negotiated an "unholy alliance" for peace with the great Ottoman *shah* ("king") Suleiman (1494–1566). In the course of a century, the Ottoman had created one of the most powerful empires in history, disrupting overland trade between Europe and the East, and establishing a pattern of theocratic Muslim rule that would persist in parts of Asia and North Africa until the early twentieth century.

The Ottoman Empire was the last great age of Muslim world power. Lasting until 1923, it left distinct marks on the culture and politics of those parts of the Near East that would become modern-day Turkey, Syria, Palestine, and Iraq. It also left, under the leadership of Suleiman, cultural landmarks that compare with those of the European Renaissance. Known to his subjects as "the Lawgiver" for his masterly legal reforms, Suleiman commissioned dozens of monumental, centrally planned mosques (Figure **7.35**), public baths, and palaces, most of which were enriched with intricately cut marble panels, mosaics, and glazed tiles. A goldsmith and a poet of some esteem, Suleiman initiated a Golden Age of literature and art that engaged the talents of Muslims from Jerusalem to Isfahan (in modern-day Iran). At his court in Istanbul he oversaw the activities of official court poets, manuscript illuminators, architects, and musicians. Pomp and luxury, achieved at staggering costs, were matched by a high degree of technical skill. Silk and wool carpets and prayer rugs, gold-embroidered textiles, ivory-inlaid furniture, and a wide variety of ceremonial objects encrusted with gems (Figure **7.36**) were among the riches of the king whom the Europeans rightly called "the Magnificent."

Figure 7.35 (left below) Sinan, Selimiye Mosque, Edirne, Turkey, 1568–1574. Sinan took as his model Justinian's great domed Byzantine church, Hagia Sophia (see Figure 4.13), which the Ottoman Turks turned into a mosque. He simplified his model by creating an octagon inscribed in a square—a plan that would have delighted the architects of High Renaissance Italy. The square base of the Selimiye Mosque is capped by a circular dome that is pierced by a ring of windows. The interior is lavishly ornamented with mosaics and exquisitely glazed tiles.

Figure 7.36 (right) Jeweled flask, Ottoman Empire, ca. 1500. Zinc decorated with jewels, 23 x 8⅞ in. Topkapi Palace Museum, Istanbul.

RENAISSANCE MUSIC

THE perception of the Renaissance as a time when secular music overtook ecclesiastical music may be due to the fact that after 1450 more secular music was committed to paper. The printing press encouraged the preservation and dissemination of all kinds of musical composition. With the establishment of presses in Venice in the late fifteenth century, printed books of lute music and part-books for individual instruments appeared in great numbers. Publishers also sold handbooks that offered instructions on how to play musical instruments.

During the Renaissance, music was composed by both professional and amateur musicians. Indeed, Castiglione observed that making music was the function of all well-rounded individuals. Music was an essential ingredient at intimate gatherings, court celebrations, and public festivals. And virtuosity in performance, a hallmark of Renaissance music, was common among both amateurs and professionals. Such Renaissance princes as Lorenzo de' Medici took pleasure in writing songs for the carnivals that traditionally preceded the Lenten season. On pageant wagons designed for holiday spectacles in Florence and other cities, masked singers, dancers, and mimes enacted mythological, religious, and contemporary tales in musical performance.

Josquin des Prez

One of the outstanding figures in High Renaissance music was the Flemish composer Josquin des Prez (ca. 1440–1521). Josquin served at the courts of France and Italy, including that of the papacy. A master of Masses, motets, and secular songs, he earned international recognition as "the prince of music." Josquin unified the polyphonic Mass around a single musical theme. In the Grand Style of the painter Raphael, he contrived complex designs in which melody and harmony were distributed symmetrically and with "geometric" clarity. He might give focus to a single musical phrase in the way that Raphael might center the Virgin and Child within a composition. And, in an effort to increase compositional balance, he might group voices into pairs, with the higher voices repeating certain phrases of the lower ones.

The expressive grace of Josquin's music followed from the attention he gave to the relationship between words and music. He tailored musical lines so that they followed the natural flow of the words, a device inspired perhaps by his appreciation of the Classical kinship of song and text. Josquin was among the first to practice **word painting**, the manipulation of music to convey the literal meaning of the text—as, for example, where the text describes a bird's ascent, the music might rise in pitch. Word painting characterized both the religious and secular music of the Renaissance.

In music, as in the visual arts, composers of the Renaissance valued unity of design. Josquin achieved a homogeneous musical texture by the use of **imitation**, a technique whereby a melodic fragment introduced in the first voice is repeated closely in the second, third, and fourth voices, so that one overlaps the next. This technique is illustrated in Josquin's elegant four-voice motet, *Ave Maria*.

Josquin, *Ave Maria* (ca. 1475)

The Madrigal

During the sixteenth century, the secular counterpart of the motet and the most popular type of vernacular song was the **madrigal**, a composition for three to six unaccompanied voices. Most Renaissance madrigals used four voices with one singer per part. Although occasionally an instrument replaced the "voice" in a four- to six-part madrigal, each "voice" had equal importance. Usually polyphonic in texture, the madrigal often included playful imitation and word painting. An intimate kind of musical composition, it could develop a romantic theme from a sonnet by Petrarch or give expression to a trifling and whimsical complaint.

Madrigals flourished in the courts of Italy and England, where they functioned as popular entertainments rather than as concert performances (see page 236). Although the lyrics of most madrigals were drawn largely from Italian poetry, the leading composers in this genre were Flemish. The most outstanding of these were the Netherlandish masters Adrian Willaert (1490–1562), who worked primarily in Venice, and Roland de Lassus (Orlando di Lasso, 1532–1594), productive in both church music and secular songs. Lassus, who graced princely courts throughout Renaissance Europe, left almost two hundred madrigals among his more than two thousand musical compositions. Less is known about the sixteenth-century composer Maddalena Casulana (fl. 1550), the first female to publish her music; her work included three books of madrigals, one of which enjoyed three reprinted editions before the year 1600.

Instrumental Music

Although most Renaissance music was composed to be sung, the sixteenth century made considerable advances in the development of instrumental music. Music for solo instruments was popular, with the lute (see Figure 5.20) still the favorite. In London, its acclaim warranted the importation of almost fourteen thousand lute strings in the one-year period 1567 to 1568. A wide variety of other instruments such as viols (string instruments), shawms, cromornes, cornets, trumpets, trombones, and drums were used for accompaniment and in small instrumental ensembles. Renaissance composers wrote music for small organs (popular in both private homes and princely courts) and for two other types of keyboard instrument: the **clavichord** and the **harpsichord** (also called the *spinet*, the *clavecin*, and the *virginal*—the last possibly after the "Virgin Queen," Elizabeth I of England, who was an accomplished musician).

During the late Middle Ages, instruments occasionally took the place of one or more voice parts. It was not until the Renaissance, however, that music for instruments alone regularly appeared. Instrumental compositions (performed independent of dance) developed out of dance tunes with strong rhythms and distinctive melodic lines. In fact, the earliest model for the instrumental suite was a group of dances arranged according to contrasting rhythms. Instrumental music was characterized by the same kind of complex invention that marked the vocal compositions of Josquin, and the skillful performance of difficult instrumental passages brought acclaim to both performer and composer.

Figure 7.37 A Gentleman Dancing with Two Ladies, from the *Trattato dell'Arte del Ballare* (*Treatise on the Art of Dancing*) by Guglielmo Ebreo, 1463. Bibliothèque Nationale, Paris.

Renaissance Dance

The Renaissance witnessed the first efforts to establish dance as an independent discipline. Guglielmo Ebreo (1439–1482), dancing master at the court of Urbino, wrote one of the first treatises on the art of dancing. He emphasized the importance of grace, the memorization of fixed steps, and the coordination of music and motion (Figure **7.37**). Guglielmo also choreographed a number of lively dances or *balli*—the Italian word from which the French *ballet* derives. The three favorite forms of Italian court dance were the *basse* (slow, solemn, and ceremonial), the *saltarello* (a vigorous, three-beat dance featuring graceful leaps), and the *piva* (in rapid tempo with double steps). In Guglielmo's day, such dances were performed by members of the court, rather than by professional dancers. The growing distinction between folk dance and courtly dance contributed to the development of dance as formal theatrical entertainment.

Afterword

A number of dramatic events accompanied the transition from medieval to early modern times: These include the Black Death, the Hundred Years' War, the rise of constitutional monarchy in England, and a schism that damaged the prestige of the Church. The arts displayed growing realism and a renewed interest in Classical models. In the prosperous city-states of fifteenth-century Italy, intense civic pride, the political ambitions of merchant princes, and the intellectual ideals of secular humanists combined to fuel a rebirth of Greco-Roman culture. Vibrant individualism, practical curiosity, and worldly optimism were hallmarks of the Age of the Renaissance. Florence led the way in the production of Early Renaissance literature, art, and architecture, while Rome and Venice enjoyed an outpouring of heroic High Renaissance masterpieces. Madrigals and court dances served a pleasure-loving society. Even as sixteenth-century Europe was threatened by the formidable Muslim empire of the Ottoman Turks, the spirit of rebirth spread from Italy to its northern neighbors.

Key Topics

- the Black Death
- the Hundred Years' War
- constitutional monarchy
- the decline of the Church
- new realism in the arts
- Italy and the Renaissance
- Petrarch: Classical humanism
- Castiglione: *l'uomo universale*
- Machiavelli: power politics
- the printing press
- Early Renaissance art
- Classical revivals in art
- High Renaissance art
- the artist as genius
- Venetian painting
- Renaissance music
- Renaissance dance
- Ottoman culture

RENAISSANCE TIMELINE

	HISTORICAL EVENTS	LANDMARKS IN THE VISUAL ARTS	LITERARY LANDMARKS	MUSIC LANDMARKS
1300	• Avignon Papacy (1309–1377) • Hundred Years' War (1337–1453) • Black Death (1347–1447)	• Giotto, frescoes for Arena Chapel, Padua (1303)		• *Ars nova* (ca. 1300–1400)
1350	• Peasant uprising in France (1358) • Great Schism (1378–1417) • Peasants' Revolt in England (1381)		• Petrarch, *Canzoniere* (*Songbook*) (ca. 1350) • Boccaccio, *Decameron* (1351) • Chaucer, *Canterbury Tales* (ca. 1390)	• Machaut, *Mass of Our Lady* (ca. 1350)
1400	• Joan of Arc burned at stake (1431)	• Early Renaissance in Italy (ca. 1400–1490) • Masaccio, Brancacci Chapel (ca. 1425) • Ghiberti, "Gates of Paradise," Florence (1425–1452) • Donatello, *David* (1432)	• Christine de Pisan, *Book of the City of Ladies* (1405)	
1450	• Gutenberg makes bulk printing possible (ca. 1450) • Ottoman Turks conquer Constantinople (1453)	• Brunelleschi, Florence Cathedral dome (1420–1460) • Verrocchio, *Bartolommeo Colleoni* (ca. 1481–1496) • Botticelli, *Birth of Venus* (after 1482) • Leonardo, *Last Supper* (ca. 1485–1498)	• Alberti, *Ten Books on Architecture* (1452)	
1500	• Vesalius, *Anatomy* (1543)	• High Renaissance in Italy (ca. 1490–1520) • Michelangelo, *David* (1501–1504) • Bramante, Tempietto, Rome (1502) • Leonardo, *Mona Lisa* (ca. 1503–1505) • Michelangelo, Sistine Chapel (1508–1512) • Raphael, *The School of Athens* (1509–1511) • Titian, *Venus of Urbino* (1538–1539)	• Pico, *Oration on the Dignity of Man* (1486) • Castiglione, *The Book of the Courtier* (1513–1518) • Machiavelli, *The Prince* (1513)	• Josquin, *Ave Maria* (ca. 1475) • Willaert; de Lassus; Casulana: Madrigals (ca. 1520–1600)
1550		• Michelangelo, dome of Saint Peter's, Rome (ca. 1546–1564) • Palladio, Villa Rotonda, Vicenza (1569) • Sinan, Selimiye Mosque (1568–1574)	• Vasari, *Lives* (1550)	

Figure 7.6
Giotto, *Lamentation over Jesus*, see p. 180

Figure 7.16
Sandro Botticelli, *Birth of Venus*, see p. 192

Figure 7.1
Leonardo da Vinci, *Mona Lisa*, see p. 172

Figure 7.17
Donatello, *David*, see p. 193

Chapter 8

Reform:

THE NORTHERN RENAISSANCE AND THE REFORMATION

ca. 1400–1650

Renaissance and Reformation were closely allied in Northern Europe during the fifteenth and sixteenth centuries. Unlike the Italian Renaissance, which took its primary inspiration from Classical Greek and Roman culture, the Renaissance in the North was marked by movements for religious change. The Protestant Reformation engaged humanist critics of the Roman Catholic Church, but the mood of reform also permeated the lives of individual Christians, now members of a broadening and increasingly wealthy middle class. A moralizing spirit motivated landmark works in art, literature, and music. Sometimes ominous, sometimes satiric, such works urged a revival of conscience, renewed religious faith, and a heightened attention to the spiritual life of the community. A hallmark of the Northern Renaissance was the observation of the human being, immortalized in painted portraits, but also depicted in literature as a creature whose humanity is debased by folly and—like Shakespeare's Hamlet—burdened by moral conflict.

A First Look

On July 6, 1535, the richly dressed Englishman depicted in this portrait was led to the scaffold and beheaded for high treason. Thomas More, humanist, diplomat, and author of the landmark political satire *Utopia* (see pages 219–220), had served as Lord Chancellor and adviser to King Henry VIII of England at a highly troubled moment in history: The religious reformation initiated in Germany by Martin Luther had spread to England, where the king had broken with the Church of Rome and established an independent Anglican Church. More was a staunch defender of Roman Catholicism. When he refused to take the oath that confirmed Henry's supremacy as leader of the Church of England, he was tried, convicted, and put to death. Less than ten years earlier, Germany's greatest portraitist, Hans Holbein the Younger, had traveled to England carrying letters of introduction to More from the famous Dutch humanist Desiderius Erasmus (see pages 215 and 219). The meeting produced the first domestic group portrait in history, a painting (now lost) of More's family from which Holbein extracted the half-length portrait pictured here. In the tradition of realistic portraiture begun by early Netherlandish painters, Holbein defined the sitter with linear precision and fine detail; he wears a fur collar, velvet sleeves, and a gold chain with the Tudor rose pendant signifying More's attachment to the royal court. This landmark painting captures the complex personality of the Christian humanist who, on the scaffold, declared he was "the King's good servant, but God's first."

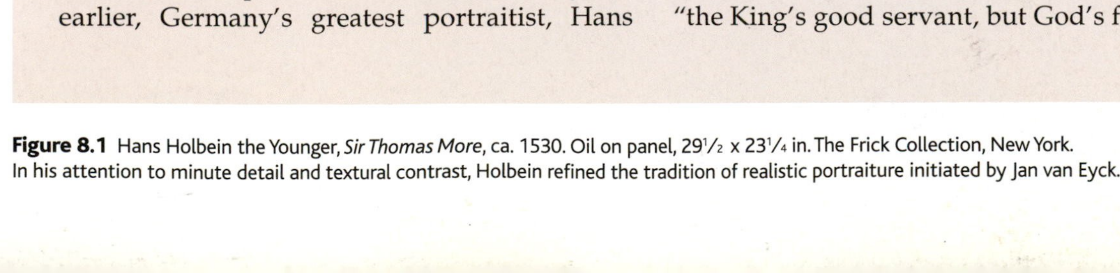

Figure 8.1 Hans Holbein the Younger, *Sir Thomas More*, ca. 1530. Oil on panel, 29½ x 23¼ in. The Frick Collection, New York. In his attention to minute detail and textural contrast, Holbein refined the tradition of realistic portraiture initiated by Jan van Eyck.

RENAISSANCE AND REFORMATION

BY the late fifteenth century, the Italian passion for Classical humanism had spread to the urban centers of the Netherlands and Germany, as well as to the burgeoning nation-states of England and France (Map **8.1**). While the North absorbed the secular spirit of the Italian Renaissance, the primary focus of the Northern Renaissance would be religious: Its twin aims were renewal and reform. For two centuries, critics throughout Europe had attacked the wealth, worldliness, and unchecked corruption of the Church of Rome. By the early fifteenth century, *anticlericalism*, that is, opposition to the influence of the Church in worldly affairs, especially politics, became closely linked to *lay piety*, a revival of devotional practice among ordinary Christians. In the Netherlands, these sentiments generated the movement known as the *devotio moderna* ("modern devotion"). Lay Brothers and Sisters of the Common Life, as they were called, organized houses in which they studied and taught Scripture. Living in the manner of Christian monks and nuns, but taking no monastic vows, these lay Christians cultivated a devotional lifestyle that fulfilled the ideals of the apostles and the church fathers. They followed the mandate of Thomas à Kempis (1380–1471), himself a Brother of the Common Life and author of the *Imitatio Christi* (*Imitation of Christ*), to put the life of Jesus into daily practice. This simply written devotional manual emphasized direct communion with God through the practice of humility, compassion, and self-renunciation. After the Bible, the *Imitatio Christi* was the most frequently published book in the Christian West until well into modern times.

Thomas à Kempis, *Imitation of Christ* (ca. 1450)

The *devotio moderna* spread quickly throughout Northern Europe, harnessing the dominant strains of anticlericalism, lay piety, and mysticism, even as it coincided with the revival of Classical studies in the newly established universities of Germany.

Christian Humanism

Although Northern humanists, like their Italian Renaissance counterparts, encouraged learning in Greek and Latin, they were more concerned with the study and translation of early Christian manuscripts than with the Classical and largely secular texts that preoccupied the Italian humanists. This critical reappraisal of religious texts is known as "Christian humanism." Christian humanists studied the Bible and the writings of the church fathers with the same intellectual fervor that the Italian humanists brought to their examination of Plato and Cicero. The efforts of these Northern scholars gave rise to a rebirth (or renaissance) that focused on the late Classical world and,

Map 8.1 Renaissance Europe, ca. 1500.

specifically, on the revival of Church life and doctrine as gleaned from early Christian literature. The Northern Renaissance put Christian humanism at the service of evangelical Christianity. This movement would feed directly into the Protestant Reformation.

The leading Christian humanist of the sixteenth century—often called "the Prince of Humanists"—was Desiderius Erasmus of Rotterdam (1466–1536; Figure **8.2**). Schooled among the Brothers of the Common Life and learned in Latin, Greek, and Hebrew, Erasmus was a superb scholar and a prolific writer—his satires are discussed later in this chapter. The first humanist to make extensive use of the printing press, he once dared a famous publisher to print his words as fast as he could write them. Erasmus was a fervent Neoclassicist—he argued that almost everything worth knowing was set forth in Greek and Latin. He was also a devout Christian who advocated a return to the basic teachings of Jesus. He criticized the Church and all Christians whose faith had been jaded by slavish adherence to doctrine and ritual. Using four different Greek manuscripts of the Gospels, he produced a critical edition of the New Testament that corrected the mistranslations in Jerome's fourth-century Latin edition. Erasmus' New Testament became the source of most sixteenth-century German and English vernacular translations of this central text of Christian humanism.

Luther and the Protestant Reformation

During the sixteenth century, papal extravagance and immorality reached new heights, and Church reform became an urgent public issue. In the territories of Germany, loosely united under the leadership of the Holy Roman emperor Charles V (1500–1558), the voices of protest were more strident than anywhere else in Europe. Across Germany, the sale of indulgences (see page 176) for the benefit of the Church of Rome—specifically for the rebuilding of Saint Peter's Cathedral—provoked harsh criticism, especially by those who saw the luxuries of the papacy as a betrayal of apostolic ideals. As with most movements of religious reform, it fell to one individual to galvanize popular sentiment. In 1505, Martin Luther (1483–1546), the son of a rural coal miner, abandoned his legal studies to become an Augustinian monk (Figure **8.3**). Thereafter, as a doctor of theology at the University of Wittenberg, he spoke out against the Church. His inflammatory sermons and essays offered radical remedies to what he called "the misery and wretchedness of Christendom."

Luther was convinced of the inherent sinfulness of humankind, but he took issue with the traditional medieval view—as promulgated, for instance, in *Everyman*—that salvation was earned through the performance of good works and grace mediated by the Church and its priesthood. Inspired by the words of Saint Paul, "the just shall live by faith" (Romans 1:17), Luther maintained that salvation was achieved only by faith in the validity of Christ's sacrifice: Human beings were saved by the unearned gift of God's grace, not by their good works on earth. The purchase of indulgences, the veneration of relics, making pilgrimages, and seeking intercession of the saints were useless. Justified by faith alone, Christians assume full responsibility for their own actions and intentions.

Figure 8.2 Albrecht Dürer, *Erasmus of Rotterdam*, 1526. Engraving, 9¾ x 7½ in. British Museum, London. A figure of great learning, the humanist is shown here at his writing desk in the quiet of his study. On a monumental tablet, a Latin inscription identifies the subject of the portrait, Erasmus of Rotterdam, and its maker, Albrecht Dürer. The Greek inscription reads, "The better image will his writings show," suggesting that the true Erasmus is to be found not in his physical person but in the products of his mind. The date, 1526, and Dürer's monogram appear below.

Figure 8.3 Lucas Cranach the Elder, *Portrait of Martin Luther*, 1533. Panel, 8 x 5¾ in. City of Bristol Museum and Art Gallery. In 1523 Luther left the Augustinian order. Two years later he married a former nun who bore him six children. Between 1530 and 1535 he published more than 150 works, some criticizing Jews, Catholics, and even other Protestants.

Ideas and Issues

LUTHER'S CHALLENGE TO THE CHURCH

"**32** Those who believe that, through letters of pardon [indulgences], they are made sure of their own salvation will be eternally damned along with their teachers.
37 Every true Christian, whether living or dead, has a share in all the benefits of Christ and of the Church, given by God, even without letters of pardon.
43 Christians should be taught that he who gives to a poor man, or lends to a needy man, does better than if he bought pardons.
44 Because by works of charity, charity increases, and the man becomes better; while by means of pardons, he does not become better, but only freer from punishment.
45 Christians should be taught that he who sees any one in need, and, passing him by, gives money for pardons, is not purchasing for himself the indulgences of the Pope but the anger of God.
62 The true treasure of the Church is the Holy Gospel of the glory and grace of God."

(from Luther, *Ninety-Five Theses*)

Q In what ways did Luther's theses challenge the authority of the Church of Rome?

In pointed criticism of the sale of indulgences, Luther posted on the door of the cathedral of Wittenberg a list of ninety-five propositions for theological dispute. The *Ninety-Five Theses*, which took the confrontational tone of the sample printed here, were put to press and circulated throughout Europe.

Luther, *Ninety-Five Theses* (1517)

Luther did not wish to destroy Catholicism but, rather, to reform it. His criticism of the institutional Church was accompanied by his assault on Church doctrine. For instance, because he found justification in Scripture for only two of the sacraments dispensed by the Catholic Church—baptism and holy communion—he rejected the other five. He attacked monasticism and clerical celibacy, but his boldest challenge to the old medieval order was his unwillingness to accept the pope as the ultimate source of religious authority. He denied that the pope was the spiritual heir to the apostle Peter and claimed that the head of the Church, like any other human being, was subject to error and correction. Christians, argued Luther, were collectively a priesthood of believers; "consecrated as priests by baptism," they needed no intermediaries between themselves and God. The ultimate source of authority in matters of faith and doctrine, held Luther, was Scripture, as interpreted by the individual Christian. To encourage the reading of the Bible among his followers, Luther translated the Old and New Testaments into German.

Luther's assertions were revolutionary because they defied both Church doctrine and the authority of the Church of Rome. In 1520, Pope Leo X issued an edict excommunicating the outspoken reformer. Luther promptly burned the edict in the presence of his students at the University of Wittenberg. The following year, he was summoned to the city of Worms in order to appear before the Diet—the German parliamentary council. Charged with heresy, Luther stubbornly refused to recant, concluding, "I cannot and will not recant anything, for to act against our conscience is neither safe for us, nor open to us. On this I take my stand. I can do no other. God help me. Amen."

The Spread of Protestantism

Luther's protests constituted an open revolt against the institution that for centuries had governed the lives of Western Christians. And that revolt was broadcast by the printing press. Perfected in Mainz in 1450 (see page 186), the printing press was essential to the success of the Reformation. Between 1518 and 1520, 300,000 printed copies of Luther's "protestant" tracts, sermons, and letters circulated throughout Europe. Within three months of its publication in 1522, the entire edition of Luther's

German Bible had sold out. Print technology proved to be the single most important factor in bringing the words of both reformers and humanists to the attention of those who could read. Not only did it provide cheap and ready access to the Bible, it also advanced the growing interest in vernacular literature, which in turn enhanced education, national pride, and the exercise of individual conscience.

Luther's defense of Christian conscience as opposed to episcopal authority worked to justify protest against other forms of dominion. In 1524, under the banner of Christian liberty, German commoners instigated a series of violent uprisings against the oppressive landholding aristocracy. The result was full-scale war, the so-called "Peasant Revolts," that resulted in the bloody defeat of thousands of peasants. Although Luther condemned the violence and brutality of the Peasant Revolts, social unrest and ideological warfare had only just begun. His denunciation of the lower-class rebels brought many of the German princes to his side; and some used their new religious allegiance as an excuse to seize and usurp Church properties and revenues within their own domains. As the floodgates of dissent opened wide, civil wars broke out between German princes who were faithful to Rome and those who called themselves Lutheran. The wars lasted for some twenty-five years, until, under the terms of the Peace of Augsburg in 1555, it was agreed that each German prince should have the right to choose the religion to be practiced within his own domain. Nevertheless, religious wars resumed in the late sixteenth century and devastated German lands for almost a century.

Calvin and Calvinism

All of Europe was affected by Luther's break with the Church. The Lutheran insistence that enlightened Christians could arrive at truth by way of Scripture led reformers everywhere to interpret the Bible for themselves. The result was the birth of many new Protestant sects, each based on its own interpretation of Scripture. The most notable of these sects was launched by John Calvin (1509–1564), a French theologian. Trained as a humanist and a lawyer, Calvin placed great emphasis on God's omnipotence. The doctrine of *predestination* was the logical consequence of Calvin's view of God as all-powerful and all-knowing, for as such, God must know who will be saved and who will be damned eternally. Further, if Christians are predestined from birth for either salvation or damnation, good works are irrelevant. Since one cannot know who is elect and who damned, Christians must live as if they are among the elect: Hard work and moral conduct must complement the unflagging glorification of God. Calvin set forth these ideas in a legalistic instrument entitled the *Institutes of the Christian Religion*, which became the most widely read theological work of its time.

Calvin, ***Institutes of the Christian Religion*** **(1536)**

Ideas and Issues

CALVIN: PREDESTINATION

"By predestination we mean the eternal decree of God, by which he determined with himself whatever he wished to happen with regard to every man. All are not created on equal terms, but some are preordained to eternal life, others to eternal damnation; and, accordingly, as each has been created for one or other of these ends, we say that he has been predestined to life or to death. . . . We say, then, that Scripture clearly proves this much, that God by his eternal and immutable counsel determined once for all those whom it was his pleasure one day to admit to salvation, and those whom, on the other hand, it was his pleasure to doom to destruction. We maintain that this counsel, as regards the elect, is founded on his free mercy, without any respect to human worth, while those whom he dooms to destruction are excluded from access to life by a just and blameless, but at the same time incomprehensible judgment. . . ."

(from Calvin, *Institutes of the Christian Religion*)

Q Do you find Calvin's world view optimistic or pessimistic? How does he envision God?

Forced to leave Catholic France, Calvin settled in Geneva, Switzerland, where he set up a government in which elected officials, using the Bible as the supreme law, ruled the community. There, under strict civic authority, Genevans were prohibited from dancing, drinking, swearing, gambling, and all forms of public display. While one's status was only known by God, Calvinists might manifest that they were among the elect by their moral rectitude and their hard work on earth. Among Calvinists, wealth was taken to be a sign of God's favor, and the "work ethic" was held in high esteem. Long after Calvin's death, Calvinism would have a far-reaching influence in such places as England, Scotland, and America.

Anabaptism

In nearby Zürich, a radical wing of Protestantism emerged: The Anabaptists (given this name by those who opposed their practice of "rebaptizing" adult Christians) rejected all seven of the sacraments (including infant baptism) as sources of God's grace. Placing total emphasis on Christian conscience and the voluntary acceptance of Jesus as the Christ, the Anabaptists called for the abolition of the Mass and the complete separation of Church and state. Holding individual responsibility and personal liberty as fundamental ideals, they were among the first Westerners to offer religious sanction for political disobedience. Many Anabaptist reformers met death at the hands of local governments—males were burned at the stake and females were usually drowned. English offshoots of the Anabaptists—the Baptists and the Quakers—would come to follow Anabaptist precepts, including the rejection of religious ritual (and imagery) and a fundamentalist approach to Scripture.

The Anglican Church

In England, the Tudor monarch Henry VIII (1491–1547) broke with the Roman Catholic Church and established a Church under his own leadership. Political expediency colored the king's motives: Henry was determined to leave England with a male heir, but when eighteen years of marriage to Catherine of Aragon produced only a daughter, he attempted to annul the marriage and take a new wife. The pope refused, prompting the king—formerly a staunch supporter of the Catholic Church—to break with Rome. In 1526, Henry VIII declared himself head of the Church in England. His actions led to years of dispute and hostility between Roman Catholics and Anglicans (members of the new English Church). By the mid-sixteenth century, the consequences of Luther's protests were evident: The religious unity of Western Christendom was shattered forever. Social and political upheaval had become the order of the day.

Religious Persecution and Witch-Hunts

For well over two hundred years following the Protestant Reformation, religious persecution and religious warfare were commonplace. Catholics persecuted Protestants, Protestants persecuted Catholics, and the Protestant sects maligned each other. Religious fanaticism transformed many Christians into foes who perceived the faith as a contest between God and Satan. Luther, Calvin, and many other learned people regarded Satan as a figure to be reckoned with on a daily basis—Luther is said to have thrown an inkpot at the devil for disturbing his work. Indeed, the witch-hunts that infested Europe (and especially Germany) during the sixteenth century were fueled by the popular belief that the devil was actively involved in human affairs.

Belief in witches dates back to humankind's earliest societies; however, the practice of persecuting witches did not begin until the late fourteenth century. The first massive persecutions occurred at the end of the fifteenth century and reached their peak approximately one hundred years later. Two theologians published the *Malleus Maleficarum* (*Witches' Hammer*), an encyclopedia that described the nature of witches, their collusion with the devil, and the ways by which they were to be recognized and punished. Since women were traditionally regarded as inherently susceptible to the devil's temptations, they became the primary victims of this mass hysteria. Women—especially single, old, and eccentric women—constituted four-fifths of the witches executed between the fifteenth and early seventeenth centuries. Among Northern European artists, witches and witchcraft became favorite subjects (Figure **8.4**). The witchcraft craze of this period dramatizes the prevailing gap between Christian humanism and rationalism on the one hand and barbarism and superstition on the other.

***Malleus Maleficarum* (*Witches' Hammer*) (1484)**

Figure 8.4 Hans Baldung ("Grien"), *Witches*, 1510. Chiaroscuro woodcut, $15\frac{7}{8} \times 10\frac{1}{4}$ in. Three witches, sitting under the branches of a dead tree, perform a black Mass. One lifts the chalice, while another mocks the Host by elevating the body of a dead toad. An airborne witch rides backward on a goat, a symbol of the devil.

SIXTEENTH-CENTURY LITERATURE

Erasmus

European literature of the sixteenth century was marked by heightened individualism and a progressive inclination to clear away the last remnants of medieval orthodoxy. It was, in many ways, a literature of protest and reform, and one whose dominant themes reflect the tension between medieval and modern ideas. European writers were especially concerned with the discrepancies between the noble ideals of Classical humanism and the ignoble realities of human behavior. Religious rivalries and the horrors of war, witch-hunts, and religious persecution all seemed to contradict the optimistic view that the Renaissance had inaugurated a more enlightened phase of human self-consciousness. It is not surprising, then, that satire, the literary genre that points up the contradictions between real and ideal situations (see page 72), was especially popular during the sixteenth century. By means of satire, Northern Renaissance writers held up prevailing abuses to ridicule, thus implying the need for reform.

Desiderius Erasmus, whom we met earlier in this chapter (see page 215), won the respect of scholars throughout Europe for his learned letters and treatises. However, his single most popular work was *The Praise of Folly*, a satiric oration attacking a wide variety of human foibles, including greed, intellectual pomposity, and pride. *The Praise of Folly* went through more than two dozen editions in Erasmus' lifetime. It influenced many other humanists, including his lifelong friend and colleague Thomas More (see Figure 8.1), to whom it was dedicated (in Latin, *moria* means "folly"). The following excerpt offers some idea of Erasmus' keen wit as applied to a typical Northern Renaissance theme: the vast gulf between human fallibility and human perfectibility. The excerpt opens with the image of the world as a stage, a favorite metaphor of sixteenth-century painters and poets—not the least of whom was William Shakespeare. Folly, the allegorical figure who is the speaker in the piece, compares life to a comedy in which the players assume various roles: In the course of the drama (she observes), one may come to play the parts of both servant and king. The lecturer then describes each of a number of roles (or disciplines), such as medicine, law, and so on, in terms of its affinity with folly. Erasmus' most searing words were reserved for theologians and church dignitaries, but his insights expose more generally (and timelessly) the frailties of all human beings:

Erasmus, *The Praise of Folly* (1516)

> Now what else is the whole life of mortals but a sort of comedy, in which the various actors, disguised by various costumes and masks, walk on and play each one his part, until the manager waves them off the stage? Moreover, this manager frequently bids the same actor go back in a different costume, so that he who has but lately played the king in scarlet now acts the flunkey in patched clothes. Thus all things are presented by shadows; yet this play is put on in no other way. . . .
>
> [The disciplines] that approach nearest to common sense, that is, to folly, are held in highest esteem. Theologians are starved, naturalists find cold comfort, astrologers are mocked, and logicians are slighted. . . . Within the profession of medicine, furthermore, so far as any member is eminently unlearned, impudent, or careless, he is valued the more, even in the chambers of belted earls. For medicine, especially as now practiced by many, is but a subdivision of the art of flattery, no less truly than is rhetoric. Lawyers have the next place after doctors, and I do not know but that they should have first place; with great unanimity the philosophers—not that I would say such a thing myself—are wont to ridicule the law as an ass. Yet great matters and little matters alike are settled by the arbitrament of these asses. They gather goodly freeholds with broad acres, while the theologian, after poring over chestfuls of the great corpus of divinity, gnaws on bitter beans, at the same time manfully waging war against lice and fleas. As those arts are more successful which have the greatest affinity with folly, so those people are by far the happiest who enjoy the privilege of avoiding all contact with the learned disciplines, and who follow nature as their only guide, since she is in no respect wanting, except as a mortal wishes to transgress the limits set for his status. Nature hates counterfeits; and that which is innocent of art gets along far the more prosperously.

More

In England, Erasmus' friend, the scholar and statesman Sir Thomas More (1478–1535), served as chancellor to King Henry VIII at the time of Henry's break with the Catholic Church. Like Erasmus, More was a Christian humanist and a man of conscience. He denounced the modern evils of acquisitive capitalism and religious fanaticism and championed religious tolerance and Christian charity. As explained in A First Look (see page 213), his refusal to support the king as head of the Anglican Church led to his execution.

More's *Utopia* (the Greek word meaning both "no place" and "a good place") is a classic political satire on European statecraft and society. The first literary description of an ideal state since Plato's *Republic*, it was inspired, in part, by accounts of wondrous lands reported by sailors returning from the "New World" across the Atlantic (see page 240). More's fictional island ("discovered" by a fictional explorer-narrator) is a socialistic state in which goods and property are shared, war and personal vanities are held in contempt, learning is available to all citizens (except slaves), and freedom of religion is absolute. Work, which More (like

More, *Utopia* (1516)

Calvin) regarded as essential to moral and communal well-being, is limited to six hours a day. More's ideal society differs from Plato's in that each citizen, rather than society's guardians, bears full responsibility for the preservation of social justice. In this commonwealth, natural reason, benevolence, and scorn for material wealth ensure peace and social harmony. More's Utopians have little use for precious metals, jewels, and the "trifles" that drive men to war. Here More draws the ironic contrast between the ideal community and his own Christian commonwealth: that is, while More's Utopians are not Christian, they are guided by the Christian principles of charity and humility.

Cervantes

The Spaniard Miguel de Cervantes (1547–1616) is a towering figure in sixteenth-century literature, a writer whose landmark novel, *Don Quixote*, was translated from Spanish into more languages than any work other than the Hebrew Bible. Like More, Cervantes treated human failings in a satiric manner. But unlike More (and Erasmus), Cervantes wrote in the vernacular—the language of everyday speech. Cervantes' *Don Quixote* recounts the adventures of a chivalrous knight who confronts reality through the lens of personal fantasy. Although the Japanese had been writing novels since the eleventh century (see page 129), *Don Quixote* is among the earliest Western examples of the *picaresque novel*, a genre of prose fiction in which a series of episodes narrate the comic misadventures of a roguish hero who lives by his wits in a corrupt society.

Cervantes, *Don Quixote* (1613)

The hero of the novel, the fifty-year-old Alonso Quixado, escapes the hypocrisy and worldliness of his own age by immersing himself in the literature of the past. Assuming the title Don Quixote de la Mancha, he sets out to defend the ideals glorified in medieval books of chivalry and romance. (Cervantes may have conceived this theme when he himself fought in the last Crusade against the Muslim Turks.) Seeking to right all social and political wrongs, the deluded Don pursues a series of heroic misadventures, including an encounter with a hostile army (actually a flock of sheep) and an armed attack on a horde of giants (in actuality, windmills). Cervantes offers up the exploits of the would-be knight and his faithful sidekick, Sancho Panza, as a tragicomedy, in effect both humorous and poignant. When his grand illusions are ultimately exposed, the disillusioned hero laments, "This world is nothing but schemes and plots, all working at cross-purposes."

The following excerpt, which recounts the Don's illusory combat with thirty "wild giants," captures the flavor of Cervantes' prose. It is also the inspiration for the English expression "tilting at windmills," which describes fighting futile battles or imaginary enemies.

The great success won by our brave Don Quixote in his dreadful, unimaginable encounter with two windmills, plus other honorable events well worth remembering

Just then, they came upon thirty or forty windmills, which (as it happens) stand in the fields of Montiel, and as soon as Don Quixote saw them he said to his squire:

"Destiny guides our fortunes more favorably than we could have expected. Look there, Sancho Panza, my friend, and see those thirty or so wild giants, with whom I intend to do battle and to kill each and all of them, so with their stolen booty we can begin to enrich ourselves. This is noble, righteous warfare, for it is wonderfully useful to God to have such an evil race wiped from the face of the earth."

"What giants?" asked Sancho Panza.

"The ones you can see over there," answered his master, "with the huge arms, some of which are very nearly two leagues long."

"Now look, your grace," said Sancho, "what you see over there aren't giants, but windmills, and what seem to be arms are just their sails, that go around in the wind and turn the millstone."

"Obviously," replied Don Quixote, "you don't know much about adventures. Those are giants—and if you're frightened, take yourself away from here and say your prayers, while I go charging into savage and unequal combat with them."

Saying which, he spurred his horse, Rocinante, paying no attention to the shouts of Sancho Panza, his squire, warning him that without any question it was windmills and not giants he was going to attack. So utterly convinced was he they were giants, indeed, that he neither heard Sancho's cries nor noticed, close as he was, what they really were, but charged on, crying:

"Flee not, oh cowards and dastardly creatures, for he who attacks you is a knight alone and unaccompanied."

Montaigne

The French humanist Michel de Montaigne (1533–1592) was neither a satirist nor a reformer, but an educated aristocrat who believed in the paramount importance of cultivating good judgment. Trained in Latin, Montaigne was one of the leading proponents of Classical learning in Renaissance France. He earned universal acclaim as the father of the personal essay, a short piece of expository prose that examines a single subject or idea. The essay—the word comes from the French *essayer* ("to try")—is a vehicle for probing or "trying out" ideas. Indeed Montaigne regarded his ninety-four vernacular French essays as studies in autobiographical reflection—in them, as he confessed, he portrayed himself. Montaigne's essays constitute the literary high-water mark of the French Renaissance. An expression of reasoned inquiry into human values, they address such universal subjects as virtue, friendship, old age, idleness, and education. They defend a learning method that poses questions instead of providing answers. In his essay on education, Montaigne criticizes teachers who pour information into their students'

Montaigne, *Essays* (1580–1588)

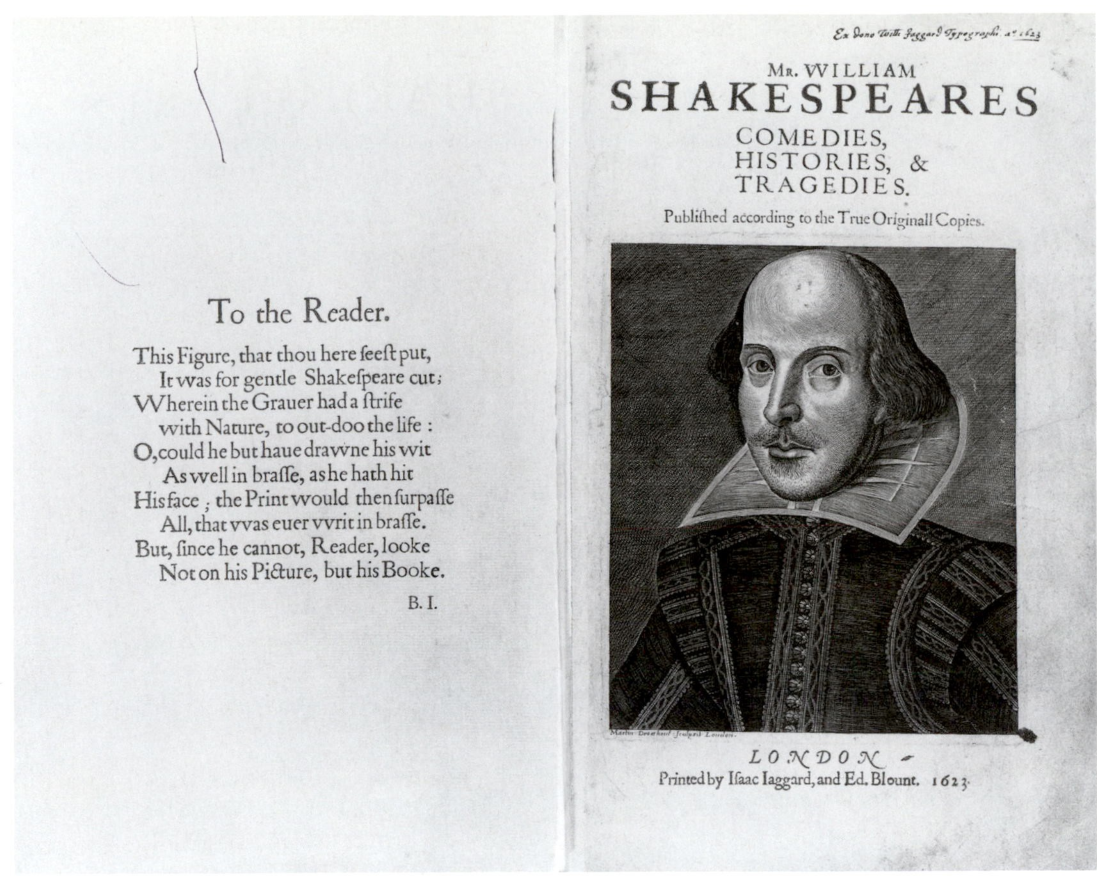

To the Reader.

This Figure, that thou here ſeeſt put,
It was for gentle Shakeſpeare cut;
Wherein the Grauer had a ſtrife
with Nature, to out-doo the life :
O, could he but haue drawne his wit
As well in braſſe, as he hath hit
His face ; the Print would then ſurpaſſe
All, that vvas euer vvrit in braſſe.
But, ſince he cannot, Reader, looke
Not on his Picture, but his Booke.

B. I.

MR. WILLIAM
SHAKESPEARES
COMEDIES,
HISTORIES, &
TRAGEDIES.
Publiſhed according to the True Originall Copies.

LONDON
Printed by Iſaac Iaggard, and Ed. Blount. 1623.

Figure 8.5 Droeshout, first Folio edition portrait of William Shakespeare, 1623. Folger Shakespeare Library, Washington, D.C.

ears ("as though they were pouring water into a funnel"), then demand that students repeat what is taught rather than exercise original thought. Montaigne balances his own opinions against those of Classical Latin writers, whom he quotes freely. He advances a wide range of fundamentally humanistic ideas: for instance, that contradiction is a characteristic human trait; that self-examination is the essence of true education; and that skepticism and open-mindedness are sound alternatives to dogmatic opinion. And, in an age when Europeans first encountered the customs and beliefs of non-Christian populations in Africa and the Americas (see Chapter 9), a forward-looking Montaigne questioned the superiority of any one culture over another.

Shakespeare

No assessment of the Northern Renaissance would be complete without some consideration of the literary giant of the age: William Shakespeare (1564–1616; Figure **8.5**). A poet of unparalleled genius, Shakespeare emerged during the Golden Age of England under the rule of Elizabeth I (1533–1603). He produced thirty-seven plays—comedies, tragedies, romances, and histories—as well as 154 sonnets and other poems. These works, generally considered to be the greatest examples of English literature, have exercised an enormous influence on the evolution of the English language and the development of the Western literary tradition. (The complete works of Shakespeare are available at the website http://shakespeare.mit.edu/works.html)

Little is known about Shakespeare's early life and formal education. He grew up in Stratford-upon-Avon in the English Midlands, married Anne Hathaway (eight years his senior) with whom he had three children, and moved to London sometime before 1585. In London he formed an acting company, the Lord Chamberlain's Company (also called "the King's Men"), in which he was shareholder, actor, and playwright. Like fifteenth-century Florence, sixteenth-century London (and especially the queen's court) supported a galaxy of artists, musicians, and writers who enjoyed a mutually stimulating interchange of ideas. Shakespeare's theater company performed at the court of Elizabeth I and that of her successor, James I (1566–1625), but its main activities took place in the Globe Playhouse (see Figure 8.7).

While Shakespeare is best known for his plays, he also wrote some of the most beautiful sonnets ever produced in the English language. Indebted to Petrarch (see page 184), Shakespeare nevertheless devised most of his own sonnets in a form that would come to be called "the English sonnet": **quatrains** (four-line stanzas) with alternate rhymes, followed by a concluding **couplet**. Shakespeare's sonnets employ—and occasionally mock—such

Figure 8.6 George Gower, *"Armada" Portrait of Elizabeth I*, ca. 1588. Oil on panel, 3 ft. 6 in. x 4 ft. 5 in. Woburn Abbey Collection, England. This image of the bewigged and bejeweled queen is one of the most famous of the many portraits of Queen Elizabeth. It was painted to commemorate the English victory over Spain in 1588. Symbolic of England's maritime ambitions, a globe of the world sits under Elizabeth's right hand.

traditional Petrarchan themes as blind devotion, the value of friendship, and love's enslaving power. Some, like Sonnet 18, reflect the typically Renaissance (and Classical) concern for immortality achieved through art and love. In this sonnet, Shakespeare addresses his lover by way of an extended metaphor: Like the summer day, his beloved will fade and die. But, explains the poet, she will remain eternal in and through the sonnet; for, so long as the poem survives, so will the object of its inspiration remain alive:

Shakespeare, *Sonnets* (1609)

Shall I compare thee to a summer's day?
Thou art more lovely and more temperate.
Rough winds do shake the darling buds of May,
And summer's lease[1] hath all too short a date.

Sometime too hot the eye[2] of heaven shines,
And often is his gold complexion dimm'd;
And every fair from fair sometime declines,[3]
By chance or nature's changing course untrimm'd,[4]

But thy eternal summer shall not fade
Nor lose possession of that fair thou ow'st,
Nor shall Death brag thou wand'rest in his shade,
When in eternal lines to time thou grow'st.[5]

So long as men can breathe or eyes can see,
So long lives this[6] and this gives life to thee.

[1] Allotted time.

[2] The sun.

[3] Beautiful thing from beauty.

[4] Stripped of beauty.

[5] Your fame will grow as time elapses.

[6] The sonnet itself.

The Shakespearean Stage

Secular drama, Renaissance England's landmark contribution to the humanistic tradition, was reborn in an era of high confidence: In 1588, the English navy defeated a Spanish fleet of 130 ships known as the "Invincible Armada." This event, a victory as well for the forces of Protestantism over Catholicism, encouraged a sense of national pride and a renewed confidence in the ambitious policies of the "Protestant Queen" Elizabeth I (Figure **8.6**). In its wake followed a period of high prosperity and commercial expansion. Stirred by a revival of interest in English history, Elizabethan poets adapted Classical and medieval literary traditions and texts to the writing of contemporary plays. The plots of these secular entertainments were based in chronicles, contemporary life, or legend, and the characters were comic, moral, or heroic.

Elizabethan London played host to groups of traveling actors (or "strolling players") who performed in public spaces or for generous patrons. Theaters, along with brothels and taverns, were generally relegated to the suburbs, but in the late sixteenth century a number of playhouses were built along the River Thames across from the city of London. Begun in 1599, the Globe, which held between two and three thousand spectators, offered all levels of society access to professional theater (Figure **8.7**). The open-air structure consisted of three tiers of galleries and standing room for commoners (known as "groundlings") at the cost of only a penny—one-sixth of the price for a seat in the covered gallery. Stage props were basic, but costumes were favored, and essential for the male actors who played all the female roles—women were not permitted on the public stage. Performances were held in the afternoon and advertised by flying a flag above the theater roof. A globe, the signature logo, embellished Shakespeare's theater, along with a sign that read, *"Totus mundus agit histrionem"* (loosely, "All the World's a Stage"). The bustling crowd that attended the theater—some of whom stood through two or more hours of performance—often ate and drank as they enjoyed the most cosmopolitan entertainment of their time.

Figure 8.7 Globe Playhouse, London, 1599–1613. Architectural reconstruction by C. Walter Hodges, 1948. British Museum, London. The projecting rectangular stage, some 40 feet wide, included balconies (for musicians and special scenes, such as required in *Romeo and Juliet*), exits to dressing areas, and a trapdoor (used for rising spirits and for burial scenes, such as required in *Hamlet*). A reconstruction of this theater, known as "Shakespeare's Globe," opened in 1997. It is located on the south bank of the River Thames.

Shakespeare's Plays

In Shakespeare's time, theater did not rank as high as poetry as a literary genre. As popular entertainment, however, Shakespeare's plays earned high acclaim in London's theatrical community. Thanks to the availability of printed editions, the Bard of Stratford was familiar with the ancient Roman tragedies of Seneca and the comedies of Plautus and Terence. He knew the popular medieval morality plays that addressed the contest between good and evil, as well as the popular improvisational form of Italian comic theater known as the *commedia dell'arte*, which made use of stock or stereotypical characters. All of these resources came to shape the texture of his plays. For his plots, Shakespeare drew largely on Classical history, medieval chronicles, and contemporary romances.

Like Machiavelli, Shakespeare was an avid reader of ancient and medieval history, as well as a keen observer of his own complex age; but the stories his sources provided became mere springboards for the exploration of human nature. His history plays, such as *Henry V* and *Richard III*, celebrate England's medieval past and its rise to power under the Tudors. The concerns of these plays, however, are not exclusively historical; rather, they explore the ways in which rulers behave under pressure: the weight of kingly responsibilities on mere humans and the difficulties of reconciling royal obligations and human aspirations.

Shakespeare, *Henry V*; *Richard III* (1593–1600)

Shakespeare's comedies, which constitute about one-half of his plays, deal with such popular themes as the battle of the sexes, rivalry among lovers, and mistaken identities. But here too, in such plays as *Much Ado About Nothing*, *All's Well That Ends Well*, and *The Taming of the Shrew*, it is Shakespeare's characters—their motivations exposed, their weaknesses and strengths laid bare—that command our attention.

Shakespeare, *Much Ado About Nothing*; *All's Well That Ends Well*; *The Taming of the Shrew* (1593–1602)

It is in the tragedies, and especially the tragedies of his mature career—*Hamlet*, *Macbeth*, *Othello*, and *King Lear*—that Shakespeare achieved the concentration of thought and language that have made him the greatest English playwright of all time. Jealousy, greed, ambition, insecurity, and self-deception are among the many human failings that Shakespeare examined in his plays, but in these last tragedies they became definitive: They drive the action of the play. Indeed, these plays are the most significant evidence of the Renaissance effort to probe the psychological forces that motivate human action.

Shakespeare, *Hamlet*; *Macbeth*; *Othello*; *King Lear* (1600–1606)

Remarkable too is the brilliance of the language with which Shakespeare brings his characters to life. Despite occasional passages in prose and rhymed verse, his plays were written in **blank verse**. This verse form was popular among Renaissance humanists because, like Classical poetry, it was unrhymed, and it closely approximated the rhythms of vernacular speech. In Shakespeare's hands, the English language took on a breadth of expression and a measure of eloquence that has rarely been matched to this day.

Hamlet (1602), the world's most quoted play, belongs to the popular Renaissance genre of revenge tragedy; the story itself came to Shakespeare from the history of medieval Denmark. Hamlet, the young heir to the throne of Denmark, learns that his uncle has murdered his father and married his mother in order to assume the throne; the burden of avenging his father falls squarely on the son's shoulders. The arc of the play follows Hamlet's inability to take action—his melancholic lack of resolve that, in the long run, results in the deaths of his mother (Gertrude), his betrothed (Ophelia), her father (Polonius), the king (Claudius), and, finally, Hamlet himself.

Shakespeare's Hamlet differs from the heroes of ancient and medieval times: He lacks the sense of obligation to country and community, the passionate religious loyalties, and the clearly defined spiritual values that drive such heroes as Gilgamesh, Achilles, and Roland. He represents a new, more modern personality—one whose self-questioning disposition and brooding skepticism more closely resemble a modern existential antihero (see page 419). Though tortured by doubt and sunk in melancholy, he shares the humanist view that human nature is freely self-formed by human beings themselves. Hamlet first marvels:

> What a piece of work is a man! How noble in reason!
> How infinite in faculty! In form and moving how
> express and admirable! In action how like an angel! In
> apprehension how like a god! The beauty of the world!
> The paragon of animals,

But then, he concludes on a note of utter skepticism.

> And yet, to me, what is this quintessence of dust?
>
> (Act II, Scene 2)

It is in the oral examination of his innermost thoughts—the *soliloquy*—that Hamlet most fully reveals himself. In a painful process of self-examination, he questions the motives for meaningful action and the impulses that prevent him from action, but at the same time he contemplates the futility of all human action:

> To be, or not to be, that is the question:
> Whether 'tis nobler in the mind to suffer
> The slings[1] and arrows of outrageous fortune,
> Or to take arms against a sea of troubles
> And by opposing end them. To die, to sleep—
> No more—and by a sleep to say we end
> The heartache and the thousand natural shocks
> That flesh is heir to. 'Tis a consummation

Beyond the West

JAPANESE THEATER

The oldest form of Japanese theater, Nō drama, evolved in the fourteenth century from performances in song, dance, and mime. Like Greek drama, the Nō play treated serious themes drawn from a legacy of history and literature. Nō drama was little concerned with character development or the realistic reenactment of actual events. Rather, it animated a familiar theme by means of a formalized selection of text, gestures, dance, and music (usually performed with flute and drum). A chorus sitting at the side of the square wooden stage might express the thoughts of the actors. As in ancient Greece, all the roles in a Nō drama were performed by men. Elegant costumes, and masks, often carved and painted, were used to portray individual characters (Figure **8.8**). A single program of Nō drama (which even to this day lasts some six or more hours) consisted of a group of plays, with selections from each of three types: warrior-plays, god-plays, and woman-plays. Comic interludes were provided between the plays to lighten the serious mood.

In the early sixteenth century, as Japan emerged from a feudal age, the new merchant class that occupied Japan's growing commercial cities demanded new forms of entertainment. From the "floating world" (*ukiyo*) of city culture—the world of sensual pleasures associated with the theaters and brothels of these towns—came a new form of staged performance known as ***kabuki***. In its late fifteenth-century origins, *kabuki* (literally, "song-dance-art") was originally a female performance genre. But within twenty years of its appearance, in 1616, the Japanese government issued an edict that forbade women to appear on stage. Thereafter, performances featuring dance, mime, and song were staged by male actors in elaborate costumes, wigs, and makeup. Dramas that drew their plots from history, myth, puppet plays, and daily life took place on a revolving stage that featured a long ramp leading from the audience to the rear of the stage (Figure **8.9**). Elegant backdrops and scenic effects embellished the performance. *Kabuki* theater flourished as day-long entertainment that, like Nō drama, included three to five plays, interrupted by intermissions to allow the audience to visit local teahouses and restaurants.

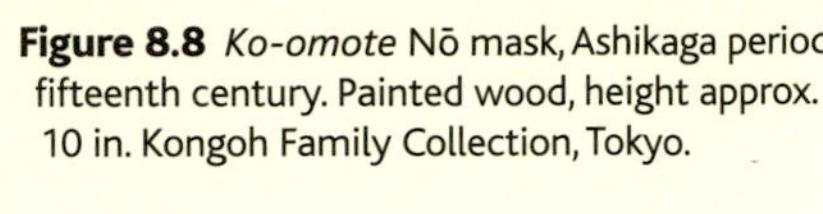

Figure 8.8 *Ko-omote* Nō mask, Ashikaga period, fifteenth century. Painted wood, height approx. 10 in. Kongoh Family Collection, Tokyo.

The similarities between Shakespearean theater in the West and Japanese theater in the East are numerous: Both addressed an audience whose worldly interests were tied to commercial advantage and urban life. Both took place in the pleasure quarters of the city, and both were subject to governmental restrictions. Both were acted by all-male casts, who performed various play types, such as history plays and domestic comedies. Japanese theater, however, was (and remains) more formally stylized than Shakespearean theater. *Kabuki* dialog is half-spoken and half-sung (often punctuated by woodwind or percussion instruments), and movements are choreographed like dances. Moreover, the Japanese play rarely seeks (as do most Shakespearean plays) to explore the psychological development of the characters, which are generally stock figures.

Despite the influence of European theater, *kabuki* survives today as a vibrant performance artform that—like Shakespearean theater—constitutes a repository of the collective imagination and a landmark in the dramatic arts.

Figure 8.9 Masanobu(?), *Kabuki* stage, ca. 1740. Colored woodblock print. British Museum, London.

Devoutly to be wished. To die, to sleep;
To sleep, perchance to dream. Ay, there's the rub,[2]
For in that sleep of death what dreams may come,
When we have shuffled[3] off this mortal coil,[4]
Must give us pause. There's the respect[5]
That makes calamity of so long life.[6]
For who would bear the whips and scorns of time,
Th' oppressor's wrong, the proud man's contumely,[7]
The pangs of disprized[8] love, the law's delay,
The insolence of office,[9] and the spurns[10]
That patient merit of th' unworthy takes,[11]
When he himself might his quietus[12] make
With a bare bodkin?[13] Who would fardels[14] bear,
To grunt and sweat under a weary life,
But that the dread of something after death,
The undiscovered country from whose bourn[15]
No traveler returns, puzzles the will,
And makes us rather bear those ills we have
Than fly to others that we know not of?
Thus conscience does make cowards of us all;
And thus the native hue[16] of resolution
Is sicklied o'er with the pale cast[17] of thought,
And enterprises of great pitch[18] and moment[19]
With this regard[20] their currents[21] turn awry
And lose the name of action.

(Act III, Scene 1)

Hamlet's internal conflict is central to the play's message: Fate may assign us a role that is inconsistent with our basic character. In Hamlet's case, a sensitive and intelligent Renaissance prince is called upon to be a ruthless avenger. The result is high tragedy.

[1] Missiles.

[2] Literally, an obstacle in the game of bowls.

[3] Sloughed, cast.

[4] Turmoil.

[5] Consideration.

[6] So long-lived, something we willingly endure for so long (also suggesting that long life is itself a calamity).

[7] Insolent abuse.

[8] Unvalued.

[9] Officialdom.

[10] Insults.

[11] Receives from unworthy persons.

[12] Acquittance; here, death.

[13] A mere dagger, unsheathed.

[14] Burdens.

[15] Frontier, boundary.

[16] Natural color, complexion.

[17] Tinge, shade of color.

[18] Height (as of a falcon's flight).

[19] Importance.

[20] Respect, consideration.

[21] Courses.

NORTHERN ART

PRIOR to the Protestant Reformation, in the cities of Northern Europe, a growing middle class joined princely rulers and Church patrons in demanding artworks that treated traditional religious themes. Wealthy middle-class patrons also commissioned portraits that—like those painted by their Italian counterparts (see Chapter 7)—faithfully preserved their physical appearance. In contrast with Italy, however, fifteenth-century artists in the Netherlands and Germany were relatively unfamiliar with Greco-Roman culture. They did not adopt, for instance, the Classical architectural ideals of their southern neighbors. Nevertheless, in both painting and the new art of printmaking, they moved in the direction of detailed realism, already evident in the illuminated manuscripts of the Limbourg Brothers (see Figure 7.4). They brought to their work a deep attachment to the physical world, a renewed zeal for devotional images, and a fondness for moralizing themes.

Jan van Eyck

The pioneer in early Netherlandish art was the Flemish painter Jan van Eyck (ca. 1380–1441), who was reputed to have perfected the art of oil painting. Jan's application of thin, translucent glazes of colored pigments bound with linseed oil achieved the impression of dense, atmospheric space and simulated the naturalistic effects of light reflecting off the surfaces of objects—effects that were almost impossible to achieve in fresco or tempera. Lacking knowledge of linear perspective, Jan was nevertheless able to achieve an extraordinary level of realism in the miniatures he executed for religious manuscripts and in his panel paintings. His oil technique brought him fame in his own lands, as well as in Italy and Spain.

In 1434 Jan painted a landmark full-length double portrait, the first in Western art to portray a secular couple in a domestic interior (Figure **8.10**). Long thought to be a document recording the marriage of the Italian merchant Giovanni Nicolas Arnolfini to Jeanne Cenami, the so-called *"Arnolfini Marriage"* has been the object of debate among scholars who question both its purpose and the true identity of the sitters (although it is generally agreed that the male figure belongs to the Arnolfini family of merchants who represented the Medici bank in Bruges). Clearly the couple are in the process of making some type of vow: witness the joined hands and the raised right hand of the richly dressed man. Above the convex mirror on the wall behind the couple is the inscription *"Johannes de Eyck fuit hic"* ("Jan van Eyck was here"), information reiterated by the reflection in the mirror of the artist and a second observer. Many other objects in this domestic setting suggest a sacred union: The burning candle (traditionally carried to the marriage ceremony by the bride) symbolizes

Figure 8.10 Jan van Eyck, *Marriage of Giovanni (?) Arnolfini and His Bride*, 1434. Tempera and oil on panel, 32¼ x 23½ in. National Gallery, London. The immediacy of the material world is enhanced by the technique of oil painting, which van Eyck brought to perfection.

the divine presence of Christ, the dog represents fidelity, the ripening fruit that lies near and on the window sill alludes to the union of the First Couple in the Garden of Eden, and the carved image of Saint Margaret of Antioch (on the chairback near the bed), patron saint of women in childbirth, signifies aspirations for a fruitful alliance. We may never know for certain whom these figures represent. However, the enduring vitality of the painting lies not with the identity of the sitters, but with Jan's consummate mastery of minute, realistic details—from the ruffles on the female's headcovering to the whiskers of the monkey-faced dog. Jan's realism captures an intimate moment: the act of marriage that (prior to Church reforms of the sixteenth century) was contracted simply by verbal vows and the joining of hands.

Bosch

The generation of Flemish artists that followed Jan van Eyck produced one of the most enigmatic figures of the Northern Renaissance: Hieronymus Bosch (1460–1516). Little is known about Bosch's life, and the exact meaning of some of his works is much disputed. His career spanned the decades of the High Renaissance in Italy, but comparison of his paintings with those of Raphael or Michelangelo underscores the enormous difference between Italian Renaissance art and that of the European North: Whereas Raphael and Michelangelo elevated the natural nobility of the individual, Bosch detailed the fallibility of humankind, its moral struggle, and its apocalyptic destiny. Bosch's most famous painting is a **triptych** (three-part painting) known as *The Garden of Earthly Delights* (Figure **8.11**). A work of astonishing complexity, its imagery has intrigued scholars for centuries. For, while it seems to present the traditional Christian theme of Creation, Fall, and Punishment, it does so with an assortment of unconventional images drawn from dozens of sources, from popular proverbs and pilgrimage badges to the pseudosciences of Bosch's time: *astrology*, the study of the influence of heavenly bodies on human affairs (the precursor of astronomy), and *alchemy*, the art of transmuting base metals into gold (the precursor of chemistry).

When the wings of the altarpiece are closed, one sees an image of God hovering above a huge transparent globe: the planet Earth in the process of Creation. An accompanying inscription reads: "He spoke, and it came to be; he commanded and it was created" (Psalms 33:9). When the wings are opened, the left one shows the Creation of Eve, but the event takes place in an Eden populated with fabulous and predatory creatures (like the cat at lower left). In the central panel, hordes of youthful nudes cavort in a variety of erotic and playful pastimes. They frolic with oversized flora and fruit, real and imagined animals, gigantic birds, and transparent beakers and tubes normally used in alchemical distillation, a process of creation and destruction analogous to the Creation and Fall. In the right wing, Bosch pictures Hell as a dark, sulfurous inferno occupied by egg-shaped vessels and infernal machines made of musical instruments. The damned, whose torments are inflicted by an assortment of sinister creatures, suffer punishments appropriate to their sins: the hoarder (at lower right) pays for his greed by excreting gold into a pothole; the nearby nude, punished for the sin of lust, is fondled by demons.

The Garden of Earthly Delights has been described as an exposition on the decadent behavior of the descendants of Adam and Eve, but its distance from conventional religious iconography has made it the subject of endless scholarly interpretation. Because the work was commissioned by a private patron, not by the Church, the Roman Catholic Bosch may have felt free to exercise his imagination. Whether perceived as a theater of perversity or a drama of innocent procreation, the "Garden" brings an unorthodox (and provocative) set of visual images to the traditional medieval view of the progress from sin to salvation.

Figure 8.11 Hieronymus Bosch, *The Creation of Eve: The Garden of Earthly Delights: The Tortures of Hell* (triptych), ca. 1510–1515. Oil on wood, 7 ft. 2⅝ in. x 6 ft. 4¾ in. (center panel), 7 ft. 2⅝ in. x 3 ft. 2¼ in. (each side panel). Prado, Madrid.

Grünewald

The German artists of the North brought to religious subject matter a spiritual intensity and emotional subjectivity unmatched elsewhere in Europe. In the paintings of Matthias Gothardt Neithardt—better known as Grünewald (1460–1528)—naturalistic detail and brutal distortion combine to produce the most painfully expressive painting style in all of sixteenth-century Northern art.

Grünewald's landmark work, the Isenheim Altarpiece, was commissioned to offer solace to the victims of disease and plague at the Hospital of Saint Anthony in Isenheim, near Colmar, France (Figure **8.14**). Like the *Imitatio Christi*, which instructed Christians to seek identification with Jesus, this multipaneled altarpiece reminded its suffering viewers of their kinship with the crucified Jesus, depicted in the central panel. Grünewald rejects harmonious proportions and figural idealization in favor of dramatic exaggeration and brutally precise detail: The body of Jesus is lengthened to emphasize its weight as it hangs from the bowed arms of the Cross, the gray-green flesh putrefies with clotted blood and angry thorns, the fingers convulse and curl in agony, while the feet—broken and bruised—contort in a spasm of pain. Grünewald places the scene in a darkened landscape and exaggerates the gestures of the lamenting attendants: John the Baptist, for instance, points an oversized finger to the prophetic Latin inscription that explains his mystical presence: "He must increase and I must decrease" (John 3:30).

The Protestant Reformation and Printmaking

Although secular subject matter such as portraiture provided abundant inspiration for Northern artists, the austerity of the Protestant Reformation cast a long shadow upon religious art. Protestants condemned the traditional images of medieval piety, rejecting relics and sacred images as sources of superstition and idolatry. Protestant iconoclasts stripped the stained glass from Catholic churches, whitewashed church frescoes, and destroyed altarpieces and religious icons. At the same time, however, Protestant reformers embraced devotional imagery—especially biblical subjects for private use. In the production of such

Making Connections

DEVOTIONAL IMAGES: PATHOS AND REMORSE

Grünewald's Jesus is not the traditional triumphant crucified Christ, but a figure whose tortured body deliberately evokes pathos and remorse (Figure **8.12**). Such renderings took their inspiration from the devotional imagery of the late Middle Ages, with its growing emphasis on Christ's human nature and his role as a suffering victim. In the carved wooden statuary designed for church altars or as part of the altarpiece itself, devotional images of Jesus—especially those from German hands—captured the torment of Christ's martyrdom with a fierce energy that is unique in European art (Figure **8.13**).

Q What do the similarities between these two images suggest about the art of the European North?

Figure 8.12 Matthias Grünewald, detail of *Crucifixion*, central panel of the Isenheim Altarpiece (see Figure 8.14), ca. 1510–1515. Oil on panel. Unterlinden Museum, Colmar.

Figure 8.13 *Crucified Christ*, from Cologne, ca. 1380–1390. Walnut, height 16¼ in., armspan 14½ in. Cleveland Museum of Art, Ohio.

Figure 8.14 Matthias Grünewald, Isenheim Altarpiece, ca. 1510–1515. Oil on panel, central panel, 8 ft. x 10 ft. 1 in. Unterlinden Museum, Colmar, France. The panel on the left shows the third-century martyred Saint Sebastian, while the panel on the right depicts the hermit Saint Anthony, said to be able to exorcize demons and evil spirits. These two figures were the principal saints invoked against affliction and disease—especially the plague.

imagery, advances in printmaking were a technological landmark. Just as movable type had facilitated the spread of the written word, so the technology of printmaking facilitated the reproduction of images more cheaply and in greater numbers than ever before.

The two new printmaking processes of the fifteenth century were **woodcut**, the technique of cutting away all parts of a design on a wood surface except those that will be inked and transferred to paper (Figure **8.15**), and **engraving** (Figure **8.16**), the process by which lines are incised on a metal (usually copper) plate that is inked and run through a printing press. Books with printed illustrations became cheap alternatives to the hand-illuminated manuscripts that were prohibitively expensive to all but wealthy patrons.

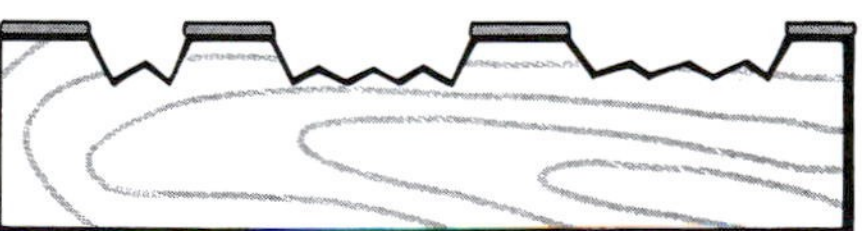

Figure 8.15 Woodcut. A relief printing process created by lines cut into the plank surface of wood. The raised portions of the block are inked and this is transferred by pressure to the paper by hand or with a printing press.

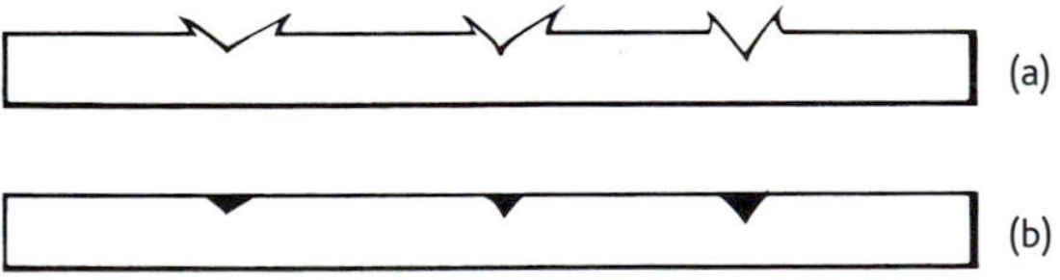

Figure 8.16 Engraving. An intaglio method of printing. The cutting tool, a *burin* or *graver*, is used to cut lines in the surface of metal plates. (a) A cross section of an engraved plate showing burrs (ridges) produced by scratching a burin into the surface of a metal plate; (b) the burrs are removed and ink is wiped over the surface and forced into the scratches. The plate is then wiped clean, leaving ink deposits in the scratches; the ink is forced from the plate onto paper under pressure in a special press.

Dürer

The unassailed leader in Northern Renaissance printmaking and one of the finest graphic artists of all time was Albrecht Dürer of Nuremberg (1471–1528). Trained as an engraver, Dürer earned international fame for his woodcuts and metal engravings. Dürer was, as well, an enthusiastic student of Italian Renaissance art. His mastery of the laws of linear perspective and human anatomy and his investigations into Classical principles of proportions (enhanced by two trips to Italy) equaled those of the best Italian Renaissance artist-scientists.

In the genre of portraiture, Dürer was the match of Raphael but, unlike Raphael, he recorded the features of his sitters with little idealization. Executed from life, his portrait engraving of Erasmus captures the concentrated intelligence of the Prince of Humanists (see Figure 8.2). Dürer's *Self-Portrait* of 1500 (Figure **8.17**) reflects his indebtedness to Jan van Eyck in its realistic treatment of hair and fur, and to Leonardo da Vinci in its psychological depth. The meditative solemnity and hieratic frontal pose

Figure 8.17 Albrecht Dürer, *Self-Portrait in a Fur-Collared Robe*, 1500. Oil on panel, 26¼ x 19¼ in. Alte Pinakothek, Munich.

are similar to representations of Jesus as *Salvator Mundi* (savior of the world), suggesting that Dürer intended the portrait as a kind of *Imitatio Christi*, that is, a self-image of the artist in the guise of Jesus.

Dürer brought to the art of his day a profoundly religious view of the world and a desire to embody the spiritual message of Scripture in art. The series of woodcuts he produced to illustrate the last book of the New Testament, The Book of Revelation (also called the "Apocalypse"), reveals the extent to which Dürer achieved his purpose. Executed two decades before Luther's revolt, *The Four Horsemen of the Apocalypse*—one of fifteen woodcuts in the series—brings to life the terrifying prophecies described in Revelation 6:1–8 (Figure **8.18**). Amid billowing clouds, Death (in the foreground), Famine (carrying a pair of scales), War (brandishing a sword), and Pestilence (drawing his bow) sweep down upon humankind; their victims fall beneath the horses' hooves, or, as with the bishop in the lower left, are devoured by infernal monsters. Dürer's image seems a grim prophecy of the coming age, in which five million people would die in religious wars.

Dürer mastered many media. His notebooks, like those of Leonardo, reflect a mind that was both curious and analytic. An avid traveler, he spent four years visiting the major cities of Germany and twice crossed the Alps into Italy, keeping travel journals in which he made a number of fine landscape studies. The genre of landscape painting had been pioneered by the Romans, who drew on nature for illusionistic frescoes and as settings for pastoral scenes (see page 83). As early as the eighth century, the Chinese made the landscape a subject in its own right (see page 140, Figure 5.24). In European art before 1490, however, landscapes appeared only as backgrounds for religious scenes and secular portraits (see Figure 7.1). Dürer established the panoramic landscape as a legitimate genre in Western art. His topographic landscapes are rendered in the elusive medium of watercolor (Figure **8.19**). To these works, as well as to his detailed studies of animals, birds, and plants, Dürer brought the pen of an engraver and the eye of a scientific naturalist.

Figure 8.18 Albrecht Dürer, *The Four Horsemen of the Apocalypse*, ca. 1496. Woodcut, 15½ x 11 in. Museum of Fine Arts, Boston. The most famous of the Apocalypse woodcuts shows the Four Horsemen—Death, War, Pestilence, and Famine—raging across the world and trampling down all creatures in their path, a prophetic vision described in the Book of Revelation.

Figure 8.19 Albrecht Dürer, *Wire Drawing Mill*, undated. Watercolor, 11¼ x 16¾ in. State Museums, Berlin. Dürer uses aerial perspective to create a sense of deep space in this delicate watercolor, probably made on his first trip to Italy in 1494. He takes a topographic approach, rendering details with precision.

Cranach and Holbein

The German cities of the sixteenth century produced some of the finest draftsmen in the history of Western art. A contemporary of Dürer, Lucas Cranach the Elder (1472–1553) was a highly acclaimed court painter at Wittenberg and, like Dürer, a devout champion of Protestant reform. Although he often worked for Catholic patrons, Cranach painted and engraved numerous portraits of Protestant leaders, the most notable of whom was his close friend, Martin Luther (see Figure 8.3). In his several other portraits of Luther, Cranach employed expressive line to define form and capture the confident demeanor of the famous reformer.

Hans Holbein the Younger (1497–1543), often celebrated as the greatest of German portraitists, was born in Augsburg, but spent much of his life in Switzerland, France, and England. His woodcut series of the Dance of Death (see Figure 7.2) brought him renown as a draftsman and printmaker. With a letter of introduction from his friend Erasmus, Holbein traveled to England, where he earned fame as a portraitist (see Figures 8.1 and 8.21). On his second trip to England, Holbein became the favorite of King Henry VIII, whose likeness he captured along with portraits of Henry's current and prospective wives. In common with Dürer and Cranach, Holbein was a master of line. All three artists manifested the integration of brilliant draftsmanship and precise, realistic detail that characterizes the art of the Northern Renaissance. Holbein, however, was unique in his minimal use of line to evoke a penetrating sense of the sitter's personality. So lifelike are some of Holbein's portraits that modern scholars have suggested he made use of technical aids, such as the ***camera lucida***, in their preparation.

Brueghel

The career of the last great sixteenth-century Flemish painter, Pieter Brueghel the Elder (1525–1569), followed that of most other Northern Renaissance masters by a generation. Like Dürer, he had traveled to Italy and embraced the humanism of the Renaissance. Unlike his

Figure 8.20 Pieter Brueghel the Elder, *Hunters in the Snow*, 1568. Oil on canvas, 3 ft. 10⅛ in. x 5 ft. 3¾ in. Kunsthistorisches Museum, Vienna. In one of the most magnificent snowscapes in Western landscape painting, the artist fuses pale greens and grays to create a frosty vista that includes a distant view of the snowcapped Alps, a winding river, local skaters on an iced valley pond, and peasants tending a blazing fire. The composition, a complex of intersecting diagonals, draws the eye from earth-bound chores to the pleasures of the season.

Making Connections

HUMANISM: EAST AND WEST

Holbein's sumptuous double portrait of the French ambassadors to Henry VIII, Jean de Dinteville and Georges de Selve, pays tribute to these dignitaries as intellectuals and humanists (Figure **8.21**). They are pictured amid an assortment of books, terrestrial and celestial globes, a lute, and the various navigational instruments that facilitated Europe's overseas expansion, such as the telescope and the astrolabe. A richly woven "Oriental" carpet, used conventionally to cover tables as well as floors, makes reference to the far-flung trading activities that characterized the commercial revolution (see page 241). The elongated foreground skull (which comes into focus only when one stands up close and at the right side of the painting) was a popular symbol of worldly vanity, while the broken lute string may refer to discord between Protestants and Catholics.

At the eastern end of the Asian continent, the tradition of the scholar-gentleman—the humanist of Chinese culture—continued into the era of the Ming dynasty (1368–1644). Such scholars, whose Confucian heritage looked back to the classical Han period (see page 86), played a major role in the administration of governmental affairs. Depicted on a silk scroll dating from the fifteenth century (Figure **8.22**), a group of richly attired dignitaries are engaged in intellectual activities. As in Holbein's double portrait, these pursuits are indicated by the inclusion of various artifacts—calligraphic writing materials, musical instruments, painted scrolls, and a chesslike board-game—enduring symbols of accomplishment among Chinese humanists.

Q What might have been the aims of each artist in depicting these figures amid the visual evidence of intellectual achievement?

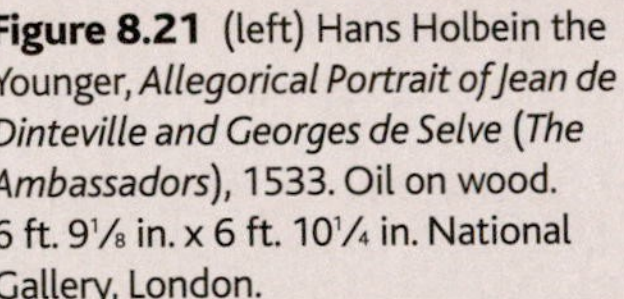

Figure 8.21 (left) Hans Holbein the Younger, *Allegorical Portrait of Jean de Dinteville and Georges de Selve (The Ambassadors)*, 1533. Oil on wood. 6 ft. 9⅛ in. x 6 ft. 10¼ in. National Gallery, London.

Figure 8.22 (below) Xie Huan, *Elegant Literary Gathering in the Apricot Garden*, detail, Ming dynasty, 1437. Handscroll, ink and colors on silk, 14¾ x 94¾ in. (entire scroll). The Metropolitan Museum of Art, New York.

older contemporary, however, Brueghel expressed only a passing interest in religious and Classical subject matter. His preoccupation with the activities of rustic life, which earned him the title "Peasant Brueghel," made him an heir to the Limbourg brothers (see Figure 7.4), while his detailed landscapes popularized the growing interest in the natural world anticipated by Dürer (see Figure 8.19). Brueghel's **genre paintings** (representations of the everyday life of ordinary people) were not small-scale renderings, but monumental transcriptions of rural activities, sometimes infused with symbolic meanings. *Hunters in the Snow*, one of a series of paintings designed to illustrate seasonal activities, renders the Flemish countryside as a cosmic setting for the ordinary labors of hunters as they trudge homeward through the bitter cold (Figure **8.20**).

Brueghel shared the Northern humanists' concern with human folly. His paintings and prints often drew on popular Northern European proverbs to illustrate the consequences of violence, prejudice, and immorality. *The Blind Leading the Blind* pictures a chain of five blind beggars led by one who has already fallen off the road; they stumble through a Flemish village served by a countryside church (Figure **8.23**). Possibly a commentary on the religious zealousness of Brueghel's time, the painting brings to life the famous biblical parable: "And if the blind lead the blind, both shall fall into the ditch" (Matthew 15:14). Like Erasmus and More, whose works he admired, Brueghel makes use of satire to address a favorite theme in sixteenth-century Northern European culture: the folly of humankind.

Figure 8.23 Pieter Brueghel the Elder, *The Blind Leading the Blind*, 1568. Tempera on canvas, 2 ft. 10 in. x 5 ft. Capodimonte, Naples. Brueghel's literal recasting of a moral message is set in a typical sixteenth-century Flemish village.

NORTHERN MUSIC

Music and the Reformation

Since the Reformation clearly dominated the religious and social history of the sixteenth century, it also touched, directly or indirectly, all forms of artistic endeavor, including music. Luther himself was a student of music, an active performer, and an admirer of Josquin des Prez (see Chapter 7). Emphasizing music as a source of religious instruction, he encouraged the writing of hymnals and reorganized the German Mass to include both congregational and professional singing. Luther held that all religious texts should be sung in German, so that the faithful might understand their message. The text, according to Luther, should be both comprehensible and appealing.

Luther's favorite musical form was the **chorale**, a congregational hymn that served to enhance the spirit of Protestant worship. Chorales, written in German, drew on Latin hymns and German folk tunes. They were characterized by monophonic clarity and simplicity, features that facilitated performance by untrained congregations. The most famous Lutheran chorale (the melody of which may not have originated with Luther) is "Ein' feste Burg ist unser Gott" ("A Mighty Fortress Is Our God")—a hymn that has been called "the anthem of the Reformation." Luther's chorales had a major influence on religious music for centuries. In the hands of later composers the chorale became a complex polyphonic vehicle for voices and instruments; however, at its inception it

Luther, "Ein' feste Burg ist unser Gott" ("A Mighty Fortress Is Our God") (1528)

was performed with all voices singing the same words at the same time. It was thus an ideal medium for the communal expression of Protestant piety.

Other Protestant sects, such as the Anabaptists and the Calvinists, regarded music as a potentially dangerous distraction to the faithful. In many sixteenth-century churches, the organ was dismantled and sung portions of the service were edited or deleted. Calvin, however, who encouraged devotional recitation of psalms in the home, revised church services to include the congregational singing of psalms in the vernacular.

Elizabethan Music

The Anglican break with Roman Catholicism had less effect on religious liturgy and church music than that which occurred among Lutheran and Calvinist Protestants. Indeed, one of the greatest English composers, the Catholic William Byrd (1543–1623), continued to write music for the Mass, as well as compositions for the Reformed Church. It was during the reign of Elizabeth I, however, and especially after the defeat of the Spanish Armada in 1588, that England enjoyed a Golden Age of music-making comparable to that of Shakespearean theater. Music held an important place in Shakespeare's plays, and informal musicmaking (although not yet public concert performance) prevailed in the royal court and in the homes of musical amateurs.

Every contemporary style and genre of music graced the age of Elizabeth, but it was the madrigal that became the rage. Usually based on Italian models, the English madrigal was generally lighter in mood than its Italian counterpart. It was also often technically simple enough to be performed by amateurs. Two of the most popular Elizabethan composers, Thomas Morley (1557–1602) and Thomas Weelkes (1576–1623), composed English-language solo songs and madrigals that are still enjoyed today. In addition to writing hundreds of popular songs, Morley edited an ambitious collection entitled *Madrigals, the Triumphes of Oriana*, works composed by twenty-four composers to pay homage to Queen Elizabeth. Each song in it addressed the "virgin queen" with the closing phrase, "Long live fair Oriana." Included in this collection is Weelkes' madrigal "As Vesta was from Latmos hill descending," which displays his facility for varied textures and artful word painting.

Morley, *Madrigals, the Triumphes of Oriana* (1601)

Afterword

By the end of the sixteenth century, the unity of Western Christendom was shattered. Religious wars between Protestants and Catholics and political rivalry among the young nation-states became the hallmarks of the early modern era. While Christian humanism and the printing press worked to advance education, bitter warfare and ruthless witch-burnings afflicted the West. Conflicts between religious and secular loyalties, the burdens of individual conscience, the consequences of human folly, and the Christian hope for salvation inspired landmark works by Erasmus, More, Montaigne, Cervantes, and Shakespeare. In Germany and the Netherlands, artists addressed some of these concerns in portraits and moralizing paintings and prints. But the drama of rebirth and reform was also played out on a larger stage, as Europeans contended for influence outside of their own lands, in parts of the world they had not known at all or had heard of only in the tales told by mariners and missionaries.

Key Topics

- Christian humanism
- Luther's reforms
- Calvin and Calvinism
- witch-hunts
- Eramus and More
- satire in Northern literature
- Montaigne's *Essays*
- Cervantes
- Shakespeare
- the Shakespearean stage
- Japanese theater
- Netherlandish painting
- printmaking
- German portraitists
- the Isenheim Altarpiece
- the Lutheran chorale
- the Elizabethan madrigal

NORTHERN RENAISSANCE TIMELINE

	HISTORICAL EVENTS	LANDMARKS IN THE VISUAL ARTS	LITERARY LANDMARKS	MUSIC LANDMARKS
1400		van Eyck, *Marriage of Giovanni (?) Arnolfini and His Bride* (1434)		
1450	Woodcuts and engravings used to illustrate books (ca. 1450) Gutenberg produces first printed version of the Bible (1454)	Dürer, landscapes (1490–1525), Apocalypse woodcuts (ca. 1496)	Thomas à Kempis, *Imitation of Christ* (ca. 1450) *Malleus Maleficarum* (*Witches' Hammer*) (1484)	
1500	Luther charged with heresy at Diet of Worms (1521) Peasant Revolts in Germany (1524–1555) Henry VIII breaks with Catholic Church (1526) Calvin establishes Protestant community in Geneva, Switzerland (ca. 1540)	Dürer, *Self-Portrait in a Fur-Collared Robe* (1500) Bosch, *The Garden of Earthly Delights* (ca. 1510–1515) Grünewald, Isenheim Altarpiece (ca. 1510–1515) Cranach the Elder, *Portrait of Martin Luther* (1533) Holbein the Younger, *Sir Thomas More* (ca. 1530)	Erasmus, *The Praise of Folly* (1516) More, *Utopia* (1516) Luther, *Ninety-Five Theses* (1517) Calvin, *Institutes of the Christian Religion* (1536)	Luther, "A Mighty Fortress Is Our God" (1528)
1550	England defeats Spanish Armada (1588)	Brueghel the Elder, *The Blind Leading the Blind* (1568); *Hunters in the Snow*	Montaigne, *Essays* (1580–1588)	
1600			Shakespeare, *Hamlet*; *Macbeth*; *Othello*; *King Lear* (1600–1606) Shakespeare, *Sonnets* (1609) Cervantes, *Don Quixote* (1613)	Morley, *Madrigals, the Triumphes of Oriana* (1601)
1650				

Figure 8.3
Lucas Cranach the Elder, *Portrait of Martin Luther*, see p. 216

Figure 8.6
George Gower, "*Armada*" *Portrait of Elizabeth I*, see p. 222

Figure 8.14
Matthias Grünewald, Isenheim Altarpiece, see p. 231

Chapter 9

Encounter:

CONTACT AND THE CLASH OF CULTURES

ca. 1400–1650

The Renaissance was Europe's first era of exploration and expansion. It was also the greatest age of trans-Eurasian travel since the days of the Roman Empire. In the years between 1400 and 1650, imperial ambition, commerce, curiosity, and maritime technology combined to ignite a program of outreach by which Europeans made direct contact with the populations of Africa and the Americas. Endowed with illustrious histories of their own, Africa and the Americas confronted the Europeans with unique traditions—many of which were radically different from those of Western Europe. Perceiving these older civilizations as backward and inferior, Westerners often misunderstood and willfully destroyed their landmarks. But out of these encounters came patterns of exchange—economic and cultural—that would transform both the West and those parts of the world in which the West established its presence. Encounter, the direct meeting of cultures, involved confrontation and conflict; but it also contributed to the rise of a global interdependence and the beginning of a Western-dominated modern world-system.

A First Look

The bronze plaque pictured here is one of hundreds showing European soldiers and merchants, and African rulers and courtiers, originally nailed to the pillars of the palace inhabited by the fifteenth- and sixteenth-century rulers of Benin in West Africa. It is a landmark, however, because it reveals the complex patterns of interaction and exchange between the vastly different cultures of Africa and the West. The soldier in the plaque represents one of the thousands of Western Europeans whose intrusion into Africa brought great wealth to the West and a radically new way of life to Africans, millions of whom were transported to Europe and the Americas as slaves. The warrior's sword symbolizes the military authority of the Portuguese, who arrived in Benin in 1486, while the trident indicates the popular regard for these invaders as semidivine creatures who arrived, like the gods, from the sea. Surrounding the figure are heavy metal horseshoe-shaped objects known as *manillas* (from the Portuguese word for "bracelets"), the earliest currency used in West Africa. First manufactured in the West, brass and copper *manillas* were exchanged for pepper, ivory, and slaves, the favored commodities of the newly established transatlantic trade system (see page 248). At the same time, the increased influx of European metals gave life to a renewed program of Benin bronze-casting. This renaissance of artistic productivity among a people who had enjoyed a long tradition of mining and smelting (see Figure 9.4) generated some of Africa's most notable bronze artworks, such as the plaque with which this chapter opens.

Figure 9.1 Benin plaque showing a Portuguese warrior surrounded by *manillas* (horseshoe-shaped metal objects used as a medium of exchange), from Nigeria, sixteenth century. Bronze, 18 x 13 5/16 in. Museum für Volkerkunde at the Kunsthistorisches Museum, Vienna. The Benin plaques may have been inspired by illustrations in books brought from Europe. Their delicately engraved background patterns are similar to those on Portuguese guns and armor.

GLOBAL TRAVEL AND TRADE

AFTER the year 1000, long-range trade, religious pilgrimage, missionary activity, and just plain curiosity stimulated cross-cultural contact between East and West. Arab merchants dominated the water routes of the Mediterranean, the Red, and the Arabian seas eastward to the Indian Ocean. Camel caravans took Arab merchants across Asia and over the desert highways of northern Africa. Muslims carried goods to and from India and Anatolia, and Mongol tribes (newly converted to Islam) traversed the vast Asian Silk Road, which stretched from Constantinople to the Pacific Ocean. The roads that sped the exchange of goods between the East and the West also took thirteenth-century Franciscans into China and made possible a vast mingling of religious beliefs: Christian, Jewish, Muslim, Hindu, Confucian, and Buddhist.

In the late thirteenth century Marco Polo (1254–1324), the young son of an enterprising Venetian merchant family, crossed the Asian continent (see Map 9.1) with his father and uncle, who had earlier established commercial ties with the court of China's Mongol emperor, Kublai Khan (1215–1294). The emperor soon proved to be an enthusiastic patron of cross-cultural dialog. Marco Polo served the Chinese ruler for seventeen years before returning to Italy, where he eventually narrated the details of his travels to a fellow prisoner of war in Genoa. The fabulous nature of his account, much of which made the West look like the poor, backward cousin of a great eastern empire, brought Marco instant fame. Embellished by the romance writer who recorded the Venetian's oral narrative, the "best-selling" *Travels of Marco Polo* came to be known as *Il Milione* (*The Million*), a nickname that described both the traveler's legendary wealth and the lavishness of his tales. Its importance as a landmark, however, is due to the fact that it opened Europeans, poised for global expansion, to an interest in the wider world.

Marco Polo, *Travels of Marco Polo* (ca. 1299)

While Marco Polo's descriptions of China's prosperity and sophistication might have been exaggerated, history bears out much of his report. Even after Mongol rule came to an end in 1368, China pursued ambitious policies of outreach: During the brief period from 1405 to 1433, as the country moved to expand its political and commercial influence, three hundred Chinese ships—the largest wooden vessels ever constructed anywhere in the world—and twenty-eight thousand men sailed the Indian Ocean to the coasts of India and Africa. Why the Chinese abandoned this program has never been determined with certainty. The future of global exploration, however, was to fall not to China, but to the West.

European Expansion

A series of unique events and developments motivated the onset of European expansion after 1450 and launched a program of outreach that would link Western Europe with

Figure 9.2 Circle of Joachim Patinir, *Portuguese Carracks off a Rocky Coast*, early to mid-sixteenth century. Oil on panel, 31 x 57 in. National Maritime Museum, London. The carrack and the caravel were fast sailing ships with a narrow, high poop deck and lateen (triangular) sails adopted from the Arabs. They were used by the Spanish and the Portuguese during the late fifteenth and sixteenth centuries to carry cargo from the East. In the right foreground is a small oar-driven galley.

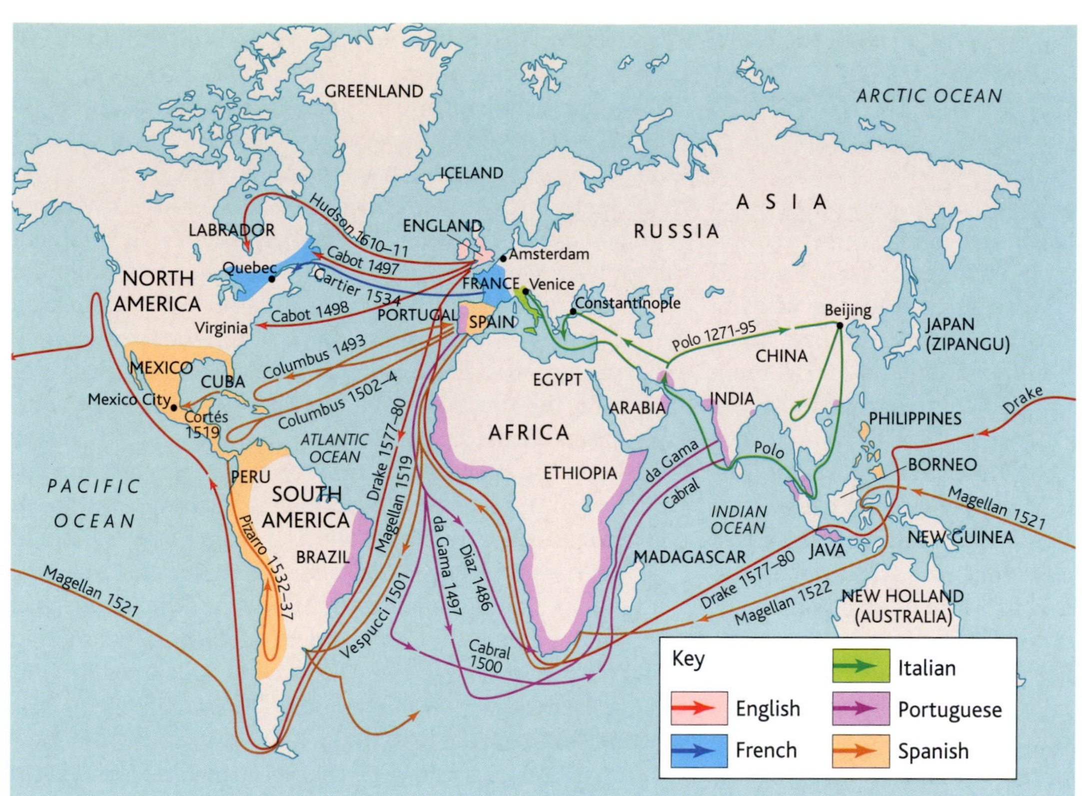

Map 9.1 World Exploration, 1271–1295; 1486–1611. Explorers are represented according to the nation for which they sailed.

the vast continents of Africa and the Americas. In 1453 the formidable armies of the Ottoman Empire (see page 208) captured Constantinople, renaming it Istanbul and bringing a thousand years of Byzantine civilization to an end. At the height of Ottoman power, as the Turkish presence in Southwest Asia threatened the safety of European overland caravans to the East, Western rulers explored two main offensive strategies: warfare against the Turks and the search for all-water routes to the East. The first strategy yielded some success when the allied forces of Venice, Spain, and the papacy defeated the Ottoman navy in western Greece at the Battle of Lepanto in 1571. Although this event briefly reduced the Ottoman presence in the Mediterranean—the Turks quickly rebuilt their navy—it did not answer the need for faster and more efficient trade routes to the East. Greed for gold, slaves, and spices—the major commodities of Africa and Asia—also encouraged the emerging European nations to compete with Arab and Turkish traders for control of foreign markets.

A second development worked to facilitate European expansion: the technology of long-distance travel. With the early fifteenth-century Latin translation of Ptolemy's *Geography*, mapmakers began to organize geographic space with the coordinates of latitude and longitude. The Portuguese, encouraged by Prince Henry the Navigator (1394–1460), came to produce maps and charts that exceeded the accuracy of those drafted by Classical and Muslim cartographers. Renaissance Europeans improved such older Arab navigational devices as the compass and the **astrolabe**.

Portugal and Spain adopted the Arab lateen sail and built two- and three-masted caravels with multiple sails—ships that were faster, safer, and more practical for rough ocean travel than the oar-driven galleys that sailed the Mediterranean Sea (Figure **9.2**). The new caravels were outfitted with brass cannons and sufficient firepower to fend off severe enemy attack. The earliest enterprises in European exploration were undertaken by the Portuguese, whose sailors had reached the Congo in West Africa by 1483. Five years later, Bartholomeu Diaz (ca. 1450–1500) opened Portugal's sea road to India by rounding the southern tip of Africa (Map **9.1**). By 1498, Vasco da Gama (1460–1524) had navigated across the Indian Ocean to establish Portuguese trading posts in India. The main obstacle to Portugal's success in India was the presence of Arab merchants, who opposed the European intrusion into their well-established and lucrative trading network. In 1509, however, by means of superior naval power, the Portuguese were able to eliminate completely their Muslim competitors in India.

While the Portuguese had reached India by sailing eastward, the rulers of Spain hired an Italian, Christopher Columbus (1460–1524), to sail West in search of an all-water route to China. Columbus' encounter with the Americas—whose existence no Europeans had ever suspected—changed the course of world history. On their way to establishing maritime empires, Portugal and Spain had initiated an era of exploration and cross-cultural encounter the consequences of which would transform the destinies of Africa and the Americas.

AFRICA

Cultural Heritage

Africa, called the "Dark Continent" by nineteenth-century Europeans because little was known of its interior geography, was unaffected by the civilizations of both Asia and the West for thousands of years. Even after the Muslim conquest of North Africa in the seventh century, many parts of Africa remained independent of any foreign influence and Africans continued to preserve local traditions and culture.

Diversity has characterized all aspects of African history, for Africa is a continent of widely varying geographic regions and more than eight hundred different native languages. The political organization of African territories over the centuries has ranged from small village communities to large states and empires.

Despite their geographic, linguistic, and political differences, however, Africans share some distinct cultural characteristics, including and especially a kinship system that emphasizes the importance and well-being of the group as essential to that of the individual. Historically, the African kinship system was based on the extended family, a group of people who were both related to each other and dependent on each other for survival. The tribe consisted of a federation of extended families, or clans ruled by chiefs or elders—either hereditary or elected—who held semidivine status. All those who belonged to the same family, clan, or tribe—the living, the dead, and the yet unborn—made up a single cohesive community irrevocably linked in time and space. While this form of social organization was not unique to Africa—indeed, it has characterized most agricultural societies in world history—it played an especially important role in shaping the character of African society and culture.

Equally important in the development of African culture was *animism*—the belief that spirits inhabit all things in nature. Africans perceived the natural world as animated by supernatural spirits (including those of the dead). Although most Africans honored a Supreme Creator, they also recognized a great many lesser deities and spirits. For Africans, the spirits of ancestors, as well as those of natural objects, carried great potency. Since the spirits of the dead and the spirits of natural forces (rain, wind, forests, and so on) were thought to influence the living and to act as guides and protectors, honoring them was essential to tribal security. Hence, ritual played a major part in assuring the well-being of the community, and the keepers of ritual—shamans, diviners, and priests—held prominent positions in African society.

West African Kingdoms

From earliest times, most of Africa consisted of villages united by kinship ties and ruled by chieftains. However, by the ninth century C.E. (encouraged by the demands of Muslim merchants and a lucrative trans-Saharan trade) the first of a number of African states emerged in the *Sudan* (Arabic for "Land of the Blacks"; see page 20): the region that stretches across Africa south of the Sahara Desert (Map **9.2**). The very name of the first Sudanic state, Ghana, which means "war chief" in Arabic, suggests how centralization came about: A single powerful chieftain took control of the surrounding villages. Ghana's rulers, who were presumed to have divine ancestors, regulated the exportation of gold to the north and the importation of salt from the desert fringes. These two products—gold and salt—along with iron, slaves, and ivory, were the principal African commodities. While gold contributed to African wealth, salt—a food preservative, a flavoring, and an early kind of antibiotic—was essential to human health. After Ghana fell to the Muslims in the eleventh century, the native kings, along with much of the local culture, came under Arabic influence.

The history of Ghana and other ancient African kingdoms is recorded primarily in Arabic sources describing the courts of kings, but little is known of African life in areas removed from the centers of power. Scholars estimate that in the hands of the Muslims, the trans-Saharan market in slaves—war captives, for the most part—increased from roughly 300,000 in the ninth century to over a million in the twelfth century.

Map 9.2 Africa, 1000–1500.

During the thirteenth century, West Africans speaking the Mande language brought much of the Sudan under their dominion to form the Mali Empire. This dramatic development is associated with the powerful warrior-king Sundiata, who ruled Mali from around 1230 to 1255. The wealth and influence of the Mali Empire, which reached its zenith in the early fourteenth century, derived from its control of northern trade routes. On one of these routes lay the prosperous city of Timbuktu (see Map 9.2), the greatest of early African trading centers and the site of a flourishing Islamic university. In Mali, as in many of the African states, the rulers were converts to Islam; they employed Muslim scribes and jurists and used Arabic as the language of administration. The hallmarks of Islamic culture—its great mosques (Figure **9.3**) and libraries and the Arabic language itself—did not penetrate deeply into the vast interior of Africa, however, where native African traditions dominated everyday life.

Prior to the fourteenth century, neither Arabs nor Europeans traveled to the parts of Africa south of the great savanna, a thickly vegetated area of tropical rainforest. Here, at the mouth of the Niger, in the area of present-day Nigeria, emerged the culture known as Benin, which absorbed the traditions of the cultures that had preceded it. By the twelfth century, Benin dominated most of the West African territories north of the Niger delta. The Benin *obas* (rulers) established an impressive royal tradition, building large, walled cities and engaging in trade with other African states. Like most African rulers, the *obas* of Benin regarded themselves as descendants of the gods (see Figure 9.4).

Figure 9.3 Grand Mosque, Djenne, Mali, 1906–1907. Originally built around 1220, the mosque pictured here is the third on this site.

African Literature

Native Africans transmitted folk traditions orally rather than in writing. As a result, the literary contributions of Africa remained unrecorded for hundreds of years—in some cases until the nineteenth century and thereafter. During the tenth century, Arab scholars in Africa began to transcribe popular native tales and stories into Arabic. Over time, several of the traditional African languages have developed written forms and produced a literature of note. Even to this day, however, a highly prized oral tradition dominates African literature.

Ancient Africa's oral tradition was the province of ***griots***, a special class of professional poet-historians who preserved the legends of the past by chanting or singing them from memory. Like the *jongleurs* of the early Middle Ages, *griots* transmitted the history of the people by way of stories that had been handed down from generation to generation. The most notable of these narratives is *Sundiata*, an epic describing the formative phase of Mali history. *Sundiata* originated in the mid-thirteenth century, in the time of Mali's great empire, but it was not until the twentieth century that it was transcribed—first to written French and then to English. Recounted by a *griot*, who identifies himself in the opening passages, the epic immortalizes the adventures of Sundiata, the champion and founder of the Mali Empire. In the tradition of such Western heroes as

Sundiata (ca. 1240)

Making Connections

TEXT AND IMAGE: THE OBA OF BENIN

This poem of praise for the *oba* of Benin employs complex rhythms that may have been accompanied by drumbeats or hand-clapping of the kind that characterize modern gospel singing. The visual counterpart of the text is the handsome portrait head shown in Figure **9.4**. As early as the thirteenth century, landmark bronze portraits like this one were displayed on the royal altars of Benin. The close-set vertical grooves may signify **scarification** (the ritual technique of incising the flesh to indicate tribal identity or rank), or they may have been introduced as an aesthetic device to enhance the shape of the head. Benin craftspeople mastered the ancient lost-wax method (see Glossary) of metal-casting.

The Oba of Benin
He who knows not the Oba
let me show him.
He has mounted the throne,
he has piled a throne upon a throne.
Plentiful as grains of sand on the earth
are those in front of him.
Plentiful as grains of sand on the earth
are those behind him.
There are two thousand people
to fan him.
He who owns you
is among you here.
He who owns you
has piled a throne upon a throne.
He has lived to do it this year;
even so he will live to do it again.

Q What does this sculpture have in common with Figure 1.14?

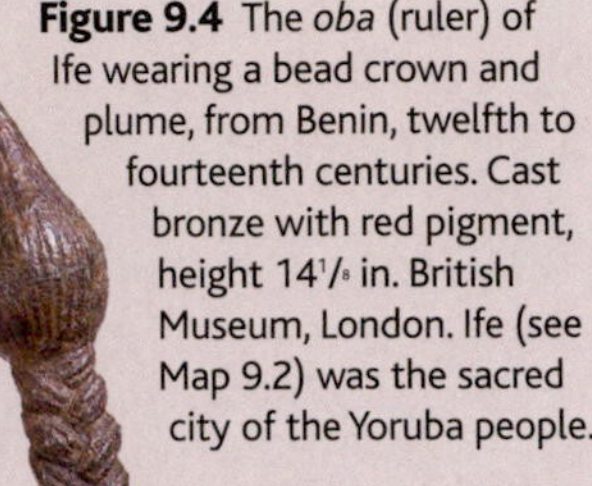

Figure 9.4 The *oba* (ruler) of Ife wearing a bead crown and plume, from Benin, twelfth to fourteenth centuries. Cast bronze with red pigment, height 14 1/8 in. British Museum, London. Ife (see Map 9.2) was the sacred city of the Yoruba people.

Gilgamesh, Achilles, Alexander, and Roland, the "lion-child" Sundiata performs extraordinary deeds that bring honor and glory to himself and peace and prosperity to his people. The landmark epic of Mali opens as follows:

> I am a griot. It is I, Djeli Mamoudou Kouyaté, son of Bintou Kouyaté and Djeli Kedian Kouyaté, master in the art of eloquence. Since time immemorial the Kouyatés have been in the service of the Keita princes of Mali [the ruling Muslim family; the Mali emperors identified themselves as descendants of the prophet Muhammad]; we are vessels of speech, we are the repositories which harbor secrets many centuries old. The art of eloquence has no secrets for us; without us the names of kings would vanish into oblivion, we are the memory of mankind; by the spoken word we bring to life the deeds and exploits of kings for younger generations.
>
> I derive my knowledge from my father Djeli Kedian, who also got it from his father; history holds no mystery for us; we teach to the vulgar just as much as we want to teach them, for it is we who keep the keys to the twelve doors [provinces] of Mali.
>
> I know the list of all the sovereigns who succeeded to the throne of Mali. I know how the black people divided into tribes, for my father bequeathed to me all his learning; I know why such and such is called Kamara, another Keita, and yet another Sibibé or Traoré; every name has a meaning, a secret import.
>
> I teach kings the history of their ancestors so that the lives of the ancients might serve them as an example, for the world is old, but the future springs from the past.
>
> My word is pure and free of all untruth; it is the word of my father; it is the word of my father's father. I will give you my father's words just as I received them; royal griots do not know what lying is. When a quarrel breaks out between tribes it is we who settle the difference, for we are the depositaries of oaths which the ancestors swore.
>
> Listen to my word, you who want to know; by my mouth you will learn the history of Mali. . . .

In ancient Africa, religious rituals and rites of passage featured various kinds of chant. Performed by shamans and priests but also by nonprofessionals, and often integrated with mime and dance, the chant created a unified texture not unlike that of modern rap and Afro-pop music. Poets addressed the fragility of human life, celebrated the transition from one stage of growth to another, honored the links between the living and the dead, praised heroes and rulers, and recounted the experiences of everyday life. African poetry does not share the satiric tone of Roman verse, the erotic mood of Indian poetry, the intimate tone of the Petrarchan or Shakespearean sonnet, or the reclusive spirit of Chinese verse; it is, rather, a frank and intensely personal form of vocal music.

Among the various genres of African literature is the mythical tale. African myths of origin, like those of the Hebrews and the Greeks, explain the beginnings of the world, the creation of human beings, and the workings of nature; still others deal with the origin of death. Such

Ideas and Issues

AFRICAN MYTHS: EXPLAINING DEATH

"One day God asked the first human couple who then lived in heaven what kind of death they wanted, that of the moon or that of the banana. Because the couple wondered in dismay about the implications of the two modes of death, God explained to them: the banana puts forth shoots which take its place, and the moon itself comes back to life. The couple considered for a long time before they made their choice. If they elected to be childless they would avoid death, but they would also be very lonely, would themselves be forced to carry out all the work, and would not have anybody to work and strive for. Therefore they prayed to God for children, well aware of the consequences of their choice. And their prayer was granted. Since that time man's sojourn is short on this earth."

(from Madagascar)

"Formerly men had no fire but ate all their food raw. At that time they did not need to die for when they became old God made them young again. One day they decided to beg God for fire. They sent a messenger to God to convey their request. God replied to the messenger that he would give him fire if he was prepared to die. The man took the fire from God, but ever since then all men must die."

(from Ethiopia)

Q What cultural values are reflected in each of these myths?

myths offer valuable insights into African culture. They generally picture human beings as fallible rather than sinful. They describe an intimate relationship between the African and the spirit world—one that is gentle and casual, rather than forbidding and formal.

African poetry is characterized by strong percussive qualities, by **anaphora** (the repetition of a word or words at the beginning of two or more lines), and by tonal patterns that are based on voice inflections. Repetition of key phrases and call-and-response "conversations" between narrator and listeners add texture to oral performance. The rhythmic energy and raw vitality of African poetry set it apart from most other kinds of world poetry.

African Music and Dance

African music shares the vigorous rhythms of poetry and dance. In texture, it consists of a single line of melody without harmony. As with most African dialects, where pitch is important in conveying meaning, variations of musical effect derive from tonal inflection and timbre. The essentially communal spirit of African culture is reflected in the use of responsorial chants involving call-and-answer patterns similar to those of African poetry. Such patterns are evident in the traditional "Gangele Song" from Angola. The most distinctive characteristic of African music, however, is its polyrhythmic structure. A single piece of music may simultaneously engage five to ten different rhythms, many of which are repeated over and over. African dance, also communally performed, shares the distinctively dense polyrhythmic qualities of African music. The practice of playing "against" or "off" the main beat provided by the instruments is typical of much West African music and is preserved in the "off-beat" patterns of early modern jazz (see pages 412–413).

A wide variety of percussion instruments, including various types of drums and rattles, are used in the performance of African ritual (Figure **9.5**). Also popular are the *balafo* (a type of xylophone), the *bolon* or *kora* (a large harp), and the *sansa* (an instrument consisting of a number of metal tongues attached to a small wooden soundboard). The latter two of these instruments, used to accompany storytelling, were believed to contain such potent supernatural power that they were considered dangerous and were outlawed among some African tribes, except for use by *griots*. Africa was the place of origin for the banjo, which may have been the only musical instrument permitted on the slave ships that traveled across the Atlantic in the sixteenth century (bells, drums, and other instruments were forbidden). African culture is notably musical, and the dynamic convergence of chant, dance, music, and bodily ornamentation generates a singularly dramatic experience that has a binding effect on the participants.

African Sculpture

The Renaissance conception of art, as represented, for instance, in Donatello's *David* (see Figure 7.17), would have been wholly foreign to the Africans whom Europeans encountered in the fifteenth century. For the African, a sculpture was meant to function like an electric circuit; it was the channel through which spiritual power might pass. The power-holding object channeled potent forces that might heal the sick, communicate with the spirits of ancestors, or bring forth some desirable state. The mask was the tangible means of drawing into the wearer the spirit of the animal, god, or ancestor it represented. Masks and headdresses, usually worn with accompanying cloth and fiber costumes, were essential to rituals of exorcism, initiation, purification, and burial. The mask not only disguised the wearer's identity; it also invited the spirit to make the wearer the agent of its supernatural power.

For centuries, the Bamana people of Mali have conducted rituals that pay homage to their ancestral man-antelope Chi Wara, who is said to have taught human beings how to cultivate the land. The ceremony pictured in Figure 9.5, which involves music and dance, requires headdresses with huge wooden crests that combine the features of the antelope, the anteater, and local birds. This three-dimensional emblem (or totem) is symbolic of Chi Wara, the mythical counterpart of the antelope. (It is also the logo for modern Mali's national airline.) The antelope headpiece epitomizes the African synthesis of expressive abstraction (the simplification of form) and geometric design (see Figure 9.7). The triangular head of the animal is echoed in the chevron patterns of the neck and the zigzags of the mane.

Figure 9.5 Bamana ritual Chi Wara dance, Mali. In the ceremony depicted here, dance movements performed to drum rhythms imitate the movements of the antelope, the totemic figure honored in this ritual (see Figure 9.7).

African art ranges in style from the idealized realism of Benin bronze portraits (see Figure 9.4) to the stylized expressionism of the Songe mask from Zaire in central Africa (Figure **9.8**). In this mask, worn at ceremonies for the installation and death of a ruler, the artist has distorted and exaggerated the facial features so as to compress energy and render the image dynamic and forbidding. As in so much African art, the aesthetic force of this object derives from a combination of abstraction, exaggeration, and distortion.

While the ancient Africans of Nok produced remarkable figures in terracotta (see Figure 1.29), the greater part of African sculpture was executed in the medium of wood or wood covered with thin strips of metal. Rarely monumental in size, wooden sculptures still bear the rugged characteristics of their medium. Like the trunks of the trees from which they were hewn, they are often formally rigid, tubular, and symmetrical (Figure **9.9**). Many images make use of the marks of scarification that held ceremonial and decorative value. Very few of Africa's wooden sculptures date from before the nineteenth century, but eleventh-century Arab chronicles indicate that the rich tradition of wood sculpture reaches far back into earlier African history. Thus most nineteenth-century examples probably reflect the preservation of long-enduring styles and techniques. Artworks in more permanent materials have survived the ravages of time—well before the end of the first millennium B.C.E., African sculptors were working in a wide variety of media, mastering sophisticated techniques of terracotta modeling, ivory carving, and metal-casting. Works in such enduring materials seem to have been produced mainly in the western and southern portions of Africa.

African Architecture

Outside of a few urban settlements, Africans seem to have had little need for monumental architecture. But at the ancient trade center of Zimbabwe ("House of Stone") in Central Africa, where a powerful kingdom developed before the year 1000, the remains of huge stone walls and towers (assembled without mortar) indicate the presence of a royal residence or palace complex—the largest structures in Africa after the pyramids.

As with the sculpture of precolonial Africa, little survives of its native architecture, which was constructed with impermanent materials such as mud, stones, brushwood, and adobe brick—a sun-dried mixture of clay and straw. Nevertheless, Africa's Muslim-dominated cities display some of the most visually striking structures in the history of world architecture. The adobe mosques of Mali (see Figure 9.3), for instance, with their organic contours, bulbous towers, and conical finials (native symbols of fertility) resemble fantastic sandcastles. They have proved to be almost as impermanent: Some have been rebuilt (and replastered) continually since the twelfth century. Their walls and towers bristle with sticks or wooden beams that provide the permanent scaffolding needed for repeated restorations. The wooden pickets, like the tree branches used in Bambara rituals, are ancient symbols of rebirth and regeneration. This fusion of Muslim and local ancestral traditions is unique to these African mosques.

Making Connections

AFRICA'S LEGACY

African sculpture had a major impact on European art of the early twentieth century. The Spanish artist Pablo Picasso was among the first to recognize the aesthetic power of African masks, which he referred to as "magical objects" (see Figures 14.10 and 14.11). But Africa's legacy continues to influence contemporary artists. For instance, for the sculpture entitled *Speedster Tji Wara* (Figure **9.6**), the African-American artist Willie Cole (b. 1955) gave an age-old African image (Figure **9.7**) a Postmodern identity by assembling scavenged bicycle parts. His sculpture recasts the Mali totem in terms that link Cole's ethnic ancestry to the industrial refuse of urban America.

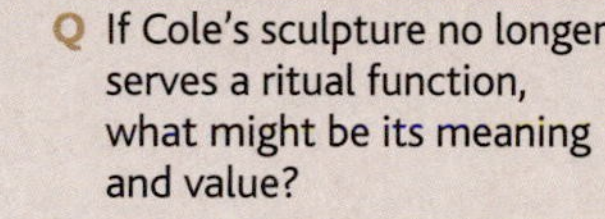

Q If Cole's sculpture no longer serves a ritual function, what might be its meaning and value?

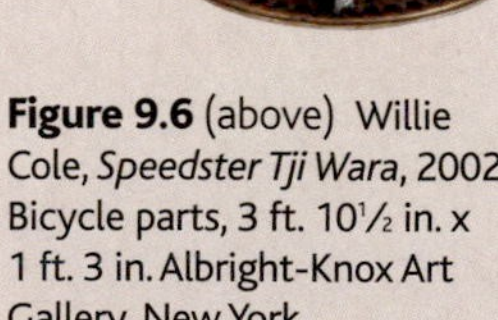

Figure 9.6 (above) Willie Cole, *Speedster Tji Wara*, 2002. Bicycle parts, 3 ft. 10½ in. x 1 ft. 3 in. Albright-Knox Art Gallery, New York.

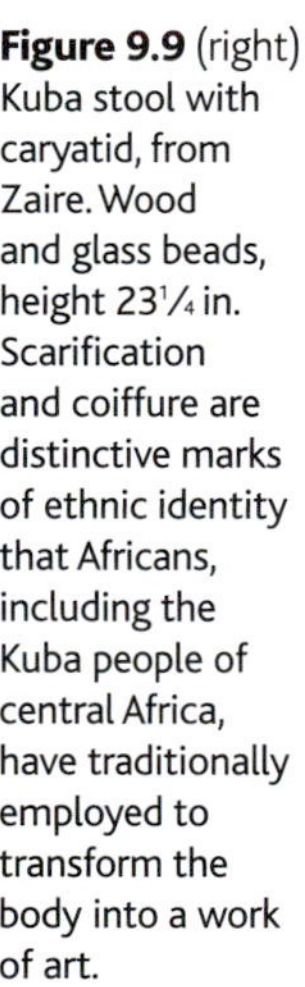

Figure 9.7 (right) Bamana antelope headpiece, from Mali, nineteenth century, based on earlier models. Wood, height 35¾ in., width 15¾ in. The Metropolitan Museum of Art, New York.

Figure 9.8 (above) Songe mask, from Zaire, nineteenth century, based on earlier models. Wood and paint, height 17 in. The Metropolitan Museum of Art, New York. The holes at the base of this mask suggest that it once was attached to some type of costume. Masks and other sculptures were often embellished with symbolic colors: red to represent danger, blood, and power; black to symbolize chaos and evil; and white to mean death. Compare the facial striation here with that in Figure 9.4.

Figure 9.9 (right) Kuba stool with caryatid, from Zaire. Wood and glass beads, height 23¼ in. Scarification and coiffure are distinctive marks of ethnic identity that Africans, including the Kuba people of central Africa, have traditionally employed to transform the body into a work of art.

The Europeans in Africa

European commercial activity in Africa resulted from the quest for new sea routes to the East, and for control of the markets in gold, salt, and slaves that had long made Africa a source of wealth for Muslim merchants. During the sixteenth century, Portugal intruded upon the well-established Muslim-dominated trans-Saharan commercial slave trade. The Portuguese slave trade in West Africa, the Congo, and elsewhere developed according to the pattern that had already been established by Muslim traders: that is, in agreement with local African leaders who reaped profits from the sale of victims of war or raids on neighboring territories. By the year 1500, the Portuguese controlled the flow of both gold and slaves to Europe.

Transatlantic slave trade commenced in the 1530s, when the Portuguese began to ship thousands of slaves from Africa to work in the sugar plantations of Brazil, a "New World" territory claimed by Portugal. The lucrative Atlantic slave trade, soon dominated by the Dutch and the English, formed a triangular loop: Europe to Africa, Africa to the Americas (the part of the journey known as the Middle Passage), and the Americas to Europe. European forms of slavery were more brutal and exploitative than any previously practiced in Africa: Slaves shipped from Africa to the Americas were branded, shackled in chains like beasts (see Figure 11.8), underfed, and—if they survived the ravages of dysentery and disease—conscripted into oppressive kinds of physical labor.

In their relations with the African states, especially those in coastal areas, the Europeans were equally brutal. They often ignored the bonds of family and tribe, the local laws, and religious customs; they pressured Africans to adopt European language and dress and fostered economic rivalry. While in a spirit of missionary zeal and altruism they introduced Christianity and Western forms of education, they also brought ruin to some tribal kingdoms, and, in parts of Africa, they almost completely destroyed native black cultural life. These activities were but a prelude to the more disastrous forms of exploitation that prevailed during the seventeenth and eighteenth centuries, when the transatlantic slave trade reached massive proportions. Between the years 1600 and 1700, the number of Africans taken captive may have reached over one million.

THE AMERICAS

Native American Cultures

As with Africa, the earliest populations of the Americas (introduced in Chapter 1) were culturally diverse, sharing deeply felt tribal loyalties and a strong sense of communion with nature. During the centuries prior to the earliest contacts with Renaissance Europeans, many of the roughly one thousand individual societies of the Americas produced illustrious histories. The indigenous peoples of North America ranged culturally from the relative simplicity of some Pacific coast tribal villages to the social and economic complexity of the Iroquois and the Zuni towndwellers (Map **9.3**). In Meso- (or Middle) America—present-day Mexico and Central America—and on the western coast of South America, villages grew into states that conquered or absorbed their rivals. Some complex communities, like Caral on the coast of the Pacific, reached back to the third millennium B.C.E. (see Figure 1.30); others, such as the Olmecs, flourished around 1200 B.C.E. (see Figure 1.31), while still others—the Maya, Inka, and Aztecs—reached the status of empire between the third and fifteenth centuries.

Native Americans fashioned their tools and weapons out of wood, stone, bone, and bits of volcanic glass. They had no draft animals and no wheeled vehicles. These facts make all the more remarkable the material achievements of the Maya, Inka, and Aztec civilizations, all three of which developed into empires of considerable authority in the pre-Columbian era.

The Arts of Native North America

There is no word for "art" in any Native American language. This fact reminds us that the aesthetically compelling artworks produced in the Americas were—like those of tribal Africa—either items of daily use or power objects associated with ceremony and ritual. A holistic and animistic view—one that perceives the world as infused with natural spirits—characterized the arts of Native America.

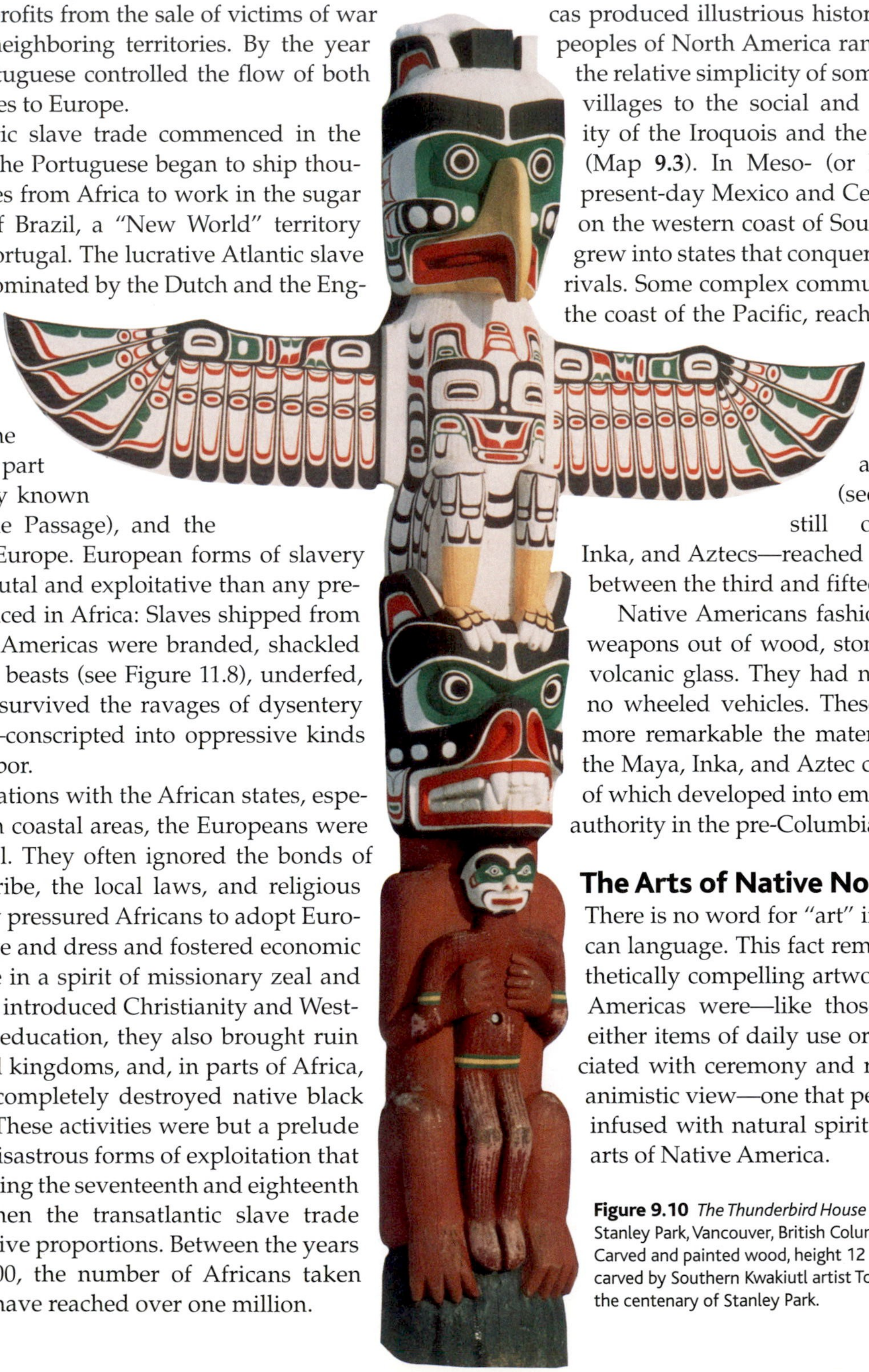

Figure 9.10 *The Thunderbird House Post*, replica totem pole, Stanley Park, Vancouver, British Columbia, Canada, 1988. Carved and painted wood, height 12 ft. This replica pole was carved by Southern Kwakiutl artist Tony Hunt to celebrate the centenary of Stanley Park.

Map 9.3 The Americas before 1500, showing tribes.

Wooden masks, painted pottery, woven textiles, sand paintings, beaded ornaments, and *kachinas* ("spirit beings") all picture gods, animals, and mythological heroes whose powers were channeled in tribal ceremonies and sacred rites. Wooden poles carved and painted with totems (heraldic family symbols) served the Southern Kwakiutl people of British Columbia as powerful expressions of social status, spiritual authority, and ancestral pride (Figure **9.10**). Also fashioned in wood, and ornamented with feathers, shells, and beads, portrait masks of spirits and ancestors (like those from Africa) worked to help the shaman or healer to cure the sick, exorcize evil spirits, and predict future events.

The more monumental landmarks of Native America are the communal villages that the Spanish called *pueblos* (towns). Located in the American Southwest, they were constructed between the eleventh and fourteenth centuries by the Anasazi (Navajo for "ancient ones"), ancestors of the Hopi and Zuni peoples. Pueblo communities consisted of flat-roofed stone or adobe multistoried living spaces arranged in terraces to accommodate a number of families. The complexes featured numerous rooms, storage areas, and circular underground ceremonial centers known as ***kivas***. Large enough to hold all of the male members of the community (women were not generally invited to attend sacred ceremonies), *kivas* served as cosmic symbols of the underworld and as theaters for rites designed to maintain harmony with nature. The Cliff Palace at Mesa Verde, Colorado, positioned under an overhanging cliff canyon wall whose horizontal configuration

Figure 9.11 (above) Cliff Palace, Mesa Verde, Colorado, inhabited 1073–1272. Mesa Verde in Colorado is the second largest of the ancient Anasazi sites in the southwest United States, the first being at Chaco Canyon in New Mexico. The pits in the floors of the *kivas* at these sites symbolize entranceways to the womb of the earth, from which the Anasazi's ancient ancestors were believed to have emerged.

Figure 9.12 Anasazi seed jar, 1100–1300. Earthenware and black and white pigment, diameter $14\frac{1}{2}$ in. St. Louis Art Museum, St. Louis, Missouri. The black and white zigzags and checkerboard patterns on this earthenware seed jar create a dynamic abstract design that may have symbolic meaning. The zigzags, for instance, may refer to lightning, associated with the rains essential to the growth of the seeds the jar contained.

it echoes, is one of the largest cliff dwellings in America (Figure **9.11**). Its inhabitants—an estimated 250 people—engineered the tasks of quarrying sandstone, cutting logs (for beams and posts), and hauling water, sand, and clay (for the adobe core structure) entirely without the aid of wheeled vehicles, draft animals, or metal tools.

The pueblo tribes of the American Southwest produced some of the most elegant ceramic wares in the history of North American art. Lacking the potter's wheel, Anasazi women handbuilt vessels for domestic and ceremonial uses. They embellished jars and bowls with elaborate designs that vary from a stark, geometric abstraction (Figure **9.12**) to stylized human, animal, and plant forms.

Native American religious rituals blended poetry, music, and dance. In many regions, the sun dance was a principal part of the annual ceremony celebrating seasonal renewal. In the Navajo tribal community of the American Southwest, shamans still conduct the healing ceremony known as the Night Chant. Beginning at sunset and ending some nine days later at sunrise, the Night Chant calls for a series of meticulously executed sand paintings and the recitation of song cycles designed to remove evil and restore good. Characterized by monophonic melody and hypnotic repetition, the chant (a section of which follows) is performed to the accompaniment of whistles and percussive instruments such as gourd rattles, drums, and rasps:

House made of dawn.
House made of evening light.
House made of the dark cloud.
House made of male rain.
House made of dark mist.
House made of female rain.
House made of pollen.
House made of grasshoppers.
Dark cloud is at the door.
The trail out of it is dark cloud.
The zigzag lightning stands high upon it.
Male deity!
Your offering I make.
I have prepared a smoke for you.
Restore my feet for me.
Restore my legs for me.
Restore my body for me.
Restore my mind for me.
This very day take out your spell for me.
Your spell remove for me.
You have taken it away for me.
Far off it has gone.
Happily I recover.
Happily my interior becomes cool.
Happily I go forth.

Native American myths and folktales were transmitted orally for generations but have been recorded only since the seventeenth century. Usually told by men and passed down to boys, tales and legends traveled vast distances and often appeared in many variant versions. As with African folklore, Native American tales feature hero-tricksters who, in the course of their adventures, may transform themselves into ravens, spiders, coyotes, wolves, or rabbits. Trickster strategies usually involve deceit and cunning, but the tale itself generally bears a moral that is meant to teach as well as to entertain. Native American myths of origins and the large corpus of tales that describe the workings of nature are among the most inventive in the folk literature of the world's civilizations.

Figure 9.13 Ceremonial knife, from the Lambayeque valley, Peru, ninth to eleventh centuries. Hammered gold with turquoise inlay, 13 x 5⅛ in. The Metropolitan Museum of Art, New York. Although sixteenth-century Europeans melted down or carried off much of the native gold, surviving pieces from Mexico, Ecuador, and Peru suggest that goldworking was one of the technical specialties of Native American artists as early as ca. 2000 B.C.E.

Ideas and Issues

MOHAWK MYTH: HOW MAN WAS CREATED

"After Sat-kon-se-ri-io, the Good Spirit, had made the animals, birds, and other creatures and had placed them to live and multiply upon the earth, he rested. As he gazed around at his various creations, it seemed to him that there was something lacking. For a long time the Good Spirit pondered over this thought. Finally he decided to make a creature that would resemble himself.

Going to the bank of a river he took a piece of clay, and out of it he fashioned a little clay man. After he had modeled it, he built a fire and, setting the little clay man in the fire, waited for it to bake. The day was beautiful. The songs of the birds filled the air. The river sang a song and, as the Good Spirit listened to this song, he became very sleepy. He soon fell asleep beside the fire. When he finally awoke, he rushed to the fire and removed the clay man. He had slept too long. His little man was burnt black. According to the Mohawks, this little man was the first Negro. His skin was black. He had been overbaked.

The Good Spirit was not satisfied. Taking a fresh piece of clay, he fashioned another man and, placing him in the fire, waited for him to bake, determined this time to stay awake and watch his little man to see that he would not be overbaked. But the river sang its usual sleepy song. The Good Spirit, in spite of all he could do, fell asleep. But this time he slept only a little while. Awakening at last, he ran to the fire and removed his little man. Behold, it was half baked. This, say the Mohawks, was the first white man. He was half baked!

The Good Spirit was still unsatisfied. Searching along the riverbank he hunted until he found a bed of perfect red clay. This time he took great care and modeled a very fine clay man. Taking the clay man to the fire, he allowed it to bake. Determined to stay awake, the Good Spirit stood beside the fire; after a while Sat-kon-se-ri-io removed the clay man. Behold, it was just right—a man the red color of the sunset sky. It was the first Mohawk Indian."

Q What ideas concerning race are suggested in this myth?

The Arts of Meso- and South America

The largest and most advanced Native American societies were those of Meso- and South America. During the four-thousand-year history of these regions, gold was the favored medium for extraordinary artworks ranging from small items of jewelry to ritual weapons (Figure **9.13**) and masks. Gold seems to have been associated both with the sun, whose radiance gave life to the crops, and with the gods, whose blood (in the form of rain) was considered procreative and essential to communal survival. In the sacrificial rites and royal ceremonies of pre-Columbian communities, human blood was shed to repay the gods and save the world from destruction. Gold, like blood, was the choice medium for the glorification of gods; it was especially important in the fashioning of objects associated with rituals at which warriors and rulers nourished the gods with their blood. Throughout Meso- and South America, the techniques of metalwork attained a remarkable level of proficiency that was passed from generation to generation.

Maya Civilization

The Maya civilization brought to a cultural climax the sacred and artistic traditions of the many Meso-American cultures that preceded it. It reached its classic phase between 250 and 900 C.E. and survived with considerable political and economic vigor until roughly 1600. At sites in southern Mexico, Honduras, Guatemala, and the Yucatán Peninsula, the Maya constructed fortified cities and elaborate religious complexes (Figure **9.14**) that look back to those of the Olmec, as well as to the extraordinary central Mexican city of Teotihuacán (ca. 100–650 C.E.). Reminiscent of both the Mesopotamian ziggurat (see Figure 1.16) and of Teotihuacán's ancient sanctuaries, such as the Pyramid of the Sun (see Figure 1.17), the Maya temple took the form of a terraced pyramid with a staircase ascending to a platform capped by a multiroomed superstructure (Figure **9.15**).

A shrine and sanctuary that also served as a burial place for priests or rulers, the Maya temple was the physical link between earth and the heavens. On the limestone façades of temples and palaces, the Maya carved and painted scenes of religious ceremonies and war, as well as images of their gods: Tlaloc, the long-snouted rain deity, and Quetzalcoatl, the feathered serpent and legendary hero-god of Meso-America. A landmark at almost all Meso-American sacred precincts was the ballpark. It was used for the performance of ceremonial games played by

Figure 9.14 Reconstruction drawing of the sacred precinct of the post-classic Maya fortress city of Chutixtiox, Quiche, Guatemala, ca. 1000. The Maya temple was the principal structure in the sacred precinct, which regularly included the ballpark (lower left) and an assortment of administrative buildings. Some precincts also had astronomical observatories.

Figure 9.15 Temple of Kukulcan (Feathered Serpent), called by the Spanish "El Castillo," with Chacmool in the foreground, Chichén Itzá, Yucatán, Mexico, Maya, ninth to thirteenth centuries. The reclining stone figure in the right foreground, known as a "Chacmool," served as an altar or bearer of sacrificial offerings.

two teams of nine to eleven men each. The object of the game was to propel a 5-pound rubber ball through the stone rings at either side of a high-walled court. Members of the losing team lost more than glory: They were sacrificed to the sun god, their hearts torn from their bodies on ritual altars adjacent to the court.

Blood sacrifice and bloodletting were also practiced by the Maya nobility. This ritual served not only to honor the gods but to confirm the political legitimacy of the rulers. Depictions of royal bloodletting appear in Maya frescoes and in carved stone sculptures adorning temples, palaces, and ballcourts. In one example (Figure **9.16**), the richly dressed King Shield Jaguar, whose feathered headdress features the shrunken head of a sacrificial victim, holds a staff above his queen, Lady Xoc, who pulls a thorn-lined rope through her bleeding tongue. Such ceremonies were performed upon the accession of a new ruler, prior to waging war, and at rituals celebrating victory in battle.

The Maya were the only known Native American culture to produce a written language. This ancient script, comprised of hieroglyphs, was decoded during the second half of the twentieth century. Indeed, only since 1995

Figure 9.16 Lintel, Yaxchilan, Chiapas, Mexico, late classic Maya, ca. 725 C.E. Limestone, height 3 ft. 8 in. British Museum, London. The blood-soaked rope runs from the queen's tongue into a basket filled with slips of paper that absorb the royal blood. These would have been burned in a large sacrificial vessel so that its smoke could lure the gods. The massive losses of blood may have produced hallucinogenic visions that enabled Maya rulers to communicate with their deities. According to the hieroglyphs on the upper part of the lintel, this ceremony took place in 709 C.E.

have the glyphs been recognized as a system of phonetic signs that operate like spoken syllables—a discovery made, in part, by studying the living language of modern-day descendants of the Maya who inhabit the Guatemalan highlands and the Yucatán. Despite the survival of some codices and many stone inscriptions, nearly all of the literary evidence of this people was destroyed during the sixteenth century by Spanish missionaries and colonial settlers. Perhaps the most important source of Meso-American mythology, however, survives in the form of an oral narrative believed to date from the Maya classic period, transcribed into the Quiche language in the sixteenth century. This narrative, known as the *Popol Vuh* (*Book of Counsel*), recounts the creation of the world. According to the Maya, the gods fashioned human beings out of maize—the principal Native American crop—but chose deliberately to deprive them of perfect understanding.

***Popol Vuh* (*Book of Counsel*) (ca. 1550)**

As if to challenge the gods, the Maya became accomplished mathematicians and astronomers. Carefully observing the earth's movements around the sun, they devised a calendar that was more accurate than any used in medieval Europe before the twelfth century. Having developed a mathematical system that recognized "zero," they computed planetary and celestial cycles with some accuracy, tracked the paths of Venus, Jupiter, and Saturn, and successfully predicted eclipses of the sun and moon. They recorded their findings in stone, on the limestone-covered bark pages of codices and on the façades of temples, some of which may have functioned as planetary observatories. At the principal pyramid at Chichén Itzá, a landmark urban site in the Yucatán (see Figure 9.15), the ninety-one steps on each of four sides, plus the platform on which the temple stands, correspond to the 365 days in the solar calendar. According to the Maya, the planets (and segments of time itself) were ruled by the gods, usually represented in Maya art as men and women carrying burdens on their shoulders. The Maya and the various Meso-American peoples who followed them believed in the cyclical creation and destruction of the world, and they prudently entrusted the sacred mission of timekeeping to their priests.

Inka Civilization

In 1000 C.E., the Inka were only one of many small warring peoples who had settled in the mountainous regions along the west coast of South America. Once established in the Andes mountains of Peru, the Inka absorbed the traditions of earlier Peruvian cultures noted for their fine pottery, richly woven textiles, and sophisticated metalwork (see Figure 9.13). But by the late fifteenth century, they had become the mightiest power in South America, having imposed their political authority, their gods, and their customs over lands that extended almost 3000 miles from present-day Ecuador to Chile (see Map 9.3). At its height in the 1500s, Inka civilization consisted of an astounding sixteen million people.

Like the ancient Romans, the Inka built thousands of miles of roads and bridges to expedite trade and communication within their empire. Lacking writing, they kept records on a system of knotted and colored cords known as *quipu*. The cult of the sun dominated religious festivals at which sacrifices—children, llamas, and guinea pigs—were offered to the gods. Ceremonial and decorative

Figure 9.17 Machu Picchu, near Cuzco, Peru, Inka culture, fifteenth to sixteenth centuries. Located near the eastern border of the Inka empire, Machu Picchu may have served as a defensive military outpost. One of the architectural marvels of the site is a masonry style that features smoothly surfaced stones laid in uniform rows.

objects were hammered from sheets of gold and silver—metals reserved for royal and religious use. With only bronze tools and without mortar, the Inka created temples and fortresses that are astonishing in their size and sophisticated in their masonry. At Machu Picchu the Inka left an elaborately constructed 3-square-mile city that straddles two high peaks some 9,000 feet above sea level (Figure **9.17**). With little more than heavy stone hammers, they raised two-story stone buildings and terraces surrounding large ceremonial plazas reminiscent of those recently uncovered at Caral (see page 21). Both the dramatic location and the superior building techniques of Machu Picchu render it a landmark in Native American history.

Aztec Civilization

Small by comparison with the Inka civilization, that of the Aztecs—the last of the three great Meso-American empires—is estimated to have numbered between three and five million people. In their earliest history, the Aztecs (who called themselves *Mexica*) were an insignificant tribe of warriors who migrated to central Mexico in 1325. Driven by a will to conquer matched perhaps only by the ancient Romans, they created in less than a century an empire that encompassed all of central Mexico and the lands as far south as Guatemala. Their capital at Tenochtitlán ("Place of the Gods"), a city of some 250,000 people, was constructed on an island in the middle of Lake Texcoco. It was connected to the Mexican mainland by three great causeways and watered by artificial lakes and dams. Like the Romans, the Aztecs were masterful engineers, whose roads, canals, and aqueducts astounded the Spaniards who arrived in Mexico in 1519. Upon encountering Tenochtitlán, with its two gigantic pyramids and countless temples and palaces connected by avenues and ceremonial plazas, Spanish soldiers reported that it rivaled Venice and Constantinople—cities that were neither so orderly nor so clean.

As with the Maya and the Inka civilizations, the Aztecs inherited the cultural traditions of earlier Meso-Americans, beginning with the Olmecs. They honored a pantheon of nature deities and extolled the sun, extending the practice of blood sacrifice to include staggering numbers of victims captured in their incessant wars. They preserved older traditions of temple construction, ceramic pottery, weaving, metalwork, and stone carving.

Figure 9.18 *Coatlique, Mother of the Gods*, Aztec, 1487–1520. Andesite, height 8 ft. 3¼ in. National Anthropological Museum, Mexico City. Spanish soldiers reported seeing statues (probably like this one) encrusted with jewels, gold, and human blood. So terrifying was this particular statue that it was reburied a number of times after its initial discovery in 1790.

Figure 9.19 Sun disk, known as the "Calendar Stone," Aztec, fifteenth century. Diameter 13 ft., weight 24½ tons. National Anthropological Museum, Mexico City. At the center of the calendar stone is the face of the sun god bordered by clawed hands that grasp human hearts, an image that symbolizes the anticipated cataclysmic end of the current world.

During the fifteenth century, the Aztecs raised to new heights the art of monumental stone sculpture. They fabricated great statues that ranged from austere, realistic portraits to ornately carved, terrifying icons of their gods and goddesses. One such example is the awesome image of Coatlique, mother of the gods (Figure **9.18**). Combining feline and human features, the over-life-sized "she-of-the-serpent-skirt" bears a head consisting of two snakes (facing each other), clawed hands and feet, and a necklace of excised human hearts and severed hands with a human skull as a central pendant. Renaissance Europeans, whose idea of female divinity was probably reflected in Raphael's idealized Madonnas (see Figure 7.27), found these often blood-drenched "idols" shocking and outrageous, and destroyed as many as they could find.

The Aztecs carried on the traditions of timekeeping begun by the Maya. Like the Maya, they adhered to a solar calendar of 365 days and anticipated the cyclical destruction of the world every fifty-two years. The "Calendar Stone," a huge votive object, functioned not as an actual calendar, but as a symbol of the Aztec cosmos (Figure **9.19**). The four square panels that surround the face of the sun god represent the four previous creations of the world. Arranged around these panels are the twenty signs of the days of the month in the eighteen-month Aztec year, and embracing the entire cosmic configuration are two giant serpents that bear the sun on its daily journey. The landmark stone is the pictographic counterpart of Aztec legends that bind human beings to the gods and to the irreversible wheel of time.

CROSS-CULTURAL ENCOUNTER

The Spanish in the Americas

Columbus made his initial landfall on one of the islands now called the Bahamas, and on successive voyages he explored the Caribbean Islands and the coast of Central America. At every turn, he encountered people native to the area—people he called "Indians" in the mistaken belief that he had reached the "Indies," the territories of India and China. Other explorers soon followed and rectified Columbus' misconception. Spanish adventurers, called *conquistadores* (Spanish for "conqueror"), sought wealth and fortune in the New World. Although vastly outnumbered, the force of six hundred soldiers under the command of Hernán Cortés (1485–1547), equipped with fewer than twenty horses and the superior technology of gunpowder and muskets, overcame the Aztec armies in 1521. Following a seventy-five-day siege, the Spanish completely demolished the island city of Tenochtitlán, from whose ruins Mexico City would eventually rise. While the technology of gunpowder and muskets had

Ideas and Issues

THE CLASH OF CULTURES

"There are three rooms within this great temple for the principal idols, which are of remarkable size and stature and decorated with many designs and sculptures, both in stone and in wood. Within these rooms are other chapels, and the doors to them are very small. Inside there is no light whatsoever; there only some of the priests may enter, for inside are the sculptured figures of the idols, although, as I have said, there are also many outside.

The most important of these idols, and the ones in whom they have most faith, I had taken from their places and thrown down the steps; and I had those chapels where they were cleaned, for they were full of the blood of sacrifices; and I had images of Our Lady and of other saints put there, which caused Mutezuma [Moctezuma II, the last Aztec monarch, who ruled from 1502 to 1520] and the other natives some sorrow. First they asked me not to do it, for when the communities learnt of it they would rise against me, for they believed that those idols gave them all their worldly goods, and that if they were allowed to be ill treated, they would become angry and give them nothing and take the fruit from the earth leaving the people to die of hunger. I made them understand through the interpreters how deceived they were in placing their trust in those idols which they had made with their hands from unclean things. They must know that there was only one God, Lord of all things, who had created heaven and earth and all else and who made all of us; and He was without beginning or end, and they must adore and worship only Him, not any other creature or thing. And I told them all I knew about this to dissuade them from their idolatry and bring them to the knowledge of God our Savior. . . ."

(from Cortés, *Letters from Mexico*)

Q How might an Aztec have reacted upon visiting a Christian house of worship such as Chartres Cathedral? (See Figures 6.1, 6.16, 6.21, and 6.25.)

much to do with the Spanish victory, other factors contributed, such as religious prophecy (that Quetzalcoatl would return as a bearded white man), support from rebellious Aztec subjects, and an outbreak of smallpox among the Aztecs.

The Spanish destruction of Tenochtitlán and the melting down of most of the Aztec goldwork left little tangible evidence of the city's former glory. Consequently, Cortés' second letter to Spain is of landmark importance: Not only does it offer a detailed picture of Aztec cultural achievement, but it also serves as a touchstone by which to assess the conflicted reactions of Renaissance Europeans to their initial encounters with the inhabitants of strange and remote lands.

Cortés, *Letters from Mexico* (1520)

The Columbian Exchange

Mexican gold and (after the conquest of the Inkas) Peruvian silver were not the only sources of wealth for the conquerors; the Spanish soon turned to ruthless exploitation of the native populations, enslaving them for use as miners and field laborers. During the sixteenth century, entire populations of Native Americans were destroyed as a result of the combined effects of such European diseases as smallpox and measles and decades of inhumane treatment. When Cortés arrived, for example, Mexico's population was approximately twenty-five million; by 1600, it had declined to one million. Disease traveled from America to Europe as well: European soldiers carried syphilis from the "New World" to the "Old." Metalworking technologies, guns, and other weaponry came into the Americas, along with Christianity and Christian missionaries.

While the immediate effect of the encounter was a dramatic clash of cultures, there were also significant (and positive) commercial, economic, and dietary consequences. The so-called "Columbian Exchange" involved the interchange of hundreds of goods and products between Western Europe and the Americas. The Europeans introduced into the Americas horses, cattle, pigs, sheep, chickens, wheat, barley, oats, onions, lettuce, sugar cane, and various fruits, including peaches, pears, and citrus. From America, Western Europe came to enjoy (and depend on) corn, potatoes, tomatoes, peppers, chocolate, vanilla, tobacco, avocados, peanuts, pineapples, various beans, and pumpkins.

Eventually, the biological and cultural mix of Europeans, Native Americans, and Africans would alter the populations of the world to include the *mestizo* (a genetic blend of Europeans and Native Americans) and the many *creole* ("mixed") populations of the Americas. The Euro-African and Euro-American exchanges opened the door to centuries of contact and diffusion that shaped the future of the world.

Afterword

Following the great age of exploration, neither Europe, nor Africa, nor the Americas would ever be the same. To the inhabitants of all three regions, the world suddenly seemed larger and more complex. The interchange of goods and customs, and the intermixture of peoples would alter the course of world culture. European outreach resulted in a more accurate grasp of world geography, a wider (if not always tolerant) appreciation of foreign customs and values, and the onset of a global economy dominated by the West. Widening commercial contacts and broadening opportunities for material wealth worked to strengthen the European nation-states, whose rivalry would intensify in the coming centuries.

Key Topics

- European expansion
- Africa's cultural heritage
- West African kingdoms
- African literature
- African music and dance
- African sculpture
- the impact of Europe on Africa
- Native North American arts
- Native American literature
- Maya civilization
- Inka civilization
- Aztec civilization
- the impact of Europe on the Americas
- the Columbian exchange

AFRICA AND THE AMERICAS TIMELINE

HISTORICAL EVENTS	LANDMARKS IN THE VISUAL ARTS	LITERARY LANDMARKS	MUSIC LANDMARKS	
• Classic Maya civilization in Meso-America (250–900 C.E.) • First African states emerge in the Sudan (by ninth century C.E.)	• Yaxchilan Maya lintel, Mexico (ca. 725 C.E.) • Chichén Itzá, Mexico (ninth to thirteenth centuries)	• *Popol Vuh* (ca. 500–800 C.E., transcribed ca. 1550)	• Navajo Night Chant (from ca. 700 C.E.)	TO 700
• Ghana falls to Muslims (1076) • Benin civilization in Nigeria (from twelfth century)	• Cliff Palace, Mesa Verde, Colorado (1073–1272) • Anasazi pottery (1100–1300)			1000
• Mali Empire in West Africa (from ca. 1230) • Aztec Empire in Meso-America (1325–1521)	• Oba of Ife, from Benin (thirteenth to fourteenth centuries) • Great Mosque, Djenne, Mali (ca. 1220)	• *Sundiata* (ca. 1240) • Marco Polo, *Travels of Marco Polo* (ca. 1299)		1200
• Inka Empire (ca. 1430–1533) • Ottoman Turks conquer Constantinople (1453) • Columbus discovers the Americas (1492) • da Gama navigates around Southern Africa (1497)	• Aztec sun disk ("Calendar Stone") (fifteenth century) • Machu Picchu, Peru (fifteenth to sixteenth centuries)		• Angola, "Gangele Song" (from ca. 1400)	1400
• Cortés subdues Aztec Empire (1519) • Transatlantic slave trade commences (1551) • Battle of Lepanto (1571)	• Benin bronze plaque (sixteenth century)	• Cortés, *Letters from Mexico* (1520)		1500
• Decline of Maya civilization (ca. 1600)	• Bamana antelope headpiece, from Mali (nineteenth century, based on earlier models) • Songe mask, from Zaire (nineteenth century, based on earlier models)			1600

Figure 9.18
Coatlique, Mother of the Gods, Aztec, see p. 254

Figure 9.9
Kuba stool with caryatid, see p. 247

Figure 9.17
Machu Picchu, near Cuzco, Peru, Inka culture, see p. 254

Chapter 10

Baroque:

PIETY AND EXTRAVAGANCE

ca. 1650–1750

The word "Baroque" describes a style that dominated the arts of Western Europe between roughly 1650 and 1750. It is characterized by dynamic movement, extravagant ornamentation, and theatrical display. These features appeared earliest in Italy and Spain in association with the Catholic Reformation. But they also flowered in the court of seventeenth-century France, where they served to advertise the opulence and power of the monarchy. The spatial grandeur of the Baroque is evident in the literature of the Protestant North and in the paintings of the Dutch Golden Age. Across Europe, the Baroque preference for contrasting effects and ornamentation gave color to new forms of vocal music, such as opera and oratorio, and to the rising tide of purely instrumental music.

Three phases of the Baroque are worthy of examination: the Italian Baroque, linked closely to the fervor of a reformed Roman Catholic Church; the Northern Baroque, typified by Protestant sentiment grounded in Scripture and fueled by the secular ambitions of Northern Europe's commercial middle class; and the Aristocratic Baroque, sponsored by the French monarch Louis XIV and widely imitated in the absolutist courts of Europe.

A First Look

If the artist who painted this picture were living today, he might have used a smartphone to capture this tumultuous scene: a company of military officers parading along the ramparts of their home town. The audio function would easily have captured the beat of the drum, the thud of boots, the barking of dogs, and the murmur of conversations taking place among the officers. However, when Rembrandt van Rijn (1606–1669), Amsterdam's leading portrait painter, was commissioned by Frans Banning Cocq to produce a group portrait of the members of Cocq's militia, the artist had at his disposal only his own great talent for putting paint to canvas (see pages 275–276). Rembrandt's genius lay in his ability to engage the viewer in the drama of the action and the lifelike exuberance of the figures, whose duty it was to protect the citizens of Holland's foremost mercantile city. Colossal in size, the painting, which was to hang in the festival hall of the militia's guild house, originally measured over eleven by seventeen feet (see Figure 10.16). Before three figures were cut from the left side of the painting in 1715, it pictured some eighteen officers, along with sixteen other figures, including Rembrandt himself. A landmark in group portraiture, the so-called "Night Watch" (the erroneous late eighteenth-century title given prior to its cleaning) draws force from its dynamic composition, theatrical gestures, and dramatic contrasts of light and dark—features that are typical of the Baroque style.

Figure 10.1 Rembrandt van Rijn, *Captain Frans Banning Cocq Mustering his Company* (detail, see Figure 10.16).

THE CATHOLIC REFORMATION

DURING the sixteenth century, as Protestant sects began to lure increasing numbers of Christians away from Roman Catholicism, the Church undertook a program of internal reform and reorganization known as the Catholic Reformation. Further, by the 1540s, in an effort to win back to Catholicism those who had strayed to Protestantism, the Church launched the evangelical campaign known as the Counter-Reformation. These two interdependent movements gradually introduced a more militant form of Catholicism that encouraged intensely personalized expressions of religious sentiment.

Loyola and the Jesuit Order

The impetus for religious renewal came largely from fervent Spanish Catholics, the most notable of whom was Ignatius Loyola (1491–1556). A soldier in the army of King Charles I of Spain (the Holy Roman emperor Charles V; 1500–1558), Loyola brought to Catholicism the same iron will he had exercised on the battlefield. After his right leg was fractured by a French cannonball at the siege of Pamplona, Loyola became a teacher and a hermit, traveling lame and barefoot to Jerusalem in an effort to convert Muslims to Christianity. In the 1530s he founded the Society of Jesus, the most important of the many new monastic orders associated with the Catholic Reformation. The Society of Jesus, or Jesuits, followed Loyola in calling for a militant return to fundamental Catholic dogma and the strict enforcement of traditional Church teachings. In addition to the monastic vows of celibacy, poverty, and obedience, the Jesuits took an oath of allegiance to the pope, whom they served as so-called soldiers of Christ.

Under Loyola's leadership, the Jesuit order became the most influential missionary society of early modern times. Rigorously trained, its members acted as preachers, confessors, and teachers: leaders in educational reform and models of moral discipline. Throughout Europe, members of the newly formed order worked as missionaries to win back those who had strayed from "Mother Church."

The Jesuit order was a fascinating amalgam of two elements—mysticism and militant religious zeal. The first emphasized the personal and intuitive experience of God, while the second involved an attitude of unquestioned submission to the Church as the absolute source of truth. These two aspects of Jesuit thinking—mysticism and militancy—are reflected in Loyola's influential handbook, the *Spiritual Exercises.*

Loyola, *Spiritual Exercises* (1548)

Loyola's affirmation of Roman Catholic doctrine anticipated the actions of the Council of Trent, the general church council that met between 1545 and 1563 to make reforms. The Council of Trent reconfirmed all seven of the sacraments and reasserted the traditional Catholic position on all theological matters that had been challenged by the Protestants. The Council revived the actions of the Inquisition and established the *Index Expurgatorius*, a list of books judged heretical and therefore forbidden to Catholic readers. The Catholic Reformation supported a broadly based Catholicism that emphasized the direct and intuitive—hence, mystical—experience of God. Although the Church of Rome would never again reassume the universal authority it had enjoyed during the Middle Ages, both its internal reforms and its efforts to rekindle the faith restored its dignity in the minds and hearts of its followers.

Ideas and Issues

LOYOLA: THE CHURCH MILITANT

"The following rules should be observed to foster the true attitude of mind we ought to have in the church militant.

1 We must put aside all judgment of our own, and keep the mind ever ready and prompt to obey in all things the true Spouse of Christ our Lord, our holy Mother, the hierarchical Church.

2 We should praise sacramental confession, the yearly reception of the Most Blessed Sacrament, and praise more highly monthly reception, and still more weekly Communion, provided requisite and proper dispositions are present.

3 We ought to praise the frequent hearing of Mass, the singing of hymns, psalmody, and long prayers whether in the church or outside; likewise, the hours arranged at fixed times for the whole Divine Office, for every kind of prayer, and for the canonical hours [the eight times of the day appointed for special devotions].

4 We must praise highly religious life, virginity, and continency; and matrimony ought not be praised as much as any of these.

5 We should praise vows of religion, obedience, poverty, chastity, and vows to perform other works . . . conducive to perfection. . . ."

(from Loyola, *Spiritual Exercises*)

Q In what ways do these rules contribute to the Jesuit ideal of "the Church militant"?

Mannerist Painting

The religious zeal of the Catholic reformers inspired a tremendous surge of artistic activity, especially in Italy and Spain. In Venice and Rome, the centers of Italian cultural life, the art of the High Renaissance underwent radical transformation. The spatial clarity, symmetry, and decorum of High Renaissance painting gave way to *Mannerism*, a style marked by spatial complexity, artificiality, and affectation. Mannerist artists brought a new psychological intensity to visual expression. Their paintings mirrored the self-conscious spirituality and the profound insecurities of an age of religious wars and political rivalry.

Figure 10.2 Parmigianino, *Madonna of the Long Neck*, 1534–1540. Oil on panel, 7 ft. 1 in. x 4 ft. 4 in. Uffizi Gallery, Florence. Mannerists like Parmigianino rejected the canonical rules of proportion and gloried in artifice and stylistic invention.

Parmigianino The traits of the Mannerist style can be seen in the *Madonna of the Long Neck* (Figure **10.2**) by Parmigianino (1503–1540). In this landmark work the traditional subject of Madonna and Child is given electric theatricality (compare Raphael's *Alba Madonna*, Figure 7.27). The Mother of God is unnaturally elongated; she is perched precariously above a courtyard adorned with a column that supports no superstructure. Her spidery fingers affectedly touch her chest as she gazes at the oversized Christ Child, who seems to slip lifelessly off her lap. Onlookers crowd into the space from the left, while a small figure (perhaps a prophet) at the bottom right corner of the canvas draws our eye into distant space. Cool coloring and an overall smoky hue make the painting seem even more contrived, yet, by its very contrivance, unforgettable.

El Greco The Mannerist passion for pictorial intensity was most vividly realized in the paintings of Domenikos Theotokopoulos, generally known (because of his Greek origins) as El Greco (1541–1614). A master painter who worked in Italy and Spain in the service of the Church and the devout Philip II (1527–1598), El Greco produced visionary canvases marked by bold distortions of form, dissonant colors, and a daring handling of space. His flamelike figures, often highlighted by ghostly whites and yellow-grays, seem to radiate halos of light—auras that symbolize the luminous power of divine revelation.

The Agony in the Garden, the scene of Jesus' final submission to the divine will, is set in a moonlit landscape in which clouds, rocks, and fabrics billow and swell with mysterious energy (Figure **10.3**). Below the tempestuous sky, Judas (the small pointing figure on the right) leads the arresting officers to the Garden of Gethsemane. The sleeping apostles, tucked away in a cocoonlike envelope, violate rational space: They are too small in relation to the oversized image of Jesus and the angel who hovers above. El Greco's ambiguous spatial fields, which often include multiple vanishing points, his acrid greens and acid yellows, and his "painterly" techniques all contribute to the creation of a personal style that captured the mystical fervor of the new Catholicism.

Music and the Catholic Reformation

In an effort to rid sacred music of secular influence, the Council of Trent condemned the borrowing of popular tunes, which had been absorbed by religious music since the late Middle Ages. It also banned complex polyphony, which tended to obscure the sacred text: The message of the text was considered primary. The Italian composer Giovanni di Palestrina (1525–1594) took these "recommendations" as strict guidelines: While polyphonic in texture, his more than one hundred Masses and 450 motets feature clarity of text, skillful counterpoint, and regular rhythms. The *a cappella* lines of Palestrina's Pope Marcellus Mass flow with the smooth grace of a Mannerist painting. Called "the music of mystic serenity," Palestrina's compositions embody the conservative and contemplative side of the Catholic Reformation rather than its inventive, dramatic aspect.

Palestrina, Pope Marcellus Mass (ca. 1561)

Figure 10.3 El Greco, *The Agony in the Garden*, ca. 1585–1586. Oil on canvas, 6 ft. 1 in. x 9 ft. 1 in. Toledo Museum of Art, Ohio. El Greco's exotic colors and elongated figures reflect his training as a painter of Byzantine-style icons. The quintessential Catholic Reformation artist, he brought the inward eye of a mystic to Christian subject matter.

THE ITALIAN BAROQUE

THE word "baroque" has a long and complex history: it probably derives from the Portuguese *barocco*, which describes the irregularly shaped pearl found in European ornamental decoration. Before the nineteenth century, "baroque" was used to mean "grotesque" or "absurd." During that century, however, the term came to describe an artistic style dominated by florid ornamentation, spatial grandeur, and theatrical flamboyance. Originating in Italy in the early seventeenth century, this style dominated artistic production between roughly 1650 and 1750. Its roots were in the Mannerist arts of Southern Europe, but it would spread much further afield, pervading Western Europe and those parts of the Americas colonized by Spain. In Italy, Baroque artists worked to increase the dramatic expressiveness of religious subject matter. Through the visual arts, they gave viewers a heightened sense of participation in the events of the Christian story and in the rituals of worship. This enhanced spirit of piety, accompanied by a delight in extravagant settings, was a prominent feature of the European Baroque.

Italian Baroque Architecture

Designed to reflect the mystical and evangelical ideals of the Counter-Reformation, Italian Baroque churches became the models for Catholic worship throughout Europe and Latin America. They featured wide naves, huge domes, and ornate altarpieces. The epitome of this flamboyant style was the monumental basilica of Saint Peter's in the city of Rome. Construction of Michelangelo's huge dome was not completed until 1590 (see page 205 and Figure 7.33), and a new façade was added to the basilica between 1608 and 1614. Funded with money from indulgences, the magnificently refurbished Saint Peter's would become a landmark symbol of Church power and prestige, celebrating its triumph over the Protestant challenge.

To design the ***piazza*** (the broad public space in front of the basilica), the Church commissioned one of the leading architects of the day, Gianlorenzo Bernini (1598–1680). A man of remarkable virtuosity, Bernini created a trapezoidal space that opened out to a larger oval—the two shapes forming a keyhole, possibly a symbolic reference to Peter, the apostle to whom Christ gave "the keys to the kingdom of heaven" (Matthew 16:15) (Figure **10.4**). Bernini ringed his courtyard with a spectacular colonnade that incorporated 284 Doric columns (each 39 feet high), as well as ninety-six sculptured saints (each 15 feet tall). In a manner consistent with the ecumenical breadth of Jesuit evangelism, the gigantic pincerlike arms of this colonnade reach out to embrace an area that can accommodate more than

Figure 10.5 (above) Gianlorenzo Bernini, *Baldacchino* (canopy), ca. 1624–1633. Bronze with gilding, height 93 ft. 6 in. Saint Peter's, Rome.

Figure 10.4 (below) Gianlorenzo Bernini, aerial view of colonnade and *piazza* of Saint Peter's, Rome, begun 1656. Travertine, longitudinal axis approx. 800 ft. Copper engraving by Giovanni Piranesi, 1750. Art Library, Berlin.

250,000 people. The Saint Peter's of Bernini's time was the locus of papal authority; then, as now, popes used the central balcony of the basilica to impart the traditional blessing: *Urbi et Orbi* ("To the city and to the world").

The proportions of this exterior setting reflect the Baroque preference for the grandiose, a preference equally apparent in the interior of Saint Peter's, for which Bernini designed an immense bronze canopy (*baldacchino*) that covers the high altar (Figure **10.5**). Following Bernini's lead, Baroque church interiors assumed a new level of sumptuousness. Ornately embellished by a combination of media—marble, painted stucco, and bronze—they became theaters for the ritual of the Mass.

Italian Baroque Sculpture

Bernini was not only the chief architect of seventeenth-century Rome, he was also one of its leading sculptors. To the rendering of a life-sized marble figure of the biblical David (Figure **10.6**) Bernini brought a daring degree of theatricality. In contrast with Donatello's languid and effeminate youth (see Figure 7.17) and Michelangelo's self-contained, Classically poised hero (see Figure 7.29), Bernini's *David* is rugged and spirited. Caught in mid-action, his adversary is left to our imagination in the space beyond the figure. As he prepares to launch his humble missile, David stretches the slingshot behind him, his torso twisting vigorously, his muscles strained with tense energy, and his face contorted with fierce determination. Insisting that he wished to "render the marble flexible," Bernini created a David who breaks into space with athletic vitality.

Two decades later, Bernini took religious art to an even more complex level of theatricality. For the Cornaro Chapel of Santa Maria della Vittoria in Rome, he created a landmark multimedia altarpiece: *The Ecstasy of Saint Teresa* (Figure **10.7**, see also Figure 10.8). The altarpiece illustrates an episode drawn from the autobiography of the Spanish Carmelite mystic Teresa of Avila (1515–1562): the moment in which she is united with God. Bernini depicted the saint with her head sunk back and eyes half closed, swooning with ecstatic surrender on a marble cloud that floats in heavenly space. A smiling angel gently lifts Teresa's bodice to insert (or remove) the flaming arrow of divine love. Bold illusionism heightens the sensuous image: The angel's marble draperies seem to flutter and billow with tense energy, while Teresa's slack and heavy gown swathes her limp body.

To capture the theatrical dimension of Teresa's divine

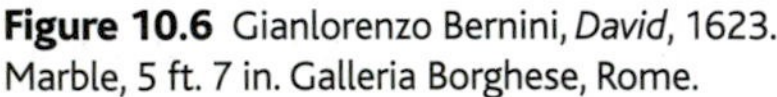

Figure 10.6 Gianlorenzo Bernini, *David*, 1623. Marble, 5 ft. 7 in. Galleria Borghese, Rome.

Making Connections

TEXT AND IMAGE: SAINT TERESA'S VISION

"It pleased the Lord that I should sometimes see the following vision. I would see beside me, on my left hand, an angel in bodily form—a type of vision which I am not in the habit of seeing, except very rarely. Though I often see representations of angels, my visions of them are of the type which I first mentioned. It pleased the Lord that I should see this angel in the following way. He was not tall, but short, and very beautiful, his face so aflame that he appeared to be one of the highest types of angel who seem to be all afire. They must be those who are called cherubim: they do not tell me their names but I am well aware that there is a great difference between certain angels and others, and between these and others still, of a kind that I could not possibly explain. In his hands I saw a long golden spear and at the end of the iron tip I seemed to see a point of fire. With this he seemed to pierce my heart several times so that it penetrated to my entrails. When he drew it out, I thought he was drawing them out with it and he left me completely afire with a great love of God. The pain was so sharp that it made me utter several moans; and so excessive was the sweetness caused me by this intense pain that one can never wish to lose it, nor will one's soul be content with anything less than God. It is not bodily pain, but spiritual, though the body has a share in it—indeed, a great share. So sweet are the colloquies of love which pass between the soul and God that if anyone thinks I am lying I beseech God, in His goodness, to give him the same experience."

(from Saint Teresa, *Visions*, 1611)

Q How literal is Bernini's rendering of Teresa's vision? What does this suggest about the Baroque style?

Figure 10.7 Gianlorenzo Bernini, *The Ecstasy of Saint Teresa*, 1645–1652. Marble, height of group 11 ft. 6 in. Altar of Cornaro Chapel, Santa Maria della Vittoria, Rome.

seduction, Bernini engages the tools of architecture, sculpture, and painting. He places Teresa beneath a colonnaded marble canopy from which gilded wooden rays appear to cast heaven's supernatural light. Real light entering through the glazed yellow panes of a concealed window above the chapel bathes the saint in a golden glow. A host of lifelike angels sculpted in **stucco** (a light, pliable plaster) miraculously descends from the ceiling, whose agate and dark green marble walls provide a somber setting for the gleaming white and gold central image. Finally, on either side of the chapel, Bernini includes the members of the Cornaro family (the chapel's patrons); executed in marble, they witness Teresa's vision from behind prayer desks resembling theater boxes (Figure **10.8**). These life-sized figures reinforce the viewer's role as witness to a staged event. It is no coincidence that Bernini's illusionistic tour de force was conceived during the first age of Italian opera, for both share the Baroque affection for dramatic expression on a monumental scale.

Figure 10.8 Gianlorenzo Bernini, Cornaro Chapel, Santa Maria della Vittoria, Rome, 1645–1652. (See also page 265 and Figure 10.7.)

Italian Baroque Painting

Visual drama and theatricality were hallmarks of Italian Baroque painting. As with Baroque sculpture, realistic detail and illusionistic effects lured the eye of the viewer into the action of the scene. To achieve these effects, artists made use of bold contrasts of light and dark, along with a perspective device known as **foreshortening**, by which figures or objects (depicted at an angle to the picture plane) appear to recede in space.

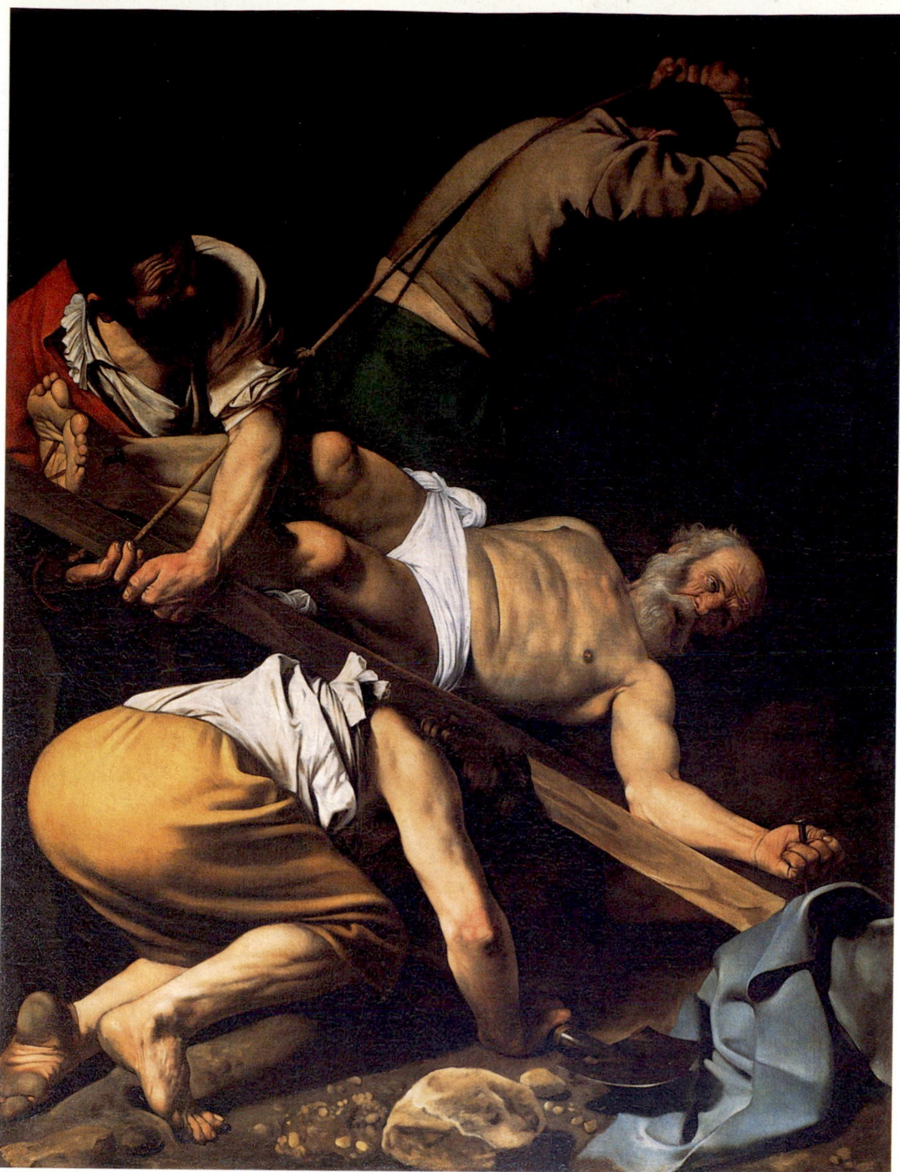

Figure 10.9 Caravaggio, *The Crucifixion of Saint Peter*, 1601. Oil on canvas, 7 ft. 6 in. x 5 ft. 9 in. Santa Maria del Popolo, Rome. Caravaggio organized traditional religious compositions like this one with unprecedented theatrical power and daring.

Caravaggio The great proponent of Baroque illusionism and the leading Italian painter of the seventeenth century was Michelangelo Merisi, better known as Caravaggio (1573–1610). This north Italian master flouted artistic conventions even as he flouted the law—he was arrested for violent acts that ranged from throwing a plate of artichokes in the face of a tavernkeeper to armed assault and murder. In his paintings, Caravaggio renounced the Grand Style—noble figures, dignified setting, and graceful symmetries—of his High Renaissance predecessors. Copying nature faithfully and without idealization, he brought to life the events of the Christian and Classical past as though they were occurring in the local taverns and streets of seventeenth-century Italy. For *The Crucifixion of Saint Peter* (Figure **10.9**), he arranged the figures in a tense, off-centered pinwheel that catches the eccentricity of Peter's torment (he was crucified upside down). By placing the vigorously foreshortened figures close to the picture plane and illuminating them against a darkened background, Caravaggio managed to thrust the action into the viewer's space—a space whose cruel light reveals such banal details as the executioner's dirty feet. True to the ideals of the Catholic Reformation, Caravaggio's paintings appealed to the senses rather than to the intellect. They also introduced into European art a new and vigorously lifelike realization of the natural world—one that inventively mingled the sacred and the profane.

Gentileschi Caravaggio's powerful style had considerable impact throughout Europe; however, his most talented follower was Italian too. Born in Rome, Artemisia Gentileschi (1593–1653) was the daughter of a highly esteemed painter, himself a follower of Caravaggio. Artemisia was trained by her father but soon outstripped him in technical proficiency and imagination. Since women were not permitted to draw from live male models, they rarely painted large-scale canvases with biblical and mythological themes, which required monumental nude figures; instead, their efforts were confined to the genres of portrait painting and still life. Gentileschi's paintings, however, challenged this tradition. Her landmark canvas *Judith Slaying Holofernes* (Figure **10.10**), which compares in size and impact with Caravaggio's *Crucifixion of Saint Peter*, illustrates the decapitation of an Assyrian general and enemy of Israel at the hands of a clever Hebrew widow. Gentileschi brought to this representation the dramatic techniques of Caravaggio: realistically conceived figures, stark contrasts of light and dark, and a composition that puts the viewer painfully close to the event. She also invested her subject with fierce intensity—the foreshortened body of the victim and foreground pattern of human limbs force the eye to focus on the gruesome action of the sword blade as it severs head from neck in a shower of blood.

Making Connections

TEXT AND IMAGE: THE BOOK OF JUDITH

A story found in the Apocrypha (the noncanonical books of the Bible), the slaying of the tyrannical Holofernes was a favorite allegory of liberty and religious defiance during the Renaissance.

"[16]Holofernes' heart was ravished with [Judith] and his passion was aroused, for he had been waiting for an opportunity to seduce her from the day he first saw her. [17]So Holofernes said to her, 'Have a drink and be merry with us!' [18]Judith said, 'I will gladly drink, my lord, because today is the greatest day in my whole life.' [19]Then she took what her maid had prepared and ate and drank before him. [20]Holofernes was greatly pleased with her, and drank a great quantity of wine, much more than he had ever drunk in any one day since he was born.

[1]When evening came, his slaves quickly withdrew. . . . They went to bed, for they all were weary because the banquet had lasted so long. [2]But Judith was left alone in the tent, with Holofernes stretched out on his bed, for he was dead drunk. . . .

[4]Then Judith, standing beside his bed, said in her heart, 'O Lord God of all might, look in this hour on the work of my hands for the exaltation of Jerusalem. [5]Now indeed is the time to help your heritage and to carry out my design to destroy the enemies who have risen up against us.'

[6]She went up to the bedpost near Holofernes' head, and took down his sword that hung there. [7]She came close to his bed, took hold of the hair of his head, and said, 'Give me strength today, O Lord God of Israel!' [8]Then she struck his neck twice with all her might, and cut off his head. [9]Next she rolled his body off the bed and pulled down the canopy from the posts. Soon afterward she went out and gave Holofernes' head to her maid, [10]who placed it in her food bag."

(from Book of Judith 12:16–20; 13:1–10)

Q Which textual details does Gentileschi recreate visually? What aspects of the painting are imagined by the artist, but *not* described in the biblical story?

Figure 10.10 Artemisia Gentileschi, *Judith Slaying Holofernes*, ca. 1614–1620. Oil on canvas, 6 ft. 6$\frac{1}{3}$ in. x 5 ft. 4 in. Uffizi Gallery, Florence.

Gentileschi's favorite subjects were biblical heroines—she painted the Judith story some seven times. The passion she brought to these depictions may be said to reflect her profound sense of victimization: At the age of eighteen, she was raped by her drawing teacher and (during the sensational trial of her assailant) subjected to torture as a test of the truth of her testimony.

Pozzo Baroque artists turned the houses of God into theaters for sacred drama. The walls and ceilings of Italian chapels and churches provided ready surfaces for illusionistic frescoes. Such is the case with the Church of Sant'Ignazio in Rome. Its barrel-vaulted ceiling bears a breathtaking *trompe l'oeil* vision of Saint Ignatius' apotheosis—his elevation to divine status (Figure **10.11**). A master of the techniques of linear perspective and dramatic foreshortening, the Jesuit architect and sculptor Andrea Pozzo (1642–1709) made the ceiling above Sant'Ignazio's clerestory appear to open up. The viewer gazes "through" the roof into the heavens that receive the levitating body of the saint. Pozzo's cosmic rendering—one of the first of numerous illusionistic ceilings found in seventeenth- and eighteenth-century European churches and palaces—may be taken to reflect a new perception of physical space inspired, in part, by European geographic exploration and discovery (see Chapter 9). Indeed, Pozzo underlines the global ambitions of Roman Catholic evangelism by adding at the four corners of the ceiling the allegorical figures of Asia, Africa, Europe, and America.

Figure 10.11 (opposite) Andrea Pozzo, *Apotheosis of Saint Ignatius*, 1691. Fresco. Nave ceiling, Sant'Ignazio, Rome. The spatial illusionism of Baroque painting and architecture gave apocalyptic grandeur to Counter-Reformation ideals.

IGNEM VENI
TERE IN TERRA

THE NORTHERN BAROQUE

THROUGHOUT France, Italy, Spain, and other parts of the West, the Baroque style mirrored the spirit of the Catholic Reformation; however, in Northern Europe, where Protestant loyalties remained strong, another manifestation of the style emerged. The differences between the two are easily observed in the arts: In Italy, church interiors were ornate and theatrical; but in England, the Netherlands, and northern Germany, where Protestants as a matter of faith were committed to private devotion rather than public ritual, churches were stripped of ornamentation. Protestant devotionalism shared with Catholic mysticism an anti-intellectual bias, but Protestantism shunned all forms of theatrical display. In Northern Europe, where a largely Protestant population prospered, the Bible exercised an especially significant influence on the arts.

If religion shaped artistic productivity, so too did the patronage of a rising middle class. Having benefited financially from worldwide commerce, merchants demanded an art that complemented their keen interest in secular life. While princely patronage did not slacken, the landmark examples of Northern Baroque art reflect the vitality of this wealthy new commercial class.

The Rise of the English Commonwealth

Following the death of Queen Elizabeth I in 1603, England experienced a period of political and social turbulence that culminated in the emergence of true constitutional monarchy. The political conflict centered on the issue of whether sovereigns governed by the grace of God and were thus unlimited in their powers, or whether such powers should be restricted by an elected legislature or parliament. This conflict between absolutism and popular rule was complicated by the emergence of a powerful middle class and, simultaneously, by the development of England's powerful Protestant element—the Puritans (English Calvinists who demanded Church reform and strict religious observance). Parliament, the Puritans, and the alliances forming in the overall political structure ultimately combined in a rebellion against royal authority. The parliamentary interests prevailed, and in the "Glorious Revolution" of 1688, the principle of constitutional government was firmly established. With the Bill of Rights (1688) and the Toleration Act (1689), England won a victory for civil rights, representative government, and freedom of worship.

The King James Bible

Closely related to the religious issues of the time was the publication of a new English translation of the Bible. Drawing on a number of sixteenth-century English translations of Scripture, a committee of fifty-four scholars recruited by James I of England (1566–1625) completed an "authorized" English-language edition of the Old and New Testaments. The new translation, known as the King James Bible, preserved the spiritual fervor of the Old Testament Hebrew and the narrative vigor of the New Testament Greek. Like Shakespeare's poetry, with which it was contemporary, the language of the King James Bible is majestic and compelling. Like the works of Shakespeare, it has had a shaping influence on the English language and on all subsequent English literature.

King James Bible (1611)

Donne

One of the most eloquent voices of religious devotionalism in the Protestant North was that of John Donne (1571–1631). Donne studied at Oxford and Cambridge and entered Parliament in 1601. Born and raised as a Roman Catholic, he converted to Anglicanism in 1615, soon becoming a priest of the Church of England.

One of the most celebrated preachers of his age, Donne held the position of dean at Saint Paul's Cathedral in London. There he developed the sermon as a vehicle for philosophic meditation. The language of his sermons is notable for its extended metaphors, or "conceits." The conceit is an elaborate metaphor that compares two apparently dissimilar objects or emotions, often with the effect of shock or surprise. In one of the most widely quoted of Donne's *Meditations*, such conceits are interwoven to picture humankind as part of a vast cosmic plan. Memorable images bind ideas together: The tolling bell, for instance, calls to mind Saint Paul's age-old tradition of ringing church bells to announce the death of a parishioner.

Donne, *Meditations* (1623–1624)

Ideas and Issues

DONNE: NO MAN IS AN ISLAND

"All mankind is of one author, and is one volume; when one man dies, one chapter is not torn out of the book, but translated into a better language; and every chapter must be so translated. God employs several translators; some pieces are translated by age, some by sickness, some by war, some by justice; but God's hand is in every translation, and his hand shall bind up all our scattered leaves again for that library where every book shall lie open to one another. As therefore the bell that rings to a sermon calls not upon the preacher only but upon the congregation to come, so this bell calls us all. . . . No man is an island entire of itself; every man is a piece of the continent, a part of the main. If a clod be washed away by the sea, Europe is the less, as well as if a promontory were, as well as if a manor of thy friend's or of thine own were. Any man's death diminishes me, because I am involved in mankind, and therefore never send to know for whom the bell tolls; it tolls for thee."

(From Donne, *Meditations*, Meditation 17)

Q Identify the extended metaphors in this excerpt. How does Donne's idea of humankind reflect the age in which he lived?

Donne's poetry was as unconventional as his prose. Because his conceits often drew on the imagery of the new learning (see page 293), critics referred to his poetry (and that of the poets who shared this style) as "metaphysical." Metaphysical poetry reflects a predisposition to dramatic contrast and frequent, unexpected shifts of viewpoint—features readily visible in Baroque painting (see pages 267–269). Such qualities dominate some of Donne's finest works, such as the nineteen religious poems known as the *Holy Sonnets*. In Sonnet 10 (reproduced below), Donne rejects the notion of Death as "mighty and dreadful." Calling Death a slave who keeps bad company ("poison, war, and sickness"), he concludes—artfully alluding to the Christian promise of salvation—that Death itself will die.

Donne, *Holy Sonnets* (1618)

Death be not proud, though some have called thee
Mighty and dreadful, for thou art not so;
For those whom thou think'st thou dost overthrow
Die not, poor Death, nor yet canst thou kill me.
From rest and sleep, which but thy pictures be,
Much pleasure, then from thee much more must flow,
And soonest our best men with thee do go,
Rest of their bones and souls' delivery.
Thou art slave to fate, chance, kings, and desperate men,
And dost with poison, war, and sickness dwell,
And poppy,[1] or charms[2] can make us sleep as well,
And better than thy stroke; why swell'st[3] thou then?
One short sleep past, we wake eternally,
And Death shall be no more; Death, thou shalt die.

[1] Opium.

[2] Sleeping potions.

[3] Puff with pride.

Milton

John Milton (1608–1674) was a devout Puritan and a staunch defender of the antiroyalist cause. His career as a humanist and poet began at Cambridge University and continued throughout his eleven-year tenure as secretary to the English Council of State. Though shy and retiring, Milton became a political activist and a persistent defender of religious, political, and intellectual freedom. He challenged English society with expository prose essays on a number of controversial subjects. In one pamphlet, he defended divorce between couples who were spiritually and temperamentally incompatible—a subject possibly inspired by his first wife's unexpected decision to abandon him briefly just after their marriage. In other prose works, Milton opposed parliament's effort to control free speech and freedom of the press. "Who kills a man kills a reasonable creature," wrote Milton, "but he who destroys a good book, kills reason itself."

Milton was already fifty years old when he resolved to compose a modern epic that rivaled the majesty of the classic works of Homer and Virgil. At the outset, he considered various themes, one of which was the story of King Arthur. But he settled instead on a Christian subject that allowed him to examine an issue particularly dear to his Protestant sensibilities: the meaning of evil in a universe created by a benevolent God. The twelve books of *Paradise Lost* retell the story of the fall of Adam and Eve, beginning with the activities of the rebellious archangel Satan and culminating in the expulsion of the First Parents from Paradise. In the opening lines of the poem, Milton calls on "the Heav'nly Muse," the divine source of inspiration, to sing:

Milton, *Paradise Lost* (1667)

Of man's first disobedience, and the fruit
Of that forbidden tree, whose mortal taste
Brought death into the world, and all our woe,
With loss of Eden, till one greater Man [Jesus]
Restore us, and regain the blissful seat

The poem concludes with the archangel Michael's explanation to Adam of how fallen humankind, through Jesus, will recover immortality. Adam's humble response (quoted below from Book XII, ll. 552–587) reflects his restored faith in good "still overcoming evil," and his optimism that humankind can ultimately obtain "a paradise within."

[. . . to the Angel] Adam [at] last replied:
"How soon hath thy prediction, seer blest,
Measured this transient world, the race of time,
Till time stand fixed: beyond is all abyss,
Eternity, whose end no eye can reach.
Greatly instructed I shall hence depart,
Greatly in peace of thought, and have my fill
Of knowledge, what this vessel can contain;
Beyond which was my folly to aspire.
Henceforth I learn, that to obey is best,
And love with fear the only God, to walk
As in his presence, ever to observe
His providence, and on him sole depend,
Merciful over all his works, with good
Still overcoming evil, and by small
Accomplishing great things, by things deemed weak
Subverting worldly strong, and worldly wise
By simply meek; that suffering for truth's sake
Is fortitude to highest victory,
And to the faithful death the gate of life;
Taught this by his example whom I now
Acknowledge my redeemer ever blest."
To whom thus also th' angel last replied:
"This having learnt, thou hast attained the sum
Of wisdom; hope no higher, though all the stars
Thou knew'st by name, and all th' ethereal powers,
All secrets of the deep, all nature's works,
Or works of God in heav'n, air, earth, or sea,
And all the riches of this world enjoy'dst,
And all the rule, one empire; only add
Deeds to thy knowledge answerable, add faith,
Add virtue, patience, temperance, add love,
By name to come called charity, the soul

Of all the rest: then wilt thou not be loath
To leave this Paradise, but shalt possess
A paradise within thee, happier far."

The august theme of the Fall and Redemption, rooted in biblical history, permitted Milton to explore questions of human knowledge, freedom, and morality and, ultimately, to "justify the ways of God to men." Considered the greatest of modern epics, *Paradise Lost* is a mirror of the Baroque imagination: vast in its intellectual sweep, theatrical in its staging, and wide-ranging in its allusions to history and literature.

The London of Christopher Wren

London at the time of Donne and Milton was a city of vast extremes. England's commercial activities in India and the Americas made its capital a center for stock exchanges, insurance firms, and joint-stock companies. While wealthy Londoners made up a growing number of its 250,000 inhabitants, many urban dwellers lived in poverty. And while English intellectuals made advances in scientific learning (see pages 294–296), one-fourth of London's inhabitants could neither read nor write.

In 1666, a devastating fire tore through London and destroyed three-quarters of the city, including thirteen thousand homes, eighty-seven parish churches, and the cathedral church of Saint Paul's, where John Donne had served as dean some decades earlier. Following the fire, there was an upsurge of large-scale building activity and a general effort to modernize London. The architect Christopher Wren (1632–1723) played a leading role in this effort. A child prodigy in mathematics, then an experimental scientist and professor of astronomy at London and Oxford, Wren was one of the founding fathers of the Royal Society of London for Improving Natural Knowledge. Following the Great Fire, Wren prepared designs for the reconstruction of London. Although his plans for new city streets (based on Rome) were rejected, he was commissioned to rebuild more than fifty churches, including Saint Paul's—the first church in Christendom to be completed in the lifetime of its architect (Figure **10.12**).

Wren's early designs for Saint Paul's featured a Greek-cross plan; however, the clergy of Saint Paul's preferred a Latin-cross structure. The final design was a compromise that combined Classical, Gothic, Renaissance, and Baroque architectural features: elegant Corinthian columns, ornate twin clock towers, and strong surface contrasts of light and dark. While Wren's dome recalls Bramante's Tempietto (see Figure 7.21), its massive scale and placement over a Latin-cross basilica look back to Saint Peter's in Rome (see Figure 10.4). Like Milton's *Paradise Lost*, Wren's Saint Paul's is a majestic synthesis of Classical and Christian traditions, while its huge size, dramatic exterior, and light-filled interior are Baroque in conception and effect.

Figure 10.12 Christopher Wren, west façade of Saint Paul's Cathedral, London, 1675–1710. Width approx. 90 ft. As at Saint Peter's (see Figure 7.33), the dome is equal in its diameter to the combined width of the nave and side-aisles. The dimensions of the cathedral are colossal: 366 feet from ground level to the top of the lantern cross (Saint Peter's reaches 452 feet).

Seventeenth-Century Holland

In 1579, after almost two decades of bloodshed, the seventeen provinces of the Netherlands expelled the armies of the invading Spanish king Philip II (1527–1598). Declaring their independence in 1581, seven of these provinces in the North Netherlands would establish a predominantly Calvinist Dutch Republic (later called "Holland"). During the seventeenth century, this self-governing state became one of the most commercially active territories in Western Europe. Dutch shipbuilders produced fine trading vessels that took goods to all parts of the world. In Amsterdam, as in hundreds of other Dutch towns, citizens profited handsomely from the thriving maritime economy.

The autonomous towns of the North Netherlands fostered freedom of thought, a high rate of literacy, and a degree of material prosperity unmatched elsewhere in the world. Their proletarian tastes, along with a profound appreciation for the comforts of home and

hearth, inspired their patronage of the arts—in particular, a preference for secular subjects such as portraits, still lifes, landscapes, and scenes of everyday life. A Golden Age of painting, marked by obsessive attention to the appearance of the natural world, flourished just as Dutch lensmakers began to experiment with the first telescopes and microscopes.

Maria van Oosterwyck (1630–1693) was one of many Dutch still-life painters. Drawing on the tradition of exacting realism initiated by Jan van Eyck (see Figure 8.10), van Oosterwyck brought a naturalist's passion for detail to every object in her landmark *Vanitas Still Life* of 1668 (Figure **10.13**): a radiant Dutch tulip, a worn book, a meticulously painted globe, a rotting skull, and a minute self-portrait reflected in the carafe on the left. These illusionistic items, as well as the moth, the fly, and the tiny mouse nibbling at some grain, make symbolic reference to the transience of temporal existence. Ostensibly a celebration of earthly life, the painting—a type known as ***vanitas***—suggests the corruptibility of worldly goods, the futility of riches, and the inevitability of death.

Figure 10.13 Maria van Oosterwyck, *Vanitas Still Life*, 1668. Oil on canvas, 29 x 35 in. Museum of Art History, Vienna. Neither this artist nor any of the many other talented seventeenth-century women who painted saleable fruit and flower pieces for the Dutch art market were permitted to enroll in the all-male local artists' guild. Nevertheless, Maria van Oosterwyck commanded top prices for her illusionistic still-life paintings.

Vermeer

The Dutch artist Jan Vermeer (1632–1675) was a master at depicting light. The soft, glowing atmosphere in his paintings inspired his admirers to describe his canvas surfaces, often stippled with small white dots, as melted pearls. Vermeer represented his immediate surroundings with a directness and intimacy that has led scholars to suggest his pictures were conceived with the aid of a ***camera obscura***, a seventeenth-century optical device that anticipated the modern pinhole camera. Whether or not he actually employed such a device, however, has little to do with his consummate ability to use light and color as subtle, unifying elements.

Vermeer's *View of Delft* (Figure **10.14**), a topographic depiction of the artist's native city, reflects the Dutch

Figure 10.14 Jan Vermeer, *View of Delft*, 1658. Oil on canvas, 3 ft. 2¾ in. x 3 ft. 10 in. Mauritshuis, The Hague. Dwarfed by their setting, two groups of tiny figures (artfully placed in the left foreground) behold the cityscape from within the painting, as we do from without.

Figure 10.15 (below) Jan Vermeer, *The Milkmaid*, ca. 1658–1660. Oil on canvas, 17⅞ x 16⅛ in. Rijksmuseum, Amsterdam. Unlike the paintings of the Italian Baroque masters, Vermeer's canvases contain no heroic narratives and little anecdotal content. They achieve monumentality by means of composition and color; witness the complementary blues and yellows. The pinpoints of light stippled on the bread suggest the use of an optical device, such as the *camera obscura*.

affection for the visible world conceived as landscape (the English word derives from the Dutch *landschap*). Vermeer lowers the horizon line to give increased attention to the dramatic sky. With Baroque expansiveness, the broad horizon of this landmark image seems to reach beyond the limits of the frame, suggesting a spatial realm that exceeds the mundane boundaries of seventeenth-century Delft.

Only thirty-odd paintings survived Vermeer's short career—he died at the age of forty-three. Many of these take as their subject a woman in a domestic interior. In *The Milkmaid*, for instance, a robust servant is occupied with a mundane task: She pours milk from a pitcher into a pot, where it will be mixed with bread to produce a sop for invalids and small children (Figure **10.15**). Her rapt concentration, the gentle lighting that pours in from a basement window, the hanging baskets, even the nail on the whitewashed wall, work to transform an ordinary scene into a memorable account of everyday life. Here, Vermeer achieves a measure of tranquility unmatched in European art.

Figure 10.16 Rembrandt van Rijn, *Captain Frans Banning Cocq Mustering his Company*, 1642. Oil on canvas, 11 ft. 9½ in. x 14 ft. 4½ in. Rijksmuseum, Amsterdam. For centuries, before layers of dirt and varnish were removed in the late twentieth century, the painting was known as "The Night Watch." Two feet of canvas (that included three more figures) were cut from the left side of the painting prior to its installation in Amsterdam's Town Hall in 1715.

Rembrandt

The unrivaled giant of Dutch Golden Age art, Rembrandt van Rijn (1606–1669), produced landmark works in almost every genre: portraiture, landscape, and religious art. A keen observer of human character and a master technician, he became the leading portrait painter in the Dutch capital of Amsterdam. The vogue of portraiture reflected the self-conscious materialism of a rising middle class. Among Rembrandt's commissions, the most lucrative was the group portrait—a genre that commemorated the achievements of wealthy families, guild members (see Figure 11.2), and civic administrators.

In 1642, Rembrandt received a commission from the civic guard of Amsterdam for a group portrait to be installed in its new meeting hall. The result was the huge painting *Captain Frans Banning Cocq Mustering his Company* (Figure **10.16** and see Figure 10.1). Rembrandt shows the harquebusiers—more a social club than an active militia—as they assemble to parade through the streets of Amsterdam. The event seems to take place on a stage, dramatically lit to create strong contrasts of dark and light. It is animated by theatrical gestures, colorful details (one can almost hear the dog barking), local "extras" (including Rembrandt himself hiding behind the flag-bearer), and dynamic energy (enhanced by the diagonally positioned lances and harquebus (long-barreled guns that gave the company its name)). A girl in a yellow dress holds the militia's goblet; hanging from her belt are the claws of a dead chicken, an emblem of the company. Captain Cocq, wearing a black uniform with a red sash, strides forward, his foreshortened left arm (which casts a strong shadow on the gold doublet of his lieutenant) reaching out to invite the viewer into the painting.

Many Dutch masters excelled in capturing the likeness of their patrons, but Rembrandt surpassed fidelity to nature to probe the inner life of his sitters. The commissions he received at the beginning of his career exceeded his ability to fill them. However, after a meteoric rise to fame, he saw his fortunes decline. Accumulated debts led to poverty, bankruptcy, and psychological depression. The history of Rembrandt's career is mirrored in his self-portraits, more than sixty of which survive. These are a kind of visual diary, a

Figure 10.17 Rembrandt van Rijn, *Self-Portrait as Saint Paul*, 1661. Oil on canvas, 35$\frac{7}{8}$ x 30$\frac{3}{8}$ in. Rijksmuseum, Amsterdam. Rembrandt's psychologically probing self-portraits have no equivalent in any non-Western culture prior to the eighteenth century.

Figure 10.18 Rembrandt van Rijn, *Christ Preaching* ("The Hundred-Guilder Print"), ca. 1648–1650. 11 x 15$\frac{1}{2}$ in. Rijksmuseum, Amsterdam. Engravings and etchings were very popular among the Dutch, both as original artworks and as copies after paintings. Rembrandt's etching of Christ preaching, sometimes titled *Christ Healing the Sick*, is more famously known as "The Hundred-Guilder Print," because it sold for that unusually large sum at a seventeenth-century Dutch auction.

lifetime record of the artist's enterprise in impassioned self-scrutiny. The *Self-Portrait* of 1661, with its slackened facial muscles and furrowed brow, engages the viewer with the image of a noble, yet utterly vulnerable, personality (Figure **10.17**). Rembrandt worked and reworked the portrait, building up layers of paint to produce a rich **impasto** that added expressive emphasis and texture.

While Rembrandt depended on his portrait commissions for financial reward, it was his religious art that brought him fame in the Protestant North. The Old Testament was especially popular among the Calvinist Dutch, who viewed themselves as God's "chosen" people. Rembrandt's Anabaptist upbringing, with its fundamentalist approach to Scripture, surely contributed to his preference for portraying biblical subjects in literal, deeply human terms. His own place and time provided him with a cast of characters for Bible narratives rendered in both monumental paintings and in small **etchings**. Etching—a printing process developed in the sixteenth century—met the needs of middle-class patrons who sought private devotional images that were inexpensive by comparison with paintings. A consummate printmaker, Rembrandt used the **burin** (a steel tool; see Figure 8.16) to develop dramatic contrasts of rich darks and theatrical lights. In the landmark print *Christ Preaching* (Figure **10.18**), Rembrandt brought to life a key episode from the Gospel of Matthew. The community of Jews—an assembly of Pharisees (far left), along with the poor, the sick, and the downtrodden—are drawn not from Rembrandt's historical imagination, but from the streets and ghettos of Amsterdam.

THE ARISTOCRATIC BAROQUE

THE "Aristocratic Baroque" describes that phase of the Baroque style that emerged in the royal courts of Western Europe during the seventeenth and eighteenth centuries. Most of Europe's ruling families at this time claimed to hold unlimited, or absolute, political power. Like the pharaohs of ancient Egypt, they governed as direct representatives of God on earth. The most notable of Europe's absolute monarchs was Louis XIV, king of France (1638–1715). During the nearly three-quarters of a century that Louis occupied the French throne, he dictated the political, economic, and cultural policies of the country, never once calling into session the Estates General, France's representative assembly. Louis controlled a centralized bureaucracy and a standing army, and he placed the Church under the authority of the state. While the King may never have uttered the famous words attributed to him, "I am the state," he surely operated according to that absolutist precept. By the end of his reign he had brought France to a position of political and military leadership in Western Europe and the arts to an unparalleled level of grandeur (Figure **10.19**).

Louis XIV and the Arts

Louis cultivated the arts as an adjunct to majesty. Following in the tradition of his father, Louis XIII (1601–1643), who had instituted the French Royal Academy of Language and Literature in 1635, he created and subsidized government-sponsored institutions in the arts, appointing his personal favorites to oversee each. In 1648, at the age of ten, Louis founded the Academy of Painting and Sculpture; in 1661 he established the Academy of Dance; in 1666, the Academy of Sciences; in 1669, the Academy of Music; and in 1671, the Academy of Architecture. The creation of the academies was a symptom of royal efforts to fix standards, but Louis also had something more personal in mind: He is said to have told a group of academicians, "Gentlemen, I entrust to you the most precious thing on earth—my fame." His trust was well placed, for the academies brought glory to the king and set guidelines that would govern the arts for at least two centuries. These standards were enshrined in "rules" inspired by the legacy of ancient Greece and Rome. Thus *Neoclassicism*—the revival of Classical style and subject matter—was a prime ingredient of France's Aristocratic Baroque style.

Supported by the academies, Louis exercised immense cultural influence. Under his leadership, the center of European artistic patronage shifted from Italy to France, and French culture—from architecture to fine cuisine—came to dominate European tastes.

As an expression of his absolute authority, Louis took as his official insignia the image of the Classical sun god Apollo, referring to himself as *le roi soleil* ("the Sun King"). Recognizing the propaganda value of the arts, the king used the French treasury to glorify himself and his office. His extravagance left France in a woeful financial condition that contributed to the outbreak of the French Revolution (see page 303).

In the vocabulary of royal power, architecture played an especially vital role. In order to exercise greater control over the French nobility, Louis moved his capital from Paris to Versailles. At this village some 12 miles from Paris, he commissioned a massive renovation of his father's hunting lodge. Almost half the size of Paris, the new complex at Versailles was connected to the old capital by a grand boulevard that ran from the king's bedroom to the center of state business in Paris. It took thirty-six thousand workers and nearly twenty years to build Versailles, but, in 1682, the French court finally established itself in the apartments of this magnificent unfortified ***château***

Figure 10.19 Hyacinthe Rigaud, *Portrait of Louis XIV*, 1701. Oil on canvas, 9 ft. 1 in. x 6 ft. 4 in. Louvre, Paris. Striking a mannered pose, the king stands in his coronation robes; he is surrounded by royal paraphernalia: two scepters, the crown (on the cushion at the left), and the sword of state.

Making Connections

ABSOLUTISM AND THE ARTS: EAST AND WEST

Comparable in size and conception to Versailles (see Figure 10.21) is Beijing's Forbidden City—the ceremonial complex that symbolized the divine authority of China's absolutist rulers (Figure **10.20**). Begun under the emperors of the Ming dynasty, this walled complex of palaces, tombs, and gardens was the most elaborate architectural monument of the Ming (1368–1644) and Qing (1644–1911) eras. For more than five hundred years, the Forbidden City—which, like Versailles, is now a park and museum—was the administrative center of China, home to the Chinese emperors (the "Sons of Heaven"), their families, their servants, and the members of their courts. All others were prohibited from entry, hence the name "Forbidden City."

The royal precinct was a sacred space, designed according to ancient principles of cosmology that had governed Chinese architecture since earliest times. Imperial buildings were arranged along the north–south axis, with the palace facing south, so as to shun the evil spirits that, according to the Chinese, originated in the north. Unlike Versailles, the buildings were constructed of wood rather than stone. Carefully arranged gardens—a hallmark of East Asian culture—were accessible from covered walkways. Objects of private contemplation rather than public display, these gardens were more intimate than those at Versailles. Yet the Forbidden City's grand avenues, broad courtyards, theaters, artificial pools, and lavish fountains rivaled those of their French counterpart.

As in France, royal patronage in China encouraged the production of luxury items that included inlaid bronze vessels, carved ivories and jades, lacquerware, embroidered silks, and brightly colored porcelain wares. Indeed, the Forbidden City was the nucleus of Chinese majesty. Its gridiron plan and ornamental splendor rivaled the magnificent landmarks of the Aristocratic Baroque in seventeenth-century France.

Q Does architecture in our own time still reflect the power and prestige of the ruling authority?

Figure 10.20 (right) Xu Yang, *Bird's-Eye View of the Capital*, 1770. Hanging scroll, ink and color on paper, 8 ft. $4\frac{1}{4}$ in. x 7 ft. 8 in. The Palace Museum, Beijing.

Figure 10.21 (below) Isidore-Laurent Deroy, *The Park and Palace of Versailles*, France, nineteenth century. Lithograph. Versailles and Trianon castles.

Figure 10.22 Parterre du Midi, Palace of Versailles. Itself a kind of outdoor theater, the royal palace provided the ideal backdrop for the ballets, operas, and plays that were regular features of court life. The formal gardens and long walkways radiating from the central building served as symbols of absolute order.

(castle). More than a royal residence, Versailles was—in its size and splendor—the symbol of Louis' majesty.

Shaped like a winged horseshoe, the almost 2000-foot-long palace—best viewed in its entirety from the air—was the focus of an immense complex of parks, lakes, and forest (Figure **10.21**). Its central building was designed by Louis Le Vau (1612–1670), while the two additional wings were added by Jules Hardouin-Mansart (1646–1708). Three levels of vertically aligned windows march across the palace façade like soldiers in a formal procession. Porches bearing freestanding Corinthian columns accent the second level, and ornamental statues at the roofline help to relieve the monotonous horizontality of the structure. In its total effect, the palace is dignified and commanding, a Baroque synthesis of Classical and Palladian elements (see Figure 7.22).

Flanking the palace were barracks for honor guards, lodgings for more than fifteen hundred servants, kennels, greenhouses, and an orangery with over two thousand orange trees. Over 7 square miles of gardens were designed by André Le Nôtre with the same compelling sense of order that Le Vau brought to the architecture (Figure **10.22**). The great park featured an array of hedges clipped into geometric shapes, sparkling fountains (that favorite of all Baroque mechanical devices), grottoes, a zoo, theaters, and outdoor "rooms" for private gatherings and clandestine meetings. When in bloom, the gardens—some planted with over four million tulip bulbs, which Louis imported annually from Holland—were a spectacular sight. On the garden side of the palace, artificial pools reflected sculptures whose subject matter glorified the majesty of the king.

If the exterior of Versailles symbolized royal grandeur, the interior was a monument to princely self-indulgence. Versailles' ***salons*** (drawing rooms) testify to Louis' success at cultivating French trades in such luxury items as crafted silver, clocks, lace, brocades, porcelain, and fine glass. During the seventeenth century, the silk industry reached its peak. French carpets competed with those of Turkey and Persia, the art of **marquetry** (inlaid wood) rivaled that of Italy, and the tapestries produced at the Gobelins factory in Paris outclassed those woven in Flanders. Versailles' *salons*/rooms were adorned with illusionistic frescoes, gilded stucco moldings, crystal chandeliers, and huge, ornate mirrors. The most splendid of these interior spaces is the 240-foot-long Hall of Mirrors, which once connected the royal apartments with the chapel (Figure **10.23**). The hall features a wall of seventeen mirrored arcades that face an equal number of high-arched windows opening onto the garden. Framing this opulent royal passageway, mirrors and windows set up a typically Baroque counterpoint of image and illusion.

Theater Arts

The court of Versailles was the setting for an extraordinary outpouring of theater, music, and dance. To provide musical entertainments for state dinners, balls, and theatrical performances, Louis established a permanent orchestra, the first in European history. All members of the court were expected to perform the basic court dances, including the very popular ***minuet***. Louis commissioned extravagant ballets in which he himself—a superb dancer—participated. Dressed as the sun, the fifteen-year-

Figure 10.23 Jules Hardouin-Mansart and Charles Le Brun, Hall of Mirrors, Palace of Versailles, ca. 1680. Length 240 ft. Mirrors were to Versailles what fountains were to Rome: vehicles for the theatrical display of changing light in unbounded space.

old king danced the lead in the 1653 performance of the *Ballet de la Nuit* (see Figure 10.28).

Of landmark significance was Louis' contribution to the birth of professional dance and the transformation of dance into an independent artform. This was achieved by way of the Royal Academy of Dance, which established rules for the five positions that became the basis for classical ballet. By 1700, there emerged a system of abstract symbols for recording specific dance steps and movements, thus initiating the art of **choreography**.

Louis' influence on theatrical performance was equally important: He granted traveling companies performance spaces that functioned as theaters in his courts at the Louvre in Paris and at Versailles. Seventeenth-century French theater rivaled that of Elizabethan England. It was in the genre of comedy and specifically in the works of Jean-Baptiste Poquelin (1622–1673)—whose stage name was Molière—that the literary landmarks of the age emerged. The son of a wealthy upholsterer, Molière abandoned a career in law in favor of acting and writing plays. Unlike Shakespeare's comedies, which depend largely on intricate plots, those of Molière bring to life the comic foibles of human society. In dramas that ridicule the hypochondriac (*The Imaginary Invalid*), religious hypocrisy (*Tartuffe*), bitter cynics (*The Misanthrope*), material greed (*The Miser*), and boorish social climbers (*The Tradesman Turned Gentleman*), he holds a mirror up to human nature. Some of Molière's plays were designed as ***comédies-ballets***—dramatic performances incorporating interludes of song and dance (in a manner similar to modern musical comedy). These were especially popular at the king's court, but even beyond Versailles Molière's comedies had wide appeal. His hilarious attack on the hypocrisy of polite society, as framed in *The Misanthrope*, is as timely today as when it was first performed in Paris.

Molière, *The Misanthrope* (1666)

The theater arts flourished in seventeenth-century Paris—the center of an urbane and glittering culture. Especially popular were dramatic tragedies, the rules of which were fixed by the French Royal Academy of Language and Literature. The Academy demanded morally uplifting drama featuring high-minded themes and noble characters drawn from Greek and Roman literature. These demands were met by the French playwrights Pierre Corneille (1606–1684) and Jean Racine (1639–1699). Their plays obey the Aristotelian unities of action and time (see page 40). To these, Racine added unity of place. The plays of Corneille and Racine pit human passions against high-minded ideals and human will against unbridled emotion—themes that attracted audiences of their own time and those of many centuries to follow.

Figure 10.24 Nicolas Poussin, *Arcadian Shepherds*, 1638–1639. Oil on canvas, 33½ x 47⅝ in. Louvre, Paris. Poussin posed his figures so that their every gesture served to narrate the story. All elements in the painting, from the position of the Muse's feet to the order of the trees in the landscape, contribute to the strict horizontal-and-vertical pictorial structure.

Academic Art

The heavy hand of the Academy of Painting and Sculpture was felt in the visual arts, where seventeenth-century painters were enjoined to follow the formalized rules of the Grand Style, inspired by the High Renaissance works of Raphael (see page 201): Artists should choose only serious and elevated subjects (such as battles, heroic actions, and miraculous events) drawn from Classical or Christian subject matter. The physical action should suit the mood of the narrative. The subject matter should be presented clearly and evenly in compositions that are harmonious and free of irrelevant and sordid details. Restraint, moderation, and decorum should govern all aspects of pictorial representation.

These academic requirements would dominate the work of one of France's finest painters, Nicolas Poussin (1594–1665). Poussin spent most of his life in Rome, absorbing the rich heritage of the Classical and Renaissance past. He revered Raphael, and, like many Neoclassicists, shared Raphael's esteem for lofty subjects drawn from Greco-Roman mythology and Christian legend. Poussin wrote an influential treatise formalizing the rules of the Academy; he also practiced them faithfully.

His *Arcadian Shepherds* (Figure **10.24**) transports us to the idyllic region in ancient Greece known as Arcadia, a place where men and women were said to live in perfect harmony with nature. Three shepherds have come upon an ancient tomb, a symbol of death; on the right, the stately Muse of History meditates upon the tomb's inscription, *"Et in Arcadia Ego"* ("I [death] also dwell in Arcadia")—that is, death reigns even in this most perfect of places. Poussin's moral allegory, at once a pastoral elegy and a *memento mori*, instructs us that death is universal. Cool, bright colors and even lighting enhance the elegiac mood, while sharp contours and the sure use of line provide absolute clarity of design. But the real power of this landmark painting lies in the elegant geometry of its composition and the faultless arrangement of its statuesque, idealized figures. Despite its Baroque theatricality, order dominates over spontaneity, intellect over the senses.

The Aristocratic Baroque Portrait

The Baroque was the great age of aristocratic portraiture. Aristocratic Baroque portraits differ dramatically from those of Rembrandt: While the latter aimed to penetrate the inner life of their sitters, aristocratic portraits favored their outward appearance, often idealizing it. The landmark example of French aristocratic portraiture is the magnificent likeness of Louis XIV by Hyacinthe Rigaud (1659–1743; see Figure 10.19). Rigaud pictures the sixty-three-year-old monarch in his ermine-lined coronation robe embroidered with *fleur-de-lis* (the stylized lily emblem of French royalty). The king wears silk stockings, a lace cravat, a well-manicured wig, and high-heeled shoes (designed by Louis to compensate for his short stature)—all of which were fashionable hallmarks of upper-class wealth. Symbolic devices enhance the themes of regality and authority: Satin curtains frame the king theatrically, and a lone column makes reference to manly fortitude. Such "props" would become standard conventions in Western aristocratic portraiture.

In England, the most accomplished seventeenth-century portraitist was the Flemish master Anthony van Dyck (1599–1641). Born in Antwerp, van Dyck moved to Genoa and then to London, where he became court painter to King Charles I of England (1600–1649). Van Dyck's many commissioned portraits of European aristocrats are striking for their polished elegance and idealized grandeur, features that are especially evident in his equestrian

Figure 10.25 Anthony van Dyck, *Charles I on Horseback*, ca. 1638. Oil on canvas, 12 ft. x 9 ft. 7 in. National Gallery, London. One usually cannot appreciate great artworks without seeing the originals. This is especially true of van Dyck's paintings, whose subtle, energetic brushstrokes are almost entirely lost even in the best photographic reproductions.

portrait of Charles I (Figure **10.25**). In this huge painting, which adopts the familiar theme of ruler-on-horseback (see Figures 3.1 and 7.20), van Dyck shows the king, who was actually short and undistinguished-looking, as handsome and regal. The combination of fluid composition and naturalistic detail, and the shimmering vitality of the brushwork, make this one of the most memorable examples of Aristocratic Baroque portraiture.

Velázquez and Rubens

In Spain, Diego Velázquez (1599–1660), court painter to King Philip IV (1605–1665), became that country's most prestigious artist. Velázquez excelled at modeling forms so that they conveyed the powerful presence of real objects in atmospheric space. For the Spanish court, Velázquez painted a variety of Classical and Christian subjects, but his landmark enterprise was the informal group portrait known as *Las Meninas* (*The Maids of Honor*; Figure **10.26**). Here, Velázquez depicted himself at his easel, alongside members of the royal court: the *infanta* (the five-year-old daughter of the king), her maids of honor, her dwarf, a mastiff hound, and the royal escorts. In the background is a mirror that reflects the images of the king and queen of Spain—presumably the subjects of the large canvas Velázquez is shown painting. Superficially, this is a group portrait of the type painted by Rembrandt (see Figure 10.16), but it is far more complex: Even as Velázquez invites the viewer into the space of the painting, he leaves uncertain

Figure 10.26 Diego Velázquez, *Las Meninas* (*The Maids of Honor*), 1656. Oil on canvas, 10 ft. 5 in. x 9 ft. Prado, Madrid. Almost all of the characters in the painting, including the painter himself, are shown gazing at the royal couple, who must be standing outside of the picture space in the very spot occupied by the viewer. With Baroque inventiveness, Velázquez expands the spatial field to invite the beholder to "enter" the scene from a variety of vantage points.

Making Connections

ARISTOCRATIC ART: EAST AND WEST

In the sixteenth century all of India was united by the Muslim dynasty known as the Moguls (the name derives from the Mongol tribes that came to dominate East Asia in the thirteenth century). Ruling India as absolute monarchs from 1526 to 1707, the Moguls established a luxurious court style and—like Louis XIV—patronized the arts as an adjunct to majesty. Mogul culture blended Muslim, Hindu, Persian, Arabic, and African traditions, and the final products were sophisticated expressions of aristocratic elegance and opulence. Gold jewelry and weaponry encrusted with gems were produced in Mogul workshops. A state-run studio of more than one hundred artists created a library of over twenty-four thousand illuminated manuscripts—painted "gems" as lavish as those in three dimensions.

Aristocratic court portraiture came into fashion during the reign of Jahangir (1569–1627), who rose to power in 1605. The portrait of Jahangir (the name means "world seizer") in Figure **10.27** reflects the royal will to glorify the absolute ruler in a realistic yet decorative style. Sitting atop an elaborate hourglass throne, the Shah ("King") Jahangir welcomes a Sufi (a Muslim mystic), a Turkish dignitary, and King James I of England. He is apotheosized by means of a huge double halo symbolizing the sun and the moon.

In an equally small format, Louis XIV is pictured as Apollo (the ancient god of light), a role he assumed as a mere teenager in one of the dances of a popular court ballet (Figure **10.28**). He wears a fancy gold corselet, a kilt made of golden rays, and an elaborate feathered headdress. The title "roi soleil" (Sun King) may have originated with this ballet. The tradition of the ruler as the sun, however, harks back to ancient Egypt.

Q What purpose is served by the elaborate adornment of the secular ruler? Why are references to divinity common in depictions of absolute monarchs?

Figure 10.27 "Jahangir Preferring a Sufi Shaikh to Kings," from the *Leningrad Album of Bichitr*, seventeenth century. Color and gold, 10 x 7 ⅛ in. Freer Gallery of Art, Smithsonian Institution, Washington, D.C.

Figure 10.28 King Louis XIV as the sun in the 1653 *Ballet de la Nuit*. National Library, Paris.

Figure 10.29 Peter Paul Rubens, *Rape of the Daughters of Leucippus*, ca. 1618. Oil on canvas, 7 ft. 3 in. x 6 ft. 10 in. Alte Pinakothek, Munich. Rubens deeply admired the flamboyant colorist Titian (see Figure 7.34), and he developed a style that, by comparison with Poussin's, was painterly in technique and dynamic in composition.

the relationships among the figures and between the viewer and these figures. *Las Meninas* becomes a Baroque "conceit" provoking a visual dialog between artist and patron and between viewer and viewed.

A contemporary of Velázquez, the internationally renowned Flemish painter Peter Paul Rubens (1577–1640) established his reputation in the courts of Europe. Fluent in six languages, he traveled widely as a diplomat and art dealer for royal patrons in Italy, England, and France. He also headed a large studio workshop that trained scores of assistants to help fill his many commissions—a total lifetime production of some 1,800 paintings.

One of Rubens' most memorable canvases, the *Rape of the Daughters of Leucippus* (Figure **10.29**), depicts the abduction of two mortal women by the Roman heroes Castor and Pollux. Rubens' portrayal of the Classical story explodes with imaginative vigor: Pressing against the picture plane are the fleshy bodies of the nude maidens, their limbs arranged in the pattern of a slowly revolving pinwheel. The masterful paintstrokes exploit sensuous contrasts of luminous pink flesh, burnished armor, gleaming satins, and dense horsehide. Probably commissioned to commemorate the double marriage of Louis XIII of France to a Spanish princess and Philip IV of Spain to a French princess (and, thus, to celebrate the diplomatic alliance of France and Spain), the landmark painting carries a subtext of (male) power over (female) privilege.

Beyond the West

ARISTOCRATIC LANDMARKS

Japan

In the seventeenth century, Japan became a centralized state ruled by members of the Tokugawa dynasty (1600–1868). Like Louis XIV, the Tokugawa *shogun* (general-in-chief) demanded that his warrior elite attend his court in Edo (modern-day Tokyo), from which center he enforced court etiquette. In the Tokugawa court artistic production reached new heights, as evidenced in handpainted scrolls, elegant ceramics (known as "Imari ware"), lacquer boxes, and multipaneled screens. Japanese screens, used to divide interior space, usually feature landscapes with birds or stylized flowers. The *Irises at Yatuhashi*, a gold-leaf screen by Ogata Korin (ca. 1658–1716), unites simplicity and luxury with breathtaking elegance (Figure **10.30**). It embodies the Japanese affection for bold, decorative shapes organized by means of a subtle balance of figure and ground (positive and negative space).

India

India's Mogul Shah Jahan (1627–1666) assumed the role of absolute ruler and patron of the arts that had brought fame to his father, Jahangir (see Figure 10.27). In addition to building sumptuous palaces, he left the world a landmark in the form of a royal tomb, dedicated to the memory of his favorite wife, Mumtaz Mahal (the name means "light of the world"). When Mumtaz died giving birth to their fourteenth child, the inconsolable Jahan commissioned a glorious mausoleum on the banks of the Jumna River. Fabricated in cream-colored marble, the Taj Mahal, flanked by four tall minarets, seems to float majestically above a tree-lined pool that mirrors its elegant silhouette (Figure **10.31**). Exquisitely carved and inlaid walls embellish the interior, while the exterior garden complex, with its four intersecting water channels, is a conscious recreation of the Muslim Garden of Paradise.

Figure 10.30 Ogata Korin, *Irises at Yatuhashi*, from the *Tale of Ise* (*Ise Monogatari*), Edo period, first half of eighteenth century. One of a pair of six-paneled screens, ink and color and gilded paper, with black lacquered frames, each screen 4 ft. 11½ in. x 11 ft. 3½ in. Nezu Institute of Fine Arts, Tokyo.

Figure 10.31 (below) Taj Mahal, Agra, India, 1623–1643.

BAROQUE MUSIC

Gabrieli

During the sixteenth century, the opulent city of Venice was the center of European musical activity. Giovanni Gabrieli (1555–1612), principal organist at Saint Mark's Cathedral in Venice and one of the most influential composers of his time, ushered in a new and dramatic style of **polychoral** and instrumental religious music. Abandoning the *a cappella* tradition favored in Rome, he composed works for two or more choruses, solo instruments, and instrumental ensembles that included trombones and **cornets** (an early type of trumpet) commonly used in Venice's ritual street processions. At Saint Mark's, where two organs were positioned on either side of the **chancel** (the space for clergy and choir surrounding the altar), Gabrieli stationed instrumental groups and up to four separate voice choirs on balconies high above the nave. The alternating bodies of sound, gloriously enhanced by the basilica's acoustics, clearly paralleled the dramatic contrasts of light and shadow found in Baroque painting and sculpture. The motet *In ecclesiis* illustrates the method of opposing or contrasting sonorities (known as **concertato**) that became basic to the music of the Baroque era.

Gabrieli, *In ecclesiis* (published 1615)

Gabrieli was among the first to specify an instrument for each part in the musical composition, earning him the name the "father of orchestration." He was also one of the first composers to write into his scores the words *piano* (soft) and *forte* (loud) to govern the **dynamics** (the degree of loudness or softness) of the piece.

Finally, Gabrieli is credited with advancing a system of major–minor tonality that came to dominate Western music. **Tonality** refers to the arrangement of a musical composition around a central note, called the "tonic" or "home tone" (usually designated as the "key" of a given composition). A keynote or tonic can be built on any of the twelve tones (the seven white and five black keys of the piano keyboard) of the **chromatic scale**. In Baroque music—as in most Western music written to this day—all the tones in the composition relate to the home tone.

Figure 10.32 Pietro Domenico Oliviero, *The Teatro Regio, Turin*, painting of the opening night, December 26, 1740. Oil on canvas, 4 ft. 2½ in. x 3 ft. 8⅞ in. Municipal Museum, Turin, Italy. Five tiers of boxes are fitted into the sides of the proscenium, one even perched over the semicircular pediment. Note the orchestra, without a conductor; the girls distributing refreshments; and the armed guard protecting against disorder.

The Birth of Opera

Opera emerged out of Renaissance efforts to revive the music-drama of ancient Greek theater. While humanist composers had no idea what Greek music sounded like, they sought to imitate the ancient unity of music and poetry. The earliest performances of Western opera resembled the Renaissance masque—a form of musical entertainment that included dance and poetry, along with rich costumes and scenery. Baroque operas were more musically complex, however, and more dramatically cohesive than most Renaissance masques.

The first opera house was built in Venice in 1637, and by 1700 Italy was home to seventeen more such houses, a measure of the vast popularity of the new genre. By the end of the seventeenth century, Italian courts and public theaters boasted all of the essential features of the modern theater: the picture-frame stage, the horseshoe-shaped auditorium, and tiers of galleries or boxes (Figure **10.32**).

Monteverdi

The first master of Baroque music-drama and the greatest Italian composer of the early seventeenth century was Claudio Monteverdi (1567–1643). Monteverdi served the court of Mantua until he became chapel master of Saint Mark's in Venice in 1621, a post he held for the rest of his life. During his long career, he wrote various kinds of religious music, as well as ballets, madrigals, and operas. His compositions reflect a typically Baroque effort to infuse music with the vocal expressiveness and emotional charge of poetry.

Monteverdi, *Orfeo* (1607)

Orfeo, composed for the duke of Mantua, was Monteverdi's first opera and one of the first full-length operas in music history. The **libretto** (literally, "little book") or text of the opera was based on a Classical theme—the descent of Orpheus, the Greek poet-musician, to Hades.

Orfeo required an orchestra of three dozen instruments, including ten viols and seven other bowed string instruments, four trombones, four trumpets, and five keyboard instruments. The instrumentalists performed the **overture**, an orchestral introduction to the opera. They also accompanied vocal music consisting of **arias** (elaborate solo songs or duets) alternating with **recitatives** (passages spoken or recited to sparse chordal accompaniment). The aria worked to develop a character's feelings or state of mind, while the recitative served to narrate the action of the story or to heighten its dramatic effect.

Monteverdi believed that opera should convey the full range of human passions. To that end, he contrived inventive contrasts between singer and accompaniment, recitative and aria, soloist and chorus. He also employed abrupt changes of key to emphasize shifts in mood and action. And he introduced such novel and expressive instrumental effects as ***pizzicato***, the technique of plucking a stringed instrument that is normally bowed. Embracing music, drama, and visual display, Italian opera became the ideal expression of the Baroque sensibility.

Music at the Court of Louis XIV

At the court of Versailles, music played a major role in all forms of royal entertainment. Extravagant theatrical productions made full use of the king's court orchestra (see page 279). Its director, the Italian-born composer Jean-Baptiste Lully (1632–1687), also administered the Royal Academy of Music. Often called the "father of French opera," Lully oversaw all phases of musical performance, from writing scores and training the chorus to staging the operas and conducting the orchestra.

Many of Lully's operas were based on themes from Classical mythology, which featured semidivine heroes—flattering prototypes of the king. Following Neoclassical principles that united words and music, Lully, like his Italian counterparts, wrote the music for his recitative to follow closely the inflections of the spoken word. Finally, Lully developed the single most characteristic feature of French opera: the inclusion of formal dance (see page 280).

Handel and the English Oratorio

Born in the Lutheran trading city of Halle, Germany, George Frideric Handel (1685–1759) was determined to pursue his childhood musical talents. When his father, who intended for him a career in law, refused to provide him with a musical instrument, he smuggled a small clavichord into the attic. After proving himself at the keyboard and as a successful violinist and composer in the courts of Hamburg, Rome, Paris, Naples, and Venice, he emigrated to London in 1710 and became a British citizen in 1726. Handel composed forty-six operas in Italian and four in his native German. He also produced a prodigious number of instrumental works. But it was for his development of the **oratorio** that he earned fame among the English, who called him "England's greatest composer."

An oratorio is the musical setting of a sacred or epic text performed in concert by vocal soloists, chorus, and orchestra. Like operas, oratorios are large in scale and dramatic in intent but, unlike opera, they are performed without scenery, costumes, or dramatic action. Soloists and chorus assume the roles of the main characters in the narrative.

Handel's oratorios are essentially **homophonic**; that is, their musical organization depends on the use of a dominant melody supported by chordal accompaniment. The homophonic organization of melody and chords differs dramatically from the uninterrupted polyphonic interweaving of voices that characterized most music prior to the seventeenth century. The chords in a homophonic composition serve to support—or, in the visual sense, to "spotlight"—a primary melody. In the seventeenth century, there evolved a form of musical shorthand that allowed musicians to fill in the harmony for a principal melody. The **figured bass**, as this shorthand was called, consisted of a line of music with numbers written below it to indicate the harmony accompanying the primary melody. The use of the figured bass (also called the "**continuo**," since it played throughout the piece) was one of the main features of Baroque music.

Handel, *Messiah* (1742)

The most famous of Handel's oratorios is *Messiah*, which was written in the English of the King James Bible. Composed, remarkably, in twenty-four days, it received instant acclaim when it was performed for the first time in Dublin. One of the most moving pieces of choral music ever written, *Messiah* celebrates the birth, death, and resurrection of Jesus. Unlike most of Handel's oratorios, it is not a biblical dramatization but rather a collection of verses from the Old and New Testaments. Handel's *Messiah* has outlasted its age: In many Christian communities, it has become traditional to perform the piece during both the Christmas and Easter seasons. The jubilant "Hallelujah Chorus" (which ends the second of the three parts of the oratorio) still brings audiences to their feet, as it did King George II of Great Britain, who introduced this tradition by rising from his seat when he first heard it performed in London in 1743.

Bach and Religious Music

Unlike the cosmopolitan Handel, Johann Sebastian Bach (1685–1750; Figure **10.33**) never strayed more than a couple of hundred miles from his birthplace in the small town of Eisenach, Germany. Nor did he stray from his Protestant roots: Martin Luther's teachings and Lutheran hymns were Bach's major sources of inspiration, and the organ—the principal instrument of Lutheran church worship—was his favorite instrument. As organ master and choir director of the Church of Saint Thomas in Leipzig, Bach composed music for the Sunday services and for holy days.

Figure 10.33 Elias Gottlob Haussmann, *Johann Sebastian Bach*, 1746. Oil on canvas. 2 ft. 6 in. x 2 ft. 4/5 in. William H. Scheide Library, Princeton University.

The most important component of Lutheran worship was the **cantata**, a multi-movement piece composed of a text sung by chorus and soloists, who are accompanied by musical instruments. Based on the simple melodies of Luther's chorales (see page 235), Bach's cantatas served as musical "commentary" on the daily scriptural lessons of the Lutheran church service. Of his 195 surviving cantatas, the most famous is No. 80, which uses the theme of the landmark Lutheran hymn "A Mighty Fortress Is Our God." Along with the organ **preludes** that set the mood for congregational singing, the cantatas are among Bach's most inspired religious compositions.

Bach, "A Mighty Fortress Is Our God" (1723) and *Passion According to Saint Matthew* (1727)

For the Leipzig congregation, Bach also wrote oratorios and settings for the Mass. His *Passion According to Saint Matthew*, an oratorio written for the Good Friday service, is a landmark in vocal music. This majestic piece—Baroque both in its complexity and in its length (some three and a half hours)—was written for two orchestras and a double chorus that alternates with a solo tenor who narrates, and other soloists who represent the main figures in the Passion (the events between the Last Supper and the Resurrection). A pious Lutheran, who in the course of two marriages fathered twenty children (five of whom became notable musicians), Bach dedicated all his sacred compositions "to the glory of God."

Instrumental Music

Until the sixteenth century, almost all music was written for the human voice rather than for musical instruments. Even during the Renaissance, instrumental music was, for the most part, the result of substituting an instrument for the portions of a text written for singing or dancing. The seventeenth century marked the rise of music that lacked an extramusical text. Such music was composed without consideration for the associational content traditionally provided by a set of sung lyrics. The idea of music as an aesthetic exercise, composed for its own sake rather than to serve a religious or communal purpose, was a notable feature of the Age of the Baroque. This concept continues to distinguish Western European music from the musical traditions of the rest of the world.

Not surprisingly, the rise of instrumental music was accompanied by refinements in tuning. By the early eighteenth century, musicians were adopting the system of tuning known as **equal temperament**, whereby the keyboard was divided into semitones of equal value, making it easy to transpose a melody from one key to another. The collection of preludes and **fugues** known as the *Well-Tempered* ["tuned"] *Clavier* (1722–1742) shows how Bach employed this uniform system of tuning to compose sublime music—he wrote two pieces in each of the major and minor keys.

The rise of instrumental music accompanied the effort to improve, refine, and standardize musical instruments: among keyboard instruments, the organ and the harpsichord (Figure **10.34**); and among stringed instruments, the violin, viola, and cello (Figure **10.35**). In the seventeenth century, northern Italy was the world center for the manufacture of violins. The Amati, Guarneri, and Stradivari families of Cremona, Italy, established the techniques of making quality violins that were sought in all of the great courts of Europe. Transmitted from father to son, the construction techniques used to produce these instruments were guarded so secretly that modern violinmakers have never successfully imitated them. As musical instruments gained greater importance, performance, especially improvisation and ornamentation, became an art in itself.

Three types of musical composition characterized instrumental music of the seventeenth century, and all three reflect the typically Baroque affection for dramatic contrast. The **sonata** (from the Italian *sonare*, "to sound"), is a musical form written for an unaccompanied keyboard instrument or for another instrument with keyboard accompaniment. Often divided into three movements of contrasting tempo (fast/slow/fast), the sonata was usually based on a popular song or dance tune. The **suite**, written for any combination of instruments, is a series of movements derived from European court or folk dances. Finally, the **concerto** (from the same root as *concertato*, describing opposing bodies of sound) features two groups of instruments—one small, the other large—playing in "dialogue."

Figure 10.34 Johannes Couchet (maker), Flemish double-banked harpsichord; compass four octaves, and a fifth F to C (each keyboard), ca. 1650. Case decorated with carving and gilt gesso work. The Metropolitan Museum of Art, New York.

The solo concerto featured an instrumental soloist and orchestra; the **concerto grosso** ("large concerto") involved a small instrumental group (the *concertino*) and a small orchestra (the *tutti*, meaning "all").

Vivaldi

The leading Italian composer of Baroque instrumental music was the Venetian-born Antonio Vivaldi (1678–1741). A Roman Catholic priest and an accomplished violinist, Vivaldi, nicknamed "il Prete Rosso" ("the Red Priest" for his flaming red hair), composed dozens of oratorios and more than forty operas. But he is best known for his 456 concertos, written for various musical instruments, including the cello, the flute, the oboe, the bassoon, the guitar, and most notably, the violin. Vivaldi held positions in Mantua and Venice, but he spent the greatest part of his career as director of the Ospedale della Pietà, a Venetian school for orphaned girls, some of whom were the illegitimate offspring of the wealthy nobility. Vivaldi's compositions were performed in concert by the young women educated at this institution, which offered them a unique opportunity to become professional musicians.

Vivaldi systematized the concerto form into three movements and heightened the contrasts between solo and ensemble groups. He made use of a recurring melody, the **ritornello** ("return"), to unify all parts of the composition. His landmark work, *The Four Seasons*, employs all of these features. *The Four Seasons* is a group of violin concertos, each of which describes a single season. The music for each season reflects the lyrics of a sonnet written by the composer himself and inscribed on the **score**. In *La Primavera* ("Spring"), musical references to birdsong, a murmuring stream, gentle breezes, and a violent thunderstorm recreate the imagery of the poem. This practice contributed to the development of **program music** (instrumental music that illustrates a story or poem), a genre that would especially become popular among Romantic composers (see page 348). While *The Four Seasons* challenges listeners to detect its extramusical references, the brilliance of the piece lies in its vibrant rhythms, its virtuoso solos, and its exuberant "dialogs" between violin and orchestra.

Vivaldi, *The Four Seasons* (1725)

Bach and Instrumental Music

Vivaldi's music received acclaim throughout Europe. In Germany, Bach studied his compositions and adopted his compositional style for his own instrumental works. Bach claimed that his study of Vivaldi had taught him to "think musically," and to endow the creative process with "order, coherence, and proportion." In the numerous concertos he composed throughout his lifetime, Bach developed the potential of the Baroque concerto form more fully than any of his predecessors. He expanded the *ritornello* sections and brought the solo episodes to new levels of complexity.

In 1721, Bach sent six instrumental works (a kind of musical resumé) to Ludwig Christian, the Margrave of Brandenburg, in the hope of obtaining a paid position. While the so-called *Brandenburg Concertos* were intended for performance by the Margrave's court orchestra, there is no evidence that they were performed during Bach's lifetime. Nevertheless, the *Brandenburg Concertos* constitute a landmark in musical achievement. Employing as soloists most of the principal instruments of the Baroque orchestra (violin, oboe, recorder, trumpet, and harpsichord), they provide rich contrasts of tone and texture between "contending" groups of instruments. In Concerto No. 4 in G major, the music of the smaller group, consisting of a violin and two recorders, makes lively conversation with the larger string ensemble. Bach spins tight webs of counterpoint between upper and lower instrumental parts, while dominant musical lines, driven by the unflagging rhythms of the continuo, unfold majestically.

The Brandenburg Concertos (1711–1721)

Over a period of five to ten years before his death, Bach undertook one of the most monumental projects of his career: a complex musical tapestry that came to be called *The Art of Fugue*. A fugue (literally "flight") is a polyphonic

Figure 10.35 Pieter de Hooch, *Portrait of a Family Making Music*, 1663. Oil on canvas, $38^{7}/_{8}$ x $45^{15}/_{16}$ in. Cleveland Museum of Art, Ohio. Holland was a center for the manufacture of musical instruments. The Dutch household pictured by de Hooch owned the bass viol, recorder, cittern (a type of lute), and violin on which the members of this family performed. Amateur music-making of this kind was widespread thanks to the availability of printed music.

composition in which a single musical theme (or subject) is re-stated in sequential phrases. (Think of the familiar round, "Three Blind Mice," in which the melody of the first voice part is imitated by successive, overlapping voices.) In the eighteen individual compositions that make up *The Art of Fugue*, Bach explored the possibilities of imitative counterpoint; for example, the musical subject might be arranged to appear backward or inverted (or both); it might be augmented (the time values of the notes doubled) or diminished (note values halved). In the last portion of the work, Bach signed his name with a musical motif consisting of the letters of his name: B flat, A, C, and B natural (pronounced as an H in German). Even the listener who cannot read music is ravished by the inventive complexity and concentrated brilliance of these landmark works.

Bach, *The Art of Fugue* (1749)

Afterword

The Baroque style prevailed in the West between the years 1650 and 1750. In Italy, it reflected the religious intensity of the Catholic Reformation; in the Protestant North, it expressed the political and spiritual loyalties of an increasingly worldly middle class; and in France, it became an expression of royal absolutism. While secular and religious circumstances differed from country to country in the European West (and beyond), the arts shared the typically Baroque characteristics of spatial grandeur and theatrical display. Ornamentation and dramatic invention dominated sacred and secular literature, vocal and instrumental music, the visual arts and architecture. Religious piety, political ambition, and royal extravagance inspired the many prominment landmarks of the seventeenth and eighteenth centuries. Already at this time, however, new developments in science and philosophy were fostering the countervailing values of the European Enlightenment.

Key Topics

- Catholic Reformation
- Mannerism
- Bernini's Rome
- Italian Baroque art
- English Baroque poets
- Wren's London
- the Protestant Baroque
- Dutch art
- the Aristocratic Baroque
- Versailles and absolutism
- court theater and dance
- academic painting
- the Aristocratic Baroque portrait
- the birth of opera
- the oratorio
- Baroque religious music
- Baroque instrumental music
- courtly arts in China, India, and Japan

BAROQUE TIMELINE

	HISTORICAL EVENTS	LANDMARKS IN THE VISUAL ARTS	LITERARY LANDMARKS	MUSIC LANDMARKS	BEYOND THE WEST
1525	• Council of Trent (1545–1563) • Dutch provinces declare independence (1581)	• Parmigianino, *Madonna of the Long Neck* (1534–1540) • El Greco, *The Agony in the Garden* (ca. 1585–1586)	• Loyola, *Spiritual Exercises* (1548)	• Palestrina, Pope Marcellus Mass (ca. 1561) • Gabrieli, Motets (ca. 1585–1612)	• Forbidden City, Beijing, China (begun fourteenth century) • Ming dynasty in China (1368–1644) • Moguls rule India (1526–1707)
1600		• Caravaggio, *The Crucifixion of Saint Peter* (1601) • Gentileschi, *Judith Slaying Holofernes* (ca. 1614–1620) • Rubens, *Rape of the Daughters of Leucippus* (ca. 1618)	• King James Bible (1611) • Donne, *Holy Sonnets* (1618); *Meditations* (1623–1624)	• Monteverdi, *Orfeo* (1607)	• Tokugawa dynasty in Japan (1600–1868) • Taj Mahal, Agra, India (1623–1643)
1625	• Reign of Louis XIV in France (1643–1715) • Great Fire of London (1666)	• Poussin, *Arcadian Shepherds* (1638–1639) • Rembrandt, *Captain Frans Banning Cocq ("The Night Watch")* (1642) • Bernini, *The Ecstasy of Saint Teresa* (1645–1652)	**Figure 10.9** Caravaggio, *The Crucifixion of Saint Peter*, see p. 267		
1650		• Velázquez, *Las Meninas* (1656) • Vermeer, *View of Delft* (1658) • van Oosterwyck, *Vanitas Still Life* (1668)	• Molière, *The Misanthrope* (1666) • Milton, *Paradise Lost* (1667)		**Figure 10.31** Taj Mahal, Agra, India, see p. 285
1675	• England's "Glorious Revolution" (1688)	• Wren, Saint Paul's Cathedral, London (1675–1710)		• Louis XIV sets up first permanent orchestra (1670s)	
1700		• Rigaud, *Portrait of Louis XIV* (1701)		• Equal-temperament tuning (early eighteenth century) • Bach, *Brandenburg Concertos* (1711–1721); Cantata No. 80 (1723)	
1725	**Figure 10.19** Hyacinthe Rigaud, *Portrait of Louis XIV*, see p. 277		**Figure 10.17** Rembrandt van Rijn, *Self-Portrait as Saint Paul*, see p. 276	• Vivaldi, *The Four Seasons* (1725) • Bach, *Passion According to Saint Matthew* (1727); *The Art of Fugue* (1749) • Handel, *Messiah* (1742)	• Korin, *Irises at Yatuhashi* (ca. 1725)

Chapter 11

Enlightenment:

SCIENCE AND THE NEW LEARNING

ca. 1650–1800

The Enlightenment marks the divide between the medieval view of the world as dominated by religion and the principles of religious faith, and the modern view of the world as governed by science and the principles of human reason. Enlightenment, meaning "illumination," describes the period between ca. 1650 and 1800, a time when educated Westerners looked to science and reason for the betterment of humankind. The Enlightenment, or Age of Reason, as it is also called, took inspiration from the Scientific Revolution, which generated new tools and experimental methods for investigating the natural world. The new learning, based in science and rational inquiry, would work—it was optimistically assumed—toward progress and human perfectibility. Across Europe and America, Enlightenment thinkers called for greater social and political equality. Reformers challenged the aristocratic culture of Europe's absolutist courts and the prevailing Rococo style, and ushered in the spirit of political revolution. A Neoclassical revival promoting the cultural values of Greco-Roman antiquity served Enlightenment ideals and inspired the artistic landmarks of this age.

A First Look

In February 1778, crowds lined the streets of Paris to welcome from twenty years of exile the superstar of the French Enlightenment, François Marie Arouet (1694–1778), better known as Voltaire. The eighty-four-year-old playwright, novelist, historian, critic, and author of the brilliant satire *Candide* (see page 307), would only live four more months. But during those months, he sat a number of times for Europe's most eminent sculptor, Jean-Antoine Houdon (1741–1828). A child prodigy, Houdon began sculpting at the age of nine. After years of academic training, and exposure to Neoclassical cultural values, he went on to become the leading portraitist of the eighteenth century, leaving memorable likenesses of the greatest figures of the Enlightenment, including Diderot, Rousseau, Napoleon, Benjamin Franklin, George Washington, and Thomas Jefferson (see Figure 11.5 and page 315). Houdon's landmark life-size likeness of Voltaire shows the aging writer enthroned in a Louis XVI-style armchair; his Classical robes and headband suggest the sitter's kinship with the philosophers of antiquity. The personality of the sitter is captured in a realistic style reminiscent of Roman portraiture (see Figures 3.3 and 3.17): Voltaire presses his lips together in a sardonic smile, his wit and intelligence indelibly engraved in the gently wrinkled brow and twinkling eyes—an effect Houdon achieved by the "trick" of leaving a small, light-catching fragment of marble hanging in front of the deeply bored hole for each pupil. So great was the demand for Houdon's portraits of Voltaire that they were produced in several versions (see Figure 11.9) and in various media.

Figure 11.1 Jean-Antoine Houdon, *Voltaire*, 1781. Marble, height 4 ft. 6 in. Hermitage Museum, St. Petersburg, Russia.

THE SCIENTIFIC REVOLUTION

THE Scientific Revolution took place over a period of 150 years: approximately 1600 to 1750. It was rooted in a long history of inquiry that began in ancient times and was advanced largely by Muslim scholarship. But it culminated in the union of three movements: 1) the effort to arrive at scientific truths by means of direct observation and experimentation, that is, empirical methods; 2) the use of mathematical theory as a method of verification; and 3) the development of new instruments by which to measure natural phenomena, test scientific hypotheses, and predict the operations of nature.

The first of these movements was already evident during the High Renaissance, in the pioneering investigations of Leonardo da Vinci (see Figure 7.26). Inspired by Leonardo's dissection of cadavers, the Flemish physician Andreas Vesalius (1514–1564) produced the first accurate descriptions of human anatomy in his *De humani corporis fabrica* (*On the Workings of the Human Body*), which became the virtual bible for seventeenth-century medical science (Figure **11.2**). At the same time, the Polish physician and astronomer Nicolas Copernicus (1473–1543) published the landmark treatise *On the Revolution of the Heavenly Spheres*. On the evidence of mathematical calculations, Copernicus had discarded the traditional **geocentric** (earth-centered) model of the universe in favor of the **heliocentric** (sun-centered) theory, according to which all the planets circled around the sun (Figure **11.3**).

Vesalius, *De humani corporis fabrica* (*On the Workings of the Human Body*) (1543)

Copernicus, *On the Revolution of the Heavenly Spheres* (1543)

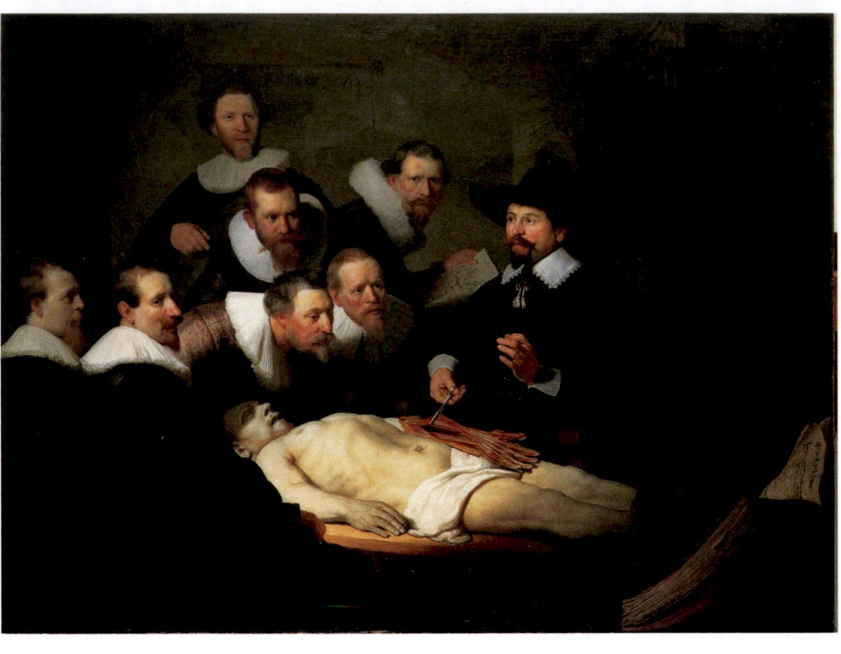

Figure 11.2 Rembrandt van Rijn, *The Anatomy Lesson of Doctor Nicolaes Tulp*, 1632. Oil on canvas, 5 ft. 3⅜ in. x 7 ft. 1¼ in. Mauritshuis, The Hague. This group portrait honors Doctor Nicolaes Tulp, the head of the Amsterdam surgeons' guild. The faces of his medical students, whose names appear on the paper held by the middle figure, carry the force of individual personalities. The book propped at the feet of the cadaver is no doubt a copy of Vesalius' *Anatomy*.

Kepler

Some fifty years later, in 1609, the German mathematician Johannes Kepler (1571–1630) published his *New Astronomy*, which set forth the laws of planetary motion and substantiated the heliocentric theory. Kepler's speculation concerning the magnetic forces emitted by the sun also indicated that the planets moved not in circles but in elliptical paths. He argued that the magnetic force emitted by the sun determined the movements of the planets and their distances from the sun.

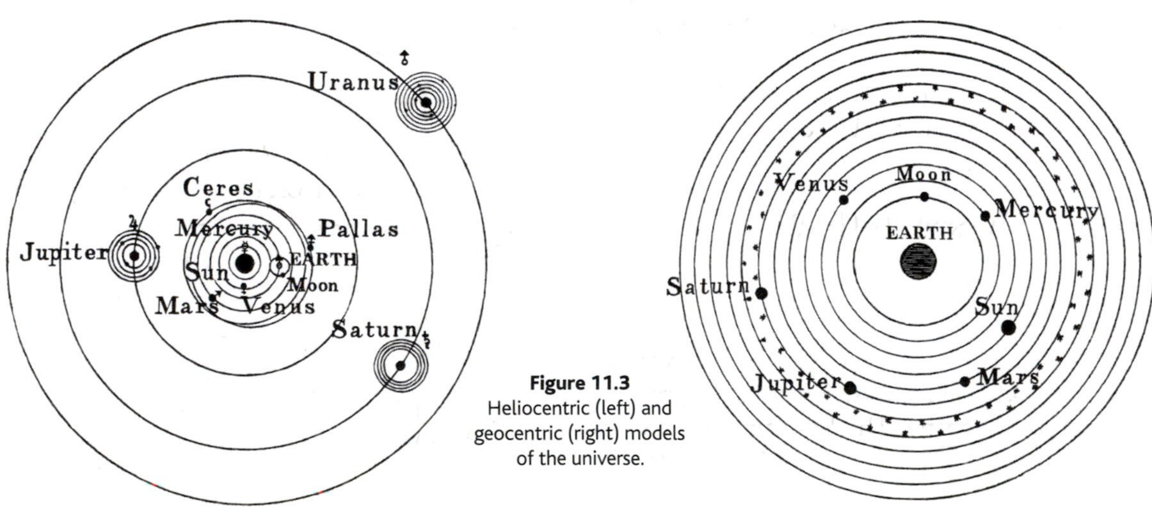

Figure 11.3 Heliocentric (left) and geocentric (right) models of the universe.

The contributions of Copernicus and Kepler stand as landmarks because they challenged the model of the universe that had prevailed from the time of Aristotle to the sixteenth century. According to Aristotle (and supported by the largely incorrect theories of the renowned second-century Hellenistic astronomer Claudius Ptolemy), the heavens consisted of concentric crystalline spheres with the planet Earth at center; planetary motion was circular, directed by a First Cause or Unmoved Mover. The new physics toppled the long-held worldview of a fixed and unchanging cosmos centering on humankind. It also generated strong opposition in religious circles. The argument for heliocentricity contradicted the Bible—where, for example, the Hebrew hero Joshua is described as making the sun stand still (Joshua 10:12–13), an event that could have occurred only if the sun normally moved around the earth. While Catholics and Protestants were at odds on many theological issues, in defending the inviolable truth of Scripture they were united. Not only did the new science deprive human beings of their central place in the universe, it contradicted divine revelation.

Galileo

Kepler's Italian contemporary Galileo Galilei (1564–1642) further advanced Kepler's model of the universe—and imperiled his freedom and his life by doing so. Galileo's inquiries into motion and gravity resulted in his formulation of the law of falling bodies, which proclaims that the earth's gravity attracts all objects—regardless of shape, size, or density—at the same rate of acceleration. Intrigued by a Dutch lens-maker's invention of an instrument that magnified objects seen at great distances, Galileo perfected a telescope that literally revealed new worlds. Through its lens, one could identify the craters of the moon, the rings of Saturn, and the moons of Jupiter, which (Galileo noted) operated exactly like the earth's moon. The telescope turned the heliocentric theory into fact.

Galileo's efforts aroused opposition from the Church, but it was not until his publication of an inflammatory tract that poked fun at outmoded theories of astronomy that he was brought to Rome on charges of heresy. After a long and unpleasant trial, in 1633 the aging astronomer was forced to admit his "errors." Condemned to reside under "house arrest" in a villa near Florence, Galileo lived out his last nine years there.

Bacon and the Empirical Method

Essential to the Scientific Revolution was the advancement of the empirical method: a process of inquiry that depends on direct observation of nature and experimentation. Natural phenomena provide evidence from which one may draw general conclusions, following a process known as **inductive reasoning**. The leading advocate of this approach to nature was the English scientist Francis Bacon (1561–1626). Bacon promoted a system of experimentation, tabulation, and record keeping that became the touchstone of modern scientific inquiry. A prophet of the new learning, he sought to eliminate errors in reasoning derived from blind adherence to traditional sources of authority and religious belief.

Bacon's *Novum Organum* (*New Method*) was an impassioned plea for objectivity and clear thinking; it remains the strongest defense of the empirical method ever written. In his strategy for the acquisition of true knowledge, Bacon warned against four false notions (or Idols, as he called them), which he condemned as hindrances to full and accurate

Bacon, *Novum Organum* (*New Method*) (1620)

Ideas and Issues

BACON: SCIENCE AND RELIGION

"... the corruption of philosophy by a combination of superstition and theology is ... widespread, and does the greatest harm both to whole philosophies and to their parts. ... Yet some of the moderns have, with the greatest frivolity, indulged so far ... as to try to found a natural philosophy on the first chapter of Genesis and the book of Job and other sacred writings. ... It is all the more important to guard against and check this foolishness, for an unhealthy mixture of the divine and the human leads not only to fanciful philosophy but also to heretical religion. The healthy course therefore is to keep a sober mind and give to faith only that which is faith's."

(from Bacon, *Novum Organum*)

Q Is Bacon's plea for the separation of science and religion still relevant? If so, how?

THE TOOLS OF SCIENCE

Seventeenth-century scientists pressed on to devise new instruments for measurement and fresh procedures for experimentation and analysis. They explored, for example, the genesis and propagation of light, thus advancing the science of optics; they accurately described the action of gases and the circulation of the blood. The slide rule, the magnet, the microscope, the mercury barometer, the air pump (Figure **11.4**), and other innovations listed below testify to the European quest to measure, investigate, and ultimately master nature.

1608 Galileo improves the design of Dutch telescopes to obtain 30-power magnification

1609 Hans Lippershey and Zacharias Janssen invent the compound microscope

1619 William Harvey accurately traces the circulation of the blood

1621 René Descartes introduces analytic geometry

1645 Otto von Guericke perfects the air pump

1650 Blaise Pascal invents the mercury barometer

1656 Christian Huygens develops the first accurate pendulum clock

1660 Anton van Leeuvenhoek discovers microscopic protozoa

1666 Isaac Newton uses a prism to analyze light

1671 Gottfried Wilhelm Leibniz invents a machine that multiplies and divides

Figure 11.4 Joseph Wright, *An Experiment on a Bird in the Air Pump*, 1768. Oil on canvas, 5 ft. 11⅝ in. x 7 ft. 11¾ in. National Gallery, London. While he earned his living as a portrait painter, Joseph Wright (1734–1797) was the first Western artist to use scientific experimentation as dramatic subject matter. The experiment shown here involves a glass bowl from which the air is removed, depriving the bird within of oxygen. The central lighting and expressions of dismay on the part of the onlookers are reminiscent of Baroque religious compositions—here, however, a scientific experiment usurps the supernatural with its own kind of "miracle."

understanding. *Idols of the Tribe* are deceptive ideas that have their foundations in human nature (such as our natural inclination to accept and believe what we prefer to be true). *Idols of the Cave* are privately held fallacies that derive from individual education and background (for example, the argument that one's own religion is "the true faith"). *Idols of the Marketplace* arise from the "ill or unfit choice of words" (for instance, the use of the noun "mankind" to designate *all* human beings). Finally, *Idols of the Theater* are false dogmas perpetuated by social and political philosophies and institutions (for instance, "divine-right monarchy"). To purge the mind of prejudice and false thinking, argued Bacon, one must destroy the Idols.

In an age dominated by fervent spirituality, Bacon called for a separation of science and religion (see Ideas and Issues on page 295). "In every age," he observed, "Natural Philosophy has had a troublesome adversary . . . namely, superstition, and the blind and immoderate zeal of religion." Bacon's clarion call for objectivity and experimentation inspired the founding in 1645 of the Royal Society of London for Improving Natural Knowledge. The first of many such European and American societies for scientific advancement, the Royal Society has, over the centuries, attracted thousands of members. Their achievements have confirmed one nineteenth-century historian's assessment of Bacon as "the man that moved the minds that moved the world."

Descartes and the Birth of Modern Philosophy

Whereas Bacon gave priority to knowledge gained through the senses, René Descartes (1596–1650) favored abstract reasoning and mathematical proof. Descartes did not deny the importance of the senses in the search for truth; however, he observed that our senses might very well deceive us. He thus advocated **deductive reasoning** as the best procedure for scientific investigation. The reverse of the inductive method, the deductive process begins with clearly established general premises and moves toward the establishment of particular truths. In the *Discourse on the Method of Rightly Conducting the Reason and Seeking for Truth in the Sciences*, Descartes set forth his rules for reasoning: Never accept anything as true that you do not clearly know to be true; dissect a problem into as many parts as possible; reason from the simple to the complex; and, finally, draw

Descartes, ***Discourse on the Method*** **(1637)**

complete and exhaustive conclusions. Descartes began the *Discourse* by systematically calling *everything* into doubt. He then proceeded to identify the first thing that he could not doubt—his own existence as a thinking individual. He expressed the truth of himself as a "thinking thing" in the proposition *"Cogito, ergo sum"* ("I think, therefore I am"). This "first principle" became the premise for all of his major arguments.

On the basis of self-evident propositions, Descartes arrived at conclusions to which empirical confirmation was irrelevant. His rationalism—like mathematical propositions—involved a process of mind independent of the senses. For instance, reasoning that the concept of divine perfection had to proceed from "some Nature which in reality was more perfect," Descartes concluded that God must exist. The idea of God, he reasoned, must come from God, since something cannot proceed from nothing. Despite his Jesuit background, Descartes identified God with "the mathematical order of nature," rather than as a supernatural being or a personal redeemer. The "father of modern philosophy" made a clear distinction between physical and psychical phenomena, that is, between matter and mind, and between body and soul. According to Descartes' dualistic model, the human body operates much like a computer, with the immaterial mind (the software) "informing" the physical components of the body (the hardware). Cartesian dualism dominated European philosophic thought until the end of the nineteenth century and still has some strong adherents today.

Newton's Synthesis

"If I have seen further," wrote Isaac Newton (1642–1727), "it is by standing on the shoulders of giants." Indeed, the work of the English astronomer and mathematician represents a practical synthesis of seventeenth-century physics and mathematics and the union of the inductive and deductive methods. Newton's monumental treatise, *Principia Mathematica* (*Mathematical Principles*) linked terrestrial and celestial physics under a single set of laws: the laws of motion and the law of universal gravitation (by which every particle of matter attracts every other particle of matter). It described the physical world by means of mathematical equations that would become the basis of modern physics. More generally, it promoted the idea of a uniform and intelligible universe that operated as systematically as a well-oiled machine.

Newton, *Principia Mathematica* (*Mathematical Principles*) (1687)

The *Principia* became the culminating thesis of the Scientific Revolution. Its fundamentals would go unchallenged until the late nineteenth century. Newton's shaping influence is best described in the lines of his contemporary admirer, Alexander Pope (see page 304), who wrote: "Nature and Nature's Laws lay hid in Night./God said, Let Newton be! And All was Light."

THE ENLIGHTENMENT

IN the year 1680, a comet blazed across the skies over Western Europe. The English astronomer Edmund Halley (1656–1742) observed the celestial body, calculated its orbit, and predicted its future appearances. Stripped of its former role as a portent of catastrophe or a harbinger of natural calamity, Halley's comet now became merely another natural phenomenon, the behavior of which invited scientific investigation. This new, objective attitude toward nature and the accompanying confidence in the liberating role of reason were hallmarks of the Enlightenment. "Theology," wrote one Enlightenment skeptic, "is only ignorance of natural causes." Just as Halley explained the operations of the celestial bodies as a logical part of nature's mechanics, so eighteenth-century intellectuals explained human nature in terms of *natural law*. This unwritten and divinely sanctioned law held that there are certain principles of right and wrong that all human beings, by way of reason, can discover and apply in the course of creating a just society. "Natural rights" included the right to life, liberty, property, and just treatment by the ruling order. Moreover, Enlightenment thinkers argued that a true understanding of the human condition was the first step toward progress, that is, toward the gradual betterment of human life. It is no wonder, then, that the eighteenth century saw the formation of the social sciences: anthropology, sociology, economics, and political science. These new disciplines, devoted to the study of humankind, optimistically confirmed that reason was the vehicle for achieving a just society and an enlightened social order.

Locke: Enlightenment Herald

The English philosopher John Locke (1632–1704) was the herald of the Enlightenment. His writings defended the empirical tradition and provided a clearly reasoned basis for centuries of philosophic debate concerning the nature of knowledge. Written seventy years after Bacon's *Novum Organum*, Locke's *Essay Concerning Human Understanding* (1690) supported his predecessor's thesis that everything one knows derives from sensory experience. According to Locke, the human mind at birth is a *tabula rasa* ("blank slate") upon which experience—consisting of sensation, followed by reflection—writes the script. No innate moral principles or ideas exist; rather, human knowledge consists of the progressive accumulation of the evidence of the senses. Since human beings are born without any preexisting qualities, their natural state is one of perfect freedom. Whether people become brutish or otherwise depends solely upon their experiences and their environment. Locke's principles of knowledge helped to shape an optimistic view of human destiny. For, if experience influenced human knowledge and behavior, then, surely, improving the social environment would work to perfect the human condition.

Locke's importance as a philosopher was second only to his influence as a political theorist. Living in a time and place in which republican ideals challenged the power of absolutist monarchs, Locke joined the debate concerning the role of government and the rights of citizens. Sixteenth-century thinkers had advanced the idea of a **social contract**—an agreement made between citizens in the formation of the state—but the mechanisms for the operation of that contract were vigorously disputed. One of England's leading thinkers, Thomas Hobbes (1588–1679), had envisioned a covenant among individuals who willingly surrendered a portion of their freedom to a governing authority (either one individual or a ruling assembly) in whom ultimate power rested. His landmark work, *Leviathan*, justified his version of the social contract with this argument: In that human beings are selfish, greedy, and warlike, a strong state is society's only hope for peace and security. Without authoritarian leadership, argued Hobbes, human life was nothing better than "solitary, poor, nasty, brutish, and short."

Hobbes, *Leviathan* (1651)

Locke's position diverged sharply from that of Hobbes: Proceeding from his view of human beings as unformed by nature, equal in potential, and capable (through reason) of defining the common good, he argued that power must remain with the people, not the ruler. Locke wrote that individuals might attain maximum development only in a society free from the restrictions imposed by absolute rulers. In *Of Civil Government*, the second of his two political treatises, he expounded the idea that government must rest upon the consent of the governed. Moreover, it should exist to protect the natural rights of its citizens. People have, by their very nature as human beings, said Locke, the right to life, liberty, and estate (or "property"). Government must arbitrate between the exercise of one person's liberty and that of the next. If a ruler is tyrannical or oppressive, the people have not only the right but the obligation to rebel and seek a new ruler. Locke's defense of political rebellion in the face of tyranny served as inspiration for the revolutions that took place in America and in France toward the end of the eighteenth century. More generally, Locke's ideas became basic to eighteenth-century liberalism, as well as to all subsequent political ideologies that held that human knowledge, if properly applied, would produce happiness for humankind.

Locke, *Of Civil Government* (1690)

Montesquieu and Jefferson

Locke's treatises became the wellspring of the Enlightenment in both Europe and America. In France, the keen-minded aristocrat Charles Louis de Secondat Montesquieu (1689–1755) championed Locke's views on political freedom and expanded on his theories. In his elegantly written thousand-page treatise *The Spirit of the Laws* (1748), Montesquieu defended liberty as the free exercise of the will and condemned slavery as fundamentally "unnatural and evil."

A proponent of constitutional monarchy, Montesquieu advanced the idea of a separation of powers among the executive, legislative, and judicial agencies of government, advising that each monitor the activities of the others in order to ensure a balanced system of government. He warned that when legislative and executive powers were united in the same person (or body of magistrates), or when judicial power was inseparable from legislative

Ideas and Issues

TWO VIEWS OF THE SOCIAL CONTRACT

"For the laws of nature—as *justice, equity, modesty, mercy,* and in sum, *doing to others as we would be done to*—of themselves, without the terror of some power to cause them to be observed, are contrary to our natural passions, that carry us to partiality, pride, revenge, and the like. And covenants without the sword are but words, and of no strength to secure a man at all. Therefore, notwithstanding the laws of nature . . . if there be no power erected, or not great enough for our security, every man will—and may lawfully—rely on his own strength and art for caution against all other men. . . .

The only way to erect such a common power as may be able to defend them from the invasion of foreigners and the injuries of one another, and thereby to secure them in such sort as that by their own industry and by the fruits of the earth they may nourish themselves and live contentedly, is to confer all their power and strength upon one man, or upon one assembly of men that may reduce all their wills, by plurality of voices, unto one will. . . ."

(from Hobbes, *Leviathan*)

"Men being, as has been said, by nature all free, equal, and independent, no one can be put out of this estate and subjected to the political power of another without his own consent. The only way whereby any one divests himself of his natural liberty and puts on the bonds of civil society is by agreeing with other men to join and unite into a community for their comfortable, safe, and peaceable living one amongst another, in a secure enjoyment of their properties, and a greater security against any that are not of it. This any number of men may do, because it injures not the freedom of the rest; they are left as they were in the liberty of the state of nature. When any number of men have so consented to make one community or government, they are thereby presently incorporated and make one body politic, wherein the majority have a right to act and conclude the rest. . . ."

(from Locke, *Of Civil Government*)

Q Which position would you defend? On what assumptions concerning human nature does each view rest?

and executive powers, human liberty might be gravely threatened. Montesquieu's system of checks and balances was later enshrined in the Constitution of the United States of America.

Across the Atlantic, on the eve of the American Revolution, a definitive expression of Locke's ideas appeared in the preamble to the statement declaring the independence of the North American colonies from the rule of the British king George III (1738–1820). Written by the leading American apostle of the Enlightenment, Thomas Jefferson (1743–1826; Figure **11.5**), and adopted by the Continental Congress on July 4, 1776, the American *Declaration of Independence* echoes Locke's ideology of revolt as well as his view that governments derive their just powers from the consent of the governed. Following Locke and Montesquieu, Jefferson justified the establishment of a social contract between ruler and ruled as the principal means of fulfilling natural law—the "unalienable right" to life, liberty, and the pursuit of happiness:

Jefferson, *Declaration of Independence* (1776)

> When, in the course of human events, it becomes necessary for one people to dissolve the political bands which have connected them with another, and to assume among the powers of the earth, the separate and equal station to which the laws of nature and of nature's God entitle them, a decent respect to the opinions of mankind requires that they should declare the causes which impel them to separation.
>
> We hold these truths to be self-evident: That all men are created equal; that they are endowed by their Creator with certain unalienable rights; that among these are life, liberty, and the pursuit of happiness; that to secure these rights governments are instituted among men, deriving their just powers from the consent of the governed; that whenever any form of government becomes destructive of these ends, it is the right of the people to alter or to abolish it, and to institute new government, laying its foundation on such principles and organizing its powers in such form, as to them shall seem most likely to effect their safety and happiness. . . .
>
> (from the *Declaration of Independence*)

Figure 11.5 Jean-Antoine Houdon, *Thomas Jefferson*, 1789. Marble, height 21½ in. Library of Congress, Washington, D.C. Jefferson was governor of Virginia and, subsequently, the third president of the United States.

The Declaration of Independence made clear the belief of America's founding fathers in equality among men. Equality between the sexes was, however, another matter: Although both Locke and Jefferson acknowledged that women held the same natural rights as men, they did not consider women—or slaves, or children, for that matter—capable of exercising such rights. In fact, the institution of slavery would persist in the United States until 1863.

If the Declaration of Independence constituted an expression of Enlightenment theory in justifying revolution against tyranny, the Constitution of the new United States of America represented the practical outcome of the Revolution: the creation of a viable new nation with its government based on Enlightenment principles. The U.S. Constitution, framed in 1787 and ratified by popular vote in 1788–1789, established a system of representative government; that is, government by the elected representatives of the people. "The people" actually meant adult white male property-owning citizens—less than 20 percent of the total population. Nevertheless, the U.S. Constitution would prove effective for over two centuries, and would serve as the model for the constitutions of most newborn republics created throughout the world.

The *Philosophes*

In writing the Declaration of Independence, Jefferson was influenced by a group of French thinkers who came to be known as ***philosophes*** ("philosophers"). Intellectuals rather than philosophers in the strict sense of the word, the *philosophes* dominated the progress of the Enlightenment. Members of the nobility and the middle class, they came together in gatherings organized by socially ambitious noblewomen, many of whom championed a freer and more public role for their gender. In the elegant *salons* of Paris, these thinkers and writers met to exchange views on morality, politics, science, and religion and to voice opinions on everything ranging from diet to the latest fashions in theater and dress (Figure **11.6**). The *philosophes* applied scientific models and the empirical method to all aspects of human life. Reason and clear thinking, they advocated, would release humankind from existing forms of intolerance, inequality, and injustice, to produce a superior social and moral order. With the banner cry *"Ecrasez l'infame"* ("Wipe out all evils"), they championed individual rights, social progress, and human perfectibility.

Antitraditional in spirit, most of the *philosophes* subscribed to Descartes'

Figure 11.6 François Dequevauviller after N. Lavréince, *Assembly in a Salon*, 1745–1807. Engraving, 15 13/16 x 19 5/8 in. The Metropolitan Museum of Art, New York.

idea of an impersonal God—a view central to the eighteenth-century doctrine known as *deism*. Deists believed God had created the world but took no part in its functioning. They envisioned God as a master clockmaker, who had flung his invention into space and allowed it to run unassisted. They rejected the Bible as revealed truth and scorned the hierarchy and ritual of organized religion. Their antipathy to irrationality, superstition, and religious dogma alienated them from the Church and set them at odds with the established authorities.

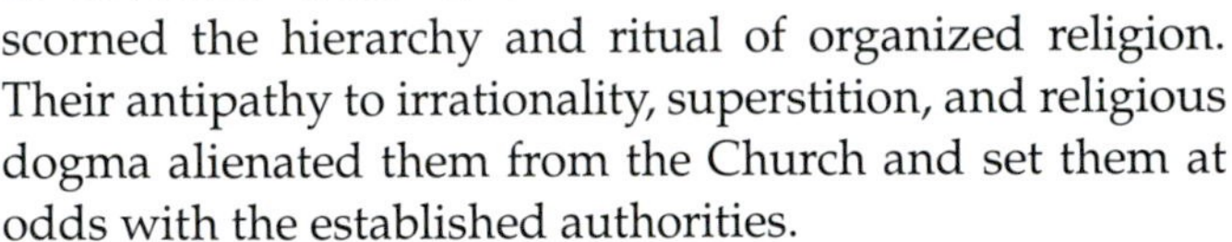

The basic ideals of the Enlightenment were summed up in a monumental literary endeavor to which many of the *philosophes* contributed: the thirty-five-volume *Encyclopédie* (*Encyclopedia*)—including eleven volumes of engraved plates—published and edited by Denis Diderot (1713–1784). Diderot's *Encyclopedia*—also known as *The Analytical Dictionary of the Sciences, Arts, and Crafts*—was the largest compendium of contemporary social, philosophic, artistic, scientific, and technological knowledge ever produced in the West. A collection of "all the knowledge scattered over the face of the earth," as Diderot explained, it manifested the ambition of the *philosophes* to dispel human ignorance and transform society. It was also, in part, a response to rising literacy and to the widespread public interest in the facts of everyday life.

Diderot, *Encyclopedia* (1751–1772)

The Crusade for Progress

Among European intellectuals, belief in the reforming powers of reason became the basis for a progressive view of human history. The German mathematician and philosopher Gottfried Wilhelm Leibniz (1646–1716) systematically defended the view that human beings live in perfect harmony with God and nature. Leibniz linked his optimistic thesis to the logic of probability: His *principle of sufficient reason* held, simply, that there must be a reason or purpose for everything in nature. In response to the question, Why does evil exist in a world created by a good God? Leibniz answered that all events conformed to the preestablished harmony of the universe. Even evil, according to Leibniz, was necessary in a world that was "better than any other possible world"—a position that came to be called "philosophic optimism."

THE ENCYCLOPEDIC CAST OF MIND

Diderot's *Encyclopedia* had a major impact on eighteenth-century culture: It put new emphasis on the accumulation, codification, and systematic preservation of knowledge. As scientific advances continued to increase, the will to collect information drove the creation of some landmark cultural contributions.

1714 The mercury thermometer and the Fahrenheit scale are invented in Germany
The first known typewriter is patented in London

1735 Carolus Linnaeus produces a systematic method for classifying plants

1756 Voltaire completes a seven-volume general history of the age of Louis XIV

1767 Georges Louis Leclerc, Comte de Buffon, publishes his *Natural History*
Samuel Johnson masterminds the first dictionary of the English language
Jean-Jacques Rousseau publishes the first Western dictionary of music

1771 John Hunter's *Natural History of Human Teeth* lays the foundation for dental science

1789 Antoine Lavoisier publishes the *Elementary Treatise of Chemistry*

The most passionate warrior in the Enlightenment crusade for progress was the French aristocrat Antoine Nicolas de Condorcet (1743–1794). A mathematician, social theorist, and political moderate amid revolutionary extremists, Condorcet believed that human nature could be perfected by the exercise of reason. All errors in politics and morals, he argued, were based in philosophic and scientific errors. "There is not a religious system nor a supernatural extravagance," wrote Condorcet, "that is not founded on ignorance of the laws of nature." Fiercely optimistic, he linked the condition of the human species to three goals: "The destruction of inequality between different nations; the progress of equality in one and the same nation; and lastly, the real improvement of man." By "man" Condorcet meant "humankind," for he stood as one of the first modern champions of sexual equality. He called for the "complete annihilation of the prejudices that have brought about an inequality of rights between the sexes, an inequality fatal even to the party in whose favor it works."

In his *Sketch for a Historical Picture of the Progress of the Human Mind,* Condorcet traced the "progress" of humankind through ten stages, from ignorance and tyranny to the threshold of enlightenment and equality. The utopian tenth stage, subtitled "The Future Progress of the Human Mind," sets forth ideas that were well ahead of their time, such as a guaranteed livelihood for the aged, a universal system of education, fewer work hours, and the refinement of a technology for the accumulation of knowledge. With buoyant faith in the future, he proclaimed:

Condorcet, *Sketch for a Historical Picture of the Progress of the Human Mind* (1793)

> The time will ... come when the sun will shine only on free men who know no other master but their reason, when tyrants and slaves, priests and their stupid or hypocritical instruments will exist only in works of history and on the stage; and when we shall think of them only to pity their victims and their dupes; to maintain ourselves in a state of vigilance by thinking on their excesses; and to learn how to recognize and so to destroy, by force of reason, the first seeds of tyranny and superstition, should they ever dare to reappear among us.

Enlightenment and the Rights of Women

While Condorcet was among the first moderns to champion the equality of the sexes, his efforts pale before the impassioned defense of women launched by Mary Wollstonecraft (1759–1797). This self-educated British intellectual applied Enlightenment principles of natural law, liberty, and equality to forge a radical rethinking of the roles and responsibilities of women. In *A Vindication of the Rights of Woman,* Wollstonecraft attacked the persistence of the female stereotype (docile, domestic, and childlike) as formulated by misguided, misogynistic, and tyrannical males, who, as she complained, "try to secure the good conduct of women by attempting to keep them in a state of childhood." Men, she argued, are anxious to turn women into alluring mistresses rather than affectionate wives and rational mothers. As a result, women are more anxious to inspire love than to exact respect. Only by the strengthening of the female mind and body might women demolish their image as "insignificant objects of desire." Calling for a "revolution of female manners," she criticized the "disorderly kind of education" received by women, who, owing to their domestic roles, learn "rather by snatches." Wollstonecraft's *Vindication* enjoyed sustained and significant influence; it remains a landmark at the threshold of the modern movement for female equality.

Wollstonecraft, *A Vindication of the Rights of Woman* (1792)

Ideas and Issues

WOLLSTONECRAFT: MAKE WOMEN FREE

"Strengthen the female mind by enlarging it, and there will be an end to blind obedience; but, as blind obedience is ever sought for by power, tyrants and sensualists are in the right when they endeavour to keep women in the dark, because the former only want slaves, and the latter a play-thing. The sensualist, indeed, has been the most dangerous of tyrants, and women have been duped by their lovers, as princes by their ministers, whilst dreaming that they reigned over them....

It appears to me necessary to dwell on these obvious truths, because females have been insulated, as it were; and, while they have been stripped of the virtues that should clothe humanity, they have been decked with artificial graces that enable them to exercise a short-lived tyranny. Love, in their bosoms, taking place of every nobler passion, their sole ambition is to be fair, to raise emotion instead of inspiring respect; and this ignoble desire, like the servility in absolute monarchies, destroys all strength of character. Liberty is the mother of virtue, and if women be, by their very constitution, slaves, and not allowed to breathe the sharp invigorating air of freedom, they must ever languish like exotics, and be reckoned beautiful flaws in nature....

Make [women] free, and they will quickly become wise and virtuous, as men become more so; for the improvements must be mutual, or the injustice which one half of the human race are obliged to submit to, retorting on their oppressors, the virtue of men will be worm-eaten by the insects whom he keeps under his feet.

Let men take their choice, man and woman were made for each other, though not to become one being; and if they will not improve women, they will deprave them!"

(from Wollstonecraft, *A Vindication of the Rights of Woman*)

Q In what ways, according to Wollstonecraft, do men enslave women? How do women comply?

Kant and Enlightenment Ethics

While Wollstonecraft emphasized the importance of education in the cultivation of virtue, her brilliant German contemporary Immanuel Kant (1724–1804) exalted rationalism as the primary guide for human conduct. The leading metaphysician of the late eighteenth century, Kant proposed an ethical system that transcended individual circumstances. In the *Critique of Practical Reason*, he proposed a general moral law called the "categorical imperative": We should act as if our actions should become the law for all humankind. In other words, we must act in ways justified by reasons so universal that they are good for all people at all times. It is not enough, argued Kant, that our actions have good effects; it is necessary that we *will* the good. Kant's notion of "good will" is not, however, identical with the Christian mandate, "Do to others as you would wish them to do to you," since for Kant, ethical conduct is based not on love, but on reason—a condition essential to human dignity. In his short essay "What is Enlightenment?" Kant defines "enlightenment" as the ability to use one's rational powers without guidance from others. For Kant, as for the *philosophes*, traditional rules and formulas were shackles that prevented people from thinking for themselves. Kant's bold motto for enlightenment was "*Sapere Aude!*" ("Dare to know!").

Kant, *Critique of Practical Reason* (1788)

Rousseau: Enlightenment Rebel

The youngest of the *philosophes*, Jean-Jacques Rousseau (1712–1778), took issue with some of the basic precepts of Enlightenment thought. Human beings may be good by nature, argued Rousseau, but, ultimately, they are corrupted by society and its institutions. This notion is voiced in the dramatic opening words of his popular treatise, *The Social Contract:* "Man is born free, and everywhere he is in chains." Influenced by writings describing the native populations of the Americas and elsewhere, Rousseau condemned the artificiality of civilized life and exalted the "noble savage" as the model of the uncorrupted individual. His writings elevate instinct over reason; they show a new appreciation of nature and the natural—ideas that would underlie the Romantic movement of the century to come.

Rousseau, *The Social Contract* and *Émile* (1762)

Rousseau's distrust of institutional authority and his wish to safeguard individual liberty dominated the content of *The Social Contract*. Unlike Hobbes, whose contract gave absolute authority to a sovereign power, or Locke, whose ruler received limited powers from the people, Rousseau defined the state as nothing more than "the general will" of its citizens. "The general will alone," he explained, "can direct the State according to the object for which it was instituted, that is, the common good." Whoever refuses to obey the general will should be constrained to do so by the whole of society; that is, citizens should "be forced to be free." For Rousseau, the social contract gave the body politic "absolute power over all its members."

Rousseau's desire to preserve the natural in human society also motivated his revolutionary vision of education. In *Émile*, his treatise on education, Rousseau suggested the then unheard-of idea that education begins at birth. He advocated "hands-on" experience as essential to early education. "Nature provides for the child's growth in her [Nature's] own fashion, and this should never be thwarted. Do not make him sit still when he wants to run about, nor run when he wants to be quiet," advised Rousseau. Rousseau's views on female education were less liberal, as he held that a woman's place was in the home; rather than raise his own five (illegitimate) children himself, he saw fit to put them in a foundling hospital. Nevertheless, *Émile* became a landmark in educational theory: Its new approach to education—particularly the emphasis on cultivating natural inquisitiveness over rote learning—influenced modern teaching methods in the West.

Adam Smith: Economic Theory

Enlightenment thinkers were primarily concerned with human liberty and equality, but they also addressed matters related to the economy of the modern state. The Scottish economist Adam Smith (1723–1790) applied the idea of natural law to the domains of human labor, productivity, and the exchange of goods and services. In his landmark work, *An Inquiry into the Nature and Causes of the Wealth of Nations*, Smith set forth the "laws" of labor, production, and trade. Smith held that labor was basic to prosperity: the labor force—not land or money—was the foundation for national wealth. He observed that self-interest guided the progress of economic life, and such natural forces as the "law of supply and demand" motivated a free market economy. Markets are driven toward the public good, argued Smith, by an "invisible hand." However, a ***laissez-faire*** (literally "allow to act") economy might invite a conspiracy of sellers against buyers. Therefore, government must play a necessary (but limited) role in protecting consumers from the fraudulent operations of wealthy dealers and producers. Modern formulations of free trade and capitalist enterprise were born in the pages of the *Wealth of Nations.* Justly called "the father of modern economics," Smith saw his *magnum opus* go through five editions in his lifetime.

Smith, *An Inquiry into the Nature and Causes of the Wealth of Nations* (1776)

Revolutions of the Late Eighteenth Century

The American and French revolutions drew inspiration from the Enlightenment faith in the reforming power of reason. In 1776, North America's thirteen colonies rebelled against the British government, claiming it had made unreasonable demands for revenues that threatened colonial liberty. The populists of the American colonies fervently sought democratic reform. Following some seven years of armed conflict, several thousand battle deaths, and a war expense estimated at over $100 million, the colonies achieved their independence. And in 1789 they began to function under the Constitution of the United States of America. The British political theorist Thomas

Figure 11.7 Briffault de la Charprais and Mme. Esclapart, *The Siege of the Bastille, July 14, 1789*, 1791–1796. Engraving, 18¼ x 12 in. Pierpont Morgan Library, New York.

Paine (1737–1809) observed that the Revolution had done more to enlighten the world and diffuse a spirit of freedom among humankind than any previous event.

The American Revolution did not go unnoticed in France. French intellectuals followed its every turn; the French government secretly aided the American cause and eventually joined in the war against Britain. However, the revolution that began on French soil in 1789 involved circumstances that were quite different from those in America. The French Revolution was, in the main, the product of two major problems: class inequality, and a serious financial crisis brought about by some five hundred years of costly wars and royal extravagance (see page 277–280). With his nation on the verge of bankruptcy, King Louis XVI (1754–1793) sought new measures for raising revenue.

Throughout French history, taxes had fallen exclusively on the shoulders of the lower and middle classes, the so-called Third Estate. Almost four-fifths of the average peasant's income went to pay taxes, which supported the privileged upper classes. In a population of some twenty-five million people, the First Estate (the clergy) and the Second Estate (the nobility)—a total of only 200,000 citizens—controlled nearly half the land in France; yet they were exempt from paying taxes. Peasant grievances were not confined to matters of taxation: Population growth and rising prices led to severe shortages of bread, the main food of the lower classes.

In October 1789, six thousand angry women marched on Versailles to protest the lack of bread in Paris. When, in an effort to obtain public support for new taxes, Louis XVI called a meeting of the Estates General—its first in 175 years—the Third Estate withdrew and formed a separate body claiming the right to approve or veto all taxation. This daring act set the Revolution in motion. No sooner had the Third Estate declared itself an independent body than great masses of peasants and laborers rioted throughout France.

On July 14, 1789, crowds stormed the Bastille (the French state prison), destroying the visible symbol of the old French regime (Figure **11.7**). Less than one month later, on August 4, the National Assembly—as the new body established by the Third Estate called itself—issued decrees that abolished the last remnants of medieval feudalism, including manorial courts, feudal duties, and church tithes. It also made provisions for a limited monarchy and an elected legislative assembly. The decrees of the National Assembly became part of a constitution prefaced by the Declaration of the Rights of Man and Citizen, modeled on the American Declaration of Independence. A Declaration of the Rights of Woman and Citizen, drafted in 1791 by a butcher's daughter, Olympe de Gouges (1748–1793), demanded equal rights for women. For the first time in history women constituted a collective revolutionary force, making demands for equal property rights, government employment for women, and equal educational opportunities.

Between 1791 and 1793, divisions among the revolutionaries themselves led to a more radical phase of the Revolution, called the Reign of Terror. This phase saw the failure of the existing government and sent Louis XVI and his queen to the guillotine. Between 1793 and 1794, over forty thousand people (including Olympe de Gouges) met their deaths at the guillotine. Finally, in 1794, a National Convention devised a system of government run by two legislative chambers and a five-man executive body of directors. One of these—Napoleon Bonaparte (1769–1821)—would turn France into a military dictatorship some five years later. If the French Revolution defended the Enlightenment bastions of liberty and equality, its foundations of reason and rationality ultimately crumbled under the forces of extremism and violence. The radicals of this and many other world-historical revolutions to follow rewrote the words of the *philosophes* in blood.

LITERATURE AND THE ENLIGHTENMENT

Pope: Poet of the Age of Reason

If any single poet typified the spirit of the Enlightenment, it was Alexander Pope (1688–1744). Pope was a British Neoclassicist who defended the value of education in Greek and Latin. Largely self-taught (in his time, Roman Catholics were barred from attending English universities), he gained recognition for his prose essays, philosophic poetry, biting satires, and for his new translations of the *Iliad* and the *Odyssey*. "A little learning is a dangerous thing," warned Pope, wittily pleading for a broad embrace of the literary past.

Pope's *Essay on Man* is a philosophical poem that explains nothing less than humankind's place in the universal scheme. A Catholic turned deist, Pope saw evil as an inherent part of God's design for a universe that, while seemingly imperfect, is actually (as Pope perceived) "A mighty maze! But not without a plan." Whatever occurs in nature has been "programmed" by God as part of a benign and rational order. Pope warns that we must not attempt to understand the whole of nature. Rather, he counsels, "Know then thyself, presume not God to scan;/ The proper study of Mankind is Man." While Pope lacked the reforming zeal of the *philosophes*, he captured the mood of philosophic optimism in his landmark poem:

Pope, *Essay on Man* (1732–1744)

Cease then, nor Order Imperfection name:
Our proper bliss depends on what we blame.
Know thy own point: This kind, this due degree
Of blindness, weakness, Heav'n bestows on thee.
Submit—In this, or any other sphere,
Secure to be as blest as thou canst bear:
Safe in the hand of one disposing Pow'r,
Or in the natal, or the mortal hour.
All Nature is but Art, unknown to thee;
All Chance, Direction, which thou canst not see;
All Discord, Harmony not understood;
All partial Evil, universal Good:
And, spite of Pride, in erring Reason's spite,
One truth is clear, WHATEVER IS, IS RIGHT.

(from *Essay on Man*, Epistle 1, Stanza X)

Newspapers and Novels

Social criticism assumed an important place in Enlightenment literature. Such commentary now manifested itself in a new literary genre: the *journalistic essay*. Designed to address the middle-class reading public, prose essays and editorials were the stuff of magazines and daily newspapers. The first daily emerged in London during the eighteenth century, although a weekly had been published since 1642. At this time, London, with a population of some three-quarters of a million people, was the largest European city, and England claimed the highest rate of male literacy in Western Europe.

With the rise of newspapers and periodicals, the "poetic" prose of the seventeenth century—characterized by long sentences and magisterial phrases—gave way to a more informal prose style, one that reflected the conversational chatter of the *salons* and the cafés. Journalistic essays brought "philosophy out of the closets and libraries, schools and colleges, to dwell in clubs and assemblies, at tea-tables and in coffee houses," explained Joseph Addison (1672–1719), the leading British prose stylist of his day. In collaboration with his lifelong friend Richard Steele (1672–1729), Addison published two London periodicals, the *Tatler* and the *Spectator*, which featured penetrating commentaries on current events and social behavior. The *Spectator* had a circulation of some twenty-five thousand readers. Anticipating modern news magazines, eighteenth-century broadsheets and periodicals offered the literate public timely reports and diverse opinions on all aspects of popular culture. They provided entertainment, helped to shape popular opinion, and cultivated a spirit of urban chauvinism best expressed by the English pundit Samuel Johnson (1709–1784): "When a man is tired of London, he is tired of life: for there is in London all that life can afford."

The most important new form of eighteenth-century literary entertainment, however, was the *novel*. The novel—a long, fictitious prose narrative—first appeared in world literature in eleventh-century Japan (see page 129), where it remained popular for centuries. In the West, the tales of Boccaccio and Chaucer and Cervantes' fictional *Don Quixote* anticipated the novel form. Nevertheless, the modern novel, with its realistic characters and settings, came to flower in England at the beginning of the eighteenth century. A landmark in this genre is the popular adventure novel *Robinson Crusoe* by Daniel Defoe (1660–1731). Defoe's narrative, based on actual experience, is sharply realistic and, thus, quite different from the fantasy-laden prose of his predecessors. Defoe's novels, and those of his somewhat later contemporaries Samuel Richardson (1689–1761) and Henry Fielding (1707–1754), feature graphic accounts of the personalities and daily lives of characters from the lower and middle classes—some perfectly average individuals, but also criminals, pirates, and prostitutes. Not surprisingly, these novels appealed to the tastes of readers who enjoyed the spicy details and journalistic gossip of the contemporary magazine and newspaper.

Defoe, *Robinson Crusoe* (1719)

Slave Narratives

A unique literary genre made its appearance in the eighteenth century: *Slave narratives* constitute a body of prose literature written by Africans who suffered the cruelties of the transatlantic slave trade. Begun in the fifteenth century (see page 248), this system of trade, by which millions of Africans were bought and shipped against their will to colonies in the "New World," reached its peak in the eighteenth century (Figure **11.8**). As England—lured by the lucrative sugar trade—became the leading player in the transatlantic traffic, some nine to twelve million slaves were transported to work on sugar plantations in the West Indies and elsewhere in the Americas. To supply this market, Africans—including African children—were frequently kidnapped by their unscrupulous countrymen, who profited handsomely by selling captives to white slave traders. The fate of the African slave who survived the perilous "Middle Passage" between Africa and the Americas (it is estimated that roughly one-third perished in transit) was a life of unspeakable suffering.

One of the earliest narrative accounts of this inhumane system is the autobiographical narrative of Olaudah Equiano (1745–1799), who was born in the West African kingdom of Benin and kidnapped and enslaved at the age of eleven. Both as a slave and after his release from slavery in 1766, Equiano traveled widely; during his stay in England (as one of only thirty thousand blacks in mid-eighteenth-century England), he mastered the English

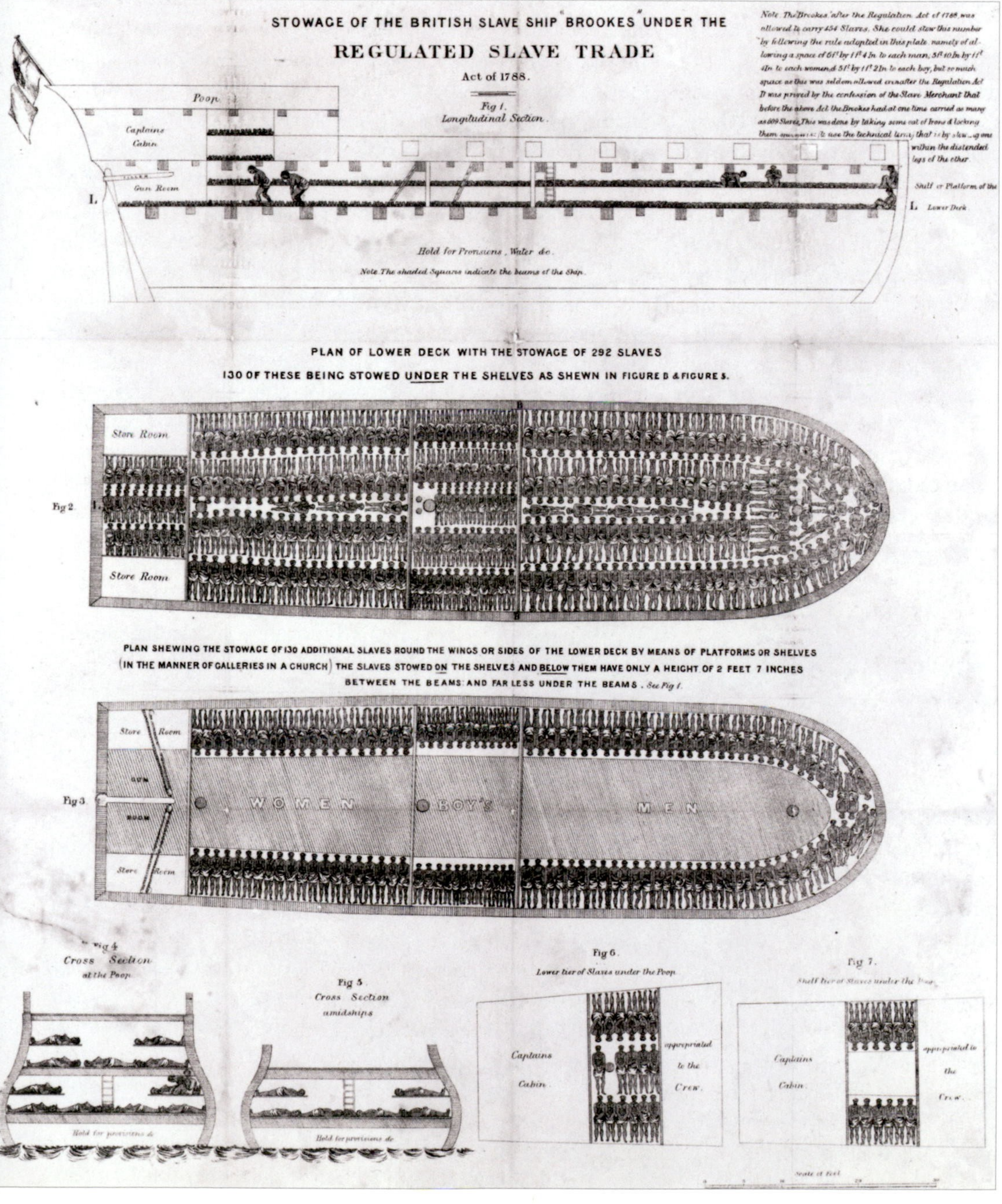

Figure 11.8 Plan of the *Brookes*, a 320-ton British slave ship of the late eighteenth century. The legend in the upper right corner reads: "Note. The Brookes after the Regulation Act of 1788 was allowed to carry 454 Slaves. She could stow this number by following the rule adopted in this plate namely of allowing a space of 6 foot by 1 foot 4 inches to each man; 5 foot 10 inches by 1 foot 4 inches to each woman & 5 foot by 1 foot 2 inches to each boy, but so much space as this was seldom allowed even after the Regulation Act. It was proved by the confession of the Slave Merchant that before the above Act the Brookes has at one time carried as many as 609 Slaves. This was done by taking some out of Irons & locking them spoonwise, to use the technical term; that is by stowing one within the distended legs of the other."

language and became an outspoken abolitionist. Equiano's autobiographic narrative, titled *Travels*, recounts with dramatic simplicity the traumatic experience of a child who was cruelly sold into bondage. Recent scholarship has cast doubt on the accuracy of Equiano's story: Baptismal records and naval rolls put his place of origin in South Carolina. If, however, Equiano fabricated his early life to fuel the abolitionist cause, the accuracy of his descriptions of the Middle Passage and the fate of the African slave are confirmed by the firsthand accounts of other slaves. The writing of slave narratives continued well into the nineteenth century, when such literature, in conjunction with the movement for the abolition of slavery (see pages 336–337), served to convince readers of the immorality of this "Peculiar Institution."

Equiano, *Travels* (1789)

Satire: Swift and Voltaire

In eighteenth-century Europe, where Enlightenment intellectuals exalted the ideals of human progress, there was clear evidence of human ignorance, depravity, and despair. Upon visiting the much-acclaimed city of Paris, Rousseau lamented its "dirty, stinking streets, filthy black houses, an air of slovenliness" and alleys filled with beggars. Indeed, outside the elegant drawing rooms of Paris and London lay clear signs of poverty, violence, and degradation.

Science and technology spawned a new barbarism in the form of machines that were potentially as destructive as they were beneficial. In England, the invention of the "flying shuttle" (1733), the "spinning jenny" (1765), and the power loom (1785)—machines for the manufacture of textile goods—encouraged the rise of the factory system and sparked the Industrial Revolution. James Watt's steam engine (1775) provided a new power source for textiles and other industries. But such technological achievements, allied with unregulated capitalism, gave rise to dangerous working conditions and the exploitation of labor. In many of London's factories, children tended the new machines for twelve- to fourteen-hour shifts, following which they were boarded in shabby barracks. And in the mines of Cornwall and County Durham, women and children were paid a pittance to labor like animals, pulling carts laden with coal. Some miners worked such long hours that they never saw the light of day.

The discrepancies between the sordid facts of eighteenth-century life and the progressive ideas of the Enlightenment provoked indignant protests, and none so potent as those couched in humor. The eighteenth century was history's greatest age of satire. The favorite weapon of many Enlightenment intellectuals, satire fused wit and irony to underscore human folly and error—and, more specifically, to draw attention to the vast contradictions between Enlightenment ideals and contemporary realities.

Swift The premier British satirist of the eighteenth century was Jonathan Swift (1667–1745). This Dublin-born Anglican priest took a pessimistic view of human nature. He once confided (in a letter to the poet Alexander Pope) that he hated the human race, whose misuse of reason produced, in his view, an irredeemably corrupt society. Yet Swift was not a man of despair, for no despairing person could have produced such a profoundly moralizing body of literature. His classic satire, *Gulliver's Travels*, is a story of travel and adventure that describes the fortunes of a hero in imaginary lands peopled with midgets, giants, and other fabulous creatures. At the symbolic level, however, it is a social statement on the whimsical nature of human behavior. In one chapter, Gulliver visits the Lilliputians—"little people" whose moral pettiness and inhumanity seem to characterize humankind at its worst. In another, he meets noble horses whose rational behavior contrasts with the bestiality of their human-looking slaves, the Yahoos. An immediate popular sensation, *Gulliver's Travels* has become a landmark in fantasy literature and social satire.

Swift, *Gulliver's Travels* (1726)

Voltaire Swift's satires were an inspiration to that most scintillating of French *philosophes* and leading intellectual of French society, François Marie Arouet (1694– 1778), who used the pen name Voltaire (Figures 11.1 and **11.9**). Born into a rising Parisian middle-class family and educated by Jesuits, Voltaire rose to fame as a novelist, historian, poet, playwright, and social critic. He quickly became a favorite figure

Figure 11.9 Jean-Antoine Houdon, *Voltaire in Old Age*, 1781. Marble, height 20 in. Versailles Museum. Voltaire is shown here wearing the customary eighteenth-century wig, ruffed collar, and vest (compare Figure 11.1). One of the first thinkers to admire the works of Confucius, which he read in Jesuit translations, Voltaire extolled the traditions of non-Western cultures.

of the French *salons*. Like most of the *philosophes*, Voltaire condemned organized religion and all forms of religious fanaticism. A declared deist, he compared human beings to mice who lived in the recesses of an immense ship without knowing its captain or its destination. Any confidence Voltaire might have had in beneficent Providence was dashed by the terrible Lisbon earthquake and tidal wave of 1755, which took the lives of more than twenty thousand Portuguese people. For Voltaire, the realities of natural disaster and human cruelty were not easily reconciled with the belief that a good God had created the universe or that humans were by nature rational—views basic to Enlightenment optimism.

In thousands of pamphlets and letters, Voltaire attacked bigotry as manmade evil and injustice as institutional evil. On two separate occasions, his controversial verse-satires led to imprisonment in the Bastille, while his assaults on royal authority forced him into frequent exile. A three-year stay in England instilled in him high regard for constitutional government, the principles of toleration, and the concepts of equality found in the writings of John Locke—whom he championed in his own writings.

Nowhere are Voltaire's incisive wit and wisdom more famously wed than in the satirical tale *Candide* (mockingly subtitled *Optimism*). In this landmark work, Voltaire addressed the age-old question: How can evil exist in a universe governed by the forces of good? His answer, which takes the form of an adventure tale, deals a major blow to the optimistic credo of Leibniz and Pope that this is "the best of all possible worlds." *Candide* follows the exploits of a naive young man through a series of terrible (and hilarious) adventures. Initially, the young hero approaches life with the glib optimism extolled by his teacher Dr. Pangloss (the name means "all tongue"), Voltaire's embodiment of Leibniz. But Candide ("candid" or "innocent") soon experiences the horrors of war, the evils of religious fanaticism, the disasters of nature, and the dire effects of human greed—the last of these an affliction derived from boredom, according to Voltaire. Candide's personal experience provides the antidote to the comfortable fatalism of Pope's "Whatever is, is right." After a lifetime of sobering misadventures, he ends his days on a farm, in the company of his closest friends. "We must cultivate our garden," he concludes with resignation. This metaphor for achieving personal satisfaction in an imperfect world relieves the otherwise devastating skepticism that underlies this moral tale. *Candide* is Voltaire's answer to blind optimism and the foolish hope that human reason can combat evil. Although it was censored in many parts of Europe, *Candide* was so popular that it went through forty editions in Voltaire's lifetime.

Voltaire, *Candide* (1759)

Hogarth's Visual Satires

"I have endeavoured to treat my subjects as a dramatic writer," wrote the English artist William Hogarth (1697–1764), "my picture is my stage, and the men and women my actors." A contemporary of Swift and Voltaire, Hogarth produced a telling visual record of the ills of eighteenth-century British society. Popular plays and novels provided inspiration for paintings he called his "modern moral subjects." He illustrated books by Defoe and Swift, among others, and he made engraved versions of his paintings, selling the prints by subscription. So popular were these prints that they were pirated and sold without his authorization. Especially successful were two landmark series based on his paintings. The first ("The Harlot's Progress") illustrates the misfortunes of a young woman who becomes a London prostitute; the second ("The Rake's Progress") reports the comic misadventures of an antihero and ne'er-do-well named Tom Rakewell.

Figure 11.10 William Hogarth, *The Marriage Transaction*, from the "Marriage à la Mode" series, 1742–1746. Engraving, 15 x 18 in. The practice of selling engravings without the permission of the artist continued even after Parliament passed the first copyright law in 1725.

Following these, Hogarth published a series of six engravings based on paintings derived from a popular eighteenth-century comedy, *Marriage à la Mode*, written by John Dryden (1631–1700). This picture cycle depicts the tragic consequences of a marriage of convenience between the son of a poverty-stricken noble and the daughter of a wealthy and ambitious merchant. The first print in the series, *The Marriage Transaction*, shows the two families negotiating the terms of the matrimonial union (Figure **11.10**). The scene unfolds as if upon a stage: The corpulent Lord Squanderfield, victim of the gout (an ailment traditionally linked with rich food and drink), sits pompously in his ruffled velvet waistcoat, pointing to his family tree, which springs from the loins of William the Conqueror. Across the table, the wealthy merchant and father of the bride carefully peruses the financial terms of the marriage settlement. On a settee in the corner of the room, the pawns of this socially expedient match turn away from each other in attitudes of mutual dislike. The earl's son, young Squanderfield, sporting a beauty patch, opens his snuffbox and vainly gazes at himself in a mirror, while his bride-to-be idly dangles her betrothal ring on a kerchief. She leans forward to hear the honeyed words of her future seducer, a lawyer named Lord Silvertongue. A combination of **caricature** (exaggeration of peculiarities or defects), comic irony, and symbolic detail, Hogarth's "stylish marriage" is drawn with a stylus every bit as sharp as Voltaire's pen.

THE VISUAL ARTS AND THE ENLIGHTENMENT

The Rococo Style

The Rococo style was the decorative finale of the Baroque era (see Chapter 10). Rich in ornamentation, but more delicate and playful than the Baroque, it provided an atmosphere of elegant refinement among the members of the French nobility who had outlived Louis XIV. The name itself fuses the Portuguese *barocco* (baroque) and the French *rocaille*, a kind of fancy shellwork commonly used to decorate aristocratic gardens and grottoes. The Rococo style flourished in the royal courts and churches of eighteenth-century Europe. But it found its ideal home in the elegant urban townhouses of Paris, where the wealthy gathered to enjoy the pleasures of dancing, dining, and socializing (see Figure 11.6).

The Salon de la Princesse is a landmark of the Parisian Rococo (Figure **11.11**). Located in the Hôtel de Soubise, a city mansion built for the prince and princess de Soubise, the oval-shaped room is rich in ornamentation, yet it has a fragile, airy look. Its brilliant white walls, accented with pastel tones of rose, blue, and lime, are ornamented with gilded tendrils, playful cupids, and floral garlands.

Beyond the *salon*, the garden was the favorite setting for the leisured elite. Unlike the geometrically ordered parks at Versailles, Rococo gardens imitated the calculated naturalism of Chinese gardens. They featured undulating paths that gave false impressions of scale and distance. They also often included artificial lakes, small colonnaded temples, ornamental pagodas, and other architectural "follies." Both outdoors and in, the fascination with Chinese objects and motifs—which began as a fashion in Europe around 1720—promoted the cult of *chinoiserie*.

Figure 11.11 Germain Boffrand, Salon de la Princesse, Hôtel de Soubise, Paris, ca. 1740. Oval-shaped, max. 33 x 26 ft. An organic pattern of curves and countercurves is repeated in the elegant mirrors and chandeliers. The walls seem to melt into ceiling vaults crowned with graceful moldings and embellished with Classically themed paintings and stucco sculpture.

Figure 11.12 Johann Michael Fischer, interior, Benedictine abbey, Ottobeuren, Bavaria, 1736–1766. Painted and gilded wood and stucco. Light floods into the white-walled interior through oval windows, and pastel-colored frescoes turn ceilings and walls into heavenly antechambers. A dazzling array of organic forms sprouts from the moldings and cornices.

Although the Rococo style originated in France, it reached spectacular heights in the courts of secular princes elsewhere in Europe. In Austria and the German states, it became the favorite style for the ornamentation of rural pilgrimage churches. The Benedictine abbey church of Ottobeuren in Bavaria, designed by the German architect Johann Michael Fischer (1692–1766), has walls that seem to disappear beneath a riot of stucco "frosting" as rich and sumptuous as any wedding cake (Figure **11.12**). Illusionism reigns: Wooden columns and stucco cornices are painted to look like marble; angels and cherubs, tendrils and leaves, curtains and clouds—all made of wood and stucco that have been painted and gilded—come to life as props in a theater of miracles.

Rococo Painting

The pursuit of pleasure dominates the paintings of the Rococo masters. In *Departure from the Island of Cythera* (Figure **11.13**), the Flemish-born Antoine Watteau (1684– 1721) paid tribute to the fleeting nature of love. The painting depicts the popular eighteenth-century ***fête galante***, a festive diversion enjoyed in an outdoor setting. Watteau shows a group of fashionable men and women on the island of Cythera, the legendary birthplace of Venus. Having paid homage to the goddess of love, whose rose-bedecked shrine appears at the far right, they prepare to board a golden boat to leave the island. With feathery brushstrokes, the artist creates a fictional moment of nostalgia in which the elegant figures linger amid fluttering cupids and billowing trees.

If Watteau's world was wistful and poetic, that of his contemporary François Boucher (1703–1770) was sensual and indulgent. A specialist in designing mythological scenes, Boucher became head of the Gobelins tapestry factory in 1755 and director of the Royal Academy ten years later. He was First Painter to King Louis XV (1710–1774) and a good friend of the king's favorite mistress, Jeanne Antoinette Poisson, the Marquise de Pompadour (1721–1764). A woman of remarkable

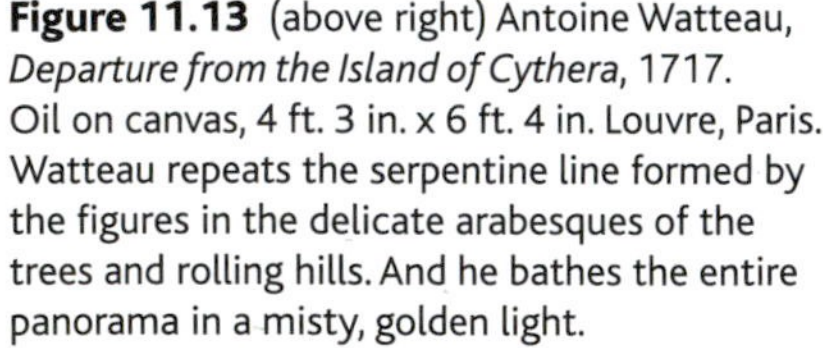

Figure 11.13 (above right) Antoine Watteau, *Departure from the Island of Cythera*, 1717. Oil on canvas, 4 ft. 3 in. x 6 ft. 4 in. Louvre, Paris. Watteau repeats the serpentine line formed by the figures in the delicate arabesques of the trees and rolling hills. And he bathes the entire panorama in a misty, golden light.

Figure 11.14 (right) François Boucher, *The Bath of Venus*, 1751. Oil on canvas, $42\frac{1}{8}$ x $33\frac{3}{8}$ in. National Gallery of Art, Washington, D.C. Boucher delighted in sensuous contrasts of flesh, fabric, feathers, and flowers. His girlish women, with their unnaturally tiny feet, rosebud-pink nipples, and wistful glances, were coy symbols of erotic pleasure.

beauty and intellect—she owned two telescopes, a microscope, and a lathe that she installed in her apartment in order to carve cameos—Madame de Pompadour influenced state policy and dominated fashion and the arts at Versailles for almost twenty years. In the idyllic *The Bath of Venus*, Boucher flattered his patron by portraying her as goddess of love (Figure **11.14**). Surrounded by attentive doves and cupids, the nubile Venus relaxes on a bed of sumptuous rosy satin draperies nestled in a bower of leafy trees and windswept grasses. In Boucher's hands, the erotic female nude became a favorite Rococo subject.

Jean-Honoré Fragonard (1732–1806), Boucher's most talented pupil, was the undisputed master of translating the art of seduction into paint. Working shortly before the French Revolution, he captured the pleasures of a waning aristocracy. In 1766, a wealthy aristocrat commissioned Fragonard to paint a scene that showed the patron's mistress seated on a swing being pushed by a friendly old clergyman. *The Swing* depicts a flirtatious encounter that takes place in a garden bower filled with frothy trees, Classical statuary, and delicate blond light. The young woman, dressed in yards of satin and lace,

Making Connections

LOVE AND LOVERS

Fragonard met the demands of his patrons for paintings that feature sensuous subjects ranging from flirtation (Figure **11.15**) to violent seduction. Love and lovers were also popular themes in Hindu art, which regarded the union of man and woman as an expression of the soul's quest for oneness with the divine. In the music, literature, and art of India, this theme is illustrated by the immortal legend of Rahda and Krishna (the incarnation of the Hindu god Vishnu). Rahda's devotion to her lover—she waited for him for decades, despite his marriages to other women—served as a model for male/female love, as well as for the union of Self and Spirit in the Hindu faith.

The final meeting of Radha and Krishna, frequently described in Indian love lyrics, was a favorite subject in Hindu painting. One anonymous eighteenth-century artist, influenced by Persian miniatures, shows the lovers wrapped in passionate embrace (Figure **11.16**). As in Fragonard's *Swing*, a remote bower sheltered by verdant trees and flowering bushes provides the romantic setting for intimate moments of tender delight. However, unlike Fragonard's vignette of amorous frivolity, the Indian image carries a deeply spiritual meaning.

Q What role does the landscape setting play in the formal and symbolic content of each painting?

Figure 11.16 *Radha and Krishna in a Grove*, from Kangra, Punjab Hills, India, ca. 1780. Opaque watercolor on paper, 4⅞ x 6¾ in. Victoria and Albert Museum, London.

Figure 11.15 Jean-Honoré Fragonard, *The Swing*, 1768–1769. Oil on canvas, 32 x 25½ in. Wallace Collection, London.

kicks her tiny shoe into the air in the direction of a statue of Cupid, while her lover, hiding in the bushes below, peers delightedly beneath her billowing skirts (see Figure 11.15). Whether or not the young lady is aware of her lover's presence, her coy gesture and the irreverent behavior of the *ménage à trois* (lover, mistress, and cleric) create a mood of erotic intrigue similar to that found in the comic operas of this period, as well as in the pornographic novel, which developed as a genre in eighteenth-century France.

Figure 11.17 Marie-Louise Elisabeth Vigée-Lebrun, *Marie Antoinette*, 1788. Oil on canvas, 12 ft. 1½ in. x 6 ft. 3½ in. Versailles Museum. Aristocratic women—especially such notable females as Marie Antoinette in France, Catherine the Great in Russia, and Maria Theresa in Austria—eagerly embraced the Rococo style. Indeed, the Rococo may be said to reflect the distinctive influence of eighteenth-century women of taste.

The widespread commercialization of the Rococo made it popular throughout most of Europe, and fashion and fashionableness—clear expressions of self-conscious materialism—were major themes of Rococo art. Marie-Louise Elisabeth Vigée-Lebrun (1755–1842), the most famous of a number of eighteenth-century female artists, produced refined portrait paintings for an almost exclusively female clientele. Her glamorous likeness of Marie Antoinette, queen consort of Louis XVI, is a tribute to the European fashion industry (Figure **11.17**). Plumed headdresses and low-cut gowns bedecked with lace, ribbons, and tassels turned the aristocratic female into a conspicuous ornament; the size of her billowing skirt required that she turn sideways to pass through doorways.

Rococo Sculpture

The finest examples of eighteenth-century sculpture are small in scale, intimate in mood, and almost entirely lacking in either dramatic urgency or religious fervor. Intended for the boudoir or the drawing room, Rococo sculpture usually depicted elegant dancers, wooing couples, or other lighthearted subjects.

One of the favorite French Rococo sculptors, Claude Michel, known as Clodion (1738–1814), worked almost exclusively for private patrons. His *Intoxication of Wine* revives a Classical theme—the ritual celebration honoring Dionysus, the Greek god of wine and fertility (Figure **11.18**). Flushed with wine and revelry, the **satyr** (a semibestial woodland creature symbolic of Dionysus) embraces a **bacchante**, an attendant of Dionysus. Clodion made the piece in terracotta, a clay medium that requires rapid modeling, thus inviting the artist to capture a sense of spontaneity.

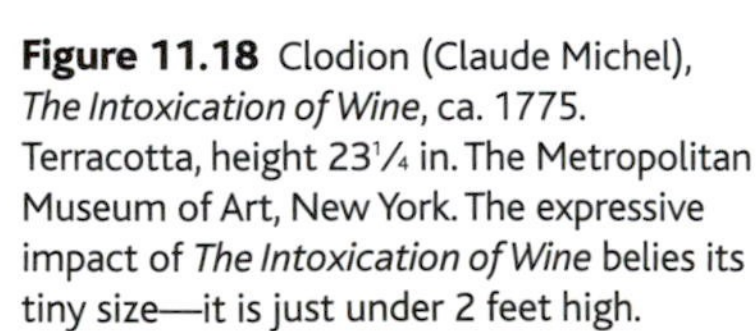

Figure 11.18 Clodion (Claude Michel), *The Intoxication of Wine*, ca. 1775. Terracotta, height 23¼ in. The Metropolitan Museum of Art, New York. The expressive impact of *The Intoxication of Wine* belies its tiny size—it is just under 2 feet high.

Figure 11.19 Jean-Baptiste Greuze, *Village Betrothal*, 1761. Oil on canvas, 3 ft. 10½ in. x 3 ft. Louvre, Paris. Greuze's painting could easily have been an illustration of a scene from a popular eighteenth-century play or novel. Such representations appealed to common emotion and sentiment.

Genre Painting

Even before the outburst of the French Revolution, Enlightenment critics attacked the Rococo style as the frivolous expression of the monied aristocracy. Diderot called for an art that made "virtue attractive and vice odious." Jean-Baptiste Greuze (1725–1805) responded with humble representations that replaced the indulgent sensuality of the Rococo with realistic scenes of everyday life. Greuze's paintings exalt the simple virtues of the middle and lower classes. His *Village Betrothal*, a landmark of genre painting, tells the story of an impending marriage in a family of simple-living rustics (Figure **11.19**). The father, who has just given over the dowry to the homely groom, blesses the couple; the mother laments losing a daughter, while other members of the family look on approvingly. A comparison of this canvas with Hogarth's *Marriage Transaction* (see Figure 11.10) reveals the extent to which eighteenth-century genre painters mirrored the social concerns of their time.

Unlike the works of Greuze, who illustrated his tales as literally (and melodramatically) as possible, those of his near contemporary Jean-Baptiste-Siméon Chardin (1699–1779) avoid explicit moralizing. The ennobling dignity of work and the virtues of domesticity are themes in such landmark works as *The Kitchen Maid* (Figure **11.20**). Reminiscent of Vermeer's *Milkmaid* (see Figure 10.15), a simple but monumental figure dominates a composition whose subtlety extends to the placement of every last potato and egg. The painting, a testament to Chardin's deep concern for commonplace humanity, evokes a mood of gentility and gravity.

Figure 11.20 (below) Jean-Baptiste-Siméon Chardin, *The Kitchen Maid*, 1738. Oil on canvas, 18⅛ x 14¾ in. National Gallery of Art, Washington, D.C. While Chardin's subjects were humble and commonplace, his patrons were often bankers, foreign ambassadors, and royalty itself—Louis XV owned at least two of Chardin's paintings.

Figure 11.21 Alexandre-Pierre Vignon, Church of Saint Mary Magdalene ("La Madeleine"), Paris, 1807–1842. Length 350 ft., width 147 ft., height of podium 23 ft. The gloomy interior of La Madeleine, which consists of a nave crowned by three low domes, presents a dramatic contrast to the majesty of the exterior.

Figure 11.22 Jean-François Thérèse Chalgrin and others, Arch of Triumph, Paris, 1806–1836. Height 164 ft. This landmark stands at the crossing of twelve avenues at the south end of the famous Avenue des Champs-Elysées. It was completed twenty-one years after Napoleon was defeated at Waterloo in 1815. (See also Figure 12.22.)

Neoclassicism

Neoclassicism—the revival of Greco-Roman culture—belonged to a tradition that stretched from the Renaissance through the age of Louis XIV. In the eighteenth century, however, the longstanding interest in antiquity was infused by a new development: the scientific study of Classical ruins. In 1738, the king of Naples sponsored the first archeological excavations at Herculaneum, one of the two Roman cities in southern Italy buried under volcanic ash by the eruption of Mount Vesuvius in 79 C.E. Excavations at Pompeii and on mainland Greece and Asia Minor would follow. Scholars assembled vast collections of Greek and Roman artifacts, many of which came to be housed in such museum repositories as the Louvre and the Vatican. The study of these works enabled artists and antiquarians to make clear distinctions—for the first time in history—between the artifacts of Greece and those of Rome.

The German scholar Johann Joachim Winckelmann (1717–1768) was active in publicizing the newly excavated Classical treasures. His magnificently illustrated *History of Ancient Art* established Winckelmann as "the father of modern art-historical scholarship." His reverence for antiquity—its "noble simplicity" and "quiet grandeur"—shaped the eighteenth-century view of Classicism as a vehicle for the elevation of human consciousness. Here, finally, was the ideal mode of expression for the Enlightenment program of reason, clarity, and order.

Neoclassical Architecture

The architecture of the Neoclassical revival was unique in its accuracy of antique detail and its purity of design. In place of Baroque theatricality and the wedding-cake fantasies of the Rococo, Neoclassical buildings made use of simple geometric masses, free of frivolous ornamentation. Neoclassical interiors consisted of clean, rectilinear wall planes, soberly accented with engaged columns or pilasters, geometric motifs, and shallow niches that often housed copies of antique statuary.

Neoclassicism, the official style of the French Revolution, became the vehicle of French imperialism. After Napoleon Bonaparte was crowned emperor in 1804, Paris was redesigned to capture the grandeur of imperial Rome: The French capital became a city of straight, wide avenues and impressive squares. Imaginary sightlines linked the various monuments raised to honor the emperor, and older buildings were remodeled in the new Empire style. Alexandre-Pierre Vignon (1763–1828) redesigned the Church of Saint Mary Magdalene (called "La Madeleine") as a Roman temple dedicated to the glory of the French army (Figure **11.21**). Fifty-two Corinthian columns, each 63 feet tall, surround the temple, which rises on a 23-foot-high podium approached by a flight of steps at the front. A popular Paris landmark, La Madeleine is the colossal sister of the Maison Carrée in Nimes (see Figure 3.11).

Figure 11.23 Thomas Jefferson, Monticello, near Charlottesville, Virginia, 1770–1784, remodeled 1796–1806. Thomas Jefferson, the main author of the *Declaration of Independence*, was a self-taught architect who popularized Neoclassicism in America. He designed Monticello, his private residence, in a style that combined a Classical temple front with a dome, but also drew on elements from Palladian and British Neoclassical models.

Perhaps the most memorable landmark of French Neoclassicism is the Arch of Triumph (Figure **11.22**). Like La Madeleine, it was designed in the style of imperial Rome to commemorate the glories of Napoleon's imperial armies. It resembles the Arch of Titus in the Roman Forum (see Figure 3.16), but at 164 feet high is larger than any arch built in ancient times.

The fledgling United States of America embraced Neoclassicism as an expression of the rationalist ideals associated with the cultures of Greece and Rome. America's impassioned apostle of Neoclassicism was Thomas Jefferson (see pages 298–299). Jefferson depended on Classical and Renaissance models for the design of the Virginia State Capitol, for the Rotunda of the University of Virginia (see Figure 3.10), and for the design of his own country estate in Monticello ("little mountain"), Virginia (Figure **11.23**). Located on a hill near Charlottesville, Monticello is a landmark that combines the clarity and symmetry of Palladian design (see Figures 7.22 and 7.23) with the key features of Roman architecture: the dome and the Doric portico. The finest architect of his generation, Jefferson envisioned architecture as a tool of the Enlightenment: He realized that harmoniously designed buildings could not only create a national image; they could also influence social conduct and human aspiration.

Neoclassical Sculpture

Jean-Antoine Houdon (1741–1828), the leading portrait sculptor of Europe, heeded the Enlightenment demand for an art that perpetuated the memory of illustrious men. Houdon's portrait busts revived the realistic tradition in portrait sculpture that had begun with the Romans. Houdon worked from life, portraying his sitters first in terracotta, then making a plaster cast (and often a life-mask), from which the final marble sculpture was produced. His talent for capturing an individual's characteristic expression gave his portraits an authentic presence. Such is the case with his likenesses of the aging Voltaire (see Figures 11.1 and 11.9), discussed at the beginning of this chapter.

Among Houdon's portraits of "virtuous men," his likeness of Jefferson (see Figure 11.5) is especially notable: It immortalizes Jefferson with the kindly smile of the pundit and the self-conscious dignity of the intellectual. In 1785 Jefferson arranged for Houdon to travel to the United States—he was one of the only eighteenth-century European artists to visit North America—where he would execute a renowned life-size statue of George Washington.

Realistic Roman portraiture was not the only source of inspiration for eighteenth-century sculptors. The idealized nude sculptures of Hellenic Greece were rivaled by the works of the internationally renowned Italian-born Antonio Canova (1757–1822). An artist of impeccable technical skill, Canova was commissioned by a galaxy of eighteenth-century patrons, including Napoleon Bonaparte. His life-sized portrait of Napoleon's sister, Pauline Borghese, is a landmark in Neoclassical refinement (see

Making Connections

THE NEOCLASSICAL VOGUE

The Neoclassical spirit touched everything from sculpture to furniture and tableware. Among the most popular Neoclassical items of the late eighteenth century were the ceramic wares of the English potter Josiah Wedgwood (1730–1795). Wedgwood's ceramics were modeled on Greek and Roman vases and embellished with finely applied, molded white clay surface designs. *The Portland Vase* (Figure **11.24**), based on a Roman model, shares with Canova's "Venus" (Figure **11.25**) the ghostlike whiteness of form that typified the work of the Neoclassicists, who seem to have been unaware that Classical sculptors painted their statues to make them look more lifelike.

Q What is the effect of the whiteness of the medium that characterized Neoclassical sculpture?

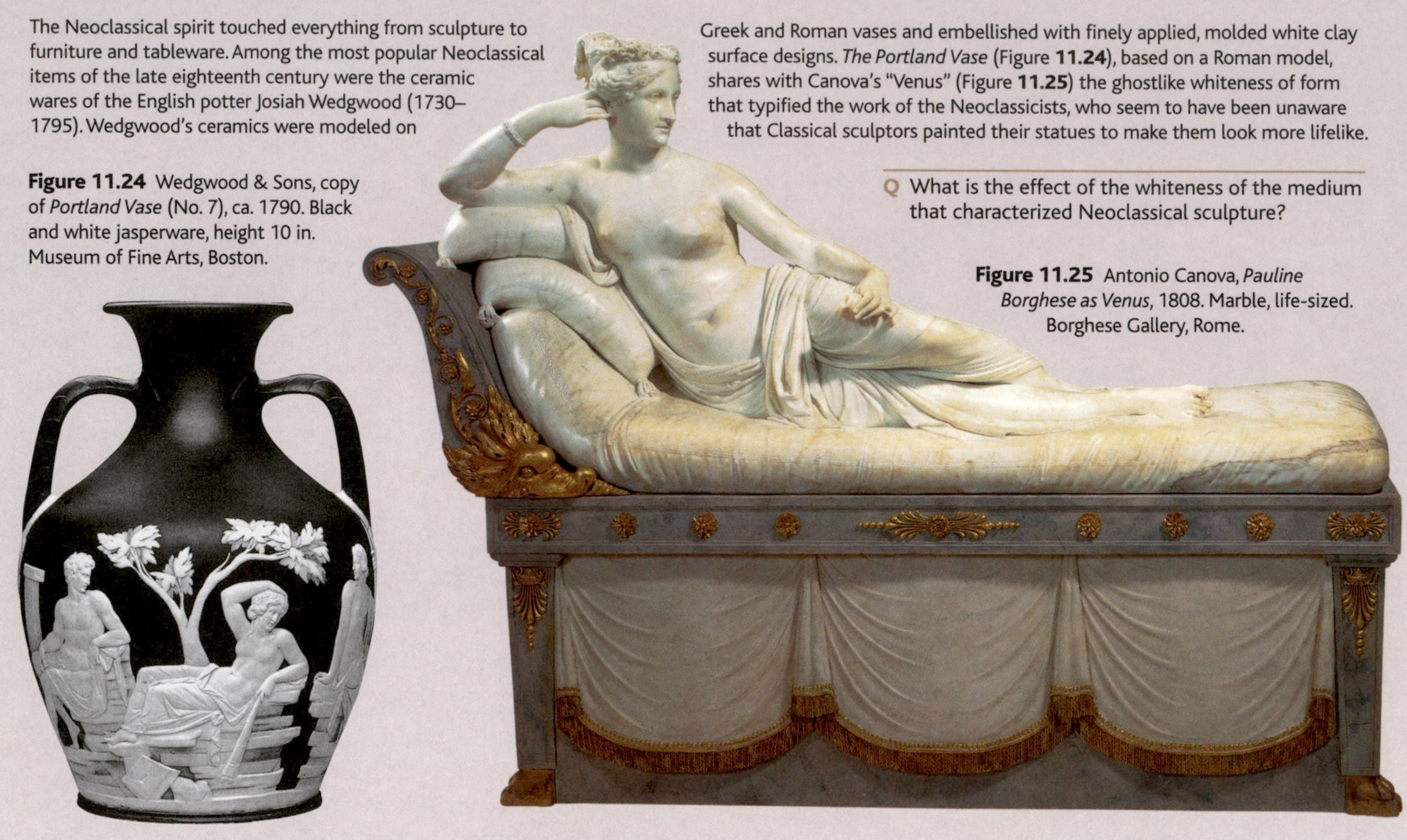

Figure 11.24 Wedgwood & Sons, copy of *Portland Vase* (No. 7), ca. 1790. Black and white jasperware, height 10 in. Museum of Fine Arts, Boston.

Figure 11.25 Antonio Canova, *Pauline Borghese as Venus*, 1808. Marble, life-sized. Borghese Gallery, Rome.

Figure 11.25). Perfectly proportioned and flawlessly elegant, Pauline appears in the guise of a reclining Venus.

Neoclassical Painting

In the last decades of the eighteenth century, as the tides of revolution began to engulf the indulgent lifestyles of the French aristocracy, the Rococo style gave way to a sober, intellectualized approach to picture-making. The pioneer of the new Classicism was the French artist Jacques-Louis David (1748–1825). After winning the coveted Prix de Rome, which sent him to study in the foremost city of antiquity, David found his place among the Classicists. In 1784 he completed the landmark painting of the late eighteenth century, *The Oath of the Horatii* (Figure **11.26**). The painting had been commissioned by the French king some five years before the outbreak of the Revolution; ironically, however, it became a symbol of the very spirit that would topple the royal crown.

The Oath of the Horatii illustrates a dramatic event recorded by Livy in his *History of Rome*: the heroic vow taken by the three sons of Horatius Proclus to meet the champions of the treacherous Curiatii family in a win-or-die battle that would determine the future of Rome. (Two of the Horatii would die in combat, but the third returned victorious, having killed his opponents.) David captured the spirit of the story in a single potent image—the moment when, resolved to defend Roman liberty even to their death, the three brothers lift their arms in a dramatic military salute.

If David's subject matter was revolutionary, so was his style: geometric shapes, hard-edged contours, and somber colors replaced the sensuous curves, delicate figures, and pastel tones of the Rococo. Bathed in golden light, the Horatii stand with statuesque dignity along the strict horizontal line of the picture plane. The figure on the far left forms a rigid triangle that is subtly repeated throughout the composition—in the arches of the colonnade and in the group of grieving women. Austere and Neoclassically precise—witness the archeologically correct Roman helmets, sandals, and swords— *The Oath of the Horatii* was an immediate success. People lined up to see the huge canvas (over 10 x 14 feet) while it hung in the artist's studio in Rome. When it arrived in Paris in 1785, it was greeted with popular enthusiasm.

David's most talented pupil was Jean-Auguste-Dominique Ingres (1780–1867). The son of an artist,

Figure 11.26 Jacques-Louis David, *The Oath of the Horatii*, 1784. Oil on canvas, 10 ft. 10 in. x 14 ft. Louvre, Paris. David's painting presented life as serious drama: It proclaimed the importance of reason and the intellect over and above feeling and sentiment, and it defended the ideals of male heroism and self-sacrifice in the interest of one's country.

Ingres rose to fame with his polished depictions of Classical history and mythology and with his accomplished portraits of middle- and upper-class patrons. He spent much of his career in Italy, where he came to prize (as he himself admitted) "Raphael, his century, the ancients, and above all the divine Greeks." Ingres shunned the weighty realism of David in favor of the purity of line he admired in Greek vase painting, in the published drawings of the newly unearthed Classical artifacts, and the engraved book illustrations for the works of Homer and Hesiod.

Late in his career Ingres turned his nostalgia for the past to exotic themes inspired by Napoleon's campaigns in Syria and North Africa. His *Grande Odalisque* represents one of the popular subjects of the day: the harem of slaves of the Ottoman Empire (Figure **11.27**). Both a revisualization of Titian's *Venus of Urbino* (see Figure 7.34) and Canova's *Pauline Borghese as Venus* (see Figure 11.25), Ingres' odalisque turns her body away from view, even as she gazes seductively at the viewer. Ingres' fine line and polished brushstrokes are typically Neoclassical, but his elongation of the body departs from Classical canons of proportion. The "incorrect" anatomy drew strong criticism, and some even objected that the subject had three too many vertebrae. Nevertheless—or perhaps because of its bold departure from the norm—the *Grande Odalisque* remains one of the landmarks of Western art.

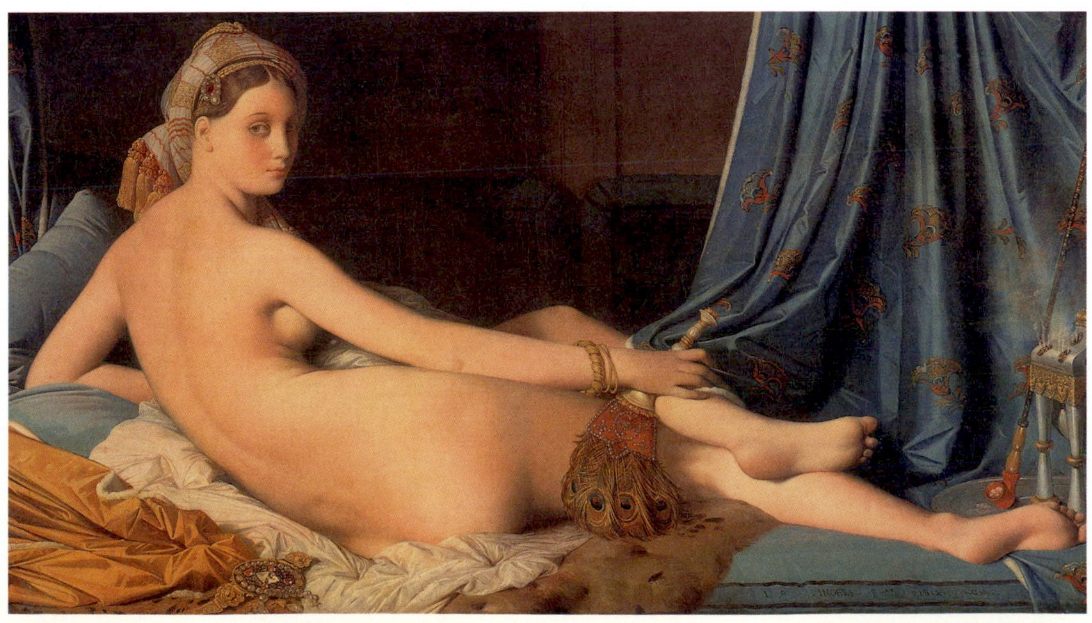

Figure 11.27 Jean-Auguste-Dominique Ingres, *La Grande Odalisque*, 1814. Oil on canvas, 2 ft. 11¼ in. x 5 ft. 3¾ in. Louvre, Paris.

MUSIC AND THE ENLIGHTENMENT

THE eighteenth century was enormously rich in musical landmarks. Music filled the courts and concert halls, the latter as a response to the rising popular demand for public recitals. While religious music was still very much in demand, it was overshadowed by vast amounts of music composed for secular entertainment. Eighteenth-century composers sought the patronage of wealthy aristocrats and often served at their courts. At the same time, many composers wrote independently for amateur performance and for the public concert hall.

During the eighteenth century certain distinctive characteristics converged to set Western musical culture apart from that of the rest of the world. These include the idea that harmony is proper and essential to music, that a musical composition should be the original product of a single composer, and that pieces should be rehearsed and performed in much the same manner each time they are played. These traits, which stress order and formality over spontaneity and improvisation, would come to characterize *classical* music—that is, "serious" or "art" music as distinct from the more ephemeral "popular" or "folk" music.

Eighteenth-Century Classical Music

The term "classical" is also used more narrowly: to describe a specific musical style that prevailed in the West between approximately 1760 and 1820. The music of that era shares the essential features of Neoclassical art: symmetry, balance, and formal restraint. Unlike Neoclassical art and architecture, however, classical music had little to do with Greece and Rome, for European composers had no surviving evidence of Greek or Roman music, and, therefore, no antique musical models to imitate. Classical music developed its own unique model for clarity of form and purity of design. Classical composers, most of whom came from Germany and Austria, wrote homophonic compositions that featured easy-to-grasp melodies, which are repeated or developed within definitive formal structures. The liberation of melody from Baroque polyphony was anticipated by the light and graceful melodies of French Rococo music, which, like Rococo art, was delicate in sound, thin in texture, and natural in feeling.

While classical composers retained the fast/slow/fast contrasts of Baroque instrumental forms, they rid their compositions of many Baroque features—replacing, for instance, the abrupt changes from loud to soft with more gently graduated contrasts. They also eliminated the unflagging rhythms and ornate musical embellishments of Baroque polyphony in favor of clear-cut musical phrases. And while counterpoint continued to play an important role in classical music, the intricate webs of sound (as heard in Bach's fugues) gave way to a new harmonic clarity. Classical music developed formal structures that parallel the Enlightenment quest for reasoned clarity and the Neoclassical artist's commitment to purity of design.

Classical composers wrote music for a variety of instrumental groupings. The largest of these was the instrumental form known as the **symphony**: an independent composition for full orchestra. In addition to the symphony, three other instrumental genres dominated the classical era: the concerto, a composition featuring one or more solo instruments and an orchestra; the **string quartet**, a piece for two violins, viola, and cello; and the sonata, a composition for an unaccompanied keyboard instrument or for another instrument with keyboard accompaniment.

All of these genres assumed the same formal structure: They were divided into three or four sections, or *movements*, each of which followed a specific tempo, or musical pace. The first movement was played ***allegro*** or in fast tempo; the second ***andante*** or ***largo***, that is, in moderate or slow tempo; the third movement (usually omitted in concertos) was written in dance tempo (usually in three-quarter time); and the fourth was again *allegro*.

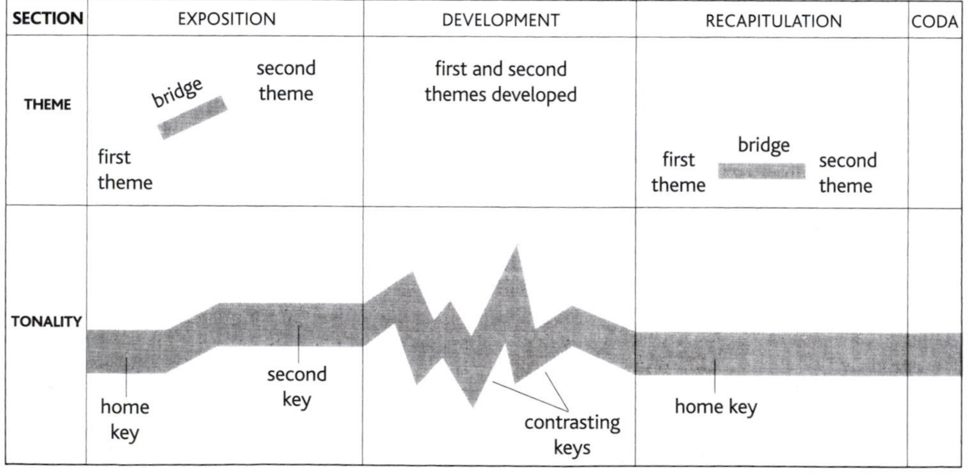

Figure 11.28 Sonata form. In the exposition, the composer "exposes," or introduces, a theme in the "home" key, then contrasts it with a second theme in a different key. Musical effect is based on the tension of two opposing key centers. In the development, the composer moves to further contrasting keys, expanding and altering the themes stated in the exposition. Finally, in the recapitulation, the themes from the exposition are restated, both now in the home key.

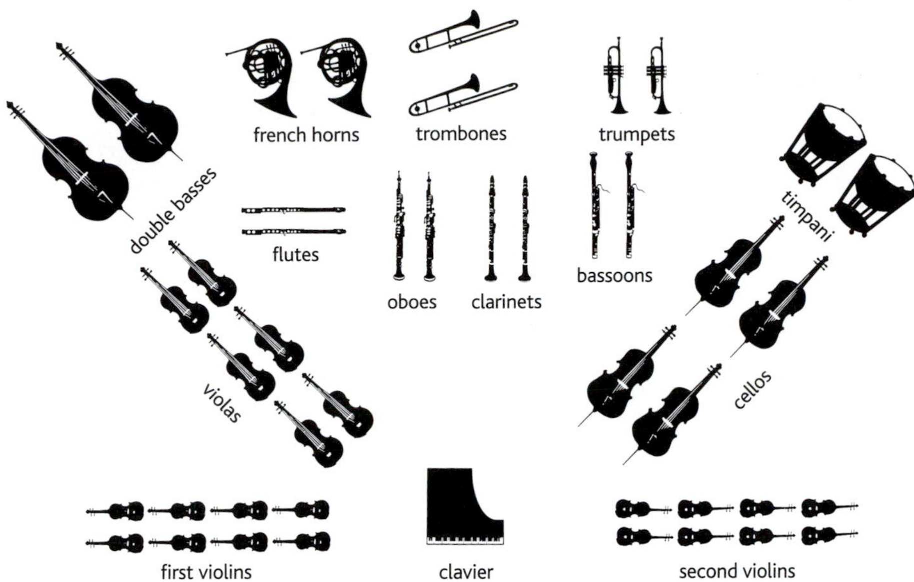

Figure 11.29 The classical symphony orchestra. The eighteenth-century orchestra was led by a musician (often the composer himself) who played part of the composition on the clavier or keyboard instrument located at the place now occupied by the conductor's podium. The string section was seated to the right and left, while the other instruments were spread across the middle distance, in a pattern that has persisted to this day.

For the organization of the first and last movements, classical composers used a special form known as **sonata form** (or **sonata allegro form**; Figure **11.28**). It calls for the division of a given movement into three parts: the exposition, the development, and the recapitulation. A **coda** ("tail") is often added as a definitive end piece. Classical composers frequently deviated from sonata form, but they looked to it to provide the "rules" of musical design—the architectural guidelines, so to speak, for musical composition.

Also popular among classical composers was the form known as **theme and variations**, which might appear as an independent piece or as a musical idea within the movement of a symphony, string quartet, or sonata. As the name suggests, theme and variations features a basic musical idea that is repeated in various ways; that is, by changes in rhythm, harmony, melody, and so on. Already evident in late Renaissance and Baroque music, this form was employed inventively by classical composers to give each variation of the theme its own identity.

The Birth of the Symphony Orchestra

Eighteenth-century instrumental music served as secular entertainment in public theaters and in the *salons* of courtly residences. The most important instrumental grouping to emerge at this time was the orchestra. It consisted of groups of related instruments, each with its own character or personality. The **strings**, made up of violins, violas, cellos, and double basses, formed the nucleus of the orchestra, since they most frequently carried the melody. The **woodwinds**, consisting of flutes, oboes, clarinets, and bassoons, specialized in mellow harmonies. The **brass** section, made up of trumpets and French horns (and, by the end of the century, trombones), added volume and resonance. Lastly, the **percussion** section, using kettledrums (otherwise known as *timpani*), functioned as rhythm markers (Figure **11.29**). The orchestra was small by modern-day standards. It included some thirty-five pieces, many of which were still rudimentary: Brass instruments lacked valves, and the clarinet was not perfected until roughly 1790. The piano, which was invented around 1720, remained until 1775 more closely related to the clavichord than to the modern grand piano. To facilitate control over the music, the orchestra used a *score*, that is, a record of musical notation that indicates every sound to be played by each instrument.

Haydn

The classical style owes its development to the Austrian composer Franz Joseph Haydn (1732–1809). In 1761, at the age of twenty-nine, he became musical director to the court of the powerful and wealthy Hungarian noble Prince Paul Anton Esterházy, who was also an accomplished musician. The magnificent Esterházy country estate (modeled on Versailles) included two theaters—one for opera and one for puppet plays—and two richly appointed concert halls. There, for almost thirty years, Haydn took charge of all aspects of musical entertainment: He composed music, trained choristers, oversaw the repair of instruments, and rehearsed and conducted an orchestra of some twenty-five musicians. At the princely court, Haydn wrote operas, oratorios, and liturgical music. But his most original works were those whose forms he himself helped to develop: the classical symphony and the string quartet. The "father of the symphony," as Haydn is often called, wrote 104 symphonies and 84 string quartets.

After the death of Prince Esterházy in 1790, Haydn was invited to perform in London, where he composed his last twelve symphonies. In the London symphonies, which he wrote for an orchestra of some sixty players, he explored an expanded harmonic range and a wealth of dramatic effects. For some of the symphonies he used folk melodies as basic themes. A landmark among his London compositions is his Symphony No. 94 in G major. In the second movement of the piece, Haydn employed the theme and variations form to novel advantage: the theme is stated, then repeated more quietly, then followed by an unexpected **fortissimo** ("very loud") instrumental crash. The device gave the symphony its nickname: "The Surprise." Tradition has it that the blaring chord was calculated to waken the drowsy members of the audience—London concerts often lasted well past midnight—and entice them to anticipate the next "surprise," which never does occur. A celebrity in his old age, "Papa Haydn" (as he was affectionately called) was one of the first musicians to attain the status of a cultural hero during his own lifetime.

Haydn, Symphony No. 94 in G major (1792)

Figure 11.30 Louis Carmontelle, *The Mozarts in Concert: Leopold, Wolfgang (age seven), and Nannerl*, 1764. Engraving. British Museum, London. It is generally acknowledged that Mozart wrote more great music in more genres than any other composer in history.

Mozart

The foremost musical genius of the eighteenth century—and, some would say, of all time—was Haydn's younger contemporary and colleague Wolfgang Amadeus Mozart (1756–1791). A child prodigy, Mozart wrote his first original composition at the age of six and his first symphony at the age of eight. His ability to sight read, improvise, and transpose music, to identify the pitch of any sound, and to transcribe flawlessly whole compositions that he had heard only once, remains unequaled in the history of music. During his brief life, Mozart produced a total of some 650 works, including 41 symphonies, 60 sonatas, 23 piano concertos, 23 string quartets, and 20 operas. (These were catalogued and numbered in the late nineteenth century by Ludwig von Köchel, hence the "K." numbers used to identify Mozart's compositions.)

Wolfgang, the son of a prominent composer, was born in Salzburg, Austria. With his father Leopold and his sister Nannerl he toured Europe, performing hundreds of public and private concerts before he was thirteen (Figure **11.30**). He often performed his own pieces, particularly his piano concertos, which constitute some of

JAPAN

The Way of Tea and Zen

The long reign of Japan's Tokugawa dynasty generated landmarks previously discussed in these pages—the *kabuki* theater and painted multifold screens (see pages 225 and 285). During the seventeenth and eighteenth centuries, a third landmark of Japanese culture reached its highest point: the ritual tea ceremony. The classic expression of Japanese elegance and simplicity, the tea ceremony emerged as a unique synthesis of art, theater, and rite. Introduced into Japan from China during the ninth century, heavily caffeinated tea served as an aid to prolonged meditation among Buddhist monks. By the sixteenth century, as better types of tea plants were cultivated in Japan, the Way of Tea (as the philosophy of tea drinking was called) became widely practiced in Japanese society. Tea drinking required a special room, a distinctive set of implements (for preparation and serving), and a highly stylized etiquette. The practice became exquisitely refined in conjunction with Zen Buddhism, a strand of Buddhism that stresses the attainment of spiritual enlightenment through intuitive illumination.

Among Zen Buddhists, the Way of Tea coincided with a revival of Zen painting. Zen calligraphers regarded brush painting as an act of meditation involving intense concentration and focus. Hakuin Edaku (1685–1768), the Zen master who penned the "portrait" *Meditating Dharuma* (Figure **11.31**), systematized the *koan* teaching method, which required meditation on a question in the form of a riddle designed to produce enlightenment. His most famous *koan* was "What is the sound of one hand clapping?" Utter simplicity and absence of detail invites the beholder to complete a Zen ink painting mentally, thus partaking of the creative, meditative process.

The verbal counterpart of the Zen exercise is the lyric verse form known as the ***haiku***. A seventeen-syllable poem arranged in three lines of 5/7/5, it achieves effectiveness by an absence of detail and a pairing of contrasting images. The unexpected contrast is designed to evoke an ineffable mood or emotion. Much like the Zen master's brush drawing (which often incorporates a poem into the composition), the *haiku* creates a provocative void between what is stated and what is left unsaid. Witness the following three poems by Japan's most famous *haiku* poet and Zen monk, Matsuo Basho (1644–1694).

The first day of the year:
thoughts come—and there is loneliness;
the autumn dusk is here.

◆

Oh, these spring days!
A nameless little mountain,
wrapped in morning haze!

◆

I'd like enough drinks
to put me to sleep—on stones
covered with pinks.

Figure 11.31 Hakuin Edaku, *Meditating Dharuma*, Edo period, ca. 1765. Ink on paper, 49½ x 21¾ in. Chikusei Collection, U.S.A. The inscription reads "Pointing directly to the human heart, see your own nature and become Buddha."

his most important musical contributions. Unlike Haydn, Mozart did not invent any new forms. However, he brought to the instrumental genres of his time unparalleled melodic inventiveness. The lyricism of popular dance tunes and folk melodies embellished the elegant compositions he wrote for garden parties, weddings, and balls. Three of his symphonies (Nos. 39, 40, and 41), written in a six-week period, remain among the landmarks of the classical symphonic form. Symphony No. 40 in G minor balances moods of unbridled excitement with tender melancholy. However, as one leading musicologist rightly observed:

Mozart, Symphony Nos. 39, 40, and 41 (1788)

> Each of these three symphonies has its own character; each is a complex but distinct personality, a personality which is defined perfectly by the music but which completely eludes verbal formulation. . . . The three works must be viewed as a summation, unusually complete and clear, of three fundamental aspects of Mozart's musical being and consequently of the whole Western musical world of the late eighteenth century.[1]

[1] Donald Jay Grout, *A History of Western Music.* 3rd edition (New York: Norton, 1980), page 513.

After leaving the service of the archbishop of Salzburg in 1781, Mozart sought appointments in the aristocratic courts of Europe, but he never received adequate patronage and had difficulty supporting himself and his family. Throughout his life, he was excessively concerned with money; when he died in Vienna at the age of thirty-five, he was buried in a pauper's grave.

During the last six years of his life, Mozart wrote four of his finest operas, receiving commissions for all but the first. These works are among the best loved in the Western operatic repertory: *Le nozze di Figaro* (*The Marriage of Figaro*), *Don Giovanni*, *Così fan tutte* (*Thus Do All Women*), and *Die Zauberflöte* (*The Magic Flute*). Mozart was a genius of musical drama: He turned the stock types of comic opera and the allegorical figures of Monteverdi and Lully into sympathetic flesh-and-blood human beings. His most beloved characters, such as the philandering Don Giovanni and the clever Figaro, convey a wide range of emotions, from grief and despair to hope and joy. In *The Marriage of Figaro*, he champions the wit and ingenuity of the lower classes over the self-serving arrogance of the nobility. Mozart's vocal music is never sentimental; it retains the precision and clarity of the classical style and invests it with unparalleled melodic grace.

Afterword

The Enlightenment was a turning point in Western history. Rooted in the Scientific Revolution, it provided the foundations for modern science and for a variety of disciplines that applied reason to social, economic, and political life. Elevating reason to the status of a religion, the *philosophes* advanced programs for human progress and perfectibility. The nature of the social contract and the rights of women were issues that inspired landmark literary contributions. Efforts to collect and systematize knowledge and to record current events and social behavior generated the encyclopedia, the newspaper, and the modern novel. The genre of satire served to bring to light eighteenth-century social and political ills. In the visual arts, the Rococo style that celebrated the world of the aristocracy gave way to Neoclassicism, which, in both Europe and the young American nation, promoted the more sober cultural ideals of Greco-Roman antiquity. The emphasis on order and formalism also appeared in eighteenth-century music: in the evolution of new instrumental forms, the birth of the symphony orchestra, and the glorious compositions of Mozart and Haydn.

Key Topics

- the Scientific Revolution
- Bacon: the empirical method
- Descartes: modern philosophy
- Locke: the social contract
- Jefferson: unalienable rights
- the *philosophes*
- the encyclopedia
- Wollstonecraft: women's rights
- Kant and Rousseau
- eighteenth-century revolutions
- newspapers and novels
- Pope: Enlightenment optimism
- the slave narrative
- Swift and Voltaire
- the Rococo style
- Neoclassicism
- Haydn and Mozart
- the Japanese Way of Tea

ENLIGHTENMENT TIMELINE

	HISTORICAL EVENTS	LANDMARKS IN THE VISUAL ARTS	LITERARY LANDMARKS	MUSIC LANDMARKS
1600	• Scientific Revolution (1600–1750) • Founding of Royal Society, London (1645)		• Bacon, *Novum Organum* (1620) • Descartes, *Discourse on the Method* (1637)	
1650		**Figure 11.13** Antoine Watteau, *Departure from the Island of Cythera*, see p. 310	• Hobbes, *Leviathan* (1651) • Newton, *Mathematical Principles* (1687) • Locke, *Of Civil Government* (1690)	
1700	• First daily newspaper published in London (1702) • First archeological excavations at Herculaneum (1738)	• Watteau, *Departure from the Island of Cythera* (1717) • Fischer, Benedictine abbey, Ottobeuren, Bavaria (1736–1766) • Chardin, *The Kitchen Maid* (1738) • Hogarth, "Marriage" series (1742–1746)	• Defoe, *Robinson Crusoe* (1719) • Swift, *Gulliver's Travels* (1726)	• Birth of the symphony orchestra (1740s)
1750		• Boucher, *The Bath of Venus* (1751) • Greuze, *Village Betrothal* (1761) • Wright, *An Experiment on a Bird in the Air Pump* (1768) • Fragonard, *The Swing* (1768–1769)	• Pope, *Essay on Man* (1732–1744) • Diderot, *Encyclopedia* (1751–1772) • Voltaire, *Candide* (1759) • Rousseau, *The Social Contract* (1762), *Émile* (1762)	**Figure 11.9** Jean-Antoine Houdon, *Voltaire in Old Age*, see p. 306
1775	• American Revolution (1775–1783) • French Revolution (1789–1799) • Industrial Revolution in Britain (end of eighteenth century)	• Clodion, *The Intoxication of Wine* (ca. 1775) • Houdon, *Voltaire Seated* (1781); *Thomas Jefferson* (1789) • David, *The Oath of the Horatii* (1784) • Jefferson, Monticello (1770–1784) • Vigée-Lebrun, *Marie Antoinette* (1788)	• Jefferson, *Declaration of Independence* (1776) • Smith, *Wealth of Nations* (1776) • Kant, *Critique of Practical Reason* (1788) • Equiano, *Travels* (1789) • Wollstonecraft, *A Vindication of the Rights of Woman* (1792) • Condorcet, *Sketch for a Historical Picture of the Progress of the Human Mind* (1793)	• Mozart, *The Marriage of Figaro* (1786), *Don Giovanni* (1787), Symphony Nos. 39–41 (1788) • Haydn, Symphony No. 94 in G major (1792)
1800	**Figure 11.22** Jean-François Thérèse Chalgrin and others, Arch of Triumph, Paris, see p. 314	• Chalgrin, Arch of Triumph (1806–1836) • Vignon, Church of Saint Mary Magdalene, Paris (1807–1842) • Canova, *Pauline Borghese as Venus* (1808) • Ingres, *La Grande Odalisque* (1814)	**Figure 11.30** Louis Carmontelle, *The Mozarts in Concert: Leopold, Wolfgang (age seven), and Nannerl*, see p. 320	

Chapter 12

Romanticism:

NATURE, PASSION, AND THE SUBLIME

ca. 1780–1880

The term "Romanticism" describes a movement, a style, and an attitude of mind. As a *movement* dominating Western culture between roughly 1780 and 1880, Romanticism was a reaction against Enlightenment rationalism, academic authority, and the depersonalizing effects of Western industrialization. Asserting the value of individual experience, it provided a vehicle for nationalism, which worked to identify a nation's unique character by way of its mythic past. Grand opera, transcendent landscapes, and captivating ballets were typical products of the Romantic era.

As a *style*, Romanticism constituted an alternative to Neoclassical formalism and the objective exercise of the intellect. The Romantics embraced spontaneity and the subjective exercise of the imagination. Glorifying the senses, the emotions, and the heroic self, they looked to nature and the political events of their own time as sources of inspiration. The Romantics were the rebels of their age. They freed themselves from exclusive dependence on the patronage of the Church and the aristocratic court; and their impassioned subjectivity often alienated them from society.

Finally, as an *attitude of mind*, Romanticism exalted the creative imagination and the primacy of feeling in personal, political, and artistic life. This aspect of Romanticism is still with us today.

A First Look

"She flies like a spirit in the midst of transparent clouds of white muslin—she resembles a happy angel," wrote a French critic of the Swedish/Italian prima ballerina, Maria Taglioni (1804–1884). The leading female dancer of the Romantic era, Taglioni was one of the first ballerinas to dance *sur les pointes* (on the toes). In her debut performance as the sylph (a mythical air-spirit) in *La sylphide*, a landmark ballet choreographed by her father, she won acclaim for her virtuoso feats, which included crossing the stage in three floating leaps (see page 349). Such ballets, which reflect the Romantic nostalgia for the mythic past, were typical of the Golden Age in European dance, a time when female dancers dominated stage performance and even began to choreograph. Women also dominated the fantastic legends and the tales of love and death that were the favorite subjects of Romantic literature (see pages 329–334). Pictured here as Flora in the ballet *Zephire* (1831), Taglioni wears a diaphanous dress with a fitted bodice and a bell-shaped skirt (the prototype of the *tutu*), shortened to display her legs and feet, and reveal the virtuoso footwork that previously was reserved for male dancers. Sensuous beauty, delicacy of movement, and elegant grace, paramount features of Romantic ballet, brought Taglioni lasting fame. Following her performances in London, dolls manufactured in the dress and hairstyle of the ballerina were in popular demand. In Russia, sweets were named after her. Legend has it that after her retirement from the stage in 1842, her fans cooked and ate a pair of her ballet shoes, covered with sauce.

Figure 12.1 Maria Taglioni in her London debut of 1830. Color lithograph. National Library, Paris. Taglioni, who brought to classical ballet the sensuous spirit of Romanticism, earned notoriety for her perfectly executed arabesques (as depicted here)—a ballet position in which the dancer stands on one leg with the other extended backward and one or both arms held to create the longest line possible from one extremity to the other.

HERALDS OF ROMANTICISM

"*EXISTER, pour nous, c'est sentir*" ("For us, to exist is to feel"), exclaimed Rousseau in the late eighteenth century. In his autobiographical *Confessions* (1782), this Enlightenment thinker exalted the commitment to personal "feeling" that would inspire artists and thinkers of the next two generations. The nineteenth century did not generate more heroes than other centuries, but it produced a set of ideals that championed heroic performance and accomplishment. The heralds of Romanticism were a varied lot: They included political figures, philosophers, mystics, scientists, and artists. Among all of these individuals, there runs a common thread—the ambition to achieve great objectives by force of will and the exercise of the imagination.

Napoleon: Romantic Hero

In 1799, the thirty-year-old Corsican army general Napoleon Bonaparte seized control of the government of France. "The Revolution is ended," announced Napoleon when he proclaimed himself emperor in 1804. In the following ten years, Napoleon pursued a policy of conquest that brought continental Western Europe to his feet. Throughout much of the West, Napoleon abolished serfdom, expropriated Church possessions, curtailed feudal privileges, and introduced French laws, institutions, and influence. Napoleon spread the revolutionary ideals of liberty, fraternity, and equality throughout his empire (Map **12.1**). He championed popular sovereignty and kindled sentiments of nationalism—the exaltation of the sovereign state. In France, Napoleon ended civil strife, reorganized the educational system, and institutionalized the system of civil law known as the *Code Napoléon*.

If Napoleon's ambitions were heroic, his military campaigns were equally stunning. Having conquered Italy, Egypt, Austria, Prussia, Portugal, and Spain, he pressed on to Russia where, in 1812, bitter weather and lack of food forced his armies to retreat. Only 100,000 of his army of 600,000 survived. In 1813, a coalition of European powers forced his defeat and exile to the island of Elba off the coast of Italy. A second and final defeat occurred after he escaped in 1814, raised a new army, and met the combined European forces led by the English duke of Wellington at the Battle of Waterloo in 1815. The fallen hero spent the last years of his life in exile on the barren island of Saint Helena off the west coast of Africa.

Napoleon, the first of the modern European dictators, became the nineteenth century's first Romantic hero, glorified in numerous European poems and paintings, and especially in the majestic portraits of Jacques-Louis David, his favorite artist (Figure **12.2**).

Nineteenth-Century Philosophers

Romanticism found its formal philosophers largely among nineteenth-century German intellectuals. The most influential of these was Georg Wilhelm Friedrich Hegel (1770–1831). A professor of philosophy at the University of Berlin, he taught that the world consisted of a single divine nature, which he termed "absolute mind" or "spirit." According to Hegel, spirit and matter were involved in an evolutionary process impelled by spirit

Map 12.1 The Empire of Napoleon at its greatest extent, 1812.

Figure 12.2 Jacques-Louis David, *Napoleon Crossing the Great Saint Bernard Pass*, 1800. Oil on canvas, 8 ft. 6 in. x 7 ft. 3 in. National Museum of Malmaison Castle, Rueil-Malmaison, France. David's equestrian portrait shows an idealized Napoleon following the path of ancient generals such as Charlemagne and Hannibal (whose names are carved in stone in the left foreground). In this painting—one of five identical versions of the subject—he suggests that Napoleon's rule was one of glory and achievement.

seeking to know its own nature. Hegel explained the operation of that process, or **dialectic**, as follows: Every condition (or "thesis") confronts its opposite condition (or "antithesis"), which then generates a synthesis. The synthesis in turn produces its opposite, and so on, in a continuing evolution that moves, Hegel explained, toward the ultimate goal of spiritual freedom. For Hegel, all reality was a process that operated on the principle of the dialectic—thesis, antithesis, and synthesis—a principle that governed the realm of ideas, artistic creation, philosophic understanding, indeed, history itself. "Change in nature, no matter how infinitely varied it is," wrote Hegel, "shows only a cycle of constant repetition. In nature, nothing new happens under the sun."

In a dense prose work entitled *The Philosophy of History*, Hegel advanced the idea that the essence of spirit is freedom, which finds its ultimate expression in the state. His view of the state (and the European nation-state in particular) as the last stage in the development of spirit, and the Hegelian dialectic in general, had considerable influence on late nineteenth-century nationalism, as well as on the economic theories of Karl Marx (see page 358).

Hegel, *The Philosophy of History* (1807)

A lone but fascinating figure in the rich history of German philosophy was Arthur Schopenhauer (1788–1860), who held that nature (and existence itself) was devoid of reason and burdened by unrelenting suffering. In his landmark treatise *The World as Will and Idea* (1819), Schopenhauer advanced the idea of a "life-will"—a blind and impersonal force whose operations are without purpose and design, and whose activities give rise to disorder and delusion. In Schopenhauer's pessimistic view, the only escape from malignant reality is selfless contemplation of the kind described in Hindu literature and the writings of Christian mystics. While humans cannot overcome nature by way of reason, they may find temporary solace in art and music, and liberation through spiritual insight.

Darwin's *On the Origin of Species*

Like Hegel, the British scientist Charles Darwin (1809–1882) perceived nature as constantly changing. A naturalist in the tradition of Aristotle, Darwin spent his early career amassing enormous amounts of biological and geological data, partly as the result of a five-year voyage to South America aboard the research vessel HMS *Beagle*. Darwin's study of fossils confirmed the view of some of his predecessors that complex forms of life evolved from a few extremely simple organic forms. The theory of evolution did not originate with Darwin; the French biologist Jean-Baptiste de Lamarck (1744–1829) had shown that fossils give evidence of perpetual change in all species. Darwin, however, substantiated the theory by explaining the process by which evolution occurs. Observing the tendency of certain organisms to increase rapidly over time while retaining traits favorable to their survival, Darwin concluded that evolution operates by means of *natural selection*.

By natural selection, Darwin meant a process whereby nature "prunes away" unfavorable characteristics in a given species, permitting the survival of those creatures most suited to the struggle for life and to reproduction of that species. The elephant's trunk, the giraffe's neck, and the human brain are evidence, he argued, of adaptations made by each of these species to its environment and proof that any trait that remained advantageous to continuity would prevail. Failure to develop such traits meant the ultimate extinction of less developed species; only the "fittest" survived.

Soon after Darwin published his landmark work, *On the Origin of Species by Means of Natural Selection, or Preservation of the Favored Races in the Struggle for Life*, a commentator observed, "No scientific work that has been published within this century has excited so much general curiosity." But curiosity was among the milder responses to this publication, for Darwin's law of evolution, like Newton's law of gravity, challenged traditional ideas about nature and the world order. For centuries, most Westerners had held to the account of the Creation described in Scripture (Genesis 1–2). Some, indeed, accepted the chronology advanced by the Irish Catholic bishop James Ussher (1581–1656), which placed earthly creation at 4004 B.C.E. Most scholars, however, perceived the likelihood of a far greater age for the earth and its species. Darwin's theory of evolution by natural selection did not deny the idea of a divine Creator—in fact, Darwin initially agreed that "it is just as noble a conception of the Deity to believe that He created a few original forms capable of self-development into other and needful forms, as to believe that He required a fresh act of creation to supply the voids caused by the action of His laws." But Darwin's theory implied that natural selection, not divine will, governed the lineages of living things. By asserting that nature and its operations were the prime source of organic design, the theory of natural selection challenged the creationist view (supported by the Bible) that God had brought into being a fixed and unchanging number of species.

Darwin, *On the Origin of Species* (1859)

Equally troubling was Darwin's argument (clarified in his later publication, *The Descent of Man*, 1871) that the differences between humans and less complex orders of life were differences of degree, not kind, and that all creatures were related to one another by their kinship to simpler forms of life (Figure **12.3**).

Figure 12.3 Spoofing evolution, a cartoon of the day portrays an apelike Charles Darwin explaining his controversial theory of evolution to an ape with the help of a mirror. The work appeared in the *London Sketch Book* in May 1874, captioned by two suitable quotations from the plays of Shakespeare: "This is the ape of form" and "Four or five descents since." The most likely ancestor for *Homo sapiens*, explained Darwin, was "a hairy, tailed quadruped, probably arboreal in its habits. . . ."

Darwin's conclusions (which nurtured his own reluctant agnosticism) toppled human beings from their elevated place in the hierarchy of living creatures. If the cosmology of Copernicus and Galileo had displaced the earth from the center of the solar system, Darwin's theory robbed human beings of their preeminence on that planet. At a single blow, Darwin shattered the harmonious worldviews of both Renaissance humanists and Enlightenment *philosophes*.

The consequences of Darwin's monumental theory were far-reaching, but his ideas were often oversimplified or misinterpreted. Among some thinkers, the theory of evolution provided the rationale for analyzing civilizations as living organisms with identifiable stages of growth, maturity, and decline. Then, too, Darwin's use of the phrase "Favored Races" in the subtitle of his major work contributed to the theory of social Darwinism, which freely applied some of his ideas to political, economic, and cultural life. The term "social Darwinism," which came into use around 1879, describes the concept that natural selection operates to determine the superiority of some individuals, groups, races, and nations over others. Social Darwinists justified European policies of imperialism, that is, Western efforts to colonize non-Western territories (see pages 356–357), by claiming that Westerners (and white people in general) were clearly the "fittest" and therefore destined to dominate the "less fit." However, since Darwin meant by "fitness" the reproductive success of the species, not simply its survival, most nineteenth-century applications of his work to social conditions represented a distortion of his ideas. Among the most threatening of these distortions was the application of *eugenics* (the study of heredity improvement by genetic control) to defend the elimination of society's "less fit" members, which was basic to the racist ideology of Adolf Hitler in Germany (see pages 389–390).

In the course of the twentieth century, modern biology—and particularly the science of molecular genetics (the study of the digital information preserved in DNA)—provided substantial evidence for the validity of Darwin's theories. Yet, to date, scientific explanations for the origins of the first life—where and how it came into being—remain the object of continued research and debate.

The Industrial Revolution

The Scientific Revolution of the seventeenth century brought with it advances in methods and technology that would feed directly into the Industrial Revolution. By the eighteenth century a variety of inventions (see Box below) and better ways of harnessing sources of energy made it possible to produce (and eventually mass-produce) goods by machine rather than by hand. The steam engine, invented by James Watt in 1765, was first employed to drain mine shafts; by the early nineteenth century, it served England's flourishing textile industry; and by mid-century, it was used to run everything from sawmills to railroads.

While industrialization began in England in the late eighteenth century (and was monopolized by that country for a half-century), by the 1830s it had spread to Europe and the United States. Industrialization would have significant social and economic effects (both positive and negative) throughout the West, but it was primarily in England that the consequences of an expanding factory system—its devastation of the British countryside and the growth of a labor force that included women and children—were painfully visible. In such cities as Leeds and London, the squalid tenements that housed a class of poorly paid urban workers drew horrified reactions from the early Romantics.

LANDMARKS OF THE INDUSTRIAL REVOLUTION

1765	James Watt builds a model of a steam engine
1769	Richard Arkwright patents a hydraulic spinning machine
1779	The world's first iron bridge is erected at Coalbrookdale, England
1785	Edmund Cartwright's water-driven power loom revolutionizes England's weaving industry
1787	Friedrich Krupp establishes a steel plant at Essen, Germany
1792	Eli Whitney (American) manufactures the first effective cotton gin
1804	Robert Fulton (American) produces the first steam-powered ship
1814	Coal is transported by locomotive for the first time in England; first use of gaslight in London
1839	Charles Goodyear (American) produces the first industrial-strength rubber
1846	Elias Howe (American) patents the sewing machine
1851	The first international industrial exposition opens in London

ROMANTIC LITERATURE

Wordsworth and the Poetry of Nature

One of the central features of nineteenth-century Romanticism was its love affair with nature and the natural. In rural settings, the Romantics found a practical refuge from urban blight, smoke-belching factories, and poverty-ridden slums. They perceived in nature, with its shifting moods and rhythms, a metaphor for the **sublime**: the power and mystery of forces that inspire awe, solace, and self-discovery. In the broadest sense, the Romantic view of nature was nothing short of religious.

The leading nature poet of the age was William Wordsworth (1770–1850). Born in the Lake District of England, he dated the beginning of his career as a poet from the time—at age fourteen—when he was struck by the image of tree boughs silhouetted against a bright evening sky. Thereafter, "the infinite variety of natural appearances" became the principal source of his inspiration and the primary subject of his poetry. Wordsworth claimed that nature could restore to human beings their untainted, childhood sense of wonder. Moreover, through nature, one might commune with the elemental and divine forces of the universe.

Together with his British contemporary Samuel Taylor Coleridge (1772–1834), Wordsworth produced the *Lyrical Ballads*—the literary work that marked the birth of the Romantic movement in England. When the book appeared in a second edition in 1800, Wordsworth added a preface that formally explained the aims of Romantic poetry. In this manifesto, Wordsworth defines poetry as "the spontaneous overflow of powerful feelings," which takes its origin "from emotion recollected in tranquillity." According to Wordsworth, the object of the poet is "to choose incidents and situations from common life [and] to throw over them a certain colouring of the imagination . . . and above all, to make these incidents and situations interesting by tracing in them, truly though not ostentatiously, the primary laws of our nature." Wordsworth championed a poetic language that resembled "the real language of men in a state of vivid sensation." This natural voice enhanced a style of lyric poetry with deep personal feeling.

Wordsworth and Coleridge, *Lyrical Ballads* (1798)

One of the most inspired poems in the *Lyrical Ballads* is "Lines Composed a Few Miles Above Tintern Abbey," the product of Wordsworth's visit to the ruins of a medieval monastery situated on the banks of the River Wye in southeast Wales (Figure **12.4**). A song of praise to nature, the 159-line poem is a joyous celebration of nature's moral value: Nature is the sublime guide that moves the poet to "see into the life of things," and hear "the still, sad music of humanity":

Figure 12.4 J. M. W. Turner, *Interior of Tintern Abbey*, 1794. Watercolor, $12\frac{5}{8}$ x $9\frac{7}{8}$ in. Victoria and Albert Museum, London. Medieval ruins served as sources of inspiration and nostalgia for Romantic poets and painters.

. . . For I have learned
To look on nature, not as in the hour
Of thoughtless youth; but hearing oftentimes
The still, sad music of humanity,
Nor harsh nor grating, though of ample power
To chasten and subdue. And I have felt
A presence that disturbs me with the joy
Of elevated thoughts; a sense sublime
Of something far more deeply interfused,
Whose dwelling is the light of setting suns,
And the round ocean and the living air,
And the blue sky, and in the mind of man:
A motion and a spirit, that impels
All thinking things, all objects of all thought,
And rolls through all things. Therefore am I still
A lover of the meadows and the woods,
And mountains; and of all that we behold
From this green earth; of all the mighty world
Of eye, and ear—both what they half create,
And what perceive; well pleased to recognize
In nature and the language of the sense,
The anchor of my purest thoughts, the nurse,
The guide, the guardian of my heart, and soul
Of all my moral being.

(from "Lines Composed a Few Miles Above Tintern Abbey," ll. 88–111)

Shelley and Keats

Like Wordsworth, the English poet Percy Bysshe Shelley (1792–1822) embraced nature as the source of sublime truth, but his volcanic personality led him to engage the natural world with greater intensity and deeper melancholy than his older contemporary. A prolific writer and a passionate champion of human liberty, Shelley had all the features of the Romantic hero. Defiant and unconventional, he provoked the reading public with a treatise entitled *The Necessity of Atheism* (1811), the circulation of which led to his expulsion from Oxford University. He was outspoken in his opposition to marriage, a union that he viewed as hostile to human happiness. He was as unconventional in his deeds as in his discourse: While married to one woman (Harriet Westbrook), with whom he had two children, he ran off with another (Mary Wollstonecraft Godwin). A harsh critic of Britain's rulers, he went into permanent exile in Italy in 1818 and died there four years later in a boating accident.

Shelley took inspiration from nature and from the inconstant state of human desire. The best of his lyric poems find in nature's moods metaphors for insubstantial, yet potent, human states. In "Ode to the West Wind" he appeals to the wind—a symbol of restless creativity—to drive his visions throughout the universe. And in "Ozymandias" (the Greek name for the oppressive Egyptian pharaoh Ramses II, whose statue stood in Thebes), he paints a memorable picture of mutability and the transience of human grandeur.

Shelley, lyric poems (1813–1822)

The poetry of John Keats (1795–1821), the third of the great English nature poets, shared Shelley's elegiac sensibility. Keats lamented the fleeting nature of life's pleasures, even as he contemplated the brevity of life. He lost both his mother and his brother to tuberculosis, and he himself

Ideas and Issues

SHELLEY: "OZYMANDIAS"

I met a traveller from an antique land
Who said: Two vast and trunkless legs of stone
Stand in the desert. Near them, on the sand,
Half sunk, a shattered visage lies, whose frown,
And wrinkled lip, and sneer of cold command,
Tell that its sculptor well those passions read
Which yet survive, stamped on these lifeless things,
The hand that mocked them, and the heart that fed;
And on the pedestal these words appear:
"My name is Ozymandias, king of kings;
Look on my works, ye Mighty, and despair!"
Nothing beside remains. Round the decay
Of that colossal wreck, boundless and bare
The lone and level sands stretch far away.

Q In what ways does this poem reflect the Romantic imagination?

succumbed to that disease at the age of twenty-five. The threat of imminent death seems to have produced in Keats a heightened awareness of the virtues of beauty, human love, and friendship. Keats perceived these phenomena as fleeting forms of a higher reality that might be made permanent only in art.

For Keats, art is the balm of the poet. A work of art is more than a response to the human experience of love and nature; it is the transmuted product of the imagination, a higher form of nature that triumphantly outreaches the mortal lifespan. These ideas are central to Keats' "Ode on a Grecian Urn." The poem was inspired by ancient Greek artifacts Keats had seen among those brought to London by Lord Elgin in 1816 and placed on display in the British Museum (see page 57). Keats describes the imaginary Hellenic urn (his metaphoric "Cold Pastoral") as a symbol of all great works of art, which, because of their unchanging beauty, remain eternally "true." The poem concludes with the joyous pronouncement that beauty and truth are one. "'Beauty is truth, truth beauty,'—that is all/Ye know on earth, and all ye need to know."

Keats, "Ode on a Grecian Urn" (1818)

Byron: Romantic Hero

The English poet George Gordon, Lord Byron (1788–1824), was one of the most flamboyant personalities of the age. Dedicated to pleasures of the senses, he was equally impassioned by the ideals of liberty and brotherhood. In his brief, mercurial life, he established the prototype of the Romantic hero, often called the Byronic hero.

As a young man, Byron traveled restlessly throughout Europe and the Mediterranean, devouring the landscape and the major sites. A physically attractive man (despite the handicap of a club foot) with dark, brooding eyes, he engaged in numerous love affairs, including one with his half-sister. In 1816, Byron abandoned an unsuccessful marriage and left England for good. He lived in Italy for a time with the Shelleys and a string of mistresses. By this time, he had earned such a reputation of dangerous nonconformity that an English woman, catching sight of the poet in Rome, warned her daughter, "Do not look at him! He is dangerous to look at." In 1824, Byron sailed to Greece to aid the Greeks in their war of independence against the Turks—one of the many episodes in the turbulent history of nineteenth-century nationalism. There, in his last heroic role, he died of a fever.

Throughout his life, Byron was given to periodic bouts of creativity and dissipation. A man of violent passions, he once described himself as "half mad . . . between metaphysics, mountains, lakes, love inextinguishable, thoughts unutterable, and the nightmare of my own delinquencies." Bound to share his innermost thoughts and feelings, he became the hero of his two great poems: *Childe Harold's Pilgrimage* and *Don Juan*, the latter written in installments between 1819 and 1824 and left unfinished at his death. The first poem narrates the wanderings of Childe Harold, Byron's fictional self, whom he describes as "the most unfit/Of men to herd with man; with whom he held/ Little in common." The disillusioned hero finds solace, however, in nature; as Byron writes in Canto Three (13):

Byron, *Childe Harold's Pilgrimage* (1819); *Don Juan* (1819–1824)

> He had the passion and the power to roam;
> The desert, forest, cavern, breaker's foam,
> Were unto him companionship; they spake
> A mutual language. . .

Begun in Venice, *Don Juan* drew on the legendary fictional Spanish libertine who had also inspired Mozart's *Don Giovanni* (see page 322). Byron's Don, however, is not the lustful womanizer of Mozart's opera; rather, he is a figure who stumbles into love in what might be called a romance of roguery and—in Byron's words—"a satire on the abuses of society." Byron's mocking disdain for his time and place is brilliantly voiced in *Don Juan*, a masterpiece that the author described as an "epic on modern life."

Blake: Romantic Mystic

The British poet, painter, and engraver William Blake (1757–1827) shared the Romantic disdain for convention and authority. Blake, however, embraced a more mystical view of nature, God, and humankind. Deeply spiritual, he claimed "To see nature in a Grain of Sand,/And Heaven in a Wild flower." This divine vision he brought to his poetry and his paintings. Indeed, his poetry was conceived along with visual images that he himself drew. He prepared all aspects of his published works, designing, illustrating, engraving, and hand-coloring each page.

Blake's early poems featured singular images with clear and vivid (and often) moral messages. "The Lamb," a short poem from his *Songs of Innocence* (1789), envisions that animal as a symbol of God's gentle goodness. In his *Songs of Experience* (1794), childlike lyricism gives way to the disillusionment of maturity: "The Tiger," reproduced in full below, demands to know whether goodness must be accompanied by evil, and whether God is responsible for both:

Blake, *Songs of Experience* (1794)

The Tiger

Tiger! Tiger! Burning bright
In the forest of the night,
What immortal hand or eye
Could frame thy fearful symmetry?

In what distant deeps or skies
Burnt the first of thine eyes?
On what wings dare he aspire?
What the hand dare seize the fire?

And what shoulder, and what art,
Could twist the sinews of thy heart?
And when thy heart began to beat,
What dread hand? And what dread feet?

What the hammer? What the chain?
In what furnace was thy brain?
What the anvil? What dread grasp
Dare its deadly terrors clasp?

When the stars threw down their spears,
And watered heaven with their tears,
Did he smile his work to see?
Did he who made the Lamb make thee?

Tiger! Tiger! Burning bright
In the forests of the night,
What immortal hand or eye,
Dare frame thy fearful symmetry.

Blake's view of an imperfect world was influenced by the evils of growing industrialism, but also by the oppression and inhumane treatment of rebellious slaves (see Figure 12.7), and by revolutionary unrest in America and France—"a tyrant is the worst disease," he proclaimed. His poetic imagination took much from the Bible and Milton's *Paradise Lost* (see page 271)—some scholars see in the fifth stanza of "The Tiger" an allusion to Milton's powerful Satan. Regardless of whether one perceives the Maker as satanic or divine or both, the poem seems to assert the typically Romantic view of the artist as sharing God's burden of creation and the creative process.

Figure 12.5 William Blake, *The Great Red Dragon and the Woman Clothed with the Sun*, ca. 1805. Watercolor, 15⁴⁄₅ in. x 14 in. National Gallery of Art, Washington, D.C.

Some of the best of Blake's artworks are illustrations to books of the Bible, and especially to such visionary landmarks as the Book of Revelation (Figure **12.5**). Trained as an engraver and studying briefly at the Royal Academy, Blake drew more from the mind than from the eye in his drawings and watercolors. (He often credited conversations with angelic emissaries as a source of his imagery.) While Blake was unappreciated in his own time, he is now regarded as a unique representative of early Romanticism.

Goethe's *Faust*

Of all literary figures of the nineteenth century, perhaps the most memorable is Goethe's Faust. The story of Faust is based on a sixteenth-century German legend. A traveling physician and a practitioner of black magic, Johann or Georg Faust was reputed to have sold his soul to the devil in exchange for infinite knowledge and personal experience. The story became the subject of numerous dramas, the first of which was written by the English playwright Christopher Marlowe (1564–1593). In the hands of the German poet Johann Wolfgang von Goethe (1749–1832), Faust became the paradigm of Western humankind and—more broadly—of the individual's quest for knowledge, experience, and power. Goethe, a student of law, medicine, theology, theater, biology, optics, and alchemy, seems to have modeled Faust after himself. The quintessential Romantic hero, he embodies the human desire to transcend all physical limitations and to master all realms of experience.

Faust was the product of Goethe's entire career. He conceived the work during the 1770s, published Part I in 1808, but did not complete Part II until the year of his death, 1832. Although ostensibly a drama, *Faust* more closely resembles an epic poem. It is written in a lyric German, with a richness of verse forms that is typical of Romantic poetry.

Goethe, *Faust* (1808–1832)

The Prologue is set in heaven, where (in a manner reminiscent of the Book of Job) a wager is made between Mephistopheles (Satan) and God. Mephistopheles bets God that he can divert Faust from "the path that is true and fit." God contends that, though "men make mistakes as long as they strive," Faust—a man of deep learning, a Christian, and a scientist—will never relinquish his soul to Satan. Mephistopheles then proceeds to make a second pact, this one with Faust himself: If he can satisfy Faust's deepest desires and ambitions to the hero's ultimate satisfaction, Mephistopheles will win Faust's soul. Mephistopheles lures the despairing Faust out of his study (Figure **12.6**) and into the larger world of experience. Having spent his life in scholarly study and in the arts of magic, Faust determines to liberate his senses and unleash his passions. Signing his pact with the Devil in blood, he declares:

Figure 12.6 Eugène Delacroix, *Mephistopheles Appearing to Faust in His Study*, 1828. Lithograph 10¾ x 9 in. The Metropolitan Museum of Art, New York.

Only do not fear that I shall break this contract.
What I promise is nothing more
Than what all my powers are striving for.
I have puffed myself up too much, it is only
Your sort that really fits my case.
The great Earth Spirit has despised me
And Nature shuts the door in my face.
The thread of thought is snapped asunder.
I have long loathed knowledge in all its fashions.
In the depths of sensuality
Let us now quench our glowing passions!
And at once make ready every wonder
Of unpenetrated sorcery!
Let us cast ourselves into the torrent of time,
Into the whirl of eventfulness,
Where disappointment and success,
Pleasure and pain may chop and change
As chop and change they will and can;
It is restless action makes the man.

(from *Faust*, Part I, Scene III, 11. 1741–1759)

The newly liberated hero soon engages in a passionate love affair with a young maiden named Gretchen. Discovering the joys of the sensual life, Faust proclaims the priority of the heart ("Feeling is all!") over the mind. Faust's romance, however, has tragic consequences, including the deaths of Gretchen's mother, illegitimate child, brother, and, ultimately, Gretchen herself. Nevertheless, at the close of Part One, Gretchen's pure and selfless love wins her salvation.

In the second part of the drama Faust travels with Mephistopheles through a netherworld in which he meets an array of witches, sirens, and other fantastic creatures. He also encounters the ravishing Helen of Troy, symbol of ideal beauty, who acquaints Faust with the entire history and culture of humankind; but Faust remains unsated. His unquenched thirst for experience now leads him to pursue a life of action for the public good. He undertakes a vast land-reclamation project, which provides habitation for millions of people, and in this endeavor the aged and near-blind Faust finds personal fulfillment. He dies, however, before fully realizing his dream. And although Mephistopheles tries to apprehend Faust's soul when it leaves his body, God's angels, led by Gretchen (Goethe's symbol of the Eternal Female), intervene to spirit his soul to heaven.

The Female Voice

The nineteenth century was the first great age of female writers. Examples include the English novelists George Eliot, a pseudonym for Mary Ann Evans (1819–1880); Emily Brontë (1818–1848), author of the hypnotic novel *Wuthering Heights*; her sister Charlotte Brontë (1816–1855), author of *Jane Eyre* (hailed as a masterpiece only after her death); Mary Godwin Shelley (1797–1851), whose novel *Frankenstein* is discussed below; and the French novelist Germaine Necker, known as Madame de Staël (1766–1817). Some of these women struck a startling note of personal freedom in their lives. In their novels, however, they tended to perpetuate the Romantic stereotype of the chaste and clinging female. Indeed, even the most free-thinking of nineteenth-century women novelists might portray her heroine as a creature who submits to the will and values of the superior male.

Brontë, *Wuthering Heights* (1847)

The novels of Jane Austen (1775–1817) represent something of an exception. In *Sense and Sensibility*, which the author published at her own expense, Austen wittily attacks sentimental love and romantic rapture. Here, as in her other novels, *Pride and Prejudice*, *Mansfield Park*, *Emma*, *Northanger Abbey*, and *Persuasion*, she turned her attention to the everyday concerns of England's provincial middle-class families and to the comic contradictions between human actions and values. Her heroines are often intelligent and generous in spirit, concerned with reconciling economic security with proper social and moral behavior. Austen's keen eye for the details of family life shows her to be the first Realist in the English novel-writing tradition.

Austen, *Sense and Sensibility* (1811)

Among French writers of the Romantic era, the most intriguing female voice was that of Amandine-Aurore-Lucile Dupin, who used the pen name George Sand (1804–1876). A woman who assumed the name (and often the apparel) of a man, Sand self-consciously examined popular Romantic stereotypes, offering not one, but many different points of view concerning male–female relations. Sand held that true and complete love involved the union of the heart, mind, and body. She avowed that "Love's ideal is most certainly everlasting fidelity," and most of her more than eighty novels feature themes of romantic love and deep, undying friendship. But for some of her novels, she created heroines who freely exercised the right to love outside of marriage. These heroines did not, however, physically consummate their love, even when that love was reciprocated. Sand's heroines were very unlike Sand herself, who enjoyed numerous love affairs with leading Romantic figures—including the poet Alfred de Musset, the novelist Prosper Mérimée, and the composer Frédéric Chopin.

Mary Shelley's *Frankenstein*

One of the most talented novelists of the Romantic era was Mary Wollstonecraft Shelley, author of the landmark work *Frankenstein; or, The Modern Prometheus*. The daughter of the feminist writer Mary Wollstonecraft (see page 301), Shelley began writing *Frankenstein* at the age of eighteen. Framed as a series of letters, the novel tells the compelling tale of the scientist-philosopher Victor Frankenstein, who, having discovered the secret of imparting life to inanimate matter, fashions a monster endowed with supernatural strength. The novel's subtitle refers to the Greek deity who challenged Zeus by giving humankind the gift of the sacred fire, source of divine wisdom and creative inspiration. As punishment for having stolen the fire from Mount Olympus, Zeus chains Prometheus to a lonely rock, where he is daily assaulted by an eagle who feeds on his liver. The modern Prometheus, Frankenstein, is punished for his ambitious project when his creation, excluded from the normal life of mortals, betrays his creator. "I was benevolent and good," mourns the creature, "misery made me a fiend." Like the fallen Lucifer, Frankenstein's creation soon becomes a figure of heroic evil.

Mary Shelley, *Frankenstein* (1818)

Frankenstein belongs to a literary genre known as the Gothic novel, a type of entertainment that brings to life elements of horror and the supernatural in a medieval ("Gothic") setting. Such novels, the earliest of which was Horace Walpole's *The Castle of Otranto* (1764), reflect the rising tide of antirationalism and a revived interest in the medieval past. Shelley's novel—actually a scientific horror tale—has become a modern classic. It is the first literary work to examine the human impact of scientific experimentation. As such, it has inspired numerous science fiction "spinoffs," literary, as well as cinematic. Ironically, however, it is the monster, not the scientist, who has captured the modern imagination, even to the point of assuming his name.

AMERICAN ROMANTICISM

ACROSS the Atlantic, along the eastern shores of the rapidly industrializing American continent, Romanticism took hold both as an attitude of mind and as a style. Romanticism infused all aspects of nineteenth-century American culture: It distinguished the frontier tales of James Fenimore Cooper (1789–1851), the mysteries of Edgar Allan Poe (1809–1849), and the novels of Nathaniel Hawthorne (1804–1864) and Herman Melville (1819–1891). It also colored the sentimental poems of America's most popular poet, Henry Wadsworth Longfellow (1807–1882). But it found its purest expression in a movement known as *Transcendentalism*.

Transcendentalism

The Transcendentalists were a group of New England intellectuals who held that knowledge gained by way of intuition transcended knowledge based on reason. They believed that the direct experience of nature united one with God. Exalting individualism and self-reliance, they urged human beings to discover their spiritual selves through sympathy with nature. While the Transcendentalists were the descendants of English Puritans, many sought instruction in Eastern religious philosophies that had reached the Boston area in the early nineteenth century. From Hinduism and Buddhism, they adopted a holistic philosophy based in pantheism (the belief that all aspects of the universe are infused with divine spirit). It followed that all living things derived their being from the same universal source and therefore shared a "universal brotherhood"—the unity of humanity, nature, and God.

The prime exemplar of the Transcendentalists was Ralph Waldo Emerson (1803–1882), whose essays powerfully influenced nineteenth-century American thought. The son and grandson of clergymen, Emerson was ordained as a

Ideas and Issues

EMERSON: I AM PART OF GOD

"In the woods is perpetual youth. Within these plantations of God, a decorum and sanctity reign, a perennial festival is dressed, and the guest sees not how he should tire of them in a thousand years. In the woods, we return to reason and faith. There I feel that nothing can befall me in life—no disgrace, no calamity (leaving my eyes), which nature cannot repair. Standing on the bare ground—my head bathed by the blithe air and uplifted into infinite space—all mean egotism vanishes. I become a transparent eyeball; I am nothing; I see all; the currents of the Universal Being circulate through me; I am part or parcel of God."

(from Emerson, *Essays*)

Q How does Emerson's approach to nature compare with Wordsworth's?

Ideas and Issues

THOREAU: NATURE AS TEACHER

"I went to the woods because I wished to live deliberately, to front only the essential facts of life, and see if I could not learn what it had to teach, and not, when I came to die, discover that I had not lived. I did not wish to live what was not life, living is so dear; nor did I wish to practice resignation, unless it was quite necessary. I wanted to live deep and suck out all the marrow of life, to live so sturdily and Spartan-like as to put to rout all that was not life, to cut a broad swath and shave close, to drive life into a corner, and reduce it to its lowest terms, and, if it proved to be mean, why then to get the whole and genuine meanness of it, and publish its meanness to the world; or if it were sublime, to know it by experience, and be able to give a true account of it in my next excursion. For most men, it appears to me, are in a strange uncertainty about it, whether it is of the devil or of God, and have *somewhat hastily* concluded that it is the chief end of man here to 'glorify God and enjoy him forever.'"

(from Thoreau, *Walden*)

Q What were Thoreau's aims and ambitions in retreating to Walden Pond?

Unitarian minister when he was in his twenties. Like Wordsworth, he courted nature to "see into the life of things" and to taste its cleansing power. In the essay entitled "Nature" (1836), Emerson sets forth a pantheistic credo: Becoming one with nature, we find true happiness.

Emerson, *Essays* (1836–1860)

Emerson's friend Henry David Thoreau (1817–1862) carried Transcendentalism to its logical end by literally returning to nature. He completed a degree at Harvard University and made his way in the world by tutoring, surveying, and making pencils. An avid opponent of slavery, he was jailed briefly for refusing to pay a poll tax to a pro-slavery government. In an influential essay on civil disobedience, Thoreau defends the philosophy of passive resistance and moral idealism that he himself practiced—a philosophy embraced by the twentieth-century leaders Mohandas Karamchand Gandhi and Martin Luther King. In 1845 Thoreau abandoned urban society to live in the Massachusetts woods near Walden Pond—an experiment that lasted twenty-six months. He describes his love of the natural world, his nonconformist attitude toward society, and his deep commitment to monkish simplicity in his "handbook for living," called *Walden, or Life in the Woods.* In this intimate yet forthright diary Thoreau glorifies nature as innocent and beneficent—a source of joy and practical instruction.

Thoreau, *Walden* (1854)

Whitman's Romantic Individualism

Though technically not a Transcendentalist, Walt Whitman (1818–1892) gave voice to the Transcendental worldview and to the Emersonian credo of self-reliance. Whitman worked as a Brooklyn editor, journalist, and teacher, and served as a nurse in an American Civil War hospital. His essays and poems, which have become an influential part of the American canon, assert his affection for the American landscape and its diverse human inhabitants: male and female, black and white, heterosexual and homosexual.

Like Wordsworth, Whitman took everyday life as his theme, but he rejected artificial poetic diction more completely than Wordsworth had. His natural voice bellowed a "barbaric yawp" that found ideal expression in **free verse** (poetry based on irregular rhythmic patterns rather than on the conventional use of meter). Whitman molded his unmetrical rhythms and sonorous cadences by means of standard poetic devices, such as **alliteration**, **assonance**, and repetition. He loved Italian opera, and his style often simulates the musical grandeur of that genre.

The prevailing themes in Whitman's poetry are nationalism and democracy. His poems celebrate ordinary people and sympathize with marginal men and women, such as felons and prostitutes. Claiming to be a poet of the body as well as the soul, he defended an honest recognition of the sexual, physical self. His pantheistic credo of unity with nature is captured in the memorable line that anticipates his afterlife: "If you want me again, look for me under your boot-soles." The American scene was the source of endless inspiration for the sprawling, cosmic images that dominate Whitman's autobiographical masterpiece, *Leaves of Grass*. Self-published as a collection of twelve poems in 1855, the book grew to almost four hundred poems over four decades. The first edition of this collection met with strident criticism for its freewheeling verse and its overt sexuality; one reviewer attacked the book as "a mixture of Yankee transcendentalism and New York rowdyism." "Song of Myself," which appeared under that title in the first edition, later became "Poem of Walt Whitman," before the poet returned it to its original title in 1881. In the opening stanza, we hear the expansive individualism of America's "poet of democracy":

Whitman, *Leaves of Grass* (1855–1892)

I celebrate myself, and sing myself,
And what I assume you shall assume,
For every atom belonging to me as good belongs to you.

I loaf and invite my soul,
I learn and loaf at my ease observing a spear of summer
grass.

My tongue, every atom of my blood, form'd from this soil,
this air,
Born of parents born here from parents the same, and their
parents the same,
I, now thirty-seven years old in perfect health begin,
Hoping to cease not till death.

Creeds and schools in abeyance,
Retiring back a while sufficed at what they are, but never
forgotten,
I harbor for good or bad, I permit to speak at every hazard,
Nature without check with original energy.

Abolitionist Literature

The abolitionist crusade against institutional slavery generated some of the most impassioned literature of the Romantic era. Although the abolitionists constituted only a small minority of America's population, their arguments were emotionally charged and their protests often dramatic and telling. Antislavery novels—the most famous of which was *Uncle Tom's Cabin* by Harriet Beecher Stowe (1811–1896)—stirred up public sentiment against the brutality and injustice of the system. Originally serialized in an antislavery newspaper, Stowe's book sold over one million copies within a year of its publication. But the most direct challenge to slavery came from the slaves themselves, and none more so than the slave rebels who mounted outright attacks against their owners and masters in their efforts to gain a prized privilege: freedom. They persisted despite the threat of horrific punishment (Figure **12.7**).

Beecher Stowe, *Uncle Tom's Cabin* (1852)

One of the most notable insurrections of the century took place in Southampton County, Virginia, in 1831: Nat Turner (1800–1831), a slave preacher and mystic, believed that he was divinely appointed to lead the slaves to freedom. The Turner rebellion resulted in the deaths of at least fifty-seven whites (and many more blacks, killed when the rebellion was suppressed) and the destruction of several area plantations. Following the defeat of the rebel slaves, the captive Turner explained his motives to a local attorney, who prepared a published version of his personal account in the so-called "Confessions of Nat Turner."

A longer, more vividly detailed autobiography—the *Narrative of the Life of Frederick Douglass: An American Slave*—came from the pen of the nineteenth century's leading African-American crusader for black freedom. Born a slave on the east coast of Maryland, Douglass (1817–1883) taught himself to read and write at an early age; he escaped bondage in Baltimore in 1838 and eventually found his way to New England, where he joined the Massachusetts Antislavery Society. A powerful public speaker, who captivated his audiences with accounts of his life in bondage and in freedom, Douglass served as living proof of the potential of black slaves to achieve brilliantly as free persons. He wrote extensively and eloquently in support of abolition, describing the "dehumanizing character of slavery" for both blacks and whites, and defending the idea that, by abandoning slavelike behavior, even slaves could determine their own lives.

Douglass, *Narrative of the Life of Frederick Douglass: An American Slave* (1845)

While Frederick Douglass was among the first African-Americans to win international attention through his skills at public speaking, his female contemporary Sojourner Truth (ca. 1797–1883) brought a

Figure 12.7 William Blake, *A Negro Hung Alive by the Ribs to a Gallows*, 1792. Line engraving, 10½ x 8 in. Private collection. John G. Stedman was a Dutch naval officer who volunteered for a military expedition to quell slave uprisings in the Dutch-owned colony of Surinam. His drawings, produced to accompany Stedman's *Narrative of a Five Years Expedition against the Revolted Negroes of Surinam*, are eyewitness accounts of the varieties of torture inflicted by colonial masters on rebellious slaves. Blake based his engravings on Stedman's drawings.

Ideas and Issues

DOUGLASS: SLAVE MORALITY

"I shall here make a profession of faith which may shock some, offend others, and be dissented from by all. It is this: Within the bounds of his just earnings, I hold that the slave is fully justified in helping himself to the *gold and silver, and the best apparel of his master, or that of any other slaveholder; and that such taking is not stealing in any just sense of that word.*

The morality of *free* society can have no application to *slave* society. Slaveholders have made it almost impossible for the slave to commit any crime, known either to the laws of God or to the laws of man. If he steals, he takes his own; if he kills his master, he imitates only the heroes of the revolution. Slaveholders I hold to be individually and collectively responsible for all the evils which grow out of the horrid relation, and I believe they will be so held at the judgment, in the sight of a just God. Make a man a slave, and you rob him of moral responsibility. . . ."

(from Douglass, *My Bondage and My Freedom*, 1855)

Q Do you agree with Douglass that "the morality of a free society can have no application to slave society"?

woman's wit and passion to the fight against slavery. Born to slave parents in Ulster County, New York, Isabella Bomefree was sold four times before the age of thirty—an inauspicious beginning for a person who would become one of America's most vocal abolitionists, an evangelist, and a champion of women's rights. After being emancipated in 1828, Bomefree traveled widely in the United States, changing her name to Sojourner Truth in 1843, and committing her life to "sharing the truth" in matters of human dignity. Although she never learned to read or write, she was determined to have her voice heard across the nation and for future generations. To accomplish the latter, she dictated her story to a friend, Olive Gilbert. The *Narrative of Sojourner Truth* recounts the major events of her life, including the tale of how she engaged in a heroic legal battle to win back her five-year-old son, who was illegally sold into slavery in New York State.

Bomefree, *Narrative of Sojourner Truth* (1850)

Sojourner Truth used her talents as an orator to communicate Christian religious visions, as well as to voice her opposition to slavery, capital punishment, and the kidnapping and sale of black children (a common practice in some parts of the country). She also supported prison reform, helped to relocate former slaves, and defended the rights of women. Sharp-tongued and outspoken (and a lifelong pipe-smoker), Sojourner Truth won popular notoriety for the short impromptu speech *Ain't I a Woman?*, delivered in 1851 to the Woman's Convention at Akron, Ohio. While scholars question the authenticity of various versions of the speech (which was published by abolitionists some twelve years later), no such debate clouds Sojourner's autobiographical *Narrative*.

ROMANTICISM IN THE VISUAL ARTS

ROMANTIC artists favored themes that gave them the opportunity to explore their feelings and intuitions. "The artist should paint not only what he sees before him, but also what he sees *in* him," advised one Romantic. Nature and the natural landscape appealed to painters (as they had to poets) as a refuge from growing industrialism and as a source of sublime inspiration. They embraced contemporary subjects, especially those involving the struggle for political independence. They looked to fantasy, medieval lore, and exotic themes that reflected nationalistic ambitions and glorified their nations' heritage. Heroic actions and events were usually central to such paintings. But heroism was also a driving force among the Romantics themselves: With a subjectivity bordering on egotism, they saw themselves as heroes—champions of the cult of the senses and of the heart.

In style, Romanticism abandoned the cool rationality and decorum of Neoclassical art in favor of temperament, accident, and emotion. While Neoclassical artists defined form by means of line, the Romantics preferred to model form by way of color, often adding dabs of complementary color to heighten visual intensity. Geometric compositions constructed in shallow space (see, for instance, David's *Oath of the Horatii*, Figure 11.26) gave way to dynamic diagonals that might draw the eye into deep space (see Figures 12.11 and 12.19). Whereas Neoclassicists smoothed their brushstrokes to leave a polished surface finish, the Romantics frequently left their brushstrokes visible, as if to underline the immediacy of the creative act. They might deliberately blur details and exaggerate the sensuous aspects of texture and tones.

The Romantic Landscape

Landscape then became a primary vehicle for expressing artists' personal feelings and shifting moods. Landscape painting was introduced in China before the eighth century C.E. (see pages 139–140) and made its appearance as an independent genre in the West during the Renaissance (see Figure 8.19). The Dutch masters rendered topographic views of specific locations (see Figure 10.14), while seventeenth- and eighteenth-century French artists painted ideal landscapes, which they assembled and composed (according to Classical principles) in the studio from sketches made outdoors. But during the nineteenth century, English artists, looking directly to nature for inspiration, took the lead in the genesis of the Romantic landscape.

"Painting," exulted John Constable (1776–1837), "is with me but another word for feeling." Constable's landscapes celebrate the physical beauty of the rivers, trees, and cottages of his native Suffolk countryside, even as they describe the mundane labors of its inhabitants (Figure **12.8**). Like Wordsworth, who embraced "incidents and situations from common life," Constable found inspiration in ordinary subjects—"water escaping from mill-dams, willows, old rotten planks, slimy posts, and brickwork," as he described them. His love of the local landscape was matched by his skill in rendering broad swaths of sun and shadow and the flickering effects of light on form. Intrigued by scientific treatises classifying clouds, Constable studied cloud formations, noting on the back of each sketch the time of the year, hour of the day, and direction of the wind. "The sky," he wrote, "is the source of light in nature and governs everything." To capture the fugitive effects of light, he often stippled parts of the landscape with white dots, which critics called "Constable's snow."

While Constable's paintings portray nature as intimate and humble, the landscapes of his English contemporary Joseph Mallord William Turner (1775–1851) render nature as vast and powerful. Turner began his career making topographic drawings of picturesque and architectural subjects; these he sold to engravers, who, in turn, mass-produced and marketed them in great numbers. One of these early drawings, the ruined monastery of Tintern Abbey, calls attention to the transience of worldly beauty and reflects the Romantic artist's nostalgia for the Gothic past (see Figure 12.4).

Turner's many tours throughout the Continent inspired hundreds of luminous studies executed in pencil and in watercolor. His mature style, however, investigated nature's more turbulent moods: the awe-inspiring grandeur associated with the Romantic *sublime*. As subjects for his large-sized canvases, Turner seized upon natural disasters—great storms, Alpine avalanches—and human catastrophes, such as shipwrecks and destructive fires. Many of his paintings treat the sea as a symbol of nature's indomitable power—a theme shared by such Romantics as Samuel Taylor Coleridge (*The Rime of the Ancient Mariner*, 1798) and Herman Melville (*Moby Dick*, 1851).

Turner's *Slave Ship* (Figure **12.9**), the original title of which was *Slavers Throwing Overboard the Dead and Dying: Typhoon Coming On*, subverts the political implications of the subject (see caption) in favor of purely visual drama. The glowing sunset, billowing waves, and fantastic fish (that appear to be devouring the shackled bodies) distract the viewer from any serious consideration of the social issue. The *Slave Ship* anticipates the daring innovations of Turner's late paintings. Layered with veils of color and increasingly abstract in form, these works were disparagingly described by critics as "tinted steam" and "soapsuds." In dozens of canvases

Figure 12.8 John Constable, *The Hay Wain*, 1821. Oil on canvas, 4 ft. $3\frac{1}{2}$ in. x 6 ft. 1 in. National Gallery, London. Constable owed much to the Dutch masters, yet his approach to nature was uncluttered by tradition. "When I sit down to make a sketch from nature," he wrote, "the first thing I try to do is to forget that I have ever seen a picture."

Figure 12.9 J. M. W. Turner, *The Slave Ship* (*Slavers Throwing Overboard the Dead and Dying: Typhoon Coming On*), 1840. Oil on canvas, 35¾ x 48¼ in. Museum of Fine Arts, Boston. While Britain had finally abolished slavery throughout its colonies in 1838, popular literature on the history of the slave trade published in 1839 described in some detail the notorious activity that inspired Turner's painting: the transatlantic traders' practice of throwing overboard the dead and dying bodies of African slaves, and then collecting insurance money on "goods lost" at sea. On the eve of rising British commercialism, Turner seems to suggest that the human capacity for evil rivals nature's cruelest powers.

that he never dared to exhibit, Turner all but abandoned recognizable subject matter; these experiments in light and color anticipated those of the French Impressionists by more than three decades.

In France, the artists of the Barbizon school—named after the picturesque village on the edge of the Forest of Fontainebleau near Paris—were the first to take their easels out of doors. Working directly from nature (though usually finishing the canvas in the studio), they painted modest landscapes and scenes of rural life that evoked an unembellished vision of the world. These Romantic Realists were highly successful in capturing nature's moods. The greatest French landscape painter of the mid-nineteenth century, Jean-Baptiste-Camille Corot (1796–1875), shared the Barbizon preference for working outdoors, but he brought to his landscapes a breathtaking sense of harmony and tranquility. In the last phase of his career, Corot painted hundreds of contemplative landscapes (Figure **12.10**). He called them *souvenirs*, that is, "remembrances," to indicate that they were recollections of previous visual experiences, rather than on-the-spot accounts.

American Painting

The landscape was a favorite subject of nineteenth-century American artists. To a remarkable degree, their canvases mirror the sentiments of the Transcendentalists, who embraced (in the words of Thoreau) "the indescribable innocence and beneficence of nature." American artists took clear delight in the beauty of nature and its fleeting moods. But they also brought to their art a nationalistic infatuation with the vast and unspoiled character of the land. Mountain ranges, broad lakes and rivers, and

Figure 12.10 Jean-Baptiste-Camille Corot, *Ville d'Avray*, 1870. Oil on canvas, 21⅝ x 31½ in. The Metropolitan Museum of Art, New York. Corot's poetic landscapes, filled with feathery trees and misty rivers, and bathed in nuances of silvery light, became so popular in France and elsewhere that he was able to sell as many canvases as he could paint. Even in his own time, forgeries of his work abounded.

verdant forests are composites of scrupulously collected and lovingly documented details. It is as if these painters felt compelled to record with photographic precision the majesty of their continent, and, at the same time, advertise the magnitude of its untamed wilderness.

Cole Panorama and painstaking precision are features found in the topographic landscapes of the Hudson River school—a group of artists who worked chiefly in the region of upstate New York during the 1830s and 1840s. One of the leading figures of the Hudson River school was

Making Connections

LANDSCAPE: WEST AND EAST

The nineteenth-century German artist Caspar David Friedrich (1774–1840) took a profoundly spiritual view of nature. His paintings feature ruined Gothic chapels and wintry graveyards, elegiac remnants of a vanished past. In *Two Men Looking at the Moon* (Figure **12.11**), he silhouettes a craggy, half-uprooted tree against a glowing, moonlit sky. Two male figures stand at the brink of a steep cliff, overlooking the edge. Somber colors contribute to the mood of poetic melancholy. Friedrich's is a universe whose mysteries are the subject of what he called "our spiritual eye."

As a comment on the eternal dialog between humanity and nature, Friedrich's painting has much in common with traditional Chinese landscapes, which often show individuals contemplating their surroundings (Figure **12.12**). Such compositions are rarely literal representations of specific places. Rather, they are expressions of a natural harmony between the individual and the setting. Typically, their vast and sweeping composition dwarfs the human presence and evokes a sense of nature's cosmic grandeur.

In Japan, as in China, landscape had always been a popular subject, but during the nineteenth century a new, more commercial, kind of landscape imagery appeared. As travel for business and pleasure increased among Japan's urban population, there arose the demand for guidebooks and scenes of popular landmarks. Woodblock prints—cheaply produced and easily duplicated—answered this demand. Japanese views of famous sites feature bold, flat colors, decorative patterns, and a dramatic layering of shapes that denies visual continuity between near and far. These features are evident in the popular series of landscapes "Thirty-Six Views of Mount Fuji" by Katsushika Hokusai (1760–1849). Mount Fuji, which had erupted in 1707, was a much-venerated volcano that was widely regarded as a symbol of immortality. In this view, the navigators (in the two boats that ride the threatening waves) were seen to represent fearless self-discipline and, at the same time, harmony with the powerful forces of nature (Figure **12.13**).

Q What is the relationship between the human figures and their natural environment in each of these artworks?

Figure 12.11 (left) Caspar David Friedrich, *Two Men Looking at the Moon*, 1819–1820. Oil on panel, $13\frac{3}{4} \times 17\frac{1}{4}$ in. Modern Masters Gallery, Dresden.

Figure 12.12 Shen Zhou, *Poet on a Mountain Top*, from the album of landscapes "Five Leaves by Shen Zhou, One Leaf by Wen Zhengming," 1496. Album leaf mounted as a handscroll: ink on paper or ink and light color on paper, $15\frac{1}{4} \times 23\frac{3}{4}$ in. Nelson-Atkins Museum of Art, Kansas City, Missouri.

Figure 12.13 Katsushika Hokusai, *Mount Fuji Seen Below a Wave at Kanagawa*, from "Thirty-Six Views of Mount Fuji," 1830–33, Tokugawa period. Full-color woodblock print, width $14\frac{3}{4}$ in. Museum of Fine Arts, Boston.

Figure 12.14 Thomas Cole, *The Oxbow (View from Mount Holyoke, Northampton, Massachusetts, After a Thunderstorm)*, 1836. Oil on canvas, 4 ft. 3½ in. x 6 ft. 4 in. The Metropolitan Museum of Art, New York. American rivers were still part of a pristine wilderness when Cole took them as subjects. The Oxbow, a loop in the Connecticut River, was a well-known Massachusetts site, which, like the Hudson River and the Catskill Mountains, provided broad expanses of magnificent scenery.

the British-born Thomas Cole (1801–1848), whose *Oxbow* offers a view of the Connecticut River near Northampton, Massachusetts (Figure **12.14**). In this landscape, Cole achieved a dramatic mood by framing the brightly lit hills and curving river of the distant vista with the darker motifs of a departing thunderstorm and a blighted tree.

Figure 12.15 Albert Bierstadt, *The Rocky Mountains, Lander's Peak*, 1863. Oil on canvas, 6 ft. 1 in. x 10 ft. ¾ in. The Metropolitan Museum of Art, New York. Panoramic landscapes with views of remote locales were popular nineteenth-century substitutes for actual travel, and viewers were known to carry binoculars to their showings. Admission usually required entrance fees.

Bierstadt Intrigued by America's drive to settle the West, nineteenth-century artists such as the German-born Albert Bierstadt (1830–1902) made panoramic depictions of that virginal territory. His landscape of the Rocky Mountains, which includes a Native American encampment in the foreground, reflects his fascination with the templelike purity of America's vast, rugged spaces along the Western frontier (Figure **12.15**). The isolated settlement, dwarfed and enshrined by snowcapped mountains, a magnificent waterfall, and a looking-glass lake—all bathed in golden light—is an American Garden of Eden, inhabited by tribes

of unspoiled "noble savages." Bierstadt gave cosmic breadth to the image of the idyllic landscape, in which human beings and nature flourish in perfect harmony. In fact, the size of Bierstadt's landmark painting (some 6 × 10 feet) heralded the official establishment of landscape as a respectable genre: Academic tradition had previously dictated that large canvases were appropriate only for the representation of historical or religious subjects.

Catlin The Romantic fascination with unspoiled nature and "natural man" also inspired documentary studies of Native Americans, such as those executed by the artist/ethnologist George Catlin (1796–1872). During the 1830s, Catlin went to live among the Native Americans of the Great Plains. Moved by what he called the "silent and stoic dignity" of America's tribal peoples, he recorded their lives and customs in literature, as well as in hundreds of drawings and paintings (Figure **12.16**). Catlin popularized the image of Native Americans as people who deeply respected nature and the natural world (see page 248). He described exotic rituals designed to honor the Great Spirit (or Great Sun) and promote health and fertility. Observing that most tribes killed only as much game as was actually needed to feed themselves, Catlin brought attention to the Indians as the first ecologists.

Figure 12.16 George Catlin, *The White Cloud, Head Chief of the Iowas*, 1844–1845. Oil on canvas, 28 x 22⁷/₈ in. National Gallery of Art, Washington D.C. Catlin's "Gallery of Indians," exhibited widely in mid-nineteenth-century Europe, drew more acclaim abroad than it did in his own country.

Unfortunately, neither Catlin nor the achievements of the Indians themselves impeded the wholesale destruction of Native American cultures. Beginning in the 1830s, under pressure from the United States government, tribes were forced to cede their homelands and their hunting grounds to white settlers and to move into unoccupied lands in the American West. The perception of the Native American as the "devil savage" ultimately prevailed over the Romantic notion of the "noble savage" and came to justify America's effort to "civilize" its indigenous populations through policies (strongly criticized by Catlin and others) that forced most tribes to take up residence on "reservations" and, more often than not, to abandon their own languages and traditions.

The Popular Hero: Goya and Géricault

Throughout the history of Western painting, heroic subjects have been drawn from Classical lore and Christian legend. However, in the nineteenth century artists looked to their own time and place for events that brought attention to contemporary heroes and heroism. Such heroism might be associated with political struggles, natural disasters, or creative enterprise—the artist engaging his or her own image as the hero-genius. The Spanish master Francisco Goya (1746–1828) initiated the turn to contemporary subject matter. He began his career as a Rococo-style tapestry designer and came into prominence as a court painter to the Spanish king Charles IV (1748–1819). But following the invasion of Spain by Napoleon's armies in 1808, Goya's art took a new direction. Horrified by the guerrilla violence of the French occupation, he became a bitter social critic, producing some of the most memorable records of warfare and human savagery in the history of Western art.

The Third of May, 1808: The Execution of the Defenders of Madrid (Figure **12.17**) was Goya's nationalistic response to the events ensuing from an uprising of Spanish citizens against the French army of occupation. In a punitive measure, the French troops rounded up Spanish suspects in the streets of Madrid and brutally executed them in the city outskirts. Goya recorded the episode against a dark sky and an ominous urban skyline. In the foreground, an off-center lantern emits a triangular beam of light that illuminates the fate of the Spanish rebels: Some lie dead in pools of blood, while others cover their faces in fear and horror. Goya invested the composition with imaginative force. His emphatic contrasts of light and dark, theatrical use of color, and graphic details heighten the visual intensity of a brutal political event.

An indictment of butchery in the name of war, *The Third of May, 1808* is restrained compared to "The Disasters of War," a series of etchings and **aquatints** that Goya produced in the years of the French occupation of Spain. The gruesome prints that make up "The Disasters of War" have their source in historical fact as well as in Goya's

Figure 12.17 Francisco Goya, *The Third of May, 1808: The Execution of the Defenders of Madrid*, 1814. Oil on canvas, 8 ft. 6 in. x 10 ft. 4 in. Prado, Madrid. Goya spotlights a young man whose arms are flung upward in a gesture, somewhat like Jesus on the Cross, that renders him as hero and victim. On the right, in the shadows, the hulking executioners are lined up as anonymously as pieces of artillery. (See also frontispiece, page ii.)

imagination. *Brave Deeds Against the Dead* (Figure **12.18**) is a shocking record of the inhuman cruelty of Napoleon's troops, as well as a reminder that the heroes of modern warfare are often its innocent victims.

Goya's French contemporary Théodore Géricault (1791–1824) broadened the range of Romantic subjects. He found inspiration in the restless vitality of untamed horses and the ravaged faces of the clinically insane—subjects uncommon in academic art, but which reflect the Romantic fascination with the life lying beyond the bounds of reason. The painting that brought Géricault instant fame, *The Raft of the "Medusa,"* immortalized a dramatic event that made headlines in Géricault's own time: the wreck of a government frigate called the "Medusa" and the ghastly fate of its survivors (Figure **12.19**). When the ship hit a reef 50 miles off the coast of West Africa, the inexperienced captain, a political appointee, tried ignobly to save himself and his crew, who filled the few available lifeboats. Over a hundred passengers piled onto a makeshift raft, which was to be towed by the lifeboats. Cruelly, the crew set the raft adrift. With almost no food and supplies, chances of survival were scant; after almost two weeks, in which most died and several resorted to cannibalism, the raft was sighted and fifteen survivors were rescued.

Géricault (a staunch opponent of the regime that appointed the captain of the "Medusa") was so fired by newspaper reports of the tragedy that he resolved to immortalize it in paint. He interviewed the few survivors, made drawings of the mutilated corpses in the Paris morgue, and even had a model of the raft constructed in his studio. The result was enormous, both in size (the canvas measures 16 feet 1 inch x 23 feet 6 inches) and in

Figure 12.18 Francisco Goya, *Brave Deeds Against the Dead*, from the "The Disasters of War" series, ca. 1814. Etching, 6 x 8¼ in.

Figure 12.19 Théodore Géricault, *The Raft of the "Medusa,"* 1818. Oil on canvas, 16 ft. 1 in. x 23 ft. 6 in. Louvre, Paris. Géricault organized his composition on the basis of a double triangle: One triangle is formed by the two lines that stay the mast and is bisected by the mast itself, the other by the mass of agitated figures culminating in the magnificently painted torso of a black man who signals the distant vessel that will make the rescue. Sharp diagonals, vivid contrasts of light and dark, and muscular nudes heighten the dramatic impact of the piece.

dramatic impact. In the decade immediately preceding the invention of photography, Géricault provided the public with a powerful visual record of a sensational contemporary event. This landmark painting elevated ordinary men to the position of heroic combatants in the eternal struggle against the forces of nature and celebrated their collective heroism in confronting deadly danger.

Revolutionary Heroism: Delacroix

While Goya and Géricault gave the commoner heroic status, Géricault's pupil and follower Eugène Delacroix (1798–1863) invested the hero with Byronic grandeur. A melancholic and an intellectual, Delacroix prized the imagination as "paramount" in the life of the artist. "Strange as it may seem," he observed in his journal, "the great majority of people are devoid of imagination. Not only do they lack the keen, penetrating imagination which would allow them to see objects in a vivid way—that could lead them, as it were, to the very root of things—but they are equally incapable of any clear understanding of works in which imagination predominates."

Delacroix loved dramatic narrative; he favored sensuous and violent subjects drawn from contemporary life, popular literature, and ancient and medieval history. A six-month visit to Morocco, neighbor of France's newly conquered colony of Algeria, was to have a lifelong impact on his interest in exotic subjects and his love of light and color. He depicted the harem women of Islamic Africa, recorded the poignant and shocking results of the Turkish massacres in Greece, brought to life Dante's *Inferno*, and made memorable illustrations for Goethe's *Faust* (see Figure 12.6). His paintings of human and animal combat are filled with fierce vitality. Such works are faithful to his declaration, "I have no love for reasonable painting."

Delacroix's landmark work, *Liberty Leading the People* (Figure **12.20**), transformed a contemporary event (the Revolution of 1830) into a heroic allegory of the struggle for human freedom. When King Charles X (1757–1836) dissolved the French legislature and took measures to repress voting rights and freedom of the press, liberal leaders, radicals, and journalists rose in rebellion. Delacroix envisioned this rebellion as a monumental drama with a handsome, bare-breasted female—the personification of Liberty—leading a group of French rebels through the narrow streets of Paris and over barricades strewn with corpses. A bayonet in one hand and the tricolor flag of France in the other, Liberty presses forward to challenge the forces of tyranny. She is champion of "the people": the middle class, as represented by the gentleman in a frock coat; the lower class, as symbolized by the scruffy youth carrying pistols; and racial minorities, as conceived in the black saber-bearer at the left. She is, moreover, France itself, the banner-bearer of the spirit of nationalism that infused nineteenth-century European history.

A hallmark of Delacroix's style, and Romantic painting in general, was *pictorial license*—the artist's freedom to romanticize form and content, and thereby enhance the expressive quality of the artwork. In *Liberty Leading the People*, for instance, the nudity of the rebel in the left foreground had no basis in reality—it is uncommon to lose one's trousers in combat—however, the detail serves to emphasize human vulnerability and the imminence of death in battle. "The most sublime effects of every master," argued Delacroix, "are often the result of pictorial license. . . . Mediocre painters never have sufficient daring, they never get beyond themselves."

Making Connections

LADY LIBERTY

Delacroix's *Liberty Leading the People* (see Figure 12.20) instantly became a symbol of democratic aspirations. In 1884 France sent as a gift of friendship to the young American nation a monumental copper and cast-iron statue of an idealized female bearing a tablet and a flaming torch (Figure **12.21**). Designed by Frédéric-Auguste Bartholdi (1834–1904), the Statue of Liberty (Liberty Enlightening the World) is the "sister" of Delacroix's painted heroine; it has become a landmark of freedom for oppressed people everywhere.

Q What symbolic features give meaning to each of these landmark works?

Figure 12.20 Eugène Delacroix, *Liberty Leading the People*, 1830. Oil on canvas, 8 ft. 6 in. x 10 ft. 7 in. Louvre, Paris.

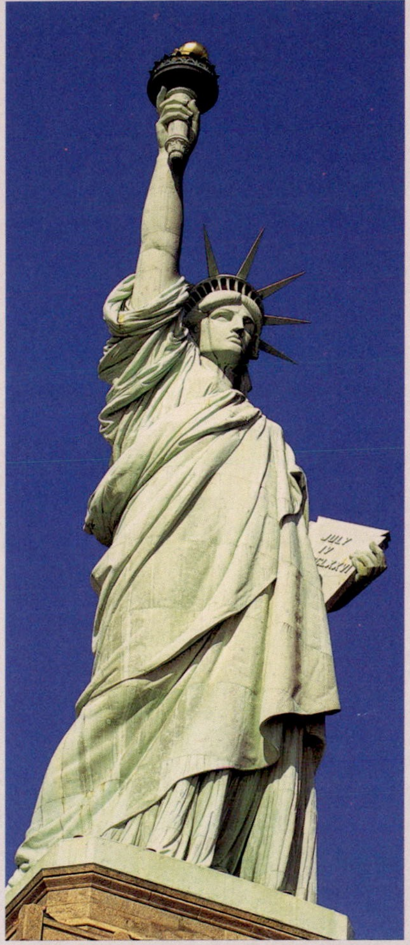

Figure 12.21 Frédéric-Auguste Bartholdi, Statue of Liberty (Liberty Enlightening the World), Liberty Island (Bedloe's Island), New York, 1871–1884. Framework constructed by A. G. Eiffel. Copper sheets mounted on steel frame, height 152 ft.

Romantic Sculpture

In sculpture as in painting, heroic subjects served the cause of nationalism. *The Departure of the Volunteers of 1792* (Figure **12.22**) by François Rude (1784–1855) embodied the dynamic heroism of the Napoleonic era. Installed at the foot of the Arch of Triumph (see Figure 11.22), which stands at the western end of the Champs-Elysées in Paris, the 42-foot-high stone sculpture commemorates the patriotism of a band of French volunteers—presumably the battalion of Marseilles, who marched to Paris in 1792 to defend the Republic. The spirited members of this small citizen army are led by the allegorical figure of Bellona, the Roman goddess of war.

Romantic Architecture

The landmarks of mid-nineteenth-century Western architecture reflect a major characteristic of the Romantic movement: the taste for medieval and other remote or exotic styles. *Neomedievalism*—the revival of medieval culture—served the ideals of nationalism, exalting the state by patriotic identification with the past. On the eve of the unification of Germany (1848) and for decades thereafter, German artisans restored their country's most notable Gothic monuments, including its great cathedrals. In England, where the Christian heritage of the Middle Ages was closely associated with national identity, many of the nation's leading artists embraced the medieval past.

Figure 12.22 François Rude, *La Marseillaise* (*The Departure of the Volunteers of 1792*), 1833–1836. Stone, approx. 42 ft. x 26 ft. Arch of Triumph, Paris. Rude universalized this allegory of war by including figures that are young and old, nude and clothed, and wearing ancient and medieval costumes.

Alfred, Lord Tennyson (1802–1892), poet laureate of Great Britain, for example, fused early British legend with the Christian mission in a cycle of Arthurian poems entitled *Idylls of the King;* while Sir Walter Scott immortalized medieval heroes and heroines in avidly read historical novels and Romantic poems.

The revival of the Gothic style assumed landmark proportions in the construction of the British Houses of Parliament (Figure **12.23**). Designed by Charles Barry (1795–1860) and Augustus Pugin (1812–1852), the Houses of Parliament are among the most aesthetically successful large-scale Neogothic public buildings in England. Neomedievalism gave rise to a movement for the archeological restoration of churches and castles throughout Europe, and it also inspired a wave of Neogothic and Neoromanesque building in North America, where many churches and universities (such as Harvard and Yale) modeled themselves on British prototypes.

Romantic architecture also drew inspiration from the "exotic" East, and especially those parts of the East where the European powers were building colonial empires. A landmark of this enterprise is the Royal Pavilion at Brighton, on the south coast of Britain (Figure **12.24**). Designed by the English architect John Nash (1752–1835), this intriguing pastiche of non-Western styles integrates Chinese, Hindu, and Islamic motifs.

Figure 12.23 (above) Charles Barry and A. W. N. Pugin, Houses of Parliament, London, 1840–1860. Length 940 ft. The picturesque combination of spires and towers fronting on the River Thames in London was the product of Pugin's conviction that the Gothic style best expressed the dignity befitting the official architecture of a Christian nation.

Figure 12.24 (right) John Nash, the Royal Pavilion, Brighton, from the northeast, 1815–1821. Nash raised bulbous domes and slender minarets over a hidden frame of cast iron, the structural medium that would soon come to dominate modern architecture. The bizarre interior décor, which includes water-lily chandeliers and cast-iron palm trees with copper leaves, produced an eclectic style that Nash's critics called "Indian Gothic."

ROMANTIC MUSIC AND DANCE

"MUSIC is the most romantic of all the arts—one might almost say, the only genuine romantic one—for its sole subject is the infinite." Thus wrote the German novelist and musician E. T. A. Hoffmann (1776–1822). Like many Romantic composers, Hoffmann believed that music held a privileged position in its capacity to express what he called "an inexpressible longing." For the Romantics, music—the most abstract and elusive of the arts—was capable of freeing the intellect and speaking directly to the heart.

The nineteenth century produced an enormous amount of music in all genres—a phenomenon that is reflected in the fact that audiences today listen to more nineteenth-century music than to music of any other time period. Its hallmark is personalized expression, a feature as apparent in large orchestral works as it is in small, intimate pieces. Like contemporary poets and painters, Romantic composers modified classical "rules" in order to increase expressive effects. They abandoned the precise forms and clear contours of classical music in favor of expanded or loosened forms, lyrical melodies, and lively shifts in meter and tempo. Just as Romantic painters exploited color to heighten emotional impact, so composers elevated **tone color** (the distinctive quality of musical sound made by a voice, a musical instrument, or a combination of instruments) to a status equal to melody, harmony, and rhythm.

During the Romantic era the orchestra grew to grand proportions. Mid-nineteenth-century orchestras were often five times larger than those used by Haydn and Mozart. While the volume of sound expanded, the varieties of instrumental possibilities also grew larger, in part because of technical improvements made in the instruments themselves. For example, modifications to the violin lent the instrument greater power—and more powerful instruments were required if the orchestra was to be heard in the ever-larger concert halls of the period. Then too, the early nineteenth-century piano, which acquired an iron frame, two or three pedals, and thicker strings, was capable of increased brilliance in tone and greater expressiveness—features that made it the most popular musical instrument of the century.

In terms of musical composition, the symphony and the concerto were the most important of the large orchestral forms. Equally significant, however, were song forms, especially songs that dealt with themes of love and death or nature and nature's moods. Composers found inspiration in heroic subjects, in contemporary events, and in the legends and histories of their native lands. Both in small musical forms and in large operatic compositions, they made every effort to achieve an ideal union of poetry and music.

As in the eighteenth century, composers were often also performers. They drew attention to their own technical abilities by writing **virtuoso** pieces (usually for piano or violin) that only highly accomplished musicians like themselves could perform with facility. They might indulge their creative whims in bouts of euphoria, melancholy, and petty jealousy. The talented Genoese composer and violinist Niccolò Paganini (1782–1840), for instance, refused to publish his own pieces, which he performed with such astounding technical agility that rumor had it he had come by his virtuosity through a pact with the devil.

The Symphony: Beethoven

The leading composer of the early nineteenth century and one of the greatest musicians of all time was the German-born Ludwig van Beethoven (1770–1827). Beethoven's lifelong residency in Vienna brought him in contact with the music of Mozart and Haydn, with whom he studied briefly. It also provided the composer with the fundamentals of the classical style that dominates his early compositions. A skillful pianist, organist, and violinist, Beethoven composed works in almost every medium and form. His thirty-two piano sonatas plumbed the expressive potential of that instrument.

Difficult as it is to imagine, Beethoven wrote much of his greatest music when he was functionally deaf. From the age of twenty-nine, when he became aware of a progressive degeneration of his hearing, he labored against depression and despair. Temperamental and defiant, he scorned the patronage system that had weighed heavily upon both Mozart and Haydn and sold his musical compositions as an independent artist. He declared contempt for the nobility and generally ignored their demands. In 1802 he confided to his family, "I am bound to be misunderstood; for me there can be no relaxation with my fellow men, no refined conversations, no mutual exchange of ideas. I must live alone like one who has been banished." In retreat from society, the alienated composer turned to nature. Outside Vienna, Beethoven roamed in the woods with his musical sketchbook under one arm, often singing to himself in a loud voice.

Beethoven's greatest achievement was his nine symphonies. These remarkable compositions generally adhere to the classical format, but they move beyond the boundaries of classical structure and are longer and more complex than any instrumental compositions written by Mozart or Haydn. As well as expanding the dimensions of the classical form, Beethoven enriched its instrumental textures. By adding piccolo, bass clarinet, trombone, bass drum, and cymbals to the scoring and occasionally doubling the number of flutes, oboes, clarinets, and bassoons, he vastly broadened the expressive range and dramatic power of orchestral sound.

The landmark Symphony No. 5 in C minor opens with the powerful four-note motif that Beethoven described as "fate knocking at the door." This motif, which unfolds in dramatic progression from movement to movement, unifies the entire symphony: It is stated dramatically in the sonata form of the first movement; appears in a theme-and-variation form in the second movement, and rises to a climax in the finale, which follows the third movement—a lively ***scherzo*** ("joke") rather than the classical minuet—without a break. Beethoven's genius is apparent in the surging rhythms that govern these shifting patterns of sound and in his use of musical dynamics (gradations of loudness and softness) to enhance the expressive impact of the piece. His daring use of dissonance and his sudden pauses and silences reflect the rule-breaking spirit of the Romantic artist.

Beethoven, Symphony No. 5 (1808)

The Art Song: Schubert

The art songs of Beethoven's Austrian contemporary Franz Schubert (1797–1828) aptly reflect the nineteenth-century composer's ambition to unite poetry and music. Schubert is credited with originating the Romantic ***Lied*** (German for "song," pl. *Lieder*), an independent song for solo voice and piano. The *Lied* is not a song in the traditional sense but, rather, a poem recreated in musical terms. Its lyric qualities, like those of simple folk songs, are generated by the poem itself. The *Lieder* of Schubert, Robert Schumann (1810–1856), and Johannes Brahms (1833–1897), which set to music the poetry of Goethe, among others, are intimate evocations of personal feelings and moods. They recount tales of love and longing, describe nature and its moods, or lament the transience of human happiness.

Among Schubert's thousand or so works (which include symphonies, operas, and chamber pieces) are six hundred *Lieder*. Of these, his musical settings for Goethe's ballads, such as the *Erlkönig* (*Erlking*), rank as landmark expressions of Romantic music.

Schubert, *Erlkönig* (*Erlking*; 1815)

Program Music: Berlioz

The *Symphonie fantastique*, the first symphony of French composer Hector Berlioz (1803–1869), is an imaginative combination of the story of Faust and Berlioz's own life. It tells the dramatic tale of Berlioz's "interminable and inextinguishable passion"—as he described it—for the captivating Irish actress Harriet Smithson. Berlioz wrote the symphony in the first flush of this romance, when he was only twenty-seven years old. Following an intense courtship, he married Harriet, only to discover that he and the woman he idolized were dreadfully mismatched—the marriage turned Smithson into an alcoholic and Berlioz into an adulterer.

Berlioz, *Symphonie fantastique* (1830)

Figure 12.25 Gustave Doré, *Berlioz Conducting Massed Choirs*, caricature published in *Journal pour rire*, June 27, 1850. The monumental proportions of Berlioz's orchestras and choirs provoked spoofs in contemporary cartoons. But Berlioz, who was also a talented writer and a music critic for Parisian newspapers, thumbed his nose at the critics in lively essays that defended his own musical philosophy.

The *Symphonie fantastique* belongs to the genre known as program music, that is, instrumental music endowed with a specific literary or pictorial content indicated by the composer. Berlioz was not the first to write music that was programmatic: In *The Four Seasons*, Vivaldi had linked music to poetic phrases (see page 289), as had Beethoven in his "Pastoral" Symphony. But Berlioz was the first to build an entire symphony around a musical motif that tells a story. In the *Symphonie fantastique*, Berlioz joins a specific mood or event to a musical phrase, or ***idée fixe*** ("fixed idea"). This recurring motif becomes the means by which the composer binds together the individual parts of his dramatic narrative.

The spiritual heir to Beethoven, Berlioz took liberties with traditional symphonic form. He composed the *Symphonie fantastique* in five movements instead of the usual four and combined instruments inventively so as to create unusual mixes of sound. In the third movement, for example, a solo English horn and four kettledrums produce the effect of "distant thunder." He also expanded tone color, stretching the register of clarinets to screeching highs, and playing the strings of the violin with the wood of the bow instead of with the hair. Berlioz's favorite medium was the full symphony orchestra, which he enlarged to include 150 musicians. Called "the apostle of bigness," Berlioz conceived an ideal orchestra that consisted of over 400 musicians, including 242 string instruments, 30 pianos, 30 harps, and a chorus of 360 voices (Figure **12.25**).

The popularity of program music during the nineteenth century testifies to the powerful influence of literature upon the other arts. Berlioz, whose second symphony, *Harold in Italy*, was inspired by Byron's *Childe Harold*, was not alone in his attraction to literary subjects. The Hungarian composer Franz Liszt (1811–1886) wrote symphonic poems based on the myth of Prometheus and Shakespeare's *Hamlet*. He also composed the *Faust Symphony*, which he dedicated to Berlioz. The Russian composer Peter Ilyich Tchaikovsky (1840–1893) wrote many programmatic pieces, including the tone poem *Romeo and Juliet*.

European political events also inspired nationalistic program music, such as Beethoven's *Battle Symphony* of 1813 (known too as *Wellington's Victory*) and Tchaikovsky's colorful *1812 Overture*, which, commemorating Napoleon's retreat from Moscow, incorporated portions of the national anthems of both France and tzarist Russia.

Tchaikovsky, *1812 Overture* (1880)

Piano Music: Chopin

If the nineteenth century was the age of Romantic individualism, it was also the age of the virtuoso: Composers wrote music that might be performed gracefully and accurately only by individuals with extraordinary technical skills. The quintessential example of this phenomenon is the Polish-born composer Frédéric Chopin (1810–1849). At the age of seven, he gave his first piano concert in Warsaw. Slight in build even as an adult, Chopin had small hands that nevertheless could reach across the keys of the piano like "the jaws of a snake" (as one of his peers observed). After leaving Warsaw, Chopin became the acclaimed pianist of the Paris *salons* and a close friend of Delacroix (who painted his portrait in Figure **12.26**), Berlioz, and many of the leading novelists of his time, including George Sand, with whom he had a stormy seven-year love affair.

Chopin composed over two hundred pieces, most of which were short keyboard works, such as dances, preludes, **nocturnes** (slow, songlike pieces), **impromptus** (pieces that sound improvised), and ***études*** (instrumental studies designed to improve a player's technique). His Étude in G-flat major, **Opus** 10, No. 5 is a breathtaking exercise that challenges the performer to play very rapidly on the black keys, which are less than half the width of the white ones. Although carefully contrived, Chopin's short compositions seem spontaneous, even improvised—the impetuous record of fleeting feeling, rather than the studied product of diligent construction. The most engaging of his compositions are marked by fresh turns of harmony and free tempos and rhythms. Chopin might embellish a melodic line with unusual and flamboyant devices, such as a rolling **arpeggio** (the sounding of the notes of a chord in rapid succession). Of his dance forms, the *polonaise* and the *mazurka* preserve the robustness of the folk tunes of his native Poland, while the waltz mirrors the Romantic taste for a new type of dance, more sensuous and physically expressive than the courtly and formal minuet. Considered vulgar and lewd when it was introduced in the late eighteenth century, the waltz, with its freedom of movement and intoxicating rhythms, became the most popular of all nineteenth-century dances.

Chopin, Étude, Opus 10, No. 5 (1830)

Figure 12.26 Eugène Delacroix, *Frédéric Chopin*, 1838. Oil on canvas, 18 x 15 in. Louvre, Paris. In his brief lifetime—he died of tuberculosis at the age of thirty-nine—Chopin created an entirely personal musical idiom linked to the expressive potential of the modern piano.

The Romantic Ballet

The theatrical artform known as "ballet" was born in nineteenth-century Paris and gained immense popularity in the Romantic era. By the year 1800, ballet had moved from the court to the theater, where it was enjoyed as a middle-class entertainment. Magnificent gas-lit theaters such as the Paris Opéra (Figures **12.27** and **12.28**), designed by Jean-Louis-Charles Garnier (1825–1878), became show-places for public entertainment.

The ballets performed on the stage of the Paris Opéra were the culmination of a Golden Age in European dance. In Paris Maria Taglioni became an instant success as **prima ballerina** (first or leading female dancer) in the ballet *La sylphide* (1830), choreographed by her father Filippo Taglioni (see Figure 12.1). Popular legends and fairytales inspired the ballets of the Romantic era. In *La sylphide*, a sylph enchants the hero and lures him away from his bride-to-be. Pursued by the hero, the sylph is nevertheless deprived of her earthly lover—she dies at the hand of a malevolent witch. The fictional heroine of this ballet (and

Figure 12.27 Jean-Louis-Charles Garnier, Façade of the Opéra, Paris, 1860–1875. The Neobaroque polychrome façade of the opera house reflects Garnier's awareness that Greek architects had painted parts of their buildings.

many other Romantic ballets) symbolizes the elusive ideals of love and beauty that were a favorite subject of the Romantic poets. Despite the growing visibility of women in important social and artistic roles, such mythical figures fulfilled the Romantic (and male-generated) stereotype of the angelic woman or the Eternal Female (see page 333).

Russian ballet came to prominence with the choreography of Marius Petipa (1818–1910), who brought to Russia in 1847 the best of French and Italian traditions in dance. For half a century, Petipa's talents dominated Russian dance at the Imperial Ballet Company in St. Petersburg and the Bolshoi Ballet in Moscow. Petipa's genius for expressive movement and his rigorous demand for technical proficiency made Russia the international center for ballet training and performance. Choreographed by Petipa, scored by Tchaikovsky, the lavishly produced full-length ballets *The Sleeping Beauty* (1889) and *The Nutcracker* (1892) became instant classics. Tchaikovsky's *Swan Lake*, first performed in 1877, but revived with Petipa's choreography and staged in St. Petersburg in 1895, joined the others as landmarks in the history of dance.

Petipa and Tchaikovsky, *The Sleeping Beauty* (1889); *The Nutcracker* (1892); *Swan Lake* (1895)

Figure 12.28 Jean-Louis-Charles Garnier, Grand Staircase at the Opéra, Paris, 1860–1875. Engraving from Charles Garnier, *Le Nouvel Opéra de Paris*, 1880. The glory of the structure is its interior, which takes as its focus a sumptuous grand staircase. Luxuriously appointed, and illuminated by means of the latest technological invention, gaslight, the Paris Opéra became the model for public theaters throughout Europe.

Grand Opera: Verdi

The quintessential expression of the Romantic sensibility was grand opera, a flamboyant spectacle that united all aspects of theatrical production—music, dance, drama, and the visual arts (in the form of stage sets and costumes). Designed to appeal to a growing middle-class audience, grand opera flourished after 1820. While Paris was the operatic capital of Europe in the first half of the nineteenth century, Italy ultimately took the lead in seducing the public with hundreds of wonderfully tuneful and melodramatic Romantic operas.

The art of singing, as it flourished in Italy through the first decades of the nineteenth century, established the ***bel canto*** tradition. Literally, "beautiful singing" (or "beautiful song"), *bel canto*-style opera emphasizes the melodic line of the music and the vocalist's ability to execute florid embellishments, such as rapid-fire runs and trills. Two of the century's most famous *bel canto* operas are Gioacchino Rossini's *Il barbiere di Siviglia* (*The Barber of Seville*, 1816), and Gaetano Donizetti's *Lucia di Lammermoor* (1835), based on a novel by Sir Walter Scott. In these works, showpiece arias with long, winding melodic lines (usually sung in the upper register) demand stunning vocal agility.

Rossini, *The Barber of Seville* (1816); Donizetti, *Lucia di Lammermoor* (1835)

The shift to operatic drama, marked by more intense and powerful singing, is evident in the music of Italy's leading composer, Giuseppe Verdi (1813–1901). In his twenty-six operas, the Italian operatic tradition that had begun with Monteverdi (see page 286) came to its peak. The heroines of Verdi's most beloved operas—*Rigoletto*, *La Traviata*, and *Aida*—are creatures of the heart, who die for love. *Aida*, which was commissioned by the Turkish viceroy of Egypt to mark the opening of the Suez Canal, made a nationalistic plea for unity against foreign domination. It is also the

Verdi, *Rigoletto* (1851); *La Traviata* (1853); *Aida* (1870)

Beyond the West

EXPLORING AFRICA

IN the nineteenth century, Africa experienced dramatic changes, many of which were due to rapidly expanding European commercial and political ambitions. Europe had been involved in Africa since the sixteenth century (see Chapter 9), but by the 1800s trade in goods and guns and slaves was clearly transforming local African culture. In some parts of Africa, the availability of guns led to violence and mayhem. While European interests in Africa focused on economic advantage, the penetration of the African interior was also the consequence of intellectual curiosity, which had been stirred by Napoleon's campaign in Egypt. Following the French invasion of Algeria in 1830, and especially after medical science had made quinine effective against the dreaded malaria, a mosquito-borne infectious disease, travel on this continent became attractive. Delacroix visited Morocco in 1831 and brought back seven sketchbooks and numerous watercolors; and the British explorers David Livingstone (1813–1873) and Henry M. Stanley (1841–1904)—among many others—spent years investigating Africa's vast terrains.

During the nineteenth century, the oral traditions of African literature and music came to be recorded in written languages based on Arabic and Western alphabets. In many regions, this was an era of high artistic productivity. The Yoruba kingdoms of Nigeria (see Map 9.2), for example, produced magnificent beaded objects that served to identify and embellish the authority of their rulers (Figure **12.29**). Beadwork had been practiced in West Africa since the sixteenth century, when the Portuguese introduced Venetian glass beads to the continent. However, the Golden Age of beadwork arrived only after uniformly sized European "seed beads" in various colors became available.

A second genre of artistic production took on landmark significance in the nineteenth century: handwoven textiles, and especially the decorative cotton cloth known as *kente* (see Figure 15.39), woven in the kingdom of Asante (modern Ghana). Like the beadwork of the Yoruba, *kente*—the name derives from the woven designs of Ghanaian baskets (*kenten*)—is associated with royal ceremony. In the seventeenth century, the Asante kings began a practice of laying claim to specific *kente* motifs through a form of royal "copyright." Individual patterns and colors continue to bear symbolic meaning, such as military prowess, spiritual purity, and courageous leadership.

Figure 12.29 Yoruba-style beaded crown, nineteenth century. Beads and mixed media, height 17¾ in. Museum of Man, Paris.

tragic love story of an Egyptian prince and an Ethiopian princess held as a captive slave. Verdi's stirring arias, vigorous choruses, and richly colored orchestral passages can be enjoyed by listening alone. But the dramatic force of this opera can only be appreciated by witnessing a theatrical performance—especially one using such traditional paraphernalia as horses, chariots, and, of course, elephants.

Music-Drama: Wagner

In Germany, the master of opera and one of the most formidable composers of the century was Richard Wagner (1813–1883). The stepson of a gifted actor, he spent much of his childhood composing poems and plays and setting them to music. This union of music and literature culminated in the birth of what Wagner called **music-drama**. Passionately nationalistic, Wagner drew almost exclusively on heroic themes from Germany's medieval past. He wrote his own librettos and composed scores that brought to life the fabulous events and personalities featured in German folk tales and legends. His aim, as he himself explained, was "to force the listener, for the first time in the history of opera, to take an interest in a poetic idea, by making him follow all its developments" as dramatized simultaneously in sound and story.

Of Wagner's nine principal operas, the landmark work is a monumental fifteen-hour cycle of four music-dramas collectively titled *Der Ring des Nibelungen* (*The Ring of the Nibelung*). Based on Norse and Germanic mythology, *The Ring* involves the quest for a magical but accursed golden ring whose power would provide its possessor with the potential to control the universe. In the course of a violent struggle between the gods of Valhalla and an assortment of giants, dragons, and dwarfs, the hero, Siegfried, secures the ring and eventually presents it to his lover Brünnhilde. However, in the end Siegfried loses both his love and his life, and Valhalla crumbles in flames, destroying the gods and eliciting the birth of a new order.

Wagner, *Der Ring des Nibelungen* (*The Ring of the Nibelung*) (1876)

Awesome in imaginative scope, *The Ring* brings to life some of the hero myths that shaped the Western, and especially Germanic, literary tradition. Equally imaginative is the music, which matches its poetry in dramatic complexity. Requiring a heroic orchestra of some 115 pieces, *The Ring* makes use of the ***leitmotif***, a short musical phrase that—like the *idée fixe*—signifies a particular person, thing, or idea in the story. No fewer than twenty *leitmotifs* weave a complex web of dramatic musical density. Wagner's *Ring* departed from operatic tradition by blending the vocal line with continuous orchestral music that engulfs the listener in a maelstrom of uninterrupted sound. In his bold handling of tonal color, Wagner anticipated some of the more radical experiments of twentieth-century music. Ultimately, in his efforts to stretch musical forms to fit his feelings, Wagner remains the most inventive of the Romantic composers.

Afterword

Romanticism dominated the culture of the West in the late eighteenth and for much of the nineteenth century. As a movement, it reacted against the rational certitudes of the Enlightenment; as a style, it rejected Neoclassical formalism. As an attitude of mind, Romanticism exalted the imagination and indulged the spontaneous expression of feeling. Heroic personalities and events (usually inspired by contemporary history and nascent nationalism), and a return to nature as an alternative to growing industrialization, were principal themes of the Age of Romanticism. The works of Byron, Blake, Whitman, Delacroix, and Chopin, reveal the rebellious individualism that favored intuition over the life of reason. The theoretical works of Hegel and Darwin have become landmarks, as have Goethe's *Faust*, Mary Shelley's *Frankenstein*, and Frederick Douglass' abolitionist writings. Concert performances of Romantic music and dance continue to attract large audiences in our own time. In the late nineteenth century, however, Romanticism (in all its manifestations) came to be challenged by growing materialism and the harsh realities of Western imperialism in Africa and elsewhere.

Key Topics

- the Romantic hero
- Hegel's dialectic
- the Industrial Revolution
- Darwin and evolution
- English Romantic poetry
- Goethe's *Faust*
- female novelists
- American Transcendentalism
- abolitionist literature
- landscape painting
- heroic themes in European art
- Neomedievalism
- nationalism and the arts
- Beethoven's symphonies
- Romantic music
- the Romantic ballet
- grand opera and music-drama
- Africa in the nineteenth century

ROMANTICISM TIMELINE

	HISTORICAL EVENTS	LANDMARKS IN THE VISUAL ARTS	LITERARY LANDMARKS	MUSIC AND DANCE LANDMARKS
1780	• Organized abolitionism begins in England (1780s)		• Blake, *Songs of Innocence* (1789); *Songs of Experience* (1794) • Wordsworth and Coleridge, *Lyrical Ballads* (1798)	
1800	• Napoleon proclaims himself emperor (1804) • Napoleon's armies invade Spain (1808) • Lamarck lays foundations of evolutionary theory (1809) • Shelley expelled from Oxford University for writings on atheism (1811) • Napoleon retreats from Russia (1812) • Battle of Waterloo: Napoleon exiled (1815)	• Goya, *The Third of May, 1808* (1814) • Nash, The Royal Pavilion, Brighton (1815–1821) • Géricault, *The Raft of the "Medusa"* (1818)	• Hegel, *The Philosophy of History* (1807) • Austen, *Sense and Sensibility* (1811) • Goethe, *Faust* (1808–1832) • Shelley, lyric poems (1813–1822) • Byron, *Childe Harold's Pilgrimage* (1818); *Don Juan* (1819–1824) • Mary Shelley, *Frankenstein* (1818) • Keats, "Ode on a Grecian Urn" (1819) • Schopenhauer, *The World as Will and Idea* (1819)	• Beethoven, Symphony No. 5 in C minor (1808) • Schubert, *Erlkönig* (1815) • Rossini, *The Barber of Seville* (1816)
1820	• France invades Algeria (1830) • Revolution of 1830 France • Start of U.S. antislavery movement (1831) • U.S. government begins to force Indian tribes from homelands (1830s)	• Constable, *The Hay Wain* (1821) • Delacroix, *Liberty Leading the People* (1830) • Rude, *La Marseillaise* (1833–1836) • Cole, *The Oxbow* (1836)	• Emerson, *Essays* (1836–1860)	• Chopin, *Étude*, Opus 10, No. 5 (1830) • Berlioz, *Symphonie fantastique* (1830) • Taglioni's debut in *La sylphide* (1830)
1840	• Darwin publishes *On the Origin of Species* (1859)	• Turner, *The Slave Ship* (1840) • Barry and Pugin, Houses of Parliament, London (1840–1860) • Catlin, *The White Cloud, Head Chief of the Iowas* (1844–1845)	• Douglass, *Narrative of the Life of Frederick Douglass* (1845) • Bomefree, *Narrative of Sojourner Truth* (1850) • Thoreau, *Walden* (1854) • Whitman, *Leaves of Grass* (1855–1892)	• Donizetti, *Lucia di Lammermoor* (1835)
1860	• American Civil War (1861–1865)	• Garnier, Paris Opéra (1860–1875) • Bierstadt, *The Rocky Mountains, Lander's Peak* (1863) • Corot, *Ville d'Avray* (1870)		• Verdi, *Aida* (1870) • Wagner, *The Ring of the Nibelung* (1876)
1880		• Bartholdi, *Statue of Liberty* (1871–1884)		• Tchaikovsky and Petipa, *The Sleeping Beauty* (1882); *The Nutcracker* (1892); *Swan Lake* (1895)

Figure 12.8 John Constable, *The Hay Wain*, see p. 338

Figure 12.17 Francisco Goya, *The Third of May, 1808: The Execution of the Defenders of Madrid*, see p. 343

Figure 12.27 Jean-Louis-Charles Garnier, Façade of the Opéra, Paris, see p. 350

Figure 12.21 Frédéric-Auguste Bartholdi, Statue of Liberty (Liberty Enlightening the World), see p. 345

Chapter 13

Materialism:

THE INDUSTRIAL ERA AND THE URBAN SCENE

ca. 1850–1900

In the decades after 1850, the industrial technologies of steam power, coal, and iron brought the West into a position of dominance over the less industrialized parts of the world. Electricity, synthetic paints, and photography provided new ways of viewing one's natural surroundings and recording everyday experience. Cast iron and mass-produced steel revolutionized building methods and designs. The age of materialism incorporated two major movements in the arts: Realism and Impressionism. Both called for an objective and unidealized record of the physical world: the bitter realities of lower-class life, and the pleasures and pastimes of the urban scene. France emerged as the center of Western artistic productivity, and Paris became a melting pot for artists, composers, and writers. Following the last Impressionist show in 1886, a rich assortment of expressive, exotic, and formal Postimpressionist styles brought the century to a close. London and Paris hosted World's Fairs that introduced the cultures of non-Western nations to many astonished Europeans. For the first time, the arts of Japan, Africa, and Oceania had a visible impact on the culture of the West.

A First Look

Georges Seurat's *Sunday Afternoon on the Island of La Grande Jatte* shows a holiday crowd enjoying a leisurely sun-filled afternoon on an island in the River Seine four miles northwest of Paris. The subject matter—the middle class at play—has replaced the gods and goddesses, saints and martyrs, kings and heroes that dominated the large-sized canvases of previous centuries. Seurat's canvas marks the attention to the realities of contemporary life that dominated the arts of the late nineteenth century. While typical of the Impressionist fascination with the activities of urban society, the painting has little of the painterly spontaneity that characterized Impressionism. Seurat shared the Impressionist's obsession with light and color, but he had little interest in the effects of fleeting sensation. *La Grande Jatte*'s orderly, geometric composition was distilled from dozens of preparatory studies (see page 376). Seurat's fervor for order may have inspired his systematic application of tiny dots of paint (in French, *points*) to heighten color intensity and emphasize form. While this novel use of color produced the style known as *pointillism,* Seurat's canvas was less than popular with the critics, one of whom wrote, "Strip his figures of the colored fleas that cover them; underneath you will find nothing, no thought, no soul . . ." Nevertheless, *La Grande Jatte,* with its brilliant atomized color and its intriguingly stylized figures, remains a landmark in the annals of French painting.

Figure 13.1 Georges Seurat, *Sunday Afternoon on the Island of La Grande Jatte* (detail, see Figure 13.27).

THE GLOBAL DOMINION OF THE WEST

Advancing Industrialism

Industrialism provided the economic and military basis for the West's rise to dominion over the rest of the world. This process is well illustrated in the history of the railroad, the most important technological phenomenon of the early nineteenth century. Made possible by the combined technologies of steam power, coal, and iron, the railroad facilitated economic and political expansion. The first all-iron rails were forged in Britain in 1789, but it was not until 1804 that the British built their first steam railway locomotive, and several more decades until "iron horses" became a major mode of transportation. The drive to build national railways spread, encompassing Europe and the vast continent of North America. By 1850, 23,000 miles of railway track crisscrossed Europe, linking the sources of raw materials—such as the coal mines of northern Germany's Ruhr valley—to factories and markets. As Western nations colonized other parts of the globe, they brought with them the railroad and other agents of industrialism.

Before the end of the nineteenth century, Western technology included the internal combustion engine, the telegraph, the telephone, the camera, and—perhaps most significant for the everyday life of human beings—electricity. In 1873, the British physicist James Clerk Maxwell (1831–1879) published his *Treatise on Electricity and Magnetism,* which explained that light waves consisting of electromagnetic particles produce radiant energy. In 1879, after numerous failures, the American inventor Thomas Edison (1847–1931) moved beyond scientific theory to create the first efficient incandescent light bulb. Edison's light bulb provided a sharper perception of reality that—along with the camera—helped to shatter the world of romantic illusion. By the year 1880, the telephone transported the human voice over thousands of miles. In the late 1880s Edison developed the technique of moving pictures. The invention of the internal combustion engine led to the production of modern motorcars in the 1890s, a decade that also witnessed the invention of the x-ray and the genesis of radiotelegraphy. Such technologies accelerated the tempo of everyday life and drew attention to the role of the senses in defining experience.

Processed steel, aluminum, the steam turbine, and the pneumatic tire—all products of the 1880s—further altered the texture of life in the industrialized world. These phenomena, along with such lethal weapons as the fully automatic "machine gun," gave Europe clear advantages over other parts of the globe and facilitated Western imperialism in less industrially developed areas. In the enterprise of empire-building, the industrialized nations of Britain, France, Belgium, Germany, Italy, and the United States took the lead.

Colonialism and the New Imperialism

The history of European expansion into Asia, Africa, and other parts of the globe dates back at least to the Renaissance. Between approximately 1500 and 1800, Europeans established trading outposts in Africa (see page 351), China, and India (see pages 240–241). But not until after 1800, in the wake of the Industrial Revolution, did European imperialism transform the territories of foreign peoples into outright colonial possessions. Driven by the need for raw materials and markets for their manufactured goods, and aided immeasurably by their advanced military technology, the industrial nations quickly colonized or controlled vast parts of Asia, Africa, and Latin America. So massive was this effort that, by the end of the nineteenth century, the West had established economic, political, and cultural dominance over much of the world (Map **13.1**).

In the race for overseas colonies, Britain led the way: The first major landmass to be subjugated was India, where commercial imperialism led to conquest and, finally, to British rule in 1858. In less than a century, the nation had established control over so much territory across the globe that it could legitimately claim that "the sun never set" on the British Empire. Nineteenth-century imperialism also brought an end to China's long history as an independent civilization. The triangular trade pattern in opium and tea between India, China, and Great Britain led to warfare and devastation among the Chinese.

The most dramatic example of the new imperialism was in Africa. In 1880, European nations controlled only 10 percent of the continent; but by 1900 all of Africa, save Ethiopia and Liberia, had been carved up by European powers, who introduced new models of political and economic authority, often with little regard for indigenous populations.

By the mid-nineteenth century, the United States (itself a colony of Britain until 1776) had joined the scramble for economic control. America forced Japan to open its doors to Western trade in 1853. This event marked the beginning of Japanese modernization under Meiji rule (1858–1912). In the Western hemisphere, the United States established its own overseas empire. North Americans used the phrase "manifest destiny" to describe and justify a policy of unlimited expansion into the American West, Mexico, and elsewhere. The end result was the United States' acquisition of more than half of Mexico, control of the Philippines and Cuba, and a dominant position in the economies of the politically unstable nations of Latin America.

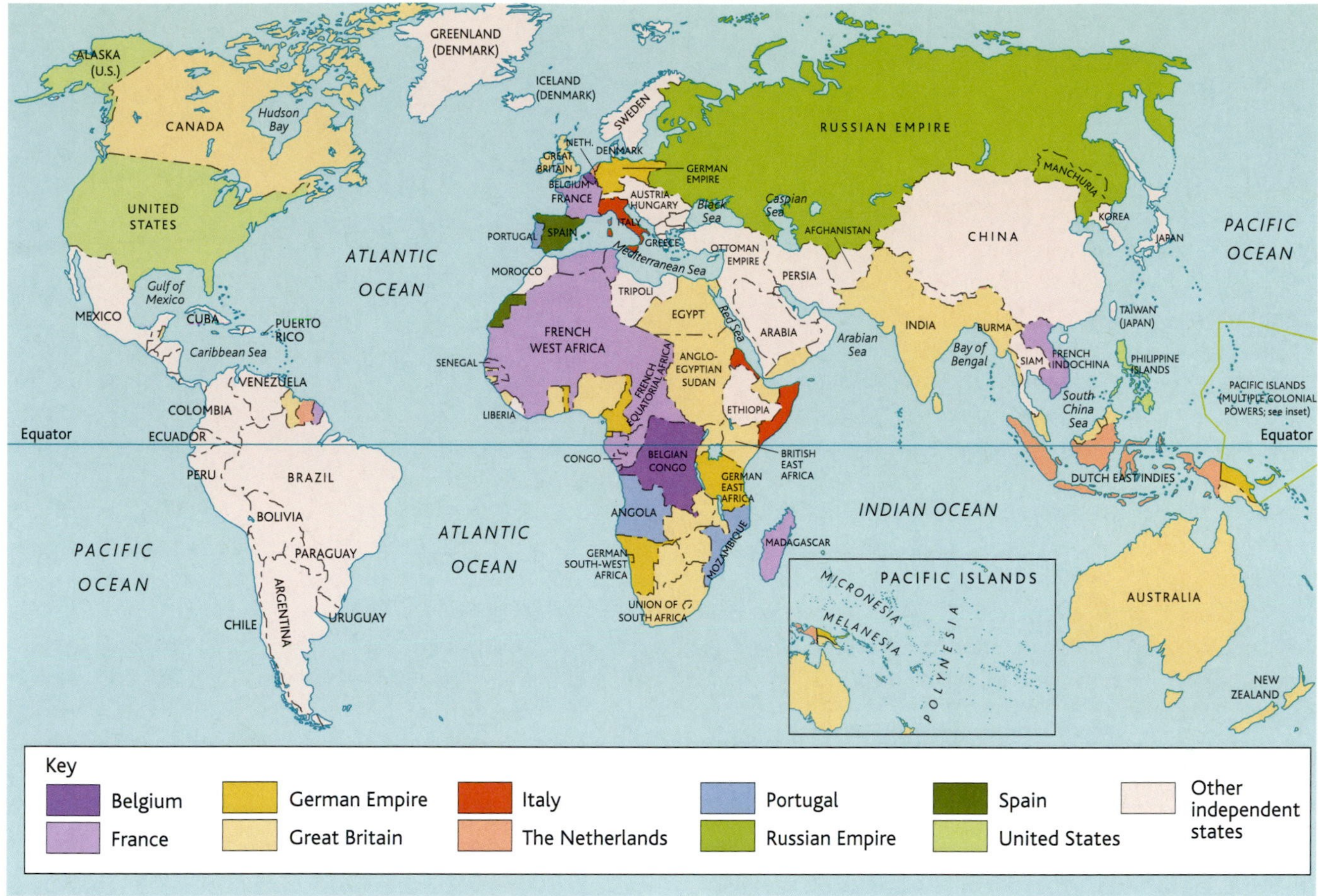

Map 13.1 Colonialism. European colonies and independent nations in 1900.

To Westerners, the benefits of science, technology, and Christianity far outweighed the destructive impact of colonialism. But the "gift" of progress did have negative consequences. In most of the colonial territories there was a marked decline in productivity and originality. The full effects of Western colonialism would not become clear until the twentieth century.

Social and Economic Realities

In global terms, advancing industrialization polarized the nations of the world into the technologically advanced—the "haves"—and the technologically backward—the "have-nots." But industrialization had an equally profound impact within the industrialized nations themselves: It changed the nature and character of human work, altered relationships between human beings, and affected the natural environment. Prior to 1800 the practice of accumulating capital for industrial production and commercial profit played only a limited role in European societies. But after the turn of the century, industrial production, enhanced by advances in machine technology, came to be controlled by a relatively small group of middle-class **entrepreneurs** (those who organize, manage, and assume the risks of a business) and by an even smaller number of **capitalists** (those who provide money to finance business). Industrialization created wealth, but that wealth was concentrated in the hands of a small minority of the population. The vast majority of men and women lived hard lives supported by meager wages—the only thing they had to sell was their labor. Factory laborers, including women and children, worked under dirty and dangerous conditions for long hours—sometimes up to sixteen hours per day.

Beginning in 1848, the lower classes protested against these conditions with sporadic urban revolts. Economic unrest prevailed not only in the cities but in rural areas. In late nineteenth-century France, the population was two-thirds rural, largely poor, and often reduced to backbreaking labor (Figure **13.2**). Wealthy landowners in some parts of Europe treated their agricultural laborers as slaves. In America, until after the Civil War (1861–1865), most of those who worked the great Southern plantations were, in fact, African-American slaves. Between 1855 and 1861, there were almost five hundred peasant uprisings across Europe (Figure **13.3**). Among these movements for economic and social reform, one of the most idealistic was *socialism*. Socialism attacked capitalism as a system that encouraged inequality and the exploitation of labor. Socialists called for the common ownership and administration of the means of production and distribution in the interest of the public good. Society, according to the socialists, should operate entirely in the interest of the people.

Figure 13.2 (above) Jean-François Millet, *Gleaners*, 1857. Oil on canvas, approx. 2 ft. 9 in. x 3 ft. 8 in. Orsay Museum, Paris. Set in golden-lit fields and against a broad sky, Millet's painting presents a somewhat romanticized view of the laboring classes. This artist's portrayals of rural women spinning, tending sheep, and feeding children idealized the female as selfless and saintly.

Figure 13.3 (below) Käthe Kollwitz, *March of the Weavers*, from "The Weavers Cycle," 1897. Etching, 8⅜ x 11⅝ in. University of Michigan Museum of Art. Kollwitz was a Social Realist and a feminist whose early prints illustrate peasant rebellions and mass protests. Reform, however, was slow in coming. Outside of England—in Germany, for instance—trade unions and social legislation to benefit the working classes did not appear until 1880 or later, while in Russia economic reform would require nothing less than a full-scale revolution.

Marx and Engels

The German theorist Karl Marx (1818–1883) agreed with the socialists that bourgeois capitalism corrupted humanity, but his theory of social reform was even more radical, for it preached violent revolution that would both destroy the old order and usher in a new society. Marx began his career by studying law and philosophy at the University of Berlin. Moving to Paris, he became a lifelong friend of the social scientist and journalist Friedrich Engels (1820–1895). Marx and Engels shared a similar critical

Marx and Engels, *Communist Manifesto* (1848)

attitude in respect of the effects of European industrial capitalism. Together they wrote the *Communist Manifesto*, a short treatise published as the platform of a workers' association called the Communist League.

Marx perceived human history in exclusively materialistic terms, arguing that the conditions under which one earned a living determined all other aspects of life. A student of Hegel, he viewed history as a struggle between "haves" (thesis) and "have-nots" (antithesis) that would resolve in the synthesis of a classless society. From Hegel, Marx also derived the utopian idea of the perfectibility of the state. The end product of dialectical change, argued Marx, was a society free of class antagonisms—the ultimate dissolution of the state itself.

The *Communist Manifesto* is a sweeping condemnation of the effects of capitalism on the individual and society at large. It argues that capitalism concentrates wealth in the hands of the few, providing great luxuries for some while creating an oppressed and impoverished **proletariat** (working class). The psychological effects of such circumstances, it claims, are devastating: Bourgeois capitalism alienates workers from their own productive efforts and robs individuals of their basic humanity. Finally, the *Manifesto* calls for revolution by which workers will seize the instruments of capitalistic production and abolish private ownership. The closing lines of the *Manifesto* convey the fervor of this revolutionary thesis:

> The Communist revolution is the most radical rupture with traditional property relations; no wonder that its development involves the most radical rupture with traditional ideas.
>
> But let us have done with the bourgeois objections to Communism.
>
> We have seen above that the first step in the revolution by the working class is to raise the proletariat to the position of ruling class, to win the battle of democracy.
>
> The proletariat will use its political supremacy to wrest, by degrees, all capital from the bourgeoisie, to centralize all instruments of production in the hands of the State, i.e., of the proletariat organized as the ruling class; and to increase the total of productive forces as rapidly as possible. . . .
>
> . . . The Communists disdain to conceal their views and aims. They openly declare that their ends can be attained only by the forcible overthrow of all existing social conditions. Let the ruling classes tremble at a Communist revolution. The proletarians have nothing to lose but their chains. They have a world to win.
>
> WORKING MEN OF ALL COUNTRIES, UNITE!

The *Communist Manifesto* had enormous influence. It brought attention to the role of economics in the larger life of a society, and it supplied the justification for working-class revolt. Although the treatise did not accurately predict the economic destiny of the modern world, it remains a landmark expression of nineteenth-century social consciousness.

Nietzsche's New Morality

If Marx and Engels offered a utopian view of society, the German philosopher and poet Friedrich Wilhelm Nietzsche (1844–1900) exalted a fierce new morality. Nietzsche was a Classical philologist, a professor of Greek at the University of Basle, and the author of such notable works as *The Birth of Tragedy* (1872), *Thus Spoke Zarathustra*, and *On the Genealogy of Morals* (1887). In these, as in his shorter pieces, Nietzsche voiced the sentiments of the radical moralist. Deeply critical of his own time, he called for a revision of all values. He rejected organized religion, attacking Christianity and other institutionalized religions as contributors to the formation of a "slave morality." He was equally critical of democratic institutions, which he saw as rule by mass mediocrity; instead he called for a "superman" or superior individual (*Übermensch*), whose singular vision and courage would, in his view, produce a "master" morality.

Nietzsche, *Thus Spoke Zarathustra* (1883–1892)

Nietzsche did not launch his ideas in the form of a well-reasoned philosophic system, but rather as aphorisms, maxims, and expostulations whose brilliance and visceral force bear out his claim to have written his works "with his blood." Reflecting the cynicism of the late nineteenth century, he asked, "Is man merely a mistake of God's? Or God merely a mistake of man's?" More dramatically, he claimed "God is dead." His view that Western materialism had generated decadence and decline, and his negation of absolute moral truth, anticipated the nihilism of many twentieth-century thinkers.

Ideas and Issues

PROGRESS: THE FALSE IDEA

"Mankind surely does not represent an evolution toward a better or stronger or higher level, as progress is now understood. This "progress" is merely a modern idea, which is to say, a false idea. The European of today, in his essential worth, falls far below the European of the Renaissance; the process of evolution does not necessarily mean elevation, enhancement, strengthening. True enough, it succeeds in isolated and individual cases in various parts of the earth and under the most widely different cultures, and in these cases a higher type certainly manifests itself; something which, compared to mankind in the mass, appears as a sort of superman."

(from Nietzsche, *The Antichrist*, 1888)

Q Is progress a modern idea? Is it a false idea, as Nietzsche claims?

LITERARY REALISM

The Novels of Dickens and Twain

Inequities of class and gender had existed throughout the course of history, but in an age that pitted the progressive effects of industrial capitalism against the realities of poverty and inequality, social criticism was inevitable. From about 1830, writers described these conditions with unembellished objectivity. This unblinking attention to contemporary life and experience was the basis for the style known as literary *Realism.*

More than any other genre, the nineteenth-century novel—through its capacity to detail characters and conditions—fulfilled the Realist credo of depicting life with complete candor. In contrast with Romanticism, which embraced heroic and exotic subjects, Realism portrayed men and women in actual, everyday, and often demoralizing situations. It examined the social consequences of middle-class materialism, the plight of the working class, and the subjugation of women, among other matters. While Realism did not totally displace Romanticism as the dominant literary mode of the nineteenth century, it often appeared alongside the Romantic—indeed, indulgent and sentimental elements can be found in generally Realistic narratives. Such is the case in the novels of Charles Dickens (1812–1870).

The most popular English novelist of his time, Dickens came from a poor family who provided him with little formal education. His early experiences supplied some of the themes for his most famous novels: *Oliver Twist* (1838) vividly portrays the slums, orphanages, and boarding schools of London; *Nicholas Nickleby* (1839) is a bitter indictment of England's brutal rural schools; and *David Copperfield* condemns debtors' prisons and the conditions that produced them. Dickens' novels are frequently theatrical, his characters may be drawn to the point of caricature, and his themes often suggest a sentimental faith in kindness and good cheer as the best antidotes to the bitterness of contemporary life.

Dickens, *David Copperfield* (1850)

While Dickens took as his locale the streets of England's industrial cities, the American writer Samuel Langhorne Clemens (1835–1910), whose pseudonym was Mark Twain, set his stories in the rural farmlands along the Mississippi River. Twain shared Dickens' sensitivity to pictorial detail, but he brought to his writing a unique blend of humor and irony. Twain's literary classic, *The Adventures of Huckleberry Finn*, is the most widely taught book in American literature. Published as a sequel to the popular "boys' book" *The Adventures of Tom Sawyer* (1876)—which, like Dickens' novels, appeared in serial format—the novel recounts the exploits of the young narrator, Huck Finn, and the runaway slave, Jim, as the two make their way down the Mississippi River on a ramshackle raft. Huck, a poor, ignorant, but good-hearted Southern white boy, experiences a crisis of conscience when he must choose between aiding a fugitive slave (a felony offense in the slave states of the South) and obeying the law by turning over his older friend and companion to the local authorities. Huck's moral dilemma was central to the whole system of chattel slavery: Historically, slaves were considered property, goods that could be bought, sold, or stolen; however, they were also human beings. In opting to help Jim escape, Huck is, in effect, an accomplice to a crime. Nevertheless, he chooses to aid Jim the *man*, even as he violates the law in harboring Jim the *slave*.

Twain, *Huckleberry Finn* (1884)

As humorist, journalist, and social critic, Twain offered his contemporaries a blend of entertainment and vivid insight into the troubled relations between blacks and whites in the American South just prior to the Civil War. These he captures in an exotic blend of dialects—the vernacular rhythms and idioms of local, untutored speech.

Russian Realism: Dostoevsky and Tolstoy

More pessimistic than Dickens or Twain, and more profoundly analytic of the universal human condition, were the Russian novelists Fyodor Dostoevsky (1821–1881) and Leo Tolstoy (1828–1910). Both men were born and bred in wealth, but both turned against upper-class Russian society and sympathized with the plight of the lower classes. Tolstoy ultimately renounced his wealth and property and went to live and work among the peasants. His landmark historical novel *War and Peace*, often hailed as the greatest example of Realistic Russian fiction, traces the progress of five families whose destinies unroll against the background of Napoleon's invasion of Russia in 1812. In this sprawling narrative, as in many of his other novels, Tolstoy exposes the privileged position of the nobility and the cruel exploitation of the great masses of Russian people.

Tolstoy, *War and Peace* (1869)

Dostoevsky pays greater attention than Tolstoy to philosophical and psychological issues. The characters in Dostoevsky's novels are often victims of a dual plight: poverty and conscience. Their energies are foiled by the struggle to resolve their own contradictory passions. Dostoevsky's personal circumstances contributed to his bleak outlook: Associated with a group of proletarian revolutionaries, he was arrested and deported to Siberia, where he spent five years at hard labor. The necessity of suffering is a central theme in Dostoevsky's writings, as

Ideas and Issues

DOSTOEVSKY: LORDS OF THE FUTURE

"... [People are] by the law of nature divided *in general* into two categories: into a lower [category] (of ordinary people), that is, into material serving only for the reproduction of its own kind, and into people properly speaking, that is, those who have the gift or talent of saying *something new* in their sphere. There are endless subdivisions, of course, but the distinctive characteristics of the two categories are fairly well marked: the first group, that is the material, are, generally speaking, by nature staid and conservative, they live in obedience and like it. In my opinion they ought to obey because that is their destiny, and there is nothing at all degrading to them in it. The second group are all law-breakers and transgressors, or are inclined that way, in the measure of their capacities. The aims of these people are, of course, relative and very diverse; for the most part they require, in widely different contexts, the destruction of what exists in the name of better things. But if it is necessary for one of them, for the fulfillment of his ideas, to march over corpses, or wade through blood, then in my opinion he may in all conscience authorize himself to wade through blood—in proportion, however, to his idea and the degree of its importance—mark that. It is in that sense only that I speak ... of their right to commit crime. (You will remember that we really began with the question of legality.) There is, however, not much cause for alarm: the masses hardly ever recognize this right of theirs, and behead or hang them (more or less), and in this way, quite properly, fulfill their conservative function, although in following generations these same masses put their former victims on a pedestal and worship them (more or less). The first category are always the masters of the present, but the second are the lords of the future. The first preserve the world and increase and multiply; the second move the world and guide it to its goal. . . ."

(from Dostoevsky, *The Brothers Karamazov*)

Q Evaluate Dostoevsky's division of humankind into two categories. Should the "lords of the future" be permitted greater liberties than the "masters of the present"?

is the hope of salvation through suffering. His landmark novels, *Crime and Punishment* and *The Brothers Karamazov*, treat matters of guilt, penitence, and the psychological consequences of moral freedom—weighty subjects that probe the human conscience. In *Crime and Punishment*, the protagonist—a young, poor student—murders an old woman and her younger sister. His crime, however, goes undetected. Struggling with guilt, he asks whether extraordinary people, by dint of their uniqueness, bear the right to commit immoral acts.

Dostoevsky, *Crime and Punishment* (1866) and *The Brothers Karamazov* (1880)

Flaubert and the Literary Heroine

The French novelist Gustave Flaubert (1821–1880) is representative of a number of nineteenth-century writers whose works examined the everyday lives of middle-class women of their time, especially as they were affected by social conventions and personal values. These literary heroines did not create the world in their own image; rather, the world—or more specifically the social and economic environment—molded them and governed their destinies.

Madame Bovary, Flaubert's landmark novel, tells the story of a woman who is afflicted by the boredom of her mundane existence. Educated in a convent and married to a dull, small-town physician, she tries to live out the fantasies that fill the pages of romance novels; but all of her efforts to escape her circumstances lead ultimately to her destruction. Flaubert, whom critics have called "the inventor of the modern novel," stripped his stories of interpretive detail and sentimentality. Aiming to describe with perfect precision both the material world and the psychological make-up of his characters, he committed himself to finding *le mot juste* ("the exact word")—a practice that often prevented him from writing more than one or two pages of prose per week.

Flaubert, *Madame Bovary* (1857)

Zola and the Naturalistic Novel

Flaubert's younger contemporary Emile Zola (1840–1902) initiated a variant form of literary Realism known as *Naturalism*. Naturalist fiction was based on the premise that life should be represented objectively and without embellishment or idealization. Naturalists differed from Realists in taking a deterministic approach that showed human beings as products of environmental or hereditary factors over which they had little or no control. Just as Marx held that economic life shaped all aspects of culture, so Naturalists believed that material and social elements determined human conduct.

In his ambition to describe the world with absolute fidelity, Zola amassed notebooks of information on a wide variety of subjects, including railroads, the stock market, and the science of surgery. He treated the novel as a carefully researched study of commonplace, material existence. He presented a slice of life that showed how social and material circumstances influenced human behavior. His subjects were as brutally uncompromising as his style. *The Grog Shop* (1877) offered a terrifying picture of the effects of alcoholism on industrial workers; *Germinal* (1855) exposed the bitter lives of French coal miners; and his most scandalous novel, *Nana*, was a scathing portrayal of a beautiful but unscrupulous prostitute.

Zola, *Nana* (1880)

Realist Drama: Ibsen

The Norwegian dramatist Henrik Ibsen (1828–1906) brought to the late nineteenth-century stage concerns similar to those in the novels of the Realists. A moralist and a student of human behavior, Ibsen rebelled against the artificial social conventions that led people to pursue self-deluding and hypocritical lives. He shocked the public by writing prose dramas that addressed such controversial subjects as insanity, incest, and venereal disease. At the same time, he explored universal themes of conflict between the individual and society, between love and duty, and between husband and wife.

Ibsen's landmark drama of female liberation, *A Doll's House*, traces the awakening of a middle-class woman to the meaninglessness of her role as "a doll-wife" living in "a doll's house." Threatened with blackmail over a debt she incurred years earlier, Nora Helmer looks to her priggish, egotistical husband Torvald for protection. When he fails to rally to her defense, Nora realizes the frailty of her dependent lifestyle. In the course of the play she comes to recognize that her first obligation is to herself and to her dignity as a human being. Her self-discovery precipitates the end of the marriage. She shuts the door on past illusions as emphatically as Ibsen may be said to have turned his back on Romantic idealism. Insisting that the playwright's responsibility is not to answer questions but to ask them, Ibsen ends the play without disclosing the outcome of Nora's decision to leave her husband and children.

Ibsen, *A Doll's House* (1879)

The unhappy dynamic of her marriage is captured in the following excerpt from the last scene in the third and last act of the play:

> **Nora**: I mean—from Father's hands I passed into yours. You arranged everything according to your tastes, and I acquired the same tastes, or I pretended to—I'm not sure which—a little of both, perhaps. Looking back on it all, it seems to me I've lived here like a beggar, from hand to mouth. I've lived by performing tricks for you, Torvald. But that's the way you wanted it. You and Father have done me a great wrong. You've prevented me from becoming a real person.
>
> **Helmer**: Nora, how can you be so ungrateful and unreasonable! Haven't you been happy here?
>
> **Nora**: No, never. I thought I was; but I wasn't really.
>
> **Helmer**: Not—not happy!
>
> **Nora**: No, only merry. You've always been so kind to me. But our home has never been anything but a play-room. I've been your doll-wife, just as at home I was Papa's doll-child. And the children, in turn, have been my dolls. I thought it fun when you played games with me, just as they thought it fun when I played games with them. And that's been our marriage, Torvald.

LATE NINETEENTH-CENTURY ARCHITECTURE

Cast-Iron Structures

In the nineteenth century, the history of architecture was revolutionized by the use of a new structural medium: cast iron. Providing strength without bulk, it allowed architects to span broader widths and raise structures to greater heights than could be achieved by traditional stone masonry. Although iron would change the history of architecture more dramatically than any advance in technology since the Roman invention of concrete, European architects were slow to realize its potential. In England, where John Nash had used cast iron in 1815 as the structural frame for the Brighton Pavilion (see Figure 12.24), engineers did not begin construction on the first cast-iron suspension bridge until 1836, and not until mid-century was iron used as skeletal support for mills, warehouses, and railroad stations.

The innovator in the use of iron for public buildings was, in fact, not an architect but a distinguished horticulturalist and greenhouse designer, Joseph Paxton (1801–1865). Paxton's Crystal Palace (Figure **13.4**), erected for the Great Exhibition of London in 1851, was the world's first prefabricated building and the forerunner of the "functional" steel and glass architecture of the twentieth century. Consisting entirely of cast- and wrought-iron girders and

Figure 13.4 Joseph Paxton, interior of Crystal Palace, 1851. Cast and wrought iron and glass, length 1851 ft. Institute for the History and Theory of Architecture, Zürich. Dismantled after the Great Exhibition and moved to a new site, Crystal Palace was hailed as a masterpiece of prefabrication and portability decades before it burned to the ground in 1930.

eighteen thousand panes of glass, and erected in only nine months, the 1851-foot-long landmark structure—its length a symbolic reference to the year of the exhibition—resembled a gigantic greenhouse. Light entered through its transparent walls and air filtered in through louvered windows. Thousands flocked to see Crystal Palace; yet most European architects found the glass and iron structure bizarre. Although heroic in both size and conception, it had almost no immediate impact on European architecture.

Like Crystal Palace, the Eiffel Tower (Figure **13.5**) began as a novelty but soon became emblematic of early Modernism (see Chapter 14). The viewing tower constructed by the engineer Gustave Eiffel (1832–1923) for the Paris World Exhibition of 1889 is, in essence, a tall (1064-foot-high) cast-iron skeleton with elevators that offer visitors magnificent aerial views of Paris. Aesthetically, the tower linked the architectural traditions of the past and future: Its sweeping curves, delicate tracery, and dramatic verticality recall the glories of the Gothic cathedral, while its majestic ironwork anticipates the austere abstractions of International-Style architecture (see page 409).

The Skyscraper

In an age of advancing industrialism, Europe's ornamental structures such as Crystal Palace

Figure 13.5 Gustave Eiffel, Eiffel Tower, Paris, 1889. Cast iron on a reinforced concrete base, original height 984 ft.

and the Eiffel Tower gave way to America's functional ones. Inevitably, the skyscraper would become the prime architectural expression of modern corporate power and the urban scene. By 1850, there were seven American cities with more than 100,000 inhabitants, and before 1900, the populations of at least three of these—New York, Philadelphia, and Chicago—swelled as a result of the thousands of immigrants who came to live and work in the metropolitan community. The physical character of the premodern city, whose buildings were no more than four stories high, changed enormously with the construction of skyscrapers.

These multistoried vertical giants were made possible by the advancing technology of steel, a medium that was perfected in 1856. Lighter, stronger, and more resilient than cast iron, steel used as a frame could carry the entire weight of a structure, thus eliminating the need for solid, weight-bearing masonry walls. By the 1880s, architects and engineers united the new steel frame with the elevator to raise structures more than ten stories high. The American architect Louis Henry Sullivan (1856–1924) designed multistory buildings such as the Guaranty Building in Buffalo (Figure **13.6**), whose exterior proudly reflects the structural simplicity of their steel frames. "Form should follow function," he argued. Within decades, the American skyscraper became an icon of modern urban culture.

Figure 13.6 Louis Henry Sullivan and Dankmar Adler, Guaranty Building, Buffalo, New York, 1894–1895. Steel made possible a whole new concept of building design characterized by lighter materials, flat roofs, and large windows.

REALISM IN THE VISUAL ARTS

The Birth of Photography

One of the most significant factors in the development of the materialist mentality was the birth of photography. While a painting or an engraving might bring to life the content of the artist's imagination, a photograph offered an authentic record of a moment vanished in time. Photography—literally, "writing with light"—had its beginnings in 1835, when William Henry Fox Talbot (1800–1877) invented the fundamental negative/positive process that allowed multiple prints to be produced from a single exposure. Talbot's French contemporary, Louis J. M. Daguerre (1787–1851), developed a different process, which used a light-sensitive metal plate and fixed the image with common chemicals. Unlike Talbot's images, Daguerre's could not be reproduced—each was unique. Nevertheless, in the next decades, his more widely publicized and technically improved product, known as a *daguerreotype*, came into vogue throughout Europe and America, where it fulfilled a growing demand for portraits. Gradual improvements in camera lenses and in the chemicals used to develop the visible image hastened the rise of photography as a medium that might record the physical world with unprecedented accuracy.

By mid-century, both Europeans and Americans were using the camera for a wide variety of purposes: They made topographical studies of exotic geographic sites, photographed the architectural monuments of the historical past, and produced thousands of portraits that offered ordinary people an affordable alternative to the painted portrait. Photography liberated artists from reproducing the physical "look" of nature. Critics proclaimed that photographs, as authentic facsimiles of the physical world, should serve artists as aids to achieving greater realism in canvas painting; and many artists did indeed use photographs as factual resources for their compositions. But it was in the genre of documentary photography that the new medium would first achieve artistic and social significance. The eyewitness photographs of the American Civil War (1861–1865) produced by Mathew B. Brady (1823–1896) and his staff testify to the importance of the documentary photographer as a chronicler of human life (Figure **13.7**). By the end of the century, the Kodak "point and shoot" handheld camera gave vast numbers of people the freedom to take their own photographic images.

Figure 13.7 Mathew B. Brady or staff, *Dead Confederate Soldier with Gun, Petersburg, Virginia*, 1865. Photograph. The Library of Congress, Washington, D.C. Brady's 3,500 Civil War photographs include mundane scenes of barracks and munitions as well as unflinching views of human carnage.

Courbet and French Realist Painting

In painting no less than in literature and photography, Realism came to challenge the Romantic style. The Realist preference for concrete, matter-of-fact depictions of everyday life provided a sober alternative to both the remote, exotic, and heroic imagery of the Romantics and the noble and elevated themes of the Neoclassicists.

The leading Realist of nineteenth-century French painting was Gustave Courbet (1819–1877). A farmer's son, he became a self-taught artist, an outspoken socialist, and a staunch defender of the Realist cause. "A painter," he protested, "should paint only what he can see." Indeed, most of Courbet's works—portraits, landscapes, and contemporary scenes—remain true to the tangible facts of his immediate vision. With the challenge "Show me an angel and I'll paint one," he taunted both the Romantics and the Neoclassicists. Not angels but ordinary individuals in their actual settings and circumstances were Courbet's subjects.

Courbet's most daring record of ordinary life was his landmark *Burial at Ornans* (Figure **13.8**). The huge canvas (over 10 x 21 feet) consists of fifty-two life-sized figures disposed around the edges of a freshly dug grave. Western representations of Christian burial traditionally emphasized the ritual aspects of death and disposal, but in this painting Courbet minimized any display of pomp and ceremony. The kneeling gravedigger and the attendant dog are as important to the picture as the priest and his retinue. With the objectivity of a camera eye, Courbet banished from his view all sentimentality and artifice.

Figure 13.8 Gustave Courbet, *Burial at Ornans*, 1849. Oil on canvas, 10 ft. 3⁵⁄₈ in. x 21 ft. 9³⁄₄ in. Musée d'Orsay, Paris. The mourners—some of Courbet's homely, hometown neighbors—play a more prominent role in the composition than the deceased, whose body is nowhere in view.

Figure 13.9 Honoré Daumier, *Nadar Raising Photography to the Heights of Art*, 1862. Lithograph. The balloonist, photographer, draftsman, and journalist Gaspard-Félix Tournachon, called Nadar, took his first photograph from a balloon.

Daumier's Social Realism

The French artist Honoré Daumier (1808–1879) left the world a detailed record of the social life of his time. He had no formal academic education, but his earliest training was in **lithography**—a printmaking process created by drawing on a stone plate. A product of nineteenth-century print technology, lithography was a cheap and popular means of providing illustrations for newspapers, magazines, and books. Daumier produced over four thousand lithographs, often turning out two to three per week for various Paris newspapers and journals. For his subject matter, he turned directly to the world around him: the streets of Paris, the theater, the law courts. The advancing (and often jarring) technology of modern life attracted Daumier's interest: pioneer experiments in aerial photography (Figure **13.9**), the telegraph, the sewing machine, the repeating rifle, the railroad, and urban renewal projects that included widening the streets of Paris. But Daumier did not simply depict the facts of modern life; he frequently ridiculed them. Skeptical as to whether new technology and social progress could radically alter the human condition, he drew attention to characteristic human weaknesses, from the hypocrisy of lawyers and the pretensions of the *nouveaux riches* to the pompous and all too familiar complacency of self-serving officials. The ancestors of modern-day political cartoons, Daumier's lithographs often depend on gesture and caricature to convey his bitter opposition to the French monarchy, political corruption, and profiteering.

Millet: "Peasant Painter"

Courbet's contemporary Jean-François Millet (1814–1875) did not share the reformer's socialist zeal; he nevertheless devoted his career to painting the everyday lives of the rural proletariat. His depictions of hard-working farm laborers earned him the title "the peasant painter." In the *Gleaners* (see Figure 13.2), three ordinary peasant women are shown in the menial task of gathering the bits of grain that are left over after the harvest. Millet delineates these stoop-laborers with ennobling simplicity. A landmark even in its own time, the painting became a symbol of the dignity of hard work, a nostalgic reference to a way of life quickly disappearing before encroaching industrialism. As such, the painting was copied, mass-reproduced, and widely sold in engraved editions.

Figure 13.10 Honoré Daumier, *The Third-Class Carriage*, ca. 1862. Oil on canvas, 25¾ x 35½ in. The Metropolitan Museum of Art, New York. Dark and loosely sketched oil glazes underscore the mood of cheerless resignation.

Figure 13.11 Edouard Manet, *Déjeuner sur l'herbe*, 1863. Oil on canvas, 7 ft. x 8 ft. 10 in. Orsay Museum, Paris. Manet defied tradition by modernizing a Classical subject—the nude in a landscape. The figures here are not woodland nymphs or Olympian gods, but his contemporaries: His favorite female model, Victorine Meurent, sits conspicuously nude alongside Manet's future brother-in-law, who reclines on the right. Manet also violated conventional practice by employing new painting techniques: Imitating current photographs and Japanese prints, he used a minimum of shading and bold lighting that tends to flatten the figures.

Primarily a graphic artist, Daumier completed fewer than three hundred paintings. In *The Third-Class Carriage*, he captured on canvas the shabby monotony of nineteenth-century lower-class railway travel (Figure **13.10**). The part of the European train in which tickets were least expensive was also, of course, the least comfortable: It lacked glass windows (hence was subject to more than average amounts of smoke, cinders, and clatter) and was equipped with hard wooden benches rather than cushioned seats. Three generations of poor folk—an elderly woman, a younger woman, and her children—occupy the foreground of Daumier's painting. Their lumpish bodies suggest weariness and futility, yet they convey a humble dignity.

The Scandalous Realism of Manet

The French painter Edouard Manet (1832–1883) presented an unsettling challenge to the world of art. A native Parisian who chose painting over a career in law, Manet admired the art of the old masters. He was equally enthralled by contemporary life: the middle-class pleasures of his fellow Parisians. In 1863, he shocked the public with a large, brilliantly painted canvas entitled *Déjeuner sur l'herbe* (*Luncheon on the Grass*). It depicted a nude woman calmly enjoying a picnic lunch with two fully clothed men, while a second, partially clothed woman bathes in a nearby stream (Figure **13.11**). Female nudity had been acceptable in European art since the early Renaissance, as long as it was cast in terms of Classical myth or allegory. However, in a contemporary setting—one that eliminated the barrier between fantasy and ordinary life—such nudity was considered indecent.

When submitted to the Paris Salon of 1863, *Déjeuner* was rejected by the jury of the Royal Academy. Nevertheless, that same year it was displayed at the Salon des Refusés ("the Salon of the Rejected Painters"), a landmark exhibition authorized by the French head of state in response to public agitation against the tyranny of the Academy. But no sooner was Manet's painting hung than visitors tried to poke holes in the canvas and critics rallied to attack its coarse "improprieties"; *Déjeuner sur l'herbe* was pronounced scandalous.

In the same year Manet offended public taste with the painting *Olympia* (see Figure 15.29). While depicting his favorite model (Victorine Meurent) in the guise of a traditional reclining Venus (see Figure 7.34), he replaced the idealized female image with that of an ordinary courtesan—a high-class prostitute. Wearing satin slippers and a black ribbon at her throat, Manet's contemporary "Venus" stares brazenly at the beholder.

Figure 13.12 Thomas Eakins, *The Agnew Clinic*, 1889. Oil on canvas, 6 ft. 2½ in. x 10 ft. 10½ in. University of Pennsylvania School of Medicine. Eakins never romanticized his subjects, and while he owed much to Rembrandt, his works communicate a fresh and stubbornly precise record of the natural world.

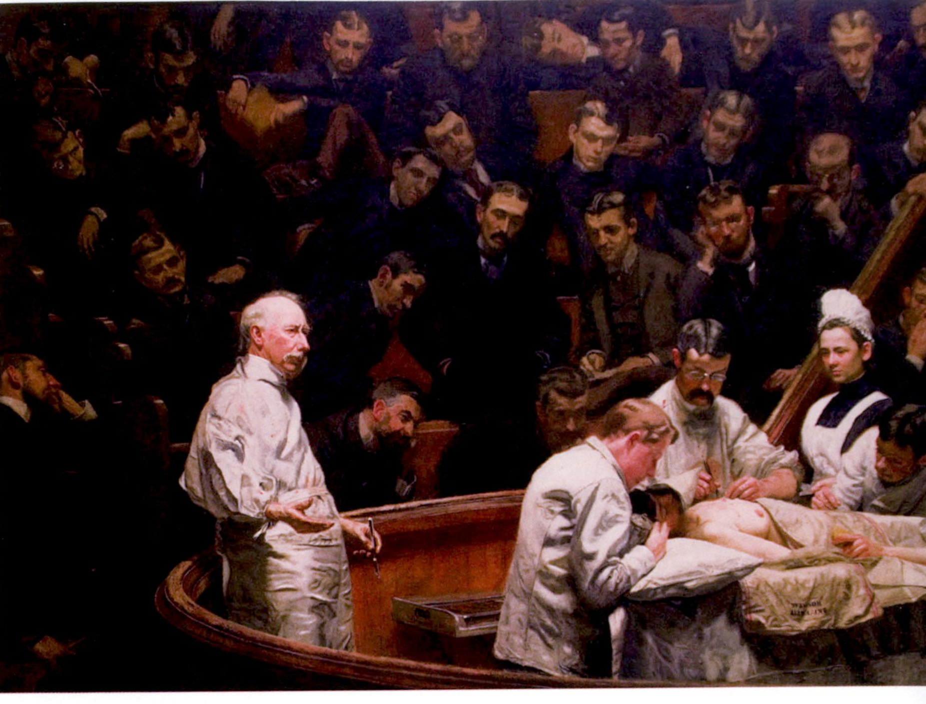

American Realists: Eakins and Homer

Although most American artists received their training in European art schools, their taste for objective reality seems to have sprung from a native affection for the material aspects of their immediate surroundings. In the late nineteenth century, an era of gross materialism known as the Gilded Age, America produced an extraordinary number of first-rate Realist painters.

The Philadepphia artist Thomas Eakins (1844–1916) spent four years of study in Europe, but he ultimately emerged as a painter of the American scene and as an influential art instructor. At the Pennsylvania Academy of Fine Arts, he received criticism for his insistence on working from nude models and was forced to resign for removing the loincloth of a male model in a class that included female students. Eakins was among the first artists to choose subjects from the world of sports, such as boxing and boating. Meanwhile his fascination with scientific anatomy—he dissected cadavers at Jefferson Medical College in Philadelphia—led him to produce some unorthodox representations of medical training and practice. Surely influenced by Rembrandt's *Anatomy Lesson of Doctor Nicolaes Tulp* (see Figure 11.2), *The Agnew Clinic* (Figure **13.12**) is a dispassionate view of a hospital amphitheater in which a doctor lectures to students on the subject of a surgical procedure. Eakins,

Figure 13.13 Winslow Homer, *The Gulf Stream*, 1899. Oil on canvas, 28⅛ in x 49⅛ in. The Metropolitan Museum of Art, New York. Compared with Géricault's more theatrical rendering of human survival in *The Raft of the "Medusa"* (see Figure 12.19), Homer's painting is a matter-of-fact study of human resignation in the face of deadly peril.

a photographer of some note, often used the camera to collect visual data for his compositions.

Nineteenth-century American Realists were also indebted to the world of journalism, which assumed increasing importance in transmitting literate culture. Winslow Homer (1836–1910) began his career as a newspaper illustrator and a reporter for the New York magazine *Harper's Weekly*. The first professional artist to serve as a war correspondent, he produced on-the-scene documentary paintings and drawings of the American Civil War, which *Harper's* converted to popular wood-engraved illustrations. Although Homer often generalized the facts of the events he actually witnessed, he never moralized on or allegorized his subjects (as did, for instance, Goya or Delacroix). His talent for graphic selectivity and dramatic concentration rivaled that of America's first war photographer, Brady (see Figure 13.7).

Apart from two trips to Europe, Homer spent most of his life in New England, where he painted subjects that were both ordinary and typically American. Scenes of hunting and fishing reveal his deep affection for nature, while his many genre paintings reflect a fascination with the activities of American women and children. Homer was interested in the role of African-Americans in contemporary culture, but he was somewhat critical of visual representations that portrayed America's slaves as merry and content. One of his most provocative paintings, *The Gulf Stream*, shows a black man adrift in a rudderless boat surrounded by shark-filled waters that are whipped by the winds of an impending tornado (Figure **13.13**). While realistic in execution, the painting may be interpreted as a romantic metaphor for the isolation and plight of black Americans in the decades following the Civil War.

IMPRESSIONISM

THE life of leisure and urban pleasures was the subject matter beloved by a group of young French painters who flourished in the 1870s and 1880s. While these artists harbored a profound attachment to their natural surroundings, they did not idealize nature, as did the Romantics. And while they rejected traditional themes from history, literature, and religion in favor of the contemporary scene—as did the Realists—they did not record reality with clinical objectivity. Rather, they invented an art of pure perception: one that intensified the immediacy of the visual experience. Their luminous canvases parallel late nineteenth-century research into the physics of light, the chemistry of paint, and the laws of optics. Treatises by French and German chemists on the properties of colors and the psychology of perception complemented the earliest appearance of synthetic pigments, which replaced traditional earth pigments with brilliant new colors. Such developments in science and technology contributed to the birth of a new art of light and color that critics would derisively call "Impressionism."

Monet: Pioneer Impressionist

In 1874 Claude Monet (1840–1926) exhibited a landmark canvas that some critics consider the first modern painting. *Impression: Sunrise* (Figure **13.14**), while patently a seascape, says more about *how* one sees than about *what* one sees. It transcribes the fleeting effects of light and the changing atmosphere of water and air into a tissue of small dots and streaks of color—the elements of pure perception.

Monet coated the raw canvas with gesso, a chalklike medium. Then, working in the open air and using the new chemical paints (available in the form of portable metallic tubes), he applied brushstrokes of pure, occasionally unmixed, color. Monet ignored the brown underglazes artists traditionally used to build up form. And, maintaining that there were no "lines" in nature, he avoided fixed contours and evoked form by means of color. Instead of blending his colors to create a finished effect, he placed them side by side, rapidly building up a radiant impasto. In order to intensify visual effect, he juxtaposed

Figure 13.14 Claude Monet, *Impression: Sunrise*, 1873. Oil on canvas, 19⅝ in x 25½ in. Marmottan Museum, Paris. In this landmark painting Monet rejected the use of browns and blacks to create shadows; instead, he applied colors complementary to the hue of the object casting the shadow, thus approximating the prismatic effects of light on the human eye.

Figure 13.15 Pierre-Auguste Renoir, *Le Moulin de la Galette*, 1876. Oil on canvas, 4 ft. 3½ in. x 5 ft. 9 in. Orsay Museum, Paris.

complementary colors, putting touches of orange (red and yellow) next to blue and adding bright tints of rose, pink, and vermilion. Monet's canvases capture the external envelope: the instantaneous visual sensations of light itself.

Monet's early subjects include street scenes, picnics, café life, and boating parties at the fashionable tourist resorts that dotted the banks of the river Seine near Paris. Following a trip to London during which he studied the works of Constable and Turner, his subjects—haystacks, poplars, and cathedral façades (obsessively recorded at different times of the day)—became increasingly formless. His late works, portraying the ponds and gardens of his personal estate in Giverny, France, are some of the most ravishing paintings in Western history.

Renoir and Degas

Impressionism was never a single, uniform style; rather, the designation (which took its name from Monet's seminal painting) embraced the individual approaches of many different artists in Europe and America. Nevertheless, the artists who met regularly in the 1870s and 1880s at the Café Guerbois in Paris had much in common. To a greater or lesser extent, their paintings reflected Monet's stylistic manner of rendering nature in short strokes of brilliant color. Above all, Impressionism brought painterly spontaneity to a celebration of the leisure activities and

Making Connections

PHOTOGRAPHS AND PAINTINGS

Degas' untiring attention to racehorses (Figure **13.16**) and ballet dancers (see Figure 13.18) expressed his lifelong fascination with matters of balance and motion. In his efforts to recreate the appearance of physical movement in space, he learned much from the British artist, photographer, and inventor Eadweard Muybridge (1830–1904), whose stop-action photographs of the 1870s and 1880s were revolutionary in their time (Figure **13.17**).

Q How would you evaluate the impact of photography on Degas and his contemporaries?

Figure 13.16 Edgar Degas, *The False Start*, ca. 1870. Oil on canvas, 12⅝ x 15¾ in. Yale University Art Gallery, New Haven, Connecticut.

Figure 13.17 Eadweard Muybridge, *Photo Sequence of Racehorse*, 1884–1885. Photograph. Library of Congress, Washington, D.C.

Figure 13.18 Edgar Degas, *Two Dancers on a Stage*, ca. 1874. Oil on canvas, $24\frac{1}{5}$ x 18 in. Courtauld Institute of Art Gallery, London. Compare the treatment of negative space in the Japanese woodblock, Figure 13.21.

diversions of urban life: dining, dancing, theater-going, boating, and socializing. In this sense, the most typical Impressionist painter might be Pierre-Auguste Renoir (1841–1919). Le Moulin de la Galette, an outdoor café and dance hall located in Montmartre (the bohemian section of nineteenth-century Paris), provided the setting for one of Renoir's most seductive tributes to youth and informal pleasure (Figure **13.15**). In the painting, elegantly dressed young men and women—artists, students, and working-class members of Parisian society—dance, drink, and flirt with one another in the flickering golden light of the late afternoon sun.

Edgar Degas (1834–1917) regularly exhibited with the Impressionists; but his style remained unique, for he never sacrificed line and form to the beguiling qualities of color and light. Whether depicting the urban world of cafés, racecourses, theaters, and shops, or the demimonde of laundresses and prostitutes, he concentrated his attention on the fleeting moment (see Figure 13.16). Degas was a consummate draftsman and a master designer. He used innovative compositional techniques that balance a sense of spontaneity and improvisation with a mood of reverie. For instance, in *Two Dancers on a Stage* he presents the subject as if seen from below and at an angle that boldly leaves "empty" the lower left half of the composition (Figure **13.18**). He also experimented with asymmetrical compositions in which figures and objects (or fragments of either) disappear off the edge of the canvas, as if the image has been caught at random. Such innovations testify to the influence of photography, with its accidental "slice of life" potential, as well as that of Japanese woodcuts, which began to enter Europe in the 1860s.

Cassatt: American Impressionist

One of the most notable of the Impressionists was the American painter Mary Cassatt (1844–1926). Cassatt was born in Philadelphia but spent most of her life in Paris, where she became a friend and colleague of Degas and Renoir, with whom she exhibited regularly. Like Degas, she painted mainly indoor scenes, cultivating a style that captured the momentary effects of light, but also integrated large areas of brilliant color and unusual perspectives—major features of the Japanese woodcuts she so admired (Figure **13.19**). Cassatt brought a unique sensitivity to domestic

Figure 13.19 Mary Cassatt, *The Bath*, 1891–1892. Oil on canvas, $39\frac{1}{2}$ x 26 in. Art Institute of Chicago. The so-called "Madonna of American art" preferred life in Paris to that in prefeminist America. "Women do not have to fight for recognition here if they do serious work," wrote Cassatt.

themes that featured mothers and children sharing everyday tasks and diversions. These gentle and optimistic paintings, which secularized the age-old subject of the mother and child, appealed to American collectors and did much to increase the popularity of Impressionist art in the United States.

Toulouse-Lautrec

The charm and gentility of Cassatt's canvases were not to the taste of Henri de Toulouse-Lautrec (1864–1901). The descendant of a wealthy aristocratic French family, Toulouse-Lautrec suffered two childhood falls that left the bones in his legs atrophied and his frame stunted. As an adult, he shunned high society for the pleasures of dance halls and brothels, where he depicted subjects so intimate that members of his own family condemned his work as unacceptable to "well-bred people." Like the novels of Zola, his paintings and drawings show the seamy side of Parisian life, a life of cabaret dancers and prostitutes. Integrating the calligraphic rhythms of *Art Nouveau* and the boldly colored, flat shapes of Japanese prints, Toulouse-Lautrec pioneered the art of modern poster design (Figure **13.20**). Alcoholism and syphilis took their toll: Toulouse-Lautrec died at the age of thirty-six.

Making Connections

JAPANESE PRINTS AND EUROPEAN PAINTINGS

When Japanese woodblock engravings arrived in the West in the mid-nineteenth century, they had an immediate impact on fine and commercial art. Their flat, unmodulated colors, calligraphic lines, daring use of **negative space**, and unusual vantage points were hallmarks of an artistic tradition that was at least four centuries old (Figure **13.21**; see also Figures 5.12, 10.30, and 12.13). In the seventeenth century, the Japanese had produced prints (made from inked blocks of wood) as substitutes for costly hand-decorated illustrations in religious and secular texts. During the eighteenth century there developed a wide market for single-leaf prints, depicting scenes from everyday life: famous male actors of the *kabuki* theater, courtesans, and other fashionable personalities. For Europeans, Japanese prints were new and inspiring, not only in their style (which suggested a way of reconciling the illusion of the three-dimensional world with the flatness of the two-dimensional canvas), but in the casual urban subject matter—much of which featured women. Monet, Degas, Cassatt, and their contemporaries collected Japanese prints. Their influence is evident in European painting, poster design (see Figure 13.20), and the decorative arts of the late nineteenth century.

Q What specific features attest to the influence of the Japanese woodcut on the style of Toulouse-Lautrec?

Figure 13.20 (left)
Henri de Toulouse-Lautrec, *Jane Avril*, 1899. Lithograph, printed in color, 22 x 14 in. The Museum of Modern Art, New York. Posters like this advertised the nightclub singers and can-can dancers of the popular Parisian café known as the Moulin Rouge ("Red Mill").

Figure 13.21 (right)
Torii Kiyonobu, *Actor as a Monkey Showman*. Woodblock print, 13¼ x 6¼ in. The Metropolitan Museum of Art, New York.

POSTIMPRESSIONISM

THE art that followed the last of the Impressionist group shows in 1886 is generally designated as "Postimpressionist." While indebted to Impressionism, the Postimpressionists gave greater emphasis to expressive color and compositional structure. They concentrated on the formal language of art, over and above its capacity to capture a fleeting, momentary impression. At the same time, there emerged a popular ornamental style known as *Art Nouveau* ("new art"). The decorative thrust of *Art Nouveau*, the influence of Japanese prints, and a concern with the value of art for art's sake motivated the Postimpressionists to move in bold new directions that anticipated twentieth-century Modernism.

Art Nouveau

Art Nouveau originated in Belgium among architects working in the medium of cast iron, but it quickly assumed an international reach that influenced painting, as well as the design of furniture, textiles, glass, ceramics, and jewelry. This seductive style shared the spirit of European movements to restore the fine artisanship of preindustrial periods, such as the Middle Ages—an era that was thought to have achieved an ideal synthesis of the functional and the decorative in the arts.

"Art in nature, nature in art" was the motto of *Art Nouveau*. The sinuous curves of blossoms, leaves, and tendrils, executed in iron and immortalized in such notable monuments as the Paris Métro (the subway), also showed up in the United States, most gloriously in the elegant glass designs of Louis Comfort Tiffany (Figure **13.22**). The son of Charles L. Tiffany, founder of the famed New York jewelry house, Louis was a great admirer of Chinese *cloisonnés* and ancient glass techniques. His inventive art glass, which featured floral arabesques and graceful geometric patterns, made him one of the masters of the international *Art Nouveau* style.

Van Gogh and Gauguin

The Dutch artist Vincent van Gogh (1853–1890) was a passionate idealist whose life was marred by loneliness, poverty, depression, and a hereditary mental illness that ultimately drove him to suicide. He produced over seven hundred paintings and thousands of drawings, of which he sold less than a half-dozen in his lifetime. Van Gogh painted landscapes, still lifes, and portraits in a style that featured flat, bright colors, a throbbing, sinuous line, and short, choppy brushstrokes. He often manipulated his heavily pigmented surfaces with a palette knife or built them up by applying paint directly from the tube. His emotional response to an object, rather than its physical appearance, often determined his choice of colors, which he likened to orchestral sound. As he explained to his brother Theo, "I use color more arbitrarily so as to express myself more forcefully." Van Gogh's landmark painting *The Starry Night* (Figure **13.23**), a view of the small French town of Saint-Rémy, is electrified by thickly painted strokes of white, yellow, orange, and blue. Cypresses writhe like flames, stars explode, the moon seems to burn like the sun, and the heavens heave and roll like ocean waves. Here, van Gogh's expressive use of color invests nature with visionary frenzy.

In the fall of 1888, van Gogh's colleague and friend Paul Gauguin (1848–1903) joined him at Arles in southeastern France, and for a brief time the two artists lived and worked side by side. Volatile and temperamental, they often engaged in violent quarrels, during one of which part of van Gogh's ear was cut off, either by van Gogh himself, or (as some historians claim) by Gauguin. Despite their intense personal differences, the two artists were fraternal pioneers in the search for a provocative language of form and color.

If van Gogh may be said to have apprehended an inner vision of nature, Gauguin tried to recast nature in its unblemished state. Abandoning his wife, his children, and his job as a Paris stockbroker, this prototype of the modern bohemian traveled to Martinique in the West Indies, to Brittany in northwest France, and to southern France before finally settling on the island of Tahiti in the South Seas. Gauguin, in his self-conscious effort to assume the role of "the civilized savage," shared the fascination with unspoiled nature that characterized the writings of Rousseau and Thoreau.

In Gauguin's *Day of the God*, nine honey-colored figures occupy the shores of a tropical island (Figure **13.24**). Flat, bright-colored shapes—blue, yellow, and pink—form rhythmic, tapestrylike patterns recalling the style of Japanese prints and *Art Nouveau* posters. A mood of ineffable serenity prevails. The organic reflections in the foreground pool of water and the fetal positions of the figures on the shore suggest birth and regeneration—motifs echoed by the totemic deity pictured at the top center of the canvas.

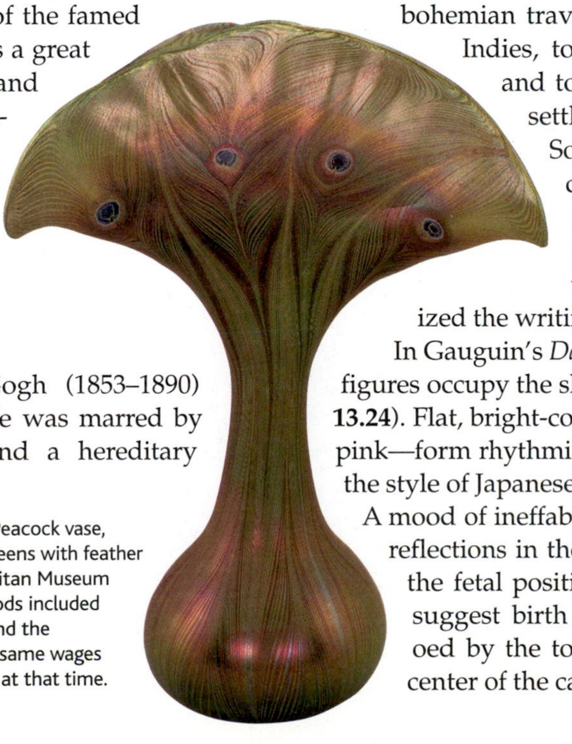

Figure 13.22 Tiffany Glass and Decorating Co., Peacock vase, 1892–1902. Iridescent "favrile" glass, blues and greens with feather and eye decorations, height 14⅛ in. The Metropolitan Museum of Art, New York. Tiffany's innovative studio methods included assembly-line production, the use of templates, and the employment of female artisans who received the same wages as males—a policy that caused great controversy at that time.

Figure 13.23 (above) Vincent van Gogh, *The Starry Night*, 1889. Oil on canvas, 29 x $36\frac{1}{4}$ in. The Museum of Modern Art, New York. In letters to his brother Theo (an art dealer by profession), van Gogh pledged his undying faith in the power of artistic creativity. In 1888, just two years before he committed suicide, he wrote: "I can do without God both in my life and in my painting, but I cannot [do without] the power to create. And if, defrauded of the power to create physically, a man tries to create thoughts in place of children, he is still part of humanity."

Figure 13.24 Paul Gauguin, *The Day of the God* (*Mahana no Atua*), 1894. Oil on canvas, $27\frac{3}{8}$ x $35\frac{5}{8}$ in. Art Institute of Chicago. Gauguin described his paintings as "arrangements of lines and colors" that "express no idea directly, but . . . make you think as music does."

THE LURE OF THE EXOTIC: OCEANIA

THE World's Fair (*Exposition Universelle*) of 1889, which was held in Paris, contributed to the Western infatuation with foreign cultures by bringing to public view the arts of Asia, Africa, and Oceania. Reconstructions of villages from the Congo and Senegal, Japan and China, Polynesia and other South Sea islands (see Map 13.1), offered most Europeans their first glimpse into the world beyond the West. Non-Western societies and their artistic achievements quickly became objects of research for the new disciplines of anthropology (the science of humankind and its culture) and ethnography (the branch of anthropology that studies preliterate peoples). For nonscholars and artists like Gauguin these exotic societies held a different kind of fascination: Their way of life suggested the innocence of preindustrial societies, and their arts—usually self-taught—reflected an authenticity of spirit that was lacking in European academicism.

Oceania (the islands of the South and Central Pacific Ocean) was both preindustrial and preliterate. Social organization was tribal, economies agricultural, and gods and spirits closely associated with nature. Reverence for deceased ancestors and for the gods was expressed through rituals involving power-objects, such as masks and spirit poles. While productivity varied from island to island, Oceania generated some of its most significant artwork during the nineteenth century. Among the Maori peoples of New Zealand, for example, the art of woodcarving flourished (Figure **13.25**). Teams of woodcarvers using European tools created elaborate wooden meetinghouses ornamented with fierce totemic images. Such wooden totems—popular throughout the South Pacific—appear in the paintings of Gauguin (see Figure 13.24) and in prints and sculpture that he produced during his stay in Tahiti. Tragically, as the cultures of Oceania came to be influenced by Western materialism and commercial exploitation, their brilliance and originality began to wane. At their finest, Maori structures were embellished with elaborate patterns of spirals and scrolls similar to those used in the decorative body art of the tattoo (from the Polynesian *tatau*).

Especially popular among the Marquesas Islanders in the South Pacific, tattooing—considered a sacred art—was performed by a specialist using a bone comb with sharp teeth. The tattoo itself, which might symbolize the specific rank and power of the wearer, served a protective function (as a kind of visual armor), but its cultural significance is open to many interpretations. Expensive and painful, all-over body tattoos were usually worn by the wealthiest and most powerful individuals in the community (Figure **13.26**).

Figure 13.25 (left) *Poupou* in the style of the Te Arawa, from New Zealand. Wood. The *poupou* is the side post in the wall of the Maori meetinghouse.

Figure 13.26 (right) *Nuku Hiva islanders with various tattoos*, 1813. Hand-colored copperplate engraving after original drawings by Wilhelm Gottlieb von Tilenau, from Carl Bertuch, *Bilderbuch für Kinder*, vol. 8, Weimar (Landes-Industrie-Comptoir) 1813, no. 2. Nuku Hiva is the largest of the Marquesas islands in French Polynesia.

Gauguin's flight to the South Seas typified the obsession with non-Western cultures that swept through the intellectual community of late nineteenth-century Europe. Intrigued by the simplicity of the native populations he encountered in what he called "the unknown paradise of Oceania," Gauguin recorded his impressions of Tahiti in his romanticized journal *Noa Noa* (*Fragrance*, 1897), where he also registered criticism of Western colonialism and foreign intrusion into non-Western societies:

> The European invasion and monotheism have destroyed the vestiges of a civilization which had its own grandeur. . . . [The Tahitians] had been richly endowed with an instinctive feeling for the harmony necessary between human creations and the animal and plant life that formed the setting and decoration of their existence, but this has now been lost. In contact with us, with our school, they have truly become "savages." . . . They themselves have remained beautiful as masterpieces, but morally and physically (owing to us) they have become unfruitful.

Seurat

Rejecting the formlessness of Impressionism, the French painter Georges Seurat (1859–1891) introduced a novel combination of pictorial construction and unorthodox technique. This academically trained Postimpressionist brought a degree of formal balance and order to compositions that rivaled those of Poussin (see Figure 10.24) and David (see Figure 11.26). The doll-like figures in Seurat's monumental canvas *Sunday Afternoon on the Island of La Grande Jatte* seem plotted along an invisible grid of vertical and horizontal lines that run parallel to the picture plane (Figure **13.27**). Strolling, lounging, or fishing, they enjoy their holiday leisure in a sun-filled island park on the outskirts of urban Paris. Each figure—even the animals, which include a popular pet of the time, the ring-tailed monkey—assumes a preordained place, isolated from the next figure as if it were frozen in time and space.

Influenced by the pioneer color theorists of his time, Seurat placed tiny dots of paint side by side (and sometimes one inside another) to intensify color and give the impression of solid form (see Figure 13.1 and page 355). This style, known as *pointillism,* called for the division of colors into their component parts. The Pointillist applied each color dot so that its juxtaposition with a nearby color would produce the desired degree of vibration to the eye. Seurat made his initial sketches outdoors, but he executed *La Grande Jatte* inside his studio, usually at night, under artificial light. More than twenty preparatory drawings and two hundred oil studies preceded the completion of *La Grande Jatte,* which, unlike the canvases of the Impressionists, left nothing to chance. Seurat died of diphtheria at the age of thirty-two, having completed barely a decade of mature work.

Figure 13.27 Georges Seurat, *Sunday Afternoon on the Island of La Grande Jatte*, 1884–1886. Oil on canvas, 6 ft. 9½ in. x 10 ft. ⅛ in. Art Institute of Chicago. Seurat's universe, with its atomized particles of color and its self-contained figures, may seem devoid of human feeling, but its exquisite regularity provides a comforting alternative to the chaos of experience.

Cézanne

Paul Cézanne (1839–1906) served as a bridge between the art of the nineteenth century and that of the twentieth. Cézanne began his career as an Impressionist in Paris, but his traditional subjects—landscapes, portraits, and still lifes—show a greater concern for the formal elements of a painting (such as line, shape, and color) than for its subject matter. Cézanne's determination to invest his pictures with a strong sense of three-dimensionality (a feature often neglected by the Impressionists) led to a method of building up form by means of small, flat planes of color. At the same time, his desire to achieve pictorial unity inspired him to take bold liberties with form and perspective. He might, for instance, tilt and flatten familiar objects; reduce them to basic geometric shapes; or depict them from different points of view. Cézanne's still lifes are not so much tempting likenesses of apples, peaches, or pears as they are architectural arrangements of colored forms (Figure **13.28**).

Cézanne's mature style developed when he left Paris and returned to his native area of southern France. Here he tirelessly painted the local landscape: Dozens of times he portrayed the stony peak of Mont Sainte-Victoire near his hometown of Aix-en-Provence. Among his last versions of the subject is a landscape in which trees and houses have become an abstract network of colored facets of paint (Figure **13.29**). All parts of the composition, like the flat shapes of a Japanese print, are equal in value. Cézanne's methods, which transformed an ordinary mountain into an icon of stability and a landmark in the visual arts, led the way to Modernist abstraction (see Chapter 14).

Figure 13.28 (above) Paul Cézanne, *The Basket of Apples*, ca. 1895. Oil on canvas, 25¾ x 32 in. Art Institute of Chicago. Cézanne's effort to "redo nature after Poussin," that is, to find the enduring forms of nature that were basic to all great art, made him the first Modernist artist.

Figure 13.29 (below) Paul Cézanne, *Mont Sainte-Victoire*, 1902–1904. Oil on canvas, 27½ x 35¼ in. Philadelphia Museum of Art. By applying colors of the same intensity to different parts of the canvas—note the bright green and rich violet brushstrokes in both sky and landscape—Cézanne challenged traditional distinctions between foreground and background.

LATE NINETEENTH-CENTURY SCULPTURE

THE leading sculptor of the late nineteenth century, Auguste Rodin (1840–1917) was a master at capturing the physical vitality of the human figure. One of his earliest works, *The Age of Bronze* (see Figure 13.31), was so lifelike that critics accused him of forging the figure from plaster casts of a live model. But Rodin augmented Realism with an unparalleled sense of organic movement and nervous energy. Modeling form rapidly in clay, he recreated the shifting effects of light and dark. His figures achieved a degree of emotional intensity absent from the Classical and Renaissance sculptures he so admired. "The sculpture of antiquity," he professed, "sought the logic of the human body; I seek its psychology."

Rodin's landmark work, *The Gates of Hell*, was a set of monumental bronze doors commissioned in 1880 for a new Paris museum. Based on the theme of Dante's *Inferno* and modeled on Ghiberti's "Gates of Paradise" (see Figure 7.18), the doors became the framework for dozens of Rodin's most imaginatively conceived images. While the commission was never completed, such individual figures as *The Kiss* and *The Thinker* (Figure **13.30**) were recast individually in both bronze and marble to become landmarks in their own right. In the rugged body language of *The Thinker*, Rodin captured the drama of intense introspection.

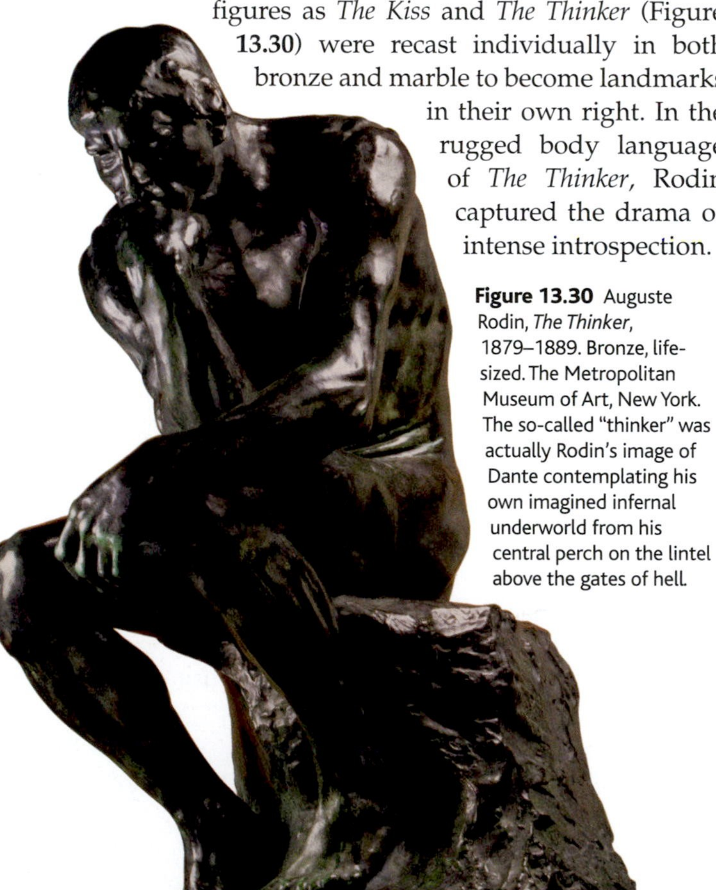

Figure 13.30 Auguste Rodin, *The Thinker*, 1879–1889. Bronze, life-sized. The Metropolitan Museum of Art, New York. The so-called "thinker" was actually Rodin's image of Dante contemplating his own imagined infernal underworld from his central perch on the lintel above the gates of hell.

Making Connections

SCULPTURE AND DANCE

Rodin was keenly interested in movement and gesture (Figure **13.31**). His drawings record the dancelike rhythms of studio models whom he directed to move about freely rather than assume traditional, fixed poses.

Rodin's close friend, the American choreographer Isadora Duncan (1878–1927), shared his desire to find a language of physical form that conveyed specific moods and mental dispositions. Duncan, who broke away from classical ballet by performing barefoot, introduced a new style of dance characterized by free form, personalized gesture, and expressive emotion (Figure **13.32**). "I have discovered the art that has been lost for two thousand years," claimed Duncan.

Q In what ways might the Duncan's new dance style have influenced Rodin's treatment of form?

Figure 13.31 Auguste Rodin, *The Age of Bronze*, 1876. Bronze, 25½ x 9⁵⁄₁₆ x 7½ in. Detroit Institute of Arts.

Figure 13.32 Isadora Duncan, photograph, ca. 1910.

LATE NINETEENTH-CENTURY MUSIC

Verismo Opera: Puccini and Bizet

In Italian opera of the late nineteenth century, a movement called *verismo* (literally, "truthism," but more generally "realism" or "naturalism") paralleled the emphasis on objectivity in literature and art. Realist composers rejected the heroic characters of Romantic grand opera and presented the problems and conflicts of people in familiar and everyday—if somewhat melodramatic—situations. The foremost "verist" in music was the Italian composer Giacomo Puccini (1858–1924). Puccini's *La Bohème*, the tragic love story of young artists (called "bohemians" for their unconventional lifestyles) in the Latin Quarter of Paris, was based on a nineteenth-century novel called *Scenes of Bohemian Life*. The colorful orchestration and powerfully melodic arias of *La Bohème* evoke the joys and sorrows of true-to-life characters. While this poignant musical drama was received coldly at its premiere in 1897, it has become one of the best loved of nineteenth-century operas.

Puccini, *La Bohème* (1897); *Madame Butterfly* (1904)

Another of Puccini's operas, *Madame Butterfly*, offered European audiences a timely view of the Western presence in Asia, one that personalized the clash of two radically different cultures. The story, based on an actual incident, takes place in Nagasaki in the years following the reopening of Japanese ports to the West (see page 356). It begins with the wedding of a young United States navy lieutenant to a fifteen-year-old *geisha* (a Japanese girl trained as a social companion to men) nicknamed "Butterfly." The American is soon forced to leave with his fleet, while Butterfly, now the mother of his three-year-old son, faithfully awaits his return. When he finally arrives, accompanied by his new American bride to claim his son, the grief-stricken Butterfly takes the only honorable path available to her: she commits suicide. Set to some of Puccini's most lyrical music, *Madame Butterfly* reflects Puccini's fascination with Japanese culture. While neither the story nor the music is authentically Japanese, its *verismo* lies in its frank (though poignant) account of the tragic consequences that befell the meeting of East and West in an age of materialism.

France also produced a landmark *verismo* opera, one that remains a favorite in the standard repertory to this day. *Carmen* (1875), composed by Georges Bizet (1838–1875) and based on a popular story by Prosper Mérimée, tells a tale of seduction, rejection, and fatal revenge set in exotic Seville. Carmen, a shameless flirt who works in a Spanish cigarette factory, lures an enamored soldier into deserting the army in order to follow her. Soon tiring of him, she abandons him in favor of a celebrity toreador, only to meet her end at the hand of her former lover. Like Zola and Puccini, Bizet drew on contemporary life, ordinary people, and violent human emotions. In contrast with the sheltered females of Romantic fare, Bizet's Carmen, a common factory worker (who brazenly smokes in public), became the late nineteenth-century symbol of faithless and dangerous womanhood.

Musical Impressionism: Debussy

Puccini's French contemporary Claude Debussy (1862–1918) moved music in a very different direction. "I would like to see the creation . . . of a kind of music without themes and motives," he wrote. Debussy admired the Romantic composers for the way they had abandoned the formal clarity of classical composition. Fascinated by the exotic music of Bali (in Indonesia), which he had heard at the World's Fair in 1889, he experimented with a five-tone scale from East Asia and with nontraditional harmonies. Debussy found his greatest inspiration, however, in contemporary Symbolist poetry and in Impressionist painting. The Symbolists, led by the French poet Stéphane Mallarmé (1842–1898), held that the visible world did not constitute a universal reality. They rejected objective forms of representation in favor of subjective images drawn from sensory experience, dreams, and myth. By means of powerful but often ambiguous images, they aimed to *suggest* rather than *describe* the ideal world of experience.

Debussy was a close friend of many of the Symbolist poets, a number of whose texts he set to music. His first orchestral composition, *Prelude to "The Afternoon of a Faun"* was (in his words) a "very free illustration of Mallarmé's beautiful poem," which had been published eighteen years earlier. The ten-minute piece is scored for a small orchestra whose predominantly wind and brass instruments recreate the mood of reverie evoked by the poem itself. A sensuous melody for unaccompanied flute provides the opening theme, which is then developed by oboes and clarinets. Harp, triangle, muted horns, and lightly brushed cymbals contribute to the creation of luminous tonal textures. Transitions are subtle, and melodies seem to drift without resolution. Shifting harmonies with no clearly defined tonal center engulf the listener in a nebulous flood of sound. Debussy's *Prelude*, which shares the dreamlike quality of Symbolist poetry and the elusive effects of Impressionist painting, became the music for the landmark Russian ballet *Afternoon of a Faun* (1912).

Debussy, *Prelude to "The Afternoon of a Faun"* (1894)

Choreographed and performed in Paris by the brilliant Russian dancer, Vaslav Nijinsky (1888–1950), the twelve-minute ballet enacted Mallarmé's sensuous evocation of a mythic faun's efforts to seduce a group of woodland nymphs. Dancing the role of the faun (Figure **13.33**), Nijinsky outraged critics by violating the formal principles of classical dance and by performing part of the work bare-footed. The ballet was attacked for its "vile movements of erotic bestiality and gestures of extreme shamelessness." A year later, Nijinksy would go on to startle audiences with his original choreography for Stravinsky's infamous *Rite of Spring* (see pages 413–414).

Figure 13.33 Vaslav Nijinsky, *Afternoon of a Faun*, 1912. The photograph documents Nijinsky's effort to capture the "look" of ancient Greek vase painting (see Figure 2.35). Although Nijinsky performed professionally for only ten years, his revolutionary choreography ushered in modern dance.

Afterword

The age of materialism, fueled by advancing industrialism and imperialism, witnessed the rise of the West to world dominance. Within Europe, nations jostled for global ascendancy, building their military and commercial bases to further their ambitions. While reformers offered utopian solutions to the social and economic consequences of Western industrialism, artists, writers, and composers left landmarks that document the realities of their time: the burdens of the laboring class, as well as the pleasures of urban life. The new technologies of photography, lithography, synthetic pigments, and cast-iron and steel construction altered the cultural landscape. Even as the spirit of heroic materialism dominated the West, an appreciation of the world beyond the West—Japan, Africa, and Oceania—inspired an exotic turn in the arts. Toward the end of the nineteenth century, Nietzsche detected in European culture "a chaos [and] an instinct of weariness"; nevertheless, the rampant materialism of the West would usher in a dynamic (and destructive) new era: the twentieth century.

Key Topics

- Western industrialism
- colonialism/imperialism
- socialism/capitalism
- literary Realism
- the Naturalistic novel
- Realist drama
- cast-iron construction
- the skyscraper
- photography
- lithography
- Realism in the visual arts
- Impressionism
- Japanese prints
- Postimpressionism
- sculpture and dance
- *verismo* opera
- Impressionism in music
- the lure of the exotic

MATERIALISM TIMELINE

	HISTORICAL EVENTS	LANDMARKS IN THE VISUAL ARTS	LITERARY LANDMARKS	MUSIC AND DANCE LANDMARKS
1800	• British build first steam railway locomotive (1804) • Birth of photography (1835)	• Courbet, *Burial at Ornans* (1849)	• Marx and Engels, *Communist Manifesto* (1848)	
1850	• America forces Japan to trade with West (1853) • Bessemer produces inexpensive steel (1856) • British rule begins in India (1858) • Meiji rule in Japan (1858–1912)	• Paxton, Crystal Palace (1851) • Millet, *Gleaners* (1857)	• Dickens, *David Copperfield* (1850) • Flaubert, *Madame Bovary* (1857)	
1860	• American Civil War (1861–1865)	• Daumier, *The Third-Class Carriage* (ca. 1862) • Manet, *Déjeuner sur l'herbe* (1863), *Olympia* (1863)	• Dostoevsky, *Crime and Punishment* (1866); *The Brothers Karamazov* (1880) • Tolstoy, *War and Peace* (1869)	
1870	• Maxwell: *Treatise on Electricity and Magnetism* (1873) • Edison creates first efficient incandescent light bulb (1879)	• Monet, *Impression: Sunrise* (1873) • Rodin, *The Thinker* (1879–1889); *The Gates of Hell* (1880–1900)	• Ibsen, *A Doll's House* (1879)	• Bizet, *Carmen* (1875)
1880	• World's Fair held in Paris (1889)	• Seurat, *La Grande Jatte* (1884–1886) • Eakins, *The Agnew Clinic* (1889) • Eiffel, Eiffel Tower, Paris (1889) • van Gogh, *The Starry Night* (1889)	• Zola, *Nana* (1880) • Nietzsche, *Thus Spoke Zarathustra* (1883–1892) • Twain, *Huckleberry Finn* (1884)	
1890	• Röntgen discovers x-rays (1898)	• Degas, *Before the Ballet* (1890–1892) • Gauguin, *The Day of the God* (1894) • Sullivan and Adler, Guaranty Building, Buffalo (1894–1895) • Homer, *The Gulf Stream* (1899)		• Debussy, *Prelude to "The Afternoon of a Faun"* (1894) • Puccini, *La Bohème* (1897)
1900		• Cézanne, *Mont Sainte-Victoire* (1902–1904)		• Puccini, *Madame Butterfly* (1904) • Nijinsky lays foundations for modern dance in *Afternoon of a Faun* (1912)

Figure 13.14
Claude Monet, *Impression: Sunrise*, see p. 369

Figure 13.5
Gustave Eiffel, Eiffel Tower, Paris, see p. 363

Figure 13.30
Auguste Rodin, *The Thinker*, see p. 378

Chapter 14

Modernism:

THE ASSAULT ON TRADITION

ca. 1890–1950

No age has broken with tradition more radically or more self-consciously than the twentieth century, which, in its opening decades, produced the movement that came to be called "Modernism." Modernists willfully rejected conventional values in favor of experimentation, innovation, and—at the most extreme—anarchy and nihilism (the view that all values are baseless). The Modernist revolution was fed by dramatic advances in science and technology, by the impact of two devastating world wars, and by the atrocities of totalitarian regimes. As the fabric of traditional moral and religious values unraveled in the West, older styles—Neoclassicism, Romanticism, and Realism—gave way to the complexities of Cubism, Expressionism, Surrealism, and Nonobjective (nonrepresentational) art. Abstraction—the reduction of recognizable form to its essence—became a hallmark of Modernism. In the visual arts, the formal elements of painting—line, color, shape—often took the place of traditional subject matter. In literature, ambiguity, absurdity, and forays into the workings of the unconscious mind challenged descriptive narrative. Modern composers abandoned conventional melody and harmony; both music and dance shocked audiences with exotic, erotic, and unprecedented candor. The unbridled will to "make it new" lay at the heart of the Modernist turn.

A First Look

The painting shown here is a landmark of Modernism. It illustrates one of the radical developments in twentieth-century art: the disappearance of recognizable subject matter. In a nonrepresentational painting, the formal elements of two-dimensional art, such as line, shape, and color, constitute the subject; the artwork's effect on the beholder rests solely with the arrangement of its formal components. The way in which Wassily Kandinsky (1866–1944), a pioneer of abstract art, arrived at this Modernist style is worth recounting. Kandinsky turned from law to art at the age of thirty. His early paintings were filled with colorful images of his native Russia: horses and riders, churches, and village festivals. One evening, upon returning to his dimly lit studio in Munich, Germany, he saw (as he wrote in his *Reminiscences* of 1913) "an indescribably beautiful picture drenched with an inner glowing." The content of the picture was incomprehensible, but its forms and colors were magnificent. Suddenly, he realized that it was a picture he himself had painted and left leaning against the wall, *standing on its side.* Recording this revelation, he concluded: "Now I knew for certain that the [pictorial] object harmed my paintings." Kandinsky went on to assemble colors, lines, and shapes without regard for recognizable objects, calling his paintings "improvisations" or "compositions." The power of color in and of itself became the subject of the treatise *On the Spiritual in Art* (see page 399), in which he defended the idea that painting was a spiritually liberating force akin to music.

Figure 14.1 Wassily Kandinsky, *Panel for Edwin Campbell, No. 2*, 1914 (detail). Oil on canvas, 5 ft. 4 1/8 in. x 4 ft. 3/8 in. The Museum of Modern Art, New York. Kandinsky usually called his Nonobjective paintings "improvisations" or "abstract compositions" and numbered them in series.

NEW DIRECTIONS

The New Physics

At the outset of the twentieth century, modern physics advanced a model of the universe that challenged the one Isaac Newton had provided two centuries earlier (see page 297). Newton's universe operated according to smoothly functioning mechanical laws that corresponded generally with the world of sense perception. Modern physicists proposed, however, that at the physical extremities of nature—in the microcosmic realm of atomic particles and in the macrocosmic world of outer space—Newton's laws did not apply.

A more comprehensive model of the universe began to emerge after 1880, when two American physicists, Albert Michelson and Edward Morley, determined that the speed of light is a universal constant. By 1900, the German physicist Max Planck (1858–1947) theorized that light waves behave as separate and discontinuous bundles of energy, or *quanta*. Alongside these and other groundbreaking discoveries in quantum physics (as the field came to be called), the great German physicist Albert Einstein (1879–1955) made public his *special theory of relativity* (1905), a radically new approach to the concepts of time, space, and motion. While Newton had held that an object preserved the same properties whether at rest or in motion, Einstein theorized that as an object approached the speed of light, its mass increased and its motion slowed. Time and space, argued Einstein, were not separate coordinates but, rather, complementary and interrelated entities.

Building on Einstein's theories, Werner Heisenberg (1901–1976) observed that since the very act of measuring subatomic phenomena altered them, the position and velocity of subatomic particles could not be measured simultaneously with absolute accuracy. Heisenberg's *principle of uncertainty* (1927)—the more precisely the position of a particle is determined, the less precisely its momentum can be known—replaced the absolute model of the universe with one based in indeterminacy.

Quantum physics gave humankind greater insight into the workings of the universe, but it made the operation of that universe more remote from the average person's understanding. The basic components of nature (subatomic particles) are inaccessible to both the human eye and the camera; they lie beyond the realm of the senses. Nevertheless, the practical and theoretical implications of the new physics were immense. Jet propulsion, radar technology, and computer electronics were but three of its long-range consequences. Atomic fission, the splitting of the atom (begun only after 1920), and the atomic bomb (first tested in 1945) confirmed the validity of Einstein's famous formula, $E = mc^2$, which describes mass and energy as different manifestations of the same thing, that is (in his words), "a very small amount of mass (matter) can be converted into a very large amount of energy." The new physics radically altered the way in which Modernists would come to view the physical world. It also paved the way for the atomic age, an era that carried with it the possibility of total annihilation.

The Freudian Revolution

While Einstein revised the established scientific perceptions of the external world, the Austrian physician Sigmund Freud (1856–1939) challenged traditional perceptions of the internal world: the human mind. Freud's work with severely disturbed patients, followed by a period of intensive self-analysis, led him to develop a systematic procedure for treating emotional illness. Pioneering the tools of dream analysis and "free association" (the spontaneous verbalization of thoughts), he founded *psychoanalysis*, a therapeutic method by which repressed desires are brought to the conscious level to reveal the sources of emotional disturbance.

Freud was the first to map the geography of the human mind. He proposed a theoretical model that became basic to *psychology* (the study of mind and behavior) and fundamental to our everyday vocabulary. This model pictures the psyche as consisting of three parts: the *id*, the seat of human instincts and the source of all physical desires; the *ego*, the manager that functions to adapt the needs of the id to the real world; and the *superego*, the moral monitor

Ideas and Issues

RELIGION AS MASS-DELUSION

"A special importance attaches to the case in which this attempt to procure a certainty of happiness and a protection against suffering through a delusional remolding of reality is made by a considerable number of people in common. The religions of mankind must be classed among the mass-delusions of this kind. No one, needless to say, who shares a delusion ever recognizes it as such. . . .

Religion restricts this play of choice and adaptation, since it imposes equally on everyone its own path to the acquisition of happiness and protection from suffering. Its technique consists in depressing the value of life and distorting the picture of the real world in a delusional manner—which presupposes an intimidation of the intelligence. At this price, by forcibly fixing them in a state of psychical infantilism and by drawing them into a mass-delusion, religion succeeds in sparing many people an individual neurosis. But hardly anything more. . . ."

(from Freud, "Civilization and Its Discontents," 1930)

Q Assess Freud's claim that religion is a form of mass-delusion.

or "conscience" that operates according to principles inculcated by parents, teachers, and social authorities. According to Freud, instinctual (id) drives—in particular the *libido*, or sex drive—govern human behavior. Guilt from repression of instinctual urges dominates the unconscious life of human beings and manifests itself in emotional illness.

In Freud's view, civilization is the product of the ego's effort to direct the primal urges of the id. Whether by dreams or by *sublimation* (the positive modification and redirection of primal urges), the ego mediates between potentially destructive desires and social necessities. In his lectures at the University of Vienna, Freud examined the psychological roots of sadism, homosexuality, fetishism, and voyeurism. His theories opened the door to the clinical treatment of previously misunderstood types of mental illness. And, by bringing attention to the central place of the libido in psychic life, they altered popular attitudes toward human sexuality.

At the turn of the century, Freud published *The Interpretation of Dreams*, in which he defined the significance of dreams in deciphering the unconscious life of the individual. In *Totem and Taboo* (1913), he examined the function of the unconscious in the evolution of religion and morality. And in the essay "Civilization and Its Discontents," he explored the relationship between psychic activity and human society. Freud's theories presented a radical new model of human behavior. Copernicus had dislodged human beings from their central place in the cosmos; Darwin had deposed *Homo sapiens* as unique among the earth's creatures; now Freud—in revealing the dark undersoul of humankind—refuted the precept that human reason governs human behavior.

Freud, *The Interpretation of Dreams* (1900)

Freud's theories drew criticism and frequent revision throughout the twentieth century. Among his immediate followers, the Swiss physician Carl Gustav Jung (1875–1961) found Freud's view of the psyche too narrow and overly deterministic. Jung held that the unconscious life rested in a deeper and more universal layer of the human mind that he called the *collective unconscious*. This realm, described in his *Psychology of the Unconscious*, belongs to humankind at large and manifests itself throughout history in the form of dreams, myths, and fairytales. The *archetypes* (primal patterns) of that realm reflect the deep psychic needs of humankind, as does religion. They reveal themselves as familiar motifs and characters, such as the hero, the wise old man, and the mother goddess. Jung's inquiries into the cultural history of humankind disclosed countless similarities between the symbols and myths of different cultures. These he took to support his theories that the archetypes were the innate, inherited contents of the human mind.

Jung, *Psychology of the Unconscious* (1916)

WAR AND REVOLUTION

AS if to confirm Freud's darkest insights, in 1914 Europe embarked on the first of two wars, both of which used the potentially liberating tools of the new science to annihilate human life. The Great War of 1914, as World War I was called, and World War II, which followed in 1939, were the first *total* wars in European history. They are called "total" not only because they involved more nations than had ever before been engaged in armed combat, but also because they killed—along with military personnel—millions of civilians. Moreover, the wars were "total" in the sense that they were fought with a "no holds barred" attitude—any and all methods of destruction were utilized in the name of conquest.

World War I

The Great War of 1914 originated in militant imperialism: specifically, in the efforts of modern European nation-states to extend their dominion in Europe, and, conversely, to protect themselves from the militant expansion of other predatory states. By the early twentieth century, Germany, having risen to power during the nineteenth century, rivaled all other European nations in industrial might. With Austria-Hungary, Germany brought military force to colonize markets for trade in Eastern Europe. In July 1914, Austria-Hungary, seeking to expand Austro-Hungarian territory to the south, used the political assassination of the archduke Franz Ferdinand (heir to the throne of Austria-Hungary) as a pretext to declare war on Serbia. Almost immediately, two opposing alliances were locked in confrontation: the Central Powers of Austria-Hungary, Germany, and the Ottoman Empire versus the Allied forces of Serbia, Belgium, France, Great Britain, and Russia.

At the beginning of the war, the Central Powers won victories in Belgium and Poland, but the Allies stopped the German advance at the first Battle of the Marne in September 1914. The two armies settled down to warfare along the Western front—a solid line of opposing trenches that stretched 500 miles from the English Channel to the Swiss border. At the same time, on the Eastern front, Russia lost over a million men in combat against the combined forces of Austria-Hungary and Germany. In the early years of the war the United States remained neutral, but in 1917, when German submarines began sinking unarmed passenger ships, the American president Woodrow Wilson resolved to support the Allies in order to "make the world safe for democracy." Fortified by American supplies and troops, the Allies moved toward victory, and in November of 1918 the fighting ended with an armistice.

The weapons of advanced technology made World War I more impersonal and more devastating than any previously fought war. Combatants made use of machine guns, heavy artillery, hand grenades, poison gas, flame throwers, armored tanks, submarines, dirigibles (airships), and airplanes. From the open cockpits of newly engineered airplanes, pilots fired on enemy aircraft, while on land soldiers fought from lines of trenches dug deep into the ground. The rapid-firing, fully automatic machine gun alone caused almost 80 percent of the casualties. The cost of four years of war was approximately $350 billion, and the death tolls were staggering. In all, seventy million armed men fought in World War I, and more than eight million of them died.

Aftermath of World War I

World War I left Europe devastated. Massive economic problems burdened both the Central Powers and the Allied nations. In the three years following the war, world industrial production declined by more than a third, prices dropped sharply, and over thirty million people lost their jobs. The United States emerged from the war as the great creditor nation, but its economy was tied to world conditions. Following the crash of inflated stock prices in 1929, a growing paralysis swept through the American economy, leading to the Great Depression. The crisis, which lasted until the 1940s, inspired literary descriptions of economic oppression and misery that were as much social documents as fictional narratives. John Steinbeck's landmark novel, *The Grapes of Wrath*, recounts in painfully detailed prose the odyssey of a family of Oklahoma migrant workers. Steinbeck's Social-Realist style, which presented subject matter with forthright objectivity, was equally apparent in the visual arts, most notably in the documentary photography of Dorothea Lange (Figure **14.2**, and see page 406).

Steinbeck, *The Grapes of Wrath* (1939)

In the tradition of American Realism (see pages 368–369), the paintings of everyday urban life by Edward Hopper (1882–1967) share the bleak outlook of Steinbeck and Lange. Hopper's melancholy studies of his native New York's gritty streets, office workplaces, filling stations, and restaurants were often inspired by American cinema and stage plays. In *Nighthawks* (Figure **14.3**), a harshly lit all-night diner is the cheerless retreat for four figures who seem estranged from their surroundings and isolated from each other.

Figure 14.2 Dorothea Lange, *Migrant Mother, Nipomo, California*, 1936. Gelatin-silver print. Library of Congress, Washington, D.C. Lange's *Migrant Mother* is a modern-day, working-class equivalent of the medieval Madonna, whose protective grief conveys a universal sentiment.

The Harlem Renaissance

Among African-Americans, economic problems were exacerbated by prevailing racism. During and after World War I, more than five million African-Americans migrated from the South to the northern states. New York City became the center of economic opportunity, as well as the melting pot for black people from various parts of the world. But white frustration and fear of black competition for jobs soon led to conflict: Race riots took place in over twenty-five American cities during the "bloody summer" of 1919 (see Figure 14.4). Nevertheless, between 1920 and 1940, the part of Manhattan known as Harlem, home to many African-Americans, became the location of an outpouring of creative expression in all the arts. The Harlem Renaissance made the self-conscious "rebirth" of the African heritage a principal part of an intellectual and cultural quest for racial identity and equality. Black poets, painters, musicians, and dancers celebrated the unique features of their race and opened a dialogue between the two Americas: white and black.

A leading figure of the Harlem Renaissance was the writer, folklorist, and anthropologist Zora Neale Hurston (1891–1960). Hurston made use of African-American dialect to bring to life some of the strongest female characters in early twentieth-century fiction. Her novel *Their Eyes Were Watching God* is widely regarded as a classic of black literature.

Hurston, *Their Eyes Were Watching God* (1937)

Hurston's contemporary Langston Hughes (1902–1967) was among the many literary voices of the Harlem Renaissance. A musician as well as a writer, Hughes was that rare poet whose powerful images—"a dream deferred," "a raisin in the sun," and "black like me"—have become enshrined as landmarks in the canon of American literature. His poems, which capture the musical qualities of the African oral tradition, fuse everyday speech with the rhythms of blues and jazz (discussed at the end of this chapter).

Figure 14.3 Edward Hopper, *Nighthawks*, 1942. Oil on canvas, $33\frac{1}{8}$ x $60\frac{1}{8}$ in. Art Institute of Chicago. No twentieth-century painter captured the condition of human loneliness more powerfully than Edward Hopper. Hopper began his career as a commercial artist for an advertising firm. A native New Yorker, he reported that this haunting scene was inspired by a corner café at Greenwich Avenue.

Making Connections

HARLEM

Langston Hughes' powerful poem "Harlem" (1951) evokes the mood of frustration and the spirit of rebellion shared by his fellow African-American Jacob Lawrence (1917–2000). One of America's foremost twentieth-century painters, Lawrence settled in Harlem in 1930. He won acclaim for paintings that deal with black history and the lives of black people. The series of sixty panels that make up "The Migration of the Negro" is a visual narrative of the great northward movement of African-Americans after World War I. Panel 50 (Figure **14.4**) depicts the riots that took place in East Saint Louis, Missouri, in 1917, when white workers rose up against blacks who were hired as strikebreakers. Lawrence lived to see violent clashes between blacks and whites (over issues of police brutality and civil rights) in the Harlem riots of 1935, 1943, and 1964.

Harlem

What happens to a dream
  deferred?

Does it dry up
like a raisin in the sun?
Or fester like a sore—
And then run?
Does it stink like rotten meat?
Or crust and sugar over—
like a syrupy sweet?

Maybe it just sags
like a heavy load.

Or does it explode?

Q What features in form and in content are shared by these two works of art?

Figure 14.4 Jacob Lawrence, "Race riots were numerous. White workers were hostile toward the migrants who had been hired to break strikes." Panel 50 from "The Migration of the Negro" series, 1940–1941; text and title revised by the artist, 1993. Tempera on gesso on composition board, 18 x 12 in. The Museum of Modern Art, New York.

Ideas and Issues

THE MEXICAN REVOLUTION

Lenin's utopian ideas fed the spirit of revolution elsewhere in the world, and nowhere more visibly than in Latin America. In Mexico, where 95 percent of the population was landless, efforts to broaden the base of landownership took the form of a violent revolution that lasted from 1911 to 1912. The Mexican Revolution was the first social revolt that united great masses of peasants and urban workers. Its spirit was captured by sympathetic Mexican artists such as Diego Rivera (1886–1957), whose paintings and public murals feature moving depictions of peasants (Figure **14.5**) and their native folk traditions. Rivera's simple yet powerful forms and bold colors reflected the vitality of the Mexican Revolution and helped to cultivate Mexico's Amerindian self-image.

Q What visual details in this painting might have incited revolutionary fervor?

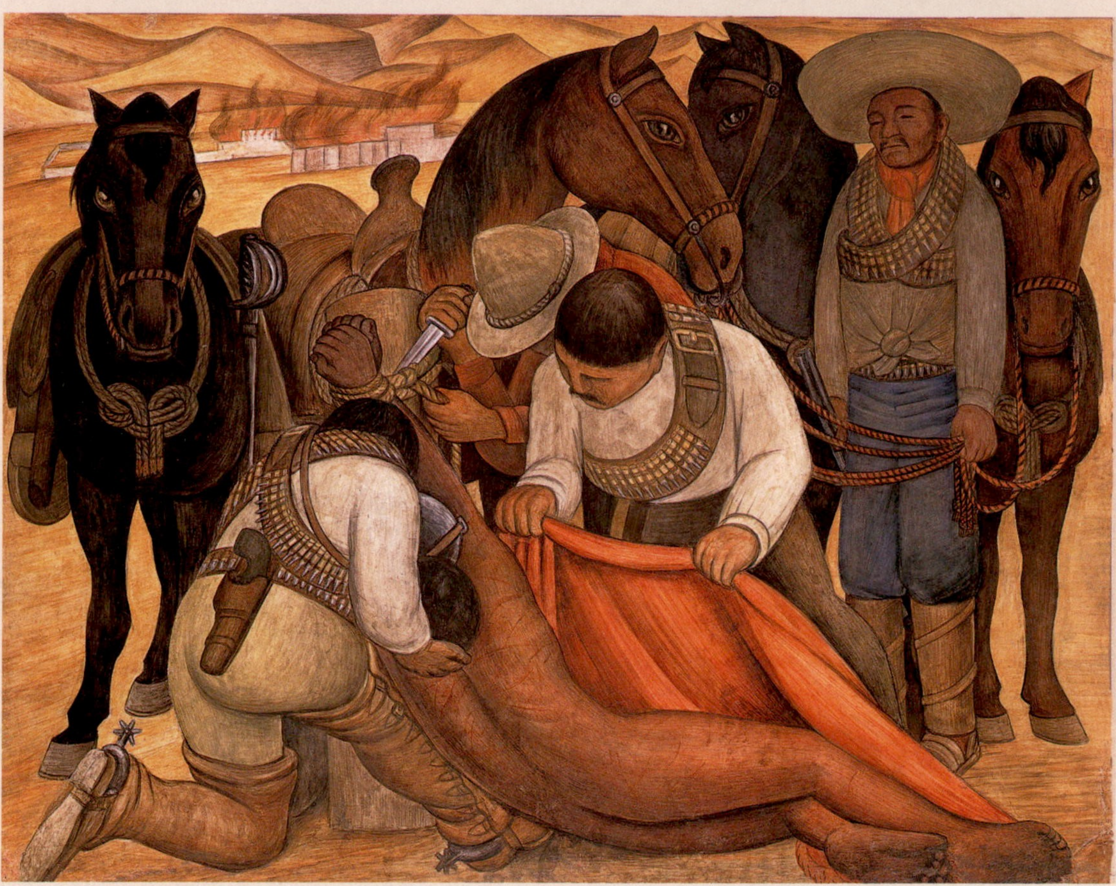

Figure 14.5 Diego Rivera, *Liberation of the Peon*, 1931. Fresco, 6 ft. 2 in. x 7 ft. 11 in. Philadelphia Museum of Art. Rivera depicts a severely whipped rural peasant, his village burning in the background.

The Russian Revolution

One of the last of the European powers to become industrialized, Russia entered World War I in 1914 under the leadership of Tzar Nicholas II (1868–1918). Within a single year, the Russian army lost over one million men and a million more soldiers deserted. Russian involvement in the war, compounded by problems of government corruption and a weak and essentially agrarian economy, reduced the nation to desperate straits. Food and fuel shortages threatened the entire civilian population. By 1917, a full-scale revolution was under way: Strikes and riots broke out in the cities, while in the countryside peasants seized the land of their aristocratic landlords. The Revolution of 1917 forced the abdication of the tzar and ushered in a new regime, which, in turn, was seized by members of the Russian Social-Democratic Labor Party under the leadership of the Marxist revolutionary Vladimir Ilyich Lenin (1870–1924).

Between 1917 and 1921, by means of shrewd political manipulation and a reign of terror conducted by the Red Army and the secret police, Lenin installed the left-wing faction of the Marxist Socialists—the Bolsheviks—as the party that would govern a nation of more than 150 million people. By tailoring Marxist ideas to the needs of revolutionary Russia, Lenin became the architect of Soviet communism. He agreed with Marx that a "dictatorship of the proletariat" was the first step in liberating the workers from bourgeois suppression. While condemning the state as "the organ of class domination," he projected a transition to a classless society in a series of

Lenin, "The State and Revolution" (1917)

phases, which he outlined in the influential pamphlet "The State and Revolution":

> The state will be able to wither away completely when society has realized the rule: "From each according to his ability; to each according to his needs," *i.e.*, when people have become accustomed to observe the fundamental rules of social life, and their labor is so productive that they voluntarily work *according to their ability*. . . . There will then be no need for any exact calculation by society of the quantity of products to be distributed to each of its members; each will take freely according to his needs.

Lenin was aware that such a social order might be deemed "a pure utopia"; yet, idealistically, he anticipated the victory of communist ideals throughout the world. The reality was otherwise. In early twentieth-century Russia, the Bolsheviks created a dictatorship *over* rather than *of* the proletariat. Russia was renamed the Union of Soviet Socialist Republics (U.S.S.R.) in 1922, and in 1924 the constitution established a sovereign Congress of Soviets. But this body was actually governed by the leadership of the Communist Party, which maintained absolute authority until the collapse of the Soviet Union in 1991.

The Communist Party established the first **totalitarian** regime of the twentieth century. Totalitarianism (a concept first formulated by Italian theorists in the 1920s) subordinated the life of the individual to the needs of the state. Through strict control of political, economic, and cultural life, and by means of coercive measures such as censorship and terrorism, Soviet communists persecuted all those whose activities they deemed threatening to the state.

Under the rule of Joseph Stalin (1879–1953), who took control of the communist bureaucracy in 1926, the Soviets launched vast programs of industrialization and agricultural collectivization (the transformation of private farms into government-run units) that demanded heroic sacrifice among the Soviet people. Stalin's secret police "purged" the state of dissidents, who were imprisoned, exiled to *gulags* (labor camps), or executed. Between 1928 and 1938, the combination of severe famine and Stalin's inhuman policies (later known as "the great terror") took the lives of fifteen to twenty million Russians. Totalitarianism, especially as described by those who witnessed it firsthand, became a riveting theme in twentieth-century literature. Aleksandr Solzhenitsyn (1918–2008), who had served in the Russian army, was arrested in 1945 for anti-Stalinist comments and sentenced to eight years of imprisonment in a Soviet labor camp. His experience in a Siberian *gulag* inspired the novel *One Day in the Life of Ivan Denisovich* (1962), a searing indictment of political oppression that became a twentieth-century literary landmark.

Hitler and World War II

In Europe, the economic decline of the 1920s and 1930s ushered in a new age of war. Following the defeat and humiliation of Germany in World War I, a group of extreme nationalists led by Adolf Hitler (1889–1945) took control of German politics. Hitler's rearmament of Germany and his pursuit of militant expansion into Poland in 1939 would trigger the next total war. In an effort to stop Nazi aggression, France and Great Britain declared war on Germany. Hitler quickly defeated and occupied France and threatened Britain, despite stubborn resistance. In 1941, Germany invaded Russia.

Blaming the post-World War I financial distress on "enemies within" (predominantly Jews), Hitler and the National Socialist ("Nazi") Party undertook to persecute Jews and other minorities. Hitler's fanatical theory of "Aryan racial superiority" inspired one of the most malevolent episodes in the history of humankind: the Holocaust—the systematic extermination of six million Jews, along with Roman Catholics, homosexuals, and other minorities (Figure **14.6**). One of the most eloquent survivors of the Holocaust is the Nobel laureate Elie Wiesel (b. 1928). At the age of fifteen, Wiesel, a Romanian Jew, was shipped with his family to the German concentration camp at Auschwitz, Poland. From there, the boy and his

Figure 14.6 Lee Miller, *Buchenwald, Germany*, April 30, 1945. Photograph. The realities of World War II were recorded by an international array of photojournalists. One of the most gifted was Lee Miller (1907–1977), an American who became the first female wartime photojournalist and an early witness to the horrors of the German concentration camps.

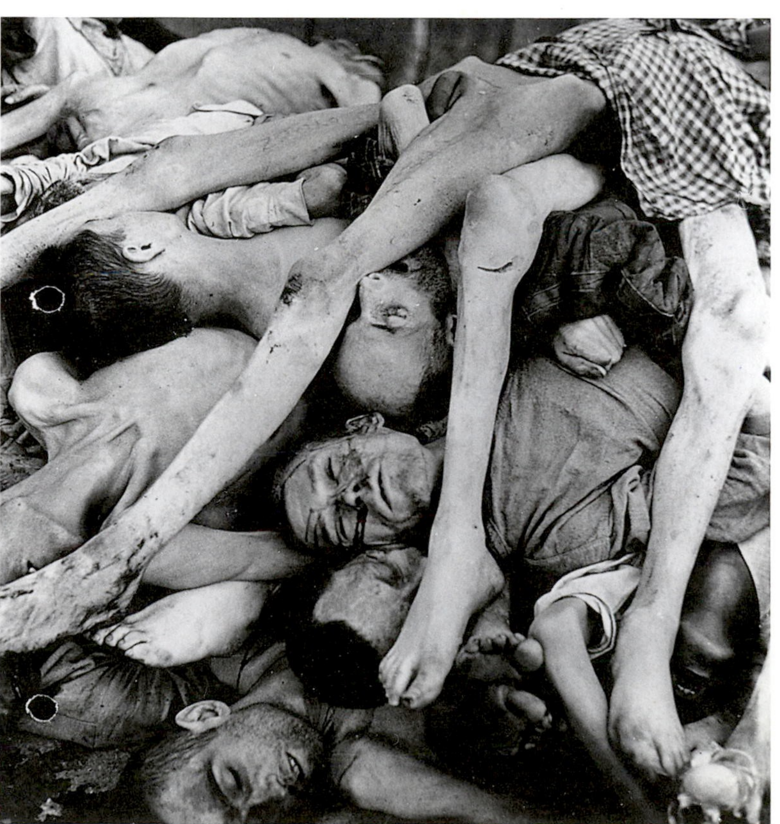

Beyond the West

MAO'S CHINA

THE history of totalitarianism is not confined to the West. In the course of the twentieth century, modern tyrants wiped out whole populations in parts of Cambodia, Vietnam, Iraq, Africa, and elsewhere. Of all the Asian countries, however, China experienced the most dramatic changes. Following World War II, communist forces under the leadership of Mao Zedong (1893–1976) rose to power, and in 1949 they formed the People's Republic of China.

Mao's ambitious reforms earned the support of the landless masses, but his methods for achieving his goals struck at the foundations of traditional Chinese culture. He tried to replace the old order, and especially the Confucian veneration of the family, with new socialist values that demanded devotion to the local economic unit—and ultimately to the state. Between 1949 and 1952, in an effort to make his reforms effective, Mao authorized the execution of some two to five million people, including the wealthy landowners themselves. To carry out his series of five-year plans for economic development in industry and agriculture, Mao also instituted totalitarian practices, such as indoctrination, exile, and repeated purges of the voices of opposition. His utopian views on cooperative social endeavor and self-discipline were broadcast by way of guidelines published in his *Quotations from Chairman Mao* (1963). Mao's "little red book" soon became the "bible" of the Chinese Revolution.

Mao directed writers to produce literature that celebrated the creative powers of the masses. The movement for a "people's literature" included the abandonment of ancient, classical modes of writing in favor of the language of common, vernacular speech—a style strongly influenced by Western literature and journalism. In the visual arts, the influence of Western printmakers contributed to the appearance of *Social Realism*—a style that presented socially significant subject matter in a lifelike manner (Figure **14.7**).

Figure 14.7 Li Hua, *Roar!* 1936. Woodcut, 8 x 6 in. Lu Xun Memorial, Shanghai.

father were sent to a labor camp in Buchenwald, Germany, where the youth saw his father and hundreds of others killed by the Nazis. Liberated in 1945, Wiesel left a graphic account of these traumatic experiences in his memoir, *Night*.

Wiesel, *Night* (1958)

By 1941, the war had become a Europe-wide conflagration. In the meantime, the Japanese, under control of a government bent on expansion and national aggrandizement, had armed itself, clearly threatening its Asian neighbors—especially China and the Pacific Islands. When Japan and Germany joined forces, it only remained to be seen how the United States would react. The Americans were reluctant to join the fray, but this reluctance vanished when, in 1941, the Japanese bombed the U.S. Pacific Fleet in Hawaii's Pearl Harbor. The sneak attack outraged and unified the American public, making it possible for President Franklin Delano Roosevelt to get a congressional declaration of war against Japan and its German ally. Four years of devastating conflict ensued, in what had become World War II.

The war against Japan was essentially a naval war, but it involved land and air attacks as well. Airplanes and aerial bombs played major roles; war costs tripled those of World War I, and casualties among the Allied forces alone rose to over eighteen million people. The terrible climax of the war was America's nuclear attack on two Japanese cities, Hiroshima and Nagasaki, in August 1945. The United States initiated the bombings as an alternative to a large-scale Allied attack on the Japanese mainland, which would have resulted in massive casualties on both sides. However, the ethical and strategical justifications for this decision are still very much debated. The bombing, which annihilated over 120,000 people (mostly civilians) and forced the Japanese to surrender within a matter of days, ushered in the atomic age. Just months before, as German forces had given way to Allied assaults on all fronts, Hitler committed suicide. World War II came to a close with the surrender of both Germany and Japan in 1945. Total war and totalitarianism, facilitated by sophisticated military technology and electronic forms of mass communication, caused the twentieth century to be the bloodiest in world history.

MODERN LITERATURE

The Imagists

Rejecting the self-indulgent sentiments of nineteenth-century Romantics and the graphic narratives of the Realists, Modernist writers sought a language of expression that was conceptual and abstract. The leaders in the search for a more concentrated style were a group of poets who called themselves *Imagists*. For the Imagist, the writer was like a sculptor whose technique required that he carve away all extraneous matter: a process of *abstraction* that arrived at intrinsic or essential form. Verbal compression, formal precision, and economy of expression were the goals of the Imagists. Unconfined by traditional verse forms and fixed meter, their free verse style became famous for its abrupt and discontinuous juxtaposition of images.

Imagism's most influential poet was the American expatriate Ezra Pound (1885–1972). Pound studied the literature of Greece and Rome, China and Japan, medieval and Renaissance Europe—often reading a literary work in its original language. A student of Asian calligraphy, he drew inspiration from Chinese and Japanese verse, and especially from the Japanese poetic genre known as *haiku* (see page 321), which employs a close succession of images to evoke a subtle, metaphoric relationship. A life-long series of poems—many of them filled with arcane historical references, foreign language phrases, and obscene jokes—makes up Pound's *Cantos*; but the terse precision of the Imagist style dominates his smaller collection, *Personae* (1926). With these early poems, Pound summoned his contemporaries to cast aside traditional modes of Western verse-making, and to "make it new"—a dictum allegedly scrawled on the bathtub of an ancient Chinese emperor. The injunction to "make it new" became the rallying cry of Modernism.

Pound, *Personae* (1926)

Modern Poetry: Eliot, Yeats, and Frost

No English-speaking poet advanced the Modernist quest for meaning more powerfully than the American-born writer T. S. (Thomas Stearns) Eliot (1888–1965). Educated at Harvard University in philosophy and the classics, Eliot was studying at Oxford when World War I broke out. He remained in England after the war, becoming a British citizen in 1927 and converting to the Anglican Church in the same year. Eliot's grasp of modern philosophy, world religions, anthropology, and the classical literature of Asia and the West made him the most esteemed literary critic of his time. His erudition also informed his poetry. His most notable poem, *The Waste Land*, draws heavily on ancient Eastern and Western myths of death and rebirth to suggest the aridity of modern life and the eternal quest for redemption. Stripped of romantic sentiment and densely packed with startling (and often obscure) images and inventive rhythms, *The Waste Land* quickly became a landmark of Modernist poetry. It established the idiom of modern verse as compressed, complex, cryptic, and serious.

Eliot, "The Love Song of J. Alfred Prufrock" (1915); *The Waste Land* (1922)

The mood of postwar despair and disillusion informed all of Eliot's work, but it is especially evident in his searching poem "The Love Song of J. Alfred Prufrock" and his verse drama *The Rock* (1934). In the latter, the poet describes a sterile Western culture afflicted with human loneliness and the absence of spiritual comforts:

All our knowledge brings us nearer to our ignorance,
All our ignorance brings us nearer to death,
But nearness to death no nearer to God.
Where is the wisdom we have lost in knowledge?
Where is the wisdom we have lost in information?
The cycles of Heaven in twenty centuries
Bring us farther from God and nearer to the Dust.

Ideas and Issues

YEATS: "THE SECOND COMING"

Turning and turning in the widening gyre[1]
The falcon cannot hear the falconer;
Things fall apart; the center cannot hold;
Mere anarchy is loosed upon the world,
The blood-dimmed tide is loosed, and everywhere
The ceremony of innocence is drowned;
The best lack all conviction, while the worst
Are full of passionate intensity.

Surely some revelation is at hand;
Surely the Second Coming is at hand.
The Second Coming! Hardly are those words out
When a vast image out of Spiritus Mundi[2]
Troubles my sight: somewhere in sands of the desert
A shape with lion body and the head of a man,
A gaze blank and pitiless as the sun,
Is moving its slow thighs, while all about it
Reel shadows of the indignant desert birds.
The darkness drops again; but now I know
That twenty centuries of stony sleep
Were vexed to nightmare by a rocking cradle,
And what rough beast, its hour come round at last,
Slouches towards Bethlehem to be born?

Q Which lines in this poem strike you as most prophetic of the twentieth century?

[1] A circular course traced by the upward sweep of a falcon. The image reflects Yeats' cyclical view of history.
[2] World Spirit, similar to the Jungian Great Memory of shared archetypal images.

Eliot's contemporary William Butler Yeats (1865–1939) was one of the great lyricists of the twentieth century. An Irish nationalist, he wrote plays and poems inspired by traditional native themes. He responded to the violence of World War I and to the prevailing mood of unrest in Ireland with the apocalyptic poem "The Second Coming." The poem, which has become a landmark in Modernist verse, alludes to the long-awaited Second Coming of Jesus, but also to the nameless force that, in Yeats' view, threatened to enthrall the world in unredeemable darkness.

Yeats, "The Second Coming" (1921)

The most popular of America's Modernist poets, Robert Frost (1874–1963), offered an alternative to Imagist abstraction and wartime pessimism. He wrote in metered verse, jokingly comparing the poet's use of free verse to "playing tennis without a net." Unlike Eliot, he disdained dense allusions and obscure symbols. In plain speech, he described his affection for the natural landscape of his native New England and his abiding sympathy for the human condition, which he perceived as uncertain and enigmatic. Written in the colloquial and direct language that became the hallmark of his mature style, "The Road Not Taken" exalts a spirit of individualism and a sparseness of expression in line with the Modernist injunction to "make it new."

Frost, "The Road Not Taken" (1916)

The Road Not Taken

Two roads diverged in a yellow wood,
And sorry I could not travel both
And be one traveler, long I stood
And looked down one as far as I could
To where it bent in the undergrowth;

Then took the other, as just as fair,
And having perhaps the better claim,
Because it was grassy and wanted wear,
Though as for that the passing there
Had worn them really about the same,

And both that morning equally lay
In leaves no step had trodden black.
Oh, I kept the first for another day!
Yet knowing how way leads on to way,
I doubted if I should ever come back.

I shall be telling this with a sigh
Somewhere ages and ages hence:
Two roads diverged in a wood, and I—
took the one less traveled by.
And that has made all the difference.

Modern Fiction and Drama

Prose fiction of the early twentieth century reflects the mood of anxiety and uncertainty generated by the writings of Freud and the outbreak of World War I. Profoundly influenced by Freud, the French writer Marcel Proust (1871–1922) perceived the literary fiction as "psychology in space and time." Between 1909 and 1922 Proust produced a sixteen-volume novel entitled *A la recherché du temps perdu* (literally "In Search of Lost Time," but usually translated as *Remembrance of Things Past*). This masterpiece, published in seven parts between 1913 and 1927, is a lengthy portrait of turn-of-the-century Parisian society, but its primary theme is the role of memory in retrieving past experience and in shaping one's private life. Proust's mission was to rediscover a sense of the past by reviving sensory experiences buried deep within his psyche: to bring unconscious life to the conscious level. In the first volume of the novel, he employs the Freudian technique of "free association" to recapture from the recesses of memory the intense moment of pleasure occasioned by the taste of a piece of cake soaked in tea. Proust's intimate literary style would have a major influence on Modernist fiction.

Proust, *Remembrance of Things Past* (1913–1927)

While for Proust the unconscious was a life-enriching resource, for the German-language novelist Franz Kafka (1883–1924) it gave conscious experience bizarre and threatening gravity. Kafka's novels and short stories take on the reality of dreams in which characters are nameless, details are precise but grotesque, and events lack logical consistency. In the nightmarish world of his prose, the central characters become victims of unknown or imprecisely understood forces. They may be caught in absurd but commonplace circumstances involving guilt and frustration, or they may be threatened by menacing events that appear to have neither meaning nor purpose. In *The Trial* (1925), for instance, the protagonist is arrested, convicted, and executed, without ever knowing the nature of his crime. In "The Metamorphosis," one of the most disquieting short stories of the twentieth century, the central character, Gregor Samsa, wakes one morning to discover that he has turned into a large insect. The themes of insecurity and vulnerability dominate this brilliant writer's prose.

Kafka, "The Metamorphosis" (1915)

Probably the single most influential novelist of the early twentieth century was the Irish-born James Joyce (1882–1941). Like Proust and Kafka, Joyce was deeply indebted to Freud, whose publications he consumed with interest. In his landmark novel *Ulysses*, Joyce made use of *interior monologue* (the private musings of a character) inspired by the free association of ideas that Freud used in psychotherapy. This challenging technique provided the basis for a literary device known as "stream-of-consciousness"—a succession of thoughts and images connected not by logical argument or narrative sequence but by the free play of the psyche. Joyce's *Ulysses*, modeled on Homer's *Odyssey*, records the adventures of his fictional protagonist, Leopold Bloom, as he moves through the streets of Dublin in a

Joyce, *Ulysses* (1922)

single day. The real "action" of the novel, however, takes place in the mind of its principal character. Joyce's modern hero is as ordinary as Homer's was heroic; his adventures seem trivial and insignificant, but his ruminations memorably capture the overwhelming sense of desolation that marked the first decades of the century.

The combined influence of Freud and Joyce is visible in the literature of the twentieth century: in the fiction of the Nobel laureates Thomas Mann (1875–1955) and William Faulkner (1897–1962) and in the stream-of-consciousness prose of Virginia Woolf (1882–1941). It is also evident in drama, especially in the works of the American playwright Eugene O'Neill (1888–1953). O'Neill's dramatic trilogy *Mourning Becomes Electra* fuses Greek myth with Freudian concepts of guilt and repression. His inventive dramatic techniques—such as two actors playing different aspects of a single individual—probe the interior life of the character. The early twentieth century saw the development of a new style of theatrical performance: *Method acting* requires the actor to harness "true emotion" to "affective memory" derived from childhood experience. The pioneer in this technique was the Russian director and actor Konstantin Stanislavsky (1863–1938).

O'Neill, *Mourning Becomes Electra* (1931)

Science Fiction and the Futurist Novel

The birth of science fiction as a modern literary genre may be traced to the works of the French novelist Jules Verne (1828–1905), whose books on adventure and popular science stirred the imagination of readers even before the turn of the century. But it was his follower, the British writer H. G. Wells (1866–1946), who produced the pioneer works in this new genre. Wells' *The War of the Worlds* (1898) tells the apocalyptic tale of an invasion of Planet Earth by Martians whose intelligence far exceeds that of the earthlings. The themes of invasion from outer space and interplanetary travel would dominate science fiction throughout the twentieth century.

During the war era, however, a more politically inspired version of Futurist fiction emerged, in which writers explored the influences of science and technology on human behavior and communal life. European totalitarianism influenced the writings of Aldous Huxley (1894–1963), whose landmark novel *Brave New World* pictures a society in which modern technology and the techniques of human engineering operate to destroy our freedom. In Huxley's futuristic society, babies are conceived in test tubes and, following assembly-line methods (initiated by Henry Ford for the manufacture of cars), individuals are conditioned to perform socially beneficial tasks. Family is eradicated, society is purged of art and religion, and human anxieties are suppressed by means of mood-altering drugs.

Huxley, *Brave New World* (1932)

A more recent flowering of the genre dates from the birth of space exploration, which triggered an energetic outpouring of literature on space travel. In 1948, Arthur C. Clarke, one of Britain's most successful writers, wrote the intriguing short story "The Sentinel," which took as its theme the fictional discovery of a four-million-year-old crystal monolith emitting powerful radio waves from its location on the Earth's moon. Whether the mysterious monument was erected by an ancient alien civilization and whether its creators intended the signals as a warning beacon remain unresolved in Clarke's story.

"The Sentinel" was the inspiration for the landmark cinematic conceptualization of the Space Age: *2001: A Space Odyssey* (Figure **14.8**). Directed by the American filmmaker Stanley Kubrick (1928–1999), the film expanded Clarke's story with epic adventures that include a contest of wills between astronauts and a supercomputer, a breathtaking encounter with the wonders of outer space, and a shattering revelation of regeneration and rebirth. Clarke's short story and Kubrick's film have influenced the production of literary and cinematic science fiction well into our own time.

Clarke, "The Sentinel" (1948)

Figure 14.8 Stanley Kubrick, *2001: A Space Odyssey*, 1968. Outfitted with a state-of-the-art spaceship called *Discovery*, engineered by a supercomputer named HAL-9000, the fictional heroes (modern counterparts of Gilgamesh or Odysseus) set out for Jupiter.

MODERN ART

THE visual art of the early twentieth century constitutes the most radical assault on tradition ever launched in the history of world art. Liberated by the camera from the necessity of imitating nature, **avant-garde** artists turned away from representation as a visual mode. They devised abstract, "stripped down" styles that—like Imagist poetry—worked to capture the intrinsic and essential meaning of their subjects. They reenvisioned the physical world by way of a new formal language that evoked (rather than described) experience.

Picasso and Cubism

The giant of twentieth-century art was the Spanish-born Pablo Picasso (1881–1973). During his ninety-two-year life, Picasso worked in almost every major art style of the century, some of which he himself inaugurated. He produced thousands of paintings, drawings, sculptures, and prints—a body of work that in its size, inventiveness, and influence, is nothing short of phenomenal.

In 1903, the young painter left his native Spain to settle in Paris. There, in the bustling capital of the Western

Figure 14.9 Pablo Picasso, *Les Demoiselles d'Avignon*, Paris, 1907. Oil on canvas, 8 ft. x 7 ft. 8 in. The Museum of Modern Art, New York.

Making Connections

"MAGICAL OBJECTS"

While scholars debate the question of exactly which tribal artworks Picasso might have seen at the Ethnographic Museum in Paris, all concur that copper-clad Kota reliquary guardians and certain ritual masks were among those he admired (compare Figures **14.10** and **14.11**). "For me," Picasso explained, "the masks were not just sculptures; they were magical objects . . . intercessors against unknown, threatening spirits."

Q What features in the Kota figure might have influenced Picasso's radical move away from realistic representation?

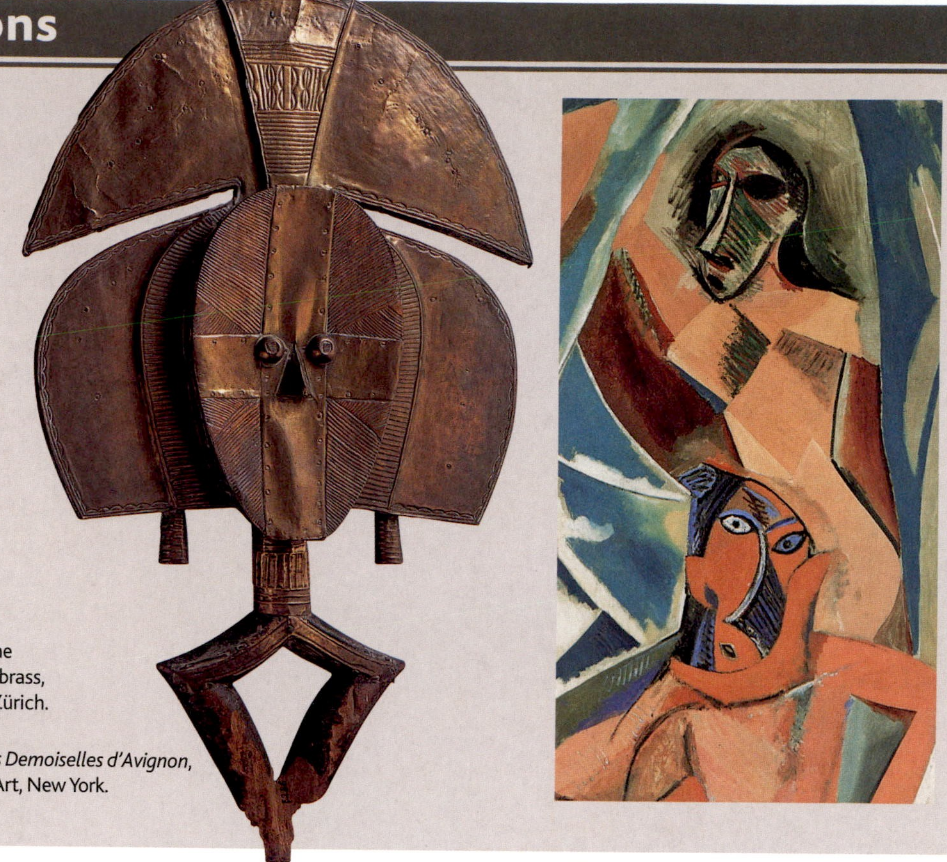

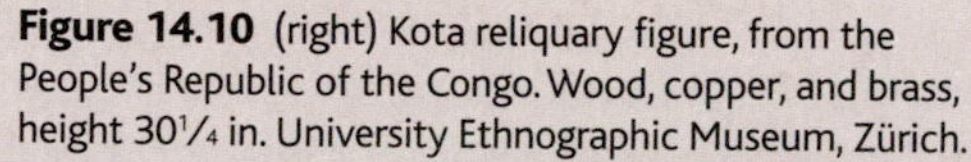

Figure 14.10 (right) Kota reliquary figure, from the People's Republic of the Congo. Wood, copper, and brass, height 30¼ in. University Ethnographic Museum, Zürich.

Figure 14.11 (far right) Pablo Picasso, detail of *Les Demoiselles d'Avignon*, Paris, 1907. Oil on canvas. The Museum of Modern Art, New York.

art world, he came under the influence of Impressionist and Postimpressionist painting, taking as his subjects café life, beggars, prostitutes, and circus folk. Picasso worked to refine form and color in the direction of concentrated expression, reducing the colors of his palette first to various shades of blue and then, after 1904, to tones of rose. By 1906, however, he began to abandon traditional Western modes of pictorial representation. Adopting the credo that art must be subversive—that it must defy all that is conventional, literal, and trite—he initiated a bold new style. That style was shaped by two major forces: Cézanne's paintings, which had been the focus of two large Paris exhibitions; and the arts of Africa, Iberia, and Oceania, examples of which were appearing regularly in Paris galleries and museums. In Cézanne's canvases (see Figures 13.28 and 13.29), Picasso recognized a rigorous new language of form that worked to define nature's underlying structure. And in African and Oceanic sculpture he discovered a unique synthesis of expressive abstraction and dynamic distortion.

Both influences contributed to Picasso's monumental *Demoiselles d'Avignon* (Figure **14.9** and see Figure 14.11), the landmark Modernist painting of the early twentieth century. The five nude women—prostitutes of a Spanish bordello—occupy a shallow space consisting of fractured planes of color—brick rose and vivid blues—that resemble shards of broken glass. At least three of the figures are rendered from multiple viewpoints—as if observed by an eye that traveled freely in time and space. The body of the crouching female on the far right is viewed from the back, while her face, savagely striated like the scarification of an African mask (see Figure 9.8), is seen from the front. The noses of the two central women appear in profile, while their eyes are frontal, a convention Picasso may have borrowed from Egyptian art (see Figure 1.26). Forbidding rather than seductive, Picasso's female nudes have been stripped of their traditional sensuous appeal. In one disquieting stroke, the artist banished the image of the alluring woman from the domain of Western art.

Les Demoiselles was the precursor of an audacious new style known as *Cubism*, which came to challenge the principles of Renaissance painting as dramatically as Einstein's theory of relativity had challenged Newtonian physics. In the Cubist canvas, the comfortable, recognizable world of the senses disappears beneath a scaffold of semitransparent planes and short, angular lines; ordinary objects are made to look as if they have exploded and been reassembled in bits and pieces (Figure **14.12**).

Cubism came to offer a new formal language, one wholly unconcerned with narrative content. Around 1912, Cubist canvases began to include fragments of wallpaper, wine labels, playing cards, and scraps of newspaper. These were pasted onto the surface of the canvas—a technique known as **collage** (from the French *coller*, "to paste"). With his colleague Georges Braque (1882–1963), Picasso produced canvases filled with hidden meanings, puns, and subtle references to contemporary events.

Figure 14.12 Pablo Picasso. *Man with a Violin*, 1911. Oil on canvas, $39\frac{1}{8} \times 29\frac{7}{8}$ in. Philadelphia Museum of Art. With *Analytic Cubism*, as the style came to be called, a multiplicity of viewpoints replaced one-point perspective. The Cubist image, conceived as if one were moving around, above, and below the subject and even perceiving it from within, appropriated the fourth dimension—time itself.

Cubism brought daring new ideas to sculpture as well. The **assemblage**, a genre invented by Picasso, made use of miscellaneous three-dimensional fragments that were built up or pieced together. Like the collage, the assemblage depended on the imaginative combination of found objects and materials. The new procedure constituted a radical alternative to traditional techniques of carving in stone, metal-casting, and modeling in clay or plaster (Figure **14.13**).

A quarter of a century after the birth of Cubism, Picasso was to paint another landmark work—one motivated not by the search for a new language of form, but by political events. On the afternoon of April 26, 1937, in the midst of the Spanish Civil War (1936–1939) that pitted republican forces against the Fascist dictatorship of General Francisco Franco, the German air force (in league with the Spanish Fascists) dropped incendiary bombs on Guernica, a small Basque market town in northeast Spain. News of the event—the first aerial bombardment of a civilian target—reached Paris, where the horrified Picasso read illustrated newspaper accounts of the attack as the death toll mounted. Earlier in the year, the artist had been invited to contribute a painting for the Spanish Pavilion of the Paris World's Fair. The bombing of Guernica provided him with inspiration for the huge mural that would become the landmark antiwar image of the twentieth century (Figure **14.14**). Picasso invests Cubism's strong, angular motifs with expressive

Figure 14.13 Pablo Picasso, *Guitar*, 1912–1913. Construction of sheet metal and wire, $30\frac{1}{2} \times 13\frac{3}{4} \times 7\frac{5}{8}$ in. The Museum of Modern Art, New York. Picasso's *Guitar* achieves its powerful effect by means of fragmented planes, deliberate spatial inversions (note the projecting soundhole), and the wedding of commonplace materials.

Figure 14.14 Pablo Picasso, *Guernica*, 1937. Oil on canvas, 11 ft. $5\frac{1}{2}$ in. x 25 ft. $5\frac{3}{4}$ in. Museo Nacional Centro de Arte Reina Sofia, Madrid. *Guernica* captures the grim brutality and suffering of the wartime era. Picasso used monochromatic tones—the ashen grays of incineration—which also call to mind newspapers, photographs, and film, the documentary media of mass communication by which Picasso learned of the event.

fervor. The bull and horse of the Spanish bullfight—Picasso's lifelong metaphor for savage discord—share the shallow stage with a broken statue of a warrior and four women, one of whom holds a dead infant. This figure, her upturned head issuing a voiceless scream, is the physical embodiment of human grief. At the center of the painting, the horse, whose body bears the gaping wound of a spear, rears its head as if to echo the woman's anguished cry. The shattered statue at the bottom of the composition symbolizes war's corrupting effects on the artifacts of high culture.

Futurism

Technology and art, linked by the Modernist mandate to "make it new," sparked the movement known as *Futurism*. The Italian poet and iconoclast Filippo Tommaso Marinetti (1876–1944) issued a series of manifestoes that attacked all forms of academic culture and linked contemporary artistic expression to industry, technology, and urban life. Marinetti demanded an art of "burning violence" that would free Italy from its "fetid gangrene of professors, archaeologists, antiquarians, and rhetoricians." "We declare," he wrote in his *Futurist Manifesto* of 1909, "that there can be no modern painting except from the starting point of an absolutely modern sensation. . . . A roaring motorcar is more beautiful than the winged *Victory of Samothrace*." The Futurists glorified the technology that had altered modern life by way of the automobile, the machine gun, and Rome's newly installed electric street lamps. Their landmark alternative to static academicism was produced by Umberto Boccioni (1882–1916). His near life-sized bronze sculpture captures the sensation of motion as it pushes forward like an automated robot (Figure **14.15**).

The radical voice of Futurism was heard beyond Italy, where it came to influence the early career of the French artist Marcel Duchamp (1887–1968). When Duchamp's

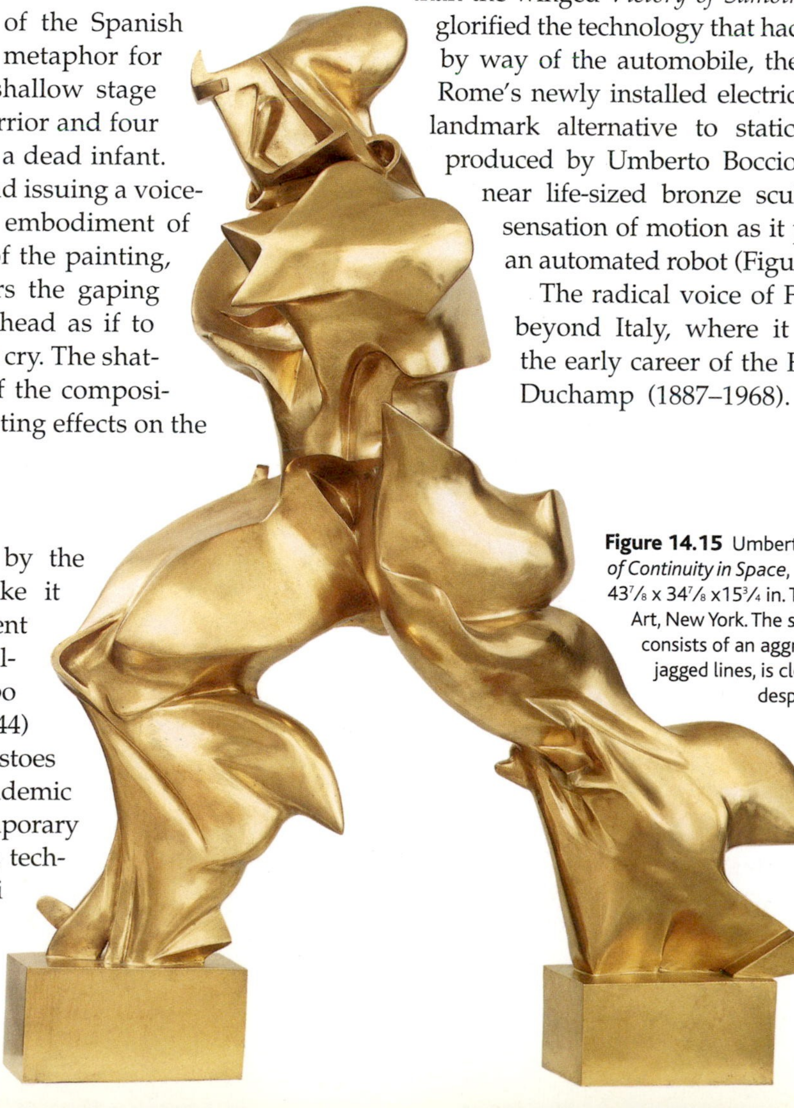

Figure 14.15 Umberto Boccioni, *Unique Forms of Continuity in Space*, 1913. Bronze (cast 1931), $43\frac{7}{8}$ x $34\frac{7}{8}$ x $15\frac{3}{4}$ in. The Museum of Modern Art, New York. The striding figure, which consists of an aggressive series of dynamic, jagged lines, is clearly human in form, despite Boccioni's assertion that artists should "abolish . . . the traditionally exalted place of subject matter."

Making Connections

THE BIRTH OF MOTION PICTURES AND THE VISUAL ARTS

As an artform that captures rapidly changing experience, cinema is *the* quintessentially modern medium. The earliest public film presentations took place in the mid-1890s. In 1895 Thomas Edison (1847–1931) was the first American to project moving images on a screen publicly, while in France the brothers Auguste and Louis Lumière (1862–1954; 1864–1948) perfected the process by which cellulose film ran smoothly in a commercial projector. These first experiments delighted audiences with moving pictures of everyday reality.

It was not until 1902, however, that film was used to create a reality all its own: In that year the French filmmaker Georges Méliès (1861–1938) completed a theatrical sequence called *A Trip to the Moon*, a fantastic reconstruction of reality based on a Jules Verne novel. One year later, the American director Edwin S. Porter (1869–1941) produced the twelve-minute silent film *The Great Train Robbery* (1903), which treated the myth of American frontier life in the story of a sensational holdup followed by the pursuit and capture of the bandits. These pioneer narrative films established the idiom for two of the most popular genres in cinematic history: the science fiction film and the "western."

Marcel Duchamp was familiar with the pioneer efforts in the new industry of motion pictures, in which "multiple profiles" gave the appearance of movement (Figure **14.16**). He was also fascinated by the "magic" of the x-ray, a technique devised in the late nineteenth century but not widely used until 1910.

Q Have motion pictures in our own time had a similar impact on contemporary art?

Figure 14.16 Marcel Duchamp, *Nude Descending a Staircase, No. 2*, 1912. Oil on canvas, 58 x 35 in. Philadelphia Museum of Art.

Futuristic *Nude Descending a Staircase, No. 2* (Figure **14.16**) was exhibited at the International Exhibition of Modern Art (known as the Armory Show) in New York City, one critic mockingly called it "an explosion in a shingle factory." Yet, from the time of its first showing in 1913, the painting (and much of the art in the Armory exhibition) had a formative influence on the rise of American Modernism. Futurism did not last beyond the end of World War I, but its impact was felt in both the United States and Russia, where Futurist efforts to capture the sense of form in motion would coincide with the first developments in the technology of cinematography.

Matisse and Fauvism

While Cubists and Futurists were principally concerned with matters of space and motion, other Modernists, led by the French artist Henri Matisse (1869–1954), made *color* the principal feature of their canvases. This group,

Figure 14.17 Henri Matisse, *Madame Matisse* (*The Green Line*), 1905. Oil on canvas, 16 x 12¾ in. State Art Museum, Copenhagen. Matisse used pure, unmixed colors for his wife's portrait. The pursuit of color abstraction—by which he chose to paint a green line down the middle of the face—would become a hallmark of modern art.

disparagingly called "Fauves" ("wild beasts") by a critic who saw their work at the 1905 Salon d'Automne in Paris, employed flat, bright colors in an arbitrary manner reminiscent of van Gogh and Gauguin (see Figures 13.23 and 13.24). But whereas the latter had used color to evoke a mood or symbolic idea, the Fauves were concerned with color as it served pictorial structure. Critics who called these artists "wild beasts" were in fact responding to the crude and savage application of paint, the spontaneous and instinctive use of pigment that they dismissed as "color madness." Matisse scorned the critics, maintaining that colors and shapes were the equivalents of feelings (Figure **14.17**). "Exactitude is not truth," he insisted. Influenced by Islamic art and Russian icons, Matisse moved in the direction of decorative simplicity; his mastery of line and color made him one of the twentieth century's most beloved painters.

Nonobjective Art

Between 1909 and 1914, three artists working independently of one another introduced a revolutionary new idea. Purging the canvas of all recognizable subject matter, they pioneered *Nonobjective art.* The Russians Wassily Kandinsky (1899–1944) and Kasimir Malevich (1898–1935) and the Dutchman Piet Mondrian (1872–1944) had all come into contact with the groundbreaking abstract styles of Picasso and Matisse; however, their own forays into pure abstraction (the elimination of *all* subject matter) were motivated not exclusively by a formal but also by a spiritual goal—to create art that remedied the soullessness of modern life.

Kandinsky moved from Moscow to Munich in 1896. His early canvases, vibrantly colored landscapes influenced by the Fauves and by Russian folk art, would impact the development of German Expressionism. Critical of his own early efforts, however, he despaired that his subject matter tended to dissolve into his colors. After the revelation that led him to abandon pictorial subject matter, he worked to develop an abstract language dependent solely on form, color, and line (see Figure 14.1 and A First Look), elements that, in his later works, he would assemble as circles, triangles, and squares.

Kandinsky's significance rests not only with his paintings, but with his theoretical writings. In the influential treatise *On the Spiritual in Art* he argues that form and color generate meaning without reference to the natural world. His insights into the effects of color on mood anticipated modern research in chromotherapy (the use of color to affect body states).

Kandinsky, *On the Spiritual in Art* (1910)

Kandinsky's contemporary Kasimir Malevich arrived at nonrepresentational art by way of Cubism. Seeking to "free art from the burden of the object," he limited his paintings to a strict geometry of ideal shapes: the square, the circle, and the rectangle (Figure **14.18**). Malevich called these shapes "suprematist elements" and his style *suprematism.*

Figure 14.18 Kasimir Malevich, *Suprematist Composition: White on White*, 1918. Oil on canvas, 31¼ x 31¼ in. The Museum of Modern Art, New York. "To the suprematist," wrote Malevich, "the visual phenomena of the objective world are, in themselves, meaningless; the significant thing is feeling . . . quite apart from the environment in which it is called forth."

The early works of the third pioneer of Nonobjective art, Piet Mondrian, reveal a search for geometric order in nature. Through a deliberate process of abstraction, Mondrian stripped his canvases of references to recognizable subjects, ultimately reducing his visual vocabulary to "pure" forms (rectangles laid out on a grid of horizontal and vertical lines), the three primary colors (red, blue, and yellow), and three values (white, gray, and black). Each of his paintings achieved a compositional balance that he called an "equivalence of opposites," similar to the satisfying equilibrium of an algebraic equation (Figure **14.19**). Mondrian emigrated to America in 1940, but the movement he had initiated in the Netherlands, called *De Stijl* ("The Style"), would have an international impact in the areas of architecture and furniture design.

Abstraction in Early Modern Sculpture

While Cubists, Futurists, and Fauves pursued their individual styles, they all shared the credo of abstract art: "What is real is not the external form but the essence of things." In the domain of Modernist sculpture, the guardian of this credo was Constantin Brancusi (1876–1957). Born in Romania, he came to Paris in 1904, where he proceeded to create an art of radically simple, organic forms—forms so elemental that they seem to speak a universal language. His landmark sculpture, *Bird in Space* (Figure **14.20**), captures at once the concept of "birdness" and the essence of flight.

Brancusi's younger American contemporary Alexander Calder (1898–1976) produced colorful **biomorphic** metal shapes that he hung with wires from the ceiling, thus inventing a new genre: the **mobile** (Figure **14.21**). Calder's mobiles (ranging from a few feet in size to enormous proportions) float freely in mid-air, taking advantage of the chance effects of air currents to create changing visual relationships between abstract solids and the spaces they occupy.

Expressionism

"Illness, madness, and death were the black angels that kept watch over my cradle," wrote the first Expressionist artist of the twentieth century, Edvard Munch (1863–1944). A contemporary of Freud, this Norwegian painter was obsessed with the traumas of puberty and sexuality, and deeply troubled by personal associations with death—tuberculosis had killed both his mother and sister. Such subjects provided the imagery for his paintings and woodcuts; but it was actually in his style—a haunting amalgam of violently distorted forms and savage colors—that Munch captured the anguished intensity of the neurosis that caused his mental collapse in 1908. *The Scream* (Figure **14.22**), a landmark painting that has become a universal symbol of the modern condition, takes its mood of urgency and alarm from the combined effects of sinuous clouds, writhing blue-black waters, and a dramatically receding pier (a popular meeting spot near Munch's summer cottage). These visual rhythms suggest the resonating sound of the voiceless cry described by Munch in the notes to a preliminary drawing for the painting: "I walked with two friends. Then the sun sank. Suddenly the sky turned red as blood. . . . My friends walked on, and I was left alone, trembling with fear. I felt as if all nature were filled with one mighty unending shriek."

Figure 14.19 Piet Mondrian, *Composition with Large Red Plane, Yellow, Black, Gray, and Blue*, 1921. Oil on canvas, 23⅜ x 23⅜ in. Gemeentemuseum, The Hague. © 2011 Mondrian/Holtzman Trust ᶜ/ₒ HCR International Warrenton, VA. Mondrian, a member of the Dutch Theosophical Society, equated spiritual progress with geometric clarity. In his view, the law of equivalence reflected "the true content of reality." "Not only science," wrote Mondrian, "but art . . . reveals itself by the mutual relations that are inherent in things. Pure science and pure art, disinterested and free, can lead the advance in the recognition of the laws which are based on these relationships."

Figure 14.20 (left) Constantin Brancusi, *Bird in Space*, 1928. Polished bronze, height 4 ft. 6 in. The Museum of Modern Art, New York. The elegant form, curved like a feather, unites birdlike qualities of grace and poise with the dynamic sense of soaring levitation characteristic of mechanical flying machines, such as rockets and airplanes. Indeed, when Brancusi's bronze *Bird* first arrived in America, United States customs officials mistook it for a piece of industrial machinery.

Figure 14.21 (right above) Alexander Calder, *Lobster Trap and Fish Tail*, 1939. Hanging mobile: painted steel wire and sheet aluminum; approx. 8 ft. 6 in. x 9 ft. 6 in. The Museum of Modern Art, New York. It was Duchamp who gave the name "mobile" to the hanging artworks Calder produced from colored shapes. While these objects evoke a sense of childlike spontaneity, they were assembled with careful deliberateness.

Figure 14.22 (right below) Edvard Munch, *The Scream*, 1893. Oil, pastel, and casein on cardboard, 35¾ x 29 in. National Gallery, Oslo. The ghostly foreground figure—Munch himself—may have been inspired by an Inka mummy the artist had seen in the Paris Exhibition of 1889.

Figure 14.23 Ernst Ludwig Kirchner, *Street, Berlin*, 1913. Oil on canvas, 47½ x 35⅞ in. The Museum of Modern Art, New York. Kirchner's angular forms reveal the influence of African sculpture, while the nervous intensity of his line style reflects his debt to the German graphic tradition.

Munch's impassioned paintings foreshadowed German Expressionism, a style that gave violent external form to intense internal feeling. The first of a number of Expressionist groups, *Die Brücke* ("The Bridge") emerged in Dresden in 1905. Its members believed their inspired paintings would constitute a bridge to the future. Influenced by Freud and by the arts of Africa and Oceania, *Die Brücke* artists Ernst Ludwig Kirchner (1880–1938) and Emil Nolde (1867–1956) used harsh colors, angular forms, and the bold application of black to create canvases (and woodcuts) filled with pathos and despair. Seized by Germany's prewar tensions, Kirchner painted ominous cityscapes that show urban life as crowded, impersonal, and threatening (Figure **14.23**).

Metaphysical Art and Fantasy

While the German Expressionists brought subjective intensity to depictions of the visible world, other artists explored the life that lay beyond the senses. Born in Greece, Giorgio de Chirico (1888–1978) moved to Italy in 1909. Rejecting the tenets of Italian Futurism (see page 397), he pioneered a style he called "metaphysical"—that is, "beyond physical reality." Using sharply delineated images, contradictory perspective, unnatural colors, and illogically cast shadows, de Chirico produced disturbing, dreamlike effects similar to those achieved by Kafka's prose. In his painting *The Nostalgia of the Infinite* (Figure **14.24**), two figures, dwarfed by eerie shadows, stand in the empty courtyard; five flags flutter mysteriously in an airless, acid-green sky. The vanishing point established by the orthogonal lines of the portico on the right contradicts the low placement of the distant horizon.

Figure 14.24 Giorgio de Chirico, *The Nostalgia of the Infinite*, 1914, date on painting 1911. Oil on canvas, 53¼ x 25½ in. The Museum of Modern Art, New York. About his disquieting cityscapes, de Chirico explained, "There are more enigmas in the shadow of a man who walks in the sun than in all the religions of past, present, and future."

Folktales and the residue of intimate dreams and memories inspired other fantasists. Marc Chagall (1887–1985) drew on childhood recollections of his native Russia for images that he combined with imaginative whimsy. Their disjunctive sizes and unexpected positions and their arbitrary colors defy the laws of physical reality (Figure **14.25**). Autobiographical motifs, such as fiddle players and levitating lovers, became Chagall's personal hallmarks in the canvases, murals, prints, and stained glass windows of his long and productive career.

Figure 14.25 Marc Chagall, *I and the Village*, 1911. Oil on canvas, 6 ft. $3\frac{5}{8}$ in. x 4 ft. $11\frac{5}{8}$ in. The Museum of Modern Art, New York. Chagall integrated romance, fantasy, and Cubist abstraction into a vividly colored, topsy-turvy world: Here, Chagall dreams of a Russian village, while the cow dreams of being milked.

The Dada Movement

The most outrageous art movement of the early twentieth century, which called itself *Dada* (French babytalk for "hobby-horse"), challenged the very nature and value of art. Founded in 1916 in Zürich, Switzerland, Dada was conceived by a loosely knit group of European painters and poets who viewed World War I as evidence of a world gone mad. Accordingly, they dedicated themselves to spreading the gospel of irrationality by way of art that was the product of chance, accident, and anticonventional behavior. The nonsensical word "dada" symbolized their irreverent stance, since it was chosen randomly, by inserting a penknife into the pages of a dictionary. The Dada spirit of denial flowered in the ashes of World War I. It infused theater and poetry. Poems made from randomly assembled words cut from newspapers celebrated the logic of chance. And the so-called *theater of cruelty* liberated deeply buried desires of the mind in performances featuring improvisation and violent, bizarre scenarios.

In the visual arts, the leading Dadaist was the French artist Marcel Duchamp, whose *Nude Descending a Staircase* (see Figure 14.16) had stirred the early twentieth-century art world. In 1917 Duchamp launched the landmark Dada work of the century: He placed a common urinal on a pedestal, signed it with the fictitious name "R. Mutt," and submitted it for exhibition. Although rejected by the jury, the piece—which he called *Fountain*—had an enormous impact. Duchamp had created *Fountain* by removing it from the context of everyday life and giving it a new identity (as art). By designating a "found object" as a work of art, he mocked the centuries-old art-making tradition and its aesthetic conventions. Even as it exalted the nonsensical and the absurd, *Fountain* removed the barrier between art and life; it introduced the revolutionary notion that a work of art was first and foremost an artist's *idea*. The nihilistic "logic" of Dada also encouraged artists to alter or "remake" existing art, as accomplished, for example, in Duchamp's revised image (Figure **14.26**) of Leonardo's venerable *Mona Lisa* (see Figure 7.1). Dada established the modern artist as maverick, self-appointed prophet, and defiler of tradition.

Figure 14.26 Marcel Duchamp, *L.H.O.O.Q.*, 1919. Rectified ready-made, pencil on a reproduction of the *Mona Lisa*, $7\frac{3}{4}$ x $4\frac{7}{8}$ in. Collection of Mrs. Mary Sisler. Duchamp called this piece a "corrected ready-made." In addition to the mustache, he added a series of letters at the bottom that, when recited rapidly (in French), describe the sitter in lusty street slang.

Figure 14.27 Salvador Dalí, *The Persistence of Memory* (*Persistance de la Mémoire*), 1931. Oil on canvas, 9½ x 13 in. The Museum of Modern Art, New York. Dalí discouraged viewers from seeking an explicit message in his art. Rather, he insisted that his paintings were designed to "stamp themselves indelibly upon the mind."

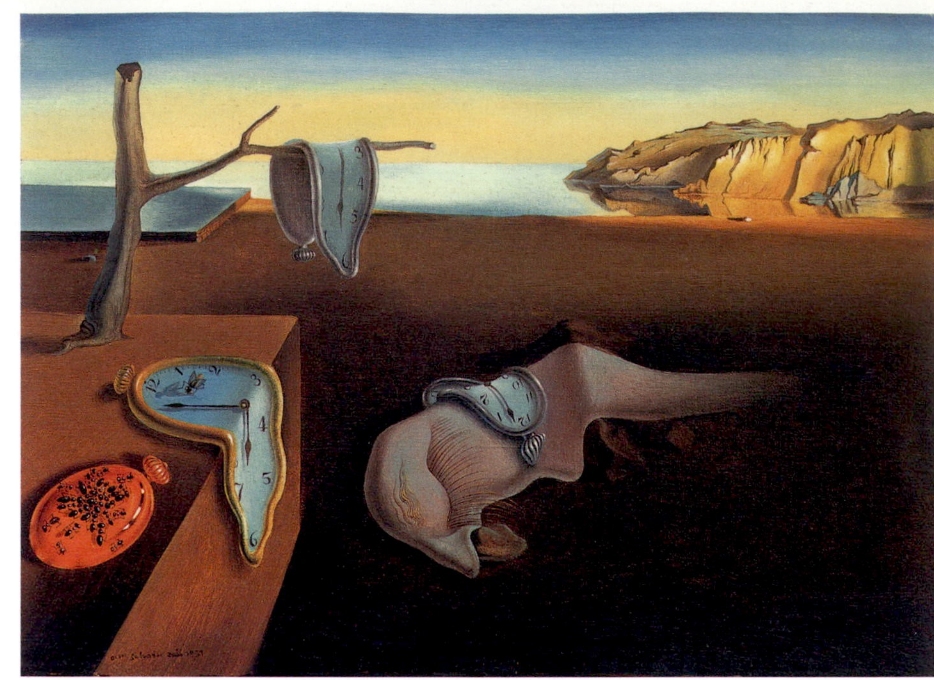

Figure 14.28 (below) René Magritte, *The Betrayal of Images*, ca. 1928–1929. Oil on canvas, 25⅜ x 37 in. Los Angeles County Museum of Art, California. Influenced by de Chirico, Magritte painted precise, realistic images with no distortions, but he juxtaposed these in ways that were irrational and fantastic, thus developing an offshoot of Surrealism known as "Magic Realism."

Surrealism

The movement that immediately followed Dada, known as *Surrealism* ("beyond reality"), gave physical expression to the world of dreams and the workings of the unconscious mind. In the first "Surrealist Manifesto" (1924), the French critic and spiritual godfather of the movement, André Breton (1896–1966), proclaimed the artist's liberation from reason and inhibition. The Surrealists paid homage to Freud and his writings on free association and dream analysis. Breton, who had visited Freud in Vienna, described art as "psychic automatism"—that is, creative effort inspired by freedom from rational control, moral inhibitions, and aesthetic restraints. Breton's emphasis on the omnipotence of the dream state became a guiding principle in the Surrealist enterprise.

Surrealist art ranged from the visionary to the abstract. The Spanish painter Salvador Dalí (1904–1989) combined meticulously painted objects—motifs from his own erotic dreams and fantasies—to evoke what he called "hand-painted dream photographs." His tiny landmark painting, *The Persistence of*

Figure 14.29 Joan Miró, *Person Throwing a Stone at a Bird*, 1926. Oil on canvas, 29 x 36¼ in. The Museum of Modern Art, New York. The "person" described in the title of this painting resembles a large, one-footed amoeba; the bird is a stick figure with a flaming cockscomb; and the stone is an egglike object whose trajectory may be traced by the curved perforated line.

Figure 14.30 Frida Kahlo, *The Broken Column*, 1944. Oil on canvas, $15\frac{3}{4}$ x $12\frac{1}{4}$ in. Frida Kahlo Museum, Mexico City. Kahlo pictures herself in the manner of popular folk images of the suffering Christ; nails and a body brace take the place of punishing thorns and the instruments of torture. The title of the painting makes reference to Kahlo's own injured spine.

Memory, illustrates a barren landscape occupied by a leafless tree, three limp watches, a watchcase crawling with ants, and a mass of brain-matter resembling Dalí's own profile (Figure **14.27**).

Dalí's Belgian contemporary René Magritte (1898–1967) also juxtaposed sharply focused, photographic images in unexpected and shocking ways, but his irrational treatments of realistically depicted objects were often done to test rational assumptions. For instance, his painting *The Betrayal of Images* features a briar pipe, accompanied by the legend "This is not a pipe" (Figure **14.28**). Here, Magritte is addressing the age-old distinction between the real world—the world of *actual* pipes—and the painted image, whose reality is the *virtual* illusion of a pipe.

In contrast with Dalí and Magritte, who depended on precisely delineated objects, the Spanish artist Joan Miró (1893–1983) made use of brightly colored biomorphic shapes and spiny, abstract forms that might constitute the denizens of a science fiction universe. Childlike images from Miró's personal mythology often interact obscurely in an ominous, airless universe (Figure **14.29**).

Perhaps more than any other Modernist movement, Surrealism attracted a number of female artists. Mexico's Frida Kahlo (1907–1954) drew on her native folk culture to produce a uniquely personal style (Figure **14.30**). The principal subject matter of her paintings—more than one-third of which are self-portraits—is Kahlo herself. Determined to present the female image as something other than the object of male desire, Kahlo recorded the experience of chronic pain, both physical (a bus crash at the age of eighteen required some thirty surgeries and ultimately resulted in the amputation of her right leg) and mental (her stormy marriage to the Mexican muralist Diego Rivera—see Figure 14.5—and repeated miscarriages were sources of grief and loss).

The most notable of the female Surrealist sculptors, the Swiss-German Meret Oppenheim (1913–1985), modified found objects in ways that were startling and irrational. Her fur-lined cup, saucer, and spoon provoke the sort of discomforting and threatening associations that informed the psychic underworld of Surrealist art (Figure **14.31**).

Figure 14.31 Meret Oppenheim, *Object* (*Le Déjeuner en fourrure*), 1936. Fur-covered cup, saucer, and spoon; cup $4\frac{3}{8}$ in. diameter; saucer $9\frac{3}{8}$ in. diameter; spoon 8 in. long; overall height $2\frac{3}{8}$ in. The Museum of Modern Art, New York. The Surrealist strategy of combining commonplace things in a disparate and unexpected manner was designed to disturb beholders, but also to disarm them of preconceived assumptions concerning the nature of the physical world.

Photography and Film

For the proponents of Dada and Surrealism, photography was the ideal medium in which to explore the layers of the unconscious mind. In an effort to achieve unusual effects, photographers experimented with double exposures, unorthodox darkroom techniques, and new ways to liberate the finished photograph from traditional pictorialism. In the 1920s, a group of Berlin artists conceived the **photomontage**, an assemblage of freely juxtaposed photographic images—including printed materials taken from books, magazines, and newspapers. These heterogeneous images were glued to a flat surface in the manner of a collage. The champion of the technique, Raoul Hausmann (1886–1971), called photomontage "the 'alienation' of photography," meaning that it worked against the role of photography as a medium for recreating physical reality. By integrating fragmentation and dislocation, photomontage struck Hausmann as "a visually and conceptually new image of the chaos of an age of war and revolution" (Figure **14.32**).

Figure 14.32 Raoul Hausmann, *Tatlin at Home*, 1920. Collage, 16⅛ in. x 11 in. Moderna Museet, Stockholm.

Early twentieth-century photography also served the practical purpose of recording the horrors of war (see Figure 14.6) and landmark events. During the Great Depression, United States federal agencies sponsored a program to provide a permanent record of economic and social conditions in rural America. Migration and rural poverty—breadlines, beggars, and the shanty towns of America's impoverished class—became significant subjects of the straightforward genre of *documentary photography.* The New York photographer Dorothea Lange (1895–1965) traveled across the country documenting the conditions of destitute farmers who had fled the Midwestern Dust Bowl for the fields of California—a phenomenon recounted in John Steinbeck's Social-Realist novel *The Grapes of Wrath* (see page 386). *Migrant Mother*, which Lange photographed at a California farm camp, portrays a gaunt thirty-two-year-old woman who had become the sole supporter of her six children (see Figure 14.2). Forced to sell her last possessions for food, the invincible heroine in this photograph became a symbol of Depression-era poverty.

No less than photography, film provided a permanent historical record of the turbulent military and political events of the early twentieth century. It also became an effective medium of political propaganda. In Russia, Lenin envisioned film as an invaluable means of spreading the ideals of communism. Following the Russian Revolution, he nationalized the fledgling motion-picture industry. In the hands of the Russian filmmaker Sergei Eisenstein (1898–1948), film operated both as a vehicle for political persuasion and as a fine art. He shaped the social and artistic potential of cinema by combining realistic narrative with symbolic imagery.

In *The Battleship Potemkin* (1925), his silent film masterpiece, Eisenstein staged the 1905 mutiny of the tzar's soldiers to resemble an on-the-spot documentary. He used to brilliant effect the technique of **montage**—the assembling of cinematic shots in rapid succession. The final sequence of the film captures with graphic force the events of a riot in the city of Odessa. Eisenstein interposed images of the advancing tzarist police with a series of alternating close-ups and long shots of civilian victims, including those of a mother who is killed trying to save her infant in a baby carriage that rolls down a broad flight of stairs (Figure **14.33**).

While Eisenstein used film to glorify the collective and individual heroism of the Soviet people, German filmmakers working for Hitler turned motion pictures into outright vehicles of state propaganda. The filmmaker and former actress Leni Riefenstahl (1902–2003) received unlimited state subsidies to produce the most famous propaganda film of all time, *The Triumph of the Will* (1934). She engaged a crew of 135 people to film the huge rallies and ceremonies staged by Hitler and the Nazi party, including their first meeting in Nuremberg (Figure **14.34**).

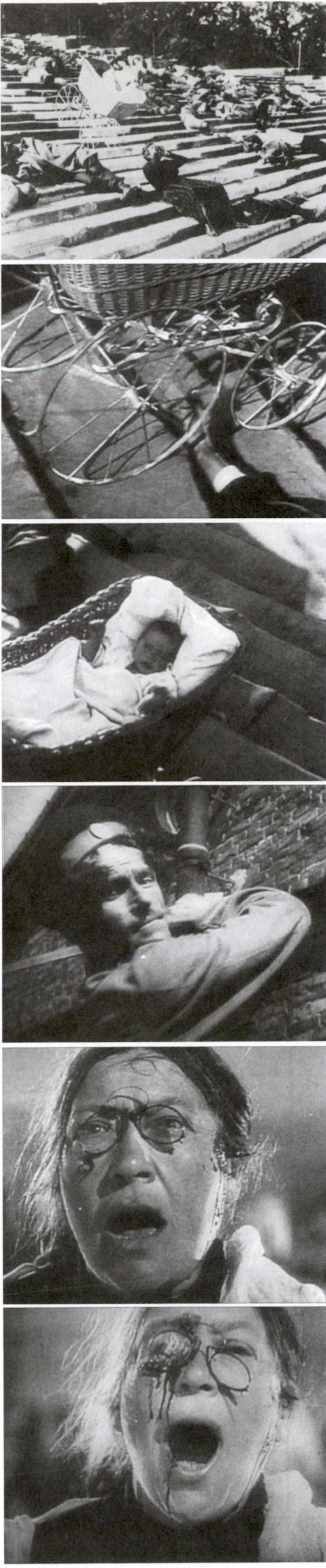

Figure 14.33 Sergei M. Eisenstein, *The Battleship Potemkin*, 1925. Film stills from Act IV, "The Odessa Steps Massacre." The so-called "Odessa Steps sequence," whose rapidly increasing tempo evokes apprehension and terror, is a landmark piece of editing that has often been imitated by modern filmmakers.

Figure 14.34 Leni Riefenstahl, *The Triumph of the Will*, 1934. Film still showing members of the Nazi hierarchy framed by columns of people as they approach the memorial monument in Nuremberg, Germany. *The Triumph of the Will* is a synthesis of documentary fact and sheer artifice. Its bold camera angles and stark compositions seem in themselves totalitarian—note the absolute symmetry and exacting conformity of the masses of troops that frame the tiny figures of Hitler and his compatriots at the Nuremberg rally.

In America, film served to inform, to boost morale, and to propagandize for the Allied cause, but it also served as entertainment and escape. At the height of the Depression as well as during the war era, millions of Americans flocked to movie theaters each week. While such prize-winning movies as *All Quiet on the Western Front* (1930) and *From Here to Eternity* (1953) were painfully realistic, numerous other films romanticized and glamorized the war. An exception to the standard war-movie fare was *The Great Dictator* (1940), which was directed by the multi-talented British-born actor and filmmaker Charlie Chaplin (1889–1977). In this hilarious satire of Fascist dictatorship, Adolf Hitler (known in the film as Adenoid Hynkel and played by Chaplin) rises to power as head of the "Double Cross Party," only to be arrested by his own troops, who mistake him for a Jewish barber.

The Surrealists looked to film as a vehicle of the nonsensical. In 1928, Salvador Dalí teamed up with the Spanish filmmaker Luis Buñuel (1900–1983) to create the landmark Surrealist film, *Un Chien Andalou*. Violence and eroticism are the dominant motifs of this film, whose more famous scenes include ants crawling out of a hole in a man's palm, a woman poking a stick at an amputated hand, and an eyeball being sliced with a razor blade. Such special techniques as slow motion, close-up, and quick cuts from scene to scene work to create jolting, dreamlike effects. It is no surprise that Surrealist film had a formative influence on some of the later twentieth century's most imaginative filmmakers, including Jean Cocteau, Jean Renoir, Ingmar Bergman, and Federico Fellini.

MODERN ARCHITECTURE

Wright and Modern Architecture

The revolution in twentieth-century architecture was made possible by the use of **ferroconcrete** (a cement building material reinforced with steel rods) in combination with the structural steel **cantilever**: a horizontal beam supported at one end and projecting beyond the point of support. In the architecture of Frank Lloyd Wright (1869–1959), the first American architect of world significance, this confluence of materials and technique attained landmark importance.

The foremost student of Louis Sullivan (see Figure 13.6), Wright visited Japan when he was in his thirties. Impressed by the grace and purity of Japanese art, he admired the respect for natural materials and the sensitive relationship between setting and structure that characterized Japanese architecture. His earliest designs embraced the East Asian principle of horizontality, by which buildings "hugged" the earth. From Japanese interiors, where walls often consist of movable screens (see Figures 5.12 and 10.30), he formulated the idea of interconnecting interior and exterior space, using the steel frame and the cantilever to create large areas of uninterrupted space. He subordinated decorative detail to the overall design and allowed the structural materials—wood, brick, glass, concrete, or natural rock—to establish the personality of the building. Wright's style featured crisp, interlocking planes, contrasting textures, and interpenetrating solids and voids—domestic architecture that was as abstract as a Cubist painting. His dramatic use of the cantilever and his integration of landscape and house reached new imaginative heights in Fallingwater, the residence he designed at Bear Run, Pennsylvania (Figure **14.35**).

The crowning achievement of Wright's long career depended on his sculptural use of ferroconcrete. The Guggenheim Museum, located in New York City's borough of Manhattan, resembles a huge snail shell (Figure **14.36**); its interior consists of a continuous spiral ramp fixed around an open central well that receives natural light passing through the glass dome at the top (see Figure 15.23). The definitive example of the modern architectural imagination, the breathtaking enclosure competes seductively with almost any artwork exhibited therein.

Figure 14.35 Frank Lloyd Wright, Fallingwater, Kaufmann House, Bear Run, Pennsylvania, 1936–1939. Reinforced concrete, stone, masonry, steel-framed doors and windows, enclosed area 5800 sq. ft. Embracing a cascading waterfall, the ferroconcrete and stone structure seems to grow organically out of the natural wooded setting.

Figure 14.36 Frank Lloyd Wright, The Solomon R. Guggenheim Museum, New York, 1957–1959. A ten-story limestone extension added in 1992 reduces the dramatic contrast between the rotunda and its urban setting, but it does not destroy the eloquence of the original design. The exterior walls of the museum have been used recently as a canvas for the electronic projection of visual art. For an interior view, see Figure 15.23.

The Bauhaus and the International Style

Wright's synthesis of art and technology anticipated the establishment of Modernism's most influential school of architecture and applied art: the *Bauhaus* ("house for building"). Founded in 1919 by the German architect and visionary Walter Gropius (1883–1969), the *Bauhaus* pioneered an instructional program that fused machine-age technology with the principles of functional design. It advocated a close relationship between form and function, whether in architecture, furniture design, typography, or industrial products. Bauhaus instructors, who included Kandinsky, Mondrian, and Gropius himself, promoted new, synthetic materials, starkly simple designs, and the standardization of parts for the production of affordable, mass-produced merchandise and large-scale housing.

Led by Gropius, the Bauhaus launched the International Style in architecture, which combined, with formal precision and geometric austerity, the materials of ferroconcrete, structural steel, and sheet glass. The four-story structure designed by Gropius for the Bauhaus school in Dessau features unadorned curtain walls of glass freely suspended on structural steel cantilevers (Figure **14.37**).

Figure 14.37 Walter Gropius, Workshop wing, Bauhaus Building, Dessau, Germany, 1925–1926. Steel and glass. First established in Weimar, the Bauhaus moved to Dessau in 1924, and then to Berlin in 1932. Its teaching program aimed to dissolve traditional distinctions between fine and applied arts and break down the barriers between painting, architecture, crafts, and industrial design.

Figure 14.38 Ludwig Mies van der Rohe, Seagram Building, New York, 1954–1958. Metallic bronze and amber glass. This sleek, unadorned slab was "the last word" in sophisticated machine engineering and a monument to the "form follows function" mandate of the International Style.

When the Nazi government closed down the school in 1933, many Bauhaus instructors emigrated to the United States, where they exercised tremendous influence on modern architecture and the industrial arts. The heroic steel-and-glass Manhattan skyscrapers of Ludwig Mies van der Rohe (1886–1969), the last director of the Bauhaus, reflect the machinelike austerity of the International Style (Figure **14.38**). "Less is more," the credo of this architect, inspired a cool, impersonal style that came to be associated with the power and authority of modern capitalism.

The Swiss architect and town planner Charles-Edouard Jeanneret (1887–1965), who called himself Le Corbusier (a pun on the French word for "raven"), was not directly affiliated with the Bauhaus but shared its precepts. Le Corbusier proposed that modern buildings should imitate the efficiency of the machine. "The house," he claimed, "is a machine for living." He realized his utopian ideal in the Villa Savoye, a residence located outside of Paris (Figure **14.39**). Considered a landmark of the International Style, the villa consists of simple, unadorned masses of ferroconcrete punctured by ribbon windows. Its open spatial plan, large areas of glass, and roof garden gave definition to the purist vocabulary of modern architecture. Le Corbusier's will to fit form to function also generated the first high-rise urban apartment buildings—structures that housed over a thousand people and consolidated the facilities for shopping, recreation, and child care under a single roof. These "vertical cities" became hallmarks of urban Modernism and—for some—symbols of its depersonalizing anonymity.

Figure 14.39 Le Corbusier, Villa Savoye, Poissy, France, 1928–1929. Ferroconcrete and glass. The house is raised above the ground on *pilotis*, pillars that free the ground area of the site. (Some modern architects have abused the *pilotis* principle to create parking space for automobiles.)

MUSIC AND DANCE

NO less than the visual arts, the music of the early twentieth century represents an assault on tradition. Modern composers rejected conventional modes of expression, including traditional harmonies and instrumentation. Melody—like recognizable subject matter in painting—became of secondary importance to formal considerations of composition. While they invented no new forms comparable to the fugue or the sonata, modern composers explored innovative effects based on dissonance, the free use of meter, and the unorthodox combination of musical instruments, some of which they borrowed from non-Western cultures. The results were as startling to the ear as modern art was to the eye.

Stravinsky

In the year 1913, a Paris audience witnessed the premiere of the ballet *Le Sacre du printemps* (*The Rite of Spring*). The piece was performed by the Ballets Russes, a company of expatriate Russians led by Sergei Diaghilev (1872–1929), and the music was written by the Russian composer Igor Stravinsky (1882–1971). Shortly after the music began, catcalls, hissing, and booing disrupted the performance, as members of the audience protested the "shocking" sounds that were coming from the orchestra. By the time the police arrived, Stravinsky had disappeared through a backstage window. What offended this otherwise sophisticated audience was Stravinsky's bold combination of throbbing rhythms and dissonant harmonies, which, along with the jarring effects of Vaslav Nijinsky's eccentric choreography (see pages 380 and 413–414), declared war on the musical precepts of the past.

Stravinsky, *The Rite of Spring* (1913)

Stravinsky was one of the most influential figures in the history of twentieth-century music. He began to study music at a young age. His family pressed him to pursue a career in law, but Stravinsky was intent on becoming a composer. At the age of twenty-eight, he left Russia for Paris, where he joined the company of the Ballets Russes. Allied with some of the greatest artists of the time, including Picasso and Nijinsky (see Figure 13.33), Stravinsky was instrumental in making the Ballets Russes a leading force in modern dance theater. His influence on American music was equally great, especially after 1939, when he moved permanently to the United States.

Russian folktales and songs provided inspiration for many of Stravinsky's early compositions, including *The Rite of Spring*. Subtitled *Pictures from Pagan Russia*, this landmark work was based on an ancient Slavonic ceremony that invoked the birth of spring with the ritual sacrifice of a young girl. *The Rite* is a pastoral piece, but its music lacks the calm grace traditionally associated with that genre. Its harsh chordal combinations and unexpected shifts of meter set it apart from earlier pastorals, such as Debussy's *Prelude to "The Afternoon of a Faun"* (see page 379). While Debussy's rhythms are gentle and ebbing, Stravinsky's are percussive and pulsing. Whereas Debussy's tonal shifts are subtle and nuanced, Stravinsky's are abrupt and disjunctive. Portions of the work are polytonal, while other passages are ambiguous in tonality. Stravinsky scored it for an unusual combination of instruments that included eighteen woodwinds, eighteen brass, and a *guiro* (a Latin American gourd that is scraped with a wooden stick).

During the 1920s, composers moved beyond the exotic instrumental forays of Stravinsky's *Rite of Spring* to explore even more unorthodox experiments in sound. A group of artists that included the French composer Erik Satie (1866–1925) incorporated into their music such "instruments" as doorbells, typewriters, and roulette wheels.

Schoenberg

Even more radical than Stravinsky was the Austrian composer Arnold Schoenberg (1874–1951). Schoenberg's early compositions were conceived in the Romantic tradition, but by 1909 he began to develop a musical language punctuated by dissonant, unfamiliar chords. Instead of organizing tones around a home key (the tonal center), he treated all twelve notes of the chromatic scale equally to create the first **atonal** (without a tonal center) compositions.

During the 1920s, Schoenberg went on to formulate a landmark unifying system for atonal composition based on **serial technique**. His type of *serialism*, called "**the twelve-tone system**," demanded that the composer use all twelve tones of the chromatic scale either melodically or in chords before any one of the other eleven notes might be repeated. The twelve-tone row might be inverted or played upside down or backward—there are actually forty-eight possible musical combinations for each tone row.

In theory, the serial technique invited creative invention rather than mechanical application. Nevertheless, to the average listener, who could no longer leave the concert hall humming a melody, Schoenberg's atonal compositions seemed forbidding and obscure. His disquieting music stirred up great controversy among audiences and critics, but he attracted a large following among composers. Even after he moved to the United States in 1933, young composers—including many associated with Hollywood film—flocked to study with him. And while critics found much of Schoenberg's music "depraved" and "ugly," movie audiences were quick to accept the jolting dissonances of scores that worked to lend emotional expressiveness to the cinematic narrative.

Modern Music-Drama and Opera

From the first decades of the twentieth century, modern music-drama and opera reflected the impact of Freud's theories. Sexuality, eroticism, female hysteria, and the life of dreams informed the musical works of the day. In the opera *Salome* (1905), a modern interpretation of the martyrdom of John the Baptist, the German composer Richard Strauss (1864–1949) dramatized the obsessive erotic attachment of King Herod's beautiful niece to the Christian prophet. Revolutionary in sound (in some places the meter changes in every bar) and in its frank treatment of a biblical subject, the opera shocked critics so deeply that a performance slated for Vienna in 1905 was canceled; in America, the opera was banned for almost thirty years after its New York performance in 1907. *Bluebeard's Castle* (1918), a one-act opera by the leading Hungarian composer of the twentieth century, Béla Bartók (1881–1945), did not suffer so harsh a fate, despite the fact that the composer had boldly recast a popular fairytale into a parable of repressed tension and jealousy between the sexes.

Schoenberg's *Pierrot Lunaire* (*Moonstruck Pierrot*), a cycle of twenty-one songs for female voice and small instrumental ensemble, brought to life the dreamworld of a mad clown. The text of this piece resembles a stream-of-consciousness monologue, while the music is atonal and harshly dissonant. The songs are performed in ***Sprechstimme*** ("song-speech"), a style in which words are spoken at different pitches. Pitches are approximated, so the voice may glide in a wailing manner from note to note.

Schoenberg, *Pierrot Lunaire* (*Moonstruck Pierrot*) (1912)

Schoenberg's foremost student, Alban Berg (1885–1935), produced two of the most powerful operas of the twentieth century. Though less strictly atonal than Schoenberg's song cycles, Berg's operas *Wozzeck* and *Lulu* make use of serial techniques and the *Sprechstimme* style. Thematically, they feature the highly charged motifs of sexual frustration, murder, and suicide.

Berg, *Wozzeck* (1921); *Lulu* (1935)

Modern Music in Soviet Russia and America

In Soviet Russia, the communist regime specified that composers write only music that "communicated" to the people. Atonality, associated with elitism and inscrutability, was censored, along with other expressions of Western "decadence." Nevertheless, two great Russian composers emerged in the first half of the twentieth century: Dmitri Shostakovich (1906–1975) and Sergei Prokofiev (1891–1953). Both wrote essentially tonal music that made dramatic use of dissonance.

Shostakovich produced fifteen symphonies, some of epic grandeur, and as many string quartets. Soviet officials criticized Shostakovich's music for its "bourgeois formalism." The composer was repeatedly denounced by the government and, in 1948, dismissed from his posts at the Moscow and Leningrad conservatories. Nevertheless, his Symphony No. 5 in D minor, appealing in its lyricism, received a half-hour ovation when it was first performed in Leningrad; it remains to this day his most celebrated work.

Shostakovich, Symphony No. 5 in D minor (1937)

Prokofiev's numerous ballet scores, his witty classic the *Lieutenant Kije Suite* (1934), and his orchestral fairytale *Peter and the Wolf* (designed to introduce all the instruments of the traditional orchestra) are melodic and rhythmically inventive. The Soviets brought pressure to bear on Prokofiev and denounced even his more tonal works as "too modern."

While the music of Shostakovich and Prokofiev prevailed over Soviet censorship, that of Aaron Copland (1900–1990) drew nourishment from Native American idioms. The New York composer spiced his largely tonal compositions with the simple harmonies of American folk songs, the clarity of Puritan hymns, and the lively and often syncopated rhythms of jazz and Mexican dance. In 1941, Copland advised American composers to find alternatives to the harsh and demanding serialism of their European colleagues: "The new musical audiences will have to have music they can comprehend," he insisted. "It must therefore be simple and direct. . . . Above all, it must be fresh in feeling." Copland achieved these goals in many of his compositions, especially in the ballet scores *Billy the Kid* (1938), *Rodeo* (1940), and *Appalachian Spring.*

Copland, *Appalachian Spring* (1944)

Jazz

The most important new musical genre of the twentieth century was called *jazz.* A unique form of modern music, jazz is a synthesis of diverse musical elements that came together in the first two decades of the twentieth century and flowered as an artform following World War I. Primarily a performer's—rather than a composer's—art, jazz combines Afro-Caribbean improvisational styles with a wide range of European and African concepts of rhythm, harmony, melody, and tone color. In its evolution, it drew upon a vocal style called *blues,* a piano style known as *ragtime,* and the musical traditions of the marching brass band and the minstrel stage.

Ragtime is a form of piano composition and performance featuring highly syncopated rhythms and simple, appealing melodies. It apparently originated in the lower Mississippi valley, but it migrated north after the Civil War and became popular during the 1890s. Its most inspired proponent (if not its inventor) was the black composer and ragtime pianist Scott Joplin (1868–1917). Early jazz performers, like "Jelly Roll" Morton (Ferdinand Joseph LaMonthe, 1885–1941), who claimed to have invented jazz, utilized ragtime rhythms in developing the essential features of the new form.

Blues, a second major contributor to the development of jazz, had begun as a vocal rather than an instrumental form of music. Native to the United States, but possibly stemming from African song forms and harmonies, it is

Figure 14.40 King Oliver's Creole Jazz Band, 1923. Honore Dutrey, Warren "Baby" Dodds, Joe Oliver, Louis Armstrong, Lillian Hardin, Bill Johnson, and Johnny Dodds.

an emotive form of individual expression for lamenting one's troubles, loneliness, and despair. A blues song may recall the wailing cries of plantation slaves; it may describe the anguish of separation and loss or the hope for deliverance from oppression. Such classics as W. C. Handy's "St. Louis Blues" begin with a line that states a simple plaint ("I hate to see the evening sun go down"); the plaint is repeated in a second line, and it is "answered" in a third ("It makes me think I'm on my last go-round")—a pattern derived perhaps from African call-and-response chants.

Handy, "St. Louis Blues" (1914)

As a performance art, jazz depends on improvisation and on the interaction of the ensemble's members as they create a composition in the very act of performing it. Although syncopated rhythms, the blues motif, certain harmonic patterns, and improvisation were not in themselves new, their combination—when vitalized by a "swinging" performance—produced an essentially new artform, one that would have a major impact on Western music for years to come.

The beginnings of American jazz are found in New Orleans, Louisiana, a melting pot for the rich heritage of Spanish, French, African, Caribbean, Indian, and Black Creole musical traditions. Here, black and white musicians drew on the intricate rhythms of African tribal dance and the European harmonies of traditional marching bands. Such parade bands performed perhaps the earliest version of what became jazz. Similar bands also played the kinds of music that were popular in nightclubs and dance halls.

Louis Armstrong (1900–1971), a native of New Orleans who began playing the cornet at the age of twelve, emerged in the 1920s as the foremost jazz musician of the period. Armstrong's innovative solos provided the breakthrough by which solo improvisation became central to jazz performance. His ability to redirect harmonies and to invent inspired reworkings of standard melodies in his solos—all performed with breathtaking virtuosity—elevated the jazz soloist to the foremost role in ensemble performance. "Satchmo" ("Satchelmouth") Armstrong was also a jazz singer with formidable musical gifts. He often embellished jazz pieces with **scat singing**—an improvised set of nonsense syllables. He is widely regarded as having turned jazz into an internationally respected musical form. "Hotter Than That," a composition by Lillian Hardin (Armstrong's wife), exemplifies the style termed "hot jazz" (Figure **14.40**).

Hardin and Armstrong, "Hotter Than That" (1927)

In the years following World War II, jazz took on some of the complex and sophisticated characteristics of "art music." The landmark suite *Black, Brown, and Beige* composed by Edward Kennedy "Duke" Ellington (1899–1974) paved the way for concert-hall jazz, a form that enjoyed a revival in the 1990s. Ellington was a prolific musician—unquestionably the foremost composer in the jazz idiom that the United States has produced.

Ellington, *Black, Brown, and Beige* (1948)

On a smaller scale, among groups of five to seven instruments, the jazz of the late 1940s and 1950s engaged the unique improvisational talents of individual performers. New forms included "bebop" (or "bop")—a jazz style characterized by frenzied tempos, complex chord progressions, and dense polyrhythms—and "cool" jazz, a more restrained and gentler style associated with the West Coast. "Ko-Ko," written by Duke Ellington and performed by the saxophonist Charlie Parker (1920–1955) and the trumpeter John "Dizzy" Gillespie (1917–1993), epitomizes the bop style of the 1940s. Since the jazz renaissance of the 1980s, the New Orleans composer, trumpet prodigy, and teacher Wynton Marsalis (b. 1961) has reconfirmed the role of jazz as America's classical music.

Modern Dance

Only a year after his daring performance in Debussy's *The Afternoon of a Faun* (see page 380), Vaslav Nijinsky aroused even greater controversy with his choreography for *The Rite of Spring* (1913). He took the rhythmic complexity of Stravinsky's score as inspiration for frenzied leaps and wild, wheeling rounds that shocked his audience—including Stravinsky himself. Nijinsky's angular movements, interrupted by frozen stillness, were reminiscent of Cubist paintings (see Figure 13.33). His choreography, according to one critic, revealed "the hidden primitive in man." Nijinsky's career ended tragically in 1917, when he became incurably insane. In his ten years as the West's first dance superstar, he had choreographed only four ballets. The original choreography for *The Rite of Spring* was lost to history. Not until 1987 was a reconstruction of this landmark work revived for the American stage.

The early history of modern dance in America owes much to the pioneer choreographer Martha Graham (1894–1991). Graham defined dance as "making visible the interior landscape." Following Isadora Duncan (see page 378) and Nijinsky, Graham rejected the rules and conventions of classical ballet and explored instead the expressive power of natural movement. Drawing on the dance traditions of Asia, Africa, and Native America, she sought in dance a direct correspondence between inner emotion and physical gesture. Dramatic abstraction and fierce, earthy expressiveness were major features of Graham's style, and of early modern dance in general.

By contrast with Graham, George Balanchine (1904–1983) developed a dance idiom that was storyless, abstract, and highly structured. Balanchine was a Russian choreographer who spent his early career in Paris with Diaghilev's Ballets Russes. In 1934, he was persuaded to come to the United States, where he helped to found the School of American Ballet. Like Stravinsky, with whom he shared a forty-five-year association, he prized pure artistic form that depended on rigorous academic dance training and the use of traditional toe-shoes for women. As impersonal as a Nonobjective painting, Balanchine's choreography brought a classical spirit to modern dance.

The development of modern dance (and its practice to this day) owes much to the genius of Katharine Dunham (1909–2006). The "Mother of Black Dance," Dunham was both a choreographer and a trained anthropologist who investigated the vast resources of the black heritage, ranging from African-American slave dances to the dance histories of Africa and the Caribbean. For centuries, dance had served African-Americans as a language of religious expression and a metaphor for physical freedom. In the late nineteenth century, when all-black theatrical companies and minstrel shows toured the United States, popular dances like the high-stepping cakewalk and tap-dance styles came to influence social and theatrical dance. Dunham created freely improvised works that drew on these traditions, as well as on the exotic dance idioms of indigenous black societies in Haiti and Africa. In the 1930s she formed her own company—the first, and for some thirty years, the only American black dance company. Touring Europe, Latin America, and the United States for decades, her company brought international stature to African-American dance. In her landmark book, *Dances of Haiti* (1983), she examined the sociological functions of dance: how, for example, communal dance captures the spirit and meaning of folk celebrations. Dunham's achievements inspired such outstanding choreographers as Alvin Ailey (1931–1989), Donald McKayle (b. 1930), and Arthur Mitchell (b. 1934), who founded the Dance Theater of Harlem, America's first black classical dance company.

Afterword

Modernism emerged in the presence of a new scientific model of time and space, a radical reassessment of the geography of the human mind, and the horrors of total war and totalitarianism. In the West, these developments fueled the rejection of traditional values and norms, and contributed to the Modernist will to "make it new." Innovation, disjunction, and abstraction were central features of a new aesthetic that pervaded early twentieth-century literature, architecture, the visual arts, music, and dance. Photography and film emerged as major Modernist art forms. By mid-century, however, at the dawn of the nuclear age, the very technologies that had promised to liberate humankind threatened its survival. In the coming decades Modernism would be absorbed in regions beyond the West and radically transformed by both globalism and the digital revolution.

Key Topics

- the new physics
- the Freudian revolution
- World War I
- the Harlem Renaissance
- the Russian Revolution
- World War II
- the Holocaust
- Imagism and modern poetry
- modern fiction and drama
- science fiction
- Cubism/Futurism/Fauvism
- Nonobjective art
- Expressionism
- Dada and Surrealism
- photography and film
- modern architecture
- modern music
- modern dance

MODERNISM TIMELINE

	HISTORICAL EVENTS	LANDMARKS IN THE VISUAL ARTS	LITERARY LANDMARKS	MUSIC AND DANCE LANDMARKS
1890	• Edison: moving images on screen (1895)	• Munch, *The Scream* (1893)		
1900	• Orville and Wilbur Wright make first successful airplane flight (1903) • Einstein: special theory of relativity (1905)	• Matisse, *Madame Matisse* (1905) • Picasso, *Les Demoiselles d'Avignon* (1907)	• Freud, *The Interpretation of Dreams* (1900)	
1910	• Mexican Revolution (1911–1912) • World War I: over 8 million die (1914–1918) • Einstein: general theory of relativity (1916) • Russian Revolution (1917)	• Duchamp, *Nude Descending a Staircase, No. 2* (1912) • Kandinsky, *Panel for Edwin Campbell, No. 2* (1914)	• Proust, *Remembrance of Things Past* (1913–1927) • Kafka, "The Metamorphosis" (1915) • Jung, *Psychology of the Unconscious* (1916) • Lenin, "The State and Revolution" (1917)	• Schoenberg, *Pierrot Lunaire* (1912) • Stravinsky, *The Rite of Spring* (1913) • Handy, "St. Louis Blues" (1914)
1920	• American women win right to vote (1920) • Stalin becomes leader of the U.S.S.R. (1926) • Heisenberg: principle of uncertainty (1927) • Great Depression (1929–1940s)	• Mondrian, *Composition with Large Red Plane* (1921) • Eisenstein, *The Battleship Potemkin* (1925) • Gropius, Bauhaus Building, Dessau (1925–1926) • Brancusi, *Bird in Space* (1928) • Le Corbusier, Villa Savoye (1928–1929)	• Yeats, "The Second Coming" (1921) • Eliot, *The Waste Land* (1922) • Joyce, *Ulysses* (1922) • Pound, *Personae* (1926)	• Schoenberg formulates twelve-tone system (1920s) • Berg, *Wozzeck* (1921) • Hardin, "Hotter Than That" (1927)
1930	• Atom is split (1932) • Spanish Civil War (1936–1939) • World War II: 11 million die in Holocaust (1939–1945)	• Dalí, *The Persistence of Memory* (1931) • Riefenstahl, *The Triumph of the Will* (1934) • Lange, *Migrant Mother, Nipomo* (1936) • Wright, Fallingwater, Bear Run (1936–1939) • Picasso, *Guernica* (1937)	• O'Neill, *Mourning Becomes Electra* (1931) • Huxley, *Brave New World* (1932) • Hurston, *Their Eyes Were Watching God* (1937)	• Shostakovich, Symphony No. 5 in D minor (1937)
1940	• Atomic bomb first used (1945) • People's Republic of China established (1949)	• Hopper, *Nighthawks* (1942)	• Clarke, "The Sentinel" (1948)	• Copland, *Appalachian Spring* (1944) • Ellington, *Black, Brown, and Beige* (1948)
1950			• Hughes, "Harlem" (1951) • Wiesel, *Night* (1958)	

Figure 14.6 Lee Miller, *Buchenwald*, see p. 389

Figure 14.30 Frida Kahlo, *The Broken Column*, see p. 405

Figure 14.17 Henri Matisse, *Madame Matisse (The Green Line)*, see p. 399

Figure 14.39 Le Corbusier, Villa Savoye, Poissy, France, see p. 410

Chapter 15

Globalism:

INFORMATION, COMMUNICATION, AND THE DIGITAL REVOLUTION

ca. 1945–the present

The second half of the twentieth century witnessed the evolution of globalism: the condition of interdependence between all parts of the world. Globalism was born in the technology of mass communication that facilitated rapidly transmitted and universally shared images and ideas. While America took the lead in the arts in the period following World War II, the rest of the planet soon shared the new styles—whether in action painting, rock music, or animated film.

Globalism represents a shift from the elitist Modernism of the early twentieth century to the populist Postmodernism of the late twentieth century. Anticolonial and cold war conflicts, existentialism, feminism, the quest for racial and ethnic identity, and a massive information explosion accelerated by digital technology are among the major developments of this era. A global quest for personal freedom, a passion for experimentation, and a fascination with the "magic" of high technology remain driving forces. While these developments have been largely positive in nature, more troubling concerns for the health of the environment and the dangers of international terrorism have come to challenge the early twenty-first century. It is too soon to determine which of the dizzying array of events, arts, and ideas will become landmarks. Nevertheless, we can be certain that they will reflect the vitality of a media-shaped world culture.

A First Look

The work of the internationally celebrated Chinese artist Yue Minjun (b. 1962) exemplifies globalism. The two grinning figures in this untitled painting, one holding the other aloft in front of the Statue of Liberty, are self-portraits of this Beijing-based artist. Here, as in most of his artworks, Yue pictures himself cloned as many different selves, touring the world's landmarks—some of which appear in the pages of this book. He often sports exotic hats or costumes and assumes the guise of famous historical or art historical characters. Working in a country that limits some forms of personal freedom, Yue draws his imagery from the global library of cultural icons accessible to anyone electronically through television and the Internet. His grinning caricatures, with too many teeth and eyes squeezed shut with the strain of smiling, share the immediacy of popular toothpaste advertisements. Their robust confidence seems to celebrate the recent economic and political reforms that have contributed to the ascendance of China on the global stage (see pages 455–456). Yue has said that his work should be understood as social commentary, but we may ask: On what is he commenting? Are these paintings intended as parodies of China's westernization, symbolized by such universally recognized icons as the Statue of Liberty? Are they mocking comments on the global accessibility of over-commercialized landmarks? Today, Yue's enigmatic grin is the most recognizable image in Chinese painting. Does it also have the potential to become a landmark of the global twenty-first century?

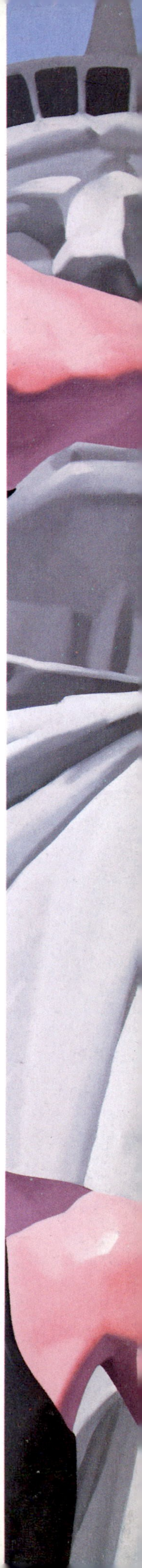

Figure 15.1 Yue Minjun. *Untitled*, 2005. Oil on canvas, 5 ft. 7 in. x 4 ft. 7in. Collection of Justin Tyler Warsh, USA.

POSTWAR CONVULSIONS

THE nightmare of World War II left the world's population in a state of shock and disillusion. The Western democracies had held back the forces of totalitarian aggression, but the future seemed as threatening as ever. The treaty settlements ending World War II left two large blocs of powerful nations ranged against each other in an effort to further their individual political, social, and ideological ends. The largest of these ideological power blocs, the nations led by the United States and its democratic/capitalistic ideology, opposed the Soviet/communist bloc, which came to include most of the Eastern European countries adjacent to Russia. Communism and capitalist democracy confronted one another in hostile distrust. And both possessed nuclear capability with the potential to extinguish the human race.

The Cold War

The contest for world domination—the cold war that followed World War II—determined the course of international relations during the second half of the twentieth century. In Europe, postwar Germany was politically divided, most visibly by the Berlin Wall that separated Soviet-dominated East Germany from West Germany's Democratic Republic. As "power vacuums" occurred in the postcolonial regions of East Asia, the cold war grew hot: in the Korean peninsula, the two "superpowers," the Soviet Union and the United States, wrestled diplomatically but unsuccessfully for dominion in what ultimately became all-out war. The Korean Conflict (1950–1953), fought virtually to a standoff with both sides suffering terrible losses (three million Koreans, mostly civilians, died), ended with the division of the country into a northern communist state (Korean People's Democratic Republic) and a southern democratic state (Republic of Korea). Within a decade, an even larger war developed along similar lines in Southeast Asia. Between 1964 and 1973, the United States succeeded France in an unsuccessful effort to defend South Vietnam from communist control. This bloody war ended with the withdrawal of the United States, and the establishment of a communist Vietnam. The instability of international relations, the threat of "the bomb," a costly arms race, and wracking fear and paranoia dictated the contours of world history until nearly the end of the twentieth century, which witnessed the collapse of Soviet communism in Russia and the fall of the Berlin Wall (1989).

Ideas and Issues

COMMUNISM VERSUS CAPITALISM

For roughly a half-century following World War II, the great powers of the world were divided into two opposing ideological camps popularly known as communism and capitalism. Each of these power blocs—one dominating in the East; the other in the West—followed its own system, and each fervently believed in the necessity of its prevailing in the world struggle for dominance. "Communism"—in reality one of several forms of Marxian socialism—described a social and political system committed to the principle that the central state should own and operate the nation's means of production and distribution of goods, with the whole population sharing the resulting wealth equally (see pages 358–359). "Capitalism" was the term employed to describe a system based on the principle that the world's market capital should function according to free market forces (see Adam Smith, page 302), and that the government should have little to do with regulation of the economic and financial world. Individual initiative and enterprise should function to produce and distribute goods among the population. Because the two systems seemed incompatible, one or the other would have to prevail. Hence, the cold war (which occasionally turned hot), a war of ideology and policies guided by those ideas, formed the basis of international relations in the postwar years.

Q Are communism and capitalism actually incompatible ideologies? How might political policy operate to combine aspects of each?

Existentialism

The pessimism that accompanied the two world wars was compounded by a loss of faith in the bedrock beliefs of former centuries. The Holocaust, the nuclear bombing of Hiroshima and Nagasaki, and the realities of the cold war made it difficult to maintain that human beings were rational by nature and that technology would work to advance human happiness. Some even wondered whether the universe was governed by a benevolent God. "Alienation," a condition of anxious estrangement from God and reason, was the governing mood of the postwar era.

The body of philosophical thought known as *existentialism* gave expression to this state of mind. Its leading proponent, Jean-Paul Sartre (1905–1980), argued that there was no preexisting blueprint for human beings, no essence to which we inevitably must conform. With this premise, Sartre challenged the fundamentals of traditional philosophy: Plato had identified "essence" with the unchanging and eternal Forms (or Ideas); Aristotle saw reason as the essential attribute that separates human beings from the lower animals. Following the ancients, Western philosophers from Descartes through Kant held that internal principles of being preceded being itself—a view metaphysically compatible with Christian theology. Sartre disagreed. Human existence, he insisted, precedes essence; that is, one's material being exists prior to and independent of any preordained factors.

Human beings, proposed Sartre, choose what they become. They have no fixed nature. They are not imbued with any special divinity, nor are they (by nature) rational. They are neither imprisoned by unconscious forces (as Freud had held) nor determined by specific economic

Ideas and Issues

SARTRE: MAN MAKES HIMSELF

"Man is nothing else but what he makes of himself. Such is the first principle of existentialism. It is also what is called subjectivity, the name we are labeled with when charges are brought against us. But what do we mean by this, if not that man has a greater dignity than a stone or table? For we mean that man first exists, that is, that man first of all is the being who hurls himself toward a future and who is conscious of imagining himself as being in the future. Man is at the start a plan which is aware of itself, rather than a patch of moss, a piece of garbage, or a cauliflower; nothing exists prior to this plan; there is nothing in heaven; man will be what he will have planned to be. Not what he will want to be. Because by the word 'will' we generally mean a conscious decision, which is subsequent to what we have already made of ourselves. I may want to belong to a political party, write a book, get married; but all that is only a manifestation of an earlier, more spontaneous choice that is called 'will.' But if existence really does precede essence, man is responsible for what he is. Thus, existentialism's first move is to make every man aware of what he is and to make the full responsibility of his existence rest on him. And when we say that a man is responsible for himself, we do not only mean that he is responsible for his own individuality, but that he is responsible for all men."

(from Sartre, "Existentialism," 1945)

Q In what ways is choice, according to Sartre, central to one's existence?

conditions (as Marx had maintained). Born into the world as body/matter, they proceed to make the choices by which they form their own natures. In Sartre's analysis, each individual is the sum of his or her actions. In that human beings must choose at every turn between a variety of possibilities, they are (in Sartre's words) "condemned to be free." Moreover, since every choice implies a choice for all humankind, each individual bears the overwhelming burden of total responsibility—a condition that Sartre called "anguish." To our profound despair, we seek meaning in a meaningless world. Yet, because human life is all there is, it must be cherished. According to Sartre, the human condition is one of anxiety experienced in the face of nothingness and the inevitability of death. Such anxiety is compounded because we alone are responsible for our actions. To disclaim responsibility for those actions by blaming external causes is to act in "bad faith." To fly from freedom and responsibility is a form of self-deception and inauthenticity. "We are alone, with no excuses," according to Sartre.

The Existential Hero

In addition to his landmark philosophic work, *Being and Nothingness*, Sartre wrote a number of significant novels, short stories, and plays. The most gripping of his plays, *No Exit*, features three characters trapped in a "hell" they have created by their efforts to justify the acts of bad faith that have shaped their lives. Sartre's secular philosophy inspired a new kind of literary hero: a hero who, deprived of traditional values and religious beliefs, bears the burden of freedom and the total responsibility for his actions. The existential hero—or, more exactly, antihero—takes up the quest for meaning: Alienated by nature and circumstance, he makes choices in a world lacking moral absolutes, a world in which no act might be called "good" unless it is chosen in conscious preference to its alternatives. Unlike the heroes of old, the modern antihero is neither noble nor sure of purpose. He might act decisively, but with full recognition of the absence of shared cultural values and moral absolutes. Trapped rather than liberated by freedom, he might have trouble getting along with others or simply making it through the day—"Hell," says one of Sartre's characters in *No Exit*, "is other people."

Sartre, *Being and Nothingness* (1943)

Although existentialism was an essentially European phenomenon, the existential hero appears in the literature of twentieth-century writers throughout the world, most notably in the novels of Sartre's French contemporary Albert Camus, Argentina's Jorge Luis Borges, and Japan's Ōe Kenzaburo. In postwar America, the existential perspective cut across regional lines, from the deep South of William Faulkner and Walker Percy to John Cheever's New England and Bernard Malamud's New York, and from the urban Midwest of Saul Bellow to California's Beat Generation, a group of writers who prized bohemian creativity, anticonformity, and a spontaneous lifestyle.

Jack Kerouac's *On the Road* (1951), a saga of youthful restlessness, and Allen Ginsberg's *Howl* (1955), a ranting lament on America's loss of values, became landmarks of the Beat Generation. *Howl*, with its notorious references to illicit drugs, sexual and homosexual acts, and the evils of American commercialism, opens with these angry lines:

> I saw the best minds of my generation destroyed by madness, starving hysterical naked,
> Dragging themselves through the negro streets at dawn looking for an angry fix;
> Angel-headed hipsters burning for the ancient heavenly connection
> To the starry dynamo in the machinery of night.

Postwar dramatists also treated the existential experience: In the Pulitzer prize-winning play *Death of a Salesman* by Arthur Miller (1915–2005), the antihero is a quintessentially American character. Miller's salesman, Willy Loman, is a "little man" who has met failure at every turn, but he cannot recognize the inauthenticity of his false claims to material success nor realize the futility of his self-deception. An American classic, *Salesman* depends on traditional dramatic structure in bringing to life a complex but ultimately sympathetic existential figure.

Miller, *Death of a Salesman* (1949)

Theater of the Absurd

The international movement known as *theater of the absurd* so vividly captured the anguish of postwar society that late twentieth-century critics called it "the true theater of our time." Abandoning classical theater from Sophocles and Shakespeare through Ibsen and Miller, absurdist playwrights rejected traditional dramatic structure (in which action moves from conflict to resolution), along with traditional modes of character development. The absurdist play, which drew stylistic inspiration from Dada performance art and Surrealist film, usually lacks dramatic progression, direction, and resolution. Its characters undergo little or no change, dialog contradicts actions, and events follow no logical order. Dramatic action, leavened with gallows humor, may consist of irrational and grotesque situations that remain unresolved at the end of the performance—as is often the case in real life.

The principal figures of absurdist theater reflect the international character of the movement: They include Samuel Beckett (Irish), Eugène Ionesco (Romanian), Harold Pinter (British), Fernando Arrabal (Spanish), Jean Genet (French), and Edward Albee (American). Of these, Samuel Beckett (1906–1989), recipient of the Nobel Prize in 1969, earned the greatest distinction with his landmark play *Waiting for Godot*, first staged in 1952. The main "action" of the play consists of a running dialog—terse, repetitious, and often comical—between two tramps as they await the mysterious "Godot" (who, despite their anxious expectations, never arrives). The progress of the play is embellished by an extraordinary blend of biblical allusions, broad slapstick, comic wordplay, Zenlike propositions, and crude jokes. Literary critics find in Godot a symbol of salvation, revelation, or, most commonly, God—an interpretation that Beckett himself rejected. Nevertheless, the absent "deliverer" (perhaps by his very absence) gives a modicum of meaning to the lives of the central characters.

Beckett, *Waiting for Godot* (1948)

Postwar Cinema

Postwar cinema took up the quest for meaning by way of films that challenged traditional moral values. The pioneer Japanese filmmaker Akira Kurosawa (1910–1998) explored the complexities of modern life by way of traditional *samurai* legends. A highly skilled director, he used unusual camera angles, flashbacks, and a stringent economy of expression in the classics *Rashomon* (1950) and *The Seven Samurai* (1954). These landmark films convey Kurosawa's view that positive social action can redeem the world's evils.

Less optimistic was the Swedish cinematic giant Ingmar Bergman (1918–2007). In his almost four dozen films, Bergman probed the troubled lives of modern men and women. The loss of God, the acknowledgment of spiritual and emotional alienation, and the anxieties that accompany self-understanding are his principal themes. Bergman's landmark film *The Seventh Seal* (1957) is an allegorical tale of despair in the face of impending death.

Figure 15.2 Willem de Kooning, *Woman and Bicycle*, 1952–1953. Oil on canvas, 6 ft. 4½ in. x 4 ft. 1 in. Whitney Museum of American Art, New York. De Kooning's wide-eyed females, taken by some to suggest the artist's negative view of women, were actually inspired by Sumerian votive sculptures and Mother Earth images (see Figures 1.3 and 1.15).

Set in medieval Europe (and inspired by the Revelation of St. John in the New Testament), it is the story of a knight who returns home from the Crusades, only to confront widespread plague and human suffering. Disillusioned, he ultimately challenges Death to a game of chess, the stakes of which are life itself.

Abstract Expressionism

During the first half of the twentieth century, almost all important new styles in painting originated in Paris or other European cities. After 1945, however, the United States took the lead. New York City was the birthplace of a radical new art style called *Abstract Expressionism*. The style ushered in the so-called "heroic age of American painting." The pioneers of the movement were a group of talented immigrants who had escaped Nazi oppression and the perils of war-torn Europe. These artists included Arshile Gorky (1905–1948), Hans Hofmann (1880–1966), and Willem de Kooning (1904–1997), all of whom moved to New York between 1920 and 1930.

Working on huge canvases and using oversized brushes, Gorky, Hofmann, and de Kooning applied paint in a loose, free, and instinctive manner that emphasized the physical gesture—the *act* of painting. Abstract Expressionist paintings were usually nonrepresentational, but where recognizable subject matter appeared, as in de Kooning's landmark series of fierce, totemic women—one of his favorite subjects—it was rendered with frenzied, subjective urgency (Figure **15.2**). Here the *process* of making art was elevated to a status almost as significant as the *product* itself.

The best known of the Abstract Expressionists is Wyoming-born Jackson Pollock (1912–1956). His early paintings reveal a coarse figural style and brutal brushwork similar to de Kooning's, but by 1945 Pollock had devised a technique that made action itself the subject of the painting. Instead of mounting the canvas on an easel, he strapped it to the floor of his studio and proceeded to drip, splash, pour, and spread oil, enamel, and commercial aluminum paints across its surface (see Figure 15.4). Layered filaments of paint—the artist's seductive "handwriting"—mingled with sand, nails, matches, bottle shards, and occasional cigarette butts. Like the currents in some cosmic whirlpool, the galactic threads in the painting *Autumn Rhythm* seem to expand beyond the limits of the canvas (Figure **15.5**). His daring, all-over technique, known as "action painting," enabled Pollock (as he explained) "to walk around [the canvas], work from the four sides and literally be in the painting," a method inspired by the healing rituals of Navajo sand painting whose union of intuition, improvisation, and rigorous control he admired.

While Pollock pioneered action painting, other mid-twentieth-century artists explored *color field painting*, a type of total abstraction that involved the application of large, often transparent, layers of paint to the surface of

Making Connections

ACTION PAINTING: EAST AND WEST

In postwar Japan, members of the radical group known as the Gutai Bijutsu Kyokai (Concrete Art Association) harnessed physical action to chance in dynamic performance-centered works. Gutai "action events," which featured the energetic and sometimes outrageous manipulation of paint (flung or hurled at the canvas), allied the random techniques of Surrealism with native Japanese traditions in spontaneous, gestural Zen painting (Figure **15.3**). In a similar manner, America's foremost action painter, Jackson Pollock, gave each of his artworks a life of its own, while insisting that he himself controlled the direction of the painting (Figure **15.4**). "There is no accident," he explained, "just as there is no beginning and no end."

Q How might Pollock's position above the canvas affect the "action" of the painting?

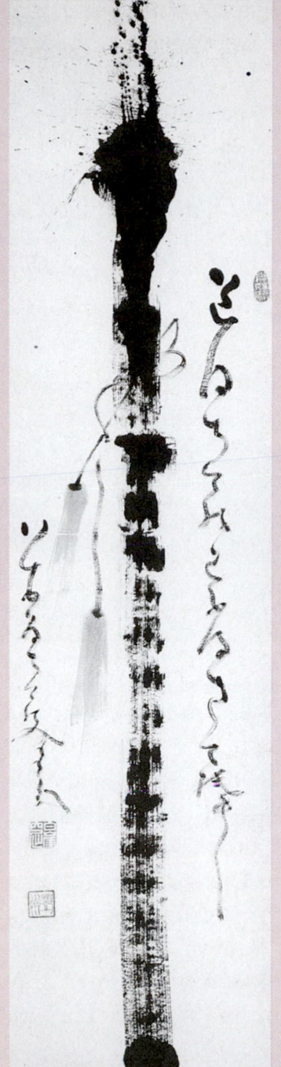

Figure 15.3 Nantembō Nakahara, *Staff* (age 85), 1923. Ink on paper, 50¼ x 13 in. Private Collection. The inscription reads, "If you speak, Nantembō. If you do not speak, Nantembō."

Figure 15.4 Jackson Pollock at work in his Long Island studio, 1950.

Figure 15.5 Jackson Pollock, *Autumn Rhythm*, 1950. Oil on canvas, 8 ft. 7 in. x 17 ft. 3 in. The Metropolitan Museum of Art, New York.

the canvas. Such is the style of Mark Rothko (1903–1970). America's leading color field painter, Rothko experienced the existential alienation of the postwar era. His art moved from figurative abstraction to nonrepresentational multiform grids of glowing, layered colors (Figure **15.6**). Beginning in 1958, a shift from bright to darker hues accompanied the deepening depression that ultimately led him to commit suicide.

Gradually, the size of Abstract Expressionist canvases expanded as if to advertise the heroic ambitions of their makers. Pollock, Rothko, and others seemed to turn their backs on bourgeois taste by creating artworks that were simply too large to hang in the average living room. Ironically, however, this style—which opposed the depersonalizing effects of capitalist technology—came to be prized by the guardians of that very technology. Abstract Expressionist paintings, which now hang in large numbers of corporate offices, hotels, and banks, have become hallmarks of sophistication.

Figure 15.6 Mark Rothko, *Untitled*, 1960. Oil on canvas, 5 ft. 9 in. x 4 ft. 21¹/₈ in. San Francisco Museum of Modern Art. The paintings of Rothko (1903–1970) consist of translucent, soft-edged blocks of color that float mysteriously on the surfaces of other fields of color. These huge, sensuous compositions derive their power from the subtle interaction of rich layers of paint, which seem to glow from within. Rothko believed that spiritual intimacy between the artwork and its viewer would be achieved if the spectator stood no more than 18 inches from the canvas.

THE QUEST FOR EQUALITY

WHILE a mood of despair pervaded the postwar era, a more positive spirit fueled the movements for equality that prevailed throughout the world. Organized efforts to reform conditions of oppression and inequality ranged from anticolonial drives for independence from foreign dominion to crusades for ethnic self-identity and demands—especially fierce in the United States—for racial and gender equality.

The End of Colonialism

The drive for liberation from colonial rule was one of the most potent themes of the twentieth century. After World War II, as weakened European nations were unable to maintain the military forces necessary to police their empires, colonial subjects increased their efforts to free themselves of imperialist control. By doing so, they hoped to reduce poverty and raise the standard of living to the level enjoyed by the more highly developed nations of the world.

One of the earliest revolts against colonial rule took place in India. During World War I, the Indian National Congress came under the influence of the Hindu Mohandas Gandhi (1869–1948). Gandhi, whose followers called him "Mahatma," or "great soul," led India's struggle for independence from Great Britain. Guided by the precepts of Hinduism, as well as by the Sermon on the Mount and the writings of Thoreau and Tolstoy, Gandhi initiated a policy of peaceful protest against colonial oppression. His program of nonviolent resistance, including fasting and peaceful demonstrations, influenced subsequent liberation movements throughout the world. Gandhi's involvement was crucial to India's emancipation from British control, which occurred in 1947, only one year before he was assassinated by a Hindu fanatic who opposed his conciliatory gestures toward India's Muslim minority.

A related drive for liberation was well under way in other parts of Asia: The pan-Islamic quest for a modern-day Muslim state on the Indian subcontinent resulted, in 1947, in an independent Pakistan. Islamist nationalism in Iraq and Iran was hampered by British and Soviet interference and by ethnic conflict among Muslim factions.

Between 1944 and 1960, many nations, including Jordan, Burma, Palestine, Sri Lanka, Ghana, Malaya, Cyprus, and Nigeria, freed themselves from British rule. Syria, Lebanon, Cambodia, Laos, North and South Vietnam, Morocco, Tunisia, Cameroon, Mali, and other African states won independence from France. And still other territories claimed their freedom from the empires of the United States, Japan, the Netherlands, Belgium, and Italy.

In Eastern Europe, the collapse of the Soviet Union in the early 1990s resulted in independence (achieved, for the most part, by way of nonviolent revolutions) in Poland, Hungary, Romania, Bulgaria, and Czechoslovakia. In Muslim Afghanistan the Soviet intervention (1978) and withdrawal (1989), and the subsequent involvement of other superpowers, has had negative consequences for the ongoing civil war among Islamic ethnic and tribal factions.

Some anticolonial movements have been very protracted. The Spanish-speaking and predominantly Catholic nations of Latin America have suffered repeated social upheaval in their attempts to cope with persistent problems of inequality, exploitation, and underdevelopment. Even after the European nations departed from the shores of many Latin American states, the intolerable conditions that had prevailed in the long era of colonialism persisted: The vast majority of Latin Americans, including great masses of peasants of Native American descent, lived in relative poverty, while small, wealthy, landowning elites held power. These elites maintained their position by virtue of their alliance with the financial and industrial interests of First World nations, including (especially since the 1890s) the United States.

Latin America's artists, allied with reformist elements in the clergy, rallied to support movements for liberation. During the 1960s, the outpouring of exceptionally powerful Latin American prose and poetry constituted a literary boom, the influence of which is still being felt worldwide. Among the literary champions of Latin American reform was the Chilean Pablo Neruda (1904–1973), one of the most prolific poets in the history of the Spanish language. The 340 poems that make up his monumental *Canto general* (1950) call attention to the bitter contrast between the proud ancient histories of Latin America and the degradation of its contemporary populations. Neruda endorsed a radical, populist ideology, one that vigorously opposed all agencies of capitalist exploitation.

Neruda, *Canto general* (1950)

The Quest for Racial Equality

The most turbulent liberation movement of the twentieth century addressed the issue of racial equality—an issue so dramatically reflected in the African-American experience that some observers have dubbed the century "The Race Era." Since the days of slavery, millions of black Americans had existed as an underprivileged minority population living within an advanced industrial state. The Dutch took the first black Africans to America in 1619, and during the late seventeenth and eighteenth centuries thousands of black slaves were imported to the American colonies, especially those in the South. For 250 years, until the end of the Civil War, slavery was a fact of American life. While the Emancipation Proclamation issued by Abraham Lincoln in 1863 facilitated the liberation of the slaves, it was not until 1865—with the Thirteenth Amendment to the United States Constitution—that all were finally freed. This and other constitutional amendments guaranteed the

Ideas and Issues

WHITE NO LONGER

"The time has come to realize that the interracial drama acted out on the American continent has not only created a new black man, it has created a new white man, too. . . . One of the things that distinguishes Americans from other people is that no other people has ever been so deeply involved in the lives of black men, and vice versa. . . . It is precisely this black–white experience which may prove of indispensable value to us in the world we face today. This world is white no longer, and it will never be white again."

(from Baldwin, "Stranger in the Village," 1953)

Q What might be the advantages of a world that is "white no longer"?

rights of black people; nevertheless, the lives of African-Americans continued to be harsh and poor by comparison with those of their former white masters. Separation of the races by segregated housing, inferior schools, and exclusion from voting and equal employment were only a few of the inequities suffered by this minority in the post-emancipation United States.

Well after World War II, racism remained an undeniable fact of American life. Ironically, while Americans had fought to oppose Nazi racism in Germany, black Americans endured a system of inferior education, restricted jobs, ghetto housing, and generally low living standards. High crime rates, illiteracy, and drug addiction were evidence of affluent America's awesome failure to assimilate a Third World population that suffered in its midst. The fact that African-Americans had served in great numbers in World War II inspired a redoubled effort to end persistent discrimination and segregation in the United States. During the 1950s and 1960s, that effort came to flower in the civil rights movement.

Civil rights leaders of the 1950s demanded enforcement of all the provisions for equality promised in the United States Constitution. Their demands led to a landmark Supreme Court decision in 1954 that banned school segregation; by implication, this undermined the entire system of legalized segregation in the United States. Desegregation met fierce resistance, especially in the American South. In response, the so-called Negro Revolt began in 1955 and continued for over a decade. It took the form of nonviolent, direct-action protests, including boycotts of segregated lunch counters, peaceful "sit-ins," and protest marches. Leading the revolt was Dr. Martin Luther King, Jr. (1929–1968), a Protestant pastor and civil rights activist who modeled his campaign of peaceful protest on the example of Gandhi. As president of the Southern Christian Leadership Conference, King served as an inspiration to all African-Americans.

The urgency of their cause is conveyed in a letter King wrote while confined to jail for marching without a permit in the city of Birmingham, Alabama. It addressed a group of local white clergy who had publicly criticized King for breaking laws that prohibited blacks from using public facilities and for promoting "untimely" demonstrations. "Letter from a Birmingham Jail" became the landmark text in a nationwide debate over civil rights: It provided philosophic justification for the practice of civil disobedience as a means of opposing injustice. King's measured eloquence and reasoned restraint stand in ironic contrast to the savagery of the opposition, who had used guns, hoses, and attack dogs against the demonstrators, 2,400 of whom were jailed along with King. Assassinated in 1968, King surely would have considered America's election of a biracial president in 2008 a landmark in the quest for racial equality.

King, "Letter from a Birmingham Jail" (1963)

Black Identity in the Arts

Two luminaries of American black protest literature were James Baldwin (1924–1987) and Ralph Ellison (1914–1994). Baldwin, the eldest of nine children raised in Harlem in conditions of poverty, began writing when he was fourteen years old. For Baldwin, it was a subversive act. "You write," he insisted, "in order to change the world, knowing perfectly well that you probably can't, but also knowing that literature is indispensable to the world. In some way, your aspirations and concern for a single man in fact do begin to change the world. The world changes according to the way people see it, and if you alter, even by a millimeter, the way a person looks or people look at reality, then you can change it." Baldwin's first novel, *Go Tell It on the Mountain*, is a sensitive exploration of his youthful experiences in the close-knit, church-dominated Harlem community.

Baldwin, *Go Tell It on the Mountain* (1953)

In his novels, short stories, and essays, Baldwin stressed the affinity African-Americans felt with other poverty-stricken populations. Yet, as he tried to define the unique differences between blacks and whites, he observed that black people were strangers in the modern world—a world whose traditions were claimed by whites.

Baldwin's contemporary Ralph Ellison, a native of Oklahoma and an amateur jazz musician, came to Harlem during the 1930s to study sculpture and musical composition. Influenced by the poet Langston Hughes (see page 387) and by the African-American novelist Richard Wright (1908–1960), he soon turned to writing short stories and newspaper reviews. In 1945, he began the novel *Invisible Man*, a fiction masterpiece that probes the black estrangement from white culture. The novel offers a glimpse into the spiritual odyssey of the protagonist, who perceives himself to be "invisible" to the white world. It broaches, with surrealistic intensity, some of Ellison's most important themes: the nightmarish quality of

Ellison, *Invisible Man* (1952)

urban life and the alienation experienced by both blacks and whites in modern American society.

Many of the most talented artists of the black revolution were female. In the tradition of such Harlem Renaissance poets as Langston Hughes, the Chicago-born Gwendolyn Brooks (1917–2000) wrote poems that employed the idioms of jazz and street slang. In 1949, Brooks was the first African-American to receive the Pulitzer Prize for poetry. Many of her poems, including the one below from 1960, bring attention to the plight of young black men and women in American society:

We Real Cool

The Pool Players.
Seven at the Golden Shovel.[1]

"We real cool. We
Left school. We

Lurk late. We
Strike straight. We

Sing sin. We
Thin gin. We

Jazz June. We
Die soon."

Continuing the tradition of Zora Neale Hurston (see page 386) and other Harlem Renaissance writers are two contemporary novelists, Toni Morrison (b. 1931) and Alice Walker (b. 1944). Morrison's *Song of Solomon* and Walker's *The Color Purple* are notable for their courageous and candid characterizations of black women facing the perils of racism, domestic violence, and sexual abuse. They stand as landmarks both in the history of black literature and in the annals of twentieth-century fiction.

Morrison, *Song of Solomon* (1977)

Walker, *The Color Purple* (1982)

In the visual arts as well, African-American women have been outspoken in dealing with the stereotypes that have perpetuated racism. Betye Saar (b. 1926) pioneered this endeavor with her attack on the icons of commercial white culture (Figure **15.7**). A more subtle and complex approach to matters of race occurs in the work of Kara Walker (b. 1969), whose trademark silhouettes explore the tangled relationships between masters and slaves, whites and blacks, in the nineteenth-century American South. Walker's images, often ambiguous or subversive, suggest that liberation is an ongoing process (Figure **15.8**).

The Quest for Gender Equality

Through the ages, the perception of females as inferior to males in intelligence and strength has enforced conditions of gender inequality. As a result, while women make up the majority of the population in many cultures, they have exercised only limited power. These anomalies inspired modern campaigns for *feminism*—the principle advocating social, political, and economic rights for women equal to those of men. The history of feminism reaches back at least to the fourteenth century, when the French poet Christine de Pisan took up the pen in defense of women (see page 177). Christine found sporadic followers among Renaissance and Enlightenment humanists, including Mary Wollstonecraft (see page 301). But it was not until the nineteenth century that reasoned pleas for female equality became central to movements that agitated for women's rights.

In his eloquent treatise *The Subjection of Women* (1869), the British intellectual John Stuart Mill (1806–1873) condemned the legal subordination of women as "wrong in itself, and . . . one of the chief hindrances to human

Figure 15.7 Betye Saar, *The Liberation of Aunt Jemima*, 1972. Mixed media, 11¾ x 8 x 2¾ in. University Art Museum, University of California at Berkeley. Since the mid-twentieth century, African-American artists have taken increasingly bold and ever more cynical approaches to themes of race discrimination and racial stereotyping. This mixed-media sculpture transforms the familiar symbol of American pancakes and cozy kitchens into a gun-toting version of the "mammy" stereotype.

[1] A Chicago pool hall.

Figure 15.8 Kara Walker, *A Work on Progress*, 1998. Cut paper and adhesive, 5 ft. 9 in. x 6 ft. 8 in. Installation view at The Walker Art Center, 2007. Adopting the cut-paper practice common to popular late eighteenth-century portrait silhouettes, Walker pictures an African-American housemaid—itself a stereotypical image—sweeping out a black female whose chains are newly broken. The liberated black woman may represent the end of slavery, but like the dust swept out of the house, she has no status in society.

improvement." In America, Angelina Grimké (1805–1879) and other *suffragettes* (women militantly advocating voting rights) were instrumental in winning women the right to vote in 1920.

Among the most impassioned advocates of feminism was the British novelist Virginia Woolf (see page 393). She argued that equal opportunity for education and economic advantage were even more important than the right to vote (British women gained the vote in 1918). In her novels and essays, Woolf proposed that women could become powerful only by achieving financial and psychological independence from men. Freedom, argued Woolf in the landmark essay, "A Room of One's Own", is the prerequisite for creativity: For a woman to secure her own creative freedom, she must have money and the privacy provided by "a room of her own."

Woolf, "A Room of One's Own" (1929)

The two world wars had a positive effect on the position of European and American women. In the absence of men, women assumed many "male" jobs in agriculture and industry. This newly found financial independence gave women a sense of freedom and stimulated their demands for legal and social equality. But the feminist movement demanded more: It called for psychological independence on the part of women themselves. The voice for the new woman was the French existentialist, novelist, and social critic Simone de Beauvoir (1908–1986). De Beauvoir urged women to shed their passivity and achieve selfhood through responsible action. In the landmark text *The Second Sex*, she dethroned the "myth of femininity"—the false and disempowering idea that women possess a unique "feminine" essence that condemns them to become the social and intellectual subordinates of men. While men define

de Beauvoir, *The Second Sex* (1949)

Ideas and Issues

DE BEAUVOIR: WOMAN AS "OTHER"

"Now, woman has always been man's dependant, if not his slave; the two sexes have never shared the world in equality. And even today woman is heavily handicapped, though her situation is beginning to change. Almost nowhere is her legal status the same as man's, and frequently it is much to her disadvantage. Even when her rights are legally recognized in the abstract, long-standing custom prevents their full expression in the mores. In the economic sphere men and women can almost be said to make up two castes; other things being equal, the former hold the better jobs, get higher wages, and have more opportunity for success than their new competitors. In industry and politics men have a great many more positions and they monopolize the most important posts. In addition to all this, they enjoy a traditional prestige that the education of children tends in every way to support, for the present enshrines the past—and in the past all history has been made by men. At the present time, when women are beginning to take part in the affairs of the world, it is still a world that belongs to men—they have no doubt of it at all and women have scarcely any. To decline to be the *Other*, to refuse to be a party to the deal—this would be for women to renounce all the advantages conferred upon them by their alliance with the superior caste. . . . When man makes of woman the *Other*, he may, then, expect her to manifest deep-seated tendencies toward complicity. Thus, woman may fail to lay claim to the status of subject because she lacks definite resources, because she feels the necessary bond that ties her to man regardless of reciprocity, and because she is often very well pleased with her role as the *Other*. . . ."

(from de Beauvoir, *The Second Sex*)

Q What might be the consequences for women who "decline to be the *Other*"? Does the world still belong to men?

women as "the Other" (the second sex), it is women themselves, observed de Beauvoir, who complacently accept that inferior position. She called on women "to renounce all advantages conferred upon them by their alliance" with men. In her fifty-year liaison with Jean-Paul Sartre, one of the most intriguing partnerships of the century, she pursued this goal. Although both enjoyed love affairs with other people, they shared a lifelong marriage of minds.

During the postwar era, new types of contraceptives gave women control over their reproductive function and greater sexual freedom. The 1960s, which culminated in the founding of the National Organization for Women (NOW) in 1966, also brought about a more vigorous effort to raise gender consciousness and win legislation to broaden political and economic opportunities for women. Two landmark books challenged the existing order: *The Feminine Mystique* by Betty Friedan (1921–2006) claimed that American society in general, and commercial advertising in particular, had brainwashed women to prefer the roles of wives and mothers to other careers. *The Female Eunuch* by the Australian-born writer Germaine Greer (b. 1939) argued that the disempowered woman could be liberated only by reclaiming her sexuality. In *The Obstacle Race: The Fortunes of Women Painters and their Work* (1979), she explained the scarcity of women artists:

Friedan, *The Feminine Mystique* (1963)

Greer, *The Female Eunuch* (1970)

> There is . . . no female Leonardo, no female Titian, no female Poussin, but the reason does not lie in the fact that women have wombs, that they can have babies, that their brains are smaller, that they lack vigor, that they are not sensual. The reason is simply that you cannot make great artists out of egos that have been damaged, with wills that are defective, with libidos that have been driven out of reach and energy diverted into neurotic channels.

Since the 1960s, there has been an outpouring of feminist artistic expression focused on the twin themes of gender equality and the search for female identity (Figures **15.9** and **15.10**). In literature, feminist writing has been confessional, autobiographical, and often—as with the voice of black liberation—strident and angry. While not all the literary works of landmark women writers address exclusively female issues, much postwar women's literature displays three recurring motifs: the victimization of the female, her effort to define her role in a male-dominated society, and her displacement from her ancient status as goddess and matriarch. Among the outstanding feminist poets of this period are Sylvia Plath (1932–1963), Anne Sexton (1928–1975), Sonia Sanchez (b. 1935), and Adrienne Rich (b. 1929).

Figure 15.9 Judy Chicago, *The Dinner Party*, 1974–1979. Multimedia, 48 x 48 x 48 ft. Elizabeth A. Sackler Center for Feminist Art, Brooklyn Museum, Brooklyn, New York. The militant American feminist Judy Gerowitz (b. 1939), who in 1969 assumed the surname of her native city (hence, Judy Chicago), has been a lifelong advocate of women's art. Between 1974 and 1979, she directed a project called *The Dinner Party*—a room-sized sculpture consisting of a triangular table with thirty-nine place settings, each symbolizing a famous woman in myth or history. The feminist counterpart of the Last Supper, *The Dinner Party* pays homage to such immortals as Nefertiti, Sappho, Queen Elizabeth I, and Virginia Woolf.

Figure 15.10 Barbara Kruger, *Untitled* (*"Your body is a battleground"*), 1989. Photographic silkscreen on vinyl, 9 ft. 4 in. x 9 ft. 4 in. Mary Boone Gallery, New York. Aware of the extent to which commercialism shapes identity, Barbara Kruger (b. 1945) creates photographs that deftly unite word and image to resemble commercial billboards. "Your body is a battleground," insists Kruger; superimposing the message over the divided (positive and negative) image of a female face, the artist calls attention to the controversial issue of abortion in contemporary society.

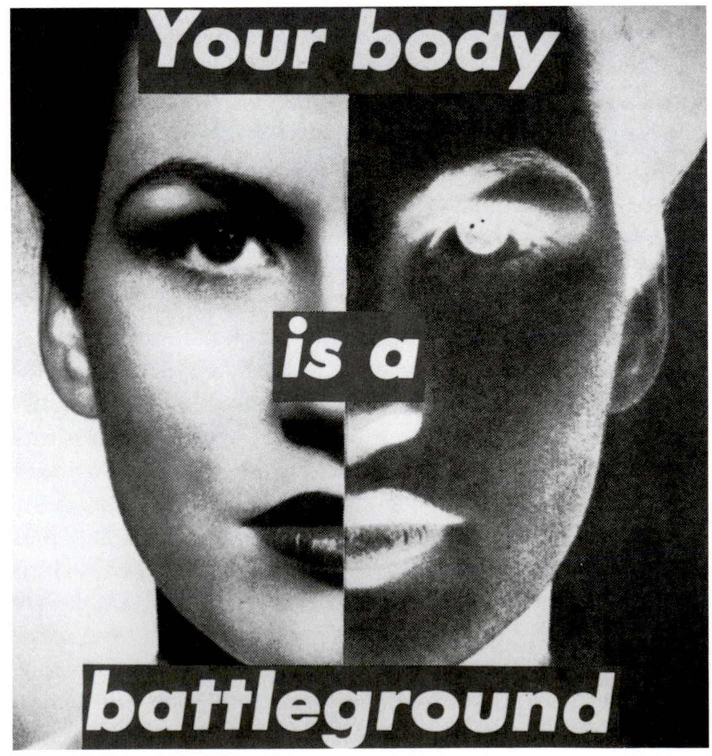

While women have played an increasingly significant role in late twentieth-century literature and the visual arts, it is only in the past two decades that they have made serious inroads into the male-dominated domains of architecture and music. The flamboyant architectural designs of Zaha Hadid (b. 1950) have won an international following; the eighty-two-story apartment tower in the center of Chicago conceived by Jeanne Gang (b. 1964) is the tallest building in the world designed by a woman.

In the sphere of contemporary music, female conductors have taken the podium in many cities of the world. Among America's most celebrated composers are Ellen Zwilich (b. 1939), the first woman to receive the Pulitzer Prize in Music; Joan Tower (b. 1935), whose *Fanfare for the Uncommon Woman* (1987) took its inspiration from the music of Aaron Copland (see page 412); and Jennifer Higdon (b. 1962), awarded the Pulitzer Prize in Music for what has been called the "dazzling virtuosity" of her Violin Concerto (2010).

Sexual Identity

The quests for racial and gender equality also worked to raise public consciousness concerning the role of sexuality in society. Assumptions concerning gender and the social roles of males and females are rooted in traditions as old as Paleolithic culture and as venerated as the Bible. For many, sexual roles are fixed and unchanging. However, these assumptions, like so many others in the cultural history of the twentieth century, have come to be challenged and reassessed. Gender issues accompanied a demand for equality on the part of those of untraditional sexual orientation—bisexuals, homosexuals (gays and lesbians), and transgendered individuals. In America homosexuals date the birth of their "liberation" to June 1969, when they openly and violently protested a police raid on the Stonewall Inn, a gay bar in New York's Greenwich Village. Thereafter, the call for protection against harassment shifted to litigated demands for social equality.

There are a number of reasons why issues of human sexuality became so visible in the culture of the late twentieth century: increasing sexual permissiveness (the consequence of improved pharmaceutical methods of contraception); the activity of the media (especially TV and film) in broadcasting sexually explicit entertainment; and the high incidence of AIDS (Acquired Immune Deficiency Syndrome) among male homosexuals in the United States. This life-threatening disease, resulting from a human immunodeficiency virus (HIV) that attacks the blood cells of the body, appeared in America in 1979 and continues to devastate many parts of the world, including and especially the black population of Africa, where it originated.

Collectively, these phenomena have had an overwhelming impact on traditional concepts of sexuality, sexual behavior, and conventional morality. Globally, they have brought attention to the ease and rapidity with which a dangerous virus might be spread. In the United States, sexual and public issues have intersected to produce highly controversial questions, such as whether homosexual marriage should be legalized, whether homosexuals should serve in the armed forces, and whether sexually explicit art should receive public funding. In the arts, there have been renewed efforts to distinguish pornography from substantial creative achievement. And, reflecting everyday life, a provocative blurring of sexual identity has pervaded commercial advertising, the popular media, and the fine arts (Figure **15.11**).

By drawing attention to the ways in which matters of sexuality affect society and its institutions, contemporary art asserts that sexuality and power are as closely related as race and power or gender and power. For example, the Pulitzer prize-winning play *Angels in America: A Gay Fantasia on National Themes* (written in two parts: *Millennium Approaches* and *Perestroika*) by Tony Kushner (b. 1957) offers a radical vision of American society set against the AIDS epidemic and the politics of conservatism. Kushner urges the old America—"straight," Protestant, and white—to look with greater objectivity at

Kushner, *Angels in America* (1990–1993)

Figure 15.11 Robert Mapplethorpe, *Lisa Lyon*, 1982. Gelatin-silver print. Robert Miller Gallery, New York. The photographs of Robert Mapplethorpe (1946–1989) reflect the artist's preoccupation with physical and sexual themes: male virility, sadomasochism, androgyny, and sexual identity. The gender-bending parody here plays on the fact that the model, Lisa Lyon, is herself a weightlifter.

Figure 15.12 The Names Project, *AIDS Memorial Quilt*, as displayed on the National Mall facing the Capitol, October 1996. Begun in 1985, the project engaged twenty thousand ordinary individuals, each of whom created a single 3 x 6-foot fabric panel in memory of someone who had died of an HIV-related disease. In 1987, AIDS activists assembled the panels in 16-foot squares and took them from San Francisco to Washington, D.C., to protest governmental inaction with regard to the AIDS crisis. Commemorating the deaths of some 150,000 Americans, the *Aids Memorial Quilt* covered 15 acres of ground between the Washington Monument and Lincoln Memorial. The Names Project continues: In 2010 the quilt panels numbered forty-five thousand, which is more than double the figure of the original.

"the fringe" (the variety of ethnic, racial, and sexual minorities), which demands acceptance and its share of power. Like Kushner's landmark drama, the *AIDS Memorial Quilt* (Figure **15.12**) represents the movement for body-conscious politics and socially responsible art that animated the last decade of the twentieth century.

Ethnicity and Identity

"Ethnic identity" refers to the manner in which individuals define themselves as members of a group sharing the same culture and values. Individual identity is a multi-dimensional phenomenon, a "cluster" of traits that form the totality of one's self-perceived image. Such traits include gender, race, language, physical appearance, and personal (including religious) values. The self-affirming significance of ethnic identity is well expressed in the ancient Yoruba proverb that asserts "I am because we are; What I am is what we are." Perceiving oneself as part of an ethnic group is a major determinant of individual identity, and the freedom to exercise that identity—as it manifests itself in language, music, and other traditional and ritual forms—has become a leading issue in contemporary society.

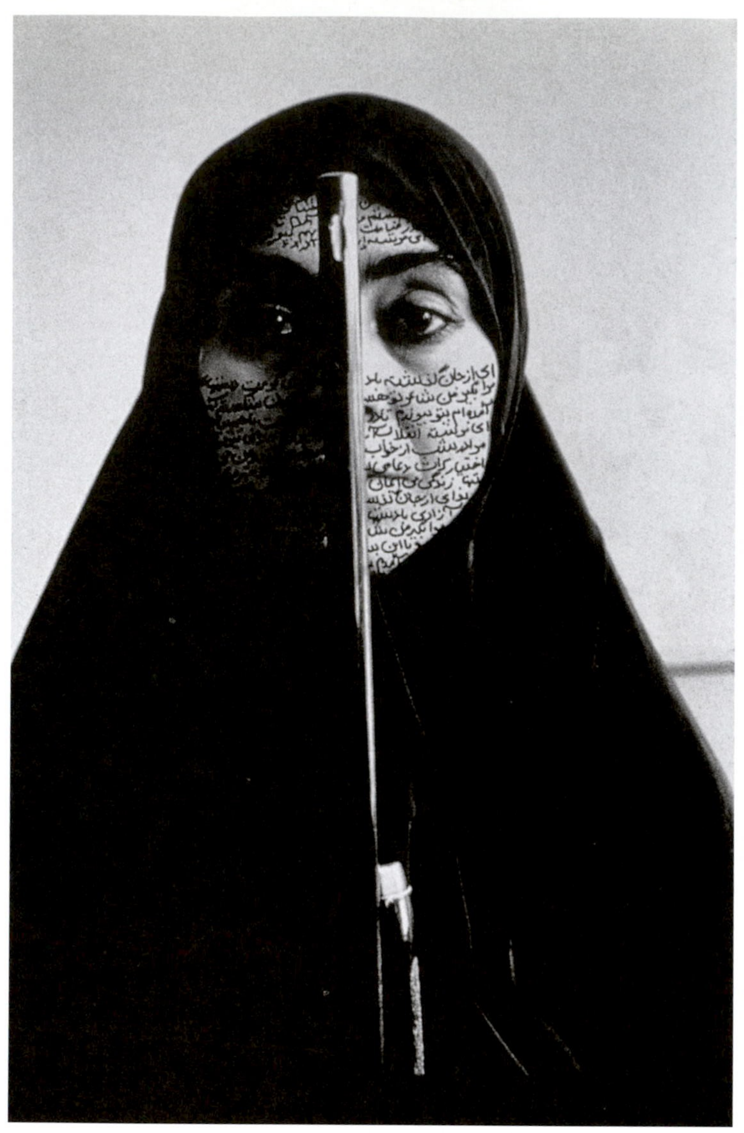

Figure 15.13 Shirin Neshat, *Rebellious Silence*, from "Women of Allah" series, 1994. Gelatin-silver print and ink. Barbara Gladstone Gallery, New York. The photographs and films of Shirin Neshat (b. 1957) deal with ethnic and feminist issues in the Muslim world, especially in her native Iran. Her photographic series "Women of Allah" (1993–1997) addresses the role of militant Muslim women who fought in the 1979 revolution that overthrew Iran's ruling dynasty. In this image from the series, Neshat makes dramatic use of the veil (the large square of black cloth known as the *chador*) to isolate her face, which—intersected by a rifle—is the site of a poem by Iran's most famous modern female poet, Forough Farrokhzad, transcribed in Farsi calligraphy.

Ethnic identity represented a powerful social and political force in the late twentieth century. Having cast off the rule of foreign powers and totalitarian ideologies, ethnic peoples sought to reaffirm their primary affiliations—to return to their spiritual roots. Efforts to revive ethnic identity coincided frequently with the quest for solidarity and political autonomy. In its most malignant guise, "identity politics"—the exercise of power by means of group solidarity—pitted ethnic groups against each other in militant opposition. Such circumstances lie at the base of many (if not most) of the world's current conflagrations in Africa, the Middle East (Figure **15.13**), the Indian subcontinent, and the former Soviet Union.

But ethnicity also underlay many of the creative projects of late twentieth-century artists and thinkers. In the United States, the quest for ethnic identity has been a central theme in the arts: Leslie Marmon Silko (b. 1948), for example (of Native American and Mexican ancestry), drew on Pueblo tribal folktales in her poetry and prose; and in *The Woman Warrior: Memoirs of a Girlhood Among Ghosts* by the Chinese-American writer Maxine Hong Kingston (b. 1940), family legends and native Chinese customs became conduits through which the author explored her identity. To these and other more contemporary writers, the oral tradition—stories handed down from generation to generation (often by and through women)—animates autobiographical themes that define a unique ethnic identity in modern society.

Hong Kingston, *The Woman Warrior: Memoirs of a Girlhood Among Ghosts* (1976)

Hispanic Voices

Ethnicity has become particularly important among vast numbers of Hispanic immigrants who made America their home. Especially in the past half-century, dramatic demographic changes (in the form of rising numbers of *Latinos*—persons from the various Latin American countries—and Asian-Americans) have changed the face of the economy, the urban environment, and the culture. Currently, Hispanics represent the largest ethnic minority in the United States. In all aspects of life, from literature and art to food and dance styles, there has been a flowering of *Latino* culture. With *The Mambo Kings Play Songs of Love*, the first novel by a Hispanic to win the Pulitzer Prize, the Cuban-American Oscar Hijuelos (b. 1951) brought attention to the impact of Latin American music on American culture and, more generally, to the role of memory in reclaiming one's ethnic roots.

Hijuelos, *The Mambo Kings Play Songs of Love* (1989)

The personal difficulties of becoming part of America's ethnic mosaic are themes pursued by one of today's leading *Chicana* (Mexican-American female) authors, Sandra Cisneros (b. 1954). Her landmark work, *The House on Mango Street*, a series of vignettes that describe the experience of a young girl growing up in the Latino section of Chicago, illustrates the shaping role of language and tradition in providing a sense of ethnic identity.

Cisneros, *The House on Mango Street* (1984)

SCIENCE AND PHILOSOPHY

SCIENTIFIC advances in the past half-century have made possible investigations into outer space—the universe at large—and inner space, the province of our own bodies. Science and technology have propelled humankind beyond planet earth and into the cosmos. At the same time, they have provided an unprecedented understanding of the genetic patterns that govern life itself. These phenomena have worked to make the planet smaller, the universe larger, and methods of navigating the two ever more promising.

String Theory and Chaos Theory

During the late twentieth century physicists began to formulate "a theory of everything," one that might explain the "fundamental of fundamentals" that governs the organization and complexity of matter. A new (but yet unproven) theory of everything proposes that all matter—from the page of this book to the skin of a peach—consists of tiny loops of vibrating strings. *String* (or *Superstring*) *Theory*, most eloquently explained by the American physicist Brian Greene (b. 1962), describes a multidimensional universe in which loops of strings and oscillating globules of matter unite all of creation into vibrational patterns. According to string theory, the universe has extra dimensions curled up in a complex manifold space. The workings of such a universe, invisible to the naked eye, can be simulated only on a computer. Language—other than the language of higher mathematics—fails to serve as an explanatory medium.

LANDMARKS: THE UNIVERSE

1957	The first artificial satellite (*Sputnik 1*) is put in orbit by the Soviet Union
1969	An American astronaut is the first person to walk on the moon
1974	Scientists prove that chlorofluorocarbons are eroding the earth's ozone layer
1981	Lasers are utilized for the study of matter
1990	The Hubble Space Telescope confirms the existence of extra-solar planets and fifty billion galaxies
2004	NASA scientists land rover probe on Mars
2005	International Space Station completed
2007	Computer imaging (CI) used to test spacecraft before production
2008	Astronomers track and intercept a meteor from space to its impact zone on Earth
2008–2010	The world's largest high-energy particle accelerator (the Large Hadron Collider) is brought online in Geneva, Switzerland

Equally fascinating are the speculations of those who analyze the behavior of discrete physical systems. The proponents of *Chaos Theory* find that universal patterns underlie all of nature and repeat themselves in physical phenomena ranging from the formation of a snowflake to the rhythms of the human heart. Chaos theorists (not only physicists, but also astronomers, mathematicians, biologists, and computer scientists) observe that while patterns appear random, unstable, and disorderly, they are actually self-similar in scale, like the zigs and zags of a lightning bolt, or the oscillations of electric currents. To Einstein's famous assertion, "God does not play dice with the universe," these theorists might respond: "Not only does God play dice; but they are loaded."

The Human Genome

One of the major projects of the late twentieth century was the successful mapping of the *human genome*. By the year 2000, molecular biologists were able (with the help of computers) to ascertain the order of nearly three billion units of DNA, thereby locating genes and determining their functions in the human cellular system. Ultimately, this enterprise is expected to revolutionize the practice of medicine, in both the preventive treatment of gene-related diseases and in the repair and regeneration of tissues. (Already such gene-related research has diminished the number of AIDS deaths internationally.) The tools of genetic engineering have given scientists the ability to clone life forms. They also promise the mitigation of what Freud described as one of humankind's greatest threats: the suffering "from our own body, which is doomed to decay and dissolution."

Language Theory

While science moves forward optimistically to reveal the underlying natural order, philosophy has entered a phase of radical skepticism that denies the existence of any true or uniform system of thought. Contemporary philosophers have fastened on the idea, first popularized by the Austrian Ludwig Wittgenstein (1889–1951), that all forms of expression and, indeed, all truths are dominated by the modes of language used to convey ideas. Wittgenstein, whose life's work was an inquiry into the ways in which language represents the world, argued that sentences (or propositions) were "pictures of reality." His groundbreaking ideas on the philosophy of language were published two years after his death under the title *Philosophical Investigations.*

Wittgenstein, *Philosophical Investigations* (1953)

LANDMARKS: THE BODY

1953 DNA discovered

1967 Christian Barnard (South African) performs the first human heart transplant

1973 American biochemists isolate genes to make genetic engineering possible

1978 The world's first test-tube baby is born

1983 The first commercial use of MRI (Magnetic Resonance Imaging)

1996 Dolly, a cloned sheep, is born in Scotland

2000 Scientists complete the mapping of the human genome

2005 First publicly available personal genetic blueprints

2007 Human skin cells are found to be reprogrammable as stem cells

2010 Neanderthal genome project: DNA is extracted from Neanderthal bones to determine the ancestry of modern humans

2010 Surgeons perform the first successful full-face transplant

Following Wittgenstein, philosophers tried to unlock the meaning of the *text* (that is, the mode of cultural expression) based on close analysis of its linguistic structure. Language theorists suggested that one must "deconstruct" or "take apart" discourse in order to "unmask" the many meanings beneath the text. The leaders of *deconstruction*, the French philosophers Jacques Derrida (1930–2004) and Michel Foucault (1926–1984), were influential in arguing that all human beings are prisoners of the very language they use to think and to describe the world. In *Of Grammatology*, Derrida examined the relationship between speech and writing, and their roles in the effectiveness of language. In a similar direction, Foucault's *The Archeology of Knowledge* suggests that language is not the servant, but the master, of those who use it: we fail to realize that we are forever submitting to its demands. Philosophers, he asserted, should abandon the search for absolute truths and concentrate on the discovery of meaning(s). Thus "deconstruction" became the primary method of analysis in philosophy, linguistics, and literary criticism of the late twentieth century. In language theory as in the sciences, the average individual confronts information that grows more accessible, but at the same time ever more arcane.

Derrida, *Of Grammatology* (1967)

Foucault, *The Archeology of Knowledge* (1969)

The American philosopher Richard Rorty (1931–2007) is deeply troubled by the limits of both linguistic inquiry and traditional philosophy. Rorty has argued that the post-philosophical age's great thinkers are not the metaphysicians or the linguists but, rather, those artists whose works provide others with insights into achieving Postmodern self-transformation. What Rorty calls the "linguistic turn" describes the move (among writers and philosophers) to rethink language as verbal coding.

THE INFORMATION EXPLOSION

THE most dramatic development of the past six decades was the shift from an industrial to an information age. In today's advanced industrial nations, more than two-thirds of the population is engaged in occupations related to high technology, rather than to farming, manufacturing, and service trades. The agents of high technology, the mass media, and electronic means of communicating, storing, and accessing information have facilitated an information explosion of vast proportions (see Box below). Electronic modes of communication have shrunk the distances between the inhabitants of the world community, creating a "global village," as the Canadian sociologist Marshall McLuhan (1911–1980) predicted in his provocative book, *The Gutenberg Galaxy* (1962). In the global village, communication between geographically remote parts of the world is almost instantaneous, and every new development—technological, political, financial, and cultural—potentially affects every villager.

Television and computers—the primary vehicles of the information explosion—have altered almost every aspect of life. The wonderchild of electronics and the quintessential example of modern mass media, television transmits

LANDMARKS: INFORMATION TECHNOLOGY

1950 Commercial color television becomes available

1953 First commercially successful computer introduced

1959 American engineers produce the first microchip from a silicon wafer

1970 Fiber optics technology is perfected to carry information thousands of times faster than copper cables

1972 First commercial video game introduced

1975 First personal computer available

1979 First portable music device (the Walkman) produced

1983 First commercial cellular (wireless) phones produced

1990 The internationally linked computer network (the Internet) becomes accessible to personal computers

1995+ Advances in nanotechnology and microprocessing make possible minicomputers, palm TVs, smart bombs, etc.

2000+ Wireless networks, broadband, digital TV, and satellite radio become mainstream

2001 Apple releases its first-generation iPod (portable digital music device)

2002 The smartphone is released commercially

2004 Facebook, a social network service, is launched

2007 Wireless electronic reading devices become available

2008–2010 First applied uses of quantum teleportation for data transmission

sound and light by electromagnetic waves that carry information instantaneously into homes across the face of the earth. TV did not become common to middle-class life in the West until the 1950s, although it had been invented decades before then. By the 1960s the events of a war in the jungles of Vietnam were being relayed via electronic communications satellite into American living rooms. In 1969, in a live telecast, the world saw the first astronauts walk on the surface of the moon. And in the early 1990s, during the Middle Eastern conflict triggered by the Iraqi invasion of Kuwait, Americans and Europeans witnessed the first "prime-time war"—a war that was "processed" by censorship and television newscasting.

The second major technological phenomenon of the information age is the computer. Digital computers—machines that process information in the form of numbers—were first used widely in the 1950s. By the 1960s, computers consisting of electronic circuits were able to perform millions of calculations per second. Smaller and more reliable than ever, computers have come to facilitate a vast range of functions from cell phone communication to rapid prototyping, a digital process that "prints" objects in three dimensions. Computers have also made possible robotics (the science and technology of robots), the creation of so-called artificial forms of intelligence, and interactive forms of **virtual reality** (computer-simulated artificial environments).

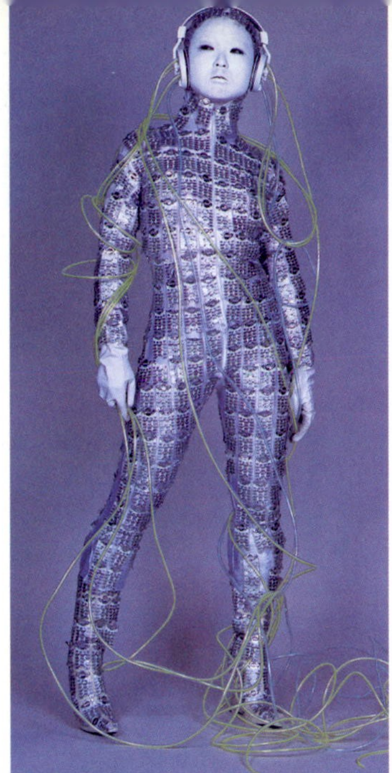

Figure 15.14 Noriko Yamaguchi, *Keitai Girl*, 2003. Performance with the artist wearing a set of large headphones and a suit of cell phone keypads and wires. Life-sized. (See also page 446.)

Media-shaped Globalism

Information-age culture is dominated by media-shaped globalism—the condition of interrelatedness and interdependence among various parts of the planet. In 1989, all parts of the global village and numberless databases were united by the World Wide Web, a system of electronically linked texts (or hypertexts), accessed by way of a series of interconnected computer networks known as the Internet. Since the 1990s, information technology has rapidly proliferated. The world's first online, nonprofit English-language encyclopedia, Wikipedia, was launched in 2001. Publicly edited and continuously updated, Wikipedia contained (in 2010) more than three million English-language articles. Equally ambitious is a current project to organize the world's information and make it universally accessible: Google, the American public corporation specializing in Internet search and online advertising, has undertaken to create a universal literary archive by putting all existing printed matter into an electronic library. The website YouTube invites a polyglot audience to post video "clips" ranging from concert performances to cooking lessons.

More recently, popular social networking websites, such as Facebook and Twitter, have elicited the exchange of information and personal opinions in the form of online postings (web logs or "blogs") on everything from current fashion fads to political policy. The second Iraq War, begun in 2003 and called "the first blog war" for the volume of online exchanges it provoked, came into our homes not only by way of television, but via the Internet on websites with on-the-spot video postings by eyewitnesses wielding handheld digital devices (Figure **15.14**). In 2011 cell phones and social networking websites were instrumental in organizing political revolutions in Egypt and the Middle East. As more and more information is electronically stored, processed, and exchanged to ever-increasing numbers of individuals at an ever-increasing speed, a global infotopia—that is, a world society dominated by information—is inevitable. Determining who controls that information and how accurately it is communicated has become a weighty task.

Postmodernism

The term "*Postmodernism*" came into use shortly before World War II to describe the reaction to or against Modernism, but by the late 1960s it had come to designate the cultural condition of the late twentieth century. Whether defined as a reaction against Modernism or as an entirely new form of modernism, Postmodernism is a phenomenon that occurred principally in the West. As a style, it is marked by a bemused awareness of a historical past whose "reality" has been processed by mass communication and information technology. Postmodern artists appropriate (or borrow) preexisting texts and images from history, advertising, and the media. They offer alternatives to the high seriousness and introversion of Modernist expression, and move instead in the direction of parody (burlesque imitation), whimsy, paradox, and irony. Their playful amalgam of disparate styles mingles the superficial and the profound and tends to dissolve the boundaries between "high" and "low" art.

In contrast with elitist Modernism, Postmodernism is self-consciously populist, even to the point of inviting the active participation of the beholder. Whereas Modernists (consider Eliot or Kandinsky) exalt the artist as visionary and rebel, Postmodern artists bring wry skepticism to the creative act. Less preoccupied than the Modernists with formal abstraction and its redeeming power, Postmodernists acknowledge art as an information system and a commodity shaped by the electronic media, its messages, and its modes of communication.

CONTEMPORARY LITERATURE

CONTEMPORARY writers have explored a wide variety of literary styles and genres, the evidence of which is global in scope. Some focus on the antirational linguistic high-jinks of *Postmodernism* or the narrative embellishments of *docufiction*; others enjoy the rich ambiguities of *Magic Realism* and the futuristic inventions of *science fiction*. Many, however, remain wedded to traditional forms of narrative. In content, the literature of the information age draws broadly on contemporary concerns, whether taken from the family dining table, the city streets, or the international scene. Profoundly influenced by the electronic media, the literature of the last sixty years freely mingles past and present, serious and frivolous, the ordinary and the bizarre.

Postmodern Fiction

Postmodern writers share the contemporary philosopher's disdain for rational structure and the deconstructionist's fascination with the function of language. In Postmodern fiction, characters undergo little or no development, plots often lack logical direction, and events—whether ordinary, perverse, or fantastic—may be described in the detached tone of a newspaper article. The novels of the Italian writer Italo Calvino (1923–1985) engage the reader in a hunt for meanings that lie in the spaces between the act of writing and the events the words describe. Further, the language of Postmodernism is often diffuse, discontinuous, and filled with innuendo and "commentary." For example, gallows humor novelist Kurt Vonnegut (1922–2007) uses clipped sentences framed in the present tense. This technique creates a kind of "videofiction" that seems aimed at readers whose attention spans have been dwarfed by commercial television programming and who require instant intellectual gratification.

While Vonnegut and Calvino are representative of literary Postmodernism, they are by no means the only writers who leave literary landmarks with a Postmodern stamp.

Lessing, *The Golden Notebook* (1962)

Doris Lessing (b. 1919), the 2007 recipient of the Nobel Prize in literature, created in *The Golden Notebook* a series of interwoven narrative fragments, diary entries, and the notes of a middle-aged female writer who struggles with political and personal traumas—all of which provide a complex portrait of postwar society. Thomas Pynchon's dense masterpiece, *Gravity's Rainbow*,

Pynchon, *Gravity's Rainbow* (1974)

is packed with an encyclopedic array of references to (and puns on) world history, chemistry, mathematics, religion, film, and popular music. Regarded as the archetypal text of American literary Postmodernism, the novel has influenced the emergence of *cyberpunk* fiction, a genre of science fiction dealing with futuristic societies dominated by computers, artificial intelligence, illicit drugs, and punk rock music.

Docufiction

It is too soon to determine which of the internationally renowned writers of the last sixty years will leave landmark works. The following are likely candidates: Joan Didion (b. 1934), Tom Wolfe (b. 1930), and Don Delillo (b. 1936). All three American authors employ the events of their time to produce *docufiction*—a literary genre that gives an original (and fictionalized) narrative context to contemporary events and situations. Delillo captures the cinematic rush of American life in the compelling novel *Underworld*, which connects major worldwide phenomena—the atomic bomb, the cold war—

Delillo, *Underworld* (1997)

to such everyday events as baseball and waste management. His style, in which the narrative moves back and forth in time, parallels a similar propensity for disordering time sequences in contemporary cinema. Delillo's concerns for international terrorism, the ecology of the planet, urban violence, and the loss of spiritual and moral values are shared by many contemporary novelists. Most English-language writers, however, such as Phillip Roth (b. 1933), John Updike (1932–2009), Margaret Atwood (b. 1939), Joyce Carol Oates (b. 1938), and Jonathan Franzen (b. 1959), have maintained a traditional narrative style.

Global concerns preoccupy some of America's younger writers: Dave Eggers' (b. 1970) docufictional novel *What Is the What: The Autobiography of Valentino Achak Deng* (2006) takes as its subject one of the "Lost Boys of Sudan," a victim of the displacement of the Sudanese population during the civil wars of 1983 to 2005. The author deliberately mixes fact and fiction to assume the voice of a young refugee who, uprooted from his native village, experiences the varieties of cruelty that have marked the recent history of East Africa.

Magic Realism

Gabriel Garcia Márquez (b. 1928) and Salman Rushdie (b. 1947) are notable exponents of Magic Realism, a style that fuses fantastic and realistic literary elements. In his landmark novel, *One Hundred Years of Solitude*, the Nobel prize-winning Márquez trans-

Márquez, *One Hundred Years of Solitude* (1967)

formed the labyrinthine history of his Colombian homeland into a fictional saga filled with irony and mythic breadth. His work is representative of the Latin American "boom" in contemporary literature.

Salman Rushdie, who was born in Bombay, India, but lives in New York, writes novels that mingle rock-and-roll lyrics with Hindu and Greek mythology. A chronicler of the global village, Rushdie joins other writers who reach back to cultural beginnings yet speak for their own time and place. Rushdie's fourth novel, *The Satanic Verses*, filled with magical sequences and dreamlike visions, was inspired in part by the life of Muhammad. The book caused immense controversy, leading Iran's religious leader to issue a *fatwa* (a Muslim legal ruling) calling on all good Muslims to kill Rushdie and his publishers.

Rushdie, *The Satanic Verses* (1988)

Science Fiction

After mid-century, the genre of science fiction responded to two major events: the Soviet Union's historic launching of an artificial earth satellite (*Sputnik 1*) in 1957, and the American moon landing in 1969. While the theme of intergalactic travel dominated much of the literature and film of these decades (see page 393), a new direction in science fiction writing focused on the impact of computers on the world's future. In the landmark novel *Neuromancer*, the American novelist William Gibson (b. 1948) anticipated many of the innovations of the digital era, including genetic engineering, virtual reality, artificial intelligence, and computer-hacking. Generally regarded as the work that launched cyberpunk as a literary genre, *Neuromancer* introduced the term "cyberspace" to describe a virtual reality in which complex data is governed by digital systems. The book has spawned a popular video game and is expected to become a film. The genre known as *cyberliterature*, which involves the creative use of electronically linked texts (hypertexts) as an alternative to the linearity of conventional prose, has yet to produce a literary landmark. However, its effort to embrace an interactive dimension (that may leave the reader to decide the outcome of the story) and its integration of graphics, sound, animation, and other media is already evident in film.

Gibson, *Neuromancer* (1984)

Poetry

The poetry of the last sixty years stands in striking contrast to the self-conscious and cryptic verse of the Modernists (see pages 391–392). It is multicultural in its concerns with global issues, and Postmodern in its claim that language shapes and articulates the self. Among the many masters of contemporary poetry, two may be singled out as representative of these themes. The global outlook is exemplified by the 1992 Nobel prize-winning poet Derek Walcott (b. 1930). Walcott writes poetry and plays that reflect his dual Caribbean and European heritage. A native of St. Lucia in the West Indies, and a world traveler, Walcott considers himself a "mulatto of styles" (biblical, Classical, Shakespearean, and Creole) and a nomad between cultures (Caribbean, European, and African). These themes he develops in the long poem *Omeros* (1990), which places the drama of Homer's epics in a Caribbean setting. Walcott's union of everyday speech, folkloristic dialect, and richly metaphorical English reaches toward a hybridized voice—the multicultural voice of the information age. At the same time, however, his verse describes his search for personal identity in the polyglot community of the global village.

Walcott, *Omeros* (1990)

The poems of Seamus Heaney (b. 1939) are already enshrined in the literary history of our time. A native of Ireland and a scholar of Classical and Anglo-Saxon literature—his 2001 translation of *Beowulf* (see page 123) breathes new life into the poem—Heaney shares with his compatriot W.B. Yeats the gift of lyric brilliance. His ability to translate the small details of everyday rural experience into transcendent ideas, though at times reminiscent of Robert Frost, is unsurpassed. While Heaney's first collection of poems, *Death of a Naturalist*, marks his deep affection for his native "bogs and barnyards," one of his most recent volumes of poetry, *District and Circle*, considers the violence of our time, specifically, the 2005 terrorist attack on London's underground (District and Circle) lines. Here, prompted by the Roman poet Horace (see page 72), he grapples with sobering, universal uncertainties:

Heaney, *Death of a Naturalist* (1966); *District and Circle* (2007)

Anything Can Happen
After Horace, Odes, I, 34

Anything can happen. You know how Jupiter[1]
Will mostly wait for clouds to gather head
Before he hurls the lightning? Well just now
He galloped his thunder cart and his horses

Across a clear blue sky. It shook the earth
and the clogged underearth, the River Styx,[2]
the winding streams, the Atlantic shore itself.
Anything can happen, the tallest towers

Be overturned, those in high places daunted,
Those overlooked regarded. Stropped-beak Fortune
Swoops, making the air gasp, tearing the crest off one,
Setting it down bleeding on the next.

Ground gives. The heaven's weight
Lifts up off Atlas[3] like a kettle lid.
Capstones shift. Nothing resettles right.
Telluric[4] ash and fire-spores boil away.

[1] Roman sky god.
[2] River in the underworld crossed by the souls of the dead.
[3] Mythic Titan condemned to support the heavens on his shoulders.
[4] Terrestrial.

ART AND ARCHITECTURE

AS with literature, no one style has dominated the visual arts since 1950. Nevertheless, four trends distinguish artistic expression of the last sixty years: First, new media, ranging from acrylic paint and neon to film and digital technology, have fueled a spirit of bold experimentation. Digitization, in particular, has had an enormous impact: It has brought a wealth of visual images to a vast global audience; it has also facilitated an outburst of independent artistic production across the globe. Second, traditional distinctions between the arts—painting, sculpture, dance, photography, and film—and traditional distinctions between high and low (elite and popular) art, have been blurred or entirely destroyed in mixed and multimedia enterprises that are often interchangeable with theatrical performance. Third, continuing a trend that began with Abstract Expressionism, art has grown to mammoth proportions: So large-scale are some artworks that the conventional sites for art—the home and the church—have given way to such commercial venues as banks, airports, and theaters, or to the physical environment itself. Finally, and most recently, art has become big business: Collectors are spending massive sums of money, not only for the landmark paintings of past centuries, but for the works of contemporary artists.

Pop Art

The term *Pop art* was coined in England in the 1950s, but the movement came to fruition in New York in the following decade. Pop art became the quintessential style of the information age in that it embraced the imagery of consumer products, celebrities, and everyday events, as mediated by TV, film, and magazines. It presented commonplace goods and popular personalities in an overtly realistic style. By departing from postwar gestural abstraction (see pages 421–422), Pop artists gave new life to the Western representational tradition.

As Andy Warhol (1931–1987), the pioneer American Pop artist, dryly pronounced: "Pop art is about liking things." Trained as a commercial artist, he took as his subject matter familiar and banal supermarket products such as Brillo, Campbell's soup (Figure **15.15**), and Coca-Cola; American superstars like Elvis Presley and Marilyn Monroe; and media-documented episodes of social violence, such as the civil rights riots of the 1960s. Warhol depersonalized images by enlarging them or by reproducing them in monotonous, postage-stamp rows that resemble supermarket displays. He employed the slick advertising techniques of **silkscreen** and airbrush, thus blurring distinctions between fine and applied art.

Warhol also pioneered some of the most novel experiments in Postmodern film. He focused a fixed camera on a single object and let it "roll" until the film ran out—thus bringing to film the (uniquely cinematic) "dead time" between "events"; and he experimented with double-screen formats to present multiple versions of his female "star" watching images of herself on televised videotape.

Among the most intriguing vehicles of Pop parody are the monumental soft vinyl and stainless steel sculptures of Claes Oldenburg (b. 1929)—gigantic versions of such everyday items as toilets, hot dogs, table fans, typewriter erasers, and clothespins (Figure **15.16**). Often enlarged ten to twenty times their natural size, these objects assume a comic vulgarity that shatters our complacent acceptance of their presence in our daily lives.

Oldenburg's contemporary George Segal (1924–2000) devised a unique method of constructing life-sized figures from plaster casts of live models—often friends and members of his own family. He installed these ghostly replicas in ordinary settings staged with uncast props: bar stools, streetlights, beds, bus seats (Figure **15.17**). Stylistically, Segal's tableaux link the tradition of Realist sculpture to the Pop and performance art movements of contemporary art. Spiritually, they share the haunting alienation conveyed in the paintings of Edward Hopper (see Figure 14.3).

Figure 15.15 Andy Warhol, *Campbell's Soup Cans*, 1962. Synthetic polymer paint on 32 canvases, each 20 x 16 in. The Museum of Modern Art, New York. Warhol's serial display of Campbell's soup cans make reference to the commercialism of contemporary life.

Figure 15.16 (left) Claes Oldenburg, *Clothespin*, Central Square, Philadelphia, 1976. Cor-ten (steel) and stainless steel; 45 ft. x 12 ft. 3 in. x 4 ft. 6 in. Oldenburg's oversized versions of everyday objects raised them to heroic status—a move that imitated billboard advertising and poked fun at Postmodern commercialization. This particular domestic icon, however, also bears ironic similarities to the human body.

Figure 15.17 (above) George Segal, *Bus Riders*, 1962. Plaster, cottongauze, steel, wood, and vinyl, 5 ft. 10 in. x 3 ft. 6⅞ in. x 7 ft. 6¾ in. Hirshhorn Museum and Sculpture Garden, Smithsonian Institution, Washington, D.C. These "assembled environments," as he called them, allowed Segal to comment—in the course of his career—on matters of alienation, social injustice, and the failure of communication in modern life.

Assemblage

Art that freely combines two- and three-dimensional elements has a history that reaches back to the early twentieth century—recall Picasso's *Guitar* (see Figure 14.13). In the 1950s, however, the American artist Robert Rauschenberg (b. 1925–2008) began to monumentalize the technique of *assemblage* in works that incorporated what he wryly referred to as "the excess of the world." By putting together old car tires, street signs, broken furniture, and other debris, he fathered landmark artworks he called "combines"—creations that attack the boundary between painting and sculpture. Rauschenberg found the stuffed angora goat that dominates *Monogram* (Figure **15.18**) in a Manhattan furniture store that was going out of business. The piece, which has become the artist's best-known work, has been widely interpreted by art critics, but, like a Dada visual prank (see page 403), its "meaning" remains personal and opaque.

A brilliant printmaker, Rauschenberg experimented with a wide variety of transfer techniques, including collage and silkscreen. As with his combines, the assembled bits and pieces of cultural debris in his prints reflect the artist's love of visual surprise and his avowal to work in "the gap between art and life."

Post-Pop Abstraction

Not all postwar artists embraced the ironic stance of Pop and Assemblage art. Some remained loyal to the variety of Nonobjective art known as *Geometric Abstraction*. In the tradition of Malevich and Mondrian, these artists achieved a machinelike purity of elemental forms and colors in artworks that often reached colossal sizes. For example, the American artist Frank Stella (b. 1936) produced brightly colored, hard-edged geometric paintings that look as though they were made with the help of a giant protractor

Figure 15.18 Robert Rauschenberg, *Monogram*, 1955–9. Freestanding combine 42 in. x 64 in. x 64 1/2 in. Moderna Museet, Stockholm, Sweden. Mounted on a rolling platform, the goat and tire stand amid a collage of printed reproductions, a rubber heel, and a tennis ball. The brashly applied paint on the face of the goat may be a sly slap at the Abstract Expressionists, from whose techniques Rauschenberg consciously departed. As a child growing up in Port Arthur, Texas, the artist witnessed the slaughter of his pet goat at the hand of his father.

(Figure **15.19**). In place of traditional square or rectangular canvases, Stella constructed chevrons or triangles, fastening them together or assembling them in groups. His more recent works, which incorporate aluminum and steel, are more baroque and three-dimensional. Nevertheless, Stella continues to favor a style that is neutral and impersonal.

Artists like Stella led the way in the development of *Minimalism* in painting and sculpture. Minimalists eliminated representation in favor of simple, geometric shapes. Minimalist sculptors developed a highly refined industrial aesthetic that made use of high-tech materials, such as fiberglass, Plexiglas, stainless steel, neon, and polyester resin. These materials have become as commonplace in the art of the past five decades as marble, clay, and oil paints were in the previous five hundred years. The elemental components of Minimalist sculpture are usually factory-produced and assembled according to the artist's instructions. A landmark example of the Minimalist's assertion of primal form on a monumental scale is *Cube* (Figure **15.20**) by the Japanese-American sculptor Isamu Noguchi (1904–1988). Poised on one corner of its steel frame, this gigantic piece shares the aesthetic purity and mysterious resonance of the Egyptian pyramids.

The Minimalist aesthetic also inspired one of the most popular landmarks of the 1980s: the Vietnam Veterans' Memorial (Figure **15.21**). Whereas traditional war monuments feature human figures in heroic poses, this unique memorial, conceived by the American artist Maya Ying Lin (b. 1959), consists simply of two granite slabs bearing the names of the 58,627 Americans missing or killed in Vietnam. Visitors to the stark, V-shaped monument, cut into a gently sloping hill near the Washington Monument, descend a walkway to see their own image softly reflected in the highly polished wall of names: a mirror of the living honoring the dead. The memorial immortalizes the deceased not by means of symbolic imagery (as with the *Aids Memorial Quilt*, see Figure 15.12), but by the affective combination of words, shapes, and space.

Figure 15.19 Frank Stella, *Tahkt-i-Sulayman I*, from the "Protractor" series, 1967. Polymer and fluorescent paint on canvas, 10 ft. 1/4 in. x 20 ft. 2 1/4 in. Menil Collection, Houston, Texas. The paintings in this series bear the exotic names of ancient circular cities in Asia Minor. Yet, the artist insists, "All I want anyone to get out of my paintings, and all I ever get out of them, is the fact that you can see the whole thing without confusion. What you see is what you see."

Figure 15.20 Isamu Noguchi, *Cube*, 1968. Steel subframe with aluminum panels, height 28 ft. Marine Midland Building, New York. Noguchi, who studied with Brancusi, was also a student of Japanese ceramics. From both he derived an appreciation of powerful, yet elegant, abstract form.

Figure 15.21 (below) Maya Ying Lin, Vietnam Veterans' Memorial, Washington, D.C., 1981–1983. Black granite, length of each wing 246 ft. An alternative to traditional war monuments, this Minimalist piece cuts open the earth like an unhealed wound.

New Realism

During the 1970s, there emerged a new version of realism that emphasized the stop-action stillness and sharp-focus immediacy of the photograph. *New Realism* (also called *Neorealism*, *Hyperrealism*, and *Photo-realism*) differs from previous realist styles (including Social Realism and Pop art) in its disavowal of narrative content and its indifference to moral, social, and political issues. Although decidedly representational, it is as impersonal as Minimal art. Neorealists do not imitate natural phenomena; rather, they recreate an artificially processed view of reality captured in the photographic image (see Figure 15.33).

High-tech materials and techniques have made possible the fabrication of New Realist sculptures that are shockingly lifelike. Duane Hanson (1925–1996) used fiberglass-reinforced polyester resin to recreate the appearance of ordinary and often working-class individuals in their everyday occupations (Figure **15.22**). He cast his polyester molds from live models, then added wigs, clothing, and accessories.

Total Art

The information age has generated creative strategies that reach beyond the studio and into the public domain. *Total art* has its origins in the performances and "happenings" of the 1960s. *Happenings*—the name coined by its founder, Allan Kaprow (1927–2006)—involved a highly structured series of actions and scripted gestures (usually based in everyday experience). While directed by the artist, the happening welcomed chance and random elements. Like a ritual or staged theatrical piece, the performance was *itself* the artwork. Regardless of whether it was performed again, the only record of a happening might be a photograph or videotape. Performance art has limited value as a saleable commodity; nevertheless, it has continued to attract artists, who frequently incorporate film, photography, dance, and other media in life-into-art displays that address personal or political issues.

Total art is essentially conceptual; that is, it is driven by ideas and concepts that take precedence over the material object. One of the purest examples of this genre consists

Figure 15.22 Duane Hanson, *Tourists*, 1970. Fiberglass and polyester polychromed, 5 ft. 4 in. x 5 ft. 5 in. x 3 ft. 11 in. Scottish National Gallery of Modern Art, Edinburgh. By comparison with George Segal's melancholic figures (see Figure 15.17), Hanson's "living dead" are symbolic of modern life at its most prosaic.

Figure 15.23 Jenny Holzer, *Untitled (Selections from Truisms, Inflammatory Essays, The Living Series, The Survival Series, Under a Rock, Laments, and Child Text)*, 1989. Extended helical tricolor LED, electronic display board; site-specific dimensions. Solomon R. Guggenheim Museum, New York. Holzer's typically Postmodern word-art wryly tests the authority of public information and commercial advertising as dispersed by contemporary electronic media.

solely of words. Barbara Kruger's billboard-style posters combine photographic images and phrases that make cryptic comments on social and political issues (see Figure 15.10). The superstar of conceptualism, the American artist Jenny Holzer (b. 1950) carves her paradoxical and subversive messages on stone slabs or broadcasts them electronically on public billboards. Her slogans are often transmitted by way of light-emitting diodes—a favorite medium of commercial advertising (Figure **15.23**). In language that is at once banal and acerbic, she informs us that "Lack of charisma can be fatal," "Myths make reality more intelligible," "Humanism is obsolete," "Decency is a relative thing," and "Ambivalence can ruin your life."

The most monumental type of Total art is the *earthwork*, a kind of installation that takes the natural landscape as both its medium and its subject. A type of *Environmental* (or *site-specific*) *art*, the earthwork is usually colossal, heroic, and temporary. Among the most impressive examples of this genre is the piece called *Spiral Jetty*, built in 1970 by Robert Smithson (1938–1973) at the northeastern edge of the Great Salt Lake in Utah (Figure **15.24**). Smithson's spiral—the snail-like symbol of eternity in ancient art—is 1500 feet wide and consists of over 6000 tons of black basalt, limestone, salt crystals, and earth—materials that were excavated from the surrounding area. A conscious reference to ancient earthworks, such as those found in Neolithic cultures (see Figure 1.8), Smithson's landmark project brought attention to the role of the artist in reconstructing the environment and its ecology. Earthworks like *Spiral Jetty*, however, were often best appreciated from the air. Tragically, it was in the crash of a plane surveying one such sculpture that Smithson was killed.

The Environmental sculptures of the American artists Christo (b. 1935) and Jeanne-Claude (1935–2010) are among the most ambitious examples of site-specific art. The Christos have magically transformed natural and human sites by enveloping them with huge amounts of fabric. They have wrapped monumental public structures, such as the Pont Neuf in Paris and the Reichstag in Berlin, and they have reshaped nature, wrapping part of the coast of Australia, for instance, and surrounding eleven islands in Miami's Biscayne Bay with over six million square feet of pink woven polypropylene fabric. One of the Christos' earliest projects, *Running Fence* (Figure **15.25**), involved the construction of a nylon "fence" 24½ miles long and 18 feet high. The nylon panels were hung on cables and steel poles and ran through Sonoma and Marin counties, California, to the Pacific Ocean. Unlike Smithson, the Christos do not seek to remake the natural landscape; rather they modify it temporarily in order to dramatize the difference between the natural world and the increasingly artificial domain of Postmodern society.

Figure 15.24 Robert Smithson, *Spiral Jetty*, Great Salt Lake, Utah, 1970. Rock, salt crystals, earth algae; coil 1500 ft. In extremely dry periods, the outline of the "jetty" is clearly visible. The red color of the water comes from salt-tolerant bacteria and algae. Smithson's documentary drawings, photographs, and films of this and other earthworks have heightened public awareness of the fragile ecological balance between culture and nature.

Video Art

The electronic media have revolutionized the arts: Computer-manipulated photographs, virtual environments, and mixed-media installations are among the innovative projects of our time. The electronic synthesis of music, video, dance, and performance opens up new kinds of experience. In the information age, the image, and especially the *moving* image, has assumed a position of power over other forms of artistic expression.

In the 1950s, the Korean artist and musician Nam June Paik (1932–2006) predicted that the television cathode ray would replace the canvas as the medium of the future. The now acclaimed "father of video art" was not far from the mark, for art that employs one or another form of electronic technology has come to dominate the current art world. Video art had its beginnings in the 1960s, shaped by Paik himself. He began his career (under the combined influence of the composer John Cage (see page 449) and Zen Buddhism) by creating performance pieces and electronic installations. These were among the first interactive experiments in sound and image. With the help of an electronic engineer, Paik designed and built one of the first videosynthesizers—a device that makes it possible to alter the shape and color of a video image.

In the 1990s, Paik assembled television sets, circuit boards, and other electronic apparatus to produce a series of "Robot" sculptures. More monumental in scope and conception, however, are the artist's multiscreen television installations. *Megatron* (1995), for instance, consists of 215 monitors programmed with a rapid-fire assortment of animated and live video images drawn from East and West (Figure **15.26**). The Seoul Olympic Games and Korean drummers, rock concert clips, girlie-magazine nudes, and quick-cuts of Paik's favorite artists alternate with the national flags of various countries and other global logos.

In contrast with the frenzied dazzle of Paik's video projects, the sound and video installations of Bill Viola (b. 1951) are profoundly subtle. Viola uses rear-projected video screens to deliver large, slow-moving visual narratives. Identity, mortality, and consciousness, Viola's central themes, find inspiration in Zen Buddhism, Christian mysticism, and Sufi poetry. The computer-controlled,

Figure 15.25 (above) Christo and Jeanne-Claude, *Running Fence*, Sonoma and Marin counties, California, 1972–1976. Nylon panels on cables and steel poles, height 18 ft., length 24½ miles. The fascinating history of this landmark piece, which cost the artists over three million dollars and mobilized the efforts of a large crew of workers, is documented in films, photographs, and books. The fence itself, meandering along the California hills like a modern-day version of the Great Wall of China, remained on site for only two weeks.

Figure 15.26 (below) Nam June Paik, *Megatron*, 1995. 215 monitors, 8-channel color video and 2-channel sound, left side 142½ x 270 x 23½ in.; right side 128 x 128 x 23½ in. The animated contour of a bird flying gracefully across a wall of screens brings magical unity to this ocular blitz, while a two-channel audio track adds booming syncopated sound to the visual rhythms. Paik's wall of video monitors dazzles viewers with a kaleidoscopic barrage of images whose fast-paced editing imitates mainstream television and film.

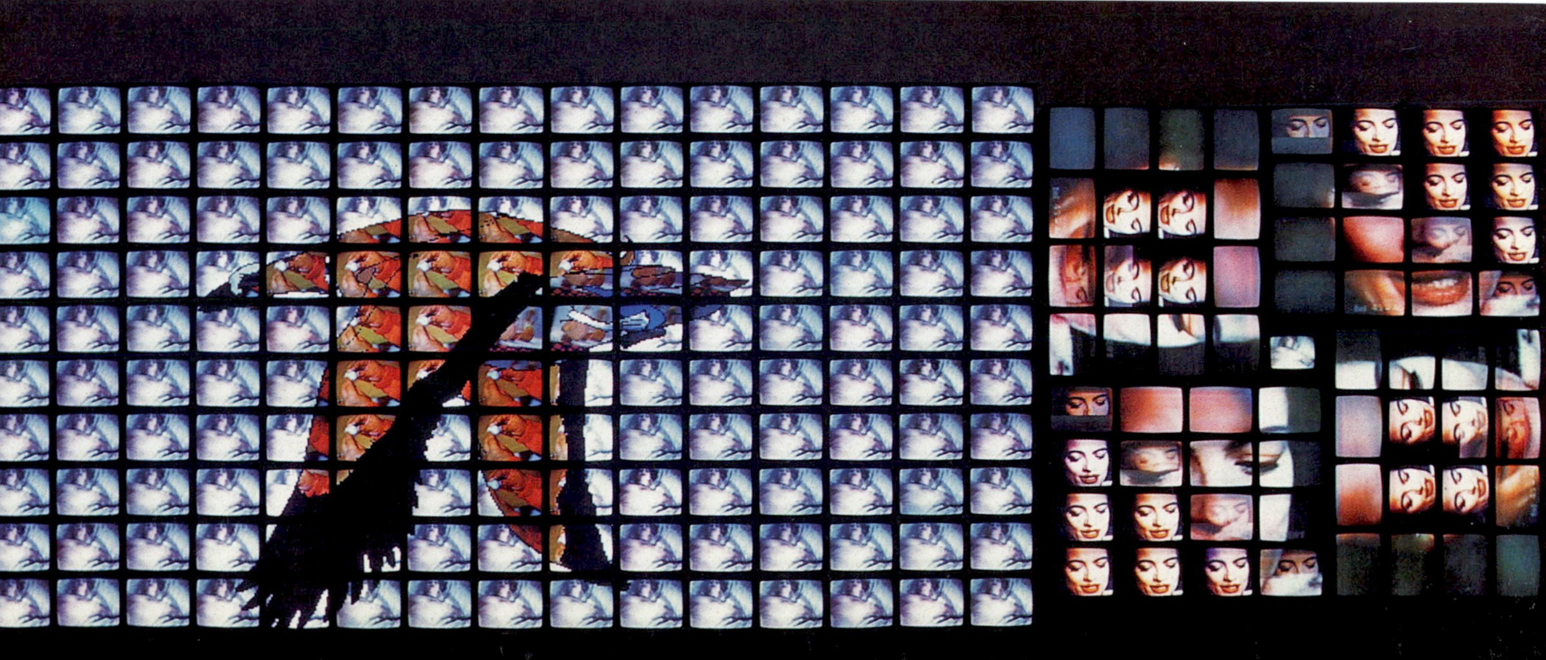

Figure 15.27 Bill Viola, *Stations* (detail), 1994. Video/sound installation with five granite slabs, five projections, and five projection screens. The Museum of Modern Art, New York.

five-channel video/sound installation called *Stations* (a reference to the Stations of the Cross, Christ's journey to Calvary), projects onto three vertical slabs of granite the image of a floating male body, which is then reflected in mirrors placed on the floor (Figure **15.27**). Viola asks the viewer to experience the piece as a "mental image" that evokes the human journey from birth to death. According to Viola, the main issue in the arts of the future is "representing information." His artworks share with contemporary film and mixed-media installations the ambition to concentrate experience by way of hauntingly memorable moving images.

Contemporary Photography

Traditional photography (discussed in Chapters 13 and 14) has undergone radical changes in the past sixty years. Pure photography (see Figures 13.7, 14.2, and 15.11) and photomontage (see Figure 14.32) still intrigue many artists; however, today's photographs are often the result of the digital manipulation of electronically accessible images. The Internet has put the world's images at the disposal of every photographer, who is then able to gather, manipulate, and produce artworks that could never have been achieved in the traditional darkroom.

There are two types of digital imaging: The first involves the use of software programs (such as Photoshop) that allow artists to manipulate existing images taken by the artist or borrowed from other sources (see

Making Connections

UPDATING MANET

Contemporary Japanese artists have been particularly successful in using computer technology to generate provocative photographs and video projects. Yasumasa Morimura (b. 1945) transforms Western masterpieces into camp spoofs in which he impersonates one or more of the central characters. In *Portrait* (*Futago*, the Japanese word for "twins") (Figure **15.28**), Morimura turns Manet's *Olympia* (Figure **15.29**) into a drag queen decked out in a blond wig and rhinestone-trimmed slippers. Using himself as the model for both the nude courtesan and the maid, he revisualizes the original, suggesting the intersecting ("twin") roles of prostitute and slave. By "updating" Manet's *Olympia* (itself an "update" of a painting by Titian), Morimura questions the authority of these historical icons, even as he makes sly reference to the postwar Japanese practices of copying Western culture and ministering to Western interests. *Portrait* is a computer-manipulated color photograph produced from a studio setup—a combination of Postmodern techniques borrowed from fashion advertising. Here, and in his more recent photographs in which he impersonates contemporary icons and film divas (Madonna, Marilyn Monroe, and Liza Minnelli), Morimura pointedly tests classic stereotypes of identity and gender.

Q In what ways does Morimura address the stereotypes of identity and gender? What Japanese motifs does he introduce into the photograph?

Figure 15.28 (above) Yasumasa Morimura, *Portrait* (*Futago*), 1988–1990. Color photograph, edition of five: 6 ft. 10½ in. x 9 ft. 10 in. NW House, Tokyo.

Figure 15.29 Edouard Manet, *Olympia*, 1863. Oil on canvas, 4 ft. 3¼ in. x 6 ft. 2¾ in. Orsay Museum, Paris.

Figures 15.10, 15.28, and 15.36). Such photographs may take the form of "historical fictions" that challenge the viewer's idea of reality. A second process involves digital imaging via various computer-graphics techniques that generate abstract simulations. Artists may give the computer a special set of instructions about the "look" of the image, which is then electronically simulated. Such purely computer-generated work is a type of *digital art* that has the appearance of a photograph.

Computers and New Media Arts

The computers of the past half-century have become a unique means of reconciling the domains of art and science. In dozens of ways, digital devices are transforming the manner in which art is made and experienced. Computers are now essential to the design and construction of architecture and art: In fiberglass sculpture, for instance, the computer makes possible the execution of otherwise unachievable three-dimensional curves. Sophisticated software programs allow artists to draw and paint electronically.

The term "New Media art" was coined in the 1990s to describe art that makes use of digital technologies, such as computer graphics, computer animation, the Internet, and a wide variety of interactive technologies. The Internet is crucial to New Media projects, but computer games, handheld cameras, and digital audio are equally important as digital sources, all of which may be sampled, mixed, and remixed. Appropriation (the borrowing and recycling of motifs) and collaboration (the sharing of tasks among individuals with different skills, often from different parts of the world) are common features of the New Media environment. While the landmarks of this essentially global movement are yet to be produced, some of its basic strategies and enterprises have enormous creative potential. For instance, current experiments in *augmented reality* add digital information to real-time images of reality on smartphone screens; Internet-based *virtual reality* may ultimately make it possible to turn one's living room into an electronic replica of a totally different space.

Contemporary communication finds a playful proponent in *Keitai Girl* (see Figure 15.14), created by the Japanese artist Noriko Yamaguchi (b. 1983). Wearing headphones and a body suit made of cell phone ("*keitai*") keypads, Yamaguchi *becomes* a human mobile phone—the telecommunication device that (in most parts of the world) also functions as a credit card, television, video, portable music device, digital camera, and more. Wires connect her to other stations in cyberspace. Her costume, futuristic in anticipating the implantation of digital devices in the human body, is part of a larger performance involving interactive lasers, fast, upbeat music, and a popular Japanese dance style known as *Para-Para* (a type of line dancing).

Contemporary Cinema

Digital technology has transformed the world of filmmaking. New technologies, such as high-definition (HD) video, which gives visual images greater immediacy, have begun to replace film itself. The ease with which digital video can be produced, reproduced from film, and downloaded via computers has raised major issues concerning copyrights, but it has also made the archive of motion pictures readily available to a worldwide audience. In response to the new technology, new film centers are developing throughout the world. The website YouTube, which invites unedited video postings, has become a forum for young and independent filmmakers, especially in the production of short and documentary films.

Computers have also revolutionized the way films are made: Computer-generated imaging (CGI) of realistic settings makes it unnecessary for filmmakers to use large-scale sets and locations. Special effects, achieved by way of computers, are used to juxtapose images in ways that distort reality. Like docufiction, films render believable what in actuality may be untrue. The 1994 film *Forrest Gump*, for instance, shows its antihero shaking hands with the long-dead president John F. Kennedy. Digital technology also makes possible entirely new and hyperreal images, such as Steven Spielberg's dinosaurs (*Jurassic Park*, 1993), James Cameron's liquid-metal cyborgs (*Terminator 2*, 1991), and Larry and Andy Wachowski's science fiction trilogy *Matrix* (1999–2003), which required more than a hundred meticulously coordinated still cameras. Just as CGI can create realistic settings, so it can replace human actors with computer-generated characters, as in the fantasy trilogy *The Lord of the Rings* (2001–2003). In the science fiction film *Avatar* (2009), James Cameron superimposed CGI over live-action imagery. The casts of this film wore skull caps and suits covered with sensors that fed body movements to a bank of computers; a virtual monitor allowed Cameron to see the motion-capture results in real time, that is, while filming. Polarized glasses allowed viewers to enjoy the film in digital 3-D. While digital artistry may not replace live-action film, it provokes questions concerning the differences between the original and the replica, the real and the virtual, truth and illusion.

Film animation has also undergone major changes. The first feature-length, entirely computerized animated film, *Toy Story*, appeared in 1995. Using even more sophisticated software for digital imaging, including three-dimensional graphics and a wider range of special effects, Hayao Miyazaki's award-winning *Spirited Away* (2001) brought Japanese *animé* to world attention.

Ironically, among the examples of contemporary cinema that may be said to have earned landmark significance, *none* depend on CGI techniques: Stanley Kubrick's *2001: A Space Odyssey* (1968) (see Figure 14.8) is a science-fiction tale of adventure not unlike that of the great Homeric epic; *Raise the Red Lantern* (1991), the work of the celebrated filmmaker Zhang Yimou (see page 456) is a ravishing treatment of Chinese concubines who remain hostage to feudal and patriarchal traditions; Steven Spielberg's powerful *Schindler's List* (1993) integrates documentary newscasts and selective color techniques to recreate a memorable episode of the Holocaust; and Steven Soderbergh's *Traffic* (2000) brings to light the gritty realities of America's drug culture.

Contemporary Architecture

Some contemporary critics link the birth of Postmodernism to the architecture of the 1960s and, specifically, to the demise of the International Style. The American Robert Venturi (b. 1925), who first introduced architectural Postmodernism in his book *Complexity and Contradiction in Architecture* (1966), countered Mies van der Rohe's dictum "less is more" with the claim "less is a bore." Venturi and others rejected the anonymity and austerity of the glass and steel skyscraper along with the progressive utopianism of Modernists who hoped to transform society through functional form. Instead, Postmodernists emphasized visual complexity, individuality, and outright fun. In contrast to the machinelike purity of the International-Style structure, the Postmodern building is a playful assortment of fragments "quoted" from architectural traditions as ill-mated as a fast-food stand and a Hellenistic temple. Postmodern architecture, like Postmodern fiction, engages a colorful mix of fragments in a whimsical and often witty manner. A prime example of this aesthetic is the Piazza d'Italia in New Orleans, designed by Charles Moore (1925–1993). The plaza, which serves as an Italian cultural center, is a burlesque yet elegant combination of motifs borrowed from Pompeii, Palladio, and Italian Baroque architecture (Figure **15.30**).

The architectural giant of the late twentieth century, Frank Gehry (b. 1930), was born in Toronto, Canada, but lives and works in California. His early buildings reflect an interest in humble construction materials such as plywood, corrugated zinc, stainless steel, and chainlink fencing. Gehry's structures, in which façades tilt, columns lean, and interior spaces are skewed, reflect his deliberate rejection of the classical design principles of symmetry and stability. More recently, in monumental projects that combine steel, titanium, glass, and limestone, he has developed a vocabulary of undulating forms and irregular shapes inspired by everyday objects: a fish, a guitar, a bouquet of flowers. The organic elegance of a Gehry building becomes a functional reality only with the assistance of a computer program that digitally maps and refines Gehry's wood-and-paper working model. The landmark of Gehry's long career is the Walt Disney Concert Hall in Los Angeles, California (Figure **15.31**). The 2265-seat hall encloses a majestic sky-lit, multilevel lobby; but it is in the breathtaking design of the exterior, with its billowing, light-reflecting stainless steel plates, that the building achieves its singular magnificence.

Another of Gehry's landmark buildings, the Guggenheim Museum in Bilbao, Spain (1997), arrived on the wave of a great boom in museum construction and expansion that is still in progress. Museums are among the global world's most popular sites, visited by millions who are awed by great art or seek a fulfilling leisure-time experience. With futuristic designs that often feature dramatically tilted walls, some of the new museums fail to provide an ideal setting for the art they display. This is not the case, however, with the daring, newly expanded Milwaukee Museum of Art, designed by the Spanish-born architect Santiago Calatrava (b. 1951). Dominating the shore of Lake Michigan like the skeleton of a bleach-boned dinosaur, the museum is entered by a 90-foot-high glass-enclosed reception hall covered by a movable winglike

Figure 15.30 Perez Associates with Charles Moore, Ron Filson, Urban Innovations, Inc., Piazza d'Italia, New Orleans, 1976–1979. The brightly colored colonnaded portico—looking every bit like a gaudy stage set—is adorned with fountains, neon lights, and polished aluminum balustrades. Moore's parodic grab-bag appropriation of Italian heritage culminates in an apron shaped like a map of Italy that floats in the central pool of the piazza.

Figure 15.31 (above) Frank Gehry, Walt Disney Concert Hall, Los Angeles, California, 2003. Metal-clad stainless steel plates connected by aluminum panels, glass curtain wall, and skylights, area 270,000 sq. ft. Like a sculptor, Gehry prefers to work out a design by a modeling process that facilitates spontaneity. Yet, like most contemporary architects, he uses a computer to realize his designs. His firm employs at least five aerospace engineers to direct the cutting and assembling of the actual building parts. The virtual building precedes the actual one.

sun screen made of 72 steel fins that control the temperature and light of the interior (Figure **15.32**). A 250-foot-long suspension bridge with angled cables links the lakefront museum to downtown Milwaukee. Two smaller museums that grace American sites are Cincinnati's Center for Contemporary Art (2003), designed by the Iraq-born Zaha Hadid (b. 1950) and the Modern Art Museum of Fort Worth (2002) by the Japanese architect Tadao Ando (b. 1941), which appears to float on an adjacent artificial lake.

Figure 15.32 Santiago Calatrava, Milwaukee Art Museum, Milwaukee, Wisconsin, 2003. Reaching out to the lake, Calatrava's birdlike structure erases the boundaries between sculpture and architecture.

MUSIC AND DANCE

Cage and Aleatory Music

The most inventive figure in mid-twentieth-century music was the American writer and composer John Cage (1912–1992). A leading spokesman for chance and experimentation, Cage described music as a combination of sounds (specific pitches), noise (nonpitched sounds), and silence, with rhythm as the common denominator. In 1953, he composed *4′ 33″*, a piece in which a performer sits motionless before the piano for four minutes and thirty-three seconds. The "music" of *4′ 33″* consists of the fleeting sounds that occur during the designated time period—the breathing of the pianist, the shuffling of the audience's feet, or, perhaps, the distant hum of traffic outside the concert hall.

Cage also produced some unusual compositions for his unique invention: the prepared piano—a traditional Steinway that he modified by attaching to its strings pieces of rubber, bamboo slats, bolts, and other objects. The results feature hypnotic tones resembling those of a Balinese orchestra, and muted percussive rhythms. Cage's works—even his more traditional compositions—are **aleatory**, that is, based on chance or random procedures. To determine the arrangement of notes in a composition, he might apply numbers dictated by the throw of a dice or by the surface stains on a blank piece of sheet music. He found inspiration for random techniques in Zen Buddhism, in the *I jing* (the ancient oracular Chinese *Book of Changes*, see page 25), and in the imperatives of Dada and Surrealism. Despite his chance methods, his compositions are fully scored; even the most unconventional passages follow explicit directions. More than his music, his radical ideas, as publicized in his numerous essays and lectures, had an enormous influence on contemporary music.

Microtonality and Minimalism

As with Cage, many twentieth-century composers took inspiration from non-Western sources. The Hungarian-born György Ligeti (1923–2006) explored musical intervals smaller than the semitones of traditional Western music. His use of **microtonality**, rich with dense clusters of sound, is evident in *Atmosphères*—featured in the film score for *2001: A Space Odyssey* (see page 393 and Figure 14.8) Such tone clusters abandon traditional rhythms and pitch in favor of shimmering currents of sound that murmur hypnotically.

Ligeti, *Atmosphères* (1961)

The Minimalist compositions of the Americans Philip Glass (b. 1937), Steve Reich (b. 1936), and John Adams (b. 1947) also draw on non-Western resources. Their *minimal music*, like minimal art, reduces the vocabulary of expression to elemental or primary components. In the "stripped-down" works of Glass (Figure **15.33**), melodic fragments are repeated in subtly shifting rhythmic patterns that reflect the influence of classic Indian music. The musical drama *Einstein on the Beach*, which Glass produced in collaboration with the designer/director Robert Wilson (b. 1941), was the first opera performed at the Metropolitan Opera House in New York City to feature electronically amplified instruments. *Einstein on the Beach* combines instrumental and vocal music, as well as recitation, mime, and dance; but it departs from operatic tradition in its lack of a narrative story line. Performed with no intermissions over a period of four-and-a-half hours, the opera is not an account of Einstein's life or work, but an extended poetic statement, whose harmonic changes occur so slowly that one must, as Glass explains, learn to listen at "a different speed"—an experience that closely resembles an act of meditation.

Glass, *Einstein on the Beach* (1976)

Historical themes have continued to inspire much of the music of Glass. His opera *Satyagraha* (1980) celebrates the achievements of India's pacifist hero Mohandas Gandhi. Sung in both Sanskrit and English, it employs a text drawn from the *Bhagavad Gita*, the sacred book of

Figure 15.33 Chuck Close, *Phil*, 1969. Acrylic on canvas, 108 in. x 84 in. Whitney Museum of American Art, New York. For this portrait of his friend, the composer Philip Glass, Close (b. 1940) used an opaque projector to transfer the photographic image to canvas after both photograph and canvas had been ruled to resemble graph paper; he then filled each square of the canvas with tiny gradations of color that resemble the pixels of a television screen. The brutally impersonal tabloid quality of Close's oversized "mug-shots" is reinforced by the monochromatic palette.

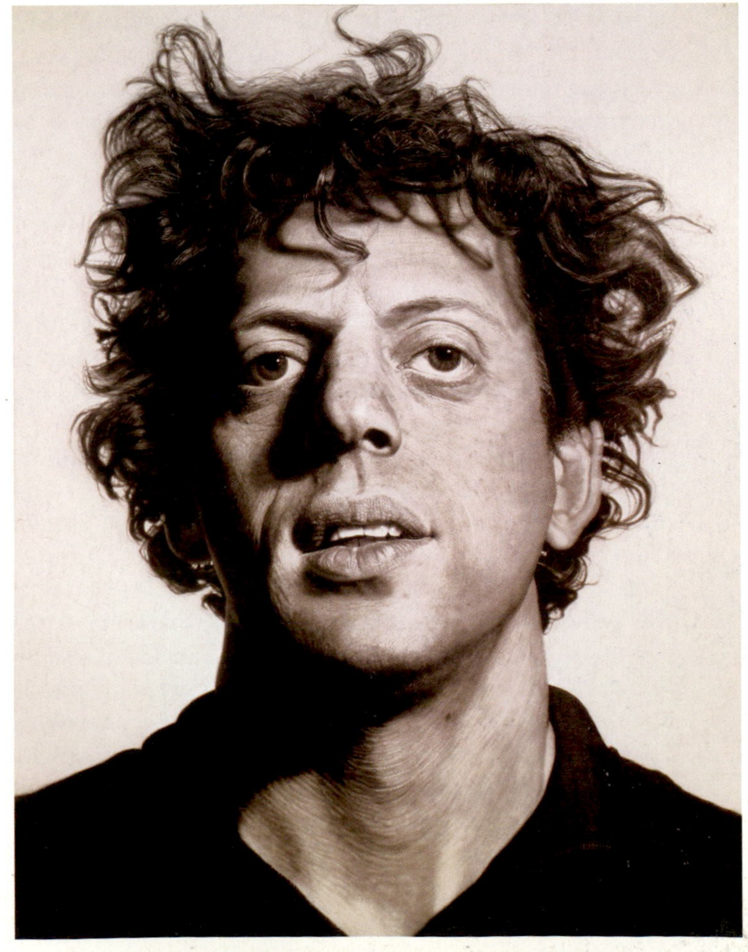

Hinduism (see page 23). Glass's *Akhenaten* (1984), based on the life of the Egyptian monotheist pharaoh, uses texts from the Egyptian *Book of the Dead* (see page 14); *The Voyage* (1992) links the heroic age of Columbian exploration to contemporary efforts in outer space and interplanetary travel; and the opera *Appomattox* (2007) moves from the American Civil War to the civil rights struggle and to the role of racism in contemporary life.

Choral Music and Opera

The outstanding choral work of the last fifty years, the *War Requiem*, was written by Benjamin Britten (1913–1976) to accompany the opening of England's new Coventry Cathedral, built alongside the ruins of the fourteenth-century cathedral that had been virtually destroyed by German bombs in World War II. For the piece, Britten—a lifelong conscientious objector and a pacifist—juxtaposed the text of the Roman Catholic Mass for the Dead with contemporary antiwar poetry. Poignant in spirit and dramatic in effect, this modern oratorio is one of the most powerful musical statements of the twentieth century.

Britten, *War Requiem* (1963)

The twentieth century's first Postmodern opera, *The Ghosts of Versailles* (1992), was composed by John Corigliano (b. 1938). Scored for orchestra and synthesizer and cast in the style of a comic opera, *Ghosts* takes place in three different (and interlayered) worlds. One is the realm of the afterlife and is peopled by the ghosts of Marie Antoinette and her court. The score of this opera commingles traditional and contemporary musical styles, alternating pseudo-Mozartian lyricism with modern dissonance in a bold and inventive (although often disjunctive) manner.

Among Corigliano's contemporaries, many have found inspiration for their operas in political events, such as international terrorism (John Adams' *Death of Klinghoffer*, 1991), and in the cult of celebrity (Adams' *Nixon in China*, 1987; Ezra Laderman's *Marilyn Monroe*, 1994; and Robert Xavier Rodriguez's *Frida* [Kahlo], 1991). Others have turned to the classics of literature and art for subject matter: Carlyle Floyd's *Of Mice and Men* (1970), based on John Steinbeck's novel, and Benjamin Britten's *Death in Venice* (1973), adapted from Thomas Mann's famous novella, are two of the most outstanding examples.

One of America's finest composers, John Adams (b. 1947) has led the way in linking popular and classical music to create a unique (though difficult to categorize) artform that has been called "music/opera." Adams' *I Was Looking at the Ceiling and Then I Saw the Sky* (1995) was written in the aftermath of the 1994 California earthquake. Unlike his operas, *Nixon in China* and *The Death of Klinghoffer*, this piece does not assume a dramatic narrative form, nor require a full orchestra. Rather, it resembles a song-cycle that tells the story of the quake as experienced by seven young Angelinos (the opera's title is based on a comment made by one of them). Performed by pop singers and a rock band, its post-minimal musical language shares the rhythmic verve of rock, pop, and jazz.

A recent landmark in contemporary opera is *The First Emperor* by the Chinese composer Tan Dun (b. 1957). Based on the life of the emperor who unified ancient China (see page 84), the opera brings together two radically different operatic styles, Western and Peking (a traditional Chinese combination of music, mime, dance, and acrobatics). Tan, who settled in America in 1985, makes brilliant use of Chinese instruments and the unique performance practices of Asian theater.

Tan Dun, *The First Emperor* (2006)

Electronic Music and Computers

Electronic technology has affected all aspects of music, from composition to performance and distribution. The ready availability of electronically reproduced sound has made music easily accessible, virtually eliminating the patronage system that supported musical composition in former eras.

While electronic technology may be used simply to record musical performance, it also provides a means of creating new types of sound, offering a range of frequencies (from fifty to fifteen thousand cycles per second) well in excess of the limited pitch range of conventional instruments. Besides this almost unlimited variability of pitch, electronic instruments provide a huge dynamic span and can execute rhythms at speeds and in patterns that are beyond the capability of live performers.

Electronic music may be created in two ways: by the electronic modification of preexisting sound or by the purely electronic generation of sound. In the first method, electronic equipment is used to modify a wide variety of natural, instrumental, and mechanically contrived sounds, while or after they are performed. In the late 1950s, John Cage and other avant-garde composers began to employ magnetic tape to record and manipulate sound. By means of such techniques as splicing and reversing the taped sounds of various kinds of environmental noise—thunder, human voices, bird calls, train whistles, and ticking clocks—they produced a genre known as *musique concrète* ("concrete music").

The second method for creating electronic music involves the use of special equipment to generate sound itself. "Pure" electronic music differs from *musique concrète* in its reliance on oscillators, wave generators, and other electronic devices. The pioneer in this type of music was the German composer Karlheinz Stockhausen (1928–2007). As musical director of the Studio for Electronic Music in Cologne, Germany, Stockhausen employed electronic devices both by themselves and to manipulate and combine pretaped sounds, including music generated by traditional instruments and voices. His compositions—atonal patterns of sounds and silence that lack any controlling frame of reference—renounce all conventional rules of rhythm and harmony. Editing taped sounds as a filmmaker edits footage, Stockhausen dispensed with a written score and composed directly on tape, thus assuming simultaneously the roles of composer and performer.

The most revolutionary musical invention of the late 1960s was the computerized **synthesizer**, an integrated system of electronic components designed for both the production and manipulation of sound. Stockhausen's American contemporary Milton Babbitt (1916–2011) was the first composer to use the RCA synthesizer to control the texture, timbre, and intensity of electronic sound. Since the 1970s, more sophisticated and portable digital synthesizers have been attached to individual instruments. These allow musicians to manipulate the pitch, duration, and dynamics of sound even as the music is being performed. The synthesizer has facilitated the typically Postmodern technique known as *sampling*. A sample is a short, "borrowed" segment of recorded sound, which may be stored digitally, manipulated at will (stretched out, played backward, and so on), then reintroduced or mixed into another musical phrase or composition.

The computer has become the definitive studio of our time. It provides an archive of universally accessible music, the software tools for cutting, mixing, mashing up, and recording music—a phenomenon that has encouraged scores of do-it-yourself composers. Computers themselves have become musical instruments. Equipped with a miniature keyboard, faders, and foot pedals, the contemporary computer is not only capable of producing a full range of sounds but of generating and reproducing sounds more subtle and complex than any emitted by human voices or traditional musical instruments. In addition to recording, reproducing, and manipulating sound, computers can be utilized to compose original music. Using a special penlike device that draws the contours of sound waves on a video screen, it is possible to create computer music.

Some composers have designed interactive musical instruments (or "hyperinstruments") that combine real-time computers and traditional instruments. Others enlarge the range of performance possibilities by way of hybrid acoustic/electronic instruments, such as Ben Neill's "mutantrumpet" with six valves, a trombone slide, and an electronic interface that functions as a synthesizer controller.

Rock and Popular Music

It is difficult to determine which of the popular musical styles of the last sixty years will leave landmarks for future generations. Nevertheless, one popular genre, jazz (see page 412), has already manifested a lasting influence and a sustaining cultural vitality. A second candidate is *rock* music. The origins of this style lie in the popular culture of the mid-1950s. The words "rocking" and "rolling," originally used to describe sexual activity, came to identify an uninhibited musical style that drew on a broad combination of popular American and African-American music, including country, swing, gospel, and rhythm and blues. Although no one musician is responsible for the birth of rock, the style gained popularity with such performers as Bill Haley, Little Richard, and Elvis Presley. In the hands of these flamboyant musicians, it came to be characterized by a high dynamic level of sound, fast and hard rhythms, a strong beat, and earthy, colloquial lyrics. A related genre, called *"soul,"* merged rhythm and blues with the emotional intensity of the gospel tradition. Originating in the black communities of the northern United States, it became popular in the 1960s with the dynamic sounds of such African-American singers as James Brown, Ray Charles, and Aretha Franklin.

From its inception, rock music was an expression of a youth culture: The rock sound, associated with dancing, illicit drugs, sexual freedom, and rebellion against restrictive parental and cultural norms, also mirrored the new consumerism of the postwar era. With the success of the Beatles—a British group of the 1960s—rock became an international phenomenon, uniting young people across the globe. The Beatles absorbed the music of Little Richard and also the rhythms and instrumentation of Indian classical music. They made imaginative use of electronic effects, such as feedback and splicing. Their compositions, which reflected the spirit of the Western counterculture, reached a creative peak in the landmark album *Sergeant Pepper's Lonely Hearts Club Band* (1967). Although the electric guitar was in use well before the Beatles emerged, it was with this group that the instrument became the hallmark of rock music, and it remains the principal instrument of the rock musician. An exception is found in the early music of the American folk singer and songwriter, Bob Dylan (b. 1941). Set to the sounds of an acoustic guitar, Dylan's lyrics to such songs as "Blowin' In the Wind" and "The Times They Are a-Changin'" are among the most overt expressions of the discontent (with racial injustice and the Vietnam War) that defined the American counterculture of the 1960s and 1970s.

Dylan, "Blowin' In the Wind" (1963)

Globalism, the spirit of international communality, colors the music of our time. The influence of Arabic chant, Indian *ragas* (traditional melody-patterns), Cuban brass, and Latino dance rhythms is evident in popular as well as classical music. To offer a few examples from the popular realm: Rock and country blues have given gospel music a new sound; *klezmer* (Jewish folk music) has been appropriated by jazz instrumentalists; and shimmering, Asian textures dominate New Age music. *Reggae*, an eclectic style that draws on a wide variety of Jamaican musical traditions—African and Christian—has become a vehicle of political criticism and social reform.

Hip-hop, a combination of loud, percussive music (often electronically mixed and manipulated by disc jockeys), jarring lyrics, and break dancing (an acrobatic dance style), has moved from its inner-city origins to a broader, international audience. A "mutating hybrid," hip-hop draws on a variety of musical traditions: disco, salsa, reggae, and rock, as well as African call-and-response chant. *Rap*, a vocal offshoot of hip-hop, born in black America's urban youth culture, launches a fusillade of raw and socially provocative words chanted in rhymed couplets over an intense rhythmic beat. Since the 1980s, hip-hop and rap have fused with local musical styles from Cuba to Senegal.

While some critics lament that Western music has split into two cultures—art music and popular music—the fact is that these two traditions are becoming more alike. More precisely, they continue to exchange various features of a global musical menu.

Dance

The single most important figure in the field of dance since 1950 is the American choreographer Merce Cunningham (1919–2009). Cunningham's contribution stems from his radical disassociation of music and dance. Rejecting the narrative style of his teacher, Martha Graham (see page 414), he focused on pure body movement and abstract form. In a Cunningham piece, dance may proceed without music; or, music may coexist with dance, but the tempo of the music may be irrelevant to the movements of the dancers. Cunningham's choreography embraces everyday actions, such as running, jumping, and falling, which may occur by way of improvisation or—as with the music of his colleague and lifetime partner, John Cage—by chance. Nevertheless, as with Cage (see page 449), even improvisation is planned (or choreographed), thus joining freedom and the control of pure movement in space. In partnership with Cage and Robert Rauschenberg (see page 438), Cunningham staged the mixed-media performance *Summerspace* (1958), which revolutionized theatrical dance. At Black Mountain College, in Asheville, North Carolina, the trio produced some of the most innovative theatrical enterprises of the late twentieth century.

Cunningham's impact on contemporary dance has been enormous. Two of today's most outstanding American dance companies, Pilobolus and Momix, incorporate acrobatics, mime, gymnastics, vaudeville, and folk dance in ever more inventive explorations of physical movement (Figure **15.34**). The choreography of Twyla Tharp (b. 1941), Paul Taylor (b. 1930), and Bill T. Jones (b. 1952) continues to reflect Cunningham's playful abstraction and quirky, improvised movements; however, these artists (and most contemporary choreographers) have restored the role of music to dance. Indeed, one of the most notable choreographers of our time, the Seattle-born Mark Morris (b. 1956), creates dance motifs specifically allied to the closely studied musical score. Morris' landmark 1988 work, *L'Allegro, il Penseroso ed il Moderato*, is set to George Frideric Handel's 1740 oratorio, which takes its text from John Milton's famous pastoral poems, "L'Allegro" and "Il Penseroso." A brilliant union of poetry, music, and dance, the piece displays the structural clarity of Baroque music and the forthright simplicity of folk dance, a genre in which Morris had early training.

Morris, *L'Allegro, il Penseroso ed il Moderato* (1988)

There is no doubt that globalism has influenced contemporary dance. Modern ballet in the tradition of the Russian-trained Balanchine (see page 414) still flourishes in America, but it may be embellished with the Expressionist influence of German *Tanztheater* ("dance theater") or Indian classical dance. Some choreographers seek to stylize movement by the adoption of traditional Asian dance styles. For instance, the influence of *butoh*, a Japanese dance form that grew out of *kabuki* theater (see page 225), is seen in performances that feature simple, symbolic movements rendered in a mesmerizingly slow and hypnotic manner. It is no surprise that dance, like all the arts since the mid-twentieth century, has been enriched by the creative imagination of both Western and non-Western cultures.

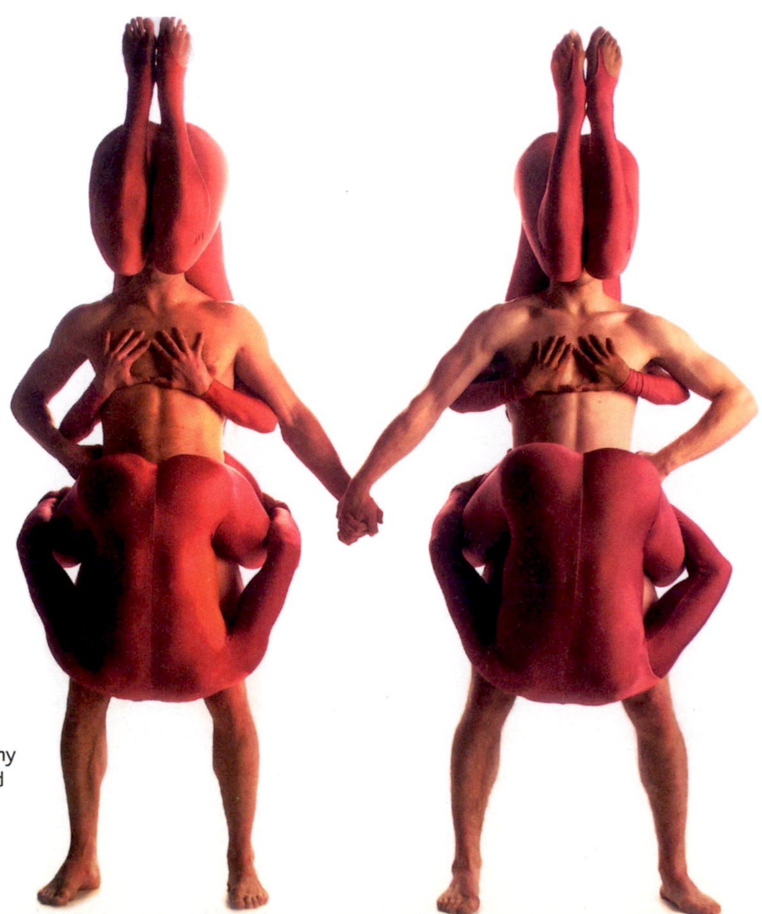

Figure 15.34 Pilobolus Dance Theatre, 2004. This remarkable dance company celebrates the strength and beauty of the human body. The dancers bend and curl, attaching to each other to create multilimbed "body-sculptures."

INTO THE TWENTY-FIRST CENTURY

AS the new millennium unfolds, two major crises challenge the global community: 1) the urgent need to preserve the environment that supports life on earth, and 2) the threat of terrorism. Both crises engage humankind in the search for expedient solutions that will ensure the healthy future of the planet. In addition to these challenges, two notable developments are likely to produce landmarks in the twenty-first century: The first, *China's global ascendance*, is as evident in the arts as it is in the economic and political spheres; the second, *interactivity in the arts*, takes inspiration from the vast array of digital phenomena that invite the active participation of the spectator. These two topics demand our attention, however brief, in the closing pages of this chapter.

The Global Ecosystem

The first great challenge of the twenty-first century is **ecological**: It concerns the relationship between organisms and their environment. While modern technology has brought vast benefits to humankind, it has also worked to threaten the global **ecosystem** (the ecological community and its physical environment). The technology of any one region on the planet affects the entire global village. Industrial pollution poisons rivers and oceans, leaks in nuclear reactors endanger populations thousands of miles from their sites, and greenhouse gases (mostly from the burning of the coal, oil, and natural gas that power the world's industries) contribute to global warming and other changes in the earth's climate. Although such realities have inspired increasing attention to the destiny of the planet, world leaders have only recently given serious attention to global warming, the steady rise in the earth's temperature. Efforts to promote energy-efficient appliances and buildings, college programs in sustainable enterprise, and recent world summits to restrict the greenhouse gas emissions are signs of heightened ecological consciousness.

One landmark figure in the study of ecological systems is Edward Osborn Wilson (b. 1929). A distinguished sociobiologist, Wilson is a leading defender of the natural environment and nature conservation. Some of his writings are visionary: In *Consilience: The Unity of Knowledge* (1998) Wilson proposes the synthesis of knowledge from a variety of fields, scientific and humanistic. He envisions a new kind of interdisciplinary research designed to improve the human condition, a pursuit that he calls "scientific humanism." His pleas for biodiversity (the preservation of all life forms in the ecosystem) and for the development of a sound environmental ethic are advanced in *The Diversity of Life* (1992) and in the more recent *Creation: An Appeal to Save Life on Earth* (2006). In the former, he writes:

> The evidence of swift environmental change calls for an ethic uncoupled from other systems of belief. Those committed by religion to believe that life was put on earth in one divine stroke will recognize that we are destroying the Creation, and those who perceive biodiversity to be the product of blind evolution will agree. . . . An enduring environmental ethic will aim to preserve not only the health and freedom of our species, but access to the world in which the human spirit was born.

The environment is a topic of major concern in the arts as well; witness the poetry of Gary Snyder (b. 1930), the prose works of Annie Dillard (b. 1945), the land art of Robert Smithson (see Figure 15.24) and Andy Goldsworthy (b. 1956), and the upsurge of art made from recycled materials: For instance, the Ghanaian artist El Anatsui (b. 1944) transforms metal food tins and bottle caps into magnificent sculptures (see Figure 15.38).

Architects have always given consideration to the environment in which they build. Now, however, in the face of rising fuel prices, fears of global warming, and the degradation of the ecosystem due to industrial growth, the job of designing structures that do the least possible damage to the environment (a practice known as "green" or "sustainable design"), has become both practical and imperative. Green buildings—structures that are both friendly to the ecosystem and energy-efficient—have been found to save money and preserve the environment. Although the United States launched the Green Building Council in 2000, fewer than eight hundred certified green buildings were constructed during the following seven years; however, the greening of architecture has become a global movement. It embraces architectural design that makes use of energy-efficient (and renewable) building materials, recycling systems that capture rainwater (for everyday uses), solar panels that use sunlight to generate electricity, insulating glass, and other energy-saving devices and techniques.

Of the green buildings that have been constructed in recent years, one has already become a landmark: The Swiss Re office building (30 St. Mary Axe), designed in 2003 by the British architect Norman Foster (b. 1935), is London's first environmentally sustainable skyscraper (Figure **15.35**). Natural ventilation, provided by windows that open automatically, passive solar heating, and a double-glazed insulating glass skin (some 260,000 square feet of glass) are some of the features that work to reduce this forty-story building's energy costs by one-half of normal costs. While Foster's tower resembles a spaceship, its tall rounded picklelike shape has inspired Londoners to call it "the Gherkin."

Figure 15.35 Norman Foster, Swiss Re building (30 St. Mary Axe), London, 2003.

Terrorism

The second challenge to the global community in the twenty-first century is the threat of **terrorism**, the deliberate and systematic use of violence against civilians to achieve political, religious, or ideological ideals. The most ruthless of terrorist attacks on American soil, the destruction of New York's World Trade Center and the assault on the Pentagon in Washington, D.C., are the paramount examples to date. On September 11, 2001, Islamic militants representing the radical Muslim group known as *al-Qaeda* ("the base") hijacked four American airliners, crashing two of them into the Twin Towers in Manhattan and a third into the United States military headquarters in the nation's capital; the fourth crashed before it could reach its target, the White House. More than three thousand civilians were killed in the coordinated attacks, which were masterminded by al-Qaeda's leader, Osama bin Laden (1957–2011). Bin Laden launched the attacks in retaliation for America's military presence and political interference in dominantly Muslim regions. Radical Islamist assaults on other primarily Western targets underline the more troubling rift between two ideologies: the modern (mostly) Western separation of church and state, fundamental to democratic republics since the eighteenth century, and traditional Islamic theocracy, by which religion and religious leaders dictate the governing order. America's intervention in Iraq in 2003 and increasing violence between Muslim religious factions (Shiite and Sunni) have complicated the already tense conflicts existing in the Middle East.

Initially, artists responded to the events of 9-11 primarily by commemorating the destruction of the World Trade Center and those who died in the assault. One year after the attack, the noted American composer John Adams (see page 449) premiered his extraordinary choral eulogy, *On the Transmigration of Souls*, which was awarded the 2003 Pulitzer Prize for Music. More recently, however, reflection on the atrocity and its aftermath has inspired some notable literary responses: Don Delillo's novel *Falling Man* (2006), and Laurence Wright's extensively researched study *The Looming Tower: Al-Qaeda and the Road to 9-11* (2007). In the visual arts, photographs and films, intensely violent in content, rehearse 9-11 and the global consequences of terrorism.

Efforts to confront the experience of those who escaped the burning buildings by jumping to their death have shaken viewers. (Eric Fischl's 2002 bronze sculpture *Tumbling Woman* was hastily removed from public view when it was first displayed in Manhattan.) One of America's most controversial artists—best known for her body-oriented performance pieces—Carolee Schneemann (b. 1939) has treated the "jumper" image in stunning mixed-media artworks. *Terminal Velocity* is a vertical grid of scanned newspaper photographs showing nine of the two hundred individuals (some still unidentified) who leaped from the upper floors of the Twin Towers before the buildings collapsed (Figure **15.36**). The anonymity of media-driven images—those seen on nightly television news—is countered here by the chilling presence and individuality of each victim.

Figure 15.36 Carolee Schneemann, *Terminal Velocity*, 2001–2005. Black-and-white computer scans of falling bodies from 9/11, inkjet on paper, 8 x 7 ft. Collection of the artist. Schneemann greatly enlarged computer-scanned newspaper photographs (including some by the American photojournalist Richard Drew). She then collaged the photos onto a grid of 8 x 7 feet. Both the huge scale of the work and the composition—a symmetrical pattern of rhythm and movement—contribute to the haunting effect of the images as a symbol of corporeal vulnerability. In the artist's own words: "The computer process allows intimate contact with each horrific isolation in the desolate shifting space. In this communal nightmare, fleeting attributes of nine lives become clearer by enlargement."

The "jumper" has become an iconic symbol of doom, one that has drawn global attention. The Nobel prize-winning Polish poet Wislawa Szymborska (b. 1923) reflected on the events of 9-11 in the collection *Monologue of a Dog* (2006). Having experienced both Nazi and communist aggression in a country that lost nearly one-fifth of its population during World War II, Szymborska is no stranger to atrocity; but her poetry never rages or sentimentalizes. It contemplates reality by way of simple, unforgettable images:

Photograph from September 11

They jumped from the burning stories, down
—one, two, a few more
higher, lower.
A photograph captured them while they were alive
and now preserves them
above ground, toward the ground.
Each still whole
with their own face
and blood well hidden.
There is still time,
for their hair to be tossed,
and for keys and small change
to fall from their pockets. They are still in the realm of
the air,
within the places
which have just opened.
There are only two things I can do for them
—to describe this flight
and not to add a final word.

China's Global Ascendance

If China experienced violent changes under the leadership of Mao Zedong (see page 456), that country has enjoyed a positive transformation in the past few decades. After Mao's death in 1976, communist officials tightened control over all forms of artistic expression; however, popular efforts to modernize China prevailed: In June 1989, at Tiananmen Square in Beijing, thousands of student activists demonstrated in support of democratic reform. With Beethoven's Ninth Symphony blaring from loudspeakers, the demonstrators raised a plaster figure of the goddess of democracy modeled on America's Statue of Liberty. The state response to this overt display resulted in the massacre of some protesters and the imprisonment of others. Nevertheless, since this landmark event, official efforts to control the arts have relaxed considerably, perhaps because reaction to it in the free world was so vocal. And, in the last decade—despite the fact that China's new wealth and power do not extend to the rural masses—the country's new quasi-capitalist policies, aggressive economic growth, and reception to mass media and information technology have transformed the People's Republic of China into a powerful world leader.

China's ascendance is visible in the arts. Contemporary Chinese novelists have described the traumatic years of Mao's Cultural Revolution (1966–1976), when thousands were shopped off to "study camps," agricultural labor centers in remote parts of China. Chinese filmmakers, most notably Zhang Yimou (b. 1951), have produced cinematic accounts of the troubling interface between ancient cultural traditions and modern ways of life (see page 447). A vigorous new wave of architecture, swelled by China's role as host of the 2008 Olympics, has dramatically transformed the landscape of China's largest cities. Painters and sculptors, most of them rigorously trained in China's notable art academies, have had the opportunity to investigate the major styles and techniques of their Western contemporaries, a phenomenon made possible by international travel and electronic networking.

Since Tiananmen Square, Chinese visual artists have generated a plurality of styles. Two related styles, however, continue to flourish in the twenty-first century's lively global art market: *Political Pop* and *Cynical Realism* both tend to seize on Western icons and popular commercial advertising techniques to satirize social and political issues of a national or global nature. In the "Great Criticism" series by Wang Guangyi (b. 1956), flat, bright colors and broad, simplified shapes (reminiscent of the communist-approved Social-Realist poster art of the early twentieth century) serve a humorous but subversive end. Three Maoist workers, armed with the red flag, Mao's "red book," and an oversized pen poised above the logo for Coca-Cola soft drinks, prepare for combat, their mission approved by official government stamps that adorn the surface of the painting (**Figure 15.37**). Here, the collective idealism of communism engages the collective consumerism generated by popular Western commodities. Wang's recent additions to the series display an ironic shift in focus: they feature elite consumer brands, such as Rolex watches, Ferrari automobiles, and Chanel perfume.

Despite China's continuing repression of public dissent, urban growth, expanding consumerism, and global economic competition are working to produce a new optimism, a sentiment clearly reflected in the art of the Beijing-based artist Yue Minjun (b. 1962). An internationally celebrated painter and sculptor, Yue uses a caricature of himself as his central pictorial motif (see Figure 15.1 and A First Look). His grinning mouth, identical teeth, and tightly shut eyes make oblique reference to the happy faces of Maoist propaganda art, China's signature smiling Buddhas, and the contrived, celebrity smiles of world-famous personalities. "A smile," says Yue, "doesn't necessarily mean happiness; it could mean something else." To Cynical Realism (or, as Yue prefers, "critical realism"), Yue brings a note of irony that questions everything, from the authenticity of commercial self-marketing to the universal illusion of happiness.

A new generation of Chinese artists, born in the late 1970s and early 80s and known as "The X Generation," has turned away from pop styles and social politics to emphasize the self. What landmarks will emerge from the more intimate narratives and experimental techniques of these younger artists is yet to be determined.

Figure 15.37 Wang Guangyi, *Coca-Cola*, from the "Great Criticism" series, 1993. Enamel paint on canvas, 4 ft. 11 in. x 3 ft. 11 in. In 1996, this painting was sold to a private collector for $1.6 million. Since 2000, Chinese art has commanded huge prices at auction.

Making Connections

TRADITION AND THE GLOBAL ENVIRONMENT

The sculptures of the Ghanaian artist El Anatsui reflect the intersection of traditional and contemporary themes. *Between Heaven and Earth* (2006) consists of thousands of aluminum seals and screw caps from bottles of wine and liquor (Figure **15.38**). The caps are flattened and woven with copper wire to create large, shimmering metal tapestries. El Anatsui recycles discarded objects into compelling artworks whose designs and colors (gold, red, and black) have much in common with the decorative African cotton-cloth textiles known as *kente* (Figure **15.39**). The handwoven *kente*—the name derives from the designs of baskets traditionally woven in the kingdom of Asante (modern Ghana)—belong to a royal textile tradition that reaches back to the eleventh century. Vibrant in color and complex in their patterns, these textiles, themselves woven from recycled silk fabric imported from China, have come to be associated with a pan-African identity.

Q In what ways does El Anatsui's work embrace globalism, environmentalism, and ethnic tradition?

Figure 15.38 (above) El Anatsui, *Between Earth and Heaven*, 2006. Aluminum, copper wire, 91 x 126 in. The Metropolitan Museum of Art, New York. Widely regarded as Africa's most significant sculptor, El Anatsui teaches at the University of Nigeria.

Figure 15.39 Detail of a Sika Futura ("Gold Dust Aweaneasa") Asante *kente* textile, nineteenth to twentieth centuries. Whole textile 5 ft. 10½ in. x 5 ft. 11 in. Fowler Museum of Cultural History, University of California, Los Angeles. The individual designs on the cloth are associated with seventeenth-century Asante kings who are said to have laid claim to specific signs and patterns.

The Interactive Spectator

More than half a century ago, Marcel Duchamp proposed that the work of art is "completed" by the spectator. Increasingly, in our own day, the rise of social networking and video games has complemented a shift to interactivity in the arts. Video games require the active involvement of the player in the navigation of a virtual world. Social networking sites, which facilitate the sharing of information, provide a platform for expanding self-expression and for democratizing social consciousness; witness the role of Facebook (see page 433) in the 2011 uprisings in Tunisia and Egypt. Spectators do not look to simply consume information; they are invited to take action.

In recent years, artworks rooted in the genre of Total art (see page 440) have expanded into increasingly larger spaces. Site-specific pieces, known as *installations*, now involve whole rooms, galleries, and vast public spaces. Video, light, sound, and even specially orchestrated odors, combine to create sensory effects in which viewers may participate or interact. In *The Weather Project* (2003), launched for the Turbine Hall of Tate Modern in London, the Danish artist Olafur Eliasson (b. 1967) used computer-controlled fluorescent lights, mirrors, and water-vapor mists to produce a sense-altering theatrical environment. The Brazilian artist Ernesto Neto (b. 1964) fills exhibition spaces with biomorphic installations that viewers can touch, poke, and walk through. Made of stretchy, colored fabrics occasionally filled with aromatic substances, these site-specific, interactive works submerge the spectator in a multisensory experience (Figure **15.40**).

The sculpture of the American artist Richard Serra (b. 1939) lures the spectator to enter and experience the intimate space created by giant rusted steel sheets, often standing more than 12 feet tall and weighing over 100 tons.

Figure 15.40 Ernesto Neto, *Anthropodino*, 2009. Installation in Park Avenue Armory, New York.

Ideas and Issues

THE DISAPPEARING ART OBJECT

Perhaps the ultimate contemporary expression of the interactive spectator is one in which social exchange and situations entirely replace the art object. Such is the objective of a new "relational aesthetics" movement. Situational art may be regarded as a unique version of conceptual art in which an artist orchestrates a specific social exchange (such as a conversation) or communal experience, but generates no tangible or material object. Similarly, with the popular phenomenon known as *Flashmob*, groups of people (usually organized via the Internet) assemble briefly in public spaces to dance, sing, or perform unusual acts. Unlike the Happenings of the 1960s (see page 440), such events are often neither photographed nor recorded. The "art" is the experience.

Q How might such artworks be judged or evaluated? Is it premature to mourn the death of the art object?

Figure 15.41 Richard Serra, *Sequence*, 2006. Weather-proof steel. Overall 12 ft. 9in. x 40 ft. 8 in. x 65 ft. 2in. Collection of the artist.

Serra's 65-foot long *Sequence* (2006) shrouds and dwarfs visitors to its narrow, undulating boundaries (**Figure 15.41**). This landmark of the twenty-first century also reflects the trend toward heroic and spectacular artworks: global enterprises that are often conceived in one country, but executed in the foundries of another, and brought to completion by the efforts of numerous studio assistants.

A pioneer in the realm of interactive music is Icelandic performer Björk Guðmundsdóttir (b. 1965). Björk's revolutionary multimedia album, *Biofilia* (2011), partly recorded on a tablet computer (the iPad) and released in the form of computer applications, including animated music scores, invites individuals to interact with both music and visuals, and even create their own version of each song.

Afterword

The last sixty years have been an extraordinary period of media-driven globalism. All the arts reflect the effects of high technology and the information explosion. In the global village, how we communicate has become as important as what we communicate. Expectations of a global utopia are marred by the sobering threat of ecological disaster and terrorism. The theater of terrorism is magnified as more nations have nuclear capability (or are seeking nuclear status), and the world's technological advances threaten to become instruments of destruction. But despite these challenges to world peace and order, human creativity will, no doubt, prevail; and a humanistic global community will work to generate tomorrow's landmarks.

Key Topics

- the cold war
- existentialism
- theater of the absurd
- anticolonialism
- racial equality
- gender equality
- sexual identity
- ethnic identity
- the information explosion
- Postmodernism
- contemporary literature
- Abstract Expressionism
- Pop and post-Pop art
- Total art/New Media art
- computers and the arts
- contemporary architecture
- contemporary music and dance
- twenty-first-century landmarks

GLOBALISM TIMELINE

	HISTORICAL EVENTS	LANDMARKS IN THE VISUAL ARTS	LITERARY LANDMARKS	MUSIC AND DANCE LANDMARKS
1940	• India emancipated from British control (1947) • Assassination of Gandhi (1948)		• Sartre, *Being and Nothingness* (1943) • Beckett, *Waiting for Godot* (1948) • de Beauvoir, *The Second Sex* (1949) • Miller, *Death of a Salesman* (1949)	
1950	• Korean Conflict (1950–1953) • First commercially successful computer is introduced (1953) • U.S. Supreme Court bans school segregation (1954) • U.S.S.R. launches Sputnik I (1957) • Vietnam War (1959–1975)	• Pollock, *Autumn Rhythm* (1950) • de Kooning, *Woman and Bicycle* (1952–1953) • Rauschenberg, *Monogram* (1959)	• Neruda, *Canto general* (1950) • Ellison, *Invisible Man* (1952) • Wittgenstein, *Philosophical Investigations* (1953)	• Cage, *4′33″* (1953) • Cunningham, *Summerspace* (1958)
1960	• First moon landing (1969) • U.S. Gay Rights Movement: Stonewall Riots (1969)	• Warhol, *Campbell's Soup Cans* (1962) • Stella, *Tahkt-i-Sulayman I* (1967) • Close, *Phil* (1969)	• Lessing, *The Golden Notebook* (1962) • King, "Letter from a Birmingham Jail" (1963) • Friedan, *The Feminine Mystique* (1963) • Heaney, *Death of a Naturalist* (1966) • Márquez, *One Hundred Years of Solitude* (1967)	• Ligeti, *Atmosphères* (1961) • Britten, *War Requiem* (1963) • The Beatles, *Sergeant Pepper's Lonely Hearts Club Band* (1967)
1970	**Figure 15.25** Christo and Jeanne-Claude, *Running Fence*, see p. 443 • World's first test-tube baby born (1978)	• Smithson, *Spiral Jetty* (1970) • Saar, *The Liberation of Aunt Jemima* (1972) • Christo and Jeanne-Claude, *Running Fence* (1972–1976) • Chicago, *The Dinner Party* (1974–1979)	• Greer, *The Female Eunuch* (1970) • Pynchon, *Gravity's Rainbow* (1974) • Morrison, *Song of Solomon* (1977)	• Glass, *Einstein on the Beach* (1976)
1980	• Demonstration at Tiananmen Square, Beijing (1989) • Berlin Wall falls (1989)	• Mapplethorpe, *Lisa Lyon* (1982) • Morimura, *Portrait (Futago)* (1988)	• Walker, *The Color Purple* (1982) • Rushdie, *The Satanic Verses* (1988)	• Morris, *L'Allegro, il Penseroso ed il Moderato* (1988)
1990	• Internet accessible to PCs (1990) • States of former U.S.S.R. achieve independence (1991)	• Wang, *Great Criticism* (1993) • Neshat, *Women of Allah* (1994) • Viola, *Stations* (1994) • Paik, *Megatron* (1995)	• Kushner, *Angels in America* (1990–1993) • Wilson, *The Diversity of Life* (1992) • Delillo, *Underworld* (1997)	• Adams, *Nixon in China* (1991) • Corigliano, *The Ghosts of Versailles* (1992)
2000	• Genome mapped (2000) • Terrorists destroy World Trade Center, New York (2001) • Pro-democratic revolutions in North Africa and the Middle East (2011)	• Calatrava, Milwaukee Art Museum (2003) • Foster, "Gherkin" Building (2003) • Gehry, Walt Disney Concert Hall, Los Angeles (2003) • El Anatsui, *Between Earth and Heaven* (2006) • Serra, *Sequence* (2006)	**Figure 15.13** Shirin Neshat, *Rebellious Silence*, see p. 430	**Figure 15.31** Frank Gehry, Walt Disney Concert Hall, Los Angeles, see p. 448 • Tan Dun, *The First Emperor* (2006)

GLOSSARY

a cappella choral singing without instrumental accompaniment

abbot (Latin, *abbas*, "father") the superior of an abbey or monastery for men; the female equivalent in a convent of nuns is called an "abbess"

aerial perspective the means of representing distance that relies on the imitation of the ways atmosphere affects the eye—outlines are blurred, details lost, contrasts of light and shade diminished, hues bluer, and colors less vivid; also called "atmospheric perspective"

aleatory (Latin, *alea*, "dice") any kind of music composed according to chance or random procedures

allegory a literary device in which objects, persons, or actions are equated with secondary, figurative meanings that underlie their literal meaning

allegro (Italian, "cheerful") a fast tempo in music

alliteration a literary device involving the repetition of initial sounds in successive or closely associated words or syllables

ambulatory a covered walkway, outdoors or indoors (see Figure 4.9)

anaphora the repetition of a word or words at the beginning of two or more lines of verse

andante (Italian, "going," i.e. a normal walking pace) a moderate tempo in music

animism the belief that the forces of nature are inhabited by spirits

antiphon a verse sung in response to the religious text

antiphonal a type of music in which two or more groups of voices or instruments alternate with one another

apostle disciple

apse a vaulted semicircular recess at one or both ends of a basilica

aquatint a type of print produced by an engraving method similar to etching but involving finely granulated tonal areas rather than line alone

arabesque in the visual arts, a type of linear ornamentation featuring plant and flower forms; in ballet, a position in which the dancer stands on one leg with the other extended behind and one or both arms held to create the longest line possible from one extremity of the body to the other

arch a curved structural device spanning an opening

archivolt a molded or decorated band around an arch or forming an archlike frame for an opening

aria an elaborate solo song or duet, usually with instrumental accompaniment, performed as part of an opera or other dramatic musical composition

arpeggio the sounding of the notes of a chord in rapid succession

ars nova (Latin, "new art") a term used for the music of fourteenth-century Europe to distinguish it from that of the old art (*ars antiqua*); it featured new rhythms, new harmonies, and more complicated methods of musical notation

ascetic one who practices strict self-denial and self-discipline

assemblage a genre (or artwork) featuring the combination of three-dimensional objects; the sculptural counterpart of collage

assonance a literary device involving similarity in sound between vowels followed by different consonants

astrolabe an instrument that measures the angle between the horizon and heavenly bodies and thus fixes latitude

Atman the Hindu name for the Self; the personal part of Brahman

atonality in music, the absence of a tonal center or definitive key

atrium the inner courtyard of a Roman house, usually colonnaded and open to the sky

aulos a wind instrument used in ancient Greece; it had a double reed (held inside the mouth) and a number of finger holes and was always played in pairs, that is, with the performer holding one in each hand; a leather band was often tied around the head to support the cheeks, thus enabling the player to blow harder (see Figure 2.17)

avant-garde (French, "vanguard") those who create or produce styles and ideas ahead of their time; an unconventional movement or style

avatar (Sanskrit, "incarnation") the incarnation of a Hindu deity

bacchante a female attendant or devotee of Dionysus

ballade a secular song that tells a story in simple verse, usually repeating the same music for each stanza

basilica a large, colonnaded hall commonly used for public assemblies, law courts, baths, and marketplaces

bay a regularly repeated spatial unit of a building; in medieval architecture, a vaulted compartment

bel canto (Italian, "beautiful singing" or "beautiful song") an operatic style characterized by lyricism and vocal embellishment

biomorphic having organic or protoplasmic form

blank verse unrhymed verse, especially that using iambic pentameters, that is, lines consisting of ten syllables each with accents on every second syllable

bodhisattva (Sanskrit, "one whose essence is enlightenment") a being who has postponed his or her own entry into *nirvana* in order to assist others in reaching that goal; worshipped as a deity in Mahayana Buddhism

Brahman the Hindu name for the Absolute Spirit, an impersonal World Soul that pervades all things

brass a family of wind instruments that usually includes the trumpet, French horn, trombone, and tuba

burin a steel tool used for engraving and incising

caliph the official successor to Muhammad and theocratic ruler of an Islamic state

calligraphy (Greek, "beautiful writing") the art of ornamental handwriting

camera lucida (Latin, "light room") a device using a prism to project onto paper an image that the artist can copy or trace

camera obscura (Latin, "dark room") a darkened box with a hole or lens used to cast an image of an object onto a glass screen or sheet of paper for the artist to copy or trace

canon a set of rules or standards used to establish proportions

canon law the ecclesiastical law that governs the Christian Church

canonic authoritative

cantata (Italian, *cantare*, meaning "to sing") a multimovement composition for voices and instrumental accompaniment; smaller in scale than the oratorio

cantilever a beam or horizontal bracket that projects beyond its support

canto (Latin, "song") one of the main divisions of a long poem

cantor the official in Judaism who sings or chants the liturgy; the official in medieval Christianity in charge of music at a cathedral, later a choir leader and soloist for the responsorial singing

capitalist one who provides investment capital in economic ventures

caricature exaggeration of peculiarities or defects to produce comic or burlesque effects

cartography the art of making maps or charts

caste system a rigid social stratification in India based on differences in wealth, rank, or occupation

catacomb a subterranean complex consisting of burial chambers and galleries with recesses for tombs

chain mail a flexible medieval armor made of interlinked metal rings

chalice a goblet; in Christian liturgy, the Eucharistic cup

chancel the space for the clergy and choir in the area surrounding the church altar

chanson de geste (French, "song of heroic deeds") an epic poem of the early Middle Ages

chateau (French, "castle") the luxurious country house or castle of French aristocrats

chatra an umbrellalike shape that signifies the sacred tree under which the Buddha reached *nirvana*

chiaroscuro (Italian, "light-dark") in drawing and painting, the technique of modeling form in gradations of light and shade to produce the illusion of three-dimensionality

chivalry a code of behavior practiced by upper-class men and women of medieval society

chorale a congregational hymn, first sung in the Lutheran church

choreography the art of composing, arranging, and/or notating dance movements

chromatic scale see "scale"

clavichord (French, *clavier*, "keyboard") a stringed keyboard instrument widely used between the sixteenth and eighteenth centuries; when the player presses down on a key, a brass tangent or blade rises and strikes a string

clerestory (also "clerstory") the upper part of the nave, whose walls contain openings for light (see Figure 4.9)

cloisonné (French, *cloison*, "fence") an enameling technique produced by pouring molten colored glass between thin metal strips secured to a metal surface; any object ornamented in this manner

coda (Italian, "tail") a passage added to the closing section of a movement or musical composition in order to create the sense of a definite ending

collage (French, *coller*, "to paste") a composition created by pasting materials such as newspaper, wallpaper, photographs, or cloth on a flat surface or canvas

comédie-ballet (French) a dramatic performance that features interludes of song and dance

common law the body of unwritten law developed primarily from judicial decisions based on custom and precedent; the basis of the English legal system and that of all states in the United States with the exception of Louisiana

concertato (derived from the Italian *concerto*, meaning "opposing" or "competing") an early Baroque style in which voices or instruments of different rather than similar natures are used in an opposing or contrasting manner

concerto (Italian, "opposing" or "competing") an instrumental composition consisting of one or more solo instruments and a larger group of instruments playing in dialog; the classical concerto, which made use of sonata form, usually featured one soloist and orchestra

concerto grosso ("large concerto") the typical kind of Baroque concerto, consisting of several movements

condottiere (plural *condottieri*) a professional soldier; a mercenary who typically served the Renaissance city-state

continuo see "figured bass"

contrapposto (Italian, "counterpoised") a position assumed by the human body in which one part is turned in opposition to another part

cornet (French, *cornett*; German, *kornett*) a Renaissance instrument made of wood; fingered like a woodwind, but blown like a trumpet; an early type of trumpet

cosmology the theory of the origins, evolution, and structure of the universe

counterpoint a musical technique that involves two or more independent melodies; the term is often used interchangeably with "polyphony"

couplet two successive lines of verse with similar end-rhymes

covenant contract; the bond between the Hebrew people and their God

crenellations tooth-shaped battlements surmounting a wall and used for defensive combat

crocket a stylized leaf used as a terminal ornament

culture the sum total of those things (including traditions, techniques, material goods, and symbol systems) that people have invented, developed, and transmitted

cuneiform (Latin, *cuneformis*, "wedge-shaped") one of humankind's earliest writing systems, consisting of wedge-shaped marks

deductive reasoning a method of inquiry that begins with clearly established general premises and moves toward the establishment of particular truths

democracy a government in which supreme power is vested in the people

dharma (Sanskrit, "law") right conduct; duties based on one's caste and station in life

dialectic in Hegelian philosophy, the process by which every condition (or "thesis") confronts an opposite condition (or "antithesis") to resolve in synthesis

dialectical method a question-and-answer style of inquiry made famous by Socrates

Diaspora (Greek, "scattering") the dispersion of the Jews after the Babylonian Captivity

dogma a prescribed body of doctrines concerning faith or morals, formally stated and authoritatively proclaimed

dolmen a stone tomb formed by two posts capped by a lintel (see Figure 1.6)

drum in architecture, the cylindrical section immediately beneath the dome of a building

dynamics the degree of loudness or softness in music

dynasty a sequence of rulers from the same family

eclogue a pastoral poem, usually involving shepherds in an idyllic rural setting

ecology relationship between organisms and their environment

ecosystem the ecological community and its physical environment

ecumenical worldwide in extent; representing the unity of Christian churches

empire a state achieved militarily by the unification of territories under a single sovereign power

empirical method a method of inquiry dependent on direct experience or observation

engraving the process by which lines are incised on a metal plate, then inked and printed (see Figure 8.16)

entrepreneur one who organizes, manages, and assumes the risks of a business

epic a long narrative poem that recounts the deeds of a legendary or historical hero in his quest for meaning or identity

epistle a formal letter

equal temperament a system of tuning that originated in the seventeenth century, whereby the octave is divided into twelve half-steps of equal size; since intervals have the same value in all keys, music may be played in any key, and a musician may change from one key to another with complete freedom

equestrian mounted on horseback

essay a short piece of expository prose that examines a single subject

etching a kind of engraving in which a metal plate is covered with resin then inscribed with a burin; acid is applied to eat away the exposed lines, which are inked before the plate is wiped clean and printed

ethics that branch of philosophy that sets forth the principles of human conduct

étude (French, "study") an instrumental study designed to improve a player's performance technique

excommunication ecclesiastical censure that excludes the individual from receiving the sacraments

faience earthenware treated with colorful glazes

fealty loyalty; the fidelity of the warrior to his chieftain

feminism the doctrine advocating equal social, political, and economic rights for women

ferroconcrete a cement building material reinforced by embedding wire or iron rods; also called "reinforced concrete"

fête galante (French, "elegant entertainment") a festive diversion enjoyed by aristocrats, a favorite subject in Rococo art

fetish an object believed to have magical power

feudalism the system of political organization prevailing in Europe between the ninth and fifteenth centuries and having as its basis the exchange of land for military defense

fief in feudal society, land or property given to a warrior in return for military service

figured bass in the Baroque period, the bass or bottom line of music with numbers written below (or above) it to indicate the required harmonies, usually improvised in the form of keyboard chords accompanying the melody; also called "continuo"

finial an ornament, usually pointed and foliated, that tops a spire or pinnacle

foreshortening a perspective device by which figures or objects appear to recede or project into space

fortissimo (Italian, "very loud") a directive indicating that the music should be played very loud; its opposite is pianissimo ("very soft")

free verse poetry that is based on irregular rhythmic patterns rather than on the conventional and regular use of meter

fresco (Italian, "fresh") a method of painting on walls or ceilings surfaced with fresh, moist lime plaster

fresco secco a variant fresco technique in which paint is applied to dry plaster

frieze in architecture, a sculptured or ornamented band

fugue ("flight") a polyphonic composition in which a theme (or subject) is imitated, developed, and restated by successively entering voice parts

gable the triangular section of a wall at the end of a pitched roof

gallery the area between the clerestory and the nave arcade, usually adorned with mosaics in early Christian churches (see Figure 4.9)

gargoyle a waterspout usually carved in the form of a grotesque figure

genre a particular category in literature or art, such as the essay (in literature) and portraiture (in painting)

genre painting art depicting scenes from everyday life

geocentric earth-centered

gesso a chalky white plaster used to prepare the surface of a panel for painting

grace the free, unearned favor of God

Greek cross a cross in which all four arms are of equal length

griot a class of poet-historians who preserved the legends and lore of Africa by chanting or singing them from memory

guild an association of merchants or craftspeople organized according to occupation

hadith (Arab, "report") a compilation of Muhammad's sayings and deeds

haiku a light verse form consisting of seventeen syllables (three lines of five, seven, and five)

hajj pilgrimage to Mecca, the fifth Pillar of the Faith in Islam

harpsichord a stringed keyboard instrument widely used between the sixteenth and eighteenth centuries; when the player presses down on a key, a quill, called a plectrum, plucks the string

heliocentric sun-centered

heresy the denial of the revealed truths or orthodox doctrine by a baptized member of the Church; an opinion or doctrine contrary to Church dogma

hieroglyphs (Greek, "sacred sign") the pictographic script of ancient Egypt

hijra (Arabic, "migration" or "flight") Muhammad's journey from Mecca to Medina in 622 C.E.

historiated ornamented with figural or decorative elements

homophony a musical texture consisting of a dominant melody supported by chordal accompaniment that is far less important than the melody; compare "monophony" and "polyphony"

hymn a lyric poem offering divine praise or glorification

hypostyle a hall whose roof is supported by columns

icon (Greek, "likeness") the image of a saint or other religious figure

iconoclast one who opposes the use of images in religious worship

iconography the study, identification, and interpretation of subject matter in art; also the visual imagery that conveys specific concepts and ideas

idealism (Platonic) the theory that holds that things in the material world are manifestations of an independent realm of unchanging, immaterial ideas or forms

idée fixe (French, "fixed idea") a term used by Berlioz for a recurring theme in his symphonic works

imam a Muslim prayer leader

imitation in music, a technique whereby a melodic fragment introduced in the first voice of a composition is repeated closely (although usually at a different pitch) in the second, third, and fourth voices, so that one voice overlaps the next; the repetition may be exactly the same as the original, or it may differ somewhat

impasto thickly or heavily applied paint

imperium (Latin, "command," "empire") the civil and military authority exercised by the leaders of ancient Rome (and the root of the English words "imperialism" and "empire"); symbolized in ancient Rome by an eagle-headed scepter and the *fasces*, an ax bound in a bundle of rods

impromptu (French, "improvised") a short keyboard composition that sounds as if it is improvised

inductive reasoning a method of inquiry that begins with direct observation and experimentation and moves toward the establishment of general conclusions or axioms

indulgence a Church pardon from the temporal penalties for sins; the remission of purgatorial punishment

infidel a nonbeliever

interdict the excommunication of an entire city, district, or state

investiture the procedure by which a feudal lord granted a vassal control over a fief

isorhythm the close repetition of identical rhythmic patterns in different sections of a musical composition

jihad (Arabic, "struggle" [to follow God's will]) the struggle to lead a virtuous life and to further the universal mission of Islam through teaching, preaching, and, when necessary, warfare

jongleur a professional entertainer who wandered from court to court in medieval Europe

joust a form of personal combat, usually with lances on horseback, between men-at-arms

Kaaba (Arabic, "cube") a religious sanctuary in Mecca; a square temple containing the sacred Black Stone thought to have been delivered to Abraham by the Angel Gabriel

kabuki (Japanese, "song-dance-art") the most popular form of drama in Japan

karma (Sanskrit, "deed") the law that holds that one's deeds determine one's future life in the Wheel of Rebirth

keep a square tower, the strongest and most secure part of the medieval castle (see Figure 5.17)

kenning a two-term metaphor used in Old English verse

kithara a large version of the lyre (having seven to eleven strings) and the principal instrument of ancient Greek music

kiva the underground ceremonial center of the Southwest Indian pueblo community

kouros (Greek, "youth"; pl. *kouroi*) a youthful male figure, usually depicted nude in ancient Greek sculpture; the female counterpart is the *kore* (Greek, "maiden"; plural *korai*)

krater a vessel used in ancient Greece for mixing wine and water

Kufic the earliest form of Arabic script; it originated in the Iraqi town of Kufa

laissez-faire a practice in which the government does not interfere or has minimal interference in economic matters to allow freedom of actions

lancet a narrow window topped with a pointed arch

lantern in architecture, a small windowed tower on top of a roof or dome that allows light to enter the interior of a building

largo (Italian, "broad") a very slow tempo; the slowest of the conventional tempos in music

Latin cross a cross in which the vertical member is longer than the horizontal member it intersects

leitmotif (German, "leading motif") a short musical theme that designates a person, object, place, or idea and that reappears throughout a musical composition

libretto (Italian, "little book") the text of a vocal work, such as an opera or an oratorio

Lied (German, "song," pl. *Lieder*) an independent song for solo voice and piano; also known as "art song"

linear perspective a method of creating the semblance of three-dimensional space on a two-dimensional surface; it derives from two optical illusions: (1) parallel lines appear to converge as they recede toward a vanishing point on a horizon level with the viewer's eye, and (2) objects appear to shrink and move closer together as they recede from view; also called "one-point perspective" or "optical perspective" (see Figure 7.14)

lintel a horizontal beam or stone that spans an opening

lithography a printmaking process created by drawing on a stone plate

liturgy the prescribed rituals or body of rites for public worship

lord any member of the feudal nobility who invested a vassal with a fief

lost wax (also French, *cire-perdu*) a method of metal-casting (originating in ancient Mesopotamia) in which a figure is modeled in wax, then enclosed in a clay mold that is fired; the wax melts, and molten metal is poured in to replace it; finally, the clay mold is removed and the solid metal form is polished

lyre any one of a group of plucked stringed instruments; usually made of tortoiseshell or horn and therefore light in weight

lyric literally "accompanied by the lyre," hence, verse that is meant to be sung rather than spoken, usually characterized by individual and personal emotion

madrigal a vernacular song, usually composed for three to six unaccompanied voices

mandala a diagrammatic map of the universe used as a visual aid to meditation and as a ground plan for Hindu and Buddhist temple shrines

manorialism the economic basis of medieval feudalism involving mutual obligations between feudal lords and serfs

marquetry a decorative technique in which patterns are created on a wooden surface by means of inlaid wood, shell, or ivory

medieval romance a tale of adventure that supplanted the older *chanson de geste* and that deals with knights, kings, and ladies acting under the impulse of love, religious faith, or the desire for adventure

megalith a large, roughly shaped stone, often used in ancient architectural construction

melismatic having many notes of music to one syllable

memento mori (Latin, "remember death") a warning of the closeness of death and the need to prepare for one's own death

menorah a seven-branched candelabrum

Messiah (Hebrew, "anointed") the promised and expected deliverer or savior of the Jewish people; in Greek, *Christos*

metallurgy the science of working or heating metals

metope the square panel between the beam ends under the roof of a structure (see Figure 2.30)

microtonality the use of musical intervals smaller than the semitones of traditional European and American music

mihrab a special niche in the wall of a mosque that indicates the direction of Mecca

minaret a tall, slender tower usually attached to a mosque and surrounded by a balcony from which the *muezzin* summons Muslims to prayer

minbar a stepped pulpit in a mosque

minuet a graceful dance in three-quarter meter and moderate tempo

miracle play a type of medieval play that dramatized the lives of, and especially the miracles performed by, Jesus, the Virgin Mary, or the saints

moat a wide trench, usually filled with water, surrounding a fortified place such as a castle (see Figure 5.17)

mobile a sculpture constructed so that its parts move by natural or mechanical means

mode a type of musical scale characterized by a fixed pattern of pitch and tempo within the octave; because the Greeks associated each of the modes with a different emotional state, it is likely that the mode involved something more than a particular musical scale—perhaps a set of rhythms and melodic turns associated with each scale pattern

module a unit of measurement used to determine proportion

monarch a single or sole ruler

monophony (Greek, "one voice") a musical texture consisting of a single unaccompanied line of melody

monotheism the belief in one and only one god

montage in art, music, or literature, a composite made by freely juxtaposing usually heterogeneous images; in cinema, the production of a rapid succession of images to present a stream of interconnected ideas (see also "photomontage")

morality play a type of medieval play that dramatized moral themes, such as the conflict between good and evil

mosaic a medium by which small pieces of glass or stone are embedded in wet cement on wall and floor surfaces; any picture or pattern made in this manner

mosque the Muslim house of worship

motet a short, polyphonic religious composition based on a sacred text

mudra (Sanskrit, "sign") a symbolic gesture commonly used in Buddhist art

muezzin a "crier" who calls the hours of Muslim prayer five times a day

mullah a Muslim trained in Islamic law and doctrine

mullion the slender vertical pier dividing the parts of a window, door, or screen

music-drama a unique synthesis of sound and story in which both are developed simultaneously and continuously; a term used to describe Wagner's later operas

mystery play a type of medieval play originating in Church liturgy and dramatizing biblical history from the fall of Satan to the Last Judgment

narthex a porch or vestibule at the main entrance of a church (see Figure 4.9)

Naturalism a style (in art) that seeks to represent objects as they actually appear in nature; often used interchangeably with **Realism**; a literary style based on the premise that life should be represented objectively and free of idealization

nave the central aisle of a church between the altar and the apse, usually demarcated from the side-aisles by columns or piers (see Figure 4.9)

negative space the background or ground area seen in relation to the shape of the figure

neume a mark or symbol indicating the direction of the voice in the early notation of Gregorian chant

niello a black sulfurous substance used as a decorative inlay for incised metal surfaces; the art or process of decorating metal in this manner

nirvana (Sanskrit, "extinction") the blissful reabsorption of the Self into the Absolute Spirit (Brahman): release from the endless cycle of rebirth

nocturne a slow, songlike piece, usually written for piano; the melody is played by the right hand, and a steady, soft accompaniment is played by the left

novel an extended fictional prose narrative

obelisk a tall, four-sided pillar that tapers to a pyramidal apex

octave the series of eight tones forming a major or minor scale

ode a lyric poem expressing exalted emotion in honor of a person or special occasion

oligarchy a government in which power lies in the hands of an elite minority

one-point perspective see "linear perspective"

opus (Latin, "work") a musical composition; followed by a number, it designates either the chronological place of a musical composition in the composer's total output or the order of its publication; often abbreviated "op."

oratorio (Latin, *oratorium*, "church chapel") a musical setting of a religious or epic text, for soloists, chorus, and orchestra; usually performed without scenery, costumes, or dramatic action

oratory the art of public speaking

order in Classical architecture, the parts of a building that stand in fixed and constant relation to each other; the three Classical orders are the Doric, the Ionic, and the Corinthian (see Figure 2.29)

organ a keyboard instrument in which keyboards and pedals are used to force air into a series of pipes, causing them to sound

organum the general name for the oldest form of polyphony: In *parallel organum*, the two voices move exactly parallel to one another; in *free organum* the second voice moves in contrary motion; *melismatic organum* involves the use of multiple notes for the individual syllables of the text

overture an instrumental introduction to a longer musical piece, such as an opera

pageant a roofed wagon-stage on which medieval plays and spectacles were performed

pantheism the belief that a divine spirit pervades all things in the universe; that nature and god are one

papyrus a reedlike plant from which the ancient Egyptians made paper

pastoral pertaining to the country, to shepherds, and the simple rural life; also, any work of art presenting an idealized picture of country life

paten a shallow dish; in Christian liturgy, the Eucharistic plate

pediment the triangular space forming the gable of a two-pitched roof in Classical architecture; any similar triangular form found over a portico, door, or window

pendentive a concave piece of masonry that makes the transition between the angle of two walls and the base of the dome above (see Figure 4.12)

percussion a group of instruments that are sounded by being struck or shaken, used especially for rhythm

philosophes (French, "philosophers") the intellectuals of the European Enlightenment

photomontage the combination of freely juxtaposed and usually heterogeneous photographic images (see also "montage")

piazza (Italian) a broad, open public space

pictograph a pictorial symbol used in humankind's earliest systems of writing

picture plane the two-dimensional surface of a panel or canvas

pilaster a shallow, flattened, rectangular column or pier attached to a wall surface

pizzicato (Italian) the technique of plucking (with the fingers) a stringed instrument that is normally bowed

polychoral music written for two or more choruses, performed both in turn and together

polychrome having many or various colors

polyphony (Greek, "many voices") a musical texture consisting of two or more lines of melody that are of equal importance

polytheism the belief in many gods

porcelain a hard, translucent ceramic ware made from clay fired at high heat

portico a porch with a roof supported by columns

post-and-lintel the simplest form of architectural construction, consisting of vertical members (posts) and supporting horizontals (lintels) (see Figure 1.6)

prelude a piece of instrumental music that introduces either a church service or another piece of music such as a fugue; also a single-movement Romantic piano piece

prima ballerina the first, or leading, female dancer in a ballet company

primogeniture the principle by which a fief was passed from father to eldest son

program music instrumental music endowed with specific literary or pictorial content that is indicated by the composer

proletariat a collective term describing industrial workers who lack their own means of production and hence sell their labor to live

prophet (Greek, "one who speaks for another") a divinely inspired teacher

psaltery a stringed instrument consisting of a flat soundboard and strings that are plucked

pylon a massive gateway in the form of a pair of truncated pyramids

qi (Chinese, "substance" or "breath") the material substance or vital force of the universe

quadripartite consisting of or divided into four parts

quatrain a four-line stanza

rabbi a teacher and master trained in the Jewish law

Realism a style (in art) that seeks truthfulness to life and fidelity to nature, often used interchangeably with **Naturalism**

recitative a textual passage recited to sparse chordal accompaniment; a rhythmically free vocal style popular in seventeenth-century opera

refectory the dining hall of a monastery

regular clergy (Latin *regula*, meaning "rule") those who have taken vows to obey the rules of a monastic order, as opposed to "secular clergy"

relief a sculptural technique in which figures or forms are carved either to project from the background surface (raised relief) or cut away below the background level (sunk relief); the degree of relief is designated as high, low, or sunken

reliquary a container for a sacred relic or relics

renaissance (French, "rebirth") a revival of the learning of former and especially Classical culture

requiem a Mass for the Dead; a solemn chant to honor the dead

res publica (Latin, "of the people") a government in which power resides in citizens entitled to vote and is exercised by representatives responsible to them and to a body of law

responsorial a type of music in which a single voice answers another voice or a chorus

ritornello (Italian, "a little return") in Baroque music, an instrumental section that recurs throughout the movement

rose (from the French *roue*, "wheel") a large circular window with stained glass and stone tracery

sacrament a sacred act or pledge; in medieval Christianity, a visible sign (instituted by Jesus Christ) of God's grace

salon (French, "drawing room") an elegant apartment or drawing room; an intellectual gathering held in such a space

sarcophagus (plural, sarcophagi) a stone coffin

satire a literary genre that ridicules or pokes fun at human vices and follies

satyr a semibestial woodland creature symbolic of Dionysus

scale (Latin, *scala*, "ladder") a series of tones arranged in ascending or descending consecutive order; the *diatonic* scale, characteristic of Western music, consists of eight tones (e.g. the series of notes C, D, E, F, G, A, B, C); the *chromatic* scale consists of all twelve tones (represented by the twelve piano keys, seven white and five black) of the octave, each a semitone apart

scarification the act or process of incising the flesh as a form of identification and rank, and/or for aesthetic purposes

scat singing a jazz performance style in which nonsense syllables replace the lyrics of a song

scherzo (Italian, "joke") a swift, light movement, commonly in triple time; established by Beethoven as an alternative to the *minuet*

score the musical notation for all of the instruments or voices in a particular composition; a composite from which the whole piece may be conducted or studied

secular clergy (Latin *seculum*, "in the world") those ordained to serve the Christian Church in the world

sequence a special kind of trope consisting of words added to the melismatic passages of Gregorian chant; also, repetition of a melodic pattern at a different pitch

serf an unfree peasant

serial technique in music, a technique that involves the use of a particular series of notes, rhythms, and other elements that are repeated over and over throughout the piece

sexpartite consisting of or divided into six parts

shaman a priestly leader or healer who mediates between the natural and the spirit world

sharia the body of Muslim law based on the *Qur'an* and the *Hadith*

shofar the ram's horn used to call the Hebrews to prayer

silkscreen a printmaking technique employing the use of a stenciled image cut and attached to finely meshed silk, through which printing ink is forced so as to transfer the image to paper or cloth; also called "seriography"

simony the buying or selling of Church office or preferment (see Simon Magus, Acts of the Apostles 8:9–24)

social contract an agreement made between citizens leading to the establishment of the state

sonata an instrumental composition consisting of three movements of contrasting tempo, usually fast/slow/fast; written for an unaccompanied keyboard instrument or for another instrument with keyboard accompaniment

sonata form (or **sonata allegro form**) a structural form commonly used in the late eighteenth century for the first and fourth movements of symphonies and other instrumental compositions (see Figure 11.28)

sonnet a fourteen-line lyric poem with a fixed scheme of rhyming

Sprechstimme (German, "speech-song") a style of operatic recitation in which words are spoken at different pitches

stele an upright stone slab or pillar

string quartet a composition for two violins, viola, and cello, with each playing its own part; a group of four such instrumentalists

strings a family of instruments that usually includes the violin, viola, cello, and double bass (which are normally bowed); the harp, guitar, lute, and zither (which are normally plucked) can also be included, as can the viol, a bowed instrument common in the sixteenth and seventeenth centuries

stucco a light, pliable plaster made of gypsum, sand, water, and ground marble

stupa a hemispherical mound that serves as a Buddhist shrine

sublime the awe and terror experienced before nature and its mysterious grandeur

suite an instrumental composition consisting of a sequence or series of movements derived from court or folk dances

syllabic having one note of music per syllable

syllogism a deductive scheme of formal argument, consisting of two premises from which a conclusion may be drawn

symphony an independent instrumental composition for orchestra

synagogue a Jewish house of worship

syncopation a musical effect that shifts the accent from the normal beat to the offbeat (or weaker beat)

synthesizer an integrated system of electronic components designed for the production and control of sound; it may be used in combination with a computer and with most musical instruments

tempera a powdered pigment that produces dry, flat colors

terracotta (Italian, "baked earth") a clay medium that may be glazed or painted; also called "earthenware"

terrorism a tactical alternative to outright war employed by minority elements aiming to demoralize or intimidate a population in order to achieve social, political, or religious goals

theme and variations a form employing a basic musical idea that is repeated with changes in rhythm, harmony, melody, dynamics, or tone color

theocracy rule by god or god's representative

tholos a circular structure, generally in Classical Greek style and probably derived from early tombs

timbre tone color; the distinctive tone or quality of sound made by a voice or musical instrument

tonality the use of a central note, called the *tonic*, around which all other tonal material of a composition is organized, and to which the music returns for a sense of rest and finality

tone color the distinctive quality of a musical sound made by a voice, a musical instrument, or a combination of instruments

Torah (Hebrew, "instruction," "law," or "teaching") the first five books of the Hebrew Bible: Genesis, Exodus, Leviticus, Numbers, and Deuteronomy

totalitarian (Italian, *totalitario*) a political regime that imposes the will of the state upon the life and conduct of the individual

totem an animal or other creature that serves as a heraldic emblem of a tribe, family, or clan

transept the part of a basilican-plan church that runs perpendicular to the nave (see Figure 4.9)

triforium in a medieval church, the shallow arcaded passageway above the nave and below the clerestory (see Figure 6.20)

Trinity the Christian doctrine of the union of the Father, the Son (Jesus), and the Holy Ghost in a single divine Godhead

triptych a picture or altarpiece with a central panel and two flanking panels

trompe l'oeil (French, "fool the eye") a form of illusionistic painting that tries to convince the viewer that the image is real and not painted

trope an addition of words, music, or both to Gregorian chant

twelve-tone system a kind of serial music that demands the use of all twelve notes of the chromatic scale (all twelve half-tones in an octave) in a particular order or series; no one note can be used again until all eleven have appeared

tympanum the semicircular space enclosed by the lintel over a doorway and the arch above it

vanitas (Latin, "vanity") a type of still life consisting of objects that symbolize the brevity of life and the transience of earthly pleasures and achievements

vassal any member of the feudal nobility who vowed to serve a lord in exchange for control of a fief

vault a roof or ceiling constructed on the arch principle (see Figure 3.5)

verismo (Italian, "realism") a type of late nineteenth-century opera that presents a realistic picture of life, instead of a story based in myth, legend, or ancient history

virtual reality the digital simulation of artificial environments

virtuoso one who exhibits great technical ability, especially in musical performance; also used to describe a musical composition demanding (or a performance demonstrating) great technical skill

Vulgate a version of the Bible in vernacular ("vulgar") Latin, translated by Saint Jerome; it became the official Bible of the Roman Catholic Church

woodcut a relief printing process by which all parts of a design are cut away except those that will be inked and printed (see Figure 8.15)

woodwinds a family of wind instruments usually consisting of the flute, oboe, clarinet, and bassoon

word painting the manipulation of music to convey a specific object, thought, or mood—that is, the content of the text

ziggurat a terraced tower of rubble and brick that served ancient Mesopotamians as a temple-shrine

zither a five- or seven-stringed instrument that is usually plucked with a plectrum and the fingertips; the favorite instrument of ancient China

FURTHER READING

Chapter 1

Aruz, Joan. *Art of the First Cities: The Third Millennium B.C. from the Mediterranean to the Indus.* New York: Metropolitan Museum of Art, 2003.

Foster, John L., trans. *Ancient Egyptian Literature.* Austin, Tex: University of Texas, 2001.

Gimbutas, Maria. *Goddesses and Gods of Old Europe, 6500–3500 B.C: Myths and Cult Images.* Berkeley, Calif: University of California Press, 1990.

Guthrie, Russell D., *The Nature of Paleolithic Art.* Chicago: University of Chicago Press, 2005.

Johnson, Anthony. *Solving Stonehenge: The Key to an Ancient Enigma.* New York: Thames & Hudson, 2008.

Johnson, Paul. *The Civilization of Ancient Egypt.* New York: HarperCollins, 1999.

Schmandt-Besserat, Denise. *Before Writing: From Counting to Cuneiform.* Austin, Tex: University of Texas Press, 1992.

Van de Mieroop, Marc. *A History of the Ancient Near East, ca. 3000–323 B.C.* Oxford: Blackwell, 2004.

Yang, Xiaoneng, ed. *The Golden Age of Chinese Archeology: Celebrated Discoveries from the People's Republic of China.* New Haven, Conn: Yale University Press, 1999.

Zimmer, Heinrich. *Myths and Symbols in Indian Art and Civilization.* Princeton, N.J: Princeton University Press, 1972.

Chapter 2

Alexander, Caroline. *The War that Killed Achilles: The True Story of Homer's Iliad and the Trojan War.* New York: Simon & Schuster, 2010.

Blundell, Sue. *Women in Ancient Greece.* Cambridge, Mass: Harvard University Press, 1995.

Chamoux, François. *Hellenistic Civilization.* London: Wiley-Blackwell, 2002.

Fullerton, Mark D. *Greek Art.* New York: Cambridge University Press, 2000.

Green, Richard, and Eric Handley. *Images of the Greek Theater.* Austin, Tex: University of Texas Press, 1995.

King, Dorothy. *The Elgin Marbles.* London: Hutchison, 2006.

Martin, Thomas R. *Ancient Greece: From Prehistoric to Hellenistic Times.* New Haven, Conn: Yale University Press, 1996.

Miller, Dean A. *The Epic Hero.* Baltimore, Md: Johns Hopkins University Press, 2000.

Neils, Jenifer. *The Parthenon: From Antiquity to the Present.* New York: Cambridge University Press, 2005.

Chapter 3

Baker, Simon. *Ancient Rome: The Rise and Fall of an Empire.* London: BBC Books, 2007.

Balsdon, J. P. *Life and Leisure in Ancient Rome.* London: Weidenfeld & Nicolson, 2002.

D'Ambra, Eve. *Roman Art.* New York: Cambridge University Press, 1998.

Fantham, Elaine. *Roman Literary Culture: From Cicero to Apuleius.* Baltimore, Md: Johns Hopkins University Press, 1999.

Schwartz, Benjamin J. *The World of Thought in Ancient China.* Cambridge, Mass: Harvard University Press, 1985.

Ward-Perkins, John B. *Roman Architecture.* New York: Phaidon, 2003.

Zanker, Paul. *Pompeii: Public and Private Life.* Cambridge, Mass: Harvard University Press, 1998.

Chapter 4

Anderson, Bernhard. *Understanding the Old Testament,* 5th ed. Englewood Cliffs, N.J: Prentice-Hall, 2006.

Armstrong, Karen. *Islam: A Short History.* New York: Modern Library, 2002.

Bloom, Jonathan M., and Sheila S. Blair. *Islamic Arts.* New York: Phaidon, 1997.

Ferguson, Everett. *Backgrounds of Early Christianity,* 3rd ed. Grand Rapids, Mich: Eerdmans, 2003.

Frye, Northrop. *The Great Code: The Bible and Literature.* New York: Harcourt, 2002.

Peters, F. E. *Muhammad and the Origins of Islam.* Ithaca, N.Y: State University of New York, 1994.

———. *The Voice, the Word, the Books: The Sacred Scripture of the Jews, Christians, and Muslims.* Princeton, N.J: Princeton University Press, 2007.

Rodley, Lyn. *Byzantine Art and Architecture.* New York: Cambridge University Press, 1994.

Smith, Huston and P. Novak. *Buddhism: A Concise Introduction.* New York: HarperCollins, 2003.

Wilson, A. N. *Jesus: A Life.* New York: Norton, 1992.

Wright, Robin. *The Evolution of God.* New York: Little, Brown & Co., 2009.

Chapter 5

Backman, Clifford R. *The Worlds of Medieval Europe.* New York: Oxford University Press, 2008.

Bury, J. B. *Invasions of Europe by the Barbarians.* New York: Norton, 2000.

Diebold, William J. *Word and Image: An Introduction to Early Medieval Art.* New York: HarperCollins, 2000.

Labarge, Margaret Wade. *A Small Sound of the Trumpet: Women in Medieval Life.* Boston, Mass: Beacon Press, 1986.

Lewis, Archibald R. *Knights and Samurai: Feudalism in Northern France and Japan.* London: Temple Smith, 1974.

Madden, Thomas F. *The New Concise History of the Crusades.* New York: Rowman & Littlefield, 2005.

Nees, Lawrence. *Early Medieval Art.* New York: Oxford University Press, 2002.

Stephenson, Carl. *Medieval Feudalism.* Ithaca, N.Y: Cornell University Press, 1973.

Watson, William. *The Arts of China to A.D. 900.* New Haven, Conn: Yale University Press, 2007.

Chapter 6

Calkins, Robert. *Monuments of Medieval Art.* Ithaca, N.Y: Cornell University Press, 1989.

Coomaraswamy, Ananda. *The Dance of Shiva,* reprint edition. New York: South Asian Books, 1997.

Fichtenau, Heinrich. *Heretics and Scholars in the High Middle Ages.* Trans. D. A. Kaiser. University Park, Penn: Pennsylvania State University Press, 1998.

LeGoff, Jacques. *The Medieval Imagination,* translated by A. Goldhammer. Chicago: University of Chicago Press, 1992.

Mazzotta, Giuseppe. *Dante's Vision and the Circle of Knowledge.* Princeton, N.J: Princeton University Press, 1994.

Oakley, Francis. *The Medieval Experience: Foundations of Western Cultural Singularity.* Toronto: University of Toronto Press, 1988.

Seay, Albert. *Music in the Medieval World,* 2nd ed. Englewood Cliffs, N.J: Prentice-Hall, 1991.

Shahar, Shulamith. *The Fourth Estate: A History of Women in the Middle Ages.* Austin, Tex: University of Texas, 2003.

Stokstad, Marilyn. *Medieval Art.* Boulder, Co: Westview Press, 2004.

Chapter 7

Adams, Laurie Schneider. *Italian Renaissance Art.* Boulder, Co: Westview Press (Icon Books), 2001.

Clark, Kenneth. *Leonardo da Vinci: An Account of His Development as an Artist.* New York: Viking, 2000.

Holmes, George. *Renaissance.* New York: Oxford University Press, 1998.

Kekewich, Lucille, ed. *The Impact of Humanism (The Renaissance in Europe: A Cultural Inquiry).* New Haven, Conn: Yale University Press, 2000.

Kelly, John. *The Great Mortality: An Intimate History of the Black Death.* New York: HarperCollins, 2005.

King, Margaret, and Catherine R. Stimpson. *Women of the Renaissance.* Chicago: University of Chicago Press, 1991.

Nuart, Charles G. *Humanism and the Culture of Renaissance Europe.* New York: Cambridge University Press, 2006.

Perkins, Leeman L. *Music in the Age of the Renaissance.* New York: Norton, 1999.

Rubin, Patricia Lee. *Images and Identity in Fifteenth-Century Florence.* New Haven, Conn: Yale University Press, 2007.

Tuchman, Barbara. *A Distant Mirror: The Calamitous 14th Century.* New York: Ballantine, 1987.

Chapter 8

Bloom, Harold. *Shakespeare: The Invention of the Human.* New York: Riverhead Books, 1998.

Eisenstein, Elizabeth L. *The Printing Revolution in Early Modern Europe.* Cambridge, U.K: Cambridge University Press, 2005.

Holden, Anthony. *William Shakespeare: The Man Behind the Genius.* Boston, Mass: Little, Brown and Company, 2000.

Kermode, Frank. *The Age of Shakespeare.* New York: Modern Library, 2004.

Pettegree, Andrew. *The Reformation World.* New York: Routledge, 2000.

Schoeck, Richard. *Erasmus of Europe: Prince of the Humanists 1501–1536*. New York: Columbia University Press, 1995.

Smith, Jeffrey Chipps. *The Northern Renaissance*. New York: Phaidon, 2004.

Strong, Roy. *The Cult of Elizabeth: Elizabethan Portraiture and Pageantry*. London: Pimlico, 1999.

Chapter 9

Bierhorst, John. *The Mythology of Mexico and Central America*. New York: William Morrow, 1990.

Coe, Michael D. *The Maya*, 7th ed. London: Thames & Hudson, 2005

Hahner, Iris and others. *African Masks: The Barbier-Muller Collection*. Munich: Prestel, 2007.

Levenson, Jay A., ed. *Circa 1492: Art in the Age of Exploration*. New Haven, Conn: Yale University Press, 1991.

Mbiti, John S. *African Religions and Philosophy*. New York: Heinemann, 1992.

Penney, David, and George Longfish. *Native American Art*. New York: Scribners, 1994.

Stannard, David E. *American Holocaust: The Conquest of the New World*. New York: Oxford University Press, 1993.

Townsend, Richard F. *The Ancient Americas: Art from Sacred Landscapes*. Chicago: Art Institute of Chicago, 1992.

Willett, Frank. *African Art: An Introduction*, rev. ed. New York: Thames and Hudson, 2002.

Chapter 10

Avery, Charles. *Bernini: Genius of the Baroque*. London: Thames & Hudson, 2006.

Carl, Klaus and Victoria Charles. *Baroque Art*. New York: Parkstone Press, 2009.

Hammond, Frederick. *Music and Spectacle in Baroque Rome*. New Haven, Conn: Yale University Press, 1994.

Lewis, W. H. *The Splendid Century: Life in the France of Louis XIV*. New York: Waveland Press, 1997.

Mitford, Nancy. *The Sun King: Louis XIV at Versailles*, reprint edition. New York: Penguin, 1995.

Mullett, Michael A. *The Catholic Reformation*. New York: Routledge, 1999.

Nevitt, H. Rodney. *Art and the Culture of Love in Seventeenth-Century Holland*. New York: Cambridge University Press, 2003.

Sternfeld, F. W. *The Birth of Opera*. New York: Oxford University Press, 1995.

Yu Zhuoyen, ed. *Palaces of the Forbidden City*, translated by Ng Mau-Sang and others. New York: Viking, 1984.

Chapter 11

Becker, Carl L. *The Heavenly City of the Eighteenth-Century Philosophers*. New Haven, Conn: Yale University Press, 1959.

Blier, Suzanne Preston. *The Royal Arts of Africa: The Majesty of Form*. New York: Abrams, 1998.

Gutman, Robert W. *Mozart: A Cultural Biography*. New York: Harcourt Brace, 1999.

Irwin, David. Neoclassicism. *New York: Phaidon*, 1997.

Jacob, Margaret C. *The Scientific Revolution: A Brief History with Documents*. New York: Bedford/ St Martin's, 2009.

Kramer, Lawrence. *Why Classical Music Still Matters*. Berkeley, Calif: University of California Press, 2005.

Levey, Michael. *From Rococo to Revolution: Major Trends in Eighteenth-Century Painting*. New York: Norton, 1985.

Porter, Roy. *The Enlightenment*. New York: Palgrave Macmillan, 2001.

Richard, Carl J. *The Founders and the Classics: Greece, Rome, and the American Enlightenment*. Cambridge, Mass: Harvard University Press, 1994.

Rosen, Charles. *The Classical Style: Haydn, Mozart, Beethoven*. New York: Norton, 1997.

Shapin, Steven. *The Scientific Revolution*. Chicago: University of Chicago Press, 1996.

Chapter 12

Bernier, Olivier. *The World in 1800*. New York: John Wiley and Sons, 2000.

Brown, Jane K. *Goethe's Faust: The German Tragedy*. Ithaca, N.Y: Cornell University Press, 1986.

Clark, Kenneth. *The Romantic Rebellion: Romantic Versus Classic Art*. New York: Harper, 1986.

Gerhard, Anselm. *The Urbanization of Opera: Music Theater in Paris in the Nineteenth Century*, translated by Mary Whittall. Chicago: University of Chicago Press, 1998.

Homans, Jennifer. *Apollo's Angels: A History of Ballet*. New York: Random House, 2010.

Honour, Hugh. *Romanticism*. New York: Harper, 1999.

Jones, Steve. *Darwin's Ghost: "The Origin of Species" Updated*. New York: Random House, 2000.

Mason, Penelope. *History of Japanese Art*. Englewood Cliffs, N. J: Prentice-Hall, 2004.

Plantinga, Leon. *Romantic Music*. New York: Norton, 1982.

Wordsworth, Jonathan, and others. *William Wordsworth and the Age of English Romanticism*. New Brunswick, N.J: Rutgers University Press, 1989.

Wu, Duncan. *A Companion to Romanticism*. London: Wiley-Blackwell, 1999.

Chapter 13

Berger, Klaus. *Japonisme in Western Painting from Whistler to Matisse*, translated by David Britt. New York: Cambridge University Press, 1992.

Clark, T. J. *The Painting of Modern Life*, rev. ed. Princeton, N.J: Princeton University Press, 1989.

Friedrich, Otto. *Olympia: Paris in the Age of Manet*. New York: Harper, 1992.

Johns, Elizabeth. *American Genre Painting: The Politics of Everyday Life*. New Haven, Conn: Yale University Press, 1994.

Kearns, Katherine. *Nineteenth-Century Literary Realism: Through the Looking Glass*. Cambridge, U.K: Cambridge University Press, 1996.

Loyrette, Henri. *Nineteenth-Century French Art: From Romanticism to Impressionism, Post-Impressionism and Art Nouveau*. Paris: Flammarion, 2007.

Nochlin, Linda. *Realism*. New York: Viking, 1993.

Thomas Nicholas. *Oceanic Art*. London: Thames & Hudson, 1995.

Chapter 14

Armstrong, Tim. *Modernism: A Cultural History*. New York: Oxford University Press, 2005.

Cork, Richard. *A Bitter Truth: Avant-Garde Art and the Great War*. New Haven, Conn: Yale University Press, 1994.

Gale, Matthew. *Dada and Surrealism*. New York: Phaidon, 1998.

Gioia, Ted. *The History of Jazz*. New York: Oxford University Press, 1999.

Huggins, Nathan I. *Harlem Renaissance*. New York: Oxford University Press, 2007.

Hughes, Robert. *The Shock of the New: Art and the Century of Change*. New York: Knopf, 1993.

Morgan, Robert P. *Twentieth-Century Music: A History of Musical Style in Modern Europe and America*. New York: Norton, 1991.

Nelson, Benjamin. *Freud and the Twentieth Century*. Whitefish, MT, 2010.

Perkins, David. *A History of Modern Poetry: Modernism and After*. New York: Belknap Press, 1987.

Vergo, Peter. *The Music of Painting: Music, Modernism, and the Visual Arts from the Romantics to John Cage*. New York: Phaidon, 2010.

Chapter 15

Elkins, James et al. *Art and Globalization*. University Park, PA: Penn State Press, 2010.

Fineberg, Jonathan. *Art Since 1940: Strategies of Being*. London: Laurence King Publishing, 2001.

Jenkins, Henry. *Convergence Culture: Where Old and New Media Collide*. New York: New York University Press, 2006.

Lucie-Smith, Edward. *Race, Sex, and Gender: Issues in Contemporary Art*. New York: Abrams, 1994.

Mazower, Mark. *Dark Continent: Europe's Twentieth Century*. New York: Vintage Books, 2000.

Powell, Richard J. *Black Art and Culture in the 20th Century*. New York: Thames and Hudson, 1995.

Rebein, Robert. *Hicks, Tribes and Dirty Realists: American Fiction After Postmodernism*. Lexington, Ky: University of Kentucky Press, 2001.

Rush, Michael. *New Media in Art*. London: Thames and Hudson, 2005.

Taruskin, Richard. *Music in the Late Twentieth Century*. New York: Oxford University Press, 2009.

Wands, Bruce. *Art of the Digital Age*. New York: Thames and Hudson, 2006.

LITERARY CREDITS

Laurence King Publishing, the author, and the literary permissions researcher wish to thank the publishers and individuals who have kindly allowed their copyright material to be reproduced in this book, as listed below. Every effort has been made to contact copyright holders, but should there be any errors or omissions, Laurence King Publishing would be pleased to insert the appropriate acknowledgment in any subsequent edition of this publication.

Chapter 1

p. 9 From *Poems of Heaven and Hell from Ancient Mesopotamia*, translated by N. K. Sandars (Penguin Classics, 1971), © N. K. Sandars, 1971.

p. 10 From *The Epic of Gilgamesh*, translated by N. K. Sandars (Penguin Classics, 1960; second revised edition, 1972), © N. K. Sandars, 1960, 1964, 1972.

p. 11 From "The Code of Hammurabi" in *The Hammurabi Code and the Sinaitic Legislation*, translated by Chilperic Edwards (Kennikat Press, 1971).

p. 23 From *The Upanishads: Breath of the Eternal*, translated by Swami Prabhavananda and Frederick Manchester (Mentor Books/New American Library, 1948).

p. 26 From Lao Tzu, *The Way of Life*, translated by Raymond B. Blakney, copyright © 1955 by Raymond B. Blakney, renewed © 1983 by Charles Philip Blakney. Used by permission of Dutton Signet, a division of Penguin Group (USA) Inc.

Chapter 2

p. 34 From *The Iliad of Homer*, translated by Richmond Lattimore (University of Chicago Press, 1965), © 1951 by the University of Chicago, used with permission of the University of Chicago Press.

p. 35 From Hesiod, *Theogony*, translated by Norman O. Brown (Bobbs-Merrill, 1953); from *The Jerusalem Bible*, edited by Alexander Jones (Darton, Longman & Todd/Doubleday, 1966), © 1966 by Darton, Longman & Todd Ltd. and Doubleday, a division of Random House, Inc., reprinted by permission.

p. 37 From Pericles' "Funeral Speech" from Thucydides, *History of the Peloponnesian War*, translated by Benjamin Jowett, in *The Greek Historian*, edited by F. R. B. Godolphin (Random House, 1942).

p. 40 From Mary Barnard, *Sappho: A New Translation* (University of California Press, 1958), © 1958 The Regents of the University of California; © renewed 1986 Mary Barnard.

p. 43 From *The Analects of Confucius*, translated by Simon Leys (W. W. Norton, 1997), © 1997 by Pierre Ryckmans. Used by permission of W. W. Norton & Company, Inc.

p. 45 From "Allegory of the Cave" from *The Republic of Plato*, edited by F. M. Cornford (Oxford University Press, 1951). 256 words. Reprinted by permission of Oxford University Press.

pp. 46 & 47 From *The Works of Aristotle*, edited by W. D. Ross, translated by Ingram Bywater (Oxford University Press, 1952), © 1952 Oxford University Press; from J. L. Ackrill, *A New Aristotle Reader* (Oxford: Clarendon Press, 1987).

Chapter 3

p. 70 From Seneca, *On Tranquillity of Mind*, in *The Stoic Philosophy of Seneca*, translated by Moses Hadas (Doubleday, 1958), © 1958 by Moses Hadas.

p. 71 From *The Aeneid of Virgil*, translated by Rolfe Humphries (Scribner, 1951), © 1951 by Charles Scribner's Sons, © renewed 1987 by Macmillan Publishing Company, reprinted with the permission of Scribner, a division of Simon & Schuster, Inc., all rights reserved; from *The Poems of Catullus*, translated by Horace Gregory (W. W. Norton, 1972), © 1956, 1972 by the Estate of Horace Gregory, used with permission.

p. 72 "*Carpe Diem*" from *Selected Poems of Horace*, translated by George F. Whicher (Van Nostrand Reinhold, 1947); from *The Satires of Juvenal*, translated by Rolfe Humphries (Indiana University Press, 1958), reprinted by permission of Indiana University Press.

Chapter 4

p. 93 Adapted from *The Egyptian Book of the Dead*, edited by E. Wallis Budge (University Books, Inc., 1977); from *The Jerusalem Bible*, edited by Alexander Jones (Darton, Longman & Todd/Doubleday, 1966), copyright © 1966 by Darton, Longman & Todd Ltd. and Doubleday, a division of Random House, Inc., reprinted by permission.

p. 99 From "Sermon on the Mount" in *The Jerusalem Bible*, edited by Alexander Jones (Darton, Longman & Todd/Doubleday, 1966), copyright © 1966 by Darton, Longman & Todd Ltd. and Doubleday, a division of Random House, Inc., reprinted by permission.

p. 111 From *The Quran* in J. R. Benton & R. DiYanni, *Arts and Culture*, Volume 1 (Prentice-Hall, 2002).

p. 116 From "Sermon on the Mount" in *The Jerusalem Bible*, edited by Alexander Jones (Darton, Longman & Todd/Doubleday, 1966), © 1966 by Darton, Longman & Todd Ltd. and Doubleday, a division of Random House, Inc., reprinted by permission; from Buddha's "Sermon on Abuse" in *The Wisdom of China and India* by Lin Yutang (Random House, 1970), copyright 1942 and renewed 1970 by Random House, Inc.

Chapter 5

p. 129 From Murasaki Shikibu, *The Tale of Genji*, translated by E. G. Seidensticker (Vintage Books, 1985), © 1976 by Edward G. Seidensticker.

p. 135 From *The Song of Roland*, translated by Patricia Terry (Macmillan Publishing Company, 1965).

p. 136 The Countess of Dia, "Lost Love" from *The Troubadours and Their World*, translated by Jack Lindsay (Frederick Muller, 1976), reprinted by permission of David Higham Associates.

p. 140 Li Bo, "Watching the Mount Lushan Waterfall" from *Gems of Chinese Poetry*, edited and translated by Ding Zuxin and Burton Raffel (The Liaoning University Press, 1987).

Chapter 6

p. 144 From "Letters of Gregory VII" in T. E. Mommsen & K. F. Morrison, *Imperial Lives and Letters of the Eleventh Century* (Columbia University Press, 1976).

p. 146 From Rumi, *Love is a Stranger*, translated by Rabir Edmund Helminski (Threshold Books, 1993).

p. 150 From Dante Alighieri, *The Divine Comedy*, translated by John Ciardi (W. W. Norton, 1970), © 1954, 1957, 1959, 1960, 1961, 1965, 1967, 1970 by the Ciardi Family Publishing Trust, used by permission of W. W. Norton & Company, Inc.

p. 152 From Thomas Aquinas, *Summa Theologica* in *Aquinas, Basic Writings: Volume 1*, edited by Anton C. Pegis (Hackett Publishing Company, 1997).

Chapter 7

p. 178 From *The Canterbury Tales of Geoffrey Chaucer*, translated by R. M. Lumiansky, © 1948 by Simon & Schuster, © renewed 1975 by Simon & Schuster.

p. 184 Petrarch, "Sonnet 134," *Petrarch: Sonnets & Songs*, translated by Anna Maria Armi (Grosset & Dunlap, 1968).

p. 185 From Giovanni Pico della Mirandola, *Oration on the Dignity of Man*, translated by A. Robert Caponigri (Regnery Gateway, 1956).

p. 186 From Baldassare Castiglione, *The Book of the Courtier*, translated by Leonard Eckstein Opdyke, © 1901, 1903, 1929 by Leonard Eckstein Opdyke.

p. 188 From Niccolò Machiavelli, *The Prince*, translated by Ninian Hill Thomson (Clarendon Press, 1987), reprinted by permission of Oxford University Press.

p. 197 From Giorgio Vasari, *The Lives of the Most Excellent Painters, Architects, and Sculptors*, edited by Betty Burroughs (Simon & Schuster), © 1946, 1973 by Betty Burroughs.

Chapter 8

p. 216 From Martin Luther, *Ninety-Five Theses*, in *Translations and Reprints from the Original Sources of European History*, II, No. 6, edited by J. H. Robinson (University of Pennsylvania Press, 1984).

p. 217 From John Calvin, "Institutes of the Christian Religion" in Harry J. Carroll, et al. (editors), *The Development of Civilization* (Scott, Foresman, 1970).

p. 219 From Desiderius Erasmus, *The Praise of Folly*, translated by Hoyt Hopewell Hudson (Princeton University Press, 1941), © 1941 Princeton University Press, copyright renewed 1969, reprinted by permission of Princeton University Press.

p. 220 From Miguel de Cervantes, *Don Quixote: A Norton Critical Edition* (W. W. Norton, 1996), edited by Diana de Armas Wilson, translated by Burton Raffel, © 1999 by W. W Norton & Company, Inc.

p. 222 William Shakespeare, *Sonnets*, in *The Complete Works of Shakespeare*, 3rd edition by David Bevington, © 1980, 1973 by Scott, Foresman & Company.

pp. 224–6 From William Shakespeare, *Hamlet*, in *The Complete Works of Shakespeare*, 3rd edition by David Bevington, © 1980, 1973 by Scott, Foresman & Company.

Chapter 9

p. 244 "The Oba of Benin" from *African Poetry: An Anthology of Traditional African Poems*, compiled and edited by Ulli Beier (Cambridge University Press, 1966); from *Soundjata ou L'Epopée Mandingue (Sundiata: An Epic of Old Mali)* (Présence Africaine, 1960), reprinted by permission of the publisher.

p. 245 From *African Myths and Tales*, introduction by Susan Feldman (Dell Publishing Company, 1963).

p. 250 "Navajo Night Chant" from *The Winged Serpents: An Anthology of American Indian Prose and Poetry*, edited by Margot Astrov (Fawcett, 1973).

p. 251 "How Man Was Created" (Mohawk) from *American Indian Legends*, edited by Allan Macfarlan (The Heritage Press, 1968).

p. 255 From *Hernán Cortés: Letters from Mexico*, edited by Anthony Pagden (Yale University Press, 1986), © 1986 by Yale University Press.

Chapter 10

p. 260 From *The Spiritual Exercises of St. Ignatius*, translated by Louis J. Puhl, S.J. (Loyola Press, 1951).

p. 265 From *The Complete Works of Saint Teresa of Jesus*, Volume 1, translated by E. A. Peers (Sheed & Ward, 1957), reprinted by permission of Rowman & Littlefield Publishing Group.

p. 268 From "Apocrypha, Book of Judith" in *New Revised Standard Version Bible with Apocryphal/Deuterocanonical Books* (HarperCollins Study Bible, 1991).

pp. 270 & 271 From John Donne, *Devotions upon Emergent Occasions and Songs and Sonnets* in *The College Survey of English Literature*, shorter edition, by Alexander Witherspoon (Harcourt Brace Jovanovich, 1951).

pp. 271–2 From John Milton, *Paradise Lost: A Norton Critical Edition*, 2nd edition, edited by Scott Elledge (W. W. Norton, 1975), © 1993, 1975 by W. W. Norton & Company, Inc.

Chapter 11

p. 295 From Sir Francis Bacon, *Novum Organum*, translated and edited by Peter Urbach and John Gibson (Open Court, 1994).

p. 298 From Thomas Hobbes, *Leviathan*, edited by Herbert W. Schneider (Macmillan, 1958), © 1985, 1958 by Macmillan Publishing Company; from John Locke, *Of Civil Government* in *The Works of John Locke* (modernized by the author) (Thomas Tegg, 1823).

p. 299 From Thomas Jefferson, *The Declaration of Independence* (1776).

p. 301 From Antoine Nicolas de Condorcet, *Sketch for a Historical Picture of the Progress of the Human Mind*, translated by June Barraclough (Weidenfeld & Nicolson, 1955), © 1955 George Weidenfeld & Nicolson Ltd.; from Mary Wollstonecraft, *A Vindication of the Rights of Woman* in *The Works of Mary Wollstonecraft*, Volume 5, edited by Jane Todd and Marilyn Butler (New York University Press, 1989).

p. 304 From Alexander Pope, *Essay on Man* in *Poetical Works of Alexander Pope* (Little, Brown & Company, 1854).

p. 321 Matsuo Basho, three haiku poems, from *An Introduction to Haiku* by Harold G. Henderson (Doubleday, 1958), copyright © 1958 by Harold G. Henderson, used by permission of Doubleday, a division of Random House, Inc.

Chapter 12

p. 330 From William Wordsworth, "Lines Composed a Few Miles Above Tintern Abbey" from *The College Survey of English Literature*, Shorter Edition, by Alexander Witherspoon (Harcourt Brace Jovanovich, 1951); Percy Bysshe Shelley, "Ozymandias" in *Complete Poetical Works*, edited by T. Hutchinson (1904).

p. 333 From Johann Wolfgang von Goethe, *Faust: Parts 1 and 2*, translated by Louis MacNeice (Oxford University Press, 1951), reprinted by permission of Doubleday, a division of Random House, Inc.

p. 334 From *The Complete Essays and Other Writings of Ralph Waldo Emerson*, edited by Brooks Atkinson (The Modern Library, 1950).

p. 335 From Henry David Thoreau, *Walden* (Airmont Classics, 1965); from Walt Whitman, *Leaves of Grass* (David McKay, 1900).

Chapter 13

p. 359 From Karl Marx and Friedrich Engels, *The Communist Manifesto*, translated by Samuel Moore, revised and edited by Friedrich Engels (London: 1888); From Friedrich Wilhelm Nietzsche, *Der Antichrist* (1888), translated by H. L. Mencken (1920; n.e. Noontide Press, 1988).

p. 361 From Fyodor Dostoevsky, *Crime and Punishment*, translated by Jessie Coulson, edited by George Gibian (W. W. Norton, 1975).

p. 362 From Henrik Ibsen, *A Doll's House* in *Six Plays*, translated by Eva Le Gallienne (Random House, 1957), © 1957 by Eva Le Gallienne.

p. 376 From Paul Gauguin, *Noa Noa*, translated by O. F. Theis (Noonday Press, 1964).

Chapter 14

p. 384 From Sigmund Freud, *Civilization and Its Discontents*, translated by James Strachey (W. W. Norton, 1989), © 1961 by James Strachey, renewed 1989 by Alix Strachey.

p. 387 Langston Hughes, "Harlem" from *The Collected Poems of Langston Hughes*, edited by Arnold Rampersad and David Roessel (Knopf, 1994), reprinted by permission of Alfred A. Knopf, a division of Random House Inc.

p. 389 From Vladimir Ilyich Lenin, *The State and Revolution* (International Publishers, 1932).

p. 391 W. B. Yeats, "The Second Coming" from *Collected Poems* (Picador, 1990); from T. S. Eliot, Choruses from "The Rock" *I. The Eagle soars in the summit of Heaven, in Collected Poems 1909–1962* (Faber & Faber, 1974), © 1936 by Harcourt, Inc. and renewed 1964 by T. S. Eliot, reprinted by permission of Houghton Mifflin Harcourt Publishing Company.

p. 392 Robert Frost, "The Road Not Taken" from *Robert Frost: Selected Poems* (The Penguin Poets, 1955).

Chapter 15

p. 419 From Jean Paul Sartre, *Existentialism*, translated by Bernard Frechtman (Philosophical Library, 1947); from Allen Ginsberg, "Howl", *Collected Poems 1947–1980*, copyright © 1955 by Allen Ginsberg, reprinted by permission of HarperCollins Publishers.

p. 424 From James Baldwin, "Stranger in the Village" in *Notes of a Native Son* (Bantam Press, 1964).

p. 425 Gwendolyn Brooks, "We Real Cool" from *Blacks* (Third World Press, 1991).

p. 426 From Simone de Beauvoir, *The Second Sex*, translated by H. M. Parshley (Knopf, 1952), © 1952 and renewed 1980 by Alfred A. Knopf Inc.

p. 427 From Germaine Greer, *The Obstacle Race: The Fortunes of Women Painters and their Work* (Farrar, Straus & Giroux, 1979).

p. 435 Seamus Heaney, "Anything Can Happen" from *District and Circle* (Faber & Faber, 2007), © 2006 by Seamus Heaney, reprinted by permission of Farrar, Straus and Giroux, LLC.

p. 455 Wislawa Szymborska, "Photograph from September 11" from *Monologue of a Dog* (Harcourt, 2005), copyright © 2002 by Wislawa Szymborska, English translation copyright © 2006 by Houghton Mifflin Harcourt Publishing Company, reprinted by permission of the publisher.

PICTURE CREDITS

Laurence King Publishing, the author, and the picture researcher wish to thank the institutions and individuals that have kindly provided photographic material for use in this book. Museum, gallery, and library locations are given in the captions; further details and other sources are listed below.

Abbreviations

ADAGP: Société des Auteurs Dans les Arts Graphiques et Plastiques, Paris
AKG: Archiv für Kunst und Geschichte, London
ARS: Artists' Rights Society, New York
BPK: Bildarchiv Preussischer Kulturbesitz, Berlin
DACS: Design and Artists Copyright Society, London
DI: Digital Image, The Museum of Modern Art, New York/Scala, Florence
MFA: The Museum of Fine Arts, Boston
MMA: The Metropolitan Museum of Art, New York
MOMA: The Museum of Modern Art, New York
NGA: National Gallery of Art, Washington, D.C.
RMN: Réunion des Musées Nationaux, Paris
SMB: Scala, Florence—courtesy of the Ministero Beni e Att. Culturali
VAGA: The Visual Arts and Galleries Association, New York

Cover and Frontispiece:

Credit information for these images appears on page iv

Preface:

1.3 Museum of Natural History, Vienna
1.4 Collection of Whitney Museum of American Art, New York. Photograph © 2000 Whitney Museum of American Art. Photography by Sandak Inc./Division of Macmillan Publishing Company. © ADAGP, Paris and DACS, London 2011

Chapter 1

1.1 © Otto Lang/Corbis
1.3 Museum of Natural History, Vienna
1.4 Collection of Whitney Museum of American Art, New York. Photograph © 2000 Whitney Museum of American Art. Photography by Sandak Inc./Division of Macmillan Publishing Company. © ADAGP, Paris and DACS, London 2011
1.5 The Metropolitan Museum of Art, Gift of Christos G. Bastis, 1968 (68.148). Photograph © 1996 The Metropolitan Museum of Art. Scala, Florence
1.7 Haldun Aydingun
1.8 © Skyscan/Corbis
1.9 Funding from the Virginia Wright Fund, National Endowment for the Arts, Washington State Arts Commission, Western Washington University Art Fund and the artist's contributions. Collection of Western Washington University, Bellingham, Washington. © Nancy Holt/ DACS, London/VAGA, New York 2011
1.10 Munich, Staatliche Museum Ägyptischer Kunst
1.11 Ashmolean Museum, Oxford
1.12 Courtesy of the C.V. Starr East Asian Library, Columbia University
1.13 Freer Gallery of Art, Smithsonian Institution, Washington, D.C. F1930.26AB
1.14 © 1990, Photo Scala, Florence
1.15 Courtesy of the Oriental Institute of the University of Chicago
1.16 © Erwin Bohm, Mainz
1.17 © Tony Morrison/South American Pictures, Woodbridge, U.K.
1.18 © Photo Josse, Paris
1.19 © Art Resource/HIP/Scala, Florence
1.20 Photo: Klaus Goeken © 2011. Photo Scala, Florence/BPK, Bildagentur fur Kunst, Kultur und Geschichte, Berlin
1.21 Excavations of MMA, 1929; Rogers Fund, 1930 (30.3.31). Photograph © 1978 MMA. Photo Scala, Florence
1.22 Dr. E. Strouhal/Werner Forman Archive, London
1.23 Sautereau/Cosmos/Woodfin Camp and Associates
1.24 © J. Paul Getty Trust. Wim Swaan Photograph Collection (96.P.21) The Getty Research Institute, Los Angeles
1.25 Photo: Margarete Buesing/Bildarchiv Preussischer Kunstbesitz/Photo Scala
1.26 © Copyright the Trustees of the British Museum
1.27 Harvard University—MFA Expedition 11.1738. Photo © 2008 MFA
1.28 Photo Jean Vertut
1.29 © Held Collection/The Bridgeman Art Library
1.30 © 2011 George Steinmetz
1.31 Werner Forman Archive/Anthropology Museum, Veracruz University, Jalapa
1.32 Robert Harding Picture Library
1.33 The Nelson Atkins Museum of Art, Kansas City, Missouri (Purchase: William Rockhill Nelson Trust) 33–81. Photo E.G. Schempf
Thumbnails: 1.18 © Photo Josse, Paris, 1.22 Dr. E. Strouhal/Werner Forman Archive, London, 1.8 © Skyscan/Corbis

Chapter 2

2.1 i-Stockphoto.com
2.2 Photo Gloria K. Fiero
2.3, 2.6, 2.22 Photo Craig & Marie Mauzy, Athens, mauzy@otenet.gr
2.4 AKG Images/Erich Lessing
2.5 © 2005 Photo Spectrum/HIP/Scala, Florence
2.7 Courtesy of the Ministero Beni e Att. Culturali. Image © 1999 MMA
2.8, 2.17, 2.31, 2.33, 2.34 © Copyright the Trustees of the British Museum
2.9 © Vincenzo Pirozzi, Rome. fotopirozzi@inwind.it
2.10 Rogers Fund, 1914 (14.130.12). Photograph © 1998 MMA. Photo Scala, Florence
2.13 Catharine Lorillard Wolfe Collection, Wolfe Fund, 1931 (31.45). Photograph © 1995 MMA. Photo Scala, Florence
2.14 From *The Great Dialogues of Plato* by Plato, translated by W. H. D. Rouse, © 1956, renewed © 1984 by J. C. G. Rouse. Used by permission of Dutton Signet, a division of Penguin Group (U.S.A.) Inc.
2.15 Rogers Fund, 1914 (14.130.14). Photograph © 1996 MMA. Photo Scala, Florence
2.16, 2.24, 2.37, 2.38 Photo Vatican Museums, Rome
2.18 Fletcher Fund, 1932 (32.11.1). All rights reserved, MMA. Photo Scala, Florence
2.19 Photo © RMN
2.20 The Art Archive/Acropolis Museum Athens /Gianni Dagli Orti
2.21 Photo © Fotografia Foglia, Naples
2.23 Photo Studio Konto Nikos, Athens
2.25 Sonia Halliday Photographs
2.28 Courtesy of the Trustees of the American School of Classical Studies at Athens
2.32 AKG Images/Peter Connolly
2.35 Fletcher Fund, 1956 (56.171.38). Photograph © 1998 MMA. Photo Scala, Florence
Thumbnails: 2.6, 2.22 Photo Craig & Marie Mauzy, Athens, mauzy@otenet.gr, 2.25 Sonia Halliday Photographs, 2.16 Photo Vatican Museums, Rome

Chapter 3

3.1 © 1990, Photo SMB. Photo: Scala/Florence
3.2 AKG Images
3.3 Photo Juergen Liepe/BPK
3.4, 3.23 The Art Archive, London
3.6 Photo © Paul M. R. Maeyaert
3.7 © Alinari Archives/Corbis
3.8 © Vincenzo Pirozzi, Rome. fotopirozzi@inwind.it
3.9 Library of Virginia
3.10 Samuel H. Kress Collection 1939.1.24. Image courtesy of the Board of Trustees, National Gallery of Art, Washington, D.C.
3.11 Photo © Paul M. R. Maeyaert
3.12, 3.21, 3.22 Spectrum Colour Library, London
3.14 © 1990, Photo SMB. Photo: Scala/Florence
3.15 © 1990, Photo Scala, Florence. Courtesy of the Ministero Beni e Att. Culturali
3.16 SEF/Art Resource, NY. Photo Scala, Florence
3.17 © Araldo De Luca, Rome
3.18, 3.20 © Fotografica Foglia, Naples
3.19 Alinari/Art Resource, New York
3.24 The Nelson-Atkins Museum of Art, Kansas City, Missouri (Purchase: William Rockhill Nelson Trust) 32–186/1–7. Photo: E.G. Schempf
3.25 Cultural Relics Publishing House, Beijing
Thumbnails: 3.4 The Art Archive, London, 3.6 Photo © Paul M. R. Maeyaert, 3.23 The Art Archive, London, 3.14 © 1990, Photo SMB. Photo: Scala/Florence

Chapter 4

4.1 Kunsthistoriches Museum, Vienna
4.2, 4.13 AKG Images/Erich Lessing
4.3 Zev Radovan/BibleLandPictures.com
4.4 Alinari/Art Resource, New York
4.5 The Art Archive/Acropolis Museum Athens/ Gianni Dagli Orti
4.6 © 1990 Photo Scala, Florence
4.8 Pontificia Commissione di Archeologia Sacra, Rome
4.10 © Canali Photobank, Capriolo (BS), Italy
4.11 Sonia Halliday Photographs
4.14 The Art Archive/Collection Dagli Orti
4.15, 4.16 © Cameraphoto Arte, Venice
4.17 Photo: Scala, Florence
4.18 Monastery of Saint Catherine, Mount Sinai, Egypt
4.19 © Reuters/Corbis
4.20 The Nelson-Atkins Museum of Art, Kansas City, Missouri (Purchase: William Rockhill Nelson Trust) 44–40/2
4.21 Harris Brisbane Dick Fund, 1939 (39.20). Photograph © 1982 MMA
4.22 Photo A. F. Kersting, London/AKG Images
4.23 Spectrum Colour Library, London
4.24 © Classic Image/Alamy
4.26 © 1990, Photo Scala, Florence
Thumbnails: 4.15 © Cameraphoto Arte, Venice, 4.6 © 1990 Photo Scala, Florence, 4.23 Spectrum Colour Library, London

Chapter 5

5.1 © 2011 Photo Scala, Florence
5.2 © copyright The Trustees of the British Museum
5.3 Ms. 58, f. 34r. The Board of Trinity College, Dublin
5.4 Photo: © RMN—J.G. Berizzi
5.5 Monastery Library of Saint-Gall, Switzerland
5.6 Photo Fotografie Maurice Cox, Cologne. Model originally constructed at Saint-Gall by Walter Horn
5.7 The Embassy of Japan, London
5.8 Ms. Lat. 9428, f. 71v. Bibliothèque Nationale, Paris
5.9 © The Pierpont Morgan Library/Art Resource, New York
5.10 H. O. Havemeyer Collection, Gift of Horace Havemeyer, 1929. (29.160.23). All rights reserved. MMA. Photograph by Schecter Lee © 2010. Image copyright The Metropolitan Museum of Art/Art Resource/Scala, Florence
5.11, 5.14 The British Library
5.12 The Art Archive, London/Private Collection, Paris/Dagli Orti
5.13 © 2010. Image copyright The Metropolitan Museum of Art/Art Resource/Scala, Florence
5.16 © English Heritage Photographic Library, London
5.17 From Patrick Rook, *The Normans*, Macdonald Education Ltd., 1977
5.18 Photo by special permission of the City of Bayeux
5.19 Ms. Fr. 13568, f. 83. Bibliothèque Nationale, Paris
5.20 Ms. E-Eb-1–2, f. 162 El Escorial de Santa Maria, Spain
5.21 Codex pal. germ. 848, f. 249v. Bildarchiv Foto Marburg
5.22 Collection of the Palace Museum, Beijing
5.23 Victoria & Albert Museum, London. V&A Images
5.24 The Nelson-Atkins Museum of Art, Kansas City, Missouri (Purchase: William Rockhill Nelson Trust) 47–71
Thumbnails: 5.18 Photo by special permission of the City of Bayeux, 5.2 © Copyright The Trustees of the British Museum, 5.23 Victoria & Albert Museum, London. V&A Images, 5.16 © English Heritage Photographic Library, London

Chapter 6

6.1 John Elk III/Bruce Coleman
6.2 Ms. 13 321 Wiesbaden Codex B, f. 1. Landesbibliothek Wiesbaden
6.3 Rogers Fund, 1918 (17.81.4). Photograph © 1986 MMA. Photo Scala, Florence
6.4 © Vincenzo Pirozzi, Rome. fotopirozzi@inwind.it
6.5 © Bulloz/RMN
6.6 Alinari/Art Resource, New York
6.8 Photo Roger Viollet, Paris
6.9 Staatliche Museen zu Berlin—Kupferstichkabinett/BPK. Photo Joerg P. Anders
6.10, 6.14, 6.15, 6.17 Photo © Paul M. R. Maeyaert
6.11 © Jean Dieuzaide
6.13 Photo Serge Chirol, Paris. © Nature Photographic Library
6.16, 6.24, 6.25 Sonia Halliday Photographs
6.21 Bob Burch/Bruce Coleman Inc
6.22 Photo Serge Chirol, Paris. © Nature Photographic Library
6.23 © Angelo Hornak
6.26 © Quattrone, Florence
6.27 The Bridgeman Art Library, London
6.28 Photo A. F. Kersting, London/Courtauld Institute of Art
6.29 Syndicated Features Limited/The Image Works
6.30 © The Cleveland Museum of Art, 2011 Purchase from the J. H. Wade Fund, 1930.331
6.31 The Nelson-Atkins Museum of Art, Kansas City, Missouri (Purchase: William Rockhill Nelson Trust) 34–10
6.32 © 1990, Photo SMB. Scala/Art Resource, New York
Thumbnails: 6.1 John Elk III/Bruce Coleman, 6.10 Photo © Paul M. R. Maeyaert, 6.5 © Bulloz/RMN, 6.26 © Quattrone, Florence

Chapter 7

7.1, 7.5, 7.6, 7.12, 7.15, 7.17, 7.19, 7.24, 7.29, 7.34 © Quattrone, Florence
7.2 Library of Congress, Washington, D.C.
7.3 Ms. 17, f. 176 Musee Dobrée, Nantes. The Bridgeman Art Library, London/Giraudon
7.4 The Bridgeman Art Library, London/ Giraudon
7.7 A. F. Kersting, © 1990, Photo Scala, Florence
7.8 Samuel H. Kress Collection (1939.1.24). Image © 2000, Board of Trustees, NGA
7.9 © Photo Josse, Paris
7.10 in P. Murray, *Renaissance Architecture*, NY (1971), fig. 22
7.11 © 1990, Photo Scala, Florence
7.13 Alinari/Art Resource, New York
7.16 © 1991, Photo SMB. Scala/Art Resource, New York
7.18 The Art Archive
7.20 a, b © 1990, Photo SMB. Scala/Art Resource, New York
7.21 Photo © Vincenzo Pirozzi, Rome. fotopirozzi@inwind.it
7.22 The Bridgeman Art Library, London
7.25 Refectory, Santa Maria delle Grazie, Milan. AKG Images, London
7.26 The Royal Collection © 2011 Her Majesty Queen Elizabeth II
7.27 Andrew W. Mellon Collection 1937.1.24. Image courtesy of the Board of Trustees, National Gallery of Art, Washington
7.28, 7.32 © Photo Vatican Museums
7.30 © Photo Vatican Museums Monumenti Musei e Gallerie Pontificie, Vatican, Rome, Italy. A. Brachetti - P. Zigrossie
7.31 From Howard Hibbard, *Michelangelo*, New York, 1974
7.33 Photo © James Morris, London
7.35 © Vanni Archive/Corbis
7.36 Topkapi Palace Museum
7.37 Bibliothèque Nationale, Paris, France/ Bridgeman Art Library
Thumbnails: 7.1, 7.6, 7.17 © Quattrone, Florence, 7.16 © 1991, Photo SMB. Scala/Art Resource, New York

Chapter 8

8.1 The Frick Collection, New York
8.2, 8.7, 8.9 © Trustees of the British Museum, London
8.3 © Bristol's Museums, Galleries & Archives
8.4 Louvre, Paris. Collection Rothschild. Photo: © R.M.N., Paris
8.5 By permission of the Folger Shakespeare Library, Washington, D.C.
8.6 © His Grace the Duke of Bedford and the Trustees of the Bedford Estates. Reproduced by kind permission of His Grace the Duke of Bedford and the Trustees of the Bedford Estates
8.8 Kongoh Family Collection, Tokyo
8.10 © The National Gallery, London. Photo Scala, Florence
8.11 Museo del Prado, Madrid. Photo Scala, Florence
8.12, 8.14 © Musée d'Unterlinden, F68000 Colmar, France. Photo O. Zimmerman
8.13 © The Cleveland Museum of Art, Andrew R. and Martha Holden Jennings Fund, 1981.52
8.17 Photo Artothek, Weilheim, Germany
8.18 Photo © 2008 MFA. Bequest of Francis Bullard, 1913. M24884
8.19 Staatliche Museen zu Berlin. Photo BPK
8.20 Kunsthistorisches Museum, Vienna/The Bridgeman Art Library
8.21 © The National Gallery, London. Photo Scala, Florence
8.22 Purchase, the Dillon Fund Gift, 1989 (1989.141.3). © 2010 Image copyright The Metropolitan Museum of Art/Art Resource/ Scala, Florence
8.23 © Fotografica Foglia, Naples
Thumbnails: 8.14 © Musée d'Unterlinden, F68000 Colmar, France. Photo O. Zimmerman, 8.3 © Bristol's Museums, Galleries & Archives, 8.6 © His Grace the Duke of Bedford and the Trustees of the Bedford Estates. Reproduced by kind permission of His Grace the Duke of Bedford and the Trustees of the Bedford Estates

Chapter 9

9.1 Museum für Volkerkunde, Vienna. Kunsthistorisches Museum, Vienna
9.2 © National Maritime Museum, London
9.3 © Gavin Hellier/JAI/Corbis
9.4 © Trustees of the British Museum
9.5 Photographic Archives, National Museum of African Art, Smithsonian Institution, Washington, D.C. Photo Eliot Elisofon
9.6 Albright-Knox Art Gallery, Buffalo, New York. Sarah Norton Goodyear Fund, 2002. Scala/Art Resource, NY
9.7 Michael C. Rockefeller Memorial Collection of Primitive Art. Gift of Nelson A. Rockefeller, 1964, MMA. Photo Scala, Florence
9.8 The Michael C. Rockefeller Memorial Collection, Bequest of Nelson A. Rockefeller, 1979 (1979.206). Photograph © 1993 MMA. Photo Scala, Florence
9.9 Boltin Picture Library, Croton-on-Hudson, NY
9.10 New York State Historical Association. Photograph by John Bigelow Taylor
9.11 Werner Forman Archive
9.12 Funds given by The Children's Art Bazaar, St. Louis Art Museum
9.13 Jan Mitchell and Sons Collection, Gift of Jan Mitchell, 1991 (1991.419.58). Photograph by Justin Kerr. Photograph © 1984 MMA. Photo Scala, Florence
9.15 AKG Images/Erich Lessing
9.16 Werner Forman Archive/British Museum
9.17 © South American Pictures/Tony Morrison, Woodbridge, UK
9.18 Art Archive/Museo Nacional de Antropologia, Mexico/Gianni Dagli Orti
9.19 Museo Nacional de Antropologia, Mexico/ The Art Archive, London
Thumbnails: 9.9 Boltin Picture Library, Croton-on-Hudson, NY, 9.17 © South American Pictures/Tony Morrison, Woodbridge, UK, 9.18 Art Archive/Museo Nacional de Antropologia, Mexico/Gianni Dagli Orti

Chapter 10

10.1, 10.16, 10.17, 10.18 Rijksmuseum, Amsterdam
10.2 © 1996, Photo SMB. Scala/Art Resource, New York
10.3 Purchased with funds from the Libbey Endowment, Gift of Edward Drummond Libbey. Toledo Museum of Art, Ohio
10.4 Kunstbibliothek/BPK/Photo Scala, Florence
10.5, 10.31 © 1990, Photo Scala, Florence
10.6 © 2000, Photo Scala, Florence, courtesy of the Ministero Beni e Att. Culturali

10.7 © Vincenzo Pirozzi, Rome. fotopirozzi@inwind.it
10.8 © 1990, Photo SMB. Scala, Florence
10.9, 10.11 © Vincenzo Pirozzi, Rome. fotopirozzi@inwind.it
10.12 Photo A. F. Kersting, London/Courtauld Institute of Art
10.13 Kunsthistorisches Museum, Vienna
10.14 Royal Cabinet of Paintings, Mauritshuis, The Hague
10.15 Rijksmuseum, Amsterdam/The Bridgeman Art Library
10.19, 10.22, 10.24 © RMN
10.20 National Palace Museum, Beijing
10.21 Photo: © RMN—Gerard Blot
10.23 Photo: © Paul M.R. Maeyaert
10.25 © National Gallery, London. Photo Scala, Florence
10.26 Museo del Prado, Madrid. Photo Scala, Florence
10.27 Freer Gallery of Art, Smithsonian Institution, Washington, D.C. Purchase, F1942.15a
10.28 Bibliothèque Nationale, Paris
10.29 Artothek/Alte Pinakothek, Munich
10.30 Nezu Institute of Fine Arts, Tokyo
10.32 Torino, Museo Civico d'Arte e Palazzo Madama. Courtesy Fondazione Torino Musei—Archivio Fotografico
10.33 The Crosby Brown Collection of Musical Instruments, 1889 (89.4.2363). William H Scheide Library, Princeton University
10.34 Image copyright The Metropolitan Museum of Art/Art Resource/Scala, Florence
10.35 © The Cleveland Museum of Art, Gift of the Hanna Fund, 1951.355
Thumbnails: 10.19 © RMN, 10.9 © Vincenzo Pirozzi, Rome. fotopirozzi@inwind.it, 10.17 Rijksmuseum, Amsterdam, 10.31 © 1990, Photo Scala, Florence

Chapter 11
11.1 © Leonid Bogdanov/SuperStock
11.2 Royal Cabinet of Paintings, Mauritshuis, The Hague
11.3 a, b Sheila Terry/Science Photo Library
11.4 © The National Gallery, London. Photo Scala, Florence
11.5, 11.8 Library of Congress, Washington, D.C.
11.6 The Metropolitan Museum of Art. Photo Scala, Florence
11.7 Alinari/Art Resource New York
11.9 © Bettmann/Corbis
11.10, 11.30 © The Trustees of the British Museum
11.11 Hervé Champollion/AKG Images
11.12 Erich Lessing/Art Resource, New York/Photo Scala, Florence
11.13, 11.27 © RMN, Paris
11.14 Chester Dale Collection. Image courtesy of the Board of Trustees, National Gallery of Art, Washington, D.C.
11.15 © By kind permission of the Trustees of the Wallace Collection, London
11.16 Photo V&A Picture Library, London
11.17 BAL Giraudon/Art Resource, New York. Photo Scala, Florence
11.18 Bequest of Benjamin Altman, 1913 (14.40.687). © 2010 Image copyright The Metropolitan Museum of Art/Art Resource/Photo Scala, Florence
11.19 Photo © RMN/Gerard Blot
11.20 © 1998 Board of Trustees, NGA. Chester Dale Collection, Samuel H. Kress Collection
11.21, 11.22 Photo © Paul M. R. Maeyaert
11.23 © Roberto Schezen/Esto
11.24 Gift of Dr Lloyd E. Hawes. Museum of Fine Arts, Boston
11.25 Galleria Borghese, Rome. © 1999, Photo Scala, Florence—courtesy of the Ministero Beni e Att. Culturali
11.26 © Photo Josse, Paris
11.29 *A Popular History of Music*, © 1956 by Carter Harmon. Used by permission of Dell books, a division of Bantam Doubleday Dell Publishing Group, Inc.
11.31 Stephen Addiss
Thumbnails: 11.22 Photo © Paul M. R. Maeyaert, 11.13 © RMN, Paris, 11.9 © Bettmann/Corbis, 11.30 © The Trustees of the British Museum

Chapter 12
12.1, 12.4 Victoria and Albert Museum. V & A Images
12.2 Photo © RMN/Franck Raux
12.3 AKG Images
12.5 Rosenwald Collection, 1943.3.8999. Image courtesy of the Board of Trustees, National Gallery of Art, Washington
12.6 Rogers Fund, 1917 (17.12). Photograph © 2008 MMA. Photo Scala, Florence
12.7 Private Collection, Archives Charmet/The Bridgeman Art Library
12.8 © National Gallery, London. Photo Scala/Florence
12.9 Henry Lillie Pierce Fund, 99.22. Photograph © 2008 Museum of Fine Arts, Boston
12.10 Catharine Lorillard Wolfe Collection, Bequest of Catharine Lorillard Wolfe, 1887 (87.15.141). Photograph © 1980 MMA. Photo Scala, Florence
12.11 Galerie Neue Meister, Staatliche Kunstsammlungen, Dresden
12.12 The Nelson-Atkins Museum of Art, Kansas City, Missouri (Purchase: William Rockhill Nelson Trust) 46–51/2. Photo: Robert Newcombe
12.13 William S. and John T. Spaulding Collection 21.6765. Photograph © 2008 MFA
12.14 Gift of Mrs. Russell Sage, 1908 (08.228). Photograph © 1995 MMA. Photo Scala, Florence
12.15 Rogers Fund, 1907 (07.123). Photograph © 1979 MMA. Photo Scala, Florence
12.16 Paul Mellon Collection, 1965.16.347. Image courtesy of the Board of Trustees, National Gallery of Art, Washington
12.17 Museo del Prado, Madrid. Photo Scala, Florence
12.19 © AKG Images/Erich Lessing
12.20 © Photo Josse, Paris
12.21 Photo: Mike Newton/Robert Harding Picture Library, London
12.22 © Leonard de Selva/Corbis
12.23 © Peter Ashworth, London
12.24 © Angelo Hornak, London
12.25 © Corbis/Bettmann, London
12.26 Photo © RMN/C. Jean
12.27 © Nathalie Darbellay/Sygma/Corbis
12.29 MA.36.21.62, Musée de l'Homme, Paris
Thumbnails: 12.27 © Nathalie Darbellay/Sygma/Corbis, 12.8 © National Gallery, London. Photo Scala/Florence, 12.21 Photo: Mike Newton/Robert Harding Picture Library, London,12.17 Museo del Prado, Madrid. Photo Scala, Florence

Chapter 13
13.1 Helen Birch-Bartlett Memorial Collection (1926.224). Photography © The Art Institute of Chicago
13.2 Photo: © RMN, Paris/Jean Schormans
13.3 Museum Purchase, 1956/1.21. The University of Michigan Museum of Art. © DACS
13.5 © Louise Psihoyos/Corbis
13.6 Collection, David R. Phillips. Chicago Architectural Photographing Company
13.7, 13.17 The Library of Congress, Washington, D.C.
13.8 Musée d'Orsay, Paris, France/The Bridgeman Art Library
13.9 Historical Pictures Service, Chicago
13.10 H. O. Havemeyer Collection, Bequest of Mrs. H. O. Havemeyer, 1929 (29.100.129). © 2010 Image copyright The Metropolitan Museum of Art/Art Resource/Scala, Florence
13.11 Photo RMN/Hervé Lewandowski
13.12 Courtesy of the University of Pennsylvania Art Collection, Philadelphia, Pennsylvania
13.13 Catharine Lorillard Wolfe Collection, Wolfe Fund, 1906 (06.1234). Photograph © 1995 MMA. Photo Scala, Florence
13.14 Photo © RMN
13.15 © Photo Josse, Paris
13.16 Yale University Art Gallery, New Haven
13.18 Courtauld Institute of Art, © The Samuel Courtauld Trust, Courtauld Institute of Art Gallery, London
13.19 Robert A. Waller Fund (1910.2). Photography © The Art Institute of Chicago
13.20 Gift of Abby Aldrich Rockefeller, 167.1946 © 2010. Digital image, The Museum of Modern Art, New York/ Scala, Florence
13.21 Rogers Fund, 1936 (JP 2623). Image © 2011 The Metropolitan Museum of Art/Art Resource/Scala, Florence
13.22 Gift of H. O. Havemeyer, 1896 (96.17.10). Photograph © 1991 MMA. Photo Scala, Florence
13.23 Acquired through the Lillie P. Bliss Bequest. 472.19. © 2003, DI. Photo Scala, Florence
13.24 Helen Birch-Bartlett Memorial Collection (1926.198). Photography © The Art Institute of Chicago
13.25 Museum of New Zealand Te Papa Tongarewa. B15248
13.26 AKG Images
13.27 Helen Birch-Bartlett Memorial Collection (1926.224). Photography © The Art Institute of Chicago
13.28 Helen Birch-Bartlett Memorial Collection (1926.254). Photography © The Art Institute of Chicago
13.29 George W. Elkins Collection (Acces 1936-1-1). Philadelphia Museum of Art
13.30 © The Gallery Collection/Corbis
13.31 Detroit Institute of Arts/The Bridgeman Art Library
13.32 © MPI/Getty Images
13.33 New York Public Library
Thumbnails: 13.5 © Louise Psihoyos/Corbis, 13.30 © The Gallery Collection/Corbis, 13.14 Photo © RMN

Chapter 14
14.1 Nelson A. Rockefeller Fund (by exchange). Digital image, The Museum of Modern Art, New York/Scala, Florence. © ADAGP, Paris and DACS, London
14.2 The Library of Congress, Washington, D.C.
14.3 Friends of American Art Collection (1942–51). Photography © The Art Institute of Chicago
14.4 Gift of Mrs. David M. Levy. 28.1942.25. © 2003, DI. Museum of Modern Art © ARS, NY and DACS, London 2011
14.5 Philadelphia Museum of Art. Given by Mr. and Mrs. Herbert Cameron Morris (43-46-1), Louise and Walter Arensberg Collection. © 2011 Banco de México Diego Rivera Frida Kahlo Museums Trust, Mexico, D.F. / DACS]
14.6 Lee Miller Archive, Penrose Film Productions, Chiddingly. East Sussex
14.8 Kobal Collection
14.9 Acquired through the Lillie P. Bliss Bequest. © 2003, DI. Photo Scala, Florence © Succession Picasso/DACS, London 2010
14.10 Völkerkundemuseum der Universität Zürich
14.11 Acquired through the Lillie P. Bliss Bequest. © 2003, DI. Photo Scala, Florence © Succession Picasso/DACS, London 2010
14.12 Louise and Walter Arensberg Collection, Philadelphia Museum of Art © Succession Picasso/DACS, London 2010
14.13 Gift of the Artist, 1973. The Museum of Modern Art, NY. Photo Scala, Florence. © Succession Picasso/DACS, London 2010
14.14 © Succession Picasso/DACS, London 2010
14.15 Acquired through the Lillie P. Bliss Bequest. 231.1948. © 2003, DI, Museum of Modern Art, NY . Photo Scala, Florence
14.16 Louise and Walter Arensberg Collection, Philadelphia Museum of Art © Succession Marcel Duchamp/ADAGP, Paris and DACS, London 2011
14.17 Photo Hans Petersen, Statens Museum for Kunst, Copenhagen © Succession H Matisse/DACS 2011
14.18 Acquisition confirmed in 1999 by agreement with the Estate of Kasimir Malevich and made possible with funds from the Mrs. John Hay Whitney Bequest (by exchange). 817.1935. The Museum of Modern Art, New York. Photo Scala, Florence © DACS 2011
14.19 Collection of the Gemeentemuseum Den Haag. © 2011 Mondrian/Holtzman Trust c/o HCR International, Warrenton, VA
14.20 Given anonymously 153.1934, The Museum of Modern Art, New York. Photo Scala, Florence © ADAGP, Paris and DACS, London 2011.
14.21 © 2003, DI, The Museum of Modern Art, New York. Photo Scala, Florence © 2010 Calder Foundation, New York/DACS London
14.22 National Museum for Art, Architecture and Design, Oslo © Munch Museum/Munch-Ellingsen Group, BONO, Oslo/DACS, London 2011
14.23 Purchase. 274.1939. © 2003, DI. The Museum of Modern Art, New York. Photo Scala, Florence
14.24 Purchase. 87.1936. © 2003, DI. The Museum of Modern Art, New York. Photo Scala, Florence © DACS 2011
14.25 Mrs. Simon Guggenheim Fund. 146.1945 The Museum of Modern Art, New York. Photo Scala, Florence © ADAGP, Paris and DACS, London 2011
14.26 Collection of Mrs. Mary Sisler © Succession Marcel Duchamp/ADAGP, Paris and DACS, London 2011
14.27 Given anonymously. 162.1934. © 2003, DI The Museum of Modern Art, New York. Photo Scala, Florence © Salvador Dalí, Fundació Gala-Salvador Dalí, DACS, 2010
14.28 Purchased with funds provided by the Mr. and Mrs. William Preston Harrison Collection. Photograph © 2008 Museum Associates/LACMA. © ADAGP, Paris and DACS, London 2011
14.29 Purchase. 271.1937. © 2003, DI The Museum of Modern Art, New York. Photo Scala, Florence © Succession Miro/ADAGP, Paris and DACS, London 2011
14.30 Museo Frida Kahlo, Mexico City. Collection Lola Olimedo
© 2011 Banco de México Diego Rivera Frida Kahlo Museums Trust, Mexico, D.F. / DACS
14.31 Purchase. 130.1946a-c. © 2003, DI The Museum of Modern Art, New York. Photo Scala, Florence © DACS 2011
14.32 Photo Moderna Museet, Stockholm. © ADAGP, Paris and DACS, London 2011
14.33 The Kobal Collection, MOMA Film Stills Library
14.34 NSDAP/The Kobal Collection
14.35 Photo Hedrich-Blessing, courtesy Chicago Historical Society © ARS, NY and DACS, London 2011
14.36 Photograph by David Heald © The Solomon R. Guggenheim Foundation, New York. © ARS, NY and DACS, London 2011
14.37 Photograph © MOMA. Photo Scala, Florence © DACS 2011
14.38 © DACS 2011
14.39 Anthony Scibilia/Art Resource, NY © FLC/ADAGP, Paris and DACS, London 2011
14.40 Hogan Jazz Archive, Tulane University
Thumbnails: 14.6 Lee Miller Archive, Penrose Film Productions, Chiddingly. East Sussex, 14.30 Museo Frida Kahlo, Mexico City. Collection Lola Olimedo © 2011 Banco de México Diego Rivera Frida Kahlo Museums Trust, Mexico, D.F. / DACS, 14.17 Photo Hans Petersen, Statens Museum for Kunst, Copenhagen © Succession H Matisse/DACS 2011, 14.39 Anthony Scibilia/Art Resource, NY © FLC/ ADAGP, Paris and DACS, London 2011

Chapter 15
15.1 Collection of Justin Tyler Warsh, USA
15.2 Photo: Geoffrey Clements. © The Willem de Kooning Foundation, New York/ARS, NY and DACS, London 2011
15.3 Photo: Audrey Yoshiko Seo
15.4 Photo © Hans Namuth, New York, 1983. Courtesy Center for Creative Photography ©1991 Hans Namuth Estate © The Pollock-Krasner Foundation ARS, NY and DACS, London 2011.
15.5 George A. Hearn Fund, 1957 (57.92). Photograph © 1998 The Metropolitan Museum of Art. Photo Scala, Florence © The Pollock-Krasner Foundation ARS, NY and DACS, London 2011
15.6 Acquired through a gift of Peggy Guggenheim. San Francisco Museum of Modern Art. © 1998 Kate Rothko Prizel & Christopher Rothko ARS, NY and DACS, London
15.7 University Art Museum, University of California at Berkeley
15.8 Photo by Dave Sweeney. Courtesy of the artist and Sikkema Jenkins & Co.
15.9 Photo Donald Woodman. © ARS, NY and DACS, London 2011
15.10 Barbara Kruger. Courtesy Mary Boone Gallery, New York
15.11 © The Robert Mapplethorpe Foundation. Courtesy Art + Commerce
15.12 Shayna Brennan, AP/Wide World Photos
15.13 Barbara Gladstone Gallery, New York
15.14 © Noriko Yamaguchi, courtesy MEM, Inc.
15.15 Gift of Irving Blum; Nelson A. Rockefeller Bequest, gift of Mr. and Mrs. William A. M. Burden, Abby Aldrich Rockefeller Fund, gift of Nina and Gordon Bunshaft in honor of Henry Moore, Lillie P. Bliss Bequest, Philip Johnson Fund, Frances Keech Bequest, gift of Mrs. Bliss Parkinson, and Florence B. Wesley Bequest (all by exchange). © 2003, DI, MOMA, NY. Photo Scala, Florence. © The Andy Warhol Foundation for the Visual Arts, Inc. /DACS, London, 2007. Trademarks Licensed by Campbell Soup Company. All Rights Reserved
15.16 Photo courtesy the Oldenburg van Bruggen Studio © 1976 Claes Oldenburg
15.17 Gift of Joseph H. Hirshhorn, 1966. Photo Lee Stalsworth. © The George and Helen Segal Foundation/DACS, London/VAGA, New York 2011
15.18 Moderna Museet, Stockholm © Estate of Robert Rauschenberg. DACS, London/VAGA, New York 2011
15.19 Menil Collection, Houston, Texas © ARS, NY and DACS, London 2011
15.20 Photo: Gloria K Fiero. © The Isamu Noguchi Foundation and Garden Museum/ARS, New York and DACS, London 2011
15.21 Frank Fournier/Contact Press Images/nb pictures
15.22 Scottish National Gallery of Modern Art, Edinburgh © Estate of Duane Hanson/VAGA, New York/DACS, London 2011
15.23 Partial gift of the artist, 1989. 89.3626. Photograph by David Heald © The Solomon R. Guggenheim Foundation, New York. © ARS, NY and DACS, London 2011
15.24 Courtesy James Cohan Gallery, New York © Estate of Robert Smithson/DACS, London/VAGA, New York 2011
15.25 © Christo 1976. Photo Jeanne-Claude, New York. Wolfgang Volz
15.26 Holly Soloman Gallery, New York
15.27 Bill Viola Studio, Photo: Charles Duprat
15.28 Courtesy of the artist and Luhring Augustine, New York
15.29 Photo RMN/Hervé Lewandowski
15.30 Norman McGrath, New York
15.31 © Rufus F. Folkks/Corbis
15.32 © Joseph Sohm; Visions of America/Corbis
15.33 © Chuck Close, courtesy The Pace Gallery. Photograph Ellen Page Wilson, courtesy The Pace Gallery. Whitney Museum of American Art, New York; purchase with funds from Mrs. Robert M. Benjamin 69.102
15.34 Photograph by John Kane, courtesy of Pilobolus
15.35 © Grant Smith/VIEW
15.36 Carolee Schneemann. Photograph by Guy L'Heureux © ARS, NY and DACS, London 2011
15.37 Photo Chinese Contemporary Gallery, London. Collection of the artist
15.38 The Metropolitan Museum of Art. Purchase, Fred M. and Rita Richman, Noah-Sadie K. Wachtel Foundation Inc., David and Holly Ross, Doreen and Gilbert Bassin Family Foundation and William B. Goldstein Gifts, 2007 (2007.96). Photo Scala, Florence
15.39 Fowler Museum of Cultural History, University of California, Los Angeles
15.40 Photo: Jean Vong Photography. Courtesy the artist; Tanya Bonakdar Gallery, New York and Galeria Fortes Vilaça, São Paulo
15.41 Collection of the Artist. Photo: Lorenz Kienzle © ARS, NY and DACS, London 2011
Thumbnails: 15.25 © Christo 1976. Photo Jeanne-Claude, New York. Wolfgang Volz, 15.13 Barbara Gladstone Gallery, New York, 15.31 © Rufus F. Folkks/Corbis

INDEX

Bold indicates an illustration

C

D